Greenhill Books

A HISTORY
OF THE
PENINSULAR
WAR

A HISTORY OF
THE PENINSULAR WAR

A HISTORY
OF THE
PENINSULAR
WAR

FERDINAND THE SEVENTH,

KING OF SPAIN AND THE INDIES

ENGRAVED BY C. S. TAYLOR. FROM THE FRENCH PRINT BY VILLAIN.

A HISTORY
OF THE
PENINSULAR
WAR

Volume VII
August 1813 to April 14, 1814
The Capture of St. Sebastian,
Wellington's Invasion of France, Battles
of the Nivelle, The Nive, Orthez and
Toulouse

SIR CHARLES OMAN

Greenhill Books, London
Stackpole Books, Pennsylvania

Greenhill Books

This edition of *A History of the Peninsular War*, Volume VII,
first published 2005 by Greenhill Books, Lionel Leventhal Limited,
Park House, 1 Russell Gardens, London NW11 9NN
www.greenhillbooks.com
and
Stackpole Books, 5067 Ritter Road, Mechanicsburg, PA 17055, USA

British Library Cataloguing-in Publication Data
Oman, Charles William Chadwick, Sir, 1860-1946
A history of the Peninsular War
Vol. 7: August 1813 to April 14, 1814 : St Sebastian's capture,
Wellington's invasion of France, battles of Nive, Orthez, Toulouse. –
(Greenhill military paperback)
Title
940.2'7

Library of Congress Cataloging-in Publication Data available

PUBLISHING HISTORY
A History of the Peninsular War, volume VII, was first published
in 1930 (Oxford), and is reproduced now exactly as the original
edition, complete and unabridged. The original maps have been
re-presented by John Richards, in the interests of clarity

For more information on books published by Greenhill, please email
sales@greenhillbooks.com or visit www.greenhillbooks.com. You can also
write to us at Park House, 1 Russell Gardens, London NW11 9NN.

Printed and bound by CPD, Ebbw Vale

PREFACE

WITH the appearance of this, the seventh, volume of a work commenced in 1902 my history of the Peninsular War at last reaches its end. The interval since the issue of the sixth volume may seem long, but it was impossible to finish the story in a conscientious fashion without two more visits to the theatre of Wellington's operations in 1813–14; and, much occupied by Parliamentary and other business, I found it hard to spare time for two more summer excursions to the Pyrenean country. After having walked carefully over the complicated battle-fields between the Bidassoa and the Adour, and having made more cursory surveys of the land eastward as far as Toulouse, I was at last in a position to issue the final volume of this history. It is a somewhat melancholy task to write the last words of a book whose compilation has been my main literary work for no less than twenty-eight years—more especially when I reflect on the fact that most of my helpers in the earlier volumes —General Arteche, General Whinyates, Colonel Gardyne, Monsieur Martinien of the French Ministry of War, Mr. E. Mayne, the Rev. Alexander Craufurd, and Rafael Reynolds, the companion of much of my Portuguese travel—have passed over to the other side.

Of those who have been my aiders from first to last three still survive. My good friend Christopher Atkinson of Exeter College with vigilant eye has looked over every line of these volumes, detecting omissions, and making suggestions always valuable, from an unparalleled knowledge of British regimental history. Colonel John Leslie, R.A., has kept me straight on artillery details from first to last. And the compiler of my seven indices has carried out her work to the end with the same loving

care and zeal with which it was begun. No one who has
not made an index for himself can realize the amount of
work required for the extraction of countless entries
from four or five hundred pages of slip-proof.

In the completion of this last volume I have to make
mention of other helpers with whom I was not acquainted
when the book was first begun—General Arzadun of
the Spanish Artillery, Colonel Olavide of the Spanish
Engineers (whose beautiful atlas of the St. Sebastian
defences proved most useful), General Teixeira Botelho
at Lisbon, author of monographs on the Portuguese
Artillery, and General J. C. Dalton, R.A., of Ripon, who
put me on the trail of the Giron papers and other Spanish
documents. It would be impossible to make a list of other
kindly correspondents, who have supplied me with isolated facts on some point of regimental history or local
topography.

While this book was being written I issued, as by-
products connected with it, yet unsuitable for inclusion
in its pages, two smaller volumes. The first, *Wellington's
Army* [1913], contained an analysis of the composition of
the Old Peninsular Army and its inner organization,
including such topics as its battalion and brigade forma-
tions, courts-martial, marching arrangements, discipline,
moral and intellectual life, and *personnel*. I added a
bibliography containing a list of all the English original
sources for the war, entered under the author's name and
corps. The second book, *Studies in the Napoleonic Wars*
[1929], contained a long article on Wellington's infantry
tactics, and a number of curious stories concerning secret
service, English and French, on which I had chanced to
hap during my excursions among original documents.
It also included some notes on French cavalry organization and tactics, which throw light on certain aspects of
the Peninsular War. To these two books I may refer

those who are interested in details of this sort: they repre-
sent a vast amount of work which could hardly be utilized
in the main history of the war, yet seemed too interesting
(when once collected) to be allowed to fall into oblivion.

If I may be allowed to lay stress on the main feature
of this last volume of my history, it is well to point out
that in Wellington's invasion of France political considerations had as important a part as strategical. All through
the six years of his command he had before him no mere
military considerations, but a politico-military problem.
His object down to 1812 was to keep up the war in
Portugal, and to 'contain' a great portion of Napoleon's
armies. He did not wish for a crisis which might
attract the Emperor himself to the Peninsula. In 1812
and the first half of 1813 this particular danger was no
longer pressing, since the Emperor was sufficiently occupied in Russia, and afterwards in Germany. But after
Vittoria, when Wellington had driven the French back
to the line of the Pyrenees, the old problem reappeared,
since it became known that the Northern Allies had
entered into peace negotiations with Napoleon during
the Armistice of Plässwitz. As long as there was any
possibility that the Allies might come to terms with the
great enemy, which Great Britain could not accept, it was
conceivable that, with his hands freed from the Northern
War, Napoleon might once more be in a position to
turn overwhelming forces against the Anglo-Portuguese.
It was not till September 3rd that Wellington heard of
the rupture of the Armistice of Plässwitz and the entry
of Austria into the war, and felt that he might strike
hard, without any danger of immediate interruption.
Hence it came that he was encouraged to force the lines
of the Bidassoa early in October and the lines of the
Nivelle early in November [see pp. 110–12 of this volume].
The news of Leipzig emboldened him to push his army

across the Nive and beset Bayonne, and the knowledge
that the Allies had crossed the Rhine on December 22nd
enabled him to begin the great manœuvre which forced
Soult to leave Bayonne and brought the invading army
to Orthez, Bordeaux, and Toulouse. But even in the last
months of his French campaign Wellington had political
problems before him. There was the chance of raising
a royalist rising in the south. But when it became known
that the Allies were once more negotiating with Napoleon
at Châtillon, Wellington realized the ignominy that would
fall upon him if he were to encourage the loyalists to raise
the White Banner, and then to be forced to tell them
that Napoleon had been granted terms, and that they were
left at their old master's mercy. Hence came the great
reluctance which he showed to forward the enterprise
of the Duke of Angoulême, and the language, almost
amounting to discouragement, which he used to the
enthusiastic Bourbon partisans at Bordeaux [see p. 398]
and at Toulouse [see p. 486]. In short, all the cam-
paigning from September 1813 to April 1814 was dictated by political even more than by military considerations. This is not always understood, and French critics
in particular are wont to drop sarcasms on 'the strategy
anything rather than Napoleonic' practised by the British
general. It is not realized that he was fully aware that
he was fighting not an isolated campaign against Soult
but a campaign that was only one section of a great
struggle, in which other things than the local successes
of the moment were in question.

In this volume, as in the earlier ones, there are points
on which I must crave the indulgence of the reader. One
is the spelling of names. When a place or a person is
mentioned at long intervals of time, and the mention of
it or him is in one case derived from a French, in another
from a Spanish source, or when two French or Spanish

authorities spell a name differently, it is quite possible
that it may appear in divergent form in two pages of this
book. I had, for example, to choose between Ainhoue,
Ainhoüe, Ainhoué, Ainhoa, Añoa, for a village by the
Nivelle, and similarly Arriverayte (to take my chosen form)
has five other spellings in different contemporary documents. General Freire, the chief of the 4th Army, wrote
his signature with an 'i', but Wellington, Soult, and nearly
all other writers called him Freyre. Daricau and Darricau seem equally well-balanced spellings for one of
Soult's divisional generals. In such cases it is easy for
the pen of the historian to be self-contradictory on
occasion. Certain names of Basque villages are never
written with the same letters by any two persons who
have occasion to mention them.

In drawing the last chapter to its end I found it hard
to avoid giving a sketch of Spanish and Portuguese
history for the years which followed 1814. But there are
limits to all things—and the chronicle of the succeeding
period was not a cheerful one.

C. O.

1 *July* 1930.

CONTENTS

SECTION XLIII

WELLINGTON ON THE ADOUR. DECEMBER 1813– FEBRUARY 1814

SECTION XLIV

END OF THE WAR ON THE EAST COAST. JANUARY– APRIL 1814

SECTION XLV

THE CAMPAIGN OF TOULOUSE. MARCH–APRIL 1814

FINIS

APPENDICES

MAPS AND PLANS

SECTION XXXIX
ST. SEBASTIAN AND SAN MARCIAL
CHAPTER I

THE SECOND SIEGE OF ST. SEBASTIAN. AUGUST 1813

THE 'Battles of the Pyrenees' were over; Soult's Army had recoiled across the frontier in a state of complete demoralization. But on the night of August 1st–2nd, 1813 Wellington had made his 'Great Refusal', and determined to give up the tempting scheme which had flitted before his vision for a few hours on the previous day for invading France in the wake of the routed enemy. He turned back to his old policy of July: St. Sebastian and Pampeluna must be reduced: when they should have fallen, it would be time enough to see whether the general situation of affairs in Europe made an advance to the Adour (or even the Garonne) advisable. If Austria came into the war on the side of the Allies, and if the German campaign of 1813 went badly for Napoleon, it might be possible to leave the Pyrenees and the Bidassoa behind, and to launch out into the plains of Southern France.

It is strange to think how different would have been the position of Wellington if he had possessed modern means of acquiring rapid information. It was on August 12th that Metternich's docile master declared war on France, and the great game recommenced on the plains of Saxony. Long before St. Sebastian fell the Armistice of Plässwitz had ended, and Wellington's hands (if he had only known it) were untied. But the news of the Austrian breach with the French Emperor only reached London on August 27th, and though Lord Bathurst sent it on by semaphore-signal to Plymouth, where a swift vessel was waiting to sail, it only reached Head-quarters at Lesaca on September 3rd. All through the month of August Wellington might fear the worst—a patched-up peace at Dresden, followed by the transference of great masses of reinforcements to the army of Soult.

Hence he concluded that the only practical policy was to resume the siege of St. Sebastian, and at least make the Spanish

356.7   B

frontier defensible, if the worst should come to the worst. Pampeluna, as he thought, would fall of itself ere long; for he had been wrongly informed as to the amount of food still remaining in its magazines. But as to St. Sebastian, he had already begun to consider its problems before Soult was well over the frontier in retreat. From the day after Sorauren onward, his correspondence with Sir Thomas Graham began to be full of details concerning guns, munitions, and transport. The disastrous failure of the first assault (July 25) had made him determine that the renewed siege should not be conducted with inadequate means—like those of Burgos and the Salamanca forts in 1812—nor hurried overmuch. Soult had received such a crushing blow in the Battles of the Pyrenees that he must obviously be out of action for some little time. So the main motive which had led to reckless haste in the first operations against St. Sebastian was no longer operative. It would have been possible to resume the battering of the place with the old train in a few days. By August 6th the guns which had been embarked at Passages were being put on shore again. But Wellington had resolved to wait for the arrival from England of the second and third consignments of the great battering train which had been promised him. It was vexatious that successive dispatches arrived, reporting that the convoy was still windbound at Portsmouth, and had not sailed on July 27th. Indeed it was one of the characteristics of military and naval co-operation, in those days, that any pledges as to time made by the Admiralty might be redeemed a fortnight or even three weeks late. In the days before steam, accurate calculation was liable to be rendered hopeless by persistent contrary winds. It will be remembered that it was this simple fact that wrecked the Walcheren Expedition in 1809, rather than the oft-quoted antagonism of the Earl of Chatham and Sir Richard Strachan.

On this occasion the first of the ships which Wellington had been expecting in the last days of July began to drop into Passages on August 18th. When they did make their appearance, it was presumably owing to 'the inherent perversity of inanimate matter' that the guns arrived first in plenty, but with hardly any of the ammunition without which they were useless[1]. The shot

[1] Cf. *Dispatches*, x. p. 604, and Jones, *Sieges of the Peninsula*, ii. p. 49.

and powder turned up in the end, but the first munition ships came in five days after the earliest consignments of artillery.

Wellington's decision to do no petty battering with his old guns, but to wait for the enormous resources which were on their way, condemned him to more than a fortnight of tiresome delays. In it he had leisure to deal with all his usual worries and problems, with some new ones added. His correspondence in the first half of August ranges over many subjects, now that he had leisure to pick up all the old threads, dropped during the distracting business around Pampeluna. The foreign troops— especially the *Chasseurs Britanniques* and Brunswick Oels—had been deserting more than ever, despite of the unpromising look of the enemy's affairs. Probably this was due simply to the fact that the army was now on the French border—desertion was less risky than in Portugal or Central Spain, where the whole civil population, including guerrilleros, was against the deserter. Here he had merely to ford the Bidassoa at night, or to slip across a steep hill-side beyond Vera, in order to find himself safe. What vexed Wellington most of all was that the epidemic of desertion affected a perceptible number of his own regulars—Irish and even British also. He thought that it was a sort of contagion caught from the foreigners[1]—but probably the explanation was the same—the easiness of absconding on a hostile frontier attracted British reprobates, who had plundered a farm, or got in the bad books of the sergeant-major; it was ridiculously easy to escape punishment by desertion. A much more serious cause of irritation was the persistent neglect of the Admiralty to provide an adequate squadron of light vessels for the protection of convoys, and the blockade of St. Sebastian and St. Jean de Luz. Wellington complained that *trincadours* and luggers ran from the French coast to St. Sebastian nearly every night, carrying not only dispatches but reinforcements, and heavy stuff like sand-bags, ordnance stores, shoes and entrenching tools. When returning they took off, with similar impunity, the sick and wounded of the garrison. The supply of men-of-war in the Bay of Biscay was so small that when the Prince of Orange was sent to London, bearing the official report of the Battles of the Pyrenees, nothing better than a cutter could be found to carry him, and he

[1] *Dispatches*, x. pp. 597 and 624.

had to wait several days for that. The want of comprehension
of the situation in Whitehall was so great, that when Wellington
had pointed out that the weekly packet with the letters, &c., for
the Army should not be sent any longer to Lisbon, the Lords of
the Admiralty had ordered it to go to Corunna, which, though
it might be nearer to Biscay, as the crow flies, than Lisbon, was
rather more inconvenient, from the point of view of roads and
mountains. Yet Bilbao, Santander, and Passages were all open[1].
In return Wellington only got explanations that the light vessels
of the British Navy were distracted to the Baltic, America, or the
Mediterranean: which was true enough, no doubt, but hardly a con-
vincing reply to one who believed that the Bay of Biscay was at this
moment by far the most interesting sphere of naval operations.

But Wellington's controversy with the Admiralty was less
bitter and less important than his contemporary controversy
with the Spanish Government, over its broken pledges concerning the supreme military command. On June 16th there
had been issued the tiresome order which displaced Castaños and
Giron from their commands in the North, and appointed Lacy
and Freire to fill their places. Wellington's protests continued to
rain down on the new regents at Cadiz. 'I shall be obliged', he
wrote to his brother Henry, the ambassador, 'if you will explain
from me to the Government, that although I think their conduct
towards Generals Castaños and Giron harsh and unjust, I do not
complain of it as a breach of engagement with me. Neither do
I complain of their refusal to promote the officers whom I
recommended after Vittoria as a breach of engagement. What I
complain of is that the Government, having made an engagement with me, without which I neither can nor will hold the
command of the army, have broken it not in one but in a hundred
instances, and that they appear to do it wantonly, because they
know of my disinclination to relinquish the command. . . . I
should lose all influence and authority if I were to submit to
these indignities without complaint, and therefore it is that
I complain, and must insist on this Government satisfying me[2].'

---

[1] To Lord Bathurst, *Dispatches*, x. pp. 631–2. Cf. x. pp. 600 and 625.
[2] Wellington to H. Wellesley, *Dispatches*, x. p. 565, and to the Minister
of War, ibid., p. 607. Cf. Bathurst to Wellington, *Supplementary Dispatches*,
viii. p. 107.

The practical compromise arrived at on the main point was that, while Castaños was not replaced, Giron was not dismissed, but transferred from the command of the Army of Galicia to that of the Andalusian Army of Reserve, *vice* Henry O'Donnell, who just at this moment chose to declare himself sick, and to ask for leave to visit the Baths of Granada. He was really suffering not so much in health as in self-esteem—he chose to regard the part that had been allotted him in the recent campaign as more fit for a general of divisions than for the commander-in-chief of an army—even though it were but an army of 11,000 men. He had suggested that he should be given a more independent command, and entrusted with the charge not of two divisions but of the whole body of Spanish troops. When this was denied him he took offence, and went on leave—to Wellington's great joy. Hard words, apparently, passed. 'He stated', wrote Wellington, 'that the Spanish nation expected that all the Spanish troops acting on this side should be joined together and act as one corps. I sent him word that I had not lately heard of any Spanish troops, acting independently as one corps, which had not been destroyed; and that the last which so acted [his brother Joseph's Army at Castalla in 1812] had been destroyed by half their own number. . . . Two days later he sent for leave to go to the Baths. I mention this because I think it probable that he will endeavour to push his objects at Cadiz, when the grand intrigue approaches, at the opening of the new Cortes in October[1].' Giron therefore took command of the army of Andalusia, and held it for the rest of the campaign, though Freire was given the charge of the larger unit, the Army of Galicia, which Giron had hitherto administered. Both were easy men to deal with in comparison with the self-assertive Henry O'Donnell, and Freire made an unexpectedly favourable impression on the commander-in-chief, soon after he took command of the 4th Army, by his handling of his troops at the battle of San Marcial on August 31st.

---

[1] Wellington to Henry Wellesley, August 16, *Dispatches*, xi. p. 6. It should be noted that in these controversies Wellington dissuaded the Home Government from intervening formally by official dispatches—holding that British protests would only embitter Spanish feeling. See *Supplementary Dispatches*, viii. p. 205.

There was also the constant necessity for keeping touch overland with Lord William Bentinck and the East-Coast Armies—
the really dangerous possibility was that Suchet might evacuate
all Catalonia save the fortresses, and march with 30,000 men to
join Soult. Hence Bentinck had to be warned to keep his eyes
open to every indication of such a movement, and to be ready to
transfer troops eastwards, to counterbalance Suchet, the moment
that he saw certain signs of his departure. Here Wellington does
not seem to have appreciated two elements in the situation which
really governed it. Soult would have liked to draw in Suchet to
join him, and often urged his removal to the West. But Suchet
cherished his independence, and had no love for the elder
Marshal; and—what was more important—the Minister of War
at Paris was obsessed with the idea that the prestige of the
French empire would be ruined if, Suchet having been withdrawn from Catalonia, Bentinck and the Spaniards should
invade Roussillon and Languedoc in force. They could not have
done so—for want of transport and food: of this Wellington was
aware, but Clarke was not.

But not only was there almost daily advice to be sent to
Bentinck, but another East-Coast matter was wasting much of
Wellington's time—the projected court-martial on Sir John
Murray. There are a large number of letters which discuss the
framing of the charges to be made at his trial, and the fixing of
the place at which it should be held—Valencia—General Head-
quarters in Biscay—or London: all of which presented geogra-
phical or moral inconveniences[1].

A more pressing matter in the early weeks of August was the
rearrangement of the positions of the various divisions, in view
of the fact that further attempts of the French to relieve
Pampeluna were unlikely, considering their recent misadventures.
But it was quite possible that one more desperate rush to save
St. Sebastian might be made—since the fortress would soon be
attacked with overpowering strength, and Soult might risk
another check rather than let it fall unsuccoured. And as the
Marshal now had his whole army—such as it was—concentrated
on the Nivelle, he was in a position to strike once more if he

[1] See especially *Dispatches*, x. p. 616, and cf. p. 611, and *Supplementary
Dispatches*, viii. p. 200.

dared. Hence provision was made for his reception, by ordering the construction of three successive lines of earthworks and redoubts between the Bidassoa and Oyarzun, which would all have to be forced by an enemy making for St. Sebastian[1]. Moreover some additional troops were gathered into Graham's wing —the first brigade of Guards, so long detained at Oporto by sickness, had at last marched up to join the 1st Division. A new brigade from England and Gibraltar, which arrived by sea on August 17th–18th was also allotted to Graham's force[2], and the detached Andalusian battalions, which Henry O'Donnell had brought up from the blockade of Pampeluna, were placed behind Vera in the valley of the lower Bidassoa, to strengthen Longa's rather weak force in that direction. Nor was this all: the 2nd Division, in consequence of its fearful losses on July 25th, was very depleted, and would not receive drafts nor recover convalescents for many weeks. Wherefore, after August 7th, Wellington moved it to Roncesvalles, at the extreme right of the line, where no further French attacks were to be expected. He replaced it at Maya by the 6th Division, while close behind at Elizondo he placed Picton's 3rd Division, which had suffered only some 120 casualties in the recent campaign. Thus the left wing of the army was decidedly strengthened: the precautions proved useful when Soult did make his last attempt to take the offensive, on the very day upon which St. Sebastian was doomed to fall. Owing to the recent arrivals the total force of the army, as Wellington observed, was only 1,500 less than it had been in mid July, despite of the 7,000 casualties of the Battles of the Pyrenees. On August 8th there were 59,524[3] British and Portuguese, of all ranks and all arms, present and fit for duty: of Spaniards somewhat under 25,000.[4]

[1] See *Dispatches*, x. p. 605, and *Supplementary Dispatches*, viii. p. 203.

[2] This anomalous brigade, always under Lord Aylmer, was never formally attached to the 1st Division but always acted with it. It consisted of the 76th, 2/84th, and 85th. Its dates of arrival are fixed by Gleig of the 85th. The 84th, which came from Gibraltar, was some days later than the other two corps.   [3] *Supplementary Dispatches*, viii. p. 176.

[4] Viz. Morillo's, Barcena's, Longa's, Porlier's, Losada's divisions of the Army of Galicia, in all 19,600. Carlos de España's division, and Giron's Army of Reserve of Andalusia were before Pampeluna: but some odd battalions of the latter had been brought up to the frontier, and one or two of Mina's battalions were not far off—the whole making about 24,500.

From July 27th—the day on which the Portuguese troops
in the trenches suffered so severely from the raid executed by
three French companies[1]—down to August 19th, there was
practically nothing to chronicle in the way of hostilities on
the side of St. Sebastian. Wellington had forbidden any attempt
to batter the place with the artillery surviving from the first
siege, and it would appear that not a single British gun was
fired for three weeks and more. The French, on the other hand,
fired frequently but intermittently, when they saw any movement in the trenches. As to musketry, there was a certain amount
of sniping always going on—the French on the walls trying to
pick off men relieving guard in the trenches—the sharpshooters
in the British lines firing at the working parties frequently more
or less visible as they carried out repairs on the old breaches.
But casualties were few, and there were no large-scale sorties
after July 27th. The really important things to note were two—
the plan for the second siege worked out by the British staff, and
the preparations against it made by the governor.

On August 7th there was a great discussion of technical
matters by the chief officers of engineers and artillery. Fletcher,
the commanding engineer, supported by Major Smith, who had
drawn up the scheme for the first siege, carried his point, that
the new attack should be a repetition of the old on a larger scale,
viz. 'to add more guns to the former breaching batteries, to
enlarge the old breach right and left; to form a new and powerful battery in the gorge of the old French redoubt [San Barto-
lomé] and to endeavour to continue the breach round to the
main front, by laying open the adjoining demi-bastion [that of
San Juan] and the end of the curtain above it'[2]. That is to say,
the water-front of the fortress was still to be the section attacked,
with the result that the assault must once more be made at low
tide, over the ground only accessible for a few hours at a time:
but the main land-front, composed of the Hornwork, was to be
left alone. This plan was sent to Wellington despite of the protests of Burgoyne, the second senior engineer, who held that the
breaches were too far from the first parallel, that the assault
across the tidal flat had already been proved inconvenient in
the highest degree, and that flank fire from the Hornwork would

[1] See vol. vi. p. 586.   [2] Burgoyne's *Diary*, i. p. 273.

have a fatal efficiency against the storming columns, as at the previous assault. Moreover the enemy had fortified an internal line cutting off the breaches from the town, as had been seen on July 25th, and would have made it much stronger during the holiday now granted him. Burgoyne advocated a formal frontal attack on the Hornwork and the curtain behind it, in the regular style[1]. But the senior engineer had his way, and Wellington approved the revised edition of the old scheme.

On the other hand Emanuel Rey, as his dispatches to Soult inform us, made the most elaborate preparations of defence[2]. He completed (as Burgoyne had foreseen) a most formidable second line of resistance behind the old breach. Taking as basis the ruined houses of the street immediately parallel with the back of the ramparts, he built up their lower stories into a continuous stone wall, very thick and 15 feet high. This immense work was carried out by aid of the débris of the fallen upper stories, and of dug up paving stones. It reached from the end of the high curtain above the demi-bastion of San Juan to the curtain beyond the Tower of Amezqueta. Rey also scarped and repaired the inner front of the walls at the breaches, making the drop sheer and lofty into the town. He built new retrenchments in the Hornwork, and repaired the part of its counterscarp which had been blown down by the mine of July 25th. He erected new traverses all along the ramparts, and perfected a system of barricades, mutually supporting each other, in the inner streets of the city. He constructed a number of covered ways in the Castle, from battery to battery, there having before been no protection on this high ground for men moving from one work to another.

The clandestine voyages of the small boats, which ran the blockade nearly every night, had permitted Rey to receive a good deal in the way of stores, a quantity of shell and shot, and a number of drafts for the garrison. He had also sent away many of his transportable wounded. The numbers of his force when the first siege began had been 3,185, the casualties down to August 15th had been over 850, but there were nevertheless 2,996 troops in the fortress on that day[3]. The place had still

[1] See Burgoyne, i. pp. 273–4. All these views were justified by the event.
[2] See Belmas, iv. p. 629, and documents to same, 13–17.
[3] See Belmas's tables on pp. 654–6, 689, and 690 of vol. iv.

60 guns on the walls, the magazines were full, and the garrison was very confident. On August 15th it treated the blockading army to an illumination: this being Napoleon's birthday, an immense inscription with letters of fire six feet long, VIVE L'EMPEREUR[1], was visible on the high slope of Monte Urgull for miles around.

On August 18th many sails were visible on the horizon, and on the 19th ships began to run into the difficult entry of the port of Passages, and continued to arrive for the next five days, till the harbour was overcrowded, and it became difficult to land anything for want of space on the quays. There were no less than four convoys—all long detained at various British harbours by contrary winds—which now ran in simultaneously. Of troops there were two battalions from Dover for the new brigade to be organized by Lord Aylmer, along with some 800 drafts, and the first complete company of sappers and miners ever seen in the Peninsula—one of the new red-coated units which were to supersede the blue 'military artificers' who had been doled out to Wellington in sixes and tens during the earlier years of the war. Much wanted at Badajoz and Burgos, the new corps appeared only just in time to see the last ten days of the last formal siege which Wellington ever conducted[2]. Besides the convoy of troops, there were no less than three separate groups of vessels with siege artillery and ordnance stores of all kinds. The first, which arrived on August 19th, consisted of the second third of the great consignment of siege pieces from Portsmouth which had been promised to Wellington in May, and which exactly duplicated in numbers and calibre the first third, which had reached him in time for the battering work in July.

To the disgust of the commander-in-chief there was hardly any ammunition sent along with the 28 new guns—about enough for one day's consumption. And irritation grew still greater when a few hours later another convoy came to hand—this was an 'uncovenanted mercy', and a most undesired one. Before the Armistice there had been a plan for occupying and fortifying Cuxhaven, at the mouth of the Elbe, in order to serve as a basis

---

[1] Or according to Burgoyne VIVE NAPOLÉON LE GRAND.
[2] See Maxwell's *Peninsular Sketches*, ii. p. 299, for the surprise of engineer officers at seeing sappers in red.

for the lively insurrection in Hanover. A quantity of garrison guns of position had been shipped for this purpose, but could not be landed when the suspension of hostilities in Germany took place. The Ordnance Board thought that Wellington might like them, fifteen 24-pounder and eight 18-pounder guns fitted on garrison carriages with traversing platforms. The accompanying ammunition included only 4,300 round shot, which 23 guns could dispose of in less than two days. Garrison guns so fitted could be of little or no use in siege operations; the store of shot, and 480 barrels of powder accompanying it, was but a trifling contribution to the general stock. Fortunately there arrived four days later the final third of the originally ordered siege-train, with all the missing ammunition, 62,000 round shot, 7,500 barrels of powder, and much more[1].

The fear which Wellington had felt from August 19th to August 23rd, that he would have plenty of guns but nothing to fire from them, was removed. And it was possible to order that the Cuxhaven consignment should be put aside, as it would not be needed[2]. The only difficulty was to get the newly arrived material ashore, when it was necessary to land much of it from ships anchored in the middle of the harbour, since all berths alongside the quays were occupied. Immense quantities of boats were wanted, and were not forthcoming, since local help was meagre, even when sturdy Basque women turned out to ply an oar, while the navy was very insufficiently represented. Wellington wrote, in anger, to the Admiralty, 'the naval force on this coast is too weak to give us aid of the description we require, and for want of it we shall now be much distressed. The soldiers are obliged to work in the transports, and unload the vessels, because no seamen can be furnished. We have been obliged to use the harbour boats of Passages, navigated by women, in landing ordnance and stores, because there is no naval force to supply us with the assistance that we have required in boats. These harbour boats being light, and of a weak construction, have, many of them, been destroyed, and there will be great delay from want of boats in the further operations of the siege. The soldiers have to load and unload the boats, the women who

[1] See Jones, *Peninsular Sieges*, ii. pp. 48–51.
[2] Wellington to Graham, *Dispatches*, xi. p. 2.

navigate them being unequal to the labour. . . . If the navy of
Great Britain cannot afford more than one frigate and a few
brigs and cutters (fit and used only to carry dispatches) to
co-operate in the siege of a maritime place, I must be satisfied,
and do the best I can without its assistance[1].'

With its own unaided resources, therefore, the army unshipped
and brought forward both ordnance and ammunition. On the
night of the 22nd the replacing of the guns in the old batteries
commenced, and by the 24th they were all in position, as on
July 25th. But many more pieces being now available, it was
determined not only to enlarge all the former works, but to
construct several new ones. Gunners to man them were obtained
by sending forward some officers and men of the field batteries
belonging to the 3rd and 4th Divisions, and by borrowing a few
seamen from Sir George Collier's minute blockading squadron[2].
The new batteries designed were two (nos. 13 and 14) on the
brow of the hill of San Bartolomé, just in front of the ruined
building, which were intended to supersede the original batteries
(4, 5, 7, 8) on that side, and to breach the demi-bastion of San
Juan, and if possible the curtain above it. On the other side of
the water, the old no. 11, the work nearest the city, was enlarged
so as to mount fifteen guns, and that next it on the north (no. 3)
was also provided with that number. Both of these were to play
on the old breach, from the Tower of Amezqueta to the demi-
bastion of San Juan. These thirty guns were intended to do the
main part of the business. The isolated battery on the top of the
lofty Monte Olia, far to the right (no. 6), was to specialize on the
Castle, and make life uncomfortable on its bare slopes. Rather
to the right of the two great breaching batteries (3 and 11) the
old battery no. 2, and a new one constructed near it (no. 15),
were fitted with six 10-inch mortars each, and the old no. 12, on
top of the Chofres sandhills, was similarly equipped with four
more. Of these mortar batteries no. 2 was intended to drop
bombs in the rear of the breaches, so as to make repairs dangerous, and the others were directed to shell the town at large.
There were altogether 63 pieces engaged, 48 on the Chofres
front, 15 on the San Bartolomé front across the water.

---

[1] Wellington to Lord Melville, *Dispatches*, xi. pp. 18–19.
[2] Eighty on the first 3 days, afterwards less were available.

Wellington expressed grave doubts as to the usefulness of the mortar batteries and the policy of 'general annoyance' against the town[1]. 'It answers no purpose whatever, against a Spanish place occupied by the French, excepting against the inhabitants. . . . If the general bombardment should set fire to the town, as it probably will, the attack on the enemy's entrenchment[2] will become impossible. I do not believe that our use of mortars and howitzers does the enemy the slightest mischief, and the conflagration which it may occasion will be very inconvenient to our friends the inhabitants, and eventually to ourselves.' Graham, charged with the duty of passing on these criticisms to Dickson and Fletcher, replied that the mortars should be used mainly to enfilade the lines of defence, but reminded his chief that bombardment at large had caused the fall of Flushing in 1809, and might have considerable effects against a garrison unfurnished with bomb-proofs[3]. With Wellington's approval or not, the mortars played a good deal on St. Sebastian 'for annoyance', incommoded the garrison a little, but half ruined the town: it was set on fire in many places, and the wretched inhabitants had to seek shelter in their cellars or the vaults of churches[4]. Against such a governor as Rey, the method, as Wellington rightly supposed, was unprofitable.

The battering began at 9 a.m. on August 26th[5] with a general salvo, the Chofres guns opening on the curtain between the towers of Los Hornos and Amezqueta and the eastern flank of the demi-bastion of San Juan, the San Bartolomé guns on the southern flank of the last-named work and the high curtain or 'cavalier' above it, while the mortars dropped a certain amount of bombs into the space in rear of the attacked front, but a much greater number into the town. The first crash was tremendous, and was followed by continuous independent firing without cessation for the whole day. The enemy replied at first with a good many pieces of all calibres, but gradually the return fire slacked off: some French guns were actually dismounted, from

---

[1] To Graham, *Dispatches*, xi. p. 32, of August 23rd.

[2] i. e. the inner defences in the streets, whose existence was well known.

[3] Graham to Wellington, August 24. *Supplementary Dispatches*, viii. p. 205.   [4] Belmas, iv. p. 634.

[5] So Jones, ii. p. 58, but Burgoyne, i. p. 276, says at 8 a.m.

others the gunners were driven away, and by night only a few distant pieces in and near the Castle were in action. It was clear that the British artillery was overpowering, and that none of that trouble from the enemy's counterfire that had been met with at Burgos and Badajoz would be experienced here.

The effect of the battering was satisfactory on the right attack: the east face of San Juan had lost all its stone facing, and was already beginning to crumble: the towers of Los Hornos and Amezqueta appeared to be much damaged, and the curtain north of the latter showed signs of grave deterioration. On the other hand there was a comparatively disappointing result from the fire of the San Bartolomé batteries: neither the front face of San Juan nor the high curtain above it had received any serious harm, though the flank of the Hornwork below them was somewhat injured. The explanation given for this by the artillery officers was that the batteries nos. 13 and 14 were too far from their mark: wherefore Wellington, after inspecting the whole front, sent orders to throw up a new battery (no. 16) in front of the parallel on the Isthmus, only 250 yards instead of 800 from the fortress. There was no great difficulty in constructing this work, as the enemy's strength was so reduced that, although he made repeated attempts to stop it by long-distance fire from the Castle, he could not much trouble the men working on it. Seeing how close they were to the Hornwork, Rey launched a sortie against them on the night of the 27th–28th, but it was easily stopped in the approaches, and never got near its goal.

As a further means of incommoding the garrison, a boat attack was made on the night of the 26th–27th upon the small rocky island of Santa Clara, out in the bay and opposite the Castle. Landing was difficult in the dark, but was accomplished, under a scattering fire. An engineer officer was killed, with two others of the party, but the French post of an officer and twenty-four men surrendered when the first two boat-loads got ashore. It was proposed to put a few guns on the island, in order to batter the flank of the Castle from it, and to fire on small craft trying to run the blockade.

All through the four days from August 27th to August 30th the breaching of the south-eastern course of the defences of St. Sebastian continued—the advanced battery in the parallel

designed by Wellington adding its services after the 29th, and
proving much more efficient against the front face of San Juan
than the remoter guns which had hitherto played on it. The
general result was to produce about the largest breach that had
ever been seen, extending continuously for nearly 300 yards,
from the Tower of Amezqueta southward to the flank of the
Hornwork. There was a much smaller and separate gap, eighty
yards further north of that tower, at the last point where access
was possible at low tide: attention had been paid to this sector
of the wall in the idea that it was outside the retrenchment or
second line of defence—which Rey was known to have built
behind the main breach. If, therefore, ingress could be secured
here, it would be possible to get into the town without having
to force any inner obstacles. But access to the foot of this
breach was difficult—assailants would have to reach it along
a strip of wet rock only a few yards broad, at the very foot of
the ramparts.

Observers describe the great breach as not looking like a
breach at all, but a long mound of sand, concrete, and broken
masonry, 'a heap of disagreeable rubbish, particles of which
sparkled brightly in the sunbeams'[1]. The mortar having been
very good, and the stones very large, much of the wall had
slipped down in great segments, still cohering, extraordinarily
slippery, and lying at a steep angle for the climber. At some
points the mass was smoking, fire lurking below among beams
and *chevaux de frise* which had been swept away and buried by
the last day's bombardment[2]. The north flank of the breach
ended at the Tower of Amezqueta, the southern one abutted on
the high curtain above the bastion of San Juan, which had been
comparatively little damaged. It was as 'practicable' a breach
as any engineer could ask, 'seeming to the amateur easy of access,
though the veteran knew it to be a deceitful slope, re-entrenched
behind, and probably cut off from communication with the rest
of the place'[3].

There only remained the details of the storm to settle. But

[1] Cooke, ii. p. 6.
[2] Frazer, p. 231. The garrison had repeatedly tried to rear barricades
and *chevaux de frise* on the lip of the breach, but the continued bombardment had smashed and buried them.   [3] Cooke, ii. p. 6.

here a very delicate problem had to be faced. The 5th Division
had hitherto been in charge of the whole business of the siege,
with some small assistance from Bradford's Portuguese. It was
their first brigade which had delivered the unlucky assault of
July 25th, and had unjustly been accused of having shown want
of pluck in it. Every man in the division from General Oswald
commanding to the youngest drummer resented this accusation
most bitterly, and was anxious to see it refuted by some
brilliant feat of arms. At the same time Oswald, both his
brigadiers, and several of his colonels, held the view that the
division had been sent to be slaughtered on July 25th, by reason
of the unskilful scheme of attack drawn up by the engineer and
artillery staff. And what was very unwise, they had not shrunk
from repeating their opinion, when it turned out that the second
storm was to be, in its essentials, a repetition of the first. Graham
wrote to Wellington on August 22nd that there seemed to be
a general opinion among all the officers of the division that a
repetition of the attack over the tidal flats at low water would
probably fail, and that the mere fact of such views prevailing
would make it fail[1]. Wellington agreed, declaring that it was
tiresome to learn of generals and colonels prophesying a failure
in the hearing of subalterns, 'which would make success quite
unattainable by the inferior officers and men who knew of such
opinions'. He suggested, with regret, that it might be necessary
to remove the 5th Division from the trenches, and send other
troops to deliver the assault[2].

The question of divisional *esprit de corps* now cropped up.
When Graham spoke of Wellington's project to the three generals
of the 5th Division, they protested with one voice that the
removal of the division would be looked upon as a humiliation,
and would cause deep mortification and resentment. The best
spirit prevailed among the troops, and they claimed a share in
reaping the results of their long labours before San Sebastian.
They would feel no slur upon them if other corps were brought
up to join in the assault. At the same time Oswald did not
deny that he and his officers had disapproved of the engineers'
plans, and thought the service a desperate one. Graham could

[1] Graham to Wellington, August 22. *Supplementary Dispatches*, viii.
p. 204.   [2] *Dispatches*, xi. p. 33.

not wholly disagree—he confessed to Wellington that he thought that the enemy had got the breaches mined, and had prepared all sorts of inner defences. 'There is reason, therefore, to expect that there may occur some very discouraging circumstances, which may make it extremely desirable to have troops in reserve for a renewal of the attack without delay[1].'

Wellington, after some consideration, thought it well to call for volunteers from the three nearest divisions, to join in the storm 'and show the 5th Division that they have not been called upon to perform what is impracticable'[2]. On the evening of the 28th he requested the general commanding the 1st Division to ask for 200 men each from the Guards and the German brigades, while the 4th Division (much thinned at Sorauren) was to provide another 200, and the smaller Light Division 150. There was much competition both among officers and men for this honourable if risky service: in some brigades a whole battalion stepped forward when 40 men were asked to fall out. William Napier the historian, then a major, failed to command the Light Division contingent, because an officer of even higher rank, Colonel Hunt of the 52nd, refused to forgo the claim of his seniority[3]. The 750 came down to the trenches on the night of the 30th to be very coldly received. The soldiers of the 5th Division were ready to pick quarrels with them, and General Leith, who had arrived on the previous day from the rear, to supersede his *locum tenens* Oswald[4], swore that so far from 'showing the 5th Division how to mount a breach' they should act as supports, and not as forlorn hope. And this was indeed to be their lot.

General Rey, finding his artillery hopelessly overmatched from the first, and for the most part destroyed, had planned a defence depending mainly on musketry and mines. The most trying part of the work of the garrison during the last five days had been the perpetual scraping away of all debris that fell inwards from the breach: it was a costly business, for the mortar batteries

---

[1] Graham to Wellington, August 28. *Supplementary Dispatches*, viii. p. 214.   [2] *Dispatches*, vi. p. 46.

[3] See Larpent's *Diary*, pp. 248–9.

[4] Wounded severely at Salamanca, a year back, Leith had been invalided to England, and was not passed fit for active service till May. He missed Vittoria, and reached St. Sebastian only on August 29th.

were intermittently lobbing bombs, which caused many casualties, into the space between the ramparts and the new stone wall behind them. But by constant attention the sheer drop at the back of the breach had been kept intact, and there was no rubbish at its foot: even the fragments of the houses once built against the inside of the wall had been almost entirely chipped away. There was still a perpendicular descent, varying from 17 to 30 feet at various points, from the lip of the breach to the ground behind. The only accessible exits from the breach were the two short fronts at each end, where it abutted on unruined ramparts—against the Tower of Amezqueta at the north end and the high curtain at the south. Here the *terre pleine* or footway of the walls had been stockaded across by traverses of solid stuff, beams or casks of earth[1], till there was only room for one man to pass: and if the first traverse was forced there were others behind. The breach was flanked and exposed to fire from both the high curtain, which looked down upon it on the left, and from the battered but still upstanding tower which was above its right or northern end. Moreover it was enfiladed from the Hornwork's eastern side, which the British artillery had never attempted to demolish. Opposite its whole length of nearly 300 yards was the new stone inner wall, fifteen feet high, and loopholed at intervals of a yard.

Of artillery on the walls there was little surviving—all the nearer guns had been disabled—there were a few heavy pieces in the St. Elmo battery and the Castle which could be used—they were well placed for enfilading fire, but very distant. Far more useful in the end were three pieces which Rey had kept concealed to the last moment, two in the casemates of the high curtain, and one behind the Hornwork. They were only brought out when the assault began. The enemy hoped to get much more profit out of a system of mines which he had devised, and which had not escaped the notice of the British engineers, and caused them many misgivings. The idea of their effect was what Graham was thinking of when he spoke of the 'discouraging circumstances' with which the storm might begin. There was

---

[1] The traverse which was first forced was composed of a cask of earth and a disabled cannon jammed between it and the curtain wall, with a three-foot gangway only left open.

one very large mine under the ruins of the tower of Los Hornos, in the middle of the Great Breach, which contained no less than 12 cwt. of powder, and was intended to blow to pieces the head of the assaulting column, when it should have reached its goal. Two smaller ones had been laid under the sea-wall at the eastern side of the Hornwork, and there were several others under that outlying defence, which the engineers of the besieged intended to blow up if it were forced, while still holding on to the main wall behind[1].

The garrison, having suffered very perceptible losses from the five days of bombardment, could put only 2,500 men under arms on September 1st. When all the fronts liable to attack had been manned, there were only 250 bayonets left for a general reserve. Every man was kept under cover till the last moment, to avoid any more loss of life: but each knew his post and his precise duty. The soldiers of the *compagnies d'élite*, told off to hold the traverses at each end of the breach, were furnished with three muskets apiece. There was a store of bombs and live shells provided for casting down from points of vantage, such as the high curtain.

Graham had handed over the details of the assault to the discretion of Sir James Leith, though the latter had only arrived from England two days before, and had been granted little time to study the problem of his task. He was instructed in them, however, by Oswald, who in a very handsome fashion offered to stay behind and act as a volunteer aide-de-camp to his successor, whose arrival had deprived him of the chance of taking his revenge for the reverse of July 25th. Leith selected as the unit which was to lead the assault Robinson's brigade of his own division (1/4th, 2/47th, 2/59th), using as support the 750 volunteers, whose arrival had given him no pleasure, and as reserve Spry's Portuguese and Hay's brigade—the unit which had been so unlucky on July 25th. He also borrowed the 5th Caçadores from Bradford's brigade, to give him sharpshooters to be employed for

[1] Jones, and some other authorities, make out five pieces, two on the high curtain or cavalier, two in the ditch between the main wall and the Hornwork, and one on the flank of the latter. Rey in his official dispatch [Belmas, iv. p. 718] only speaks of three, and I rather fancy that the third gun in the flank of the Hornwork is what some English writers call 'the *two* guns in the ditch below the main wall'.

sniping from the trenches during the assault—a duty to which some of the volunteers were also told off, to their immense discontent. Robinson's brigade was divided into two columns, of which the first was to make for the old breach, the second for the ruined corner of the bastion of San Juan. It was hoped that this column might get on to the high curtain over the ruins of the bastion, and so be able to outflank the second line of defence which the French were known to have built behind the breach[1].

Meanwhile the small breach, beyond the Tower of Amezqueta, was to be attempted by Bradford's Portuguese, in a fashion which it was hoped might surprise the enemy, viz. by a sudden attack of troops fording the Urumea at its mouth—a thing which had been discovered to be quite possible by the nightly prowlings in the water of several officers, one of whom had even ended his wade by climbing up the face of the smaller breach without being discovered[2]. For this adventure Bradford had succeeded in getting 300 volunteers from each of his two line regiments, the 13th and 24th Line. The best ford was only three feet deep at the lowest ebb—but the channel was 200 yards broad, and the point of passage lay immediately under the undisabled guns of the enemy on Monte Urgull. This attack was to be made after the main assault had developed, and when the attention of the enemy, as it was hoped, would have been entirely drawn off to the southern breaches. Another distraction was to be provided for him, by the appearance in the bay, opposite the sea-front of the Castle rock, of a couple of cutters and a number of launches carrying some companies of the 85th Regiment. They were to simulate a purpose of disembarcation, but never to come within range, their only object being to pin down a certain number of the enemy to the protection of the lofty La Mota.

The last preparation made for the storm was that at 2 a.m. on the night of the 30th–31st, measures were taken to obviate

---

[1] Explanation of this is to be found in Graham to Wellington of the night of August 30th, *Supplementary Dispatches*, viii. p. 216.

[2] The first to discover this was Captain Macdonald, R.A. (Jones, ii. p. 67). Snodgrass of the 52nd (then serving as a major with the 13th Portuguese, see Morrison's *History of the 52nd*, p. 201) was the man who climbed the breach. A third officer is said to have gone even farther, and to have got some way up the Castle rock.

the difficulty that had been found at the assault of July 25th in getting the troops out of the trenches, and on to the tidal flats, on a sufficiently broad front, and without delay. To secure this, three mines were run out from the advanced sap, in front of the battery no. 16, under the sea-wall, which impeded egress on to the beach below. When fired they blew it down for a distance of seventy feet, leaving a broad road of exit on to the ground over which the assault would have to be delivered.

Low tide on August 31st was at noon—this fact fixed the hour for the assault at 11 a.m., since it had been determined that it must be by daylight, and not (as at Badajoz or Rodrigo) under cover of the night. It resulted from this circumstance that the storm of St. Sebastian was viewed by such a multitude of spectators as was never before collected for such an occasion. Not only officers from the newly arrived brigade at Passages, and from the convoys which had brought the ordnance, but others who had ridden over from the Bastan on a day's leave, commissaries, doctors, clerks, and quarter-masters, orderlies and servants, were sitting in serried rows on the slopes of Monte Olia, which provided convenient tiers of stony seats, mixed with hundreds of the inhabitants of Passages, Renteria, Oyarzun, and Hernani, who had come out dressed in their holiday attire to see the show[1]. Those present long remembered the curious effect of emotions sweeping over the mixed multitude, as long hours of hope and disappointment went by, and most particularly the way in which every man and woman rose and shouted for joy when the stormers finally burst into the town and the big French flag on the high curtain was seen to come down. But that was at 1.15 and the deadly panorama had begun at 10.55.

It is fortunate for the historian that, not among the mere spectators, but in the front breaching battery on the Chofres sandhills, there was an intelligent artillery officer with his watch

[1] Cooke of the 43rd, on a day's leave from Vera, records that he witnessed the storm seated between two very charming young ladies of the neighbour-hood, who were eating sugar-drops all the time, some of which they gave him. 'They kept ejaculating (while shedding a few pearly tears, and unfolding the little papers containing their sweetmeats) "poor St. Sebastian! Oh, poor St. Sebastian!" We asked them why they did not rather say "poor soldiers". To which they replied, *oh, si, si! Pobres soldados también*.' Cooke, ii. pp. 11–12.

in his hand, making notes, from minute to minute, of what he saw and of the orders which he gave—this was Lieutenant-Colonel Augustus Frazer, commanding the batteries of the right attack, whose accurately dated table of things seen and things done enables us to fix the exact sequence of events, in a fashion that exposes the curious inaccuracy of the memories of most of the gallant officers and men who took part in the actual assault. Their impressions were vivid, but their estimates of time vague, and they often invert the order of incidents in the strangest way. I adhere to Frazer's dating all through the succeeding narrative[1].

[1] For Frazer's *Minutes* taken during the assault of St. Sebastian, see pp. 236-9 of his *Letters written during the Peninsular and Waterloo Campaigns*, published in 1859.

NOTE

The Towers in the breach at St. Sebastian.

It will be noted that in my plan and my narrative, I speak of the northern tower as that of Amezqueta, and the southern as Los Hornos. Jones in his *Sieges of the Peninsula* calls them merely A and B. Napier, and most other English writers, following him, make Amezqueta (or 'Mezquitas' or 'Minguetas') the southern tower. But in reversing the nomenclature I am following the very elaborate map in the Spanish official publication by Colonel Olavide, which puts Amezqueta next the lesser breach, and Los Hornos right in the middle of the great breach. Colonel Olavide's beautiful atlas of maps and plans seems conclusive evidence. No help is to be got from Belmas, Rey's dispatches, or Frazer or Burgoyne. It may be noted that Napier (v. p. 269) calls Los Hornos the 'middle of the great breach' though his plan puts it at the northern side.

SECTION XXXIX: CHAPTER II

THE STORM OF ST. SEBASTIAN. AUGUST 31, 1813

THE morning of August 31st was one of dull heat and sweltering haze: it was impossible to see a hundred yards ahead. Only at 8 a.m. did the haze clear off, showing a lowering sky, that obviously portended a thunderstorm before dark. The moment that the fortress became visible all the batteries opened upon it, and kept up a continuous fire till 10.55 when—about an hour before full ebb tide—the assault began. As the garrison stayed very close under cover, it did not suffer many casualties, and the breach was already so much knocked about that little further damage seems to have been done. But one thing of importance the bombardment did effect—it broke or cut the *saucisson* of the great mine under the tower of Los Hornos, which was lying in wait for the first rush of the stormers. A chance ball or a falling stone severed the train, and it was never fired—or some hundreds more of casualties would have had to be recorded in Robinson's brigade.

At 10.55 the first stormers bounded out of the trenches—Lieutenant Maguire of the 1/4th with twenty men of his own regiment forming the 'forlorn hope'. This young officer was clearly visible to all the spectators beyond the Urumea—he outran his men by several yards[1], waving a large old-fashioned cocked hat with a plume, which he had picked out instead of the shako of 1813 to make himself easily recognizable. He reached the foot of the central breach, and had climbed one step up it before he was shot dead. Three seconds later the forlorn hope and the head of its supports went up over his prostrate body. There was at this moment a tremendous explosion a little further back—the French mine under the sea-wall opposite the north end of the Hornwork had been fired—its existence had been known by the British engineers, and a devoted party of a sergeant and twelve men had been told off to find and cut its *saucisson*.[2] All perished—but few others of the stormers, for they had been

---

[1] Cooke, ii. p. 9.　　　　[2] Jones, ii. p. 74.

directed to keep away from the sea-wall and well out on the tidal flats.

When the forlorn hope first appeared, the French started out of the shelters where they had been lurking for the last three hours, and ran to occupy their appointed posts—observers across the water saw the previously empty defences suddenly black with men. The two guns in the casemates of the high curtain were run out, and began to open with canister in less than two minutes. Long-distance fire from the Castle, the Mirador, and one surviving gun in the St. Elmo battery also began—it was not rapid, though very accurate. But the enemy's musketry was his real defence; it came fast and furious from both flanks, and when the head of Robinson's brigade reached the crest of the breach, the troops manning the counterwall behind opened out with a sounding volley from their loopholes.

The breach was singularly hard to climb—there was no soft rubble, but only big blocks of stone and concrete on its face. The assaulting columns were seen to reach its lip in several places by painful clambering, and then to stop. There was a sheer drop of twenty feet or more in front of them[1], facing the retrenchment from which the French musketry was playing. The front ranks halted, and were immediately shot down: officer after officer brought up a fresh party, was checked at the sight of the gap in front, and fell with his men. One reckless leader jumped down and broke his neck, though untouched by any bullet. For half an hour unceasing attempts were made by successive waves of stormers to no effect. At 11.35 the observer in the Chofres battery no. 3 wrote down in his note-book, 'Much firing—the troops do not advance—though the bugles keep sounding the advance'. The survivors had realized by this time that the only spots at which they could possibly get forward were the two places where the breach-ends abutted on the intact part of the ramparts—under the High Curtain at the south, under the Tower of Amezqueta at the north. Each of these was blocked by traverses, one behind the other: not more than three or four men abreast could get at them. All who tried to do so were shot down. Charges at the High Curtain traverse were

---

[1] An intelligent officer a few days later tried its height with an 18-foot scaling ladder, from inside, and found that it did not reach the top.

particularly deadly, for one of the guns above had been trained on the approach, and fired canister into each party that surged up: and there was soon a second gun at the back of the Hornwork playing diagonally on the same narrow point of access.

Meanwhile reinforcements continued to arrive—General Leith, with his predecessor Oswald at his elbow, stood on the beach outside the sea-wall, opposite the advanced trench, directing from time to time the sending out of new reserve companies from the approaches. For a short time Sir Richard Fletcher, the commanding engineer, stood with them, but he was shot through the neck early in the day, and killed on the spot. Some time later Oswald was hit in the face and taken to the rear. Leith, though once knocked down and stunned by a stone, which had been sent flying by a round shot from the Mirador, kept his place for two hours, feeding the assault first with the rear companies of Robinson's brigade, then with the 'Volunteers', till he too was finally disabled by the splinter of a shell which broke his arm in two places[1]. The observer on the Chofres wrote down 'More reinforcements from the trenches. This duty is being well performed—whoever may direct it[2].'

At 11.35, the firing at the main breaches being at its hottest, the minor attack by Bradford's Portuguese brigade upon the lesser breach was set going, in the hope that the attention of the enemy was by now distracted from this secondary point of danger. It was delivered by two small columns, the first composed of 300 volunteers from the 13th Line, led by their Major Snodgrass, the discoverer of the ford, the second of six companies of the 24th Line under Major MacBean. They had 900 yards to go, the first 700 across the rocks and pools of the tidal flats, the last 200 through the shallow water of the estuary of the Urumea, about three feet deep. 'They took it nobly at the double quick'[3], covering the whole distance in ten minutes, so rapidly that the enemy's guns on the Castle and in the St. Elmo battery could be turned on them only in time to get in two salvoes during their

---

[1] Frazer, p. 257. Cf. Leith Hay [Leith's nephew and aide-de-camp], ii. p. 247.

[2] He was carried off just as the right wing of the 1/9th, the last of all his regiments, went into action.

[3] Frazer's *Minutes*, p. 236.

passage—these, however, were sufficiently deadly—one dis-
charge into Snodgrass's column knocked over fourteen men. By
11.45 all the Portuguese were across the shallow water—the
13th Line went straight for the lesser breach, the greater part
of the 24th Line got drawn into the attack under the Tower of
Amezqueta, joining in with the right of Robinson's brigade.
Snodgrass's people failed to carry the lesser breach at their first
rush, but established themselves upon it, and found (as had
been calculated) that it outflanked the French second-line wall,
and looked straight into the town; but it was traversed, and
held against them for some time.

This was a useful distraction, especially in drawing off the
fire from the upper French guns—and it was a most gallant
advance—900 yards across absolutely open ground—the last
quarter of it with the men thigh-deep in the water. But it had
failed to carry the lesser breach by its first impact, and meanwhile matters at the Great Breach looked desperate. The surviving men of Robinson's brigade and the Volunteers had been
forced to throw themselves down among the stones of the
breach-slope—where they were safe from the fire from within,
but not from that of the men in the traverses on their flanks,
and in the east flank of the Hornwork, which enfiladed the whole
left side of the breach. A party of sappers had been attached
to the column, with orders to throw up a lodgement under the
face of the breach. But they found this impossible, since they
had no earth or small stones to build with, but only vast blocks
of stone or broken concrete. And—it may be asked—what would
have been the use of a lodgement, when in three hours the tide
would have been full again, the water cutting off the breaches
for many hours from any access from the British trenches?

It was at this moment that Graham issued the surprising and
abnormal order which had much to do with the success of the
storm. Seeing the assailants beaten back from the crest, and
taking cover below it, he ordered all the guns in the Chofres
batteries, which had hitherto been confining their attention to
the French guns on the Castle Hill, to open on the High Curtain,
over the heads of his own men. The range was known from long
practice, and as the stormers had recoiled some way from the
crest, it is said that hardly a man was killed that day by British

fire[1]. This battering of the High Curtain continued for about
twenty minutes, apparently from about 12.15 to 12.35: it was
most effective, because the whole angle of the defence on which
the fire was concentrated was now packed with Frenchmen, and
the slaughter among them was terrible. Those who visited the
curtain next day report that they saw long lines of dead under
the parapet, whose heads had been taken off as they fired over it,
and the artillerymen of the two guns all lying mangled beside
their pieces. At 12.35 the siege-batteries turned off their fire
to the more distant defences, and the assaulting troops gathered
themselves together for another rush, and this time succeeded
in passing the first two or three traverses, which had been
damaged by the recent battering, and got a footing on the east
end of the High Curtain. The French still held stubbornly on
to the central bastion and the part of the curtain immediately
adjoining it. But the defence was slackening: at 12.40 Frazer
marked down in his invaluable *Minutes* 'They are getting down
from the old breach into the town. It will do! They wave their
hats from the *terre pleine* of the curtain.' At 12.45 it is 'The
Hornwork apparently deserted. Our men are now firing from
the right of the right round tower [Amezqueta]; this bounds our
ground to the right.' At 12.55 we read 'enemy still holds the
end of the curtain next the Cavalier'. But at 1 p.m. 'More
reinforcements from the trenches. Our men are entering the
town—principally by the end of the old breach next the round
tower [Amezqueta].'

The interpretation of these hasty and rather cryptic notes is
that three separate successes were being scored between 12.40
and 1 o'clock. When the British got possession of the east end
of the high curtain, they were dominating the French garrison
of the Hornwork below them, who saw that their line of retreat
might be cut off ere long, and therefore flinched, running off for
escape to the postern gate by which alone they could take refuge
behind the main wall. At the same time, by their capture of
many yards of the High Curtain, the stormers had got behind the
end of the French retrenchment, the second wall which cut off
the breaches. They began to drop down into the town behind it,

[1] Napier says a sergeant of the 1/9th [v. p. 282], but it would seem that
this battalion had not gone up the breach so early as 12.15–12.35.

and to enfilade its defenders. But simultaneously, three hundred
yards away to the north, a separate entry was being made: the
Light Division 'volunteers' had found, adjoining the Amezqueta
tower, a ruined house built against the back of the ramparts,
which had not been so carefully chipped away and demolished
as the rest. By risky jumps and glissades down its broken stairs
they began to pour into the street below.

At about this time—apparently one o'clock—there occurred
the accident which Rey and Graham in their reports to their
respective chiefs name as the cause of the final collapse of the
French defence. By some chance the store of bombs and musket
cartridges, which was serving the French who were still holding
the traverse below the 'cavalier', or central bastion in the High
Curtain, got on fire and blew up, scorching or killing some sixty
of the men of the *compagnies d'élite* who had made such a gallant
defence in this quarter. Both of the generals say that the explosion was caused by a British shell, but there is good evidence
that it was not—the fire on the high curtain having ceased some
twenty-five minutes before the catastrophe took place[1]. This
explosion happened just as a new reinforcement was being put
in by Sir James Leith. Having already sent up all the Volunteers,

---

[1] I agree with Napier, v. p. 282, in thinking that we must reject Rey's
and Graham's theory that a shell did the mischief. There is clear evidence
against it (as Napier says) in the narrative of Cooke of the 43rd, who
looking on, 'an undisturbed spectator', from the slopes of Monte Olia,
particularly noted that the affair took place half an hour after the cannonade
had been turned off, and must have been due to 'sparks or burning cartridge
paper' [Cooke, ii. p. 26]. A narrative by an officer of the 3/1st who was
'in at the death' says oddly enough that the French fired a mine prema-
turely, in order to blow up the head of his regiment, 'instead of which it
considerably facilitated the attack'. This is first-hand evidence that the
explosion was not caused by a British shell. Jones, the most careful official
chronicler of the siege, specially avoids [ii. p. 79] asserting that the bombardment set the combustibles aflame, saying that '20 minutes after it
began the live shells, hand grenades, &c., of the garrison *caught fire*'.
Frazer, whose *Minutes* ought to settle the matter, has by some odd chance
omitted the explosion altogether, though so full on all other points. At
1 o'clock his attention was being engrossed by affairs at the lesser breach,
to which he devotes himself for ten minutes. At 1.15 he notes that the
enemy 'still holds the curtain next the cavalier, but must be forced from
it'. Burgoyne, i. p. 280, says that 'by accident or mismanagement a
quantity of powder, &c., was exploded by the enemy'. And this is, I think,
the true story.

and Spry's Portuguese, he was now playing his last card—Hay's brigade, his final reserve. The 3/1st, the leading regiment of this unit, had just reached the high curtain when the crash was heard, and covered by the smoke its leading files ran in upon the traverses and carried them one after the other. Even then the enemy, grenadiers and *Chasseurs des Montagnes*, put in a last desperate resistance on the cavalier: once they bore back the head of the Royal Scots to the last traverse, and the high step from the curtain on to the *terre pleine* of the cavalier was defended for a few minutes. But numbers prevailed, when desperate courage was equal, and the French were finally bayoneted down the broad flight of steps which leads from the back of the bastion down into the town, which their pursuers entered with them. The eviction of the garrison from the cavalier, and their evacuation of the Hornwork, would have settled the whole affair in any case. But even if they had held on longer there, the game was already up, for some of the British had by now pushed along the rampart from the tower of Amezqueta northward, towards the little breach. Driving out the French who were manning the traverses which were keeping Snodgrass's Portuguese back, they liberated his column from the long detention which it had suffered. It burst into the town at once, followed by many stray men of the 5th Division from the right corner of the great breach[1]. And further south a considerable number of the Light Division stormers had now got down through the ruined house, and were beginning to work along the streets.

At 1.20 Frazer, from his observation post on the Chofres, begins to note 'very heavy fire inside the town'. At 1.35 we have 'many prisoners are being brought out of the town into the trenches'. At 1.45 it is 'Heavy musketry fire in the town, our

---

[1] Frazer notes on this '1 p.m. One man of the Guards runs alone to the part of the parapet on the right of the right tower [Amezqueta]: a sergeant and a few Portuguese at the right breach of all. [The lesser breach.] The enemy lines the stockade. The enemy runs from the rampart behind that stockade: all goes well! 1.10. Two of our shots go through that stockade, the enemy abandons it. One brave French officer and two men alone remain: now they are gone.'

Cooke of the 43rd evidently noticed the same men as Frazer, as he writes 'At last I saw several soldiers quitting the large breach, and running to the right, to assist the Portuguese at the small one', ii. p. 13.

bugles sound the advance in all parts of it'. At 1.50 'with judgement the town is securely ours, our men are pulling prisoners
out by the breach'. At 2 'town seems on fire near the right
breach': at 2.15 'Musketry fire from the Mirador: firing in town
continues, but is decreasing. Our guns in the batteries cease
firing by order.'

Rey's intended defence of the town by means of the system of
internal barricades had been a complete failure. It was not that
the barricades were not strong, but so many of the garrison had
by now been destroyed, that there were not nearly enough men
to hold all points of this elaborate system of defence. When
checked at one street corner, the stormers sought about for
a side street, whence the barricades could be turned, or broke
into houses and fired down from above into the small parties
which were trying to hold on. It took no more than an hour to
evict the French from the streets, the time between 1.20 when
Frazer first began to note heavy musketry fire inside the town,
and 2.15 when the enemy was having to defend the Mirador,
i.e. the walls on the lower part of the Castle Rock, and the convent
of Sta Teresa above the harbour, by infantry fire. Many of the
French were cut off and captured in corners which they tried to
defend too long—Wellington reported 750 prisoners, of whom
some 350 were wounded. Rey escaped to the Castle with perhaps
1,000 men to join the small garrison left there, and manned the
old walls which cut it off from the town; he also held on to the
convent of Sta Teresa and some houses in its neighbourhood,
on the lower slopes at the western end of Monte Urgull. It was
generally held in the allied army that the Castle might have been
carried in the final rush that cleared the town, if only there had
been fresh troops to put in, and any guiding mind to direct the
assault. But at 1.30 the last unit left in the trenches, the left
wing of the 1/9th, had been sent up to assist in clearing the town.
And, as to direction, Leith had been disabled during the last
minutes of the storm, Oswald was wounded also, so was Robinson
who commanded the brigade that had led the assault. Hay was
the only general officer surviving, and he found it impossible
to organize any attack.

The troops were all mixed up—the town was on fire in more
than one place, owing to the bombardment—and about two

o'clock the storm that had been threatening since the morning burst. There came first a whirlwind which caught up the sand and sent it flying in dense clouds, then thunder, and drenching rain, which lasted all the afternoon and night—the same deluge that was to have no small effect on events that were taking place a few miles away on the banks of the Bidassoa. A certain number of the good soldiers followed their officers up to the lines held by the French on Monte Urgull, and engaged in a bickering fire with their defenders. The majority, it must be confessed, appear to have turned to that which armies of those days, whatever their nationality, considered the stormer's perquisite. 'Having succeeded,' writes a disgusted officer, 'the troops were, of course, admitted to the immemorial privilege of tearing the town to pieces. It was already on fire in many places, and a dreadful scene of devastation ensued, additionally to be deplored because the unfortunate inhabitants were the friends and allies of the lawless soldiery who now revelled in any species of excess[1].'

In a previous volume something has already been said about the psychology of the men who have just gone through a specially bloody and exhausting storm[2]. The circumstances at St. Sebastian were in a way even more distressing than those at Badajoz, for at the latter there was no street fighting, and the town was not on fire. Even without the conflagration, the lot of the citizens would have been sufficiently dreadful—they had been cowering in their cellars for some days to escape the bombardment, many houses were already destroyed, and others had been broken into by both sides during the hour of struggle, while the French were being evicted from their barricades. The sufferings of the civil population must have been very great even if no subsequent disorder had taken place. Unfortunately all the scenes of Badajoz were here repeated, with the additional horror of a storm-wind urging the flames from street to street. An eloquent passage in Napier[3] and an often-quoted manifesto by the local Junta have spread a general idea that the atrocities at St. Sebastian were the worst known during the whole war. I am inclined to doubt this—at any rate the impression made by the detestable scenes which they witnessed on officers of

---

[1] Leith Hay, ii. p. 257. [2] See above, vol. v. pp. 257–60.
[3] Napier, v. pp. 277–8.

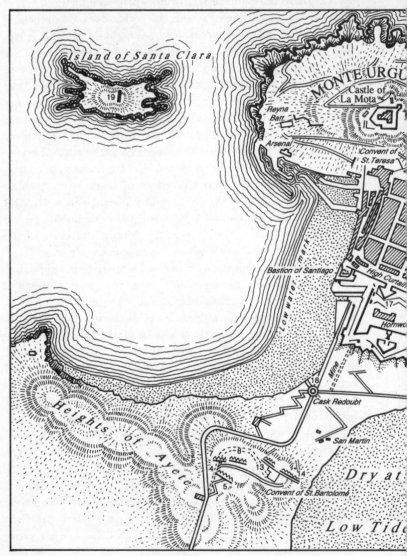

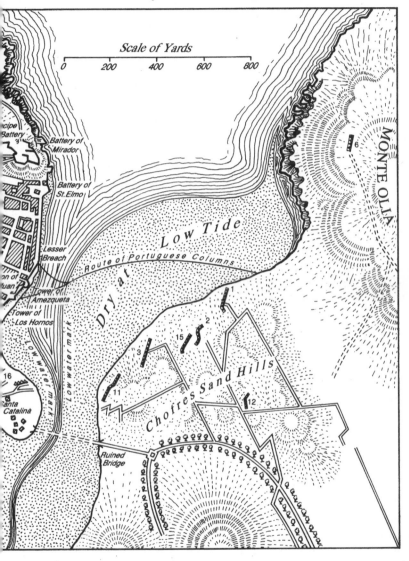

Scale of Yards

0   200   400   600   800

MONTE OLIA

Príncipe Battery

Battery of Mirador

Battery of St. Elmo

Low Tide

Route of Portuguese Columns

Lesser Breach

Dry at Low Tide

Tower of Amezqueta

Tower of Los Hornos

Low water mark

16

Santa Catalina

Chofres Sand Hills

Ruined Bridge

experience and strong moral rectitude does not seem to have been so distressing as in the Estremaduran disgrace of 1812. Gomm, a very distinguished 5th Division officer, who had been at both the storms, wrote four days after in his diary: 'The day closed, as it always has done since the first town was taken, in riot and tumult: and although many of the excesses committed at Badajoz were avoided here, St. Sebastian is a more melancholy story than either Badajoz or Rodrigo. For, with the exception of ten or twelve fortunate buildings, there is nothing left of St. Sebastian but the blackened walls of its houses, and these are falling every instant with a tremendous crash. How the fire was started is uncertain—I think there is little doubt of its having been done intentionally by the enemy. In a town so constructed as this, there was little chance of its being got under when kindled—particularly by our soldiers, who were busy about anything else. Imagine what the scenes were that passed under our eyes during the last four days. We have been driven almost to the ramparts by the fire, while the people rushed in crowds where certain destruction seemed to threaten them, in search of their property, great part of which they had concealed and buried. Much certainly has been saved: we have done what was in our power to assist them: a great deal however has been plundered, and a vast proportion must lie buried under the ruins. Never surely was there a more complete picture of desolation than the place presents. I do not know that it is not more distressing in its present quiet than when the fire was raging at its height, and every effort was being made not only by the people to save their property, but by all ranks and conditions to save the hundreds of wounded, French and English, from the flames, which every instant gained ground[1].'

Despite of this evidence by a very sensitive and high-minded officer, I think there can be no doubt that there was much drunkenness, much plunder of houses not yet reached by the fire, and some isolated cases of rape. Wellington mentions, with indignation, that a Portuguese officer was killed by looters whom he tried to drive off[2]. Of the wholesale murder and debauchery which the Junta's manifesto alleges, and at which Napier hints, I have found no trace in any eyewitness's

---

[1] Gomm, pp. 319–20.   [2] *Dispatches*, xi. p. 166.

record. An officer of the 47th—one of the five out of twenty-two of that much-tried corps who were neither killed nor hurt—describes disgusting scenes—drunken soldiers lying incapable between corpses, plundering parties breaking into churches as well as private houses, the soldiers' wives sitting in circles dividing the watches and silver which their men brought them, Portuguese soldiers robbing drunken English and Irish of their loot—but saw nothing of murder, though a friend told him one dreadful tale of a rape which he had been unable to prevent[1]. In fact the more horrible stories come from authors like Napier and Gleig who were not at St. Sebastian on August 31st or September 1st, and who possessed strong descriptive talent, or else from the rhetorical and most unconvincing tirades of Spanish politicians. What the eyewitnesses relate is bad enough, but much less lurid stuff[2].

It may be worth while to give the official reply of General Hay, the responsible officer in command, to Wellington, when the latter asked him to specify the extent of the disorders which were beginning to provoke such acrid comment, not only in Spain but in London. Hay said that when he entered the place street-fighting was still going on in the upper end of the town, that he found it on fire in several places, and that his first efforts had to be directed to saving the powder magazine and the hospital from the flames. The wind being very high and gusty, no appliances to fight fire being available, and the men employed on roofs being fired on by the French from the Castle defences, all efforts to fight the fire were useless. A certain amount of plunder he does not deny—there were so few officers left that there was hardly any one available to keep an eye on the stragglers. This is certainly true—as the casualty lists show, 106 officers had fallen in the 5th Division alone out of about 200 who were present at the storm—in the 47th there were only five surviving, in the 59th only four. The survivors did what they could—but the regiments were so completely dispersed that no

[1] Captain Harley's *The Veteran, or Forty Years in the British Service*, ii. pp. 83–7.

[2] I think that the worst indictment that can be made against the management of affairs at St. Sebastian is that the storming troops were not got out of the town next morning, and replaced by Lord Aylmer's Brigade—as Wellington suggested to Graham.

one could find his own men, and those of other corps ignored discipline. On the whole he thought that there had been less disorder than might have been expected—there were exceptions, but on the whole the men had been fairly well behaved. Any one detected with plunder had been seized and flogged at once[1]. He enclosed a certificate from the Provost Marshal of the 5th Division that he had arrested and flogged about thirty men on the 1st and as many on the 2nd of September, and that he had not had a single instance of personal violence to a civilian brought to his notice, though many of pillaging. He had cleared marauders out of several houses, but had never seen any of them setting fire to anything—which indeed would have been against their own interest[2]. Hay also enclosed letters from the officers left in command of the 3/1st, 9th, 38th, and 59th regiments to the effect that they and their juniors had done their best to stop looting, and absolutely scouted the silly allegation that the town had been deliberately set on fire by the stormers[3]. 'As to plundering having been *permitted*', wrote the Major commanding the 59th, 'I can assure you that every exertion was made by me and the officers to prevent anything of the kind, and that I sent frequent patrols, by your order, to arrest any man found in the town, and to afford assistance to any inhabitant who might ask for it[4].'

It must be confessed that this packet of six or seven statements by responsible persons, who do not deny that a certain amount of disorder took place, weighs much more heavily than the rhetoric of Napier about atrocities or the picturesque paragraphs of Gleig [both many miles away on September 1]. And nothing can be more absurd than the Spanish manifestoes, which take as their thesis the ludicrous notion that St. Sebastian was deliberately destroyed by the order or connivance of Wellington, for reasons of commercial jealousy! The civil prefect [Jefe Politico] of Guipuzcoa[5] charged General Graham with deliberate intention to burn the town, because its former trade had been exclusively with France and to the disadvantage of Great

---

[1] Hay to Wellington, October 18, *Supplementary Dispatches*, viii. pp. 309–10.   [2] Ibid., p. 314.
[3] Ibid., pp. 312–13.   [4] Major Hoysted to Hay, ibid., p. 314.
[5] A certain Conde de Villa Fuentes.

Britain. Wellington, when this document came before him,
remarked that he had discouraged Dickson's schemes for
'general annoyance' and bombardment at large—as was perfectly true[1]—and that if he had ever harboured so infamous a
wish as to destroy a town from motives of commercial revenge,
a long and continuous bombardment, which he had prohibited,
would have been the way to carry it out[2]. The soldiers had done
some plundering: 'I am concerned to say that I never saw or
heard of a town so taken, by troops of any nation, that was not
plundered.' As to personal injury to inhabitants, if any really
occurred, it was probably during the street-fighting, when French
and English balls were flying about in all directions. As to the
variations made on the theme of the Jefe Politico by the Spanish
newspapers and the Junta of St. Sebastian, it is sufficient to say
that their violent rhetoric and their vague declamation serve to
prove that the whole is largely political propaganda by the
Liberal party against the British alliance. The writers did well
to be angry; they had good cause to be disgusted at such
behaviour by the troops of an allied nation; but they spoiled
their case by trying to insinuate that the destruction of St.
Sebastian was deliberate and malicious—when it was clear from
the evidence that it was mainly the result of the conflagration,
which had come to pass in the ordinary course of military operations. Graham, writing to Wellington on ultimate responsibilities, was probably putting the brutal truth correctly, when he
observed that he was under the impression that if Dover
happened to be in French hands, and to be retaken by a British
force with storm and conflagration, he did not think that shops
or cellars would be much respected[3].

Before passing on from this unpleasant topic to the battle on
the Bidassoa, which ended Wellington's last campaign in Spain,
or detailing the final surrender of General Rey, it may be well
to note the terrible losses of the 5th Division in the storm of
August 31st—losses which can only be compared to those of
Albuera in all the Peninsular record, and which serve in some
degree to explain the wild doings of the distraught survivors.

[1] See above, p. 13.   [2] *Dispatches*, xi. p. 171.
[3] Graham to Wellington, October 9, *Supplementary Dispatches*, viii.
p. 301.

Robinson's brigade had gone in about 1,500 strong, and had lost in the two awful hours which it spent on the breach-slope 20 officers and 312 men killed and 28 officers and 502 men wounded, a loss of 57 per cent. for the whole, but of something like 72 per cent. among the officers. Hay's brigade, the last unit put in, and the one whose leading battalion made the final thrust which broke the French defence, brought about 1,400 men to the breaches, of whom it lost 9 officers and 125 men killed and 22 officers and 330 men wounded—or a general total of about 35 per cent. Spry's Portuguese, who went in after Robinson's brigade but before Hay's, lost nearly 400 out of the 1,600 men present. The utterly abnormal thing in these appalling figures is the disproportion of killed to wounded, 664 to 1,047, instead of the normal one to six. This came from the fact that the majority of the losses were from artillery fire at close range—it was the grape and canister from the three guns firing into the mass, at a range of only 50 or 100 yards, which did the mischief, not the musketry. If the defence had relied on that alone, the proportion of dead would have been nothing like so large. But all the successive bands which tried to break into the traverses were swept down by grape fired point-blank—hence the excessive mortality.

Among the 'Volunteers' and Bradford's Portuguese the losses were in comparison moderate—no unit save that from the Guards brigade (which lost 112 men out of 200) had anything like the dreadful proportion of casualties which fell to the 5th Division troops. The whole list seems to have amounted to about 520 casualties among 1,700 volunteers—but the proportion of dead to wounded was again portentous, about 200 to 320—showing once more that the grape killed where musketry would only have wounded.

SECTION XXXIX: CHAPTER III

THE BATTLE OF SAN MARCIAL: SURRENDER OF THE CASTLE OF ST. SEBASTIAN. AUGUST 31–SEPTEMBER 9, 1813.

EVEN before the 'forlorn hope' had issued from the British trenches in front of St. Sebastian, the thunder of many guns had begun along the lower Bidassoa. It was inaudible to the troops engaged in the storm, because the preliminary bombardment of the fortress by their own siege artillery drowned all other sounds. But to listeners at Oyarzun or Passages it was doubtful whether the cannonade to the east or the west was the heavier. There was a general action of the first class going on at San Marcial and on the Heights of Salain, at the precise moment when the 5th Division hurled itself at the great breach. And, while the strife was at its height, Graham was disturbed by receiving a message from Wellington asking whether it would be possible to spare Bradford's Portuguese, who were at that moment starting out to ford the shallows of the Urumea, for the purpose of reinforcing the Spanish lines on the Bidassoa[1]. Seldom can a general have been so distracted as the British commander-in-chief, who, standing on the heights that overlooked the French frontier, was directing the episodes of a battle, and at the same time receiving from half-hour to half-hour hurried reports of the progress of the storm of St. Sebastian—reports by no means of a pleasant kind. All through the hours of noon the mental stress must have been acute: but on either side the afternoon brought a turn of the tide; and the stormy evening witnessed not only one but two French disasters.

Soult, as Wellington had foreseen, considered himself in honour bound to make one more effort for the relief of St. Sebastian. He was in touch, day by day, with the stubborn

---

[1] Frazer's *Letters from the Peninsula*, p. 237. The messenger swam the Urumea in order to get more quickly to Graham. The Portuguese entered the ford at 11.45—the messenger had passed Frazer at 11.15, but evidently did not get to Graham early enough to allow of the latter countermanding the attack of Bradford's brigade.

governor, who sent him constant appeals for help by means of the blockade-running *trincadours*, which slipped in and out despite of Sir George Collier's squadron. He was aware that since the second bombardment began on August 25th the place was in peril every hour. The Emperor had signified his interest in the garrison, and his appreciation of its obstinate defence. Had not Rey's report of the repulse of the British attack on July 25th received a place of honour in the *Moniteur*?

Earlier in the month of August it would have been impossible to do anything to help Rey; the army had trailed back into Sare and Ainhoue and Espelette low in numbers and low in morale. But Wellington—most inexplicably as Soult thought—had chosen not to follow up his victory, but to grant his adversary four precious weeks of repose. Soult had recovered no less than 8,000 stragglers, who had not been with their eagles on August 2nd. Many battalions which had shown 100 rank and file on that day were now up to 400 and 500 bayonets. Some drafts had been taken in from the conscript reserve at Bayonne: promotion* of deserving sergeants had done something to fill up the dreadful gaps in the commissioned ranks. The two divisions which had been most cut up at Sorauren, those of Maucune and Vandermaesen, had shed their most depleted units, and had been made up afresh by intact regiments from Villatte's reserve[1]. The gross total of the army was, no doubt, 15,000 short of what it had been on July 25th, owing to the losses in the Pyrenees, but the nine active divisions had been brought up again to 45,000 men, and there was still some good fighting stuff left in Villatte's reserve— such as the veteran German brigade and the King's French Guards. The depleted regiments went back to do garrison duty in Bayonne, till they could be recruited up to a respectable strength.

Soult was quite aware that the thing that was wrong with the army was not so much insufficient numbers as the sensation of

[1] Maucune's division sent to the rear the skeletons of the 66th, 82nd, 86th Line and 34th Léger, while the 15th Line was cut down from two battalions to one. In compensation it received the 10th Léger, 102nd, and 105th (each two battalions strong), and the one battalion of the 3rd Line. Vandermaesen's division shed the 1st Line and the 25th Léger, and received the 34th and the 40th Line, and the 4th Léger. Both divisions, as reconstructed, were somewhat stronger numerically than on July 25th.

recent defeat. The impression of Sorauren was still very deeply rooted—wherefore in his new stroke he used as far as possible the divisions which had not seen the worst of the Pyrenean fighting. There was nothing alluring in the prospect of making another stroke at Wellington, but he was aware that the Emperor would take the fall of St. Sebastian very badly, while the Minister of War kept repeating to him that the place must not be abandoned, that the integrity of the soil of France must be preserved at all costs, but that he must depend on his own resources and not expect reinforcements. This was a disappointing reply to an appeal which the Marshal had made early in the month, asking that the effective infantry of the Army of Spain should be brought up to 100,000 bayonets!

After making allowance for flank-guards, and for the garrison of Bayonne, Soult considered that he would not be able to use more than 45,000 men. He knew that he must deliver his blow on a short front and in a rapid fashion. The lower Bidassoa was the only practicable line on which he could operate—a fact that Wellington knew quite as well as he did. There was neither time nor numbers available for a complicated turning manœuvre, such as that which had led to the battles of the Pyrenees. St. Sebastian was only a day's march from the Bidassoa; the allied army was once more strung out from the sea as far as Roncesvalles, and therefore the one obvious policy was to deliver a fierce blow which should settle matters in twenty-four hours, before Wellington could call up his more distant divisions, from the back of the Bastan or the passes beyond Pampeluna. The Marshal took every possible means of discovering the situation of each British division, and expressed pleasure at seeing that the line from Vera to the Bay of Biscay was still held only by the Army of Galicia and Longa's Cantabrians. This was the actual front that would be attacked. On the other hand there was an uncomfortable fact to be faced when it was realized that from Vera to the Maya Pass, in a position beyond the Bidassoa and flanking the fords over which the attack would be delivered, the British were in considerable force, the Light and 6th and 7th Divisions in first line from the Heights of Santa Barbara to the Col de Maya, while other troops (the 3rd and 4th Divisions) were suspected to be behind them.

A very large proportion of the French Army would have to be detailed as a flank-guard, to protect the units that were to make the attack from being assailed from their left, when they should have committed themselves to an advance.

Soult had begun to gather in his fighting force on the 27th, bringing up even the most outlying of his divisions, that of Foy, from St.-Jean-Pied-du-Port, so that the whole nine were concentrated between Espelette and St. Jean de Luz. The south bank of the Bidassoa is not an inviting objective—a great part of it is composed of rugged slopes coming down precipitously to the water from the spurs of the great 'Mountain of the Four Crowns', the Peña de la Aya, which overlooks the narrow valley from the Spanish side, just as the less lofty but equally picturesque Grande Rhune does from the French. The more accessible sections of the south bank are two, the one nearer the sea by Fuenterabia and Irun, and the burnt bridge of Béhobie, where the high road from France to Spain takes the easiest line of passage. Here there is a comparatively low-lying gap, between the Jaizquibel—the long narrow mountain by the sea, 2,000 feet high—and the wide spreading shoulders of the Peña de la Aya, whose four parallel crests rise to the greater height of 3,200 feet. About Irun there is a small plain extending for a mile or so on either hand; behind it the road climbs a low *col*, half hidden by the steeps on either side, and goes on to Oyarzun and Hernani. This is the front door of Spain, not one of hospitable aspect—the entry that has been fought over in a score of campaigns of all ages. It was the obvious place for Soult's frontal attack, for, though the bridge of Béhobie had been destroyed two months back, there were four or five fords perfectly practicable at low water not far from its charred pillars. The road after passing the bridge turns to its right, and runs for nearly a mile parallel with the river bank, before turning up inland towards the *col*. Overhanging its course to east and south there is a bold under-feature of the Peña de la Aya range, separated from it by a well-marked dip, called the Hill of San Marcial. It is 600 feet high or a little more, has a prominent hermitage chapel at its western and highest point, is moderately steep (but nothing compared to Bussaco or Sorauren), and about two miles long. As this height commands the route into Spain for a good mile, where the high road runs between its foot and the river, it is the obvious position for any force to take up, which has to stop an advance into Biscay by an enemy who wishes to cross at the bridge of Béhobie or the fords around it. It had been occupied for that purpose in the last Spanish-French war, that of 1793–5, when its storming in August 1794 by the Jacobin general Fregeville had formed part of a combined operation for the forcing of the line of the Bidassoa, exactly similar to that which Soult was now about to undertake in August 1813. Indeed it is practically certain that the Marshal modelled his attack on that which the old Republican army made nearly twenty years before.[1] For the frontal attack on San Marcial, across the fords, in 1794 had been accompanied by a strong turning movement higher up the Bidassoa, directed by General Moncey—the same who was destined to become one of Napoleon's marshals, and to conduct a second and less happy Spanish campaign in 1808. Moncey in the old war had crossed the Bidassoa at Vera, had circumvented the great *massif* of the Peña de la Aya by the mountain road which turns its right flank by Lesaca, and had appeared in the rear of the Spanish defenders of San Marcial, while they were being assailed by Fregeville in front, causing their disastrous rout.

This was now precisely the manœuvre that Soult had sketched out. Three divisions under Reille were to cross the Bidassoa by the fords in front of Irun and Béhobie, and to deliver the frontal attack on San Marcial; while four, led by Clausel, were to cross up-stream, below Vera, to break the allied line, and to turn westward across the rear of the Peña de la Aya so as to come down on the high road at Oyarzun, in the rear of San Marcial. If this could be done, the force holding the heights above Irun would have to fly in haste, or it would be surrounded and captured. But the line of attack marked out for Clausel would be passing diagonally in front of the allied divisions known to be holding the heights of Santa Barbara, the Ivantelly peak, and the rest of the positions as far as the Pass of Maya. These might

[1] For the operations of 'Thermidor Year III', see the *Mémoires sur la dernière guerre entre la France et l'Espagne*—interesting for old fights on places more familiar to us by events of 1813—such as the Alduides, Roncesvalles, and the fords of Béhobie.

descend on the flank and rear of the turning column; wherefore it was necessary to give it a strong protective flank-guard, to hold back any such movement on Wellington's part. For this purpose D'Erlon was told off, with two divisions [Abbé's and Conroux's] placed at Sare, Ainhoue, Urdax, and Espelette.

It cannot be said that the prospect was a very cheerful one for Soult. Though a lodgement might be made on San Marcial, it would be of no great use, unless the turning column under Clausel played its part with complete success. For, if beaten off the heights of San Marcial, the Army of Galicia had two more positions behind it, both eminently defensible, and both strengthened with field works during the last month, as Wellington had advised. Of course they would neither of them serve, supposing Clausel's attack brought in a French force on the Spanish rear. But the turning column had very stiff ground to face, and it was not certain that the Allies might not be found in heavy force in this direction. Moreover what would Clausel do, if after he had committed himself to the adventure, a great allied column were to debouch against his flank and rear driving in D'Erlon's covering force?

It would have added much to Soult's searchings of heart on the 28th–30th of August if he had known that Wellington had not only discovered the general movement of French troops westward, which was a necessary preliminary to the projected attack, but had realized that, in addition to the obvious frontal attack on San Marcial, there would be another launched against his centre from the direction of Vera. The day before the attack Murray, the Quartermaster-General, was writing to all the commanders of divisions that 'the enemy appears to have assembled a very considerable force towards Irun, opposite our left, and also to have added something to their strength near Vera, opposite the position of the Light Division. All rumours from them also agree that they mean to make an attempt for the relief of St. Sebastian.' Then followed the consequential order to each commanding officer[1]. The general scheme was to receive the brunt of the attack on San Marcial with Freire's Galician divisions, who had been holding those heights ever since their first arrival on the Bidassoa in June, but to have them

[1] Murray to Lord Dalhousie, &c., *Supplementary Dispatches*, xiv. p. 281.

supported by two English divisions behind their left rear and right rear, to bring help if it should be needed. On the left Fuenterabia was held by some Biscayan volunteer battalions of Mendizabal's recent levy[1]—the estuary was so broad here that an attack was unlikely. Next came the town of Irun, on its knoll, barricaded and held by three Spanish battalions, but with four British brigades concealed behind it, on its rear and its right—the Guards and Germans of the 1st Division, and Lord Aylmer's newly arrived battalions from England. Then came, somewhat advanced, three Galician divisions—those of Losada, Barcena, and Porlier, occupying the two miles of the San Marcial heights with their 10,000 bayonets. Porlier's division, a mere fragment of three battalions, was placed at the west end of the heights, under the hermitage chapel, Losada's division had the centre, Barcena's the right or eastern end, opposite Biriatou on the French side. To the right rear of the San Marcial position, but on a separate and higher spur of the Peña de la Aya, were Longa's Cantabrians, recently drawn in from Lesaca and the gorge of the Bidassoa, where they had been replaced by some of Wellington's own troops. All the Spanish divisions were weak—there were less than 15,000 bayonets in the field—Porlier's and Longa's had under 2,500 men apiece—each of the others less than 5,000. All the Galicians had been suffering greatly from famine, they received little or nothing from their own commissariat, and General Freire was reduced to soliciting uncovenanted and casual aid from Wellington's magazine[2]. But the men's spirit was good, and Longa's mountaineers, the only corps which had yet been seriously engaged, had behaved excellently at Vittoria, Tolosa, the bridge of Yanzi, and various recent skirmishes along the Bidassoa. In general support of the Galicians Wellington had placed Cole, with the two British brigades of the 4th Division, on a high spur of the Peña de la Aya behind Freire's extreme right, and above Longa's position.

All these troops looked toward the expected French attack

---

[1] 1st, 2nd, and 3rd of Guipuzcoa, 2,000 men. These were the levies of the winter of 1812–13, the old bands of El Pastor, &c., reorganized into permanent units, like the similar Biscayan and Alavan troops raised at the same time. Later they were called the 7th Division of the Galician Army.

[2] See *Dispatches*, xi. p. 25.

from the direction of the broken bridge of Béhobie and the fords east of it. To their right there was a long stretch of the river without a good ford, where the spurs of the mountains on both sides came down to the water's edge, forming a sort of miniature cañon. There is no convenient access to this part of the banks, and they required to be watched but not guarded. Accordingly the next section of Wellington's army was three miles up-stream from the end of the Spanish line on San Marcial. It was looking after the four fords at the angle below Vera, where the Bidassoa makes its sudden change of direction, and flows west instead of north. The best of the fords—broad and only a foot deep in normal weather—was that of Enderlaza near the village of Salain de Lesaca; the others were up-stream—one quite close to the Enderlaza ford, under the other Salain [de Vera, as it is called to distinguish it from the lower Salain de Lesaca], the other two close below the bridge of Vera, the only communication left between the two banks of the river since the great bridge of Béhobie had been burned.

Vera village and bridge were held by pickets of the Light Division, which was encamped above, on the heights of Sta Barbara. The bridge was barricaded, and more effectively stopped by the placing of a company of the 95th in a group of fortified houses at its northern exit. The fords of Enderlaza and Salain de Vera, very obvious crossing-places for an enemy wishing to turn the Peña de la Aya position, were guarded by the Portuguese brigade of the 4th Division—now under Colonel Miller, as its former chief Stubbs had been invalided after Sorauren[1]. To support this brigade Wellington had on the 30th sent across the Bidassoa Inglis's brigade of the 7th Division, as an immediate reserve, while he had warned the generals of the other divisions in the Bastan, including Giron, that they were to be ready to move at short notice. But his main measure of defence on this wing was an indirect, though, as it turned out, a most effective one. The 6th Division on the Maya Pass, and the 7th Division on the Puerto de Echalar, were ordered to make lively demonstration of an intention to attack D'Erlon's troops at Sare and Zagaramurdi, who formed the French flank-guard

[1] This move had been made as early as the 26th, *Supplementary Dispatches*, viii. p. 278.

that was to protect Clausel's great stroke. And the troops behind them, Giron's Andalusians and the 3rd Division, were to make ready to move up in support. The generals were told not to commit themselves to a real attack, but to 'disquiet' the enemy by lively and threatening movements[1]. It was still uncertain whether the Light Division at S[ta] Barbara would join in this feigned flank attack on Soult's whole position, or whether it would have to be used on the other bank of the Bidasssoa, to aid Miller and Inglis[2]. It is thus obvious that Wellington had understood, before the crisis came, the irresistible moral pressure that he could use against any French attempt to come across the Enderlaza and Salain fords, by a demonstration against its flank and rear, on the north bank of the river.

Soult, much alarmed by the letters which he continued to receive from the Governor of St. Sebastian, had originally intended to move on the 30th. But he was forced to defer the attack till the next day, by the non-arrival at the front of indispensable material for the bridges which he intended to throw across the Bidassoa, after his troops should have passed by the designated fords, and also by the fact that some of his divisions had not received the two days' rations which had been ordered for them. The troops, who had all reached their positions by the 29th, were told to keep under cover as much as possible, Clausel's divisions behind the crest of the Bayonette mountain, the long ridge opposite Vera, Reille's behind the lower rising ground above the estuary of the Bidassoa. In neither case was the concealment perfect. British observing officers on the Peña de la Aya and the Peak of Ivantelly caught sight of masses of troops, whose existence was duly reported.

The dawn of August 31st, as we have seen when dealing with the storm of St. Sebastian, was one of dense haze and dull heavy air. This was fortunate for the French, as it enabled them to bring down all their columns to their destined points of passage on the Bidassoa unnoticed by the enemy. It also permitted

---

[1] See especially Q.M.G. to Colville [now again in command of the 6th Division], *Supplementary Dispatches*, xiv. p. 281. Pakenham, who had relieved Pack on the latter's being wounded at Sorauren, had now been superseded by a regular 6th Division general.

[2] Wellington's orders left both alternatives open to the officer in command of the division.

Soult to place in position, unseen and at leisure, the mass of
artillery which was to protect the crossing of the infantry—
thirty-six guns on Reille's front from Hendaye to Biriatou,
twelve on Clausel's front above the fords of Enderlaza and Salain.
The haze had not yet begun to clear off when the infantry
entered the water at 6 a.m., and it was only when they emerged
on the southern bank and began to drive in the Spanish pickets
opposite them that the Allies got the alarm. From one point of
view this was an immense advantage for Soult, as the columns
while crossing the shallows were incommoded neither by infantry
nor by artillery fire: on the other hand when they had come to
land, and wished to deploy for the attack on the heights opposite,
the thick weather made it very difficult for them to form in any
orderly line, or to make out their exact objectives. Indeed till
the haze had lifted by 8 a.m. it was impossible to go forward,
and the enemy had ample time to take up his chosen positions.

As the fighting was on a larger scale upon the San Marcial
front than on the hill-sides toward Vera and Lesaca, it may be
well to dispose of Reille's attack before dealing with Clausel's.
Here the advance began by the passage of Lamartinière's
division at three fords under the village of Biriatou; it was
accomplished without loss, and the leading regiment occupied
without difficulty a wooded knoll, half a mile long, just above
the Spanish end of the fords, which made an admirable lodgement for a *tête-de-pont*. From the passage-point the division
spread out, more to the east than the west, ready to attack the
much loftier San Marcial heights above, when other troops
should have crossed. Maucune's division followed, using the
same fords, and began to deploy west of Lamartinière's. Sappers
started off in haste to build a trestle bridge and a boat bridge
between the fords, by which the troops beyond the river would
have a permanent communication at high tide with their base.
Meanwhile Villatte's reserve, or that part of it which was used
this day as a fighting force—two French brigades, with King
Joseph's Guards, and the Rheinbund regiments—was visible when
the haze lifted, waiting at the water's edge for the falling tide to
make the lower fords near the broken bridge of Béhobie practicable. During the night Soult had determined to borrow Foy's
division from D'Erlon's covering force; it had now arrived

and was waiting in reserve behind Villatte. It was still only eight o'clock, and full ebb tide was not till noon. When the day cleared the French guns on the north bank began to shell Irun and the Spanish positions on San Marcial. The reply was feeble—Giron had only twelve guns, and many gunners of Graham's divisional batteries were absent at the siege of St. Sebastian.

Having made up his mind that it would be wasting time to wait until Villatte and Foy had crossed, Soult, who was watching affairs from the hill named after Louis XIV, resolved at about 9 o'clock to attack with the troops that were already in hand. Lamartinière's division was to storm the central sector of the San Marcial heights, Pinoteau's brigade of Maucune's division their western end, where lies the hermitage chapel. The other brigade of this Division (Montfort's) remained below, to act as reserve, and to guard the building of the bridges.

The slopes of San Marcial are thickly sprinkled with bushes and underwood, which gave some cover, but prevented the formed battalions from keeping their order, as they climbed the hill. It had been intended that they should attack with a screen of *tirailleurs* supported by solid columns. But before they were half-way up the slope the whole had dissolved into one broad and irregular mass, like a dense swarm of skirmishers. General Freire, using the Wellingtonian style, kept the Spaniards in a line of columns two-thirds up the hill, along the front of an old trench of 1794, only sending out his light companies to skirmish. When the disordered enemy had got near his position, he ordered his whole force to charge, which it did with complete success, rolling the French mass downhill, with such an impetus that it never stopped till it reached Montfort's reserve brigade, on the knoll by the river. The Spaniards did not pursue far, but returned and took up their old position.

This affair would seem to have been ended by 10 o'clock. An hour later the falling of the tide enabled Villatte's reserve to make an easy crossing, under cover of artillery fire, some brigades by the fords near the broken bridge of Béhobie, others nearer the troops already on the Spanish bank. Only St. Pol's Italian brigade remained behind by Hendaye. Soult then repeated at noon his first attack with much superior strength; Lamartinière's rallied troops assailing the eastern sector of the

heights, Maucune's the centre, and Villatte's the western, the
hill crowned by the Hermitage. The result, however, was the
same as in the morning. The Spaniards awaited the attack high
up the slope, and charged when the enemy rolled up to their
front. The French left and centre, probably broken in spirit
already by their first repulse, gave way without any great
resistance. The fresh troops of Villatte made a much more
determined assault, and the extreme right brigade[1], that of
General Guy, which contained King Joseph's French Guards,
seized part of the crest of the Hermitage height, one battalion
actually reaching the chapel and driving off Porlier's men from
the summit.

Wellington, watching all this from the Peña de la Aya, had
ordered up Lord Aylmer's brigade from Irun to support the
Spanish left. They were not yet, however, near their destination,
and General Freire sent an aide-de-camp to ask for the loan of
the 4th Division also. It was refused—Wellington had noted
that all the rest of the French attack had failed completely, and
judged that the local success of the enemy at one end of the line
could not be maintained[2]. He was quite right: after a few
minutes the French battalions which saw themselves abandoned
high on the hill by the retreat of all their comrades, gave way at
the first Spanish counter-attack, and joined in the general recoil.
This partial and temporary success cost King Joseph's men
dear—the casualty lists show 25 officers of his Guard and 12 of
his *Royal Étranger* killed and wounded[3].

The routed French divisions fell back with such disorder that

---

[1] Composed of the four battalions of the Royal Guard, one battalion of
foot-gendarmes, and the king's foreign regiment , 'Royal Étranger', into
which he had been wont to draft German and Irish deserters from Wellington's army. It was the successor of his earlier 'Royal Irlandais'.

[2] It is said that he handed his telescope to the Spanish officer who
brought Freire's appeal, and asked him to look through it and see whether
he thought such succour was necessary. A glance through the glass showed
the French already dislodged and in full retreat. Wellington added 'If
I sent you British troops, it would be said that they had won the battle.
But as the French are already retiring, you may as well win it by yourselves',
Stanhope's *Conversation with Wellington*, p. 22.

[3] The whole of Villatte's division in Soult's official report is credited
with only 30 officers and 453 men in casualties. But Martinieu's invaluable lists show 37 officer-casualties in Guy's brigade only.

many of them rolled into the Bidassoa and broke the bridge of boats by overcrowding. It was several hours before they could be rallied. Soult wrote to the Minister of War that he had been intending to deliver a third attack in the afternoon, bringing up Foy's reserve to support the discomfited divisions. He was prevented from doing so, as he alleged, by two unexpected developments. One was that he received such disquieting news from D'Erlon, on the left, that he had to detach Foy to help him, the other that the same tempest of rain which had swept down on St. Sebastian, just after the breaches were carried, had also fallen on the Bidassoa, blotting out the landscape, swelling the river, and damaging the bridges. We may safely disregard this tale of a projected third assault—the troops were not in a condition to fight again—there had been at least 2,500 casualties; and Soult confesses that it took three hours to rally them. Many of them had recoiled to the north bank of the Bidassoa, and could not be got forward again, now that the tide was beginning to rise[1]. There was little more left on the south bank than a line of skirmishers holding the knoll above the bridges. The Marshal did the only possible thing when he withdrew every man into France after dark, well screened by the rain, which never ceased to fall during the night.

Clausel's attack up-stream had been less costly but equally ineffective. Before dawn his immensely long column emerged from behind the Bayonette ridge, and marched down unobserved to the two fords near Salain, where the artillery were in position to cover their passage. Not a round, however, needed to be fired, as the morning haze concealed their advance: Taupin's division crossed at the ford of Enderlaza, Darmagnac's, followed by Vandermaesen's, at the neighbouring ford farther north. Clausel left his fourth division, that of Maransin, on the French bank, as a precaution to guard against any attempt which might be made to cut his communications with D'Erlon by the British force known to be on the heights of Santa Barbara. And Vandermaesen's was halted soon after it had crossed the river, and directed to take up a similar covering position on the south bank, to ward off any possible attack from the side of Lesaca.

<hr/>

[1] For a discussion of the unreality of Soult's account both of what he did, and what he had hoped to do, see Vidal de la Blache, i. pp. 310–11.

Thus the attack was only delivered by Taupin and Darmagnac, whose advance parties, going forward slowly in the haze, had at last run against the pickets of Miller's Portuguese, and were beginning to interchange shots with them on the slopes leading up from the fords.

Between 7 and 8 o'clock the haze gradually thinned off, and revealed the combatants to each other. The British saw clearly four French divisions committed to the attack—one halted on the north bank, one a little way up the slope on the south bank, two ascending on two separate spurs of the Peña de la Aya, and obviously about to press forward. Clausel, on the other hand, could see what he described as a 'black mass' on the heights of Santa Barbara—the Light Division—but in front of him only the Portuguese brigade with which he was already in touch. There seemed, however, to be other troops in movement on the side of Lesaca—these were Inglis's brigade, hastily marching off to support Miller[1]. It is doubtful if the 4th Division on the other side of the Peña de la Aya can have been visible.

The French guns beyond the Bidassoa opened so soon as the haze had lifted. One battery shelled Vera, from which the pickets of the Light Division withdrew; some of Maransin's men entered it, but did not stay there, nor take possession of the bridge. The other battery tried some shots at Miller's Portuguese—so badly directed at first that the shells fell among Taupin's skirmishers. But as the French infantry could now see their way, and had room to begin deploying battalion after battalion, Miller was soon driven off the first ridge and pushed uphill, and beyond artillery range. The enemy pursued, and presently at about 11 o'clock came across Inglis's brigade, on which the Portuguese fell back, drawn up on a second height. Here there was a good position, and a very severe struggle took place, which endured till Darmagnac's division, coming up through woods on Inglis's right, forced him and Miller to abandon their ground. The 51st and 68th made some very daring counter-attacks during this fight, and lost heavily—the former had no less than eleven officers disabled out of a very

---

[1] By the narrative of Green of the 68th, the brigade passed through 'Head-Quarters', i.e. Lesaca, at 7. By that of Wheeler of the 51st it was in action before 11.

small battalion[1]. Still hanging together, however, the two
brigades rallied on a third ridge a mile to the south, and once more
stood to fight[2]. Clausel followed them, but with great caution:
he was getting very nervous about his rear, and had been
hearing ominous noise of battle from the hills east of Vera,
though neither Maransin nor Vandermaesen's division had yet
been attacked. But he could see more allied troops beginning
to appear in the direction of Lesaca, above Vandermaesen's
position. This was a detachment of the Light Division—a wing
of the 43rd and three companies of the 1/95th—accompanied by
three battalions of Giron's Andalusians. Kempt, in command
this day owing to the temporary absence of Charles Alten—had
sent them over the Bidassoa by the bridge of Lesaca, in exercise
of the discretion left to him by Wellington's orders[3]. He afterwards followed himself, with the rest of his brigade. They got
engaged in trifling long-range bickering with Vandermaesen's
flank-guard, and were shelled by two mule-guns which the
French division had brought over—but to no effect[4]. These
allied troops showed no offensive purpose as yet; but, though
no attack was being made here, Clausel could not be sure that
it might not begin at any moment. It would seem also that he
got about this time—2 o'clock in the afternoon—into touch with
the two British brigades of the 4th Division, which Wellington
had moved to the right, when he saw Soult's second attack on
San Marcial. They were now on a spur above the foundry of
St. Antonio, high up on the right shoulder of the Peña de la Aya.
The skirmishers on their flanks were beginning to bicker with
those of Taupin's division[5].

It seems clear that by this time Clausel felt it dangerous to
go on—two of his four divisions were now detached as mere
flank and rear guards—the other two were somewhat exhausted.
They might have pushed Inglis and Miller another mile backward—but to what purpose, when allied detachments were
gathering all around them? It appeared to the French general

---

[1] One 51st diarist, Wheeler, notes that they fought mainly with the
French 51st, of Darmagnac's division.
[2] See Inglis's Report, *Supplementary Dispatches*, viii. p. 221.
[3] See above, p. 45.   [4] Surtees of the 95th, p. 235.
[5] This I deduce from finding 42 casualties in Anson's brigade.

that it would be little use to make another thrust, if he thereby got farther from his reserves and more liable to be cut off. He halted on a wooded hill in front of Inglis's position. An hour later he received a dispatch from Soult bidding him recross the river, as the San Marcial operation had failed, and D'Erlon was being attacked in flank. Clausel is said to have shown some anger at the order, crying 'Mais que veut donc le Maréchal? L'opération est à moitié faite[1]!' His tentative conduct during the last hour causes reasonable doubt whether there was more than simulated indignation, intended to show his staff and Soult's messenger that he considered his own troops to have been victorious up to this moment. But anyhow he could have gone on no longer; for at this moment (3 o'clock) the storm swooped down, rain fell in blinding torrents, and the battle-field became invisible. The two fighting divisions, on getting their order to go back to the fords, lost their way in the darkness, on the pathless spurs of the mountain on which they had been fighting since 8 o'clock in the morning.

There can be no doubt that a considerable operating cause, both in Clausel's indecision and in Soult's resolve to give up the game altogether, was the simulated attack on D'Erlon which had been carried out, according to Wellington's orders of the 30th, even before the moment when the haze had lifted. Soon after dawn Lord Dalhousie had sent out Le Cor's Portuguese of the 7th Division to demonstrate against the French brigade at Zagaramúrdi (Rémond's of Abbé's division), and Colville from the Maya front had, in the same way, ordered Madden's Portuguese to feel the front of the French on the side of Urdax. Meanwhile Giron's Andalusians skirmished with Conroux's outposts in front of Sare. The supporting troops in each case showed themselves behind the deployed brigade, and it looked as if D'Erlon's two divisions were about to be attacked with vigour. He sent back to Soult appeals for help without delay. Probably he might soon have discovered that the enemy had no

---

[1] Lemonnier-Delafosse, p. 240. He was the aide-de-camp who brought the order, and is an interesting witness, as showing that Soult's supposed intention to make a third attempt at San Marcial was a mere figment. Fording the Bidassoa on his way back, in the storm, Delafosse had a narrow escape from drowning.

serious intentions, if Lord Dalhousie had not ordered (or allowed)[1] Le Cor's brigade to make a very real attack on Zagaramurdi, with complete success—Rémond's troops being driven out of the place with loss, and retiring on Ainhoue. The French by Urdax, hotly pressed by Madden's brigade, thereupon retired also, and the whole of Abbé's division massed in front of Ainhoue. Madden and Le Cor, whether with or without Dalhousie's approval, attacked them, and were driven back, with a loss of about 250 men. Thereupon Dalhousie brought up Barnes's British brigade, and rallied his Portuguese upon it. Abbé did not take the offensive, but stood on his position in front of Ainhoue—he had lost rather more than the Portuguese, 325 casualties in all.

All this was strictly contrary to Wellington's orders, for he had limited Dalhousie to a mere demonstration; but it had the desired effect of making D'Erlon think that he was to be attacked in good earnest. The French brigadier on the Mondarrain lines, north of Maya, confirmed him in this idea, by reporting that the advance of Madden's Portuguese towards Urdax was being supported by many columns, which were commencing a turning movement. This was, in reality, Colville demonstrating with the British brigades of the 6th Division. But the general effect made on D'Erlon's mind was such that he wrote to Soult declaring that he was to be attacked all along his line, and that he would not answer for the safety of the army, unless Foy's division was at once sent back to him.

Dalhousie had got to such close quarters with Abbé, that when he received a dispatch from Wellington at 10 a.m., ordering him to break off his demonstration and march to join Inglis on the Peña de la Aya, he was unable to disentangle himself for some hours, and it was only at 4 p.m. that Barnes's brigade got off towards Lesaca. Le Cor's Portuguese were still left to look after Abbé. Wellington was very naturally discontented with

[1] Dalhousie, in his report to Wellington, *Supplementary Dispatches*, viii. p. 221, acknowledges that he authorized Le Cor to drive out the enemy from Zagaramurdi—which was already a piece of disobedience to Wellington's orders, but all Le Cor's further proceedings were owing 'to the too forward gallantry of the Portuguese troops'. Remembering what Dalhousie did with Barnes's brigade at Echalar on August 2nd, I cannot help suspecting that Le Cor was not so irresponsible as his chief tried to make out.

Dalhousie's whole conduct this day—but it probably served him well enough, by scaring D'Erlon much more than mere bloodless manœuvring would have done.

Soon after noon had passed, D'Erlon sent a report to Soult that the enemy's attack seemed to be slackening—but by the time that it came to hand the damage had been done at San Marcial—Foy's division had started off to reinforce the left wing, and there was nothing left but broken troops in front of the Spaniards. And Clausel, warned of fighting far in his rear, had been kept in a state of mental discomfort all through his very cautious and slow advance on the Vera side.

It remains only to speak of Clausel's disastrous retreat from the Peña de la Aya. His two fighting divisions retired on the fords, Vandermaesen's being left out to cover their passage. But when, after much fruitless wandering in the blinding rain, they got to the Bidassoa at dusk, it was found that the water was rising so rapidly that the river was growing impassable. Clausel himself got over, and the leading brigade of each division had the same luck, Taupin's at Enderlaza, Darmagnac's at Salain, though each lost a good many men drowned. But presently the fords grew absolutely useless—there was six feet of rushing water, and the banks were overflowed. The rear brigade of each division, and the whole of Vandermaesen's men, who were covering the passage, were left stranded on the wrong bank. It was a sufficiently desperate position. Vandermaesen took command and, seeing that he must be overwhelmed in the morning, unless he got the troops across the river in some way or other, marched them along the road by the river to Vera, hoping to find the bridge there available. It was not: Maransin, after the departure of the Light Division pickets in the early morning, had never thought of occupying Vera or securing its bridge. He had remained above, on the heights of Alzate Real, facing the Light Division on the opposite heights of Santa Barbara.

The barricaded bridge and the fortified houses beside it were occupied by the party of riflemen of the 2/95th—the company of Captain Cadoux, with a platoon of the company of Captain Hart, about 100 men in all. Vandermaesen, after wandering for many hours of drenching rain along the loops of the Bidassoa, on slopes occasionally lit up by the lightning, ran at about 2 a.m., still in complete darkness, against this picket. The two sentries at the bridge-barricade were bayoneted, without having been able to give the alarm—their priming was wet and their rifles missed fire. But the passage was not forced, for the riflemen in the fortified houses were on the alert, and opened with a volley from their loopholes, which brought down many men at the head of the column and stopped it completely. Party after party of the French tried to break into the houses, but in vain. The noise of the continuous firing was heard above the rattling of the storm all around the hills above. Skerrett, commanding the Light Division brigade on the heights of Santa Barbara, only half a mile away, failed to see the opportunity thus offered in the dark. He refused to listen to all suggestions that he should rein-force the picket, though Cadoux twice reported that he was holding his own well, and had the French column blocked—with reinforcements the bridge could easily be maintained[1]. For more than an hour the strife continued, and the enemy made no progress—General Vandermaesen himself was killed while lead-ing one desperate charge to break through. But numbers pre-vailed in the end, and just before dawn the houses were forced, and Cadoux and his little force cut to pieces—he and 16 men were killed, three other officers and 43 men wounded out of 100 rifle-men or less. The few survivors were brought off by another company, which Skerrett sent down, all too late, for that purpose. The brigadier was never forgiven by any officer or soldier of the 95th for this cold-blooded sacrifice of willing men: it was universally held that a single battalion more could have blocked the passage of the French with ease, since they could only attack on a small front across a narrow bridge. In that case four French brigades would have had to surrender in the morning, when the

---

[1] There are two versions of this incident—one given by Harry Smith, Skerrett's aide-de-camp, merely makes the brigadier refuse to send down any succour to Cadoux; the other told on the authority of Colonel Thomas Smith, another eyewitness, in Cope's *History of the Rifle Brigade*, adds the allegation that Skerrett twice ordered Cadoux to retire, and that he and his company were cut to pieces when executing a retreat against which he had vehemently protested. As Harry Smith's account is consistent with the narratives of Surtees, Kincaid, Simmons, and Leach, I accept it, rather than Cope's.

allied troops from all sides descended on them. For the river
was still quite unfordable on the first of September. Two
hundred killed and wounded of Vandermaesen's division were
found lying at the bridgehead at dawn. But his regiments,
followed by those of the rear brigades of the other two divisions,
were in safety at Sare long before Skerrett realized the chance
he had lost. He appears to have succeeded in concealing the facts
from Wellington, whose only note of them in his dispatch is that
'the nature of the ground rendering it impossible to prevent
entirely the passage of the bridge after daylight, it was made
under fire of a great part of Major-General Skerrett's brigade,
and the enemy's loss in the operation must have been very
considerable'[1].

So ended Soult's last battle in Spain—one whose management
does not show his talents at their best. It would seem to
have been a cardinal error to attack the Allies with two columns
of approximately equal strength, on two points separated from
each other by five miles of impassable mountain. There was no
way in which Reille and Clausel could have co-operated, unless
one or the other of them had achieved a complete success on
his own sector of the front. This being so, it would have been
well to give one column—Reille's for choice—overpowering
numbers, and to have made the other little more than a demonstrating force. It may be said that the whole adventure was too
hazardous, so long as Wellington had a strong corps on the other
side of the Bidassoa, between Santa Barbara and the Col de
Maya, with which he could attack the whole French frontier in
flank. The mere threat to do so wrecked Clausel's offensive.
Logically, no doubt, the Marshal ought to have begun by evicting
the British from the Col de Maya, the Puerto de Echalar, and
Vera—if this had been done the threat to his flank would have
been removed. But with only 45,000 troops in hand, he could
hardly have found enough men to execute this movement and
also to attack frontally across the Bidassoa. Moreover there was
no time for a three days' campaign, such as this scheme would
have required. He had to strike at once, or to see St. Sebastian
fall. The actual plan adopted was unsatisfactory, and deserved
to fail: yet it is hard to see how on that ground, with those

[1] *Dispatches*, xi. p. 69.

numbers, and with only one day at his disposition, he could have produced any really satisfactory scheme of attack.

As to Wellington—the battle was not of his seeking: he regarded it as a purely defensive operation, and fought merely to cover the siege of St. Sebastian. If he had been prepared to utilize success, and to take the offensive, it is clear that he might have destroyed Reille, by launching at his beaten columns the five British brigades which were in reserve behind San Marcial. Or a real instead of a feigned attack on D'Erlon's flank-guard could hardly have failed to produce a tremendous effect—the 3rd, 6th, and 7th Divisions with Giron's Andalusians were all available for it. But such a blow would have involved a victorious advance into France, and this was precisely what Wellington was not prepared to undertake at the moment.

He was content to have foiled Soult with the minimum of effort—only Freire's three Galician divisions, one British brigade (that of Inglis), and three Portuguese brigades[1] were really put into action: they sufficed to win the battle—45,000 men were checked by 12,000 Spaniards and 8,000 Anglo-Portuguese. And nearly half the French army was really 'contained' all day and kept from doing serious mischief by a mere tactical threat— the demonstration against D'Erlon's covering force.

Soult's loss was over 4,000 men—3,808 by his own report[2]. He had one general killed—Vandermaesen; one mortally wounded, Lamartinière; three less severely hit, Menne, Rémond, and Guy. Lamartinière's division with 1,643 casualties was the unit which suffered most. Of the 350 'missing' a great proportion were men drowned in the fords of the Bidassoa: Wellington made no claim to any serious number of prisoners.

The Allies had 2,524 casualties, of which no less than 1,679 were Spaniards killed or hurt in their very gallant and successful defence of San Marcial, which Wellington praised in the most glowing terms in his official dispatch. The 304 casualties of Inglis's brigade were a light price to pay for the keeping back of

---

[1] And two of these brigades (Le Cor and Madden) fought against Wellington's orders, when they had been told to do no more than demonstrate.

[2] See Appendix at end of this volume for losses on both sides on August 31st. As Mr. Fortescue remarks, Soult's figures are wrongly cast up, and produce only 3,607, the real correct addition being 3,808 [*British Army*, ix. p. 371].

BATTLE OF SAN MARCIAL, AUGUST 31ST 1813

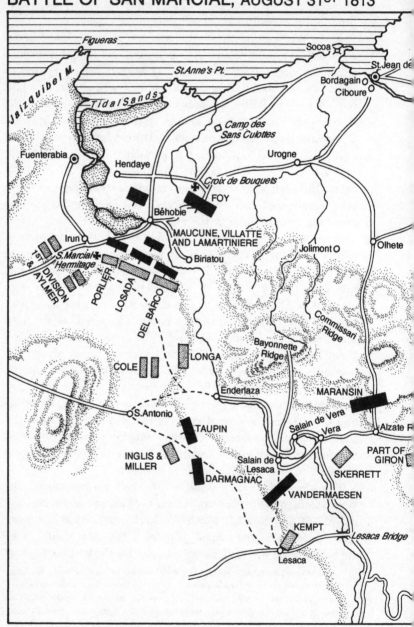

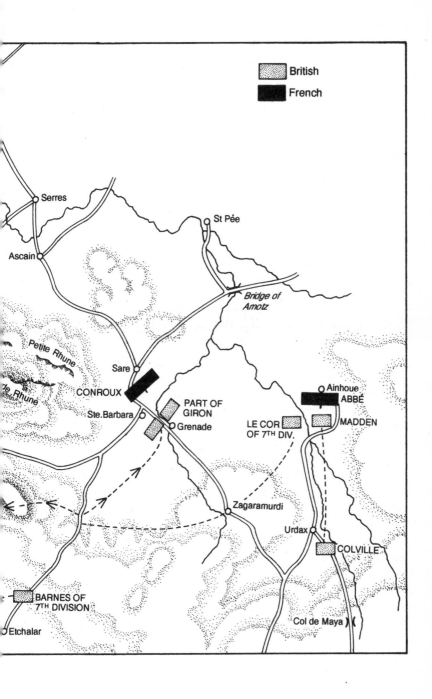

British

French

Serres

St Pée

Ascain

*Bridge of
Amotz*

Petite Rhune

Sare

e Rhune

CONROUX

Ste.Barbara

PART OF
GIRON

Grenade

Ainhoue
ABBÉ

LE COR
OF 7TH DIV.

MADDEN

Zagaramurdi

Urdax

COLVILLE

BARNES OF
7TH DIVISION

Etchalar

Col de Maya

Clausel's two divisions for many hours, while reinforcements were coming up. The fighting of this brigade was certainly most obstinate and praiseworthy—it held off five times its own numbers from 8 a.m. till 3 p.m., suffered heavily, yet was in full fighting trim at the end of the engagement. Probably Wellington would have regarded the 250 men lost by the Portuguese brigades at Zagaramurdi and Urdax as unnecessary casualties—their generals had been told not to fight, but only to demonstrate. Of Skerrett's sacrifice of Cadoux's company at Vera bridge, he had evidently not heard the full story.

Soult had spent a restless night after the action of August 31st, being still uncertain whether Vandermaesen and the four brigades with him had not been destroyed or taken. Soon after dawn he heard of their safety. But at the same time he learnt that St. Sebastian had been stormed, so that his battle had been useless, even as a mean of distracting Wellington's attention from the siege. There was nothing to do save to replace the troops in their old positions, and to order them to resume the work of fortifying strong points along the north bank of the Bidassoa and the slopes of the Bayonette and the Rhune, on which they had started before the unlucky offensive of August 31st.

It only remains to tell of the last nine days' agony of Rey and the obstinate remnant of the St. Sebastian garrison, now lodged high up on the rocky summit of Monte Urgull. The general had about 1,300 sound men left—they were hampered by the care of 450 wounded, and of nearly 350 English and Portuguese prisoners, the men captured at the unsuccessful assault of July 25th and in the great raid on the trenches on the night of July 27th. The buildings on the crest were few—the only one of any military use was the old castle, whose vaults served as the main powder magazine. Its upper stories were not proof against artillery fire, and when they should have been demolished there would be imminent danger of an explosion. The other defences were open batteries without casemates. There were some huts and barracks in the enceinte, but many were of wood, and none were capable of resisting the impact of an 18-pounder ball. Even in these there was not sufficient shelter for the whole garrison, many of whom, along with the prisoners, had to lie out in the open, taking shelter in cracks and clefts of the rock. Of guns there were hardly any remaining of the thirty-one which had stood on the upper defences before the bombardment began— only four heavy pieces on the sea-front, and four smaller ones and three mortars on the land front looking towards the town[1].

Wellington had at first hoped to reduce the Castle by merely continuing the bombardment. On the 1st, 2nd, and 3rd of August the mortars and howitzers in the Chofres batteries and on Monte Olia continued to pound the whole surface of the rock, and by no means without effect. All the flimsy buildings on the summit were knocked to pieces: not only was no cover left for the enemy save in the Castle, but there too the upper works began to fall in. Casualties were numerous, including thirty-eight killed and wounded among the unlucky prisoners, to whom Rey refused leave even to build themselves stone shelters, justifying himself by saying that the bombardment was not respecting his hospital, and that they should be parked outside it to get their share of the shells[2].

On the morning of September 3rd Graham judged that the bombardment would probably have broken the spirit of the governor, and sent up a flag of truce and a formal summons to surrender. Rey refused to accept it, though he was by now aware of the results of the battle of San Marcial, and knew that there was no hope of relief from outside. His means of defence were exhausted, and further resistance could only lead to further casualties before the inevitable end. Apparently this obduracy, when all hope was gone, came partly from personal pride, partly from a blind obedience to the military theory which holds that it is the duty of a good officer to detain as many of the enemy before him as he can, down to the last possible moment. Every French general knew the story of the surrender of the Prussian fortresses after Jena, and had contemned the slackness of the numerous governors, who gave up strong places uncompelled, merely because their king's field-army had been annihilated.

Wellington therefore had to bring Rey to reason. If the

---

[1] See Major Brian's Report to General Rey, printed in Belmas, iv. pp. 734-5.

[2] See Belmas, iv. p. 649. Cf. Graham's note in *Supplementary Dispatches*, viii. p. 232.

bombardment by the mortar batteries on the Chofres had not broken his spirit, still further pressure must be applied. Hitherto there had been no attempt to construct approaches towards the Castle: the town had been burning steadily since the day of the storm, and the flames had not yet entirely died down. The conflagration had prevented the establishment of any large body of troops at the foot of the Monte Urgull, and pickets had been kept with difficulty in the narrow belt of houses that still stood unconsumed, immediately under the Castle. Now it was determined that the place should be not merely bombarded but battered down and assaulted. The engineers chose two sites for heavy batteries, as close in as was prudent—and on the 3rd their construction was begun—one was for seventeen 24-pounders in the central space of the Hornwork, the other for three more a little further back on the isthmus, on the site of the so-called 'Cask Redoubt' taken from the French on July 20th. In addition two guns were got across to the island of Santa Clara, from which the sea-front of the Castle could be enfiladed. The artillery of the defence was so entirely subdued that fifteen pieces for the great battery in the Hornwork were dragged across the fords of the Urumea in full daylight on September 4th, without drawing a shot from the Castle. One got lost in a quicksand—the rest arrived safely at their destination. The other pieces required for the new batteries were obtained from the old works on the Isthmus front.

On September 8th the whole scheme of attack had been completed, and sixty-one guns and mortars opened on the Castle defences—twenty-six from the left attack, thirty-three from the old batteries on the Chofres and Monte Olia, and two from the island. After two hours only of bombardment General Rey hoisted the white flag—every inch of the crest of the rock had been searched by the converging fire, and all the defences levelled with the ground. In a few hours more the magazine in the castle vaults would been found by some shell, and the siege would have ended in a general explosion. The necessity for instant surrender had been foreseen, for on September 5th Rey had authorized the holding of a council of war, at which the commanding officers of artillery and engineers and the surviving battalion-commanders drew up a formal statement that further resistance was impossible[1]. His responsibility therefore was completely covered, and he only waited for the efficiency of the bombardment to be proved before hoisting the white flag.

Graham and Wellington granted the usual military terms—the garrison marched out with the honours of war and laid down its arms among the still smoking ruins of the Plaza Vieja, while the band of a Portuguese regiment played somewhat discordantly. The scene was dismal, many of the garrison wept, others broke their arms before casting them on the heap: a thin circle of the burnt-out inhabitants glowered with equal hate on the vanquished and the victors, as they stood on the heaps of shattered stones that represented their lost houses. The French officers were permitted to keep their swords—baggage was not to be searched—women and children were allowed to return to France. As a special mark of favour, Rey was allowed to send an officer to Soult, bearing his last dispatch, and charged with the giving of personal explanations. But the whole garrison was shipped off to England—the suggestion that they should be put on parole and allowed to go to their homes being of course ignored.

So ended a siege which brought much honour to a very gallant and obstinate governor[2] and garrison, and very little credit to British engineering science. Indeed there is little to commend in the whole conduct of the siege save the desperate courage of the regimental officers and the rank and file. It is clear that the whole plan of attack was a mistake—and Wellington and Graham must take a certain share of the responsibility that falls mainly on Fletcher and Smith. The generals showed persistence in approving a misguided scheme, in face of the protests of those who like Burgoyne, the second in command of the engineers, and Oswald, the commander of the 5th Division, pleaded for a regular siege, and deprecated the reckless form of attack which was bound to be costly in human life. It is easy to understand

---

[1] It may be found in Belmas's Appendix, No. 40, vol. iv. pp. 737-8.

[2] British officers did not like Rey—they thought him no gentleman—a sulky Jacobin. Gomm describes him as 'a coarse fellow' (p. 321), Frazer as 'a great fat fellow, not pleasing in appearance' (p. 265). He 'used opprobrious and vulgar terms' and was 'altogether brutal'. His subordinate, Colonel de Sentuary, on the other hand, seems to have impressed every one favourably.

the feeling that haste was necessary, when Soult was close at hand and likely to interfere at any moment. But in this instance, as in so many others, it was a case of 'more haste less speed', and it is impossible to differ from the verdict of Burgoyne and John Jones that 'the operations against St. Sebastian afford a most impressive lesson on the use of science and rule in a siege. The effort made to overcome and trample on these restrictions caused an easy and certain operation of twenty days to extend over sixty, and cost the besiegers a loss of 3,500 officers and men[1].' If anything was wanting to complete the unhappy impression that the name of St. Sebastian left on the mind of contemporaries, it was the story of the disgraceful sack which followed the storm.

Fortunately the present generation has forgotten and forgiven that sad story—as was shown by the splendid ceremony in October 1925 at which the Queen of Spain presided over the erection of the new monument placed above the grave of Sir Robert Fletcher and other British dead on the slope of Monte Urgull. A handsome group of statuary rises above the little graveyard and its garden, and looks out from the cliff on the stormy waves of the Bay of Biscay. Standing by the castle of La Mota it is hard to recognize the outlines of the old St. Sebastian of 1813 among the wide-spreading houses of the new town below, which extends all over the isthmus, and runs up to the foot of the Convent of San Bartolomé. The old ditch and walls of the landward front have completely disappeared, and where the Hornwork lay there is now a busy public square. The little commercial port of 1813 has become a big pleasure town—the favourite watering place of Northern Spain, ringed round with villas and gardens on the beautiful blue sweep of the 'Concha' bay. A single house by the church of Santa Maria bears on its front an inscription, telling that it stood intact when all its neighbours perished in the flames. There is nothing else in the town itself to recall unhappy memories.

[1] Jones, ii. p. 97.

SECTION XL

THE EAST COAST IN THE AUTUMN

CHAPTER I

SUCHET EVACUATES VALENCIA AND ARAGON. JULY 1813

WHILE Murray had been absent on his Tarragona expedition from May 31st till June 22nd, the Spanish generals in the Kingdom of Valencia had been not very much less blameworthy in Wellington's eyes than their Anglo-Sicilian colleague. It is true that Suchet had taken away with him to the Ebro a much smaller proportion of his army than might have been expected: he had marched with only 8,600 men, leaving 14,000 behind him under Harispe to defend his much-cherished viceroyalty[1]. But the front was a very long one, from Severoli's posts on the right on the upper Guadalaviar and watching the pass of Las Cabrillas, to Habert's on the left at Alcira, not far from the sea. And of the 14,000 men under Harispe over 2,000 were locked up in the garrisons of Saguntum, Denia, Peniscola, and Morella, and only 12,000 or so available for operations in the field.

Del Parque's troops were, in Wellington's estimation, the best Spanish force existing, with the exception of Copons's small army in Catalonia. They had been three years continuously in movement under Ballasteros, during Soult's occupation of Andalusia, and were adepts in mountain warfare. But there were not very many of them—12,000 infantry with 700 horse and four batteries of artillery, by their morning state of June 1st[2]. Elio's troops were much more numerous—on paper. But of the 30,000 men on his muster rolls 10,000 were not really under his control, or available for a campaign in Valencia: they consisted of the guerrillero bands of the Empecinado and Duran, which infested the one New Castile, and the other

---

[1] Napier, v. p. 162, much understates Harispe's force at 8,000 men. He certainly had his own infantry division, 4,000 men by the return of May 15th, Habert's 4,200 bayonets, Severoli's 2,000, and the cavalry 1,000 sabres, over and above the garrisons—making with artillery, sappers, &c., over 12,000 men, ready for the field, and not including garrisons.

[2] Divisions of the Prince of Anglona (5,000 men), Las Cuevas (4,000), and Cruz Murgeon (2,800).

Southern Aragon. They were always on the move, and occupied with petty enterprises of their own: if they could have been caught and brought in to head-quarters, they would not have been troops who could safely be put in line of battle. In the oncoming campaign they did not count. There remained really under Elio's command four divisions of infantry, those of Mijares, Villacampa, Sarsfield, and Roche—about 17,000 bayonets, with a cavalry brigade of 900 sabres, and hardly any artillery (perhaps two batteries). Roche's regiments had (like Whittingham's better-known division) been armed, and paid for the last two years with British money, and trained by British officers: they passed for good troops. The rest of the infantry had a bad record—they were the survivors of the disasters of Saguntum, Valencia, and the first Castalla (O'Don-nell's rout of July 29th, 1812). These unfortunate corps had a consistent tradition of defeat: and, as Wellington held, they were not to be trusted. Between them Del Parque and Elio could produce 32,000 men, including a wholly insufficient provision of artillery and cavalry—1,600 sabres, six batteries. But the mounted arm could be made up to a much higher figure by Whittingham's two strong cavalry regiments, Almanza and Santiago, and by the Sicilian squadrons: all of these belonged to the Anglo-Sicilian Army, but had been left behind for want of horse-transport—between them they had 1,200 sabres.

The Spanish generals had considerably more than double Harispe's force, and the inestimable advantage of being able to choose their point of attack, since the French general was tied down by his orders to the defensive. Wellington, in his famous 'Instruction of April 14th for the Operations on the East Coast', had laid down the policy which was to be pursued in general terms. The French were to be manœuvred out of their lines on the Xucar by a flank attack, and this attack was to be delivered by Del Parque, since he had an army that could both fight and march, while Elio was to demonstrate along the front of the Xucar lines, and to commit himself as little as possible; he was to be lent the three unattached cavalry regiments, to enable him to provide himself with a screen, and was not to endeavour to close till Del Parque had got the enemy well engaged.

Unfortunately Elio disliked this arrangement, and in a most

blameworthy fashion, persuaded Del Parque to exchange roles, urging that if he himself took the inland work and turning movement as his share, he would be operating on ground which he knew, and would be able to get in touch with his outlying subordinates, the Empecinado and Duran. To induce the Duke to make the exchange he offered him the loan of Roche's division. And so it came to pass that the exact opposite of Wellington's scheme was carried out—there was a rather weak flank movement carried out by the worst troops, while the better ones pushed hard in front against strong positions, and were checked with severe loss. The campaign started late, because the two armies had to change places, Del Parque coming down to Castalla from the interior, while Elio went up to Almanza from his original front near the coast. Hence the advance began on the 9th of June only, though Murray had sailed on May 31st, and it had been intended that the Spanish attack should synchronize with his descent on Catalonia.

Elio sent Villacampa's division to turn the extreme northern flank of the line which Severoli held, while he himself with the other two divisions (Mijares and Sarsfield) drove out the small French garrison of Requena, and seized the defile of the Cabrillas (June 15). He then attacked rather feebly the positions of the Italians around Liria, and gained some advantage, which was not unnatural, as he had a superiority in numbers of at least three to one. But this mattered little, as Del Parque's frontal attack on the Xucar miscarried entirely.

The Duke had marched in person with two of his divisions and most of his cavalry, by Villena and Fuente Higuera, on Moxente, the right of the position which Suchet had entrenched many months back. His third division and Roche went by Alcoy and the pass of Albayda to attack the *tête-de-pont* at Alcira, which was the most central and most important of the French works. Having evacuated Moxente and Jativa, and drawn in every available man from his right towards his left, Harispe sallied out and attacked the Spanish columns, when they drew near him and began to demonstrate against his bridgeheads. He caught them advancing on a rather wide front, on two roads which made lateral communication between the units difficult. A vigorous assault by Habert's division and Delort's cavalry

356.7   F

broke up at Carcagente in front of Alcira (June 13) three of
the Spanish brigades[1], which were routed with the loss of
1,000 killed and wounded and 500 prisoners. Del Parque, with
the other half of his army and the bulk of the cavalry, was
completely out of the game that day. Indeed, only 8,000 of
his troops were under fire, so that Harispe fought with very
nearly an equality of numbers. But the results of the combat
of Carcagente were decisive; seeing his centre so badly mauled
Del Parque drew back, and abandoned the offensive, waiting to
see whether Elio's turning movement would have any effect
on the French in front of him.

That general, after some inconclusive fighting with Severoli,
slipped Villacampa's division round his enemy's flank; it got on
June 19th on to the high road to Valencia, in the rear of the
Italians, and might have threatened the city itself. But at
this moment Suchet who (as it will be remembered) had commenced his retreat from the Ebro on the 17th, came into play.
Musnier's division, descending from Amposta by the coast road,
turned off against Villacampa and hunted him back into the
inland. Having cleared his flank, and brought down Pannetier's
troops from the north also, Suchet concentrated his main
force on the Xucar, and, leaving Severoli to look after Elio,
was ready to sally out against Del Parque, who had now taken
up Murray's old defensive position at Castalla. Meanwhile the
Anglo-Sicilians, much delayed by the results of the storm at
sea[2], were reorganizing at Alicante, and preparing to get forward
to the Duke's assistance. Lord William Bentinck, in his dispatches to Wellington, complained bitterly of an additional
hindrance to the mobilization of his army, caused by an inex-
cusable act on the part of his predecessor. Murray, on sailing
for Tarragona, had issued orders for the dismissal of nearly all
the land-transport which he had left behind him. Six hundred
mules and 200 country carts, collected with great difficulty
during the spring, had gone back to their villages, and could
not be replaced[3]. Though the army had embarked at the Col

---

[1] Four of Roche's battalions, four of Cruz Murgeon's, and three of Las
Cuevas's, the remainder of each of these divisions not being on the spot.
[2] See vol. vi. p. 521.
[3] Bentinck to Wellington, June 30, *Supplementary Dispatches*, viii. p. 38.

de Balaguer on June 18th, and though its last straggling units had got to Alicante on the 28th, there was no prospect of its being able to move forward till July should be well advanced. Meanwhile Suchet, who had left the Ebro on the 17th, was back on the Xucar in a menacing posture by the 25th, with his whole army collected. He had completely outpaced his enemy.

What would have happened on the East Coast but for the news of the battle of Vittoria it is difficult to say. For Bentinck, having visited Del Parque at Castalla on the 29th, and seen his troops, sent back a very downhearted report to Wellington. The '3rd Army' had been much shaken by the late reverse: 'they seem to understand perfectly their real condition. They do not disguise it, and seem anxious not to commit their troops.' It would be madness for them to advance without British support: 4,000 French could stop and beat them in their present state of morale. Wherefore Bentinck held that Del Parque and the Anglo-Sicilians must move together: and as it would be reckless to attack Suchet's entrenched lines on the Xucar, held by his whole army, in any frontal fashion, a turning movement was the only chance. But this would be a long business: the only roads by which the French inland flank could be circumvented were the high road from Madrid by Utiel and Requena, on which Elio had been operating, and the still more circuitous route by Cuenca and Teruel, which passes over the worst defiles of the Sierra de Albaracin. Bentinck, ignorant from his entire want of Peninsular experience of the meaning of a march over secondary roads among uninhabited mountains, proposed to Wellington that this dreadful detour should be taken —though he submitted his resolve for approbation to the commander-in-chief. He acknowledged that it would take a fortnight before he could get a reply; but as the harvest in the mountainous province of Cuenca would not be gathered in till mid-July, and the armies could not move till it was available, the delay would not be of crucial importance[1]. This was a very bad scheme; fortunately it was never put into operation, for (as Wellington wrote to Bentinck after the whole face of affairs had changed) the Anglo-Sicilian Army had no proper provision of transport or commissariat, and would have starved if it had

[1] Ibid., p. 37.

thrown itself into the most barren region of Central Spain, in
the vain hope of living on the harvest[1]. Its sole power of movement depended on its free communication with the sea, which
would have been abandoned by a march into the province of
Cuenca; and its operations, therefore, must always be restricted
to regions in which it could remain in touch with the fleet, and
could count on sea-borne supplies.

But all this, though perfectly sensible and correct, was a
lecture of an academic sort, since by the time that Wellington
wrote his reply the news of the battle of Vittoria had flown all
round Spain, and the plan for marching the Anglo-Sicilian Army
through the central sierras had become obviously unnecessary.
For Bentinck grasped the new situation at once, and wrote
that the first result of the glorious victory in the North would
be that Suchet must evacuate Valencia, and recross the Ebro,
under pain of getting cut off from the rest of the French armies
in Spain. Wherefore he intended to march on Valencia by the
direct road, and to press Del Parque to make a parallel movement farther inland, while Elio, who had retired far back on
the Madrid road, should come forward again, and close on
Valencia from the rear.

Bentinck's views were quite correct. Suchet, the moment
that the disastrous news from the King's Army began to reach
him, was thinking of evacuation. His information was very
scanty, for of all the dispatches which Joseph and Jourdan had
sent him during their long retreat only one, written from
Torquemada on June 6th, reached him, and that only on
July 2nd, so well did the guerrilleros do their work of blocking
communications. The Marshal had become anxious at receiving
no news, and had sent officers of his own to seek for the King,
but they had to make intolerable detours, and were so late in
returning that the news of Vittoria got in by other sources long
before they reappeared. Learning from the dispatch from
Torquemada that the King had lost the line of the Douro, and
was retreating to Burgos or perhaps even farther, Suchet had
realized that his position at Valencia was hazardous, and made
preparations for a retreat to the lower Ebro, where his front,
as he supposed, would be parallel to that of the King's Army

[1] Wellington to Bentinck, July 8, *Dispatches*, x. p. 515.

defending the upper course of that river, with Saragossa as their point of connexion.

This conception had hardly been formed when there arrived at Valencia, on July 3rd, a dispatch from General Paris, commanding at Saragossa, with the news that Clausel's corps had just fallen back on him in hurried retreat (June 30), bringing the news that the King and Jourdan had lost a decisive battle at Vittoria, and were retiring to Pampeluna, or even farther, abandoning all their guns and transport. Clausel, driven off in an eccentric direction, thought it probable that he was being pursued by Wellington himself, or at least by a large fraction of his army. But as he was still out of touch with the King, he did not know the exact details of the lost battle, or the further intentions of the head-quarters of the Army of Spain. The information received by Suchet was vague and incomplete, but it could not be doubted that a catastrophe had occurred, and that the line of the Ebro could no longer be maintained. He must retreat behind that river, and promptly, if it were true that the British were marching on Saragossa. The main problem was to discover whether Clausel and his 15,000 men could be counted on for the defence of Aragon, or whether that general would think it his duty to rejoin the King, by crossing the Pyrenees. In the former case, the Army of Valencia would move on Saragossa, and take up a campaign against Wellington: Suchet hoped that this, 'le parti le plus sage', would be the one adopted. But if Clausel should march for the mountains, and withdraw himself from Spain, Aragon must be abandoned, and Catalonia only could be defended. Orders were sent to General Paris, bidding him to be ready to retire on Mequinenza if he was abandoned to his own resources, and to leave a garrison in the citadel of the Aljafferia[1].

Whatever might be Clausel's decision, the first thing necessary was to get out of Valencia as quickly as possible. 'This awful catastrophe', as Suchet wrote to the Minister of War, 'takes from me by a single blow all that has been won by five years of hard work and devoted service[2].' His decision was

---

[1] This order was sent off also on July 3rd, and reached Paris on the night of the 7th–8th.

[2] Suchet to Clarke, July 3, 1813.

rapid—as it had need to be. On July 2nd Habert, Harispe, and the cavalry had been about Jativa and Moxente, on the south side of the Xucar, Musnier at Requena, from which he had recently driven Elio. By the 4th they had fallen back to the environs of Valencia, leaving nothing but a cavalry screen behind them. On the 5th they marched through the city, where all the civil administrators, French residents, and prominent *Afrancesados* had packed up, and fell into the column with more than 150 coaches beside other vehicles. The citadel was blown up before the Marshal departed—the outer defences had never been restored since the capitulation of January 1812. That night the army slept in Murviedro and the neighbouring villages, under the walls of the fortress of Saguntum.

From this point the main body pursued the coast road, and reached the Ebro opposite Tortosa on July 9th in four marches. But Musnier's division turned inland, in order to pick up Severoli's Italians, who had been forming the flank-guard of the army against any possible return of Elio and Villacampa to the scene of their former operations. No trouble was suffered on this side, and having even gathered in the outlying garrisons of Teruel and Alcaniz, Severoli and Musnier reached Caspe on the Ebro on July 12th.

The evacuation of the Kingdom of Valencia, therefore, had been carried out with order and rapidity, and on July 12th the army held a position from which it could either fall back on Catalonia or march on Saragossa. No molestation whatever had been suffered from the enemy, who only entered Valencia on July 9th, four days after Suchet had abandoned it. There is only one thing to criticize in the Marshal's operations—but this was a very fatal error—the same error which his great master was committing on a vaster scale in Germany during this same summer campaign of 1813. Just as Napoleon, in a mood of over-great optimism, believed in the ultimate triumph of his own arms, and therefore deliberately left strong garrisons in all the fortresses whose neighbourhood he was temporarily obliged to quit, intending to come back at leisure to relieve them, so did Suchet. Napoleon dealt in thousands where his Marshal dealt in hundreds, but the hundreds were just as important to the moderate strength of the Army of Aragon as the thousands to the Imperial host in Germany. And if Napoleon fought a hopeless game in Champagne, because he had left behind him the enormous garrisons of Königsberg and Wittenberg, of Magdeburg and Dresden, of Hamburg and Torgau, and never could rally them for his final effort, so Suchet condemned himself to impotence in the autumn and winter campaigns that were to come, because he locked up nearly half his veteran infantry in fortresses that he was never to see again.

He began on a small scale: in the Kingdom of Valencia he left a single company in Denia, a battalion in Peniscola, two battalions in the rocky fastness of Saguntum, another single company in Morella. All these were strategic points, and the total of men left behind was only 2,000. But this was only the beginning of a ruinous policy—ere long he was to leave 4,800 men to be shut up in the great fortress of Tortosa, 2,000 in Lerida, still greater numbers in Barcelona—all in the end presents to the enemy. For it is the field-army that counts—as Wellington saw in 1810, when he refused to shut up a single British soldier in Ciudad Rodrigo, or Almeida, or Badajoz, or Elvas, important as they all were. And a general who has reduced his field-army to a half will never succeed in relieving the strongholds in which he has locked up the other half. Suchet defended himself by saying that his garrisons detained in front of them a much larger number of Spanish troops, conducting the siege or blockade: that they could hold out for a very long time: that they blocked lines of communication valuable to the enemy: and that he had a reasonable hope of saving them when the turn of the tide should come. Napoleon expressed much the same ideas[1]. But what if the tide of fortune has ebbed for good, and no turn ever comes? All Suchet's future troubles resulted from the ruinous policy which he first displayed when, on quitting Valencia, he left behind him the unlucky garrisons of Denia, Saguntum, Morella, and Peniscola.

Meanwhile he had still a field-army on July 12th, though it had but 18,000 men in its four infantry divisions and its cavalry brigade. And he could count on some assistance from Catalonia, whose army would come under his command, since Decaen was his junior, whenever he entered that province. But the

---

[1] Napoleon to Mortier, January 12, 1814.

moment was not a particularly favourable one for drawing help from Catalonia, since after Murray's departure Decaen had contrived to entangle himself in unsuccessful operations, though he had now no enemy to contend against save Copons's very small, if ubiquitous, 'First Army'. Before the final embarkation of the Anglo-Sicilians had taken place, Decaen had at last got together a complete brigade, by much shifting of garrisons, and had marched from Gerona to Barcelona on June 17th with a little over 2,000 men: next night he reached his destination, and heard that Maurice Mathieu was now at Villurodena on the Gaya. He went out to join him, with his column and a large convoy of powder for Tarragona, whose stores were low after the siege. They met at Villafranca, and after throwing the convoy into Tarragona, started out in search of Copons with their united forces, some 8,000 strong. They advanced to Reus, the Spaniard's old head-quarters, on June 23rd, but found (of course) that he had retired into the mountains after Murray's departure. After visiting the site of the fort of Balaguer, and noting its complete destruction, Decaen and his subordinate returned to Barcelona on July 1st. The news of Vittoria had not yet come to hand, and Decaen thought the moment a favourable one, now that he had a field force collected, for falling upon Vich, the central rallying point of the Spanish Army of Catalonia, and the only large town of which Copons was in possession. Eroles (it will be remembered) had been lying there during the absence of the rest of the Catalan force in the south, and had been doing his best with his two battalions to give trouble to the French garrisons in the Ampurdam[1]. But his chief was now back, with the 6,000 men who had been co-operating with Murray, and the 'First Army' was concentrated, some 8,000 strong, at its head-quarters.

Decaen's scheme was to attack Vich himself from the south with his field force of ten battalions, breaking through the defiles of the Congost, while Lamarque was to strike from the east, with a column of 2,000 men from Gerona, along the course of the river Ter, and to fall on the rear of the Catalans. The operation was timed to commence on July 6th. But just as both

[1] He had a hot fight with Maximilien Lamarque at Bañolas on June 23rd, and was beaten, but the French lost nearly 200 men.

forces had started, Decaen received the untoward news of the battle of Vittoria. He saw that this was not the time for offensive operations, and that he must at once recast all his plans, get into touch with Suchet, and think of the defence of the high road to France. He halted near Hostalrich, and sent triplicate orders to Lamarque to abandon the enterprise and return to Gerona, to which he himself now directed his march. But Lamarque had started punctually, and had forced his way up the Ter as far as Roda, only three miles from Vich, after much skirmishing with three battalions under Eroles, who tried to stop him (July 8). He received none of the dispatches which ordered him to turn back. Now Copons had been watching Decaen with the bulk of his force; but seeing the latter turn aside from the passes, he sent another brigade to help Eroles. This concentrated triple numbers against the Gerona column, which was beaten back, and intercepted during its retreat, on the heights of La Salud, and surrounded on three sides. It would have been destroyed if Decaen, who was growing anxious at its non-appearance on the Gerona road, had not sent Beurmann's brigade forward, up the valley of the Ter, in search for the missing detachment. Beurmann arrived just in time to save Lamarque, whose guns were silenced, and whose ammunition was nearly exhausted. The Gerona column had lost over 400 men, and the astounding number of 31 officers, before it was rescued, and the Catalans looked upon the combat of La Salud as a success. For Vich had been saved and the enemy's operations had failed completely[1].

This affair ruined Decaen's credit at Paris: coming on top of his tardiness in joining Maurice Mathieu at Barcelona during Murray's invasion, it gained him the repute of being an irresolute commander, who gave orders to his subordinates, and then failed to do his own part in co-operating with them. And there was some foundation for the rebukes which the Minister of War

[1] Some curious details of this little campaign may be had in Vidal de la Blache's *Évacuation de l'Espagne*, i. pp. 382–4. One of the oddest of them was already known to Napier—viz. that Lamarque's determination on July 8th to continue pushing towards Vich, despite of all opposition, was caused by hearing gunfire in the town: he deduced that it came from Decaen's attack on the other side. But it was really a salute of 100 guns for the victory of Vittoria, of which the news had just arrived at Vich.

lavished upon him and reported to the Emperor. But the daily
work of a general in Catalonia was particularly hard—how
could he deal with a situation in which three separate messages
to a column only twenty miles away might all fail to arrive?
And how could he keep a field force concentrated for any length
of time, if it had to be scraped together from garrisons, of which
any one that was brought down too low in strength might be
set upon by the enemy's main body, while the field force was
occupied a hundred miles away? After the abortive movement
on Vich was over, Decaen returned one of the brigades of his
marching column to Lamarque, and another to the garrison of
Barcelona. But the only result was that when Suchet, later in
the month, ordered him to collect a fighting force once more, its
elements had to be gathered in as before, and all the normal
arrangements for keeping roads open and convoys safe had to
be abandoned, in order to concentrate 10,000 men.

But to return to Suchet, whom we left approaching the Ebro
five days after his departure from Valencia, and waiting for
news from Saragossa. He had hoped to hear that Clausel, after
joining Paris's division in the Aragonese capital, would halt
there, and concert with him plans for threatening Wellington's
flank. And the first letters that he received from that general
gave him some reason to think that his expectation might be
fulfilled, for Clausel wrote to say that he was taking up a position on the Gallego river, from which he could join the Marshal
if Wellington came down the Ebro in force, or on the other
hand move up to meet the King in the Pyrenees, if he were so
ordered[1]. Suchet thereupon sent a dispatch to the Minister of
War, expressing his intention of throwing his impedimenta into
Lerida, and marching with all available units on Saragossa.
'If we can gain some marches on the enemy who is opposite us
(Bentinck and Del Parque), and find Wellington with his army
divided, it would be a glory for the Army of Aragon to meet and
beat him, with the aid of General Clausel's corps[2].'

But the hope of a campaign on the central Ebro only lasted
for a day. On July 9th Suchet received a second dispatch from
Clausel, to say that, since he had heard that Wellington's

[1] Suchet to Clarke, quoting Clausel (July 17).
[2] Suchet to Clarke, July 8.

columns had turned back towards Pampeluna, and that there was no hostile force in the neighbourhood of Saragossa which need cause the Marshal any apprehension, he had made up his mind to seek for the King's army, and was marching for the Pyrenees, by the valley of Roncal and Ochagavia[1]. There was no further hope of a concentration at Saragossa, and all chances of preserving Aragon were gone. The Marshal sent orders to Paris that he must abandon Saragossa at once, and march down the Ebro to Mequinenza to join the main body, which would reach that fortress on the 12th or 13th.

But Paris never received this dispatch, for he had been driven out of Saragossa before it could reach him. Clausel had been much in the wrong when he wrote to Suchet that, since the English had turned back, there was no enemy in Aragon of whom he need be afraid. Paris had in all some 6,000 men[2], and there were closing in upon him Duran's so-called '5th Division of the 2nd Army', which was really a vast guerrillero band of over 5,000 men, and Mina with all his nine Navarrese and Aragonese battalions and his own horse, strengthened by Julian Sanchez's Castilian lancers. His corps was at least 9,000 strong. Now in an ordinary way 6,000 French troops need not have feared 14,000 guerrilleros. But Mina was not the sort of leader who would commit the usual faults of his less-experienced compeers, and allow himself to be surprised, or brought to action when he did not desire it. Long experience had made him a formidable enemy. He himself kept south of the Ebro, and got in touch with Duran, while he detached his lieutenant Chaplangara, with three battalions, to threaten Saragossa from the north bank. Paris sallied out with the bulk of his forces, and gave battle to Mina's own column on the Torrero heights to the south-west of the city on July 9th. He checked the Navarrese after some sharp fighting, but was chagrined to receive the news that in his absence the south front of Saragossa was being attacked by Duran's men, and its transpontine suburb by Chaplangara's

[1] Suchet to Clarke, quoting Clausel (July 17). For all these foiled hopes see Vidal de la Blache, i. pp. 370–2.

[2] Two battalions each of the 10th and 81st Line, one Neapolitan battalion, some companies of Gendarmes and miquelets, three squadrons of the 12th Hussars, and various details.

detachment. This compelled him to come back, to reinforce the inadequate garrison which he had left in the city. It was evident that the enemy was upon him in great strength, and that he stood some risk of being cut off and blockaded in his fortress. Indeed, he would have done well to obey Suchet's original orders of July 3rd, and to have evacuated Saragossa the moment that he received them on the 7th. For Clausel had abandoned him by marching north from the Gallego, and he had been told to depart without delay, and fall off down the Ebro, if this should happen.

Obeying his orders three days too late, Paris marched out at 9 p.m. on July 10th, after blowing up the city bridge in order to detain Mina, and throwing a garrison of 500 men into the Aljafferia, the old Moorish citadel outside the walls. This was a useless sacrifice, but done under the Marshal's direct command —another example of Suchet's persistent habit of making presents of isolated garrisons to the enemy. The troops marched off by Alcubierre and the road to Lerida, which Paris preferred to the Mequinenza road, because the latter ran for many miles through the open Llanada de Santa Lucia, where Mina's numerous cavalry would have him at an advantage. For the column was escorting an immense train, and the vehicles of several thousand *Afrancesados*—many of them Madrid refugees, who had accumulated in Saragossa. Its length was therefore preposterous and its progress slow.

Having a night's start, and being at first pursued by Chaplangara's men only, Paris made good time for the first twelve hours, but before the 11th was over he had been overtaken by Mina's cavalry, and was forced to fight for every mile that he gained. The convoy fell into disorder, six guns had to be spiked and abandoned in a pass, and the loss of men was becoming serious. At Alcubierre, 30 miles from Saragossa, Paris made up his mind that it was hopeless to think of continuing his march on the Lerida road, for detachments of the enemy had got across it in front of him. Sacrificing all hope of joining Suchet, he waited till dark, and turned the column off northward on to the road to Huesca and Jaca, which was unobstructed. Marching all night he reached Huesca at noon next day, not much troubled by the pursuing Spaniards, but strewing the road with wagons, coaches, worn-out refugees, and foot-sore soldiers.

On the 13th he reached Jaca and the Pyrenean passes by another forced march, having lost only 300 men, but all his wheeled transport and hundreds of unfortunate *Afrancesados*. The troops, as we are told, systematically plundered the vehicles of the civilian fugitives, and even their persons, all discipline having been lost in the hurried and disorderly flight. But Paris brought 4,400 infantry and 680 horse to safety, which was more than could have been expected.

At Jaca he learned that Clausel had passed through on the previous day (July 12), and having thrown a battalion into the fortress to strengthen its garrison, he halted to guard the passes. Paris's troops never rejoined Suchet—a serious loss to the Marshal, who could ill spare 5,000 men. For after a long halt at Jaca, where they faced and contained the pursuing battalions of Mina, they were ultimately ordered to descend into France; they joined the main army, and served out the rest of the war as a brigade of Soult's left wing.

While Mina was observing Paris at Jaca, Duran undertook the siege of the citadel of Saragossa, which he conducted in a leisurely way. For though it was surrounded on July 10th, he did not begin to bombard it till August 1st. The brick-built walls soon began to crumble, and the commandant, Captain Bouquet, seeing that his garrison was growing demoralized, took the desperate resolve of blowing up the magazine rather than hoist the white flag. The explosion destroyed a bastion, and killed some men, whereupon the survivors, despite of the efforts of their chief, surrendered in a disorderly and individual fashion (August 5). The place ought never to have been held, and the 500 men in it were a useless sacrifice to Suchet's mistaken theory of holding strategic points.

On July 12th the Marshal's main body was near Tortosa, his minor column (Musnier and Severoli) at Caspe. He was impatiently awaiting the arrival of Paris, but could get no news of him till the 14th, when he heard of the evacuation of Saragossa, and the retreat of its garrison, not towards Mequinenza, according to his order, but towards Huesca and the Pyrenees. On receiving this disappointing intelligence, he resolved that he must retire into Catalonia, and after gathering in all the smaller garrisons of the lower Ebro, he directed his march on Tarragona.

His own column went by Tortosa and the Col de Balaguer, where it was much incommoded by the fire of British warships close inshore, that of Musnier by Mequinenza, Lerida, and Mont-blanch. From Tarragona on July 17th Suchet wrote long explanatory dispatches to the Minister of War, contending that all his troubles were the result of the battle of Vittoria, for which he had no responsibility, and that the conduct of Clausel, Paris, and Decaen had been anything rather than helpful during the crisis. His policy of dropping heavy garrisons in strategic points was now fully developed—General Robert being placed in Tortosa with 4,800 men—the equivalent of a full division, Isidore Lamarque in Lerida with 2,000; a battalion was also left in Mequinenza, and a company in Monzon, the two minor fortresses in front of Lerida. Allowing for the fact that there had already been garrisons in all these places, and that the extra troops dropped behind were largely those that had been saved from the smaller evacuated posts in Aragon and Valencia, there was still a solid deduction of 8,000 men from the strength of the field-army—and they were never to be seen again. But Suchet had now assumed command in Catalonia over the head of Decaen, and his first order to his junior was that he must reconstitute his army of operations, and have 8,000 or 10,000 men ready to join in the campaign which would certainly begin when Bentinck, Del Parque, and Elio made their inevitable appearance on the lower Ebro. Decaen did not see how this could be done, without either cutting down the northern garrisons to a figure which would make them dangerously weak, in face of the incursions of Copons and Eroles, or reducing the large force which was required to keep down the turbulent city of Barcelona. But, protesting all the time, he nevertheless produced 8,000 men when they were wanted. Meanwhile Suchet first inspected Tarragona, which he condemned as altogether too dilapidated to be held against a serious attack—a good commentary on Murray's recent proceedings. He ordered preparations to be made to dismantle it, and to remove or destroy all surplus guns. But it was to be held meanwhile, till the enemy began to press, as it was a useful half-way-house on the way to Tortosa, which was to be held in strength. He then made a flying visit to Lerida and Monzon, also for purposes of inspection (July 18–23), while his weary army rested about Tarragona. But he was back in five days to await the expected invasion from the south.

It was long in coming. Bentinck, as he complained to Wellington, had not a quarter of the land-transport required for an army of 16,000[1] men about to undertake a long campaign. Suchet's rearguard had vanished from the Xucar on July 3rd; Bentinck had the best will in the world to get forward, but it was not till July 9th that his advanced guard entered Valencia, four days after Suchet's departure. Villacampa's division of the 'Second Army' came up on the same day from the inland, but Elio himself and his other divisions were still far off, and Del Parque had hardly moved. However, on the 13th, when Suchet was already beyond the Ebro, Bentinck got the two Spanish generals to his head-quarters, and drew up a plan of campaign. Elio was to be set the task of besieging the Valencian fortresses, with the divisions of Roche, Mijares, and Sarsfield. He would not, therefore, have to move far from his present position: but his fourth division, that of Villacampa, was to follow the Anglo-Sicilians to Catalonia. Del Parque, who professed entire inability to advance unless food were given to him, was sent 100,000 rations of flour to induce him to move forward[2]. The Anglo-Sicilians started from Valencia on July 16th— just as Suchet was entering Tarragona—and advanced by slow stages along the coast road as far as Vinaroz (July 20), fifteen miles south of the Ebro. Here Bentinck halted them, partly because Del Parque and Villacampa were still some marches behind him, partly because he was anxious to get more accurate news concerning Suchet, partly because he had not quite made up his mind between a simple frontal advance to the Ebro followed by the siege of Tortosa, and the bolder plan of shipping his army round to the beaches where Murray had landed in June, and throwing himself into the middle of the French for a sudden stroke. There were strong (but false) rumours that Suchet was about to evacuate Catalonia altogether, and that large bodies of

---

[1] He had now picked up the Sicilian cavalry and Whittingham's horse, which had not gone to Tarragona.

[2] Wellington told him that the flour would be wasted, 'they will not know how to get it baked, how to carry it, or how to issue it, and they will never repay the supply'. *Dispatches*, x. p. 554.

troops had been moving towards the Pyrenees[1]. If this were true, why should not a blow be made at Barcelona itself, the centre of all French power? By a malicious chance none of Wellington's letters written after that of July 1st reached Bentinck for four weeks, and he was left to his own inspirations, without any further help than could be got from a document dictated when the commander-in-chief could know neither of Suchet's retreat, nor the evacuation of Aragon, and therefore sadly out of date. It merely directed Bentinck to overrun the kingdom of Valencia: after which 'your lordship will be the best judge whether it is more expedient to embark and again attack Tarragona, or to cross the Ebro and attack Tortosa, or to endeavour to obtain possession of the enemy's fortresses on the coast of Valencia[2]'.

Bentinck, wrongly believing that Suchet was ready to abandon Catalonia, and would give way when pressed, opted for the most ambitious programme—he would embark and attack Tarragona. And if (as he was informed wrongly) that fortress was already evacuated, he would attack Barcelona also. Meanwhile Del Parque should come up and besiege Tortosa, and Copons should be asked to descend from his mountains, and join the disembarking force in the Campo of Tarragona. What Bentinck did not know was that Suchet had 15,000 of his own men close to Tarragona, quite ready to fight when they should be joined by Decaen and 10,000 more. It was rash to challenge the Marshal with the Anglo-Sicilians alone—16,000 men of five different nationalities, including only 5,000 British troops.

[1] Apparently a late echo of Decaen's march of July 6th–9th from Barcelona to Gerona.

[2] From Huerta, July 1, *Dispatches*, x. pp. 478–80.

SECTION XL: CHAPTER II

BENTINCK'S INVASION OF CATALONIA: CONTROVERSIES BETWEEN SUCHET AND SOULT. AUGUST–SEPTEMBER 1813

By July 23rd Suchet had brought down his army to the coast of Catalonia, and cantoned it for a much-needed rest in the valleys of the Llobregat and the Gaya. He was in full touch with the garrison of Barcelona, and had issued to Decaen orders that a field-force should be collected for his assistance, as it had been before, at the time of Murray's wretched Tarragona expedition. He was still in communication with his all-too-large garrisons at Lerida (which he had just visited) and Tortosa, and was waiting for the next move of the enemy. His chief fear was that Wellington might detach a large force down the valley of the Ebro, to join up with the accumulation of Spanish troops about Saragossa, and that he might be attacked in flank as well as in front[1].

Lord William Bentinck meanwhile, having decided to invade Catalonia by the sea-coast route along the Col de Balaguer, was inspired by an unjustified optimism as to the condition and intentions of the enemy. He had made up his mind that it was quite clear that Suchet was about to draw back his whole front in Catalonia, probably as far as the Llobregat, so as still to cover Barcelona, perhaps even as far as the Fluvia and the Ampurdam, on the very borders of France. It seemed to him, and the hypothesis was quite reasonable, that one of the results of Vittoria would be that an immense proportion of the army of Catalonia would be withdrawn, to reinforce the troops under Soult, which were gathering at Bayonne and on the Bidassoa in face of Wellington. And unluckily for him persistent rumours were coming in, through spies, that large columns were marching north from Barcelona towards the Pyrenees. The same rumours got to Wellington[2]. It was even reported that Tarragona had been blown up and evacuated: for this story there was a certain

---

[1] Suchet to Clarke, July 25.

[2] Wellington to Bentinck, August 25, *Dispatches*, xi. pp. 29–30, and August 14, *Dispatches*, x. p. 634.

foundation of truth, for Suchet had (as a matter of precaution) caused some of its bastions to be mined; on inspection he had thought the place too weak, and he was prepared to dismantle it if necessary. But it was a good half-way-house to Tortosa, and he was prepared to hold it unless the attack upon him was made in great force.

Having concerted measures with his Spanish associates, Bentinck determined to push on. He put Clinton's division on shipboard, and ordered it to land at Tarragona, if it should prove to be true that it had been evacuated. With the rest of his own force, McKenzie's division, Adam's brigade, Whittingham's Spanish horse and foot, and the three regiments of his own cavalry, he began on July 26th to cross the Ebro at Amposta, five miles down stream from Tortosa, and then to march by the coast road over the Col de Alba and the Col de Balaguer for the plain of Tarragona. Clinton had to come back, reporting that Tarragona was held, and that he had seen numerous troops moving around it: there was as a matter of fact a change of garrison going on. The passage at Amposta was tedious—there was no bridge but only a ferry-pontoon worked on ropes, and a few fishing boats. It took several days for the army to dribble across, thread the defiles of the Col de Alba, and reach the pass of Balaguer, where Clinton landed and joined his chief. Bentinck had in all about 16,000 men—including Whittingham's *División Mallorquina*, but only six British and one German Legion battalions of infantry, and four squadrons of British and German cavalry. The rest were Sicilians, Calabrese, the once mutinous Anglo-Italian levy[1], or foreign corps. The only Spanish division near him was Villacampa's, from Elio's army, which crossed the Ebro after the Anglo-Sicilians. The Duque Del Parque with his '3rd Army'—only about 10,000 strong since its misfortunes at Carcagente in June—was a march or two behind Villacampa. Of the bulk of the '2nd Army', the divisions of Roche and Mijares were blockading Saguntum and Peniscola, Duran was still besieging the Aljafferia at Saragossa, which did not fall till August 5th. The Empecinado's division was at Madrid, which it had seized after the departure of the French in June, and which it continued to occupy till September, when troops from

1 See vol. vi. p. 279.

Andalusia came up to replace it[1]. There remained only the
division of Sarsfield, which ultimately moved up from the
Valencian coast in the wake of Del Parque. The little army of
Catalonia under Copons was for the most part in the north, since
its success over Lamarque at La Salud, but had a battalion or
two watching Barcelona under Manso.

On July 30th Bentinck, affronting a greater danger than
he realized, marched straight on Tarragona by the coast-road,
and shut it in on all sides with his two Anglo-Sicilian divisions.
The Spanish auxiliary corps under Whittingham was dropped
at Reus, partly as flank-guard, to watch the inland roads from
Barcelona, but more for the reason that it had no transport,
had exhausted the little food that the men were carrying, and
had, for the moment, to live on the country-side[2]. Suchet, with
his head-quarters at Villafranca, and all his four divisions
cantoned close in to them, along the lower Llobregat, could
have marched on Tarragona with 20,000 men within two days,
if he had made some slight borrowings from the garrison of
Barcelona. But he took Bentinck's over-boldness for conscious
strength, and waited for the return of Decaen, whom he had
recently sent off northward, to escort to Gerona an accumulation
of sick, wounded, and of Spanish refugees, whom he had brought
with him from Valencia. At Gerona Decaen was to pick up a
large convoy of cattle and foodstuffs, destined to replenish the
magazines of Barcelona. This he did successfully; but having
to accommodate the marching-pace of his columns to that of
ox-wagons and sheep, he only got back to Barcelona on August
12th. He led out 8,000 men and 19 guns to join Suchet on
August 13th.

Thus Bentinck lay for fourteen days unmolested below the
walls of Tarragona, under constant menace of being attacked
by Suchet, but never actually assailed. Soon after his first
arrival he had discovered that things were not so easy as he had
expected—that Suchet was in force on the Llobregat, and as
yet showing no signs of an intention to retreat, and that, though
Del Parque and Villacampa had drawn up to his neighbour-

[1] Though Wellington had sent the Empecinado orders to march for
Aragon as early as August 7th. *Dispatches*, x. p. 618.

[2] See Wellington to Bentinck. *Dispatches*, xi. p. 40.

hood, it was difficult, or impossible, to keep them concentrated, for mere reasons of commissariat. The country round Tortosa, as far as the pass of Balaguer, is among the most arid, rough, and forbidding tracts of Spain[1]. Del Parque had to leave one of his divisions to 'observe' the large garrison of Tortosa, in company with that of Villacampa, but could neither place them near the fortress, nor keep them fed, when he had disposed them at a distance from it. He brought his first and third divisions (Anglona's and Berenguer's)[2] to Constanti not far in Bentinck's rear, and in a good position for supporting him. Meanwhile Whittingham's division was moved forward from Reus to occupy the Col de Santa Cristina and the Col de Liebra, the two passes from the upland country to the plain of Tarragona. But its general complained that the men were starving in the mountains, and they had to be fed, under protest, from Bentinck's own stores landed by the fleet.

Bentinck, under these circumstances, thought it best not to disembark his battering train—the ignominy of Murray's loss of guns in June was fresh in his memory. He merely blockaded Tarragona, and fortified 'strong points' in his front of circumvallation. Perhaps he was waiting for what he considered the practical certainty that Suchet would, in the end, draw back northward, perhaps for the completion of his arrangements with Copons for Catalan co-operation. For he had been assured that the '1st Army' had an admirable capacity for distracting the French, and was capable of such rapid movement as no other Spanish corps could rival. Copons did indeed come down from Vich towards Barcelona, and signalized his arrival by a raid into the midst of Suchet's cantonments, cutting up at San Sadurni on August 7th a battalion of the Italian 1st Léger, only ten miles from the Marshal's Head-Quarters. But he seemed loath to commit himself to a junction with the Anglo-Sicilians—probably because of an evil memory of the way in which Murray had left him in the lurch six weeks back, but possibly also because

---

[1] I have seen many unhappy-looking regions in Spain, but none more rocky, desolate, and unpeopled than the Tortosa–Caspe country, about the lower Ebro.

[2] This officer had replaced Cruz Murgeon in command of the 3rd Division after the affair of Carcagente.

Bentinck had hurt his feelings by sending orders to his subordinate (and rival) Baron Eroles, now commanding the first Catalan division[1]. At any rate he was heard of at Tarragona, but no close touch with him was secured. And meanwhile the battering train remained on shipboard.

This was fortunate, for on August 14th Suchet executed one of those concentric forced marches of several columns for which he had a well-deserved reputation. On that morning he sent Harispe's and Musnier's divisions forward by Vendrils to cross the Gaya, by the coast-route to Tarragona; he led himself Habert's and Severoli's divisions by Villarodona and the Col de Liebra pass, and dispatched Decaen, with his two divisions of the *Armée de Catalogne*, to force the Col de Santa Cristina pass, and come down upon Reus, in Bentinck's rear. The British general, getting the news of all these moves simultaneously, with a report from Whittingham that he was far too weak to hold the passes against 15,000 men, gave orders for a general retreat, and not a moment too early. For if he had offered to hold the line of the Gaya against the coast-column, the other two would have come down to Valls and Reus, and have cut off his retreat southward. The alternative of calling in Whittingham and Del Parque, and offering battle, would have been far too hazardous. Villacampa and the detached divisions of Del Parque's army could not possible have come up in time to help. And Copons had been completely isolated from the Anglo-Sicilians by Suchet's last move.

Accordingly on the night of August 15th Bentinck fell back by the coast-road to Cambrils, and was joined in the morning by Whittingham's force dropping in from the side of Reus. Del Parque, by order, had already started off in full retreat, and was some way ahead. Thus it came that all Suchet's columns joined successfully, but found nothing in front of them save a cavalry rear-guard, which they pushed before them all day, without succeeding in doing it much harm. Suchet halted Decaen's column at Valls, but pushed on his own cavalry on the 17th till it came in sight of Hospitalet, and the north entry of the Col de Balaguer. Here the British fleet was discovered lying off the shore in great force, while upon the sea-cliff inland

---

[1] This was Wellington's idea, *Dispatches*, xi. p. 85.

Bentinck's infantry could be seen in position holding the pass and the rugged hills above.

The temptation to attack must have been considerable—as Suchet had with him a force such as he would find it hard to collect again, and a victory would have meant the relief of Tortosa, and a chance of rolling the beaten army against the bridgeless course of the lower Ebro. But Bentinck's ground was very strong; he could only be attacked along the shore-road, and the attacking force would be exposed to a terrible cannonade from the fleet. The Marshal resolved that he must be content with the relief of Tarragona, and the complete check inflicted on Bentinck's offensive move.

The British commander was obviously disappointed: he had drawn wrong conclusions from imperfect premises overcharged with optimism, and had (very rightly) to submit with patience to Wellington's inevitable 'I told you so'. His chief had written to him, before the event, 'You may depend upon it that Suchet will endeavour to interrupt any operation of this kind [sieges] that you may attempt, and you will do well to be prepared accordingly[1].' After the failure came, 'I was quite certain that Suchet would move upon you to interrupt your operations—and you were fortunate to be able to raise the siege without loss of guns or stores[2].' Then followed a warning that more caution must be shown in the future. It was not unneeded—as Bentinck's operations in September were to show.

Meanwhile the fortified position at the mouth of the Col de Balaguer had its disadvantages—the army had to subsist entirely on food from the fleet, and there was not enough to supply the Spanish troops as well as the Anglo-Sicilians. Del Parque had to be asked to drop back across the Ebro, and Whittingham's horse (though not his infantry) accompanied the 3rd Army to the crossing-place at Amposta, where a new bridge was found to have collapsed, and the pontoon-ferry alone to be available. On August 19th, when most of Del Parque's infantry and all the cavalry but two squadrons had been ferried over, with interminable delays, Robert, the governor of Tortosa, made a sally with five battalions and 100 dragoons against the last Spanish unit which had still to cross—the weak division of Berenguer—

---

[1] *Dispatches*, x. p. 617.   [2] Ibid. xi. p. 40.

and threw it into some confusion, but was beaten off by the accurate fire of Whittingham's horse-artillery battery, which averted a disaster[1]. The Spanish division lost 400 men in this 'Combat of Amposta', the sallying force probably about half that number[2].

Suchet, on returning from the pursuit of Bentinck, carried out what had apparently been his original intention, the evacuation and dismantling of Tarragona. He thought that its fortifications, never thoroughly repaired since the siege of 1811, were imperfect, and would require, to keep them safe, a larger garrison than the two battalions with which General Bertoletti had defended them against Murray in June and Bentinck in August. Accordingly he used the powder in store to blow up all the bastions of the more accessible front, that which looks towards the Lower Town. The ancient Cyclopean walls—Iberian or Punic—along the cliff-front were inaccessible to any besieger, and so were left intact—as they remain to this day. After executing this destruction, Suchet retired to his old headquarters at Villafranca, sent his four divisions into cantonments, and gave Decaen permission to disperse his field-force, and send its fractions northward, to deal with the incursions of the Catalans. The departure of Decaen's forces caused rumours of the approaching evacuation of Catalonia to spread abroad once more; these were transmitted to Bentinck by spies, in the shape of an assurance that half Suchet's army was in march for France —a most dangerous delusion.

For it was on this untrustworthy hypothesis that Bentinck thought himself compelled to carry out an order of Wellington's given on August 14th[3], by which he was directed to send the Duque Del Parque's '3rd Army' to join the commander-in-chief on the upper Ebro, if Suchet were detected detaching troops to join Soult. As a matter of fact Suchet had sent nothing to Soult —as we shall see—but Del Parque's three divisions marched for Saragossa on August 28th, and were at Tudela in Navarre by

---

[1] The best account of this is in Whittingham's *Diary*, pp. 211-12. He accuses Berenguer of being 'as drunk as a beast' that afternoon.

[2] There are 9 officer-casualties in Martinien's list for the combat of Amposta, in 3rd Léger and 11th and 114th Line—probably some 180, therefore, in rank and file.   [3] *Dispatches*, x. p. 635.

September 15th. Wellington had no need of them there, and only found use for one of the divisions by sending it to assist in the tedious blockade of Pampeluna—which endured till the last day of October. To replace Del Parque in Catalonia there were now available Villacampa's division observing Tortosa, Sarsfield's division, recently come up from Valencia, and Duran's division (or rather great guerrillero band), to which the blockade of Lerida and Mequinenza was entrusted, after the fall of the Saragossa citadel early in August.

Bentinck's abortive invasion of Catalonia having been warded off, Suchet had some leisure in the second half of August to envisage the whole military situation in the Principality. He had, looking at the total of his muster-rolls only, a large force at his command, 67,000 men, or allowing for 5,000 sick about 62,000. This figure, however, included Paris's brigade, which had been driven off to Jaca, and was in touch with Soult rather than with its own army. If these 5,000 men[1] are deducted, there were 57,000 sabres and bayonets available, without counting the National Guards and *Chasseurs des Montagnes* who were guarding the Pyrenean passes on the French side, nor a depôt of conscripts, neither trained nor armed, at Perpignan.

Now 57,000 men under arms make a respectable army. But as we have already explained in other places, the French in Spain were obliged to be at once an army of occupation and an army for the field. Copying their master, the commanders tried to hold down the country-side, because any district not occupied became at once a focus of insurrection. Of Suchet's total of 57,000 men no less than 27,000 were tied up in garrisons, ranging from small posts (like Monzon) held by a single company, to large towns, where a whole division was immobilized—e.g. 4,800 men at Tortosa and 6,400 at Barcelona. Nor were these the only troops who were cancelled for effective field service— at least two brigades, sometimes three, were constantly circulating with convoys, keeping the roads open, and provisioning each garrison as its stores grew low. They could only be called in to join the operating army for a few days, as in their absence communications were cut between place and place, and the

---

[1] They had started from Saragossa 6,000 strong, but had lost men by the way, and placed a garrison of one battalion in Jaca.

miquelets and *Somatenes* attacked, and sometimes annihilated, the smaller posts. If the system of garrisons placed at every strategic point was to continue, Suchet could never hope to assemble more than 25,000 men for a serious and prolonged operation. And this was about the sum total of the force that he had collected to throw back Bentinck on August 14th.

To the critic of to-day, who cannot help knowing what was to be the final result of this system, it seems obvious that Suchet's correct game was to abandon all Catalonia, after withdrawing the garrisons, up to the line of Rosas and Figueras, or that of the Fluvia river. Leaving a small field-force—say 15,000 or 18,000 men—to hold that line, he could have assembled a fine army 40,000 strong, entirely composed of war-tried troops, with which he could have exercised a predominant influence on the general aspect of the war in the Peninsula. This was Wellington's notion of what was likely to happen[1]: he was expecting news of the evacuation of all Southern and Central Catalonia, and of the arrival of Suchet with a formidable force to join Soult, by the route of Perpignan, Tarbes, and Pau, inside the French frontier. His orders to Bentinck are full of provisions for what was to be done, when it was ascertained that much, or most, of Suchet's army had gone northward, and disappeared from the Catalan front. Not only Del Parque's '3rd Army' but Whittingham's division were to march at once, via Saragossa, for the Western Pyrenees, when quite certain intelligence of the withdrawal of the French towards their own frontier should come to hand. At a later time he thought of bringing over the Anglo-Sicilians also. Wellington had no notion whatever of a counterstroke into Roussillon or Languedoc, if the enemy should weaken his eastern front. He would trust Copons and Elio to bicker with whatever force Suchet might leave behind on the frontier. An invasion on a large scale, with a mainly Spanish army, did not seem attractive to him. Firstly, he did not consider that transport and commissariat arrangements for a large force could ever be organized: and secondly he believed that if a Spanish army should succeed

---

[1] See especially *Dispatches*, xi. pp. 39–41, and 83–4. But it was not his *first* opinion, as see *Dispatches*, x. p. 553, of July 20th, when he thinks Suchet may hold on to all Catalonia. But by August 14th he thought it fairly certain. *Dispatches*, x. p. 635.

in penetrating far beyond the Eastern Pyrenees, it would ravage the country-side, and provoke a wave of national wrath in France which he was anxious to avert.

Now Suchet was perfectly well aware that it was an absurd misuse of strength for him to have 27,000 men in garrisons and only 25,000 in the field. But he was obsessed with the idea that if he evacuated Southern Catalonia, and then the Emperor achieved a crowning victory in Saxony, and dictated peace to the Allies, his position before his master would be humiliating, and the imperial thunders would play upon him heavily. 'Je suis trop pénétré', he wrote to the Minister of War, 'des consé-quences graves qui pourraient en être la suite. S'il arrivait que Sa Majesté pût amener les ennemis à une bataille générale, et changer par une grande victoire la face des choses, n'aurais-je encouru aucun reproche en prenant sur moi de détruire les clefs de l'Ébre?' Moreover the minister kept warning him at intervals that it would be contrary to the prestige of the empire to allow Spanish armies to approach too near the frontier. And when the transference of Suchet's army to Tarbes and Pau, by a march north of the Pyrenees, through French soil, was suggested, Clarke opined that such a concentration would be 'onéreuse pour le Trésor, et fertile en incidents fâcheux pour la discipline des troupes et le bon esprit du pays[1]'. That is to say, the army would plunder, and the sight of the army in what looked like a retreat would produce a fatal effect in the depart-ments of the South. We need not be surprised that Suchet made up his mind that nothing, save a definite order from the Emperor himself, bidding him draw in his garrisons, evacuate Catalonia, and march to join Soult, would induce him to take these steps. The responsibility would be too great, and he detested the idea of putting himself under Soult's orders.

Meanwhile there ensued a long correspondence, full of cross questions and crooked answers, between Soult at St. Jean de Luz and Suchet at Barcelona. On August 10th, when his army was still reeling under the effects of the disaster of Sorauren, the Duke of Dalmatia wrote to the Duke of Albufera that 'dire necessity demands that the army of Aragon and Catalonia should

[1] For all these arguments see Vidal de la Blache's admirable summary of the correspondence in vol. i. pp. 452–69 of his *Évacuation de l'Espagne*.

make a great diversion, to bring back the theatre of war to the
banks of the Ebro, and remove it from the Bidassoa '. Let
Suchet march across Northern Aragon, making for Jaca, where
he would find the garrison left by Paris still in position, and he
himself would come over the Somport [or the pass of Canfranc],
and join him, leaving only a covering force to face Wellington.
They would have 80,000 men between them, and the 'prompt
and astonishing' result of their junction would be to remove
the war far from the frontiers of France[1]. Soult said nothing
about the results of Sorauren, or the state of his own army, save
that he congratulated himself that his recent offensive on
Pampeluna had forced Wellington to draw in westward many
troops hitherto opposed to his colleague. The statement was
simply untrue—on August 10th not a single allied unit had
moved from the Catalan front towards Soult's sphere of
operations[2].

This was well known to Suchet, and was one of many causes
which induced him to treat Soult's proposal with grave suspicion.
Misstatement for misstatement, he wrote to the Minister of
War that, so far from Soult having drawn off allied troops from
Catalonia, Sir Rowland Hill and the Andalusian Army of Reserve
were at the moment on the march to join Bentinck[3]. This was
indeed 'a Rowland for an Oliver'! To Soult he replied that his
colleague 'must evidently be unaware of the small number of
his troops, if he supposed that a disaster like that of Vittoria
could be repaired by a little army enfeebled by numerous
garrisons'. He was at present barely able to keep up his communication with France, and was soliciting reinforcements. To
Clarke Suchet wrote in the most unmeasured terms about Soult's
proposal. It was a mere snare, intended to sacrifice the Army of
Aragon: the Duke of Dalmatia owed him old grudges[4], and was

[1] Soult to Clausel, August 10.
[2] Del Parque's move, which had nothing to do with Soult's operations,
was only *ordered* on August 14th, and executed on August 28th. And it
took place in consequence of a mistaken rumour about Suchet's departure
from Catalonia.
[3] Suchet to Clarke, August 23.
[4] Suchet goes back to 1812, to detail his quarrels with Soult at Valencia
[see vi. p. 89], when he had refused several proposals of his colleague, and
had been insulted by him.

prepared to wreck him, for a most problematical advantage to himself: 'il méditait mon déshonneur.' Soult had kept silence about the deplorable state of his own troops, who were incapable at the moment of executing the march which he proposed. He wanted to see the Army of Aragon destroyed in a hopeless thrust across a country-side where every bridge was broken, and every road cut, if it tried the route Lerida–Huesca–Jaca: while if it went by Saragossa it would be beset by triple numbers, and something like a second Baylen might ensue. If it were checked and turned off into the Pyrenees, there was no pass open to it save that of Venasque, a mule-track 8,000 feet above sea-level. The enemy could turn 70,000 men upon him without drawing upon Wellington's aid. But—as mentioned above—he declared that Hill and O'Donnell also were on the move against him. Altogether Soult's project was 'sans objet, et manifestement dangereux[1]'.

The Duke of Dalmatia, on receiving his colleague's peremptory refusal, wrote to Paris to acknowledge that there had, perhaps, been something hazardous in the project of a march by Suchet's army across the whole breadth of Aragon. He therefore submitted a second plan—and this was one which was undoubtedly more feasible, and something like that which Wellington had expected to see put in execution. Let Suchet abandon all Lower Catalonia, draw in its garrisons, and march with all his own and Decaen's disposable troops through French soil, from Perpignan to Pau and Tarbes, where he would meet him with the bulk of his own army. He would leave 8,000 men only in front of Wellington, placing them in the fortifications of Bayonne: Suchet might leave another 8,000 at Gerona, in front of Bentinck and Copons. They would then have 80,000 men united, and would advance into Spain by the pass of the Somport. He would collect enormous magazines, sufficient for both armies, at Pau. There was nothing hostile blocking the Somport save some of Mina's guerrilleros, engaged in the siege of Jaca.

There was only one serious defect in this project from the purely military point of view—the proposal to use the Somport pass, which was unsuited for any wheeled traffic. Clausel and Paris had both crossed it, but without guns or wagons, which

[1] Suchet to Clarke, Aug. 23.

they had been forced to abandon. The French ascent was difficult, but as Soult alleged, capable of being made 'carossable' by a few days of vigorous engineering, and work there would be safe and secret. But what about the Spanish descent, which was known to be difficult also, and where Mina's guerrilleros were in occupation? No repairs could be executed there till the enemy had been driven off—and the pushing back of the Spanish outposts would tell its own tale to the enemy. All chance of a surprise would be made impossible. Why was the Somport route chosen by Soult? Possibly because the names of Maya and Roncesvalles, both obviously better passes, were now connected with memories of disaster. Possibly because the Somport was far from Wellington's front, and was not guarded by any regular unit of his army. But Suchet suspected—and we cannot be sure that he was wrong—that Soult was now making offers which he knew were impracticable, merely in order to put the blame of refusing co-operation on his colleague, when their master's eye should look over the file of their correspondence. To support this suspicion we may remember that the Somport was 6,000 feet above sea-level, and liable to be blocked by snow as early as October. Moreover the civil engineers declared that it would take two months' hard work to make the French side passable for guns, while Suchet added that the route was well known to many of his officers, and that they thought a year's toil would be required to set it right. Soult's reply to the objection about snowdrifts is also very suspicious. He said that artillery could be taken over the Somport, in the same way in which the Emperor had taken it across the St. Bernard in 1801—sledge-carriages could be made for the guns—if not on the spot then in Paris—and then sent by express post to the Pyrenees[1]. With sufficient goodwill and patience a hundred guns could be hauled over the pass.[2] This wild solution for the difficulty hardly seems sincere[3]. How long would it take to get the orders to Paris, to have the sledges planned and manufactured there, and then to

---

[1] Soult to Clarke, September 1.   [2] Soult to Suchet, September 4.

[3] Vidal de la Blache (i. p. 462), in his admirable synopsis of Soult's correspondence, observes: 'Il est assez difficile de prendre ces combinaisons au sérieux, quand elles émanent d'un homme qui avait fait la guerre de montagne en Suisse (1800).'

transport them on wheeled vehicles to the foot of the passes?
Obviously it would not be till winter had set in, when all cam-
paigning was impossible in those high altitudes.

Suchet's answer to the Somport proposition turned largely
on the impracticability of the pass—at all seasons, and especially
in this particular season. His memory reminded him, that
infantry, without guns or wagons, had been stopped there for
three consecutive days by a blizzard in early autumn. He had
hints, also, from Paris that the march of the Armies of Catalonia
and Aragon through the southern departments would be highly
objectionable to the authorities. Wherefore he would make a
counter-proposition. If and provided that (1) he got formal
leave from the Emperor himself to cut down the Catalan
garrisons and evacuate territory, and (2) he were allowed time to
thrust Bentinck's Anglo-Sicilians across the Ebro as a preliminary
precaution, he would undertake to collect at least 30,000 men
from his two armies. With these, a force large enough to brush
aside all local opposition, he would undertake to march via
Lerida and Huesca to the Gallego river, making for the point
where that stream emerges into the plains, after leaving the
defiles which lead to Jaca and the Somport pass. Here Soult
might join him with every man that he could spare: the Duke of
Dalmatia need not bring guns, as the Army of Catalonia could
supply batteries enough for both armies. But it was necessary
to point out that, when the two armies should have met, there
would be a terrible food-problem, as North-Western Aragon was
a bare desolate country: also that the roads from the Gallego
river to Pampeluna might prove impracticable for guns. He
presumed that the relief of Pampeluna was the primary object
of the expedition; it might be secured, but beyond achieving
that end, and occupying Saragossa, the power of the united
armies would not go. And Soult must bear in mind that two
days mistiming, at the rendezvous on the Gallego, might mean
ruin and destruction for one of the two armies.

It seems that Suchet's answer was as insincere as Soult's
proposition. He wrote his letter on September 4th. To get the
plans sent to Paris and forwarded to the Emperor would take
many days. The Emperor's answer would require many more to
reach Barcelona. Suchet would then require time to cut down

or evacuate his garrisons, and when he had accomplished this tedious business, and collected his large field-army, he would want at least a week to cast Bentinck over the Ebro, and some days more to march to Lerida. Clearly the complicated arrangement could not be carried out before October had made the mountains of Aragon impassable. And Suchet quite understood this; but like Soult he was playing for a plausible situation in face of their common master, lest he should be accused of turning down all plans for a junction of their two armies. He wrote privately to Decaen to tell him of the plan, with the comment that he thought the propositions astounding—they were *mouvements étonnants*. Decaen agreed: if they were carried out, the enemy would use his fleet to land troops in the rear of the French line in Northern Catalonia—even perhaps in Languedoc, which was absolutely defenceless.

Soult received Suchet's counter-propositions on September 22nd, and wrote to the Minister of War that he was prepared to accept them—indeed they were but a variant on his own scheme sent to Suchet on August 10th. The dispatches of both marshals were forwarded from Paris for the Emperor's consideration and approval. They reached the front in Saxony in the early days of October, when Napoleon was engaged in the whirl of unsatisfactory operations which led up to the battle of Leipzig. Either he had not time to read them at all, or he had not time to turn his mind from his own all-engrossing problems to the complicated situation in Spain, and to dictate a reply. At all events no answer was sent to Paris or the Pyrenees: the disaster of Leipzig supervened on October 16th–19th, and on October 31st the Emperor reached Frankfort, a broken man, with scarcely 70,000 men of the vast army which he had raised in the spring. But long before the news of Leipzig came to Bayonne or the Bidassoa, Wellington had settled Soult's problems for him, and raids over the Somport had become dreams of the past. It is doubtful whether they had ever been more than dreams.

SECTION XL: CHAPTER III

BENTINCK'S SECOND INVASION OF CATALONIA. THE COMBAT OF ORDAL. AUGUST–OCTOBER 1813

The Duke of Wellington being once asked what was the special faculty which had brought him through so many difficulties, and led him to so many victories, replied that he thought that he could guess what was going on 'upon the other side of the hill' better than most men. By this he meant that long experience and acute insight had made him a good judge of what each particular general, among the many who had been opposed to him, would be likely to be doing under the special circumstances of the moment. His little epigram also implied that he had learnt to test, by his own standards, the amount of reliance to be placed on each of the various reports and rumours, official and unofficial, which were being brought in to him all day long. Here, as in the other case, critical psychology came into play: he knew precisely what amount of credence should be given to information volunteered by a trusted intelligence officer like Colquhoun Grant, a nervous brigadier, a French deserter, or a Spanish alcalde of an optimistic frame of mind.

It would appear that Lord William Bentinck, though an enterprising officer, and a man of some capacity, was singularly destitute of Wellington's power of making accurate inductions as to what the enemy was doing, from the various items of information supplied to him. Otherwise, after his first unfortunate experience before Tarragona on August 14th–15th—the result of putting overmuch confidence in optimistic reports—he would not have repeated his error in September, from precisely the same causes. He had found that Suchet was far stronger than he had been led to believe, and that the very justifiable idea which he had entertained concerning the likelihood of a prompt evacuation of Catalonia by the French had been inaccurate. It is odd therefore that the intelligence which reached him at the end of August was not discounted, when it exactly repeated that which he received at the end of July. He was told by emissaries of good faith in Barcelona that Decaen had marched north with at

least 10,000 or 15,000 men, and that there was reason to believe
that Suchet was about to follow. Now it was quite true that
Decaen had broken up his field-force on August 20th, and had
marched off, with the best part of a division, to reopen the roads
in the direction of Gerona. And a few days later Suchet lent
his colleague Severoli's small Italian division, to be used for
convoy and escort work in Northern Catalonia. But there was
no certainty that these troops were bound for France, and leaving
Spain altogether. They were only serving the ordinary work
of the French army of occupation, and had not gone out of call.

Unfortunately for himself, Bentinck chose to regard the
perfectly correct news that Decaen and Severoli had passed out
of sight northward, as a proof that the evacuation of Catalonia
had really begun. He sent off Del Parque to march for Saragossa,
as we have already explained[1], holding that he was thereby
obeying Wellington's orders. And he then prepared to undertake a second invasion of Central Catalonia. He would seize
and repair the dismantled Tarragona, and use it as a naval base
for further operations. If it were true that an immense proportion of the French army had gone off to reinforce Soult, he
could even dare to think of the siege of Barcelona. At least he
would assume a forward and menacing position, for he would
be quite capable of challenging Suchet in the field, now that the
latter had sent away 10,000 or 15,000 men[2]. Accordingly on
August 27th he sallied out from his fortified position at the Col de
Balaguer, and in two marches reached Tarragona, to which the
fleet also transferred itself. A summary inspection of the ruined
fortifications convinced him that they could be repaired so as
to resist a *coup de main*, and many spiked guns were found
among the debris, which his artillery officers assured him could
be drilled and remounted with no great difficulty. On September 1st General Copons paid him a flying visit, confirmed the
news that Decaen had gone off with 15,000 men, and promised
to bring down the bulk of his own little army from the north, at
least as far as Igualada, for concerted operations against the
French positions in front of Barcelona.

[1] See above, p. 87.
[2] Bentinck to Wellington, September 1, from Tarragona. *Supplementary
Dispatches*, viii. pp. 219–20.

Bentinck had with him, beside his own Anglo-Sicilians, Whittingham's Spanish infantry—but not the cavalry of the 'Majorcan division'—and Sarsfield's division of the 2nd Army —altogether about 22,000 men. Villacampa's division was observing Tortosa, where the Empecinado's division, coming from Madrid (but very late), was due to join it. Duran's division was blockading Lerida and Mequinenza; those of Roche and Mijares were besieging Saguntum and Peniscola. Thus of all Elio's '2nd Army' only one division—Sarsfield's—was available to co-operate with Bentinck. His total force for attacking Suchet was somewhat less than it had been in the end of July, when the whole of Del Parque's '3rd Army' had been at his disposition. Copons was in touch, with some 6,000 men, and promised co-operation, but was working from his own base, and with his own scheme of operations. That he was an effective helper was shown on September 10th, when one of his brigades came right down to the Llobregat, and destroyed a French battalion at Palleja[1], near Molins de Rey, not ten miles from Barcelona.

On September 5th, having landed stores at Tarragona, and set his engineers to draw up plans and start repairs on its walls, Bentinck marched out of Tarragona with the Anglo-Sicilians, and occupied Villafranca, fifteen miles forward on the inland Barcelona road. He did not at first bring up either Sarsfield or Whittingham, who were left at Valls and Reus, from the usual difficulty of transport for their food. But he was hoping, when the critical moment came, to give them at least some supplies from the fleet: and they could join him in two marches if the enemy proved dangerous. It cannot be denied that to take only 12,000 Anglo-Sicilians into easy striking distance of Suchet's cantonments on the Llobregat was a risky move—but Bentinck had wrongly persuaded himself that the Marshal could not put 10,000 men in line. In an *ex-post-facto* dispatch, written after the combat of Ordal, he owns that he had begun to doubt the estimates of his informants—but if so his doubts came much too late.

For on the morning of September 12th he ordered forward his

[1] This was one of Manso's raids. He pounced right down among Suchet's cantonments, and cut up completely the 2/7th Line within a few miles of Barcelona.

'Advanced Guard Brigade'—still under Adam, as it had been at Biar in the spring[1]—and bade it occupy the defile of Ordal, by which the Barcelona high road crosses the mountain ridge between the valleys of the Noya and the Foix. This small force consisted of two battalions and two light companies of foot, a four-gun battery of light artillery, and a troop of the Brunswick Hussars. The battalions were the 2/27th and the Calabrese Free Corps, the rifle companies those of the 4th K.G.L. and De Roll. The third battalion which had formed part of the 'advanced guard' in earlier months—the 1st Italian Levy—had been transferred to Mackenzie's division, to replace the 6th K.G.L. Line, which had been sent back to Sicily. The whole of Adam's force amounted to between 1,500 and 1,600 men.

Bentinck conducted his vanguard in person to the Ordal defile, and placed it in position on the down-slope of the pass, where there were three ruined lines of trenches flanking the road, relics of fortifications thrown up by Reding against St. Cyr three years before. Below the trenches, but three-quarters of a mile in advance of them, the *chaussée* is carried across a deep ravine by a bridge, or rather a very high viaduct, of fourteen arches. This ravine covers the whole front of the position, and it can only be crossed at the bridge, and at one other point, far to its right, where there is a scrambling path down one steep bank and up the other, which could not bear two men abreast. A safer position could hardly be found, and so Bentinck thought— he told Adam that he was perfectly secure in it, and assured him that the whole army would be marching up from Villafranca that afternoon. A cavalry reconnaissance went five miles down the road, and saw no trace of the French in any direction. On the other hand touch was established with Manso's brigade of Copons's army, five miles to the north, which was holding San Sadurni on the banks of the Noya. Late in the afternoon there came up to the Ordal position the leading brigade of Sarsfield's Spanish division, which had just marched up from Valls, consist- ing of three battalions—Badajoz, Tiradores de Cadiz, and Voluntarios de Aragon, under Colonel Torres of the last-named corps—about 2,300 bayonets, with a squadron of horse attached. Bentinck's very short dispatch gives no explanation of whether

[1] See vol. vi. p. 289.

this addition to Adam's force was an afterthought, or a matter of chance. Perhaps, however, it may have been their arrival which determined him not to move up his whole army from Villafranca that afternoon, as he had told Adam that he intended to do.

Adam had to change his dispositions when this considerable reinforcement came up. He moved the Calabrese Free Corps sideways to the hill on the left of the bridge, placed his four guns across the high road some way up the slope, occupied the front trench near the guns with his two rifle companies and two companies of the 27th, placed the Spaniards in line along the centre of the position, to the right of the road, and put the remaining eight companies of the 27th on his extreme right, above the only spot where the lower course of the ravine could be crossed. Having done this, he and his whole force went to sleep. The story is almost incredible, but it is a fact that although he had 150 cavalry with him, and 1,500 yards in his front a most defensible defile—the great bridge-viaduct—he neither kept a cavalry vedette a mile or two out along the road, nor placed a picket at the bridge. It could—as Napier truly remarks[1]—have been blocked with an abattis or a loose stone barricade, and would have been impregnable against anything short of an artillery bombardment. There would appear to have been no watch kept of any sort, beyond the line of sentries in front of the bivouacs of the troops half-way up the hill.

Now Suchet had been given a week of warning since Bentinck made his forward move from Tarragona to Villafranca on September 5th, and this week had enabled him to collect from various quarters an army almost as large as that with which he had scared away his enemies in August. He got together at the bridge of Molins de Rey, where the main road crosses the Llobregat, the whole of the available infantry of the Army of Aragon, and he had called back Decaen and Severoli, and added to their force a battalion or two from the garrison of Barcelona. His own column had some 10,000 infantry and 1,500 horse, while Decaen's was somewhat less—7,000 infantry and a squadron or two of chasseurs. His intention was to make a sudden descent upon Bentinck, with the two columns converging—he himself

[1] *Peninsular War*, vi. pp. 179–80.

marching by the high road and bridge of Ordal, while Decaen, crossing the Llobregat higher up, at Martorel, was to sweep the Catalan detachments out of the valley of the Noya, and then turn in on the flank of the Anglo-Sicilians by the road San Sadurni–Villafranca. His scheme must have been formed before he knew that Bentinck had occupied the pass of Ordal, for this was only done at noon on the 12th, and the two French columns were massed and ready to move at that same moment. Probably Suchet had intended originally to seize the pass of Ordal himself, and descend on Bentinck at Villafranca. But he informs us in his dispatch that he received prompt information of the occupation of the defile, and resolved to retake it by surprise. Success would stop any further advance of the enemy, and might lead to a definite victory, if the turning movement by Decaen's column should work happily. It has been observed with justice[1] that the Marshal's plan was a risky one: if Adam had been awake, and the bridge of Ordal had been blocked, he would have run the chance of suffering much the same check as Ney received from Craufurd at the combat of the Coa in 1810. For 4,000 men, with artillery to back them, could have held such a defile for ever—there was little hope of crossing the ravine or turning the bridge on either flank. And operations in the dead of night are proverbially dangerous.

However, Suchet resolved to take the risk, and was rewarded by what can only be called undeserved success. He was forced to march in one long column on the high road, only a single battalion being detached on the left, to try to utilize the goat-path which led to the lower course of the ravine[2]. It is ten miles from Molins de Rey to the bridge of Ordal, and this distance the head of the marching column covered in $3\frac{1}{2}$ hours, arriving at the viaduct at a little after 11 p.m.—not at all a bad pace for a night march[3]. The bridge was crossed without a shot being fired or an enemy seen: but apparently the noise of the moving multitude over the stones must have roused somebody—

[1] Both by Napiér and by Sir John Fortescue.

[2] This was the 2/116th under Bugeaud, then a chef-de-bataillon—afterwards a Marshal of African celebrity.

[3] Two and a half miles an hour is good for a large body under night conditions.

CATALONIA

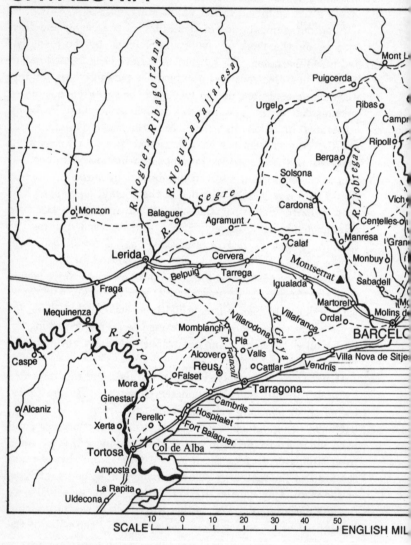

SCALE 10 0 10 20 30 40 50 ENGLISH MIL

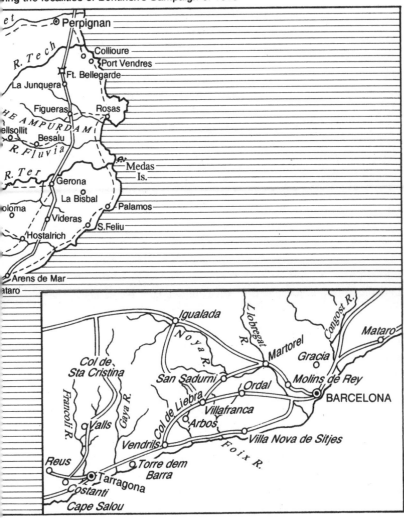

T:- THE COUNTRY BETWEEN BARCELONA AND TARRAGONA
ving the localities of Bentinck's Campaign of 1813

a patrol of Spanish horse came trotting down the road, and was fired at point-blank by the leading company of the 7th Line of Mesclop's brigade of Harispe's division, which led the advance of Suchet's interminable column. A minute later the whole hill-side above the bridge was ablaze with musketry. Each French battalion, as it passed the defile, deployed to its left and prolonged the line in that direction. Adam's troops had been sleeping in their fighting positions—this is the only thing that can be said in favour of his arrangements. As they woke, each found itself in succession attacked from the front, save the Calabrese Free Corps on the defenders' left, for none of the French turned in that direction, all the effort being made 'down-stream' and not 'up-stream' of the meagre river at the bottom of the ravine.

The first clash seems to have been the storming of the entrenchment half-way up the pass by the French 7th Line, who evicted the four companies which held it, and drove them uphill. They rallied at the second trench, were joined by some of the nearest battalion of Spaniards, and made a sudden counter-attack. The French were expelled for a moment, but rallied on the 44th Line, retook the earthwork, and went up the hill again, always extending their left. They were now engaged mainly with the three Spanish battalions, which by the agreement of every English eyewitness fought admirably, and counter-attacked twice with success. But Suchet kept slipping more troops to his left, putting in Habert's division and the reserve brigade of Harispe's. These bore back the Spaniards, and pressed round the flank of the 27th, on the extreme Allied right, which was presently also turned and completely outflanked by the detached battalion under Bugeaud, which had crossed the ravine by the difficult path in its lower course. Four battalions could not hold out for ever against fifteen, fought they never so fiercely. Moreover all command had ceased—Adam had been wounded early in the fight; Colonel Reeves of the 27th, who succeeded to the command, was also disabled, just as he was preparing to order a retreat, and sending off the guns to the rear. The next senior officer, Colonel Carey of the Calabrese, was bringing his battalion in from the left, where he had never been molested, and endeavouring to distract the French by a flank-attack, when he was simultaneously informed that he was in charge of the troops, and that the right wing was turned and broken. The game was up—the remains of the 27th and of the three Spanish battalions lurched past his flank in a confused mass, closely pursued by Habert's men from the right and Harispe's from the front: they dispersed over the hill-side, losing many prisoners, as was natural. Carey drew off the Calabrese by the path along the crest by which he had arrived, with hardly any loss, and made for San Sadurni.

The four British companies, which had formed the original garrison of the front entrenchment, cut their way out along the main road, and reached Villafranca only 150 strong. The four guns of Arabin's battery, and the Spanish squadron which was escorting them, were overtaken some way from the field by Suchet's cavalry [4th Hussars], which he had pushed out in pursuit. The guns were captured, but the gunners, all save twelve, escaped by leaving their horses, and scrambling down the hill-side, where they could not be followed by mounted men.

The bulk of the Spaniards, and the survivors of the eight companies of the 27th which had fought along with them, reached the outposts of Manso's brigade at San Sadurni in a confused mass, some 2,000 strong, of whom 200 were of the Inniskillings. The darkness of the night was their salvation, as it also was of Carey's Calabrese. This last corps had a curious experience—it had almost reached San Sadurni when it ran into the head of Decaen's column, which was marching on that place, and had to turn aside, when it was fired upon. Evading this attack, Carey took the hazardous step—only possible in the dark—of striking for the sea, across the hills in the rear of Suchet's army, and was fortunate enough to reach the fishing town of Villanueva de Sitjes, where he got boats, and brought his men round to Tarragona, only one officer and fifty men short of their original total.

The rest of the defenders of the pass had of course suffered terribly—the rifle companies who held the first entrenchment had 45 per cent. losses, 87 casualties out of about 180 of all ranks, the 2/27th, when all its scattered members had dropped in, was found to have lost 364 men, including one officer and 247 other ranks missing: out of these many were dead, and only

92 unwounded prisoners were in Suchet's hands: just half the battalion had been destroyed. The Spaniards, whose table of losses chances (an exceptional thing) to have been preserved, counted 87 dead, 239 wounded, and 132 missing[1]. The total casualty list of all nations was just over 1,000, of whom 464 were prisoners (mostly wounded) in the hands of the enemy. On the whole a loss of 26 per cent. of the troops present was less than might have been expected, when Bentinck's carelessness and Adam's neglect of common precautions are taken into consideration. The night, if it had permitted of a surprise, had also permitted easy evasion on the dappled hill-sides.

What were Suchet's losses we cannot tell—he gave a total of 271 only for this fight and that on the Villafranca road on the following morning, in which his cavalry lost at least 100 men. But 171 seems too low a figure for a desperate close-quarters engagement, lasting over two and a half hours, more especially when we note in the official lists 14 officer-casualties in Harispe's and Habert's divisions. This should rather mean nearly 300 losses of all ranks—possibly more—but calculations based on percentages are always dangerous. Officer-casualties are some-times exceptionally heavy, just as sometimes they are exception-ally light [e.g. in the British losses at Maida and certain other fights].

Having treated his infantry to a long night march and nearly three hours of fighting, Suchet was naturally forced to give them a rest. But he sent on his intact cavalry, when daylight appeared, to report on the condition of affairs at Bentinck's camp in front of Villafranca, and to see if there were any signs of Decaen's column on the San Sadurni–Villafranca road. It was possible that the Anglo-Sicilians might have marched off at once, on hearing the loss of the pass of Ordal. If they had so done, they would be out of reach—unless indeed Decaen—of

---

[1] All British narratives, official and unofficial, speak in warm terms of the splendid stand made by the three Spanish battalions. One of them—Cadiz—had recent experiences of an unhappy sort, having been one of the two units cut to pieces at the combat of Yecla on April 11th, and filled up with the remains of the Malaga regiment destroyed at Villena on the day after. But it gave an excellent account of itself, under a gallant Irish-Spanish colonel, Antony Bray, who received the Cross of San Fernando for his conduct on this night.

whom nothing had yet been heard—had been rapid in his marching and was already pressing on their flank. In that case something might be accomplished against them.

Neither of these possibilities had occurred: Bentinck was found drawn up in a neat and regular order of battle—two lines and a reserve[1]—between San Culgat and Villafranca, and with his front covered by the ravine of the Foix river. He had evacuated the town and broken its bridge. No signs whatever were to be seen of Decaen's column. That general indeed had made, of necessity, a very slow march. On his start he had been delayed by a demonstration of three Catalan battalions of Eroles' division in front of Martorel. When these were thrust back, he had a curving and difficult road to San Sadurni—it crosses the Noya four times in ten miles. When nearing his destination, he had been distracted by the unexpected appearance of Carey's fugitive Calabrese on his flank, at 3.30 in the morning, and lost an hour in scaring them off. It was dawn before he reached San Sadurni, out of which he drove Manso's brigade after a little fighting. It retired up the river towards Igualada, accompanied by the wrecks of the English and Spanish troops from Ordal, who had dropped in before Decaen's arrival.

At 5 a.m. San Sadurni was occupied, but the French column was absolutely exhausted. It had marched all night, and been engaged in three separate skirmishes. Some hours of rest were required before it could move, and tackle the mountain road from San Sadurni to Villafranca, which it was ordered to follow. Hence, when Suchet's cavalry appeared in front of Bentinck's lines, there was no sign of any movement on the San Sadurni road. But Manso had sent news of Decaen's march to the British head-quarters; and Bentinck, when he saw that he was not about to be attacked at dawn, and that Suchet's infantry was still far off, resolved to retire towards Tarragona, and to put himself out of any danger of being caught between two hostile forces.

He spent the morning in two formal movements of retreat in fighting order—division retiring behind division in turn, covered by his cavalry and horse artillery. Suchet in his dispatch allows that the operation was carried out in a precise and orderly

---

[1] Very possibly with his two Anglo-Sicilian divisions each in a line, and Sarsfield's second brigade (which had not gone to Ordal) behind them.

manner. The French infantry being far behind, the Marshal tried the experiment of throwing his cavalry in mass against the Anglo-Sicilians. As he had a superiority of three to two in this arm, he counted perhaps on repeating his achievement at Margalef in 1810[1], when, with some of these same veteran squadrons, he had cut up a whole Spanish division caught re-treating across a plain. While Delort's brigade [4th Hussars and 13th Cuirassiers] came down the main road with a horse-artillery battery, and threatened and cannonaded Bentinck's centre, Meyer's brigade [24th Dragoons and Westphalian Chev-aux-légers] cut in upon the western flank of the Allied line. This was what Bentinck had been expecting, and when the French charged, they were promptly met by four squadrons of the Brunswick Hussars and the 20th Light Dragoons, who were waiting for them. There was a furious clash—for a moment the two brigadiers Meyer and Lord Frederick Bentinck (the brother of the commanding general) who had each ridden some paces ahead of his front line, were seen exchanging thrusts and passes, before their men came up. The attack was checked with loss; the flank battalion of the British infantry (the 1/10th) formed square and threw in a useful volley.

Bentinck then drew back to his second position, behind a ravine, near the isolated inn called the Venta de Monjos. While he was forming up anew, Suchet threw in all his cavalry again on the western flank of his opponent's line—Bentinck did the same, putting in even his two Sicilian squadrons and his miscellaneous 'troop of Foreign Hussars'. There was very fierce fighting, in which the Allied horse, much outnumbered, suffered severely. But it achieved its purpose—the enemy never got a chance of breaking in upon the infantry, and finally drew off. Each side lost about a hundred men—the Anglo-Sicilians 4 officers and 102 troopers—the French 7 officers and 100 other ranks. Twenty-six wounded and dismounted men (mostly of the Brunswick Hussars) were left on the ground by the Allies, and became prisoners: on the other hand the Hussars carried off General Meyer's aide-de-camp Bondurand, who had cut in too deep among them. This was a most creditable achievement on the part of Lord Frederick and his miscellaneous following. How

[1] See vol. iv. p. 303.

completely they gained their end is shown by the fact that the Anglo-Sicilian infantry only lost 21 men in its long retreat across open country, and these by the fire of the French horse battery which followed them up, and not by the sabre. Of the French infantry only one battalion of the 116th Line got near the fighting line. When Bentinck was taking up his third position, there was some difficulty with his last guns—two Portuguese 6-pounders—and their escort from the troop of Foreign Hussars. A bridge, roughly mended with fascines, got on fire before the rear-guard was all over, and guns and troopers had to gallop across, half smothered with smoke, only a minute before the flames blazed up. The French pursuit stopped here, in front of the village of Arbos. It had cost Bentinck 134 men only—106 from the gallant cavalry—Suchet lost perhaps a score less.[1] It is unfortunate that Bentinck wrote a laconic dispatch—the French Marshal a most insincere one, in which he pretended that his cavalry had won a great success, and ended up with estimating that the total loss in the campaign of his enemy—Spanish and Anglo-Sicilian—had been 3,500 men! It was actually 1,229, including all the casualties of the unhappy affair at the pass of Ordal. There are hardly any personal narratives of the admirable retreat in fighting-order from Villafranca to Arbos [2]— though an officer of the 1/10th has left an interesting personal impression of the exciting, but rather exhilarating, sensation of retreating in square across open ground with enterprising hostile cavalry hovering about, and occasionally asking for, and getting, a volley from the rear face. The combat in its main features somewhat resembles the long self-sacrificing fight of the British cavalry at Fuentes de Oñoro,[3] which held back Montbrun's overpowering force of squadrons till Wellington's right wing had got into position.

Suchet, though the afternoon was still before him, and though

[1] See tables in Appendix V. Perhaps we should add the odd 70 to make up 1,000, as an allowance for Eroles' and Manso's losses at the skirmishes in front of Decaen's advance.

[2] Beside the reminiscence above, quoted from an anonymous writer in Lee's *History of the 10th Foot*, p. 30, I only know the narrative of Landsheit of the 'Foreign Hussars' (pp. 192–6), which is interesting, but (like much of the rest of his autobiography) certainly inaccurate in many details.

[3] See vol. iv. p. 323.

he had now got into touch with Decaen, whose cavalry had ridden through from San Sadurni, made no attempt to meddle with Bentinck any longer. His own infantry and Decaen's were both very tired, and could not have got into action that day. His explanation given to the Emperor was that Bentinck had now got close to the sea, and could offer battle in front of Vendrils, with the fire of his fleet covering his flank. The Marshal made the most of his success at Ordal, exaggerated the exploits of his cavalry, and boasted that he would not again be troubled by offensive movements on the part of the Anglo-Sicilians, who had been given a lesson. As a matter of fact he was lucky not to have met with a disastrous check. His plan for marching on Villafranca by two separate defiles, with no possible communication between his two columns, was risky in the extreme. He might have met Bentinck's whole force entrenched in the Ordal positions, and have received a decisive repulse—a second Castalla. And even if Bentinck had not brought his army up, yet Adam, using the simplest and most obvious precautions, could have blocked Ordal bridge, and held his own long enough to allow the whole of the Anglo-Sicilians to come up from Villafranca.

The over-optimistic Bentinck left Catalonia only ten days later—subordinating his interests on the East Coast to those in Sicily. For the brand-new constitution on the Whig model, which he had recently inflicted on the unwilling King Ferdinand and the astonished Sicilians, was not working well. Troubles and riots—something like civil war—were on foot, and he thought that only the maker of the constitution could set it right. After learning that Suchet had again dispersed his army, and was not thinking (as Wellington and others feared) of making a push to carry off the garrisons of Tortosa and Lerida, Bentinck sailed for Palermo on September 22nd. He turned over the command to William Clinton, the senior divisional general with the Anglo-Sicilian army, who did not want to take it up. We have noted elsewhere[1] how he explained to Wellington that Clinton was so diffident and nervous that he ought not to be trusted with an army, and how that general wrote to head-quarters at Lesaca, to confirm this estimate of his own capacities—one of the oddest letters ever indited by a British lieutenant-general.

[1] See below, p. 113.

But Wellington had no substitute to send to Tarragona, and continued Clinton in command—on the same principle that he had avowed with regard to the East-Coast army in the early spring, viz. that a subordinate who risked nothing was better, on the whole, than a subordinate with ideas and ambitions. Bentinck had been pursuing a policy of considerable danger, William Clinton

'Did nothing in particular—and did it pretty well',

as we shall see in a later (and a very tedious) chapter on the end of the war in Catalonia. Bentinck, in the next spring, carried out his long-cherished scheme for invading Italy; he conquered Tuscany and Genoa from a skeleton enemy, and promised freedom and constitutions to a number of unfortunate Italians. His proclamations got many worthy Milanese, Tuscan, and Genoese patriots into sad trouble, for the Austrians quashed his projects, and the British Government was obliged to disavow and recall the unlucky constitution-maker, just as his splendid dreams seemed to have reached fruition. A very short-lived parliamentary régime in Sicily—lasting till the Bourbon King suppressed it—was the sole memorial that he left behind him.

SECTION XLI

WELLINGTON ENTERS FRANCE

CHAPTER I

THE CROSSING OF THE BIDASSOA
OCTOBER 7, 1813

THE more important of the two Spanish fortresses which barred the way into France had now fallen: the other—Pampeluna—was known to be drawing near the end of its resources. But it was not the capture of the one or the other which would solve the great politico-strategical problem that lay before Wellington, ever since the battle of Vittoria. Now, for the third time in three months, the French army had recrossed the frontier beaten and in disorder—if not so hardly hit as at Vittoria or Sorauren yet much broken in spirit. Soult—as in July—was reproaching his generals; his generals were criticizing their commander's strategy, and reporting that they could do no more than they had done with battalions who expected to be beaten. Undoubtedly there was a fine opening for a counterstroke, a bold move forward into France.

But again Wellington put any such project aside; he had no intention of following Soult across the Bidassoa, or to the gates of Bayonne, until he should find out what had happened at Dresden, and whether the Armistice of Plässwitz still ran on. As a matter of fact hostilities in Saxony had recommenced; and, on the day before that of the storm of St. Sebastian and the battle of San Marcial, Napoleon's armies had received such an affront as they had not known since Baylen. On August 30th Vandamme had surrendered, with the wrecks of his battered corps, at Kulm. On August 26th Macdonald's Army of Silesia had suffered a less spectacular, but an even more important, disaster at the passage of the Katzbach, which cancelled the effect of Napoleon's victory at Dresden.

It was only on September 3rd, despite of Lord Bathurst's endeavours to send speedy news, that Wellington got tidings of the Austrian declaration of war on France[1]. It was followed soon after by blurred reports of the battle of Dresden, received through spies and French deserters, which represented it as a complete and decisive victory for Napoleon[2]. Then there came ten days of uncertainty, and first-hand information was absolutely wanting. It was not till the 15th that the full report of Kulm came to hand—though none as yet of the more important, and even more bloody, disaster on the Katzbach[3].

With his usual perspicacity Wellington discounted the French report of Dresden; and, regarding the mere fact of the Austrian intervention as the governing feature in the situation, he resolved to abandon his defensive attitude, and to cross the frontier. On September 19th he wrote to Lord Bathurst that he had made up his mind to move forward:

'We have here reports that the allies were defeated between the 26th and the end of August, to which I do not give entire credit. And indeed it appears that the [French] 1st Corps was cut off and destroyed. Yet it appears certain that the allies were defeated in their attack on Dresden. However I shall put myself in a situation to menace a serious attack, and to make one immediately if I should see a fair opportunity, or if I hear that the allies have been really successful, or when Pampeluna shall be in our power.

'I see that (as usual) the newspapers on all sides are raising the public expectation, and that the Allies are very anxious that we should enter France, and that the Government has promised that we shall do so, as soon as the enemy has been finally expelled from Spain. So I think that I ought, and I will, bend a little to the views of the Allies, if it can be done with safety to the Army. Notwithstanding, I acknowledge that I should prefer to turn my attention to Catalonia, as soon as I shall have secured this frontier[4].'

With some reluctance, then, and purely in the interest of the general cause of the Allies, Wellington made up his mind that the long-deferred invasion of France might at last begin. A note to the secretary at the Horse Guards, dated September 19th, throws a curious light on his private inclinations. Acknow-

---

[1] *Dispatches*, xi. p. 74.
[2] On September 5, see *Dispatches*, xi. p. 87, for this rumour.
[3] *Dispatches*, xi. p. 115.
[4] Wellington to Bathurst, *Dispatches*, xi. p. 124.

ledging the receipt of a bundle of French large-scale maps, he asks for more, including those of the country about the Upper Garonne and of the Bordeaux region. '*I wish I may not require them*—but it is as well to have them, at all events[1].'

The invasion, then, shall begin, 'but the superiority of numbers which I can take into France will consist of about 25,000 Spaniards, neither paid nor fed, who *must* plunder, and will set the whole country against us'. That this last factor in the problem was a very real one is shown by half a dozen contemporary letters exchanged with Generals Freire and Giron, and even with the Duke Del Parque, who was far off in the valley of the Ebro. All were reporting absolute starvation, due to the complete inefficiency of the Spanish Commissariat, and the apathy of the remote Spanish Regency. Freire's troops, who had fought so well at San Marcial, had 8,000 men in hospital to 15,000 present with the colours. Their general wrote that for several days his men had subsisted on a half ration of bread and eight ounces of rice—meat had not been seen for weeks.

Freire's military chest was empty, his transport practically non-existent. Many of the wounded of San Marcial had died with their wounds undressed, because it was impossible to get them back a few miles to hospital. The provincial officials sent nothing to the front, ignoring government orders. 'Pour remédier à tant de maux, je fais ce que je puis: mais crier, écrire, représenter, ça suffit à rien[2].' Grumbling terribly at the necessity for depleting his own magazines, Wellington had to issue reluctant permission for the Spaniards to draw on the British sea-borne food at Passages, and on the general reserve depots at Tolosa and Vittoria, for a limited number of rations[3]. But he felt that this was only 'giving sops to Cerberus'; famine would recur again in a few weeks, unless the Regency showed a will to punish malingering provincial intendants. And the Regency was so much occupied with its own private troubles[4]—

[1] Wellington to Bunbury, *Dispatches*, xi. p. 122.

[2] Freire to Wellington, *Supplementary Dispatches*, viii. p. 227.

[3] *Dispatches*, xi. p. 119.

[4] See Henry Wellesley to Wellington, *Supplementary Dispatches*, viii. pp. 201–2 and 262–3. Wellesley's amusing second letter gives a vivid account of 'a disgraceful scene of lying and prevarication' between the Ministers, the Regency, and the Liberal Party in the Cortes.

its fall might come any day—that complaints from the Bidassoa seemed to it 'a tale of little meaning, though the words were strong'. Moreover the story of the sack of St. Sebastian, repeated in most exaggerated terms by the Liberal press (though it needed no exaggeration), was doing the British interest at Cadiz no good. It was hinted that Giron was a mere satellite of Wellington, and that Freire seemed likely to become another.

There were plenty more daily worries for Wellington, at the moment when he was making up his mind to cross the Bidassoa. One of the worst we have already mentioned: the erratic Lord William Bentinck, after taking over the charge of the East Coast Army from the wretched Murray on June 18th, announced his intention of throwing up the command and returning to his proper sphere in Sicily on September 1st, and actually sailed off for Palermo on the 22nd. His letter reporting his departure contained the cheering information that Sir William Clinton, whom he had left in command, was an individual of such a nervous and retiring character that he was a public danger in charge of an army. 'A more honourable man cannot exist: but diffidence makes him unfit for command: his fear of responsibility and the anxiety and uneasiness he suffers under, would in a short time ruin his constitution[1].' So Wellington had better appoint a new commander for the East Coast Army—or something untoward might happen. But Wellington had no one to send of sufficient seniority to outrank Clinton. It was not possible to think of divorcing Beresford from his Portuguese responsibilities. Graham's eyes had again given out, and he was just on the eve of sailing for England to get medical advice. Rowland Hill was too valuable to be spared—he was the one impeccable lieutenant to whom his chief could trust any task, with the certainty that it would be carried out with perfect accuracy. Picton had procured himself a seat in the House of Commons, and was demanding leave to go home and take it up. Moreover he was not in Wellington's good books—his conduct on the two days before Sorauren had led to some caustic comment[2]. Cole had shared in the same censure on that occasion. Lord Dalhousie had not given satis-

[1] Bentinck to Wellington, *Supplementary Dispatches*, viii. p. 219.

[2] Picton thought that his merits were not being recognized, and wrote stormy letters. See Wellington's reply in *Dispatches*, xi. pp. 97–8.

faction either at Vittoria, or quite recently on the day of San Marcial. The other divisional generals were junior to William Clinton, so could not supersede him. Wellington would have liked to go himself to Catalonia and set things right, as he hinted to the Horse Guards[1]. This being impossible, if France was to be invaded, he resolved to let matters stand—Clinton was at least unlikely to do anything rash: and despite of a querulous letter from him, begging that a senior officer might be sent to Tarragona, he was continued in command[2].

The usual minor worries continued to drag on—correspondence with Lord Melville about the inadequate naval force in the Bay of Biscay—with the Duke of York on the old topic of provisional battalions[3]—with the Spanish Minister of War as to promotions—with the Foreign Office as to politico-strategical schemes —mostly unwise—on other theatres of war. But to such distractions Wellington was now inured, and they did not divert his mind from the new purpose. The invasion, however, started a few days later than he had originally intended[4]. One governing hindrance was the delay in bringing up his great pontoon train from Vittoria, where it had long been parked[5]. Another was a meteorological one—the chief feature in his new scheme of operations was to be the passage of the Bidassoa by the little-known fords near its mouth, where no troops had ever crossed before. It would be well to wait till the lowest possible tides, and these fell inconveniently late—a week after everything else was ready. The blow was only delivered on October 7th, and the very elaborate preliminary arrangements for it were only sent to the officers commanding divisions two days before.

Meanwhile Soult, much surprised that he had not been followed into France on the day after his defeat at San Marcial, was devoting himself to a policy of building defensive lines behind the frontier, covering the whole space from the sea to the upper Nive, quite in the style of the early eighteenth century. He was

---

[1] See above, pp. 108–9.

[2] W. Clinton to Wellington, *Supplementary Dispatches*, viii. p. 265.

[3] See vol. vi. pp. 232–3.

[4] The elaborate reports on the fords of the Lower Bidassoa were sent in to Wellington as early as September 15th. See *Supplementary Dispatches*, viii. p. 254.

[5] See *Supplementary Dispatches*, xiv. p. 292.

under the impression—yet was by no means certain—that Wellington would not attack him by the difficult upland passes leading down to St.-Jean-Pied-du-Port, since autumn was verging toward winter, but would probably confine his operation to those nearer the ocean, from the Col de Maya westward. His main design was to cover the ground, from Cambo on the upper Nive to Hendaye on the estuary of the Bidassoa, with a series of redoubts—supplemented by minor fortifications—on which he would be able to check any attack from the south. This front of more than twenty-three miles in length was divided into two sections by the monstrous hump of the Grande Rhune, which rises to a height of 2,800 feet above the town of Vera, where the Bidassoa makes its sudden twist from a northerly to a north-westerly direction. This mountain is the one dominating object on the French side of the frontier; visible from incredible dis-tances to the north, it stands out decisively as the sentinel of the main line of the Pyrenees, which show in dim lines behind it to the spectator on the heights above Biarritz or Bayonne. It is no craggy cone, but a high straggling mass, like many a Scottish mountain of the secondary sort, with long steep slopes covered by gorse and brushwood, and occasional naked out-crops of rock. On most sides it is perfectly accessible to a vigorous pedestrian, and there are well-marked foot-tracks to its top, from whence a complete panorama of Soult's chosen lines of defence—east and west—can be mastered by the eye. But here and there on its fronts there are long stretches of bare cliff or of 'scree', up which no man can climb, least of all a soldier with musket and accoutrements. Such patches have to be turned at their ends.

From the Great Rhune eastward, there runs out a chain of much inferior heights—that of the Little Rhune, separated from its greater namesake by a chasm only, is the steepest—whose intermittent summits run to no more than 600 or 900 feet in height. Through a crack in the middle of them the river Nivelle forces its way. At the extreme eastern end of this line of upland the ground rises again to the Mondarrain—2,000 feet over sea-level, close above the river Nive and the 'Pas de Roland'—the defile that leads to St.-Jean-Pied-du-Port and Roncesvalles. Between the eastern side of the Rhune and the Mondarrain

there are twelve miles of hill-sides, mostly quite accessible. And
here Soult had set the spade to work in the most vigorous style,
and had placed the larger half of his army. Foy was out to
the east, beyond the Nive, at St.-Jean-Pied-du-Port, watching the upland roads from Roncesvalles. For, though Soult
thought that it was unlikely that any attack would come from
that direction, he was aware that the 2nd Division was still on
the Linduz and at Altobiscar. If, by any chance, it should move,
Foy could draw in to his help the brigade from Saragossa[1] under
Paris, which had since July been blocking the pass from Jaca
to Oloron, where no enemy had appeared save roving parties
of Mina's guerrilleros. The 8,000 men of Foy and Paris were
a mere outlying flank-guard. But from the Mondarrain to the
Rhune Soult had alined six out of his nine fighting divisions,
and they were entrenched up to the eyes. D'Erlon with three
divisions—Abbé, Darmagnac, Daricau—held the sector from
the Mondarrain to Ainhoue on the Nivelle, some six or
seven miles—with five closed redoubts on the more important
summits, and lines of trench linking them together in an almost
continuous series. If this front line were lost, there was a second
behind it, from Espelette to Amotz, of somewhat lower heights,
on which a less complete line of fortifications was beginning
to arise.

Clausel, with the three divisions of Conroux, Maransin, and
Taupin, had the next sector, from the Nivelle up to and including the Rhune, for his right-hand division was on the
western under-features of that mighty hump, the Insola, Commisari, and Bayonette ridges. The Rhune was lightly held, it
was almost a defence for itself, but the two divisions of Conroux
and Maransin were thoroughly well entrenched on the eastern
side of it on the hills by Sare—with two big redoubts (Grenade
and Sainte Barbe) in front line and plenty of supporting trenches.
The third division (Taupin), on the western side below the
Rhune, was equally well protected by three redoubts and an
elaborate system of trenches.

Behind Clausel's line, at Ascain in the valley of the Nivelle,
just below the north front of the Rhune, lay Soult's reserve, the
troops under Villatte of which we have so often heard—one

[1] See p. 77.

French, one German, one Franco-Spanish, and one Italian brigades of infantry, still (despite of their losses at San Marcial) a solid force of 8,000 bayonets.

Finally the tidal estuary of the Bidassoa, six miles of bank from Biriatou to the ocean, was given in charge of Reille, who had only two of his three normal divisions, the third (that of Foy) having been detached far to the eastward. Reille was directed to keep one division (Maucune's) in front line: the other, that long commanded by Lamartinière, but since his death entrusted to Boyer, being kept in reserve, five miles back, at the camps of Urrogne and Bordagain in front of St. Jean de Luz.

Looking at these dispositions, we see that Soult provided 14,000 bayonets for the protection of the left or inland sector of his lines [1], 15,000 for the defence of his centre on both sides of the formidable Rhune [2], and 10,000 for the sector nearest to the ocean [3]. The reserve of 8,000 men was behind the centre, conveniently placed for reinforcing it, but very remote from the lower Bidassoa and the sea—some twelve miles indeed, if allowance be made for the curves of roads in the hills, above Hendaye. The Marshal evidently looked for an attack on his centre and left, and regarded the right as least likely to be assailed, the broad tidal bed of the Bidassoa seeming a very complete barrier to enterprises near the sea. A second criticism, made by several French students of the battle, is that the front line absorbed four-fifths of the army, and that the reserve was not only proportionately weak, but badly placed. Wellington, it will be noted, when defending the line of the Pyrenees in July, had kept heavy reserves behind his outpost-line.

To Soult's misfortune, his arrangements were precisely those which Wellington had hoped that he would make. The main nature of the British general's plan was surprise, by an attack on the part of his adversary's front which was regarded as most impregnable—his extreme right flank, near the sea. And while he also proposed to assail the French centre, he left the whole eastward wing, D'Erlon's front, unmolested save by demonstrations. And this was precisely the front which Soult had con-

[1] Abbé 6,054 of all ranks, Darmagnac 4,447, Daricau 4,092.
[2] Conroux 4,962, Maransin 5,575, Taupin 4,478.
[3] Maucune 3,996, Boyer 6,515.

sidered the most likely to attract attention. The danger which
the Marshal had feared was a great turning movement to the
east, which might roll up his whole line and drive him seaward,
with some danger of seeing his right wing pinned against the
coast and cut off. Wellington's plan was much less ambitious;
it was a mere commencement of his invasion scheme, by estab-
lishing himself in force beyond the Bidassoa, and manœuvring
his adversary out of his all-dominating advanced post on the
Great Rhune. After that should be accomplished, there would
be plenty of time to plot out the next decisive advance.

As a preliminary move, with the deliberate intention of lead-
ing Soult to think that the danger lay eastward and inland,
Wellington rode to the Roncesvalles passes on October 1st,
showed himself there, and inspected the outposts of the 2nd
Division, who were beginning to be vexed by snow in the defiles.
On his way to Roncesvalles he looked in upon the camp of
A. Campbell's Portuguese brigade in the Alduides valley on
September 30th, and, turning out the troops, directed them to
drive in the French posts covering the neighbouring valley of
Baigorrey. This was a mere demonstration, but very successful:
Campbell captured a French picket on the peak of Airola,
swept down the valley, and drove off 2,000 sheep. The note of
alarm ran along the whole inland front, and Soult rode over in
haste from Ascain on October 2nd, as far as St.-Jean-Pied-du-
Port, and directed Foy to throw up more works in front of his
position there, and to be prepared for a serious attack[1]. As
Wellington had intended, the Marshal was confirmed in his
notion that the coming blow would be struck at the east end of
his all-too-extended line of defence; he paid little attention to
reports from deserters and others as to the presence of a British
pontoon train at Oyarzun, behind the Peña de la Aya range.
Fortunately these tales had been coupled with a rumour that
Wellington intended to attack on September 27th—which had
not been far from the truth. But as no such move took place, the
whole theory of British activity in the seaward sector was dis-
credited. There was far more evidence for projected movements
at the inland end of the line.

Wellington's plan of operations, issued to the divisional

[1] Girod de l'Ain's *Life of Foy*, p. 225.

generals on October 5th, was as follows. Hill's front line divisions, the 2nd at Roncesvalles, the 6th on the northern debouches of the Maya pass, were to stand firm. But behind them all the second line and reserve divisions were to move westward. The Portuguese brigades in the Alduides [A. Campbell and Da Costa[1]] handed over their outpost line to some of Mina's irregulars, and marched over the pass of Ispegui to the upper Bastan valley, where they relieved at the village of Maya, on the south end of the famous pass, Picton and the 3rd Division. Picton then moved over the 'Chemin des Anglais' along the top of the hills to Zagaramurdi. Here the 7th Division had been lying; on the arrival of Picton's leading unit it was to move in successive brigades to the Puerto de Echalar, where the left division of Giron's Andalusians had been posted. Giron, collecting all his troops, was to make ready to attack the eastern sector of the Rhune, after driving in first all the French outposts on its under-features. The 7th Division would be behind him as a reserve, if it were needed, and the 3rd behind the 7th.

The southern sector of the Rhune front was to be tackled by the Light Division, assisted by Longa's small Cantabrian division [only four battalions and 2,500 bayonets]—the Spanish troops in which Wellington had the most confidence, from their previous record. Alten was to attack in two columns; Kempt's brigade, in touch with Giron's left, was to begin by driving in the enemy's outposts in the 'Puerto de Vera', the pass up which the road from Vera goes, and then outflank the Rhune behind it; Colborne, more to the west, was to attack the French trenches visible above Vera town, on the Bayonette and Commisari heights, under-features of the Great Rhune, and to turn that great hill from the south-west. Two of Longa's four battalions were extended in a thick line of skirmishers to connect the two British columns. The other two were placed on the left, to provide a flank-guard, or, if they found it possible, to turn the flank of the high-lying redoubts which Colborne's brigade was about to attack. A solid reserve was provided for the Light

---

[1] Hamilton had just arrived and taken charge of these two brigades, which had formed Silveira's division since the spring. Silveira had gone off on sick leave. Hamilton arrived looking so ill that Wellington presciently wrote that 'he would not last'.

Division, the 4th Division being brought across the Bidassoa, and established on the height just south of Vera town.

This front of attack formed by Giron, the Light Division, and Longa's men, was about four miles long, and covered the sector of the French lines held by Taupin's division on the western and Conroux's on the eastern slopes below the Rhune. There was no attempt made to assail the positions of Daricau's division, close to the Nivelle, or of D'Erlon's divisions beyond that river. But Colville's 6th Division was demonstrating in front of them, and the 3rd and Hamilton's Portuguese were within supporting distance of the 6th, if D'Erlon should dare to come out of his lines and counter-attack the British flank.

Thus three Spanish and one British divisions were to attack Soult's centre[1], with four more British and one Portuguese divisions as flank-guard and supports[2]. They had in front of them all Clausel's three and D'Erlon's three French divisions, not to speak of Villatte's reserve, placed in rear of Clausel at Ascain. But on the western end of the battle front, nearer the sea, forces were not balanced in any such fashion, and Wellington had secured himself an immense preponderance of strength, with which he was about to execute the great surprise of the day—the turning of Soult's right wing by the passage in over-whelming force of the tidal estuary of the Bidassoa. Between the fords of Salain, just west of Vera, and those above Biriatou, four miles lower down, there lies the 'Gorge of the Bidassoa', a stretch of that river where it is practicably uncrossable, the north bank (formed by a considerable ridge with the difficult Basque names of Chouhille and Choldogogagna[3]) dropping precipitously to the water's edge, and having no path along it. On the south or Spanish bank the hills, though rough, are not so steep or high, and there was a bad track along the stream, where now the Irun–Vera railway runs. The existence of this petty cañon caused both Soult's operations on the day of San Marcial, and Wellington's on October 7th to be divided into two

---

[1] Light Division, two divisions of Giron, and Longa.

[2] The 3rd, 4th, 6th, 7th Divisions and Hamilton's Portuguese.

[3] I take this uncouth name from the French staff map. But contemporary narrators on both sides seem to have been frightened by it, and speak of the Col du Poirier and the Chouhille redoubt, and the Mandale

completely separate sections. Communication between them could only be kept up by a long detour inland on the north bank, where the ridge called the Mandale lies behind the Choldogogagna, and joins the Commisari and Bayonette heights to those above Biriatou, ending at the spot called the Croix des Bouquets, where the high road from the bridge of Béhobie and Irun crosses the sky-line on its way to Urrogne and St. Jean de Luz. It is impossible to see anything happening on the Vera front from Béhobie, or vice versa, owing to the high crests of the intervening hills above the winding river. The French had put up a semaphore on the south end of the Choldogogagna, to pass news from one point to another. But of course (like all semaphores) it was useless, not only at night, but during fogs and heavy rain, both frequent contingencies in the lower Pyrenees.

But we must now examine the seaward section of Soult's front. That the Bidassoa was fordable at several places, near the spot where the charred pillars of the wrecked bridge of Béhobie rose above the water, was well known. Here the French had crossed during their unhappy attack on the heights of San Marcial on August 31st, and what could be done from one side could be done from the other. Soult had ordered redoubts to be thrown up on the modest heights along the French bank, at Biriatou, on the knoll known from a reminiscence of 1659 as the height of Louis XIV, and on the Café Républicain—an old look-out post of the war of 1794. The last two works had not yet received their guns. But lower down no precautions whatever had been taken—the estuary for half the day showed a breadth of 1,000 yards of salt water. For the other half-day, when it was feeling the effects of the tide, low water exhibited a broad belt of sands, with the comparatively narrow freshwater channel of the Bidassoa meandering through their midst. To venture out upon the flats, during the few hours of the lowest possible tide, did not look a tempting venture. And no one save a few fishermen and shrimpers of Irun and Fuenterabia knew how shallow the freshwater breadth of the Bidassoa was at certain places.

From the time of the fall of St. Sebastian onward Wellington had been collecting information as to the fords up and down the river. He had his reports in hand as early as September 15th,

and the great secret which he had discovered was that not only
were there three fords at Irun passable by infantry at low tide,
but also three more, far nearer the sea, at the port of Fuenterabia,
where the immense breadth of the estuary seemed to make such
things incredible. Only shrimpers had ever explored them[1].
The French had no fortification down-stream from the Café
Républicain redoubt: only a picket or two supervised the last
three miles of the estuary, down to the Bar of the Bidassoa,
where now the villas of Hendaye Plage line its eastern shore.
There was an old sea-coast battery round the corner, at St.
Anne's Point, but this looked at the ocean, not at the estuary.

From Biriatou to the edge of the Bay of Biscay the division
of General Maucune was in charge. It chanced to be the
weakest division in the French army—only 4,000 bayonets in
eight battalions. And its weaker brigade—three battalions under
General Pinoteau—was at the seaward end—one battalion on
the knoll of Louis XIV opposite the broken bridge of Béhobie,
one strung out in companies between Béhobie and Hendaye,
the third in reserve at the Café Républicain. The other brigade
—Montfort's—had two battalions opposite the fords of Biriatou,
one above, at the Calvaire on the Mandale ridge, two in reserve
at the high-lying cross roads of the Croix des Bouquets with a
field battery. The nearest reserve was five miles back—Boyer's
(late Lamartinière's) division in and about Urrogne and Bordagain, some 6,000 strong. But two battalions of it had been
lent to Maucune, and were prolonging his line at the Col du
Poirier, beyond the Calvaire.

Against this thin line Wellington was about to let loose
some 24,000 men, twenty-three English, nine Portuguese, and
thirteen Spanish battalions—an irresistible mass.

His arrangements were as follows. Under cover of the night
the three brigades of the 5th Division were to leave their camp
at Oyarzun, and hide themselves in and behind the ruined and
deserted town of Fuenterabia. One brigade lay in the ditch of
the old enceinte, two behind a long dyke south of the walls,
which had served to keep sea-water out of the low meadows along
the shore. They were to wait till 7.15, when it was calculated
that the three newly discovered fords across the permanent

[1] See Batty's *Campaign in the Western Pyrenees*, p. 22.

channel of the Bidassoa would have only three feet of water. They were then to dash across the sands and strike for Hendaye on the French side. Their divisional battery and a squadron of the 12th Light Dragoons were to follow. When across the river, the division was to drive forward, seize the heights above Hendaye, and then turn to the right and sweep along the crests, so as to take in flank and rear the position on the Croix des Bouquets, which the French were known to be holding as their rallying point.

The three brigades of the 1st Division were to come down in the night to Irun, and place themselves under cover of the long low ridge below the heights of San Marcial which the French had held with their reserves during the battle of August 31st. On seeing the 5th Division start from Fuenterabia, the 1st Division was to make for the three fords allotted to them, one at the broken bridge of Béhobie, two (known as Nasas de Arriba and Nasas de Abaxo) just below it. When across the river they were to make for and storm the hill known as the Montagne de Louis XIV. Wilson's Portuguese unattached brigade, two squadrons of the 12th Light Dragoons, and two batteries were to accompany them. To cover the crossing three batteries were to open from the lower slopes of San Marcial against the Louis XIV hill, the moment that the troops were over the water; the engineers were to proceed to throw their pontoons across the river near the ruined bridge. Guns and pontoons were to be hidden carefully behind Irun, till the moment when the infantry advance began.

Further up-stream General Freire was to cross with two divisions of the Army of Galicia[1] at all the six fords which existed above the broken bridge, one division at those used by the French at the battle of San Marcial, the other by the three fords opposite Biriatou, much further up-stream. The first column was to seize the ridge called the Green Hill, the second to establish itself upon the Mandale heights. A second pontoon-bridge would be thrown across the water for the use of the

---

[1] The 3rd and 4th Divisions, now commanded by Del Barco and Barcena, Losada having been wounded at San Marcial. Of the other divisions of Freire's army one (Longa) was operating on the other wing, Morillo's was with Hill at Roncesvalles, Carlos de España's was besieging Pampeluna, and Mendizabal's had been sent back to besiege Santoña.

Spanish troops as soon as the opposite bank had been secured.

As reserves, Lord Aylmer's brigade—the newly arrived battalions from England now seeing their first action—was to wait above Irun as a support for the 1st Division, and Bradford's Portuguese brigade was to take position above the crossing-place of the right-hand Spanish column opposite Biriatou. If all went well, both might cross the Bidassoa later on.

The early hours of the night of the 6th–7th were disturbed by a severe thunderstorm—it was hoped that its din might cover the rumbling noise of the pontoons and artillery coming down to Irun by the paved chaussée. This was—according to French narratives—not fully achieved: Maucune's pickets reported continuous movements. But as their easy-going commander took no precautionary measures in consequence, this did not much matter. The storm ceased after midnight, and the troops, crouching under cover, had time to get dry before the dawn.

The sun was up, and the horizon clear by 7.25[1], when the elaborate arrangements of Wellington began to work. No large-scale operation ever went off with more perfect timing and more complete success. When the heads of the 5th Division columns ran out upon the sands in front of Fuenterabia, the guns on San Marcial spoke at once, and the Guards and Germans started out for their shorter dash across the waters from Irun. A few minutes later the Spaniards were streaming down to the upper fords. So complete was the surprise that the light companies of the 5th Division were actually across the channel of the Bidassoa before a shot was fired at them, and the Guards and Germans were half-way to the north bank before the enemy opened. There were no mistakes made in the guiding, save that the column of the German Legion brigade was, for one moment, in danger of getting over the edge of a rather curving ford into deep water—but the error was easily repaired without loss by drowning.

The force thrown out against the thin French line upon the north bank was so overwhelming that no serious resistance could be made. The 5th Division had only to hunt a picket of

---

[1] Hay found the fords of Hendaye not quite ready by the appointed 7.15. See his Dispatch, *Supplementary Dispatches*, viii. p. 303.

40 men out of Hendaye, and then to sweep along one disjointed battalion of the 3rd Line across the hills toward the Croix des Bouquets. General Hay, who was in command this day, for both Leith and Oswald had been wounded at St. Sebastian, had his troops in three brigade columns. That to the left—Robinson's brigade—kept near the coast, to guard against any possible advance of French troops from St. Jean de Luz. It captured from the rear an old shore-battery with four guns of position looking out on the headland of St. Anne, and later got into contact with a single French battalion[1] coming along the coast-road, which it pushed back as far as an old redoubt of 1794, the 'Sans Culottes' which lies half-way from Hendaye to St. Jean de Luz. Here the brigade halted by order.

The two other columns of the 5th Division, Greville's British and De Regoa's Portuguese brigades, when they had mounted the heights above Hendaye, turned south and swept the crests parallel to the river, driving off a battalion and a battery from the Café Républicain, and then making for the flank of the main French fighting position, the cross-roads at the Croix des Bouquets, which the 1st Division was already attacking from the front[2].

Meanwhile, the 1st Division and Wilson's Portuguese had plunged at the enemy's defences at and above Béhobie, deploying their light companies on a broad front the moment that they had reached the shallows on the opposite bank. The French battalion in Béhobie[3], seeing itself about to be enveloped, abandoned its trenches and fortified houses, and recoiled to the redoubt upon the hill of Louis XIV, uphill and to their left, where there was a battery in action. But the four attacking brigades, spreading out as fast as they could, enveloped this position also, and the French were only able to make head at the top of the main crest, at the cross-roads of the Croix des Bouquets, where an infantry reserve[4] and a battery from the

---

[1] This was the 2/105th sent down by Reille from the Croix des Bouquets.

[2] See Hay's and Greville's reports, *Supplementary Dispatches*, viii. pp. 303–4. Hay evidently exaggerates the force opposed to him—which was only a battalion of the 3rd regiment, one of the 15th, which had been driven from the Café Républicain, one of the 105th, left at the Croix des Bouquets, and another of the 17th which had fallen back from before the 1st Division.

[3] 17th Léger of Maucune's division.

[4] The 1/105th of Montfort's brigade.

other brigade of Maucune's division were awaiting them. Here also the troops driven in by Hay's movement had sought refuge.

There was sharp fighting here for a short time, for Reille, who was present in person, having come up from Urrogne in haste, tried to hold his ground till Boyer's division should arrive from the rear. But ere more than one of the reserve battalions had arrived, the Croix des Bouquets was stormed, its right flank having been turned by the head of Hay's column coming along the heights from Hendaye. Four battalions of Boyer's brigade from Urrogne arrived only in time to cover the retreat of the fugitives, and were themselves much hustled by the attack of the leading 5th Division unit, the 9th Foot, under Colonel Cameron, which struck in upon their flank. Reille then drew back to the outskirts of the fortified camp at Urrogne, where Boyer's other brigade, that of Gauthier, had just arrived, having been very late in starting from its billets in Bordagain, the southern suburb of St. Jean de Luz. Wellington, whose scheme did not extend beyond the seizure of all the heights of the Bidassoa, forbade any attack on Urrogne, and by noon Reille was strengthened there by the arrival of the leading brigade of Villatte's reserve, brought over from Ascain in haste. Thither also came Soult himself, in great wrath and dismay. 'I had many reasons', he wrote to the Minister of War at Paris, 'to think that the enemy's main attack would be on Ainhoue [D'Erlon's wing], and was there at 7 a.m. when the action commenced. But finding that there was but a demonstration in that quarter, I hurried to my right—only to find that everything was over [1].'

The whole matter, indeed, had gone off with almost incredible quickness. The crossing of the river had commenced at 7.25, the Croix des Bouquets was carried by 9 o'clock, ere Boyer's first brigade, which had only five miles to go, could reinforce the front line. And Reille's whole force had been tumbled back into Urrogne before noon, when Villatte's reserve began to turn up, after a nine-mile march from Ascain to Urrogne by hilly cross-roads.[2]

[1] Soult to the Minister of War. Report of October 18th.
[2] The distance is less as the crow flies, but over country roads it was, as Clerc truly remarks, a *forte étape*, over three hours' marching.

Meanwhile Freire's Spaniards, at the upper fords of the Bidassoa, had been as successful as the 5th and 1st Divisions on the lower waters. The left-hand columns, at the Biriatou fords, had been held back for some time by the redoubt and the two French battalions opposite them[1], but the right-hand columns crossed higher up, only finding pickets opposite them, and gaining the crest of the Mandale ridge fell on the flank and rear of the force at Biriatou, and enabled the other columns to get across the water. The whole then extended to right and left— one brigade linked up with the Guards at the Croix des Bouquets, the others, pushing along the crests, dislodged the single French battalion at the Calvary on the Mandale ridge[2], and finally the two isolated battalions at the Col du Poirier much farther east. These (the 2nd Léger) were so completely out of touch with any other French troops, that they went off in haste for fear of being enveloped. Some of Freire's light troops followed them for many miles.

Thus Wellington was in possession of the whole of the heights above the Bidassoa, and at an absurdly small cost—some 400 casualties [3]—the only serious losses being in the light companies of the German Legion brigade (9 officers and 129 men) and in the 9th Foot from Hay's turning column (10 officers and 72 men). The French had been hustled out of their positions rather than badly hurt—they left four field guns and several more heavy pieces in the redoubts behind them, but only 60 prisoners, and their total loss was only about 450 in Maucune's and Boyer's divisions.

While this easy victory, over an enemy taken completely by surprise and outnumbered, was being won on the lower Bidassoa, there was much heavier and more costly fighting in progress on the side of Vera and the Great Rhune, where—as has been already explained—the Light Division, Giron's Andalusians, and Longa's four battalions were about to assail the formidable position in front of them. Their flank was to be protected against any possible interference on the part of Soult's left wing

[1] Two battalions of the 10th Léger, of Montfort's brigade of Maucune's division.

[2] The 101st Line, of Montfort's brigade.

[3] See tables in Appendix.

PASSAGE OF THE BIDASSOA, OCTOBER 7TH 1813

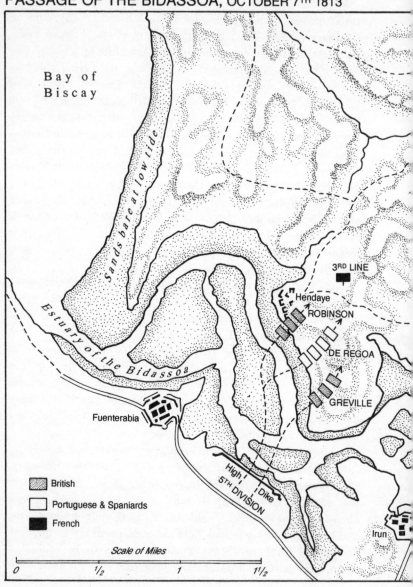

Bay of Biscay

Sands bare at low tide

Estuary of the Bidassoa

3RD LINE

Hendaye

ROBINSON

DE REGOA

GREVILLE

Fuenterabia

High
Dike

5TH DIVISION

Irun

British

Portuguese & Spaniards

French

Scale of Miles

0   ½   1   1½

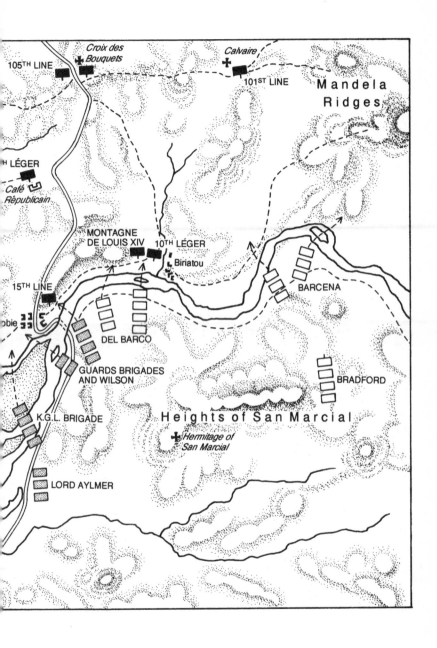

105TH LINE

Croix des
Bouquets

Calvaire

101ST LINE

Mandela
Ridges

ᴴ LÉGER

Café
Républicain

MONTAGNE
DE LOUIS XIV

10TH LÉGER

Biriatou

BARCENA

15TH LINE

obie

DEL BARCO

GUARDS BRIGADES
AND WILSON

BRADFORD

K.G.L. BRIGADE

Heights of San Marcial

Hermitage of
San Marcial

LORD AYLMER

by demonstrations carried out against D'Erlon's front by the
6th and 7th Divisions, which Colville and Dalhousie were forbidden to turn into a serious attack.

The advance began, according to Wellington's time-table,
at a little after 7 o'clock, when Colville drove a French picket
out of the village and foundry of Urdax, and carried out his
orders by noisy skirmishing in front of D'Erlon's centre. It
had the desired effect—the attention of the enemy's troops in
this direction was duly attracted to him. Meanwhile Giron,
Alten, and Longa made their prescribed movements. The
former, leaving one brigade deployed on his right in the low
ground, to face any possible counter-attacks from the direction
of Sare and the Nivelle, went up the slopes in front of him.
One battalion, on his right, worked upwards through the woods
on the lower southern slopes of the Rhune, to see if it could
reach the summit under cover of ravines and dead ground. The
bulk of the division—eight battalions—ascended in two columns,
with deep skirmishing lines in front, up the ridge called the
Fagadia, which forms the immediate under-feature descending
from the west side of the Rhune. It met with opposition at
once, from four of Conroux's battalions (12th Léger and 32nd
Line) which held this section of the French front, spent several
hours in slowly forcing them uphill, and finally reached the
crest, some little time after the attack of Alten, further to
the left, had won similar success. The isolated battalion on the
far right, when it got out of the woods after long climbing, found
the crest and the Hermitage on top of the Rhune held by two
battalions sent up by Clausel from his reserve (Maransin's
division)[1], and could not get anywhere near its objective.

Meanwhile Alten, farther to the left, had started from the
low ground at Vera in two brigade columns. That on the right
under Kempt, included the first and third battalions of the
95th, along with the 43rd, and the 17th Portuguese line. That on
the left, Colborne's[2] brigade, was composed of the 2nd battalion
of the 95th, with the 52nd, and the 1st and 3rd Caçadores.
Kempt's attack was directed against the steep path of the Puerto

[1] 1/34th and 1/50th Line.
[2] Colborne had replaced Skerrett, who had gone home, to the delight of
all members of the 95th.

de Vera, which crosses the main ridge at its lowest point between the Commisari and Fagadia slopes; it was then a mere mule-track, but the only way of reaching the valley of the Nivelle from Vera without a lengthy detour to the east[1]. Its foot was guarded by a low knoll called the Alzate Real—but better known to the Light Division as the Hog's Back—which was held by the most outlying French pickets.

The left attack, by Colborne's brigade, was obviously a more formidable business. It was to be directed against the Bayonette, a long narrow straight spur sticking out at right angles from the main ridge above, and blocked at three successive points by solid fortification. Half-way up it was a star fort called St. Benôit, a closed work, spanning the whole crest; half a mile higher was a second entrenchment; and at the end, where the spur joined the main ridge, a second closed work, the Redoute de la Bayonette. Between the two lines of advance of the 1st and 2nd brigades was a broad wooded ravine, up which were sent in skirmishing order the two battalions of Longa's Canta-brians, which had been told off by Wellington to link the front. Longa's other two units went up the hill-side to the left of Colborne, except three companies detached to destroy the French semaphore on Mount Choldogogagna.

Taupin's whole division was in line to oppose Alten's attacks. Béchaud's brigade was on the Bayonette and to each side of it. Cambriel's[2] was farther east, with one battalion on the Hog's Back below, and the other four in trenches above it, as far as the crest, facing Kempt. Ten battalions, 4,700 bayonets, entrenched up to the eyes on commanding ground, and with artillery, were about to be assailed by five British, four Portu-guese, and four Spanish battalions, 6,500 men in all, so that the numbers here had no such hopeless disproportion as had been seen in the fighting on the lower Bidassoa.

The operations commenced by the evicting of the French battalion on the Hog's Back, mainly by the 3/95th, at the head

---

[1] A better road has now been cut over these slopes, and has usurped the name of the Puerto de Vera in modern times. The pass which Kempt stormed is now known as the Puerto de Insola.

[2] Colonel of the 47th, acting as brigadier *vice* Lecamus, wounded at Sorauren.

of Kempt's column. This preliminary push being accomplished, the two brigades diverged to their separate tasks. That of Kempt's brigade proved the easier, though no child's play, as the mule-path up to the Puerto was cut in half a dozen places, and commanded by several successive trenches. They were carried mainly by flanking attacks; the Rifles and Portuguese spreading out on a long front, while the 43rd delivered the blow in the centre. The ground on each side of the path was not impracticable, but covered with scrub and thorns, so that wide turning movements were possible though tiresome. By a series of successive thrusts the brigade finally reached the crest of the Commisari in half a dozen places, with no excessive losses— the two rifle battalions had only 31 casualties, the 17th Portuguese 20, the 43rd only 27. Officers on the spot thought the defence feeble; 'had they fought as French troops *have* fought, and as they *ought* to have fought here, we should have lost a vast number, or even been repulsed'[1].

The work of Colborne's brigade was much harder, the ground being much more rugged, and the Bayonette ridge so narrow that flank movements were very difficult, while not only mere trenches but two closed works had to be stormed. The first clash at the Star Redoubt, half-way up the hill, was fierce and prolonged; Colborne first attacked it with the riflemen of the 2/95th, who failed to get in, and were cast back by an unexpected counter-attack, which sent them rolling back on to the 52nd. He then sent this battalion, when rallied, round by the steep slope on the left, and the Caçadores similarly to the right, and bringing up his own regiment on the narrow crest ordered the two flanking corps to make a second attack. The French battalion in the redoubt made a stiff defence, and was holding its own when Colborne bade the 52nd charge in the centre; they went over the stone wall with a rush, and the garrison was thrust uphill, and pursued by the light corps not only as far as but over the second trench line, which was weakly defended. But the second closed redoubt, at the head of the spur, was held by fresh troops, and there was more fighting here. An eyewitness writes—

[1] From an interesting letter of a 43rd officer in Levinge's history of that corps, p. 191, far the best narrative from Kempt's column. But that of Cooke of the 43rd is also interesting.

'We again advanced, with the swarm of riflemen and caçadores in skirmishing order, keeping up a murderous fire. Firing
up-hill is more destructive than firing down, as the balls in the
latter case fly over. The 52nd advanced under a most heavy
fire, but it was not near so destructive as we expected. Still
more to our astonishment the enemy did not defend their well-
constructed work so determinedly as we had anticipated. They
stood behind their parapets, until we were in the very act of
leaping on them, they then gave way, and precipitated themselves into the ravine behind, and fled down almost out of
sight as if by magic[1].'

Colborne's brigade won the redoubt just after Kempt's brigade
had reached the head of the Puerto on their right; the two
columns saw each other, and were linking up, when a rush of
French infantry came up the broad gorge between them. This
was the battalion of the 9th Léger which had been holding back
Longa's men, in the gap between the two British brigades.
Seeing the line above them broken, they tried to escape before
they were cut off, but were too late, and 300 surrendered in
a body to Colborne himself, who rode across their front and
summoned them to lay down their arms, though he had only ten
riflemen with him at the moment. However, there were plenty
more about him by the time that the short colloquy was over.

The left brigade had suffered very heavily—the 2/95th had
111 casualties, nearly a quarter of its strength, the 52nd lost
80, the Caçadores Algeo, colonel of the 1st battalion, 10 other
officers, and well over 100 men. But they had inflicted far more
loss on the French brigade opposite them[2] and captured four
guns. The routed troops retired in complete disorder across the
hills, pursued for three miles by some of Kempt's men, and did
not halt till they ran into the arms of one of Villatte's reserve
brigades near Ascain. Only the two battalions opposite the
extreme right of Alten's attack[3], cut off from the rest by the loss

---

[1] There are good accounts of this in Colborne's *Diary* [in his life by Moore
Smith], pp. 186–7; in Harry Smith's *Autobiography*, i. pp. 132–5; Surtees,
p. 241; Kincaird, *Random Shots*, pp. 258–9; and Castello, p. 254. The
quotation above is from Harry Smith.

[2] Béchaud's brigade shows in Martinien's lists 24 casualties of officers.

[3] These were the 70th and 86th Line of Cambriel's brigade.

of the ridge, retired separately and joined the troops of Conroux, who were defending the Fagadia ridge and the Great Rhune against Giron's Spaniards[1].

The breaking up of Taupin's division enabled the Andalusians to establish themselves on the upper slope of that great hill, and in the afternoon, and even far into the evening, they made repeated attempts to win their way to its crest. But this was beyond their power—Clausel had sent up in succession five battalions to strengthen this part of the position[2], till his reserves were almost exhausted. Long after fighting in all other directions had ceased, there was heavy musketry fire on the upper slopes of the Rhune. But all attempts to win it were fruitless—the ground was so strong that only immense superiority of numbers could have carried it, and this Giron in the later hours of the day did not possess[3].

It was not till the next night that the Rhune passed into Wellington's hands—and then not by a direct assault, but by means of operations on its flanks. On the 8th there was dense fog all the morning; when it dispersed, after midday, orders were given to Freire to push forward from the Mandale and the Croix du Poirier over the hills toward Olhete and Ascain. This advance reached as far as the isolated upland farm of Jolimont, only three miles from Ascain, the place of the French central reserve. At the same time the 6th and 7th Divisions were directed to demonstrate again opposite Clausel's left and D'Erlon's right, as if the actual attack threatened on the previous day was about to be delivered. Colville showed himself in front of D'Erlon's lines at Ainhoa. Dalhousie advanced on the works in front of Sare—the redoubts called Ste. Barbe and Grenade. Meanwhile Giron's reserve brigade in the valley, and the right wing of his troops on the slopes of the Rhune pushed eastward, driving in Conroux's posts in that direction, capturing the redoubt of the Chapelle d'Olhain[4], and finally coming in

---

[1] 50th and 59th Line.　　　　[2] 32nd and 34th Line, 12th Léger.

[3] Having left a brigade below as reserve, he had only nine battalions.

[4] Wellington, who did not often specify operations by Spanish units, makes particular mention in his dispatch of October 8th of the fine way in which the regiment of Ordenes Militares, led by Colonel Hore, carried this fort. *Dispatches*, xi. p. 178.

upon the flank of that of Ste. Barbe. Clausel, thinking that the 7th Division also was about to throw itself in on this direction, evacuated all his works in front of Sare, including the Ste. Barbe redoubt, and drew back to the level of that village and his second line of fortified posts[1]. He still, however, clung to the Rhune, whose summit Giron's left battalions had once more attacked without success.

But after dark the colonels of the two regiments on the chief summit of the Rhune[2], seeing their position threatened with envelopment on both sides, evacuated it on their own responsibility, retiring by the path leading to the Col of St. Ignace. Clausel, in his dispatch, declares that they acted without orders, and contrary to his intention. But he made no attempt to replace them, and the Spaniards were in possession of the 'Hermitage' on the highest point ere dawn. Wellington ascended it next day, and got a wonderful panorama from its summit of the whole of Soult's complicated lines of fortification from the Mondarrain to the ocean.

The whole operation had been singularly successful, and had cost few casualties, when the difficulties of the ground and the large numbers of troops put in motion are considered. The total loss was but 1,600, of whom 573 were from British units, 242 from Portuguese, and nearly 800 were Spaniards. The losses of the latter were almost entirely among Giron's troops, who had fought so long upon the Rhune; Freire's and Longa's had suffered little. The British casualties were mainly in the 2/95th and 52nd on Alten's front, and in the 9th and the two Light Battalions of the German Legion at the Croix des Bouquets.

If Soult's statistics are to be trusted[3], the French losses about

---

[1] Clausel's report implies that the Ste. Barbe was evacuated without his orders.

[2] These were the 12th Léger and 34th. The regiments which had been driven off the lower eastern slopes were the 32nd and 50th. The 70th and 88th were on the other side of the Rhune, the 4th Léger and 40th were on the little Rhune. The 4th Léger, 34th, and 50th were of Maransin's division, sent up from the reserve. Eight battalions in all were on the position.

[3] I am not sure that Soult's figures *can* be trusted. For while his official table of losses shows 4 officer-casualties in Boyer's division, Martinien's invaluable and absolutely certain lists show 8. And in Conroux's division Martinien names 5 officers while Soult only gives 4. One remembers the falsification of the Albuera losses. See vol. iv. p. 395.

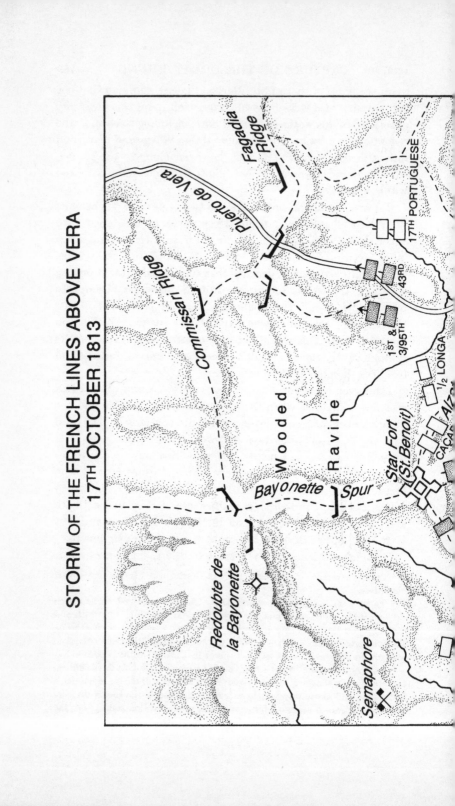

STORM OF THE FRENCH LINES ABOVE VERA
17TH OCTOBER 1813

Fagadia Ridge

Puerto de Vera

Commissari Ridge

17TH PORTUGUESE

43RD

1ST & 3/95TH

½ LONGA

AIZ

CAÇA

Wooded Ravine

Bayonette Spur

Star Fort (St Benoit)

Redoubte de la Bayonette

Semaphore

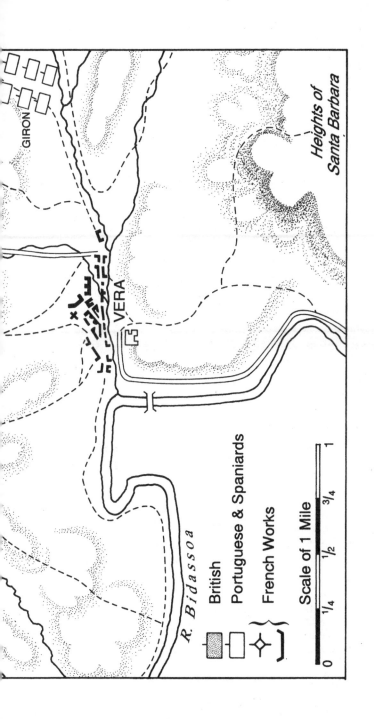

GIRON

Heights of
Santa Barbara

VERA

R. Bidassoa

British

Portuguese & Spaniards

French Works

Scale of 1 Mile

0   1/4   1/2   3/4   1

equalled those of the allies, they ran to 1,673, including 22 officers and 576 rank and file prisoners—nearly all from Taupin's battalions, who could not get away easily when their line on the Bayonette was pierced. Half the total French casualties were in this division. Maucune had been hustled back so rapidly on the other wing that he only lost 357 men, of whom some 60 were prisoners. D'Armagnac in fending off the demonstrations of the 6th Division had as many as 200 casualties. Conroux, who fought Giron's men on the Rhune, returned the unaccountably small total of only some 100 men lost[1]. Nine small calibre field-guns and mountain-guns had been captured, at the Croix des Bouquets, Biriatou, and on the Bayonette, besides some heavy pieces of position taken in redoubts.

Soult blamed everybody but himself for the lost battle. He wrote to Paris that the crossing of the lower Bidassoa could not have taken place if Reille and Maucune had exercised ordinary powers of observation, and had taken certain precautions which he had recommended[2]. Reille replied that he had given very minute directions for the watching of the river, and had started off his reserves at the earliest possible moment to reinforce Maucune. The mischief was that he had too few troops to cover such a long sector, and that his supporting division was placed too far back from his front-line division, when a lightning-swift surprise was carried out by the enemy. For this he was not responsible. Soult then concentrated his wrath on Maucune, who most certainly *had* been negligent, and ought to have detected that something was afoot early on October 7th—the surprise, as Soult pointed out, was made in broad daylight, and the defenders of the Bidassoa had not fired a shot till many of the enemy were across the water. Maucune was sent to the rear in disgrace, but was afterwards utilized in Italy[3]. He was a good fighter, but habitually rash and careless. Once before he had been surprised and routed for want of taking proper precau-

[1] This *must*, I think, be wrong: many battalions of the division were seriously engaged. But Martinien only shows five officer-casualties.

[2] Soult to Clarke, Dispatch of October 18th.

[3] Vidal de la Blache (i. p. 512) says that he retired to Paris and became one of the 'militaires déchus' who haunted the gaming-houses of the Palais Royal. But he was serving in Italy in January–March 1814.

tions—when he was fallen upon by the Light Division at the combat of San Millan[1]. And his tendency to hazardous attacks had been shown at Villa Muriel in 1812[2].

There can be no doubt, however, that the main fault lay with Soult himself. The system of entrenched lines of vast length, which absorb a whole army, and leave only small reserves available when an attack is delivered on one or two points of those lines, is vicious. From Hendaye to the Mondarrain Soult was trying to hold a continuous line with a front of some 23 miles, if salients and re-entrant angles are allowed for. Despite of his fortifications the front was too long; and, misled by Wellington's threats against its inland sector, he concentrated his attention on D'Erlon's part of the line, and left the lower Bidassoa undermanned. When the blow came, his reserves were both too small and too distant from the line of resistance. He himself was present at the least important sector in his whole front, and by the time that he got to the crucial point 'the game was over', as he ingenuously confessed in his dispatch to Paris.

As to Wellington's scheme, it worked precisely as he had intended—'planmässig' in the language of the last Great War. But the astonishing thing about it is that it aimed at nothing more than it accomplished. As Soult observed, the English left wing might have got into St. Jean de Luz by dusk on October 7th[3]. Maucune's division was scattered, Boyer's was holding a very long line; the French head-quarters could have spared no more reinforcements, after sending up Villatte's leading brigade; the other three had been told off to 'stop the rot' on the side of the Bayonette and the Col de Vera, and were covering Taupin's fugitives on the slope by Olhete. The whole army was 'bien décousue', as said Villatte in a downhearted letter of the 8th, ordering quarters for himself and staff to be looked for in Bayonne[4].

One of the three ingenious French specialists who have described Soult's campaign in the Pyrenees criticizes Wellington as having exposed himself to a counter-attack on his right wing

[1] See vol. vi. pp. 375–6. [2] See vol. vi. pp. 80–2.
[3] Soult to Clarke, Dispatch of October 18th.
[4] Villatte to Thouvenot on the night after the battle.

by the united forces of D'Erlon and Clausel. But two of Clausel's three divisions and a fraction of the third were already tied up by the necessity of opposing Alten and Giron. And if D'Erlon had taken the offensive, he had in front of him Picton's, Colville's, and Cole's divisions close at hand, with Hamilton's Portuguese on the Col de Maya within calling distance. It is quite erroneous to say that Wellington had 'no reserves' on this wing[1].

It is true that a passive defensive, without any attempt to meet the enemy by counter-attacks, generally leads to defeat in detail. But where could Soult have found it possible to counter-attack, with his troops in the precise positions in which he had placed them? The battle was lost before a shot had been fired, owing to Wellington's prescient strategy, and his opponent's misconception of the whole situation.

[1] See Clerc's *Campagne du Maréchal Soult*, p. 117.

SECTION XLI: CHAPTER II

BETWEEN THE BIDASSOA AND THE NIVELLE. THE
FALL OF PAMPELUNA. OCTOBER 8–NOVEMBER 7, 1813

ON the day after the evacuation of the Great Rhune every
officer in the French Army, and all those in the British Army
who were not in the confidence of the commander-in-chief,
expected to see the advance continue—certainly to the Adour,
perhaps even farther. Anything seemed possible after the events
of October 7th–8th, when the French line had been driven in
with such ease, and its most prominent strong-point captured.
'This is a fine fertile country, and offers every temptation to
get a little more of it', wrote an intelligent officer on the staff
to his relatives at home. 'I think we shall shortly throw the
French Army behind the Adour, and I hope that my next
letter will be at least from St. Jean de Luz[1].' At the same time
Soult was writing to the Minister of War that the English
might easily have got into St. Jean de Luz on the evening of the
7th, and was pressing the governor of Bayonne to multiply his
outer fortifications. 'It is probable that to-morrow the affair
will be more serious. I hope the works at Bordagain may make
a good resistance, but I must impress on you that the line of
the entrenched camp in front of Bayonne must be strengthened
by every imaginable means. Throw up works commanding all
the roads, so that the troops which may, in case of something
happening [en cas d'événement] have to form up upon them,
may find shelter behind them without delay. This is of the
highest importance. Every one must be set to work, even the
civil population, and work even at night. Arm all the recently
arrived conscripts, and make them dig also[2].'

Villatte wrote on that same night to the same recipient:
'The men are fighting badly. They are no good [ils ne vaillent
rien]. At the head of such troops we shall certainly come to
shameful grief [on ne peut que se déshonorer]. God knows
what will happen to-morrow.'

[1] Letters of Sir W. M. Gomm, p. 325.
[2] Soult to Thouvenot, night of October 7th–8th.

But the 9th of October came and passed, and Wellington showed no signs of intending to push on. Indeed he forbade further offensive moves. Early on that day Dalhousie, as it would seem, permitted the Portuguese brigade of the 7th Division to make a lodgement in the outer houses of the village of Sare. Clausel drove them out again, and their retreat had to be covered by some of Giron's Andalusian battalions. Wellington wrote a letter of rebuke for the benefit of their brigadier Madden. ' I am sorry to have to express disapprobation of the conduct of an officer of whom I have always entertained a good opinion. But I must say that it is unworthy of one of his reputation to get his brigade into scrapes, for the sake of the little *gloriole* of driving in a few pickets, knowing that it was not intended that he should engage in a serious affair[1].' On the 12th there occurred a more grave incident, which bore still clearer witness to Wellington's determination to hold back for the present.

The extreme point which the Allies had occupied, when Clausel drew back to his second line of defence, was the redoubt of Ste. Barbe, close under the French position. It was so marked a salient into Soult's line that, having recovered his confidence after three days, he resolved to make a *coup de main* upon it. He could see that the two companies of Andalusian troops which formed its garrison were keeping no good watch; indeed French vedettes had approached within twenty yards of them without being fired at[2]. Accordingly Clausel enveloped the work at dead of night with three battalions of Conroux's division, and stormed it by escalade, with hardly a shot fired. Not a man of the garrison of 200 escaped—one of the attacking battalions having entered by the gorge of the redoubt and stopped all exit. At dawn the brigade of La Torre's division, which had charge of this sector of the Allied front, made a counter-attack and tried to recover the Ste. Barbe. It was completely beaten off, and when Giron repeated the attempt, later in the morning, with five battalions, Clausel turned out the rest of Conroux's units to support the captors of the redoubt, and the Andalusians were completely foiled. Cole had deployed a brigade of the

---

[1] Wellington to Colville, *Dispatches*, xi. p. 189.
[2] Larpent (p. 277) says that the garrison had no outlying sentries, and that the men had not their arms by them.

4th Division to support Giron, but Wellington refused to allow
it to engage in the fight, holding that the Ste. Barbe was too
much in a salient, and not worth keeping[1]. So Clausel, to the
surprise of both friends and enemies, was allowed to retain the
work, and linked it up by trenches with the rest of his front.
The losses in the three successive combats had been fairly
heavy—the Spaniards had 500 casualties, including about
200 prisoners—Conroux probably half as many, if we may take
as basis of calculation the fact that 12 officers in his division
were hit[2].

What were the reasons for Wellington's acceptance of the
situation on October 9th, and his halt of several weeks on the
positions which he had gained with such skill and ease? A
glance at his official dispatches to the Secretary of State in London
shows that the main one was the same which had held him
back, on August 2nd, from pursuing Soult into France after the
battles of the Pyrenees. He was keeping a wary eye on the news
from the theatre of war in Germany, and even after the reports
of the Katzbach and Dennewitz reached him, he still did not
consider Napoleon definitely beaten, or the general prospect of
the future so satisfactory, as to tempt him to make a stroke far
into France. It was not, indeed, till he had heard of the results
of Leipzig (October 16–18), which did not reach him in detail
till after the battle of the Nivelle (November 10), that he began
to consider the French cause as definitely lost, and the ultimate
victory of the Allies as certain. 'The system of my operations
must depend a good deal on what is doing in the North' was
still his verdict on October 12th[3]; and six days later, 'I am very
doubtful indeed about the advantage of going any further
forward here at present. I see that Buonaparte was still at
Dresden on September 28th, and unless I could fight a general
action with Soult, and gain a *complete* victory, which the nature
of this country scarcely admits of, I should do but little good
to the Allies. . . . It is impossible to move our right wing (Hill, &c.,
at Roncesvalles) till Pamplona shall have fallen, which I think

---

[1] This he explains at length in his dispatch to Lord Bathurst of
October 18th, *Dispatches*, xi. p. 206.

[2] Four each in the 32nd and 34th Line, three in the 55th, one in the 58th.

[3] *Dispatches*, xi. p. 188.

will be within a week. I shall then decide according to the
state of affairs at the moment[1].'

The allusion to the Right Wing and Pampeluna means that,
so long as the siege of that fortress was still lingering on,
Wellington felt compelled to keep Hill, with Stewart's and Hamilton's divisions and their auxiliaries the Spanish troops of Morillo,
fixed in the Roncesvalles positions, in order to guard against
a sudden dash to relieve Pampeluna on the part of Foy and
Paris, from St.-Jean-Pied-du-Port. But when the place should
fall, the Spanish corps now besieging it, under Carlos de España,
could replace Hill in the passes, and the latter could bring up
his two divisions to join the main army. For after the surrender
of Pampeluna, Foy would have no object left for an incursion into
Navarre. It was most unlikely that he would move, with winter
coming on, over the inland passes; and Carlos de España's troops
would suffice to guard them. The fall of Pampeluna, therefore,
would mean the addition of 10,000 bayonets to the force on the
Bidassoa and the Nivelle.

But undoubtedly another consideration, which had much
weight with Wellington, was that there was grave danger that
a move deep into France would provoke the outbreak of a
national insurrection. The troops might plunder, especially the
Spaniards, who were in such a dire state of starvation that they
could hardly be expected to refrain from snatching at food
wherever they saw it. Their commissariat had failed completely,
owing to the apathy of their civil administration, and they
were kept alive by frequent and much grudged doles from the
British magazines. Moreover, both the Spanish and the Portuguese troops had so many French atrocities to remember, that
revenge on the hostile country-side was an inevitable temptation.
And on the very first day of the advance on to French soil some
untoward things had happened[2] in the way of 'eye for eye, and

[1] To Bathurst, October 18, *Dispatches*, xi. p. 207.
[2] A British officer, marching near a Portuguese brigade recounts that
he arrived too late to prevent a caçador from perpetrating the business-like
murder of a French family, in the first farm that he came to. The man then
handed himself into arrest. He explained that his father, mother, and sister
had all been killed by the French during Masséna's retreat in 1811, and he
had made a vow to revenge them. He was tried and hanged, apparently
satisfied to have redeemed his pledge. Gleig, p. 145.

tooth for tooth'. If this went on upon a large scale, as Wellington argued, he would find the whole civil population in arms against him, and would suffer from 'guerrilleros', just as the French had been doing in Spain for the last five years. 'For in France every man is or has been a soldier. If we were five times stronger than we are, we ought not to enter France, if we cannot prevent the men from plundering[1].' In the end, as we shall see, he took the heroic measure of sending back the Spaniards to their own country, thereby sacrificing his numerical advantage over Soult. And he kept the English and Portuguese in order by the most stringent use of punishments. The result was satisfactory to an unexpected degree, for after a few weeks the French peasantry became more friendly to the invaders than to their own troops. For Soult's men, from old habits formed in Spain, had become such irreclaimable marauders that they could not be restrained from plunder by the mere fact that they had come into their own country. Already the stragglers of August had, after their defeat in the Pyrenees, sacked many an upland farm round St.-Jean-Pied-du-Port. And on October 7th Maucune's and Taupin's routed troops did untold and wanton damage about Urrogne and Ascain. Soult's correspondence is full of complaints from mayors and sub-prefects, and he did his best to restore order—but with imperfect results. In one case he court-martialled and shot a captain of the 45th Line, decorated with the Legion of Honour, who was caught supervising the sack of a farm by his company, and struck a military policeman who tried to hinder him. Many more examples were made among the rank and file, but nothing could stop marauding. In 1417 a French chronicler once remarked that the passage of the well-disciplined army of Henry V across Normandy was less dreaded than the advent of one of the roving bands of the loyalist Dauphinois—and the same was the case in Béarn and Gascony in 1813[2].

In October Wellington could not foresee the immense success which his policy was destined to achieve, nor realize that a few weeks later an isolated English soldier, lost on a by-road, was likely to be far safer in France than he had ever been in Spain.

[1] To Sir John Hope, *Dispatches*, xi. pp. 169–70.
[2] Vidal de la Blache, i. p. 513.

Nor had he yet discovered the intensity of the passive disloyalty to the Emperor which had been bred by the conscription and the *droits réunis*. He rightly distrusted reports brought to him by *émigrés* concerning the existence of a large royalist party in the South[1]; but had not yet discovered that if there were few Frenchmen ready to take arms against Napoleon, there were an infinite number who would not raise a finger for him, and only desired his fall. It was not till November, after he had occupied a good deal more French territory, that he came to the conclusion that the general wish of the country was to be quit of the Emperor for good, 'from a conviction that so long as he governs them they will have no peace', and that 'he has no real adherents save the superior officers of his army, the civil functionaries, and possibly some of the new proprietors; but even these last I consider doubtful[2]'. Here Wellington was perhaps overstating the case, but it is clear that a month before he was somewhat underrating it He was still under the impression that the sight of the Allies on French soil might raise the whole nation to patriotic fury.

Meanwhile the weeks of waiting in late October had brought several of Wellington's habitual worries to a head. His relations with the Spanish Government were worse than ever. At the end of August he had sent the Regency a letter stating that as the promotions which he made, as Spanish Commander-in-Chief, were persistently turned down, while officers whom he dismissed in disgrace were given other posts of importance, and as all his suggestions concerning organization, commissariat, &c., were treated with contumely, he had better resign a title which had become meaningless. He thought that this conditional resignation would have scared the Regents into giving him more real authority. But they, willing to disoblige, and not sure that they themselves were not about to disappear—for the new General Cortes had just been elected, and might clear them out—wrote him back that his resignation was noted, and should be referred to the Cortes. It was given in to the last meeting of

---

[1] See Bathurst to Wellington, September 9, for an astounding statement by the Duc de Berri, that 20,000 royalists would take arms the moment Wellington crossed the frontier. *Supplementary Dispatches*, viii. p. 245.

[2] To Bathurst, November 21, *Dispatches*, xi. p. 305.

the old Cortes on September 24th; the moribund assembly naturally refused to decide upon it, and referred it to the new Cortes, which was to meet on October 1st.

This was a body which was much more representative of Spain as a whole than its predecessor, for the greater part of its members had been really chosen in their own districts, precisely because Wellington had liberated the whole country save Catalonia. The late 'extraordinary' Cortes had been a farce so far as real representation went, and was overstocked with 'Liberals' who had practically nominated themselves. In the new one there was a bare 'Liberal' majority, and the 'Serviles' were very strong. Moreover, they resolved that they would move from Cadiz, and the sinister influence of its democratic mob, to Madrid. Then came an outbreak of yellow fever which put all business out of gear for some weeks.

But the new Cortes decided that the affair of the military command should be referred to the Council of State, not to the Regents, and the Council issued [November 8] a most satisfactory report, censuring the Regents, and more especially their minister of war—Wellington's old enemy O'Donoju[1]—and declaring that all the original conditions granted to Wellington nearly a year back must be kept. So the problem came to a satisfactory end[2]. The Cortes voted, before setting out for Madrid, that the conditions must be observed[3]. And, the day after they reassembled at the old capital, they dismissed O'Donoju from his official post[4]. The Regents, much vexed, tried to tone down his disgrace by promoting him from Major-General to Lieutenant-General on his enforced resignation—an insult to the Cortes which gave rise to much comment.

It will be noted, therefore, that from the beginning of September to the end of November Wellington's position as Spanish Commander-in-Chief was most precarious and unsatisfactory; he had offered to resign and his resignation was not

---

[1] See vol. vi. p. 347.

[2] H. Wellesley [minister at Cadiz] to Wellington, November 1, *Supplementary Dispatches*, viii. pp. 355–6.

[3] Henry Wellesley to Castlereagh, November 3, *Supplementary Dispatches*, viii. p. 406.

[4] H. Wellesley to Wellington, *Supplementary Dispatches*, viii. p. 518.

refused for nearly three months! It might conceivably have been accepted, if the Regency and O'Donoju had felt themselves stronger, and if the new Cortes had been as full of anti-British members as the old one. And what then would have been the effect on the conduct of the war on the Bidassoa and the western Pyrenees?

All through these three months the propaganda against Wellington in the Cadiz press had been irritating him into outbursts of anger, which interrupt the usual calm and sardonic tenor of his observations on pressmen. There was too much truth in the comments on untoward events at San Sebastian—but what could excuse the repeated statement that Wellington had given deliberate orders for the destruction of the place for reasons of commercial rivalry[1]? A wilder statement was that Castaños had offered to make him King of Spain, by means of a military *coup d'état*[2], if only he would adopt the Catholic religion. Considering his views on Spanish politics this seems an almost incredible suggestion; though Liberal readers did not know their commander-in-chief's private sentiments on this point. But newspaper libels were of less practical harm than petty interferences by Spanish local officials in the concerns of the army. Wellington found the landing of his military stores at Passages and Bilbao delayed by the Customs House officials claiming to search every vessel, for contraband concealed among the powder barrels and the flour sacks[3]! The couriers bearing his dispatches were denied billets and food; storage-room for his supplies was refused, in places where there were many empty buildings. A case which irritated him especially was that of the military hospital at Fuenterabia; having requisitioned it for the wounded of the recent fights, it was handed over to him swept bare of all fittings, the plank-beds and tables having been carried off to be burnt as firewood. British wounded sent to Bilbao were thrust into an empty rope-walk, without beds, bedding, or utensils of any kind, and so lay for weeks[4], many dying from privation. For all this, not the people of Spain but

---

[1] See repeated letters on this point all through October in *Dispatches*, xi. especially that on pp. 214–15.   [2] *Dispatches*, xi. p. 199.

[3] See Wellington to Alava, *Dispatches*, xi. pp. 192–5.

[4] Journal of Hale of the 9th Foot, p. 117.

arrogant petty bureaucrats were responsible—with the Regency
at their back. 'The officers of the Government would not dare
to conduct themselves in this manner, if they did not know
that their conduct was agreeable to their employers [1].'

The Portuguese Government contributed a secondary list of
worries. Here the fundamental cause of evils was that the war
had now moved so far from the national frontier that the
imminent danger of French invasion was no longer present, to
keep the Regency active. Only the burden and not the profit
of supporting an army, large in proportion to the total population,
of the realm, was now felt. The recruiting laws were allowed
to grow slack, and even such conscripts or convalescents as
accumulated at the depots were not forwarded to the front.
The battalions in the Pyrenees were growing very attenuated,
because no losses were replaced—some were down to less than
350—even to less than 300 bayonets [2]. They were fighting well—
better, as Wellington said, than he had ever seen before; but
they were dwindling to skeleton units. The winter was at hand,
and it had always proved very deadly to the Portuguese troops,
unless they were comfortably stowed away in winter quarters.
Meanwhile the drafts to complete them failed to appear. It is
easy to note that a land march from Elvas to St. Sebastian, or
a sea voyage from Lisbon round to Passages, was a long business
—very much more tedious than a move to join the winter
quarters of an army cantoned on the frontier of Beira or
Alemtejo. But the drafts were not simply late—they were not
appearing at all. Beresford was sent back to Lisbon in September to stir things up, but found the Regency in a perverse and
captious temper.

For this there were many reasons—not the least was the fall
in revenue recently caused by the transference of the military
base of the whole British army in the Peninsula from Lisbon
to Passages, Bilbao, and Santander. The Tagus quays, recently
crammed with merchantmen no less than with government
transports, were growing deserted, and customs receipts were
naturally dwindling. This made the financial burden of the

---

[1] Wellington to Bathurst, *Dispatches*, xi. p. 326.

[2] The two battalions of the 17th Line on the Rhune had only 700 present;
the 10th Caçadores in Campbell's brigade less than 300.

356.7   L

war press more heavily than before. A more secret cause of stinted reinforcements for the Army in the Pyrenees, and one that could never be avowed openly, was that Portugal was—as always—somewhat afraid of Spanish designs. The contested possession of Olivenza was a standing grievance; there was an angry correspondence going on concerning shelter given in Portugal to the exiled bishop of Orense, and there were claims and counter-claims for very large war-expenses in dispute between the two countries. Now that Spain was practically free from the French, and had large bodies of troops in the interior, which had not gone up to the front, Portugal did not feel quite safe—she had only at home some dismounted cavalry, two regiments of the line, and her militia, only half of which was kept under arms this year.

A plausible grievance, much enlarged on by Forjaz—the very capable minister of war—was that Wellington had been somewhat reticent in his dispatches as to the services of the Portuguese, while he had emphasized what Forjaz considered the infinitely less valuable help of the Spanish armies. But the remedy proposed for this alleged neglect was that Wellington should mass all the ten brigades of Portuguese infantry at the front, and form them into a separate national army, under a general of the Portuguese service, complete with cavalry and artillery from the same establishment. It is not clear whether this was a bid for greater opportunities by the ambitious Silveira—who had not particularly distinguished himself in the command of a single division in the recent campaign—or whether Forjaz (who had a good conceit of his own military capacity) would have liked to take on the job himself. But Wellington was aghast at the proposal—the Portuguese infantry had been doing admirably of late, but divorced from their old divisions, and worked by a native staff, and with native commissariat, he was sure that they would come to grief. 'Separated from ourselves they could not keep the field in a respectable state, even if the Portuguese government were to incur ten times the expense they now incur. . . . Not only can they acquire no honour in, but they cannot come out of, the contest without dishonour[1].' This decision sent to the British Minister at Lisbon

[1] To Sir Chas. Stuart, October 11, *Dispatches*, xi. p. 185.

had to be conveyed in more diplomatic terms to Forjaz, and naturally left him discontented. But Wellington took care in the future to be more explicit in his commendation of the very real merits of the Portuguese infantry in his later dispatches[1]. And Beresford stirred up the depots, and succeeded in sending off some much needed drafts to the front.

The Home Government continued, as before, to provide the commander-in-chief in Spain with some legitimate causes of complaint. But since Vittoria he had certainly acquired an ascendancy over them, which enabled him to voice his grievances in a firmer tone, and to meet unwise suggestions with more blunt refusals. One mark of consideration for his demands deserves a word of special notice: since 1799 the coinage of the British guinea had stopped, and that handsome coin grew scarcer year by year, till it could command 26s. in Bank of England paper. By a great effort in 1813 gold enough was collected to strike, for the benefit of the army in Spain, the so-called 'military guinea', otherwise the 'Garter Guinea'. The bulk of this handsome issue was sent direct to the Peninsula, where it was welcomed as an earnest of good things to come. But this was the last guinea ever coined in London: none appeared in 1814 or 1815, and in 1816, with peace conditions at last restored, was struck the first of the modern St. George sovereigns, with the graceful reverse by Pistrucci, which has endured down to our own day. Dollars remained hard to procure: the silver famine which had endured for so many years still continuing, and the five-shilling tokens, which the Bank of England was producing since 1804, having no currency on the Continent[2].

The Admiralty appears to have provoked Wellington's ire during this autumn more than any other department of the Home Government. We may discount somewhat his complaint of lack of ships on the Biscay station, for the First Lord could argue, plausibly, that the expedition to the Baltic had now been added to the American War as a cause for the distraction of war-vessels from the nearer seas. But no excuse could be found

---

[1] But the concession is made in rather sarcastic terms, see *Dispatches*, xi. p. 257, to Beresford.

[2] In November many regiments had not received their pay for June. *Dispatches*, xi. p. 302.

for such carelessness as the failure to warn masters of transports that the port of Santoña was still in the hands of a French garrison: several vessels ran into it and were captured. And the fact that, when new clothing was being sent out, the uniform coats were delivered in one ship at Passages, but the knapsacks and cross-belts at Corunna in another ship, needs no comment, and reminds us of Crimean days[1]. It was more vexatious still that the great-coats of certain regiments, left at Oporto in May, and shipped for transport, had not reached their owners in November, for lack of convoy[2]. And by November they were bitterly wanted.

The Duke of York still continued to harp upon his old grievance that the 'Provisional Battalions' had not been sent home to England for reconstruction. But Wellington as obstinately kept them back—they were too valuable to him, and he retained them till the end of the war[3]. More discomposing was an offer from Lord Bathurst that, if these battalions were reclaimed by the Duke, the army might receive instead a number of battalions of militia—there seemed to be some prospect that whole units might volunteer for foreign service. This proposal provoked Wellington, usually most courteous in all his communications with the Minister of War, to an explosion of sarcastic disapproval.

'I have never had under my command more than one regiment of English militia. I found that, however, to be so entirely divested of interior economy and real discipline, that however well the soldiers may be disciplined as regards their exercises and movements, I should very much doubt that a large militia army could be useful in the field for more than a momentary exertion. My notion of them is that their officers have all the faults of those of the Line to an aggravated degree, and some more peculiarly their own[4].'

He asked that the militia might only be utilized for drafts for the regiments at the front; and if volunteering for active service was slack, it might be stimulated by promising a susten-

---

[1] See *Dispatches*, xi. p. 218.   [2] Ibid., xi. p. 240.
[3] See Ibid., xi. p. 140.
[4] To Bathurst, *Dispatches*, xi. p. 140, also see Bathurst to Wellington, *Supplementary Dispatches*, viii. p. 249.

ance-allowance for the wives of militiamen offering themselves for the line. 'The women in Ireland, when I was there, took the utmost pains to prevent the men from volunteering—naturally enough, because from that moment of enlisting they themselves went not "upon the parish" but upon the dunghill, to starve. It is astonishing that any Irish militia soldier was ever found to volunteer: they must certainly be the worst members of society; and I have often been inclined to attribute the enormity and frequency of crimes committed by the soldiers here, to our having so many men who left their families to starve, for the inducement of getting a few guineas to spend on drink.' It was certainly true, as court-martial statistics show, that crimes of violence and robbery in the Peninsular army were committed by soldiers with Irish names in a surprising predominance, even when it is realized what a considerable percentage of the whole army was Irish. Scottish names, when due allowance is made for the comparatively moderate total of Scots in the army, are decidedly scarce in proportion[1].

The Government did not give up the idea of inducing militia units to volunteer *en masse*, but the scheme worked badly, for various reasons, and but one militia brigade of 2,800 men ever set sail—only to arrive at Bordeaux just after Napoleon's abdication. So no chance was given them to disprove Wellington's indictment. Those who care to study the scheme in detail will find it set forth very sufficiently in Sir John Fortescue's *History of the British Army*, vol. ix, Chapter XII. It concerns the general story of organization in Great Britain rather than the Peninsular War.

In half a dozen of his letters to Lord Bathurst and other correspondents, Wellington mentions the fall of Pampeluna as a desirable contingency, which would allow him to make another move, even if the news from Germany were not conclusive or satisfactory. The long-awaited event came upon the final day of October, after much negotiation, for Baron Cassan held out till the garrison had used up its last ration.

---

[1] I once, for a paper read before the United Services Institution, worked out the figures for the whole court-martial record of 1808–14. There could be no doubt of the result. I left out in my calculation men with names probably but not certainly Irish.

It may be worth while to give here some account of this blockade—a siege it never became and no battering took place—which we have so often had occasion to mention in a passing fashion. When Clausel set out on June 18th, upon his luckless march toward Vittoria, with the intention of joining King Joseph in time for battle, he left Pampeluna in charge of three battalions of the Army of the North, and 800 men of the 'legions' of Gendarmerie, which had been used in 1811–12 for garrison duty in Northern Spain[1]. The place had been the central arsenal of the Army of the North, and contained a good store of munitions, and no less than 54 field guns—the equipment of all the four divisions which Clausel had taken with him on his long hunt after Mina in the mountains—as well as 80 guns of position on the ramparts. The weak point was food—the store was very low, till on June 15th a convoy from Bayonne brought in 77 days' rations of biscuit and flour, calculated for a garrison of 2,500 men. But when King Joseph's army swept by in rout on June 24th, after Vittoria, the governor had thrust in upon him by Gazan a great number of foot-sore or sickly men, who could not follow the army in its retreat[2], and hundreds more of lost and strayed individuals dropped in of their own accord. This gave Cassan a full hospital, but allowed him in time to organize a 'battalion of detachments' to aid in his defence. He had altogether some 3,800 combatants at his disposition. On the day after the Army of the South moved on, the head of Wellington's marching columns appeared, hastening down the valley of the Arga in pursuit.

It has been already related in the last volume of this book[3] that Wellington established on June 25th a cordon of blockade around Pampeluna, formed by the 3rd, 7th, and Light Divisions. They were soon replaced by Hill's corps (2nd Division and Silveira's Portuguese), when the first comers were drawn off in the pursuit of Clausel. When that ineffective movement came to an end, Hill marched northward to force the passes, leaving the 3rd, 4th, and 6th Divisions opposite Pampeluna, till they were relieved on July 12th by Henry O'Donnell's 'Andalusian

---

[1] 1st and 2/52nd, 4/117th, 3rd legion of Gendarmerie.
[2] As also 40 unlucky prisoners of the 71st British Foot. See vol. vi. p. 416.
[3] Vol. vi. pp. 528–9.

Reserve', which came up after the capitulation of Pancorbo, and took over the British line of posts. Wellington left orders that there was to be no attempt at a formal siege—he was not going to send thither any of his own battering-train, which was to be reserved for St. Sebastian, and O'Donnell had only 12 field-guns with him, while the fortress was bristling with heavy pieces of position. The system adopted was to form an inner cordon of light pickets close in to the town, and an outer circle of strong posts, partly established in villages a couple of miles out, which were put in a state of defence, partly in field-works, thrown up in sectors where there was no convenient village to fortify. Of these there were nine, each armed with two of the French pieces captured at Vittoria.

The city is built on a flat-topped plateau of no great height, with the river Arga running immediately under its walls on the north and north-east sides, where it acts as an impassable ditch. On the south and south-east sides there was a bastioned enceinte, with the strong citadel projecting from it to the due south. Two outlying forts at some distance from the walls were 'slighted', being judged by Cassan to have dangerously long communications with the main fortress, and to require inordinately large garrisons. The country-side on both banks of the Arga was flat and fertile, covered, even quite close in to the walls, with market-gardens, and with wheatfields, whose produce had not been ripe for the sickle when the blockade began. This open ground was the scene of numerous skirmishes all through July, August, and September, as Cassan sent out many sorties, to cover reaping and potato-digging activity, in the fields outside cannon shot from the walls, and not too close to the main Spanish fortified posts. The front line of blockading pickets was often driven in by a sudden sally of 400 or 500 men, and food-seeking went on till the Spaniards came up in force. Very perceptible benefit to the stores of the garrison was got in this way, and Wellington held that there had been negligence shown by the blockading army, in not burning the wheatfields, and systematically digging up the market-gardens, in the early months of the siege. The place might have been starved out three weeks earlier, if all outlying foodstuffs had been destroyed. And precisely those last three weeks were important, for if Pampeluna had surrendered

early in October instead of on its very last day, it would have
been possible to push the advantage of the crossing of the
Bidassoa and the capture of the Great Rhune, without any
further delay. Three October weeks spent under canvas on the
windy hills north of the Bidassoa, in perpetual rain, gave Wellington's army many sick : and on the Roncesvalles front snow had
already begun, and Hill's and Morillo's divisions suffered from
frostbite, and from losing men in blizzards on the more outlying
posts.

The first month of the blockade (June 25th–July 26th) was
diversified by many sorties, but by no event of outstanding
importance. Cassan judged that Soult might try to relieve him,
but had no certainty of his hope. For every messenger that he
sent out was intercepted, either by the blockading cordon, or by
Mina's bands pervading the country up to the foot of the
Pyrenees[1]. The only information that he got was by a few
deserters from the *Chasseurs Britanniques*, who could tell him
something of Wellington's dispositions, but nothing of Soult's
intentions. And the Marshal was equally unlucky in trying to
send emissaries into the town. It was only therefore by the
evidence of his own eyes and ears that the governor got knowledge of the great endeavour to free him from blockade, which
culminated in the battle of Sorauren.

On the 26th of July distant musketry and a certain amount
of artillery-fire was heard toward the north-east, in the direction
of Roncesvalles. This came from Cole's rear-guard action with
Clausel in front of Linzoain[2]. On the 27th it became still more
clear that the relieving army must be drawing near to Pampeluna.
Though the line of the San Cristobal heights hid Sorauren and
the hill of Oricain from Cassan's view, he noted the arrival of
Picton's and Morillo's divisions on the heights beside Huarte,
where they took position facing north only a mile or two away
from the city. And, what was equally good evidence, in the
afternoon one of Henry O'Donnell's two divisions from the
blockading force—that which faced the south side of the city—
was seen to march off in a wide circuit, and extend itself along

[1] For one of Cassan's cipher letters to Soult, captured and sent to
Major Scovel for interpretation, see Jones's *Sieges of the Peninsula*, ii.
pp. 350–1.   [2] See vol. vi, p. 653.

the heights of St. Cristobal, continuing Picton's and Morillo's
line[1]. The governor thought it worth while to send out a sortie,
and to demonstrate against the village of Villaba, in the hope
that the army of relief might already be appearing on the other
side. But there was such a strong barrier of troops between
him and his friends that nothing came of the effort.

That night [July 27], however, the fires of the bivouacs of
Foy's division on the French left were distinctly visible to the
garrison, on the hills beyond the Arga—not more than five
miles away. Next day the decisive fight must obviously take
place, and Cassan hoped to be relieved by the afternoon of the
28th. Instead there came bitter disappointment: on the visible
side of the battle-field Foy and Picton faced each other all day
without coming to blows. But a din lasting for many hours
showed that a bitter contest was going on upon precisely that
part of the hills which was invisible from Pampeluna. It died
down at nightfall, and the French columns did not appear over
the crests. Cole's and Pack's divisions had completely beaten off
the main attack of Soult, and it was in vain that Cassan held all
his disposable men ready to sally out, to fall upon the Allied rear
when the French column-heads should show on San Cristobal.
Meanwhile new troops from the south, the division of Carlos de
España, came up, and occupied all the posts that O'Donnell had
evacuated on the afternoon of the 27th.

On the 29th the garrison of Pampeluna waited for the renewal
of the general action. But hardly a shot was fired all day, and
the visible part of the Allied army lay unmoved in its old positions.
The situation looked disheartening, and the dawn of the next
day brought the conviction of disaster. The whole Allied second
line, from Picton on the right to Henry O'Donnell's division on
the left, was seen to descend from its posts on the hills, and to
strike northward. A loud outburst of cannon and musketry
fire began, and continued for many hours—but always growing
more distant and continuing to die away to the north-west. This
was the second battle of Sorauren, and the complete rout of
Soult's army. All chance of relief was over for Pampeluna.

We can now see that Cassan might conceivably have got
away eastward on the 27th, and saved his garrison by slipping

[1] See map of Sorauren facing p. 640 of vol. vi.

off through the gap left in the Spanish blockading lines—this was his only chance. He might have joined Foy with luck, though not with certainty. But of course he was not intending merely to carry off his garrison, but to give Pampeluna intact into the victorious hands of Soult, with all its guns and stores. Evasion was not his game at the moment. And he cannot be blamed for not foreseeing the incalculable.

It says much for the quality of Cassan as a leader of men that, having gone through this heart-breaking experience on July 26th–29th he was able to keep his men to their duty for three months longer, though every week that passed made it more certain that no relief was likely to come. Indeed the generals in charge of the blockade contrived to let him know, by means of *parlementaires,* of the results of the battle of San Marcial (August 31) and the crossing of the Bidassoa (October 7). He knew that it was the duty of a good officer to detain in front of him, for the longest possible time, the largest possible enemy force: and on this principle he held out till his last ration had been consumed. He cannot have known, however, what good service he was doing to his master, by reason of Wellington's resolve not to move deep into France until Pampeluna should have fallen. The actual force which was locked up in the blockade was not a very large one—from July 28th to the end of September it consisted of one of Henry O'Donnell's Andalusian divisions and of Carlos de España's five Castilian battalions, with the cavalry regiment that belonged to the Andalusian corps—not more than 9,500 men[1]. Late in September Wellington ordered the remaining Andalusians to the front, replacing them by a division of the Duque del Parque's '3rd Army'—that of the Prince of Anglona, about 5,000 strong—which had just come up by a very long march from the lower Ebro. But it was not the 9,000 Spanish troops immobilized in front of Pampeluna which counted in Wellington's calculation, but Hill's corps on the Roncesvalles positions, which had to be maintained there, so long as there was a chance that Soult might make one last sally from the side of St.-Jean-Pied-du-Port, to relieve Cassan's much-

[1] Morning states of July show Don Carlos with 3,200 men, the Andalusian division with about 5,000 bayonets and cavalry 700, artillery, &c., 300.

enduring garrison. He wanted to have Hill and his auxiliaries on the Bidassoa and the Nivelle for the grand advance: when Pampeluna should have fallen, the force lately engaged in blockading it could replace Hill in the passes—where there would be no danger, since Soult would no longer have any inducement for a stroke toward Navarre.

All through August and September Cassan kept up the spirits of his garrison by sorties for foraging purposes, which nearly always got through the weak inner line of Spanish observation posts, and sometimes brought in useful supplies—after foodstuffs could no longer be got, even firewood and stubble for horse-fodder were useful. On September 9th a sally, pushed farther than usual, so irritated Carlos de España that he charged the retreating French at the head of his own cavalry escort, was beaten off, and was badly wounded in the thigh at close quarters. This was quite in consonance with his reckless courage displayed on many occasions, but the charge was not an appropriate exploit for a responsible commander-in-chief! He soon resumed command of his troops—but not (as subsequent negotiations proved) of his temper.

By the end of September Cassan's troops were on half rations, and no adventitious aid by foraging could be got from the autumn fields. The whole of the horses of the legion of Gendarmerie, which formed part of the garrison, were gradually killed and eaten. An attempt had been made to expel the much diminished civil population, but it failed, as Carlos de España fired upon the fugitives and drove them back. Low living began to tell upon the garrison, which had now sent 1,000 sick to the hospitals—scurvy broke out in them and claimed many victims. By the third week in October all the horses and mules had been finished, and in the vain search after green food the soldiers were devouring roots dug up outside the walls—some of which turned out to be hemlock, and poisonous. Cats, dogs, and rats were hunted and eaten. Desertion began on a considerable scale—the evaders being mostly Spanish *Juramentados*, or Germans, Italians, and Belgians from the *départements réunis*. Under these circumstances Cassan sent out *parlementaires* to Carlos de España on October 24th.

The negotiations for surrender were a curious example of

'bluffing' on both sides. Cassan began with the absurd proposal
that he should be allowed to march out with the honours of war
and six pieces of cannon, taking bag and baggage, and all the
dependants of the army, French and Spanish, and should join
Soult on the frontier. The Spanish general demanded uncon-
ditional surrender. Cassan replied by announcing that he should
blow up all the works and cut his way to France—mere *fanfa-
ronnade*—as he acknowledges, in his report to Paris, that his men
could not have marched three miles, and that he had not a
beast of burden left. Don Carlos answered that there were
25,000 men between Pampeluna and the French frontier, that
all roads and bridges had been cut up, and that he should regard
the destruction of Pampeluna as 'an unworthy resolution
suggested by vile despair'. Wherefore, if the French sallied out,
there should be no quarter given—he had issued orders that
any Spanish soldier accepting the surrender of a prisoner should
be shot. And if by chance any fugitive should escape the fury
and vengeance of the regular troops, he would infallibly fall into
the hands of an enraged peasantry[1]. On this Cassan, knowing
that his own threat was an empty one, proposed that the
garrison should surrender on condition of being 'exchanged',
and not serving against the Allies for a year and a day. His sick
in the hospitals should have the same conditions, and go to
France as soon as they could travel. And civil employees,
French or Spanish, were to go free. Again Don Carlos returned
a blank refusal: it was notorious that 'exchanges' with the
imperial government had never been worked honestly; if not
drafted into Soult's ranks, the garrison would probably be sent
off to fight the Allies in Germany. And the Spanish nation had
no intention of letting *Afrancesado* traitors go free.

In the end Cassan had to accept a rather rigorous form
of capitulation. His men might march out with the honours of
war, but must lay down their arms 300 yards from the gates of
Pampeluna and go into captivity in England by ship. Normans
Cross and Stapleton and Porchester prison-camps were at any
rate better than the Isle of Cabrera. The sick were also to be
prisoners, but, if permanently disabled, might be exchanged
against Spanish or British invalids of the same sort. Civil

---

[1] See the letter in Belmas's *Sièges dans la Péninsule*, iv. p. 784.

employees of French nationality might be exchanged against some of the many Spanish civilians unjustifiably detained in France. Women, children, and men over 60 years of age of French nationality might be given passports for France. *Afrancesados* should be left behind, to be dealt with by 'the wise laws which govern Spain'[1]: this clause to include women as well as men of Spanish nationality. Deserters from the Spanish or British armies were to be given up, with no provision of immunity[2]. These last clauses led to some executions, though many *Afrancesados* are said to have been smuggled away in the French uniform, and some Spanish ladies to have successfully played the part of Frenchwomen.

Wellington gave his full approval to the stern attitude adopted by Carlos de España. He had written to him: 'You tell me that the enemy had mined the fortifications of Pampeluna, and that he proposes to attempt to escape after blowing up the works. The destruction of the city and an attempt to escape can only be considered as a scheme for doing a sensible damage to the Spanish nation, and then throwing themselves upon the generosity of the allied army. I may tell you that I feel no inclination to treat generously those who behave in such a way. If the garrison of Pampeluna does the least damage to the city, I order you to grant them no capitulation, and no terms of grace. You may shoot the governor and his officers, and decimate the rank and file[3].' Wellington was well aware that Cassan could not really attempt to break out, and that his threats were merely 'bluffing', for he had been informed by many deserters that the garrison was absolutely exhausted, and unable to move three miles. So his authorization to Don Carlos was probably intended only to hearten him up for the conduct of the oncoming negotiations. But, as Napier remarks[4], the proposal to decimate the rank and file would have been contrary to all the rules of war. To be decimated, a body of men must

---

[1] A queer expression, 'les lois sages qui gouvernent l'Espagne'.

[2] There is an interesting trial of a British deserter found at Pampeluna in *Peninsular Court-Martials*, 1813, p. 395, of a man of the 28th found in French uniform, who was condemned to death, but pardoned, as having been long 'subject to mental derangement'.

[3] Wellington to Carlos de España, *Dispatches*, xi. p. 210.

[4] *Peninsular War*, v. p. 338.

first have been taken prisoners: and to shoot prisoners in cold blood for the doings of their commander would have been inadmissible. The Spanish general improved on his chief's formula, when he said that 'no quarter should be given'. For to refuse quarter altogether, though more bloodthirsty, would have been more in accordance with the code of contemporary warfare than cold-blooded decimation. The horrid story of the executions at Quiberon may be remembered; and Napoleon himself shot the whole garrison of Jaffa after surrender, on the pretext that it consisted of paroled troops, who had been found in arms again, after engaging not to serve further in the war. It was lucky for everybody concerned in the negotiation that Cassan's threat was never carried out, for Carlos de España— as his conduct in Catalonia during the later Spanish Civil Wars showed—was quite capable of wholesale massacre. And Wellington's dispatch certainly contained some orders which English public opinion would never have condoned.

SECTION XLI: CHAPTER III

THE BATTLE OF THE NIVELLE. NOVEMBER 10, 1813. THE PRELIMINARIES

WHILE Wellington was waiting for the fall of Pampeluna, and while his men were shivering under sleet-showers on the Rhune, or under snow-blizzards above Roncesvalles, Soult had fallen back on his old plan of continuous linear fortification—though the events of October 7th should have warned him of its fundamental unsoundness. It was evident enough to his opponent. One of the most lively narrators of the campaign, Harry Smith of the Light Division, has left us a story which explains the situation well enough, though it may not be a word for word reproduction of the dialogue which took place[1].

On a morning of exceptional bright weather Wellington was lying down near the Hermitage on the Rhune, with his telescope to his eye, watching the whole French army toiling like strings of ants upon every hill-side below, each man bearing his stone for the erection of walls and redoubts. Colborne, the brigadier in charge of the sector, and several staff officers were sitting or standing around. Turning on his elbow, Wellington remarked to Colborne, 'those fellows think themselves invulnerable, but I shall beat them out, and with great ease.' 'That we may beat them out, when your lordship attacks, I have no doubt', replied Colborne, 'but as to the great ease—?' 'Ah, Colborne, with your local knowledge only you are perfectly right: it appears difficult. But the enemy have not men enough to man all those works and lines they occupy. I can pour a greater force on certain points than they can concentrate to resist me.' 'Now I see it, my lord', says Colborne. And this puts the case in a nutshell.

Soult had at first not wholly resigned himself to the idea of passive linear defence. Despite of the awful rebuffs of Sorauren and San Marcial, he had still in the early autumn some hankering, as it would seem, after that rather chimerical irruption into Aragon which he had proposed to Suchet in August. Though his colleague had refused to accept his plans—as we have seen

[1] See Sir Harry Smith's *Autobiography*, i. p. 142.

in a previous chapter[1], and had put in a counter-scheme of his own—correspondence went on as late as October[2]. By that time it was obviously futile, as snow had begun to close all the upper passes from Roncesvalles eastward.

But these arguments about the impracticable had become, by the time of the crossing of the Bidassoa, a mere academic discussion. Soult had resolved to stand firm on his second line, after his first had fallen, and he began to cast his eyes behind him, and to give serious attention to his third line—along the course of the Nive from Cambo to Bayonne—which had hitherto taken up less of his attention. For the events of October 7th had already revealed to him the fact that it was at least conceivable that another thrust on Wellington's part might pierce very deep—his own dispatches acknowledge that, on the day of the passage of the Bidassoa, the enemy might, if he had chosen, have gone far beyond St. Jean de Luz[3]. It is a little difficult to arrive at the Marshal's inmost thoughts in the weeks that followed. Only a few days after the loss of his first position he was trying to prove on paper that he had lost little or nothing, and was writing to the Minister of War at Paris in an optimistic strain. 'It has been advantageous rather than otherwise to lose the heights along the Bidassoa, which would have been hard to hold in winter, owing to the difficulty of keeping the troops supplied. If the enemy tries to occupy them during the rainy season, he will soon see that he has lost rather than gained by pushing forward[4].' Still more astonishing is it to find that 'the possession of the Little Rhune is most advantageous, and is quite as profitable to us as if we were occupying the summit of the Greater Rhune'. And 'militarily speaking, I consider the events of October 7th as profitable to us, because the army is now more concentrated, and has its right wing resting in a much better position than before'[5].

Finally Soult, being pressed by the Minister to try one of those counter-attacks which the Emperor had repeatedly recommended in his earlier orders, replied that he intends to receive

---

[1] See above, pp. 90–5.
[2] The last letter on the subject seems to be that to Suchet of October 19th.
[3] See above, p. 137.   [4] Soult to Clarke, October 28.
[5] Soult to Clarke, October 18.

battle in his chosen position, not to undertake any offensive movements. 'I consider that in the actual state of affairs, I ought rather to fight a general action in a good position, than to take the risks of partial attacks upon ground which I could not hold if I succeeded in winning it, on account of the broad spaces involved. If I were to receive a check in a local attack, I might next day have to recross the Nive, perhaps even the Adour[1].' He said later that he had fortified himself so well from the Mondarrain to the port of St. Jean de Luz 'that the enemy ought not to have been able to break through without losing 25,000 men'[2]. And such a loss would have ruined Wellington's army, and made it incapable of any further advance.

On the whole I am inclined to think that the true explanation of Soult's mental attitude at this period is to be found in the character-sketch of him left by his sarcastic contemporary Lamarque. 'Proud of his reputation, he was full of assurance the day before a battle—and recovered that same assurance the day after a defeat. And when he had conceived and written down at his desk a scheme, he seemed to regard it as an inevitable decree from heaven[3].' His not inconsiderable literary power was always utilized to prove not only that he had acted for the best, though he had been betrayed by his generals, or his soldiers, or the weather, but also that no practical harm had resulted from his last disaster or failure. So he had dealt with Sorauren, San Marcial, and the Passage of the Bidassoa, and so he was about to deal with the battles of the Nivelle, the Nive, and Orthez. A good deal could be accomplished by a judicious mixture of *suppressio veri* and *suggestio falsi*, when reporting to a distant Minister of War at Paris.

For the present Soult was staking everything on the power of passive resistance given by scientific fortification. He did not, of course, trust to one continuous line of forts and trenches any more than Wellington had done at the lines of Torres Vedras. Long stretches of wall or *abattis* were not frequent in his plan, though a few of them were to be seen. He relied upon what modern engineers call 'strong points', redoubts, flanking and

---

[1] Soult to Clarke, November 8.
[2] Soult to Clarke, November 19.
[3] Max. Lamarque, *Memoires*, ii. p. 182.

supporting each other, closed forts armed with guns on very crucial points, 'sungahs' of loose stones commanding the paths which crossed the position, or the narrow saddles between knoll and knoll. There was some approach to the 20th-century idea of 'defence in depth'; the first-line trenches or redoubts could be lost without any fatal result, since they all had second- or third-line works behind them, to which the garrison could retire, and rally on its reserves. The whole system is impossible to realize without a very detailed map, and most difficult to describe, because of the innumerable works scattered over very rough and irregular ground.

Roughly speaking, however, we may say that the position of the Nivelle fell into three sectors. Their total length was somewhat over 20 miles. The first, or seaward, sector lay along, or rather in front of, the lower tidal course of the Nivelle river, from the port of St. Jean de Luz to Ascain, the point beyond which the tide does not ascend. Above Ascain the river is merely a fine mountain stream, flowing in a narrow valley (much haunted by trout-fishers in these days). But from the high-tide mark to the sea there are six miles in which the Nivelle is for half the day almost as broad an obstacle as the Bidassoa itself. Here Soult did not place his line of defence along the river, but on the commanding heights upon its south bank, which is far higher than the northern one. The whole of these heights were turned into a fortified camp, so thickly were the redoubts set upon them, and so frequent were the trenches between the redoubts. There were something like fifteen redoubts for infantry, and six big closed works armed with guns of position on this group of hills. On the extreme right, above the sea, was the old fort of Socoa, a seventeenth-century shore-battery: for a mile south of Socoa an inundation had been contrived, and behind it were several closed works and the fortified village of Ciboure, the transpontine suburb of the town of St. Jean de Luz. Above the head of the inundation, the village of Urrogne, the most projecting point in this part of the line, had been crenellated and loopholed—its streets were stopped with barricades, partly of sandbags, partly of barrels filled with earth. There was a big redoubt armed with heavy guns looking down into the village from the hill of Urtubia above—it was the out-lying feature of a complicated group of enclosed works which French narrators of the campaign call the 'Fortified camp of Bordagain'.

The other half of the western sector of Soult's front consisted of a second group of redoubts, trenches, and batteries on the northern side of the Nivelle, which makes a sharp turn west of the Bordagain positions, so that these lines, though continuing the general direction of those nearer the sea, are on the opposite bank of the river. The whole are called the 'Fortified camp of Serres', from the name of a village enclosed in their midst. The central works were on high ground immediately above the north bank of the Nivelle, but there were advanced redoubts on the south bank covering the village and bridge of Ascain, and forming a first line of defence, a sort of broad *tête-de-pont*, which would have to be forced before the position on the further bank of the Nivelle could be approached.

Soult would appear to have been so much impressed by the fact that on October 7th his enemy had turned his seaward flank, by the crossing of the Lower Bidassoa, finding there only two divisions opposing him, that he had determined that nothing of the kind should happen again. He loaded up the Serres–Bordagain positions with work on work, placed many guns of position upon them, and garrisoned them with no less than four of the ten infantry divisions which he had at his disposal. In the Bordagain lines he placed 11,000 men—the divisions once led by Lamartinière and Maucune, but now by Boyer and Laval, since the death of the one and the disgrace of the other of their former commanders. And in the Serres lines he had concentrated all Villatte's Reserve, except the weak Italian brigade of St. Pol, with the division of Daricau, borrowed from D'Erlon's corps—another 12,000 men. Thus on the strongest and shortest sector of his line he had accumulated 23,000 men, leaving a very inadequate force for the maintenance of his much longer positions in the inland sectors.

It may be noted that since the crossing of the Bidassoa Soult had drafted into all his divisions those of his conscript-reserve whom he now considered fit for service. The result was that the losses of San Marcial and of the Bidassoa fighting had been made up, so far as numbers went. Laval's and Boyer's divisions had a slightly greater strength on November 7th than on October 7th

—Daricau's had 1,500 men more in line. Only the foreign brigades in Villatte's Reserve had not been reinforced—German, Italian, and Spanish recruits for them were (of course) unprocurable. And so with the rest of the army—even Taupin's division, so badly cut up upon the Rhune and the Bayonnette, had replaced the whole of the 900 men lost on October 7th. Soult's general total of infantry in line in his nine fighting divisions and his reserve was in November 57,243 as against the 52,067 of a month before. This figure, of course, does not include gunners, cavalry, engineers, train, &c., of whom there were 16,749 in November to 14,706 in October—nor the outlying force of Paris in the Eastern Passes, nor the National Guards under arms in the Pyrenees, nor the local garrison of Bayonne, nor the undistributed conscripts still remaining in that fortress. Adding to his field force of infantry the gunners of the numerous batteries and the sapper companies in the works, Soult stood to fight on the line of the Nivelle with about 62,000 men. The cavalry of course counted for nothing in the game—much of it was cantoned far to the rear. Only a brigade or so had been brought up to the further bank of the upper Nive in the direction of Cambo and Hasparren, far beyond the outer flank of the Nivelle positions.

The central sector of Soult's line of defence differed in character from the seaward sector, in that it was not on the most commanding ground of the region, but was dominated by the massive heights of the Great Rhune, from which Wellington could overlook the whole position, and count every trench and redoubt. Like the Bordagain sector, but unlike the Serres sector, it was entirely on the south bank of the Nivelle, from the bridge of Ascain to the bridge of Amotz. There were two lines of works; the first and more formidable one consisted of an entrenched camp about and around the village of Sare, with strong advanced forts on each side of it. To the west lay the lofty jagged ridge of the Lesser Rhune, with three redoubts upon it, and adjacent a star-fort on the hill of Mouiz: to the south the redoubts of Ste. Barbe and Grenade, each a closed fort furnished with artillery. From Sare to the bank of the Nivelle north of it there was an immense *abattis* more than a mile long. The second line consisted of a chain of trenches and closed works, of which the chief were the redoubts of Saint-Ignace, the Signals Redoubt, the redoubt called after Louis XIV, and that of La Madeleine— the first and last of these were furnished with artillery. The long *abattis* in the front line covered and protected the Louis XIV and Madeleine works.

Clausel's corps, consisting of the three divisions of Conroux, Taupin, and Maransin [late Vandermaesen][1], was in charge of this sector, being about 15,000 strong. Taupin had the right, Maransin the centre, Conroux the left. But all Taupin's troups were in the second or reserve line—the front line being held by a brigade each of Maransin's and Conroux's divisions, of which the second brigades were, along with Taupin's whole division, on the second line of defence. Clausel had 28 battalions in all —of these 14 were shut up as garrisons in one or other of the works, the remainder, three brigades, was available for reserves, and could be moved to any point required. But the ground was so extraordinarily rugged and difficult that movement in many directions was bound to be slow, and was in some localities almost impossible. The Little Rhune, for example, looked almost impregnable in itself, with its scarped front and three stone redoubts overhanging precipitous slopes, but to reinforce it would be difficult, and if (contrary to expectation) the enemy should make a lodgement on its crest, the garrison would find retreat a hard matter, egress being almost as impracticable as assault, on such a rocky position.

Beyond the Nivelle to the left D'Erlon's corps occupied the continuation eastward of the French defences. Here also there were two lines. The front one consisted of a series of 'strong points' and trenches extending uphill from the banks of the Nivelle in front of Ainhoue, where a large closed work, with guns, the battery of Arbonne, lay close above the river. To the east of Ainhoue a very lofty set of works extended over successive crests of well-marked heights growing loftier as the line ran east: Mount Atchulegui (1,600 feet), Mount Chapura (1,900 feet), and the culminating summit of the Mondarrain (2,300 feet). A little east of the Mondarrain the Nive—a considerable river while the

---

[1] The change of commanding officers of divisions needs noting. After Aug. 31 Maransin replaced Vandermaesen, after Oct. 7 Boyer replaced Lamartinière, and Leval replaced Maucune.

upper Nivelle is but a trout-stream—bounded the field of possible operations.

The final position consisted of a formidable range of entrenched hill-sides, running along a well-marked upland, from the bridge of Amotz—in front of which there was a double line of *abattis*— to the Col de Finodetta, the depression or pass which separates this group of hills from the loftier Mondarrain group. Along it were six redoubts for infantry and several connecting lines of trenches; two of the redoubts had guns of position. The hill-sides here were only some 400 to 700 feet above sea-level, the range being not a third so high as that of the Mondarrain–Atchulegui heights in the eastern sector. D'Erlon had for the manning of these positions only the two divisions of D'Armagnac and Abbé, 11,000 bayonets: his third division (Daricau's) had been taken from him, to strengthen the entrenched camp of Serres in the distant central sector of the lines. The garrisoning of the redoubts and closed works absorbed eleven of his sixteen battalions, so that he had only the equivalent of one brigade— five battalions—disposable as reserve along the six-mile front of his positions.

But D'Erlon was informed by Soult that he might count on assistance from the long-detached division of Foy, which had at last been brought westward from its isolated position at St.-Jean-Pied-du-Port, and had come into touch with the main army. This move—which only took place two days before the battle of the Nivelle—requires a word of explanation. It will be remembered that the Marshal had always been anxious as to the possibility of an attack on his left flank from the Ronces- valles passes, and that so long as Hill's and Morillo's divisions were known to be lying in a menacing position on this line, with their outposts on the Linduz and Altobiscar, he considered it necessary to have a strong blocking force opposite them. Foy had been told to fortify all the defiles in front of St. Jean, and had been authorized to call in Paris's brigade from the Val d'Aspe, and all the national guards who had been watching the minor eastern passes. He calculated himself that he had 10,000 bayonets at his disposal, if Hill should show any signs of de- bouching from Roncesvalles. But by the first days of November any attack over this defile, which was beginning to be snowed up, was growing daily less probable, and if Hill should have been moved westward to join Wellington's main army, it would be only reasonable that Foy should shift himself on a parallel line to connect himself with Soult.

About the beginning of November Foy received many reports from the national guard pickets on the frontier, to the effect that Hill's force had marched for the Bastan and the upper Nivelle. And there was good foundation for the news, as we shall presently see. But, thinking it necessary to verify the reports, Foy marched out upon November 7th with a brigade on the Roncesvalles road, on a day when fine weather had at last made observation easy. He ran upon Spanish scouts on the lower crests, and pushing them aside, came on a blockhouse garrisoned by a strong British picket at the ridge of Altobiscar. Finding that there was evidence of Hill's troops being still in position, he turned back after a few shots had been fired[1]. As a matter of fact the 2nd Division had just marched westward, save one single brigade, that of Walker, but Foy was justified in drawing the conclusion that some at least of Hill's forces were still at Roncesvalles—and, for all he could tell, the whole might have remained there. Walker's brigade went off after the rest of the 2nd Division on the next morning, having turned over the blockhouses and trenches on the pass to some of Mina's men.

Nevertheless Foy received orders from Soult that same night to march with his own division from St.-Jean-Pied-du-Port, and to come into touch with D'Erlon's wing of the main army. The news of the arrival of Hill's corps in the Bastan had been confirmed, and the troops of Paris and the National Guards would suffice to protect the defiles on the Roncesvalles side from any Spanish force which remained on that front. Accordingly Foy made on the 8th of November a long march from St. Jean to Bidarray on the upper Nive, which brought him within ten miles of D'Erlon's posts on the Mondarrain. Soult intended that he should act as a flank-guard, if the enemy should try to turn D'Erlon's defences by a long detour; but if the attack were made frontally, then Foy was to fall upon the flank and rear of the troops menacing the line from Amotz to the Mondarrain. His position was intended to be something like that which

[1] The picket belonged to the 92nd, and had 3 casualties.

Wellington gave to Pakenham's division at Salamanca,—one which would enable him to demonstrate against, or to attack seriously, the extreme right wing of Wellington's army, if it should have committed itself to an advance against D'Erlon's front.

Wellington had intended to deliver his blow against Soult's positions as soon as the fall of Pampeluna should be reported to him: and as early as October 29th had caused detailed directions to be sent out to each general commanding a division[1]. His arrangements provided for the concentration of every English and Portuguese brigade that was at his disposition against the lines of the Nivelle. Of the Spaniards he was intending to use Morillo's and Longa's small divisions, two of Freire's Galician divisions (those of Barcena and Del Barco), and Giron's much depleted 'Army of Reserve of Andalusia' which now numbered less than 8,000 bayonets. The whole made up a force of about 82,000 infantry, of whom 38,000 were British, 22,000 Portuguese, and 22,000 Spaniards[2]. On a great part of the front that was to be attacked artillery could not move, so that only seven batteries were brought forward—one of them of mountain guns. Wellington had also called up from their cantonments three of his nine brigades of cavalry—on the bare chance that they might be useful for pursuit, if he should achieve (what he hardly expected) a complete breach in the French lines, followed by a *débandade* across the lower lands north of the Nivelle. These brigades—those of Grant, Bock, and Victor Alten—need no more be counted in the statistics of the day than Soult's cavalry, which had come up to the further bank of the Nive. The general balance of force was that Wellington had 82,000 infantry and gunners to use against Soult's 62,000, and that he intended, while showing assaulting columns along the whole of the hostile front, to throw in his surplus of 20,000 men on one section of it, the centre on both sides of the Nivelle, from the Little Rhune to Ainhoue. While making a false attack on the seaward sector, and demonstrating against, rather than attacking, the high-lying positions of D'Erlon's left, he intended to pour such overwhelming forces against the divisions in the French centre, that all their trenches

---

[1] See Wellington to Freire, *Dispatches*, xi. p. 229.
[2] See tables in Appendix at end of the volume.

and redoubts should fail to counter-balance the inequality of numbers. His dispatches written after the victory show that he had some hope of breaking through Soult's line so rapidly, that the troops locked up in the complicated works in front of St. Jean de Luz would be outflanked, and pinned against the sea, before they could disentangle themselves from their fortifications. In this hope he was foiled by the shortness of November days—he did all in the way of penetration that he had intended, but night fell, and the outflanked French right wing escaped along the road by the sea, under cover of the friendly darkness.

The sixteen-mile front on which the allies were to attack was so long, and so sharply divided, that Wellington on this occasion arranged his force into what he might well have called army-corps, if he had been wont to use the term. On the right Hill was to command and to be responsible for, the 2nd and 6th Divisions, Hamilton's Portuguese, and Morillo's Spaniards. In the centre Beresford was put in charge of the Light, 3rd, 4th, and 7th Divisions, of Bradford's independent Portuguese brigade, and of Giron's and Longa's Spaniards. Near the sea there were deployed the 1st and 5th divisions, Aylmer's independent British and A. Campbell's independent Portuguese[1] brigades, and Freire's two Galician divisions. These were under an officer of whom we have not heard since 1808—Lieutenant-General Sir John Hope[2]—not to be confounded with the Major-General John Hope, who had commanded the 7th Division in 1812, and had gone home invalided in the September of that year. Sir John was an officer who had a good military reputation won in Holland, Malta, and Egypt, and had been sent out to replace Graham, when the latter's eyesight finally gave out, and caused him to apply for leave, which was long overdue. For he had stayed on duty to the last moment that his health allowed, and only departed on the day after he had guided the left wing successfully across the fords of the Bidassoa. Hope was so senior that he outranked Beresford, Hill, Stapleton Cotton, and all the other lieutenant-generals, and would have been left in supreme command if some untoward accident had befallen

---

[1] A. Campbell had just succeeded Wilson, wounded at the passage of the Bidassoa, October 18.

[2] He had served under Moore in the Corunna Retreat.

Wellington. This was probably the reason why the latter welcomed his appointment, though he generally deprecated the drafting out to his army of generals with no recent Peninsular experience. Hope's appearance removed any danger of the conduct of the campaign falling into the hands of Beresford, whose unpopularity was well known to Wellington, or of Cotton whom no one but himself considered competent to direct an army[1]. Sir John was a most gallant soldier, and a good leader of troops, but whether he was more able to conduct the 'great game' than Beresford or Cotton might be disputed, and certainly none of them approached Rowland Hill in strategic insight: but Hill was unfortunately junior to all the other three.

The divisions on the Nivelle were in many cases under new commanders, so that familiar names are associated with new numbers. Hope had succeeded Graham in the 1st Division—Colville was acting for Picton—on leave in England—in the 3rd Division; Hay had the 5th, *vice* Leith wounded at St. Sebastian; Clinton (absent since June) had just returned to take over the 6th Division, which Pack had commanded at Sorauren, and Colville at the Bidassoa; the 7th Division was under the Portuguese general Le Cor, since Lord Dalhousie had gone home in October; the independent Portuguese division, which Silveira had commanded at Vittoria and Sorauren, had reverted to its old leader Hamilton a few days before the battle of November 10th. Le Cor's case is a curious one—there seems to be no other case since 1800 of an officer without a British commission commanding a British division. The nearest parallel is that of the Sicilian general La Tour, who had charge of one of Bentinck's brigades in the Army of the East Coast.

Before he could strike, Wellington had to arrange for the bringing up of Hill's outlying divisions from the Roncesvalles front to join the main body of his army. The first orders to march were given to these divisions on November 4th[2]; they were to be relieved by the bulk of Mina's battalions, which had hitherto been watching Paris in the direction of Jaca and the Col de Somport. Only so many of the Navarrese volunteers were

---

[1] For the question of the 'second in command' or destined successor, see vol. vi. pp. 229–30, where all the difficulties are discussed.

[2] *Dispatches*, xi. pp. 255 and 260.

to remain behind as would suffice to maintain the blockade of
Jaca. It was intended that in a few days Carlos de España
should bring up his division from the lines round Pampeluna, to
reinforce Mina's battalions in the passes.

But Hill was unable to move on November 5th owing to
furious weather in the high-lying positions where his brigades
were distributed—the outposts were up to their knees in snow,
the roads blocked. And it was wholly impossible for him to be
in position at Maya on the 7th, as had been intended, for the
general attack to be delivered on the 8th according to Wellington's original plan. It was not till the morning of the 7th that
a sudden fall in the temperature and brilliant sunshine made
the start possible. Hill's own troops—the 2nd Division—and
Morillo's Spaniards, started on the 7th, save Walker's brigade
of the 2nd, which did not get off till the 8th. On their arrival in
the upper Bastan, under the pass of Maya, they found Hamilton's
Portuguese waiting for them, who had moved on from the
Alduides, when the general shift began, while the 6th Division
had already been on the ground for some time.

Thus Hill's striking force was collected. To hold the front
hitherto occupied by Hamilton, he dropped one of Morillo's
battalions, and two of Mina's[1], who were to watch the Ispegni
pass and the *Chemin des Anglais*, in case of any hostile inter-
ruptions from the side of St.-Jean-Pied-du-Port. This turned
out a very useful precaution on the 10th. The rest of the corps—
26,000 men in all—was kept on the south side of the passes till
the moment for attack should come, and the outposts toward
Soult's position were held by the 6th Division only. This did
not prevent the enemy from learning, through the peasantry of
the French frontier, that a considerable shift had been going on.

It will be the easiest fashion of explaining the very complicated
operations of the battle of the Nivelle if we take its three sectors
in succession—the fighting on the west end and the east end of
the line was singularly disconnected from the main break-
through in the centre, on both sides of the Nivelle.

To take the seaward sector first—Hope's orders were to
demonstrate with great show of earnestness against the formid-

[1] Jaen, and 3rd and 4th Volunteers of Navarre—brigaded under Colonel
Andrade.

able entrenched camps in front of St. Jean de Luz, but not to commit himself to a general action, or to throw away men's lives in attacking the continuous and heavily manned line of redoubts in front of him. These directions he carried out perfectly—as the casualty lists of his corps show—he only engaged three brigades out of his eight, and in these the total loss was about 250 men. Next the sea the 5th Division under Hay drove in the French outlying pickets from the Camp des Sans Culottes, a decayed remnant of an old entrenchment of 1794, but halted before the main line, and indulged in noisy skirmishing for the rest of the day—its total casualties were 13 killed and 31 wounded. Further inland the 1st Division demonstrated against the formidable front of the camp of Bordagain. Only the German Legion brigade was seriously engaged, and in this the two Light Battalions took most of the knocks. They pressed back the rather slenderly held French first line, carrying an outlying entrenchment, called after the neighbouring chapel of Bons Secours, while two battalions of Lord Aylmer's newly arrived brigade—the 2/84th and 85th—stormed the neighbouring village of Urrogne, which was barricaded and loopholed, but not very strongly maintained. There was no attempt made to assail the line of heights above Urrogne, which bristled with redoubts and guns of position, but skirmishers pressed up against them—a little too closely at one point, where the German Light Battalions crossed the end of the inundation and came under artillery fire. Bickering went on for the whole morning, and Hope displayed his main force on a long front, several times making dispositions as if for a general attack all along the line. But it was never delivered, nor intended to be delivered, though the object of keeping the French divisions opposite in a state of apprehension was duly carried out. The character of the demonstration will be sufficiently understood when it is recorded that the two Guards brigades lost ten men between them, Aylmer's brigade 22, Wilson's Portuguese had eighteen casualties: the K. G. L. brigade alone showed appreciable losses—174 of all ranks of whom 109 were in the two Light Battalions.

To the right of the 1st Division the eastern sector of Wellington's false attack was entrusted to the two Galician divisions of Freire's army, one of which approached the French front line in the direction of Jolimont, the other showed itself at a discreet distance from the bridges in front of the great entrenched camp of Serres. Both columns made a pretence of deploying for attack, when Hope's skirmishing fire on their left was especially noisy. But neither, of course, committed itself to any such adventure. The eastern column pushed forward skirmishers toward Ascain, who got engaged with Villatte's outlying pickets, but the losses —under 100 in all—were negligible. Oddly enough, Spaniard was here fighting Spaniard—as the section of the French front in this direction was being held by the forlorn remnant of King Joseph's defunct army.

The casualties in Soult's right wing were as trifling as those in the allied divisions which demonstrated so noisily in front of it —90 men in Villatte's 'Reserve' brigades, 390 in the three divisions of Boyer, Laval, and Daricau, which held the line between the camp of Serres and the sea. Soult, in his dispatch on the battle, declared that his defence of this part of his line had been successful and most creditable to the troops. A glance at the casualty figures sufficiently shows that this front was never attacked at all, and that Wellington had the advantage of containing two-fifths of Soult's army with one-third of his own. Nor was he risking any danger from a counter-attack: the enemy was tied up in his elaborate line of trenches and redoubts, and unlikely to quit these. If he did, Wellington's left wing had behind it a very good position along the hills above the Bidassoa, and ample reserves, since Hope had only engaged three brigades out of eight, and those very lightly.

But all this bickering on the hill-sides toward the sea was mere stage-play—the real attack was to be on the centre, under the shadow of the Great Rhune, and by the central gorge of the Nivelle, where it passes between the two lines of heights held by Clausel and D'Erlon.

SECTION XLI: CHAPTER IV

THE BATTLE OF THE NIVELLE: THE MAIN ENGAGEMENT

FOR the real attack on Soult's lines Wellington had brought together nearly 60,000 men—seven of his nine old divisions, and the Spaniards of Giron, Morillo, and Longa. The westward corps—nominally under Beresford, but Wellington himself was present with it—was to assail Clausel's rugged positions on each side of the Lesser Rhune, between the camp of Serres and the upper Nivelle. The eastward corps, under Hill, was destined in part to co-operate with the central attack, by carrying the lower section of D'Erlon's position, near the gorge of the Nivelle, but also in part to 'contain' the troops in the eastern and loftier half of D'Erlon's works, as far as the Mondarrain, by demonstrations in force.

The connexion between the two halves of Wellington's battle-front was entrusted to Longa's Spaniards, who were to get into touch with their compatriots of the army of Galicia opposite Ascain on the left, but also to link on with the flank of Beresford's corps on the right. They were not to commit themselves to any serious engagement—and it was almost incredible that the French should ever think of making an irruption in this steep and broken country-side.

The first thrust of the attack on Clausel's position was to be made by the Light Division, who, on their eyrie of the Great Rhune, were far nearer to the French advanced line than any other part of the army. They were to storm the Lesser Rhune, though the ravines before them were rugged and hard to cross. On their right were Giron's Spaniards of the Andalusian army, whose objective was the French works to the west of the Lesser Rhune and to the east of the Sainte Barbe redoubt. They were to spare two or three battalions to cover the flank of the Light Division, when it should pounce down from its heights. To the right of Giron again was Cole's 4th Division, whose assigned objective was first the Sainte Barbe and the works in front of Sare, and then the fortified village behind them. Going eastward the 7th Division under Le Cor was to storm the Grenade redoubt, and then press forward on to Sare, where it would be in touch with the 4th, converging on the same point from a different direction. The 3rd Division, coming from Zagaramurdi—a point more distant from its objective than those of the divisions further to the west—would strike in somewhat later, and probably after Sare had been already cleared by Cole and Le Cor. It was to aim at the fords of the Nivelle and the bridge of Amotz, with the French works to the left of them, in Clausel's second line.

Here it was, as Wellington hoped, to be assisted in making the breach in the hostile centre by the operations of Hill's column, or at least by those of the leading division—the 6th—of that corps, to whom there was assigned for attack the works on the other side of the Nivelle, overlooking the bridge of Amotz from the east or right bank. Hill had a long way to come, his camps on the previous night having been pitched on the south side of the pass of Maya, in the head of the Bastan valley. After debouching from the Col, his troops were to be arranged in *échelon* fashion, the 6th Division—leading the advance and most to the westward—was to aim at the bridge of Amotz and the works immediately to its right; Hamilton's Portuguese division had as its objective the French works on the heights next to the east of those which the 6th would tackle. The large and formidable 2nd Division, with all its four brigades, would come into line somewhat after Hamilton, against Ainhoue and the redoubts on the hill-side above it. Lastly, Morillo (short of the one battalion which he had left on the Gorospil path to look after his flank and rear) would extend to the right of the 2nd Division, and threaten the French lines along the Atchulegui and Mondarrain heights—not attacking, unless it was clear that the enemy was shaken by the progress of events farther west, and was preparing to abandon his positions.

It has been noticed by French critics that the whole of this attack by Beresford's and Hill's corps was made in a single line of divisions, with no general reserve in the rear save Bradford's Portuguese brigade, which came up behind the Light and 4th Divisions a long way to the rear. But this comment ignores the fact that each division advanced in two lines, furnishing its own reserve of one, two (or in the case of the 2nd), three brigades. This fact accounts for the extreme difference in the casualty lists of the brigades; in each division one or two which were forming the second line or reserve, had hardly any losses at all. In the second division this was the case with three brigades—Walker's, Pringle's, and Ashworth's. These reserves were never engaged, and always remained at the disposition of the corps-commander, in case there had been any serious counter-attack by the French[1]. Supposing that Foy had come in directly on the eastern flank of Hill's corps, there were three absolutely intact brigades of the 2nd Division waiting for him, not to speak of those in the rear line of the 6th and Hamilton's divisions, neither of which had lost fifty men. And if Clausel had been reinforced from the reserve at Serres—which might well have been the case—there were five intact brigades of the 3rd, 4th, and 7th Divisions ready to check any counter-attack. They were not employed at all in the actual battle. In each divisional unit, save the Light Division, all the fighting was done by the first-line brigade. More than half of the battalions of Hill's and Beresford's columns never fired a shot, and only lost a few men by artillery-fire, while advancing far to the rear of the front line.

The signal for the general advance was given by three guns fired from the lofty Atchubia peak at day-break, which fell a little after six o'clock. A very few minutes later the sun appeared—it turned out to be a bright cold day, with no trace of fog, and splendid visibility on all sides—spectators on the Great Rhune could easily descry the sea beyond St. Jean de Luz and the ships upon it, ten miles away. The enemy in his lines could clearly mark column-heads appearing from every direction, those on his right quite close to his outer works,

[1] Compare the figures, 2nd Division: Byng's Brigade, 118 casualties; Pringle's, 10; Ashworth's, 11; Walker's, none.

3rd Division: Keane's Brigade, 355 casualties; Power's Portuguese, 90; Brisbane's, 1.

4th Division: Anson's, 291 casualties; Vasconcellos's, 34; Ross's, 24.

6th Division: Lambert's, 159 casualties; Douglas's, 69; Pack's, 44.

7th Division: Inglis's, 308 casualties; Barnes's, 17; Doyle's Portuguese, 25.

Hamilton's Division: Campbell's, 90; Buchan's, 32.

The Light Division was the only unit in which both brigades were seriously engaged and suffered heavy casualties.

those on his left, where Hill was coming on, still very far away. But it was clear that every section of Soult's long front had hostile forces advancing toward it.

The first clash in the main attack was opposite the Lesser Rhune, where the advanced posts of the Light Division were within a few hundred yards of the outlying French pickets, and were engaged almost before the echoes of the signal-cannon had died away. For Alten had been directed to get his troops forward as far as was possible before daylight—despite of all the difficulties of a steep and stony hill-side. The men had taken a meal in the dark at 2 a.m., and had then been moved, by officers who had been set to study the ground, down to the line of the foremost pickets. That no errors of direction were made, and that each unit arrived at its destined post without confusion or mishap, is a fine testimonial to the guidance of the picked officers who carried out the move. Only one musket was discharged by a stumbling soldier, and this was evidently taken by the French as an accident occurring to a nervous sentry, when it was followed by no further noise of any sort. The hill-side remained quiet for the hour that still remained before the 'zero' moment. When they had reached their destined places the Light Division troops lay down flat, and covered themselves with their blankets. An observer who got the first glimpse of them, before dawn was fully come, describes them as looking more like lines of dirty-white sheep rather than anything else[1].

The front which the Lesser Rhune presents to observers on the Greater Rhune is absolutely precipitous, and the attack which the Light Division was directed to deliver was not launched from the summit of the higher mountain, but from ground some way down upon its north-western slope. And it was not to be made upon the front of the French position but upon its flank, though this was only to be reached by making a detour to the more accessible slope on its south-western side. The Lesser Rhune was indeed a formidable problem. Its front was composed of small precipices in irregular juxtaposition, often twenty feet perpendicular. Its crest was guarded against

---

[1] The comparison is in a letter of Maclean of the 43rd, printed in Levinge's history of that corps, p. 195.

attacks from the south or west by three successive fortifications, a stone wall, well loop-holed, enclosed a space called the 'Place d'Armes'. Above this was a closed work called the Magpie's Nest (*Nid de Pie*), and on the culminating point of the rock another large square work named the Keep (*Donjon*). Running down the slope parallel with the 'Donjon' was a long stone wall, crossing the bottom which separated the Lesser Rhune from the next height within the French position, and ending in a star-fort, the *Étoile de Mouiz*. The group of works was in charge of the brigade of Barbot, belonging to Maransin's division. One battalion (4th Léger) held the star-fort of Mouiz and the neighbouring trenches; two (40th Ligne) were on the Lesser Rhune; one (34th Ligne) lay to the north of its culminating point the 'Donjon', where there is a down-slope, up which assault is barely possible, on a front of only sixty yards[1], where the line of precipice is broken for a space. At the foot of this gap, in the bottom between the two Rhunes, was an outlying advanced 'strong-point', on a clump of rocks in the hollow, which was held by one company from the regiment above it on the main height. The fifth battalion of Baurot's brigade, the 1/50th Ligne, prolonged the line northward towards Sare, but was outside the sphere of the attack of the Light Division; it was opposite Giron's Spaniards.

The position was a formidable one: the 2,500 men placed in it were a not inadequate garrison for what was really a group of forts, rather than a battle front. Large sections of it were absolutely inaccessible; all the rest was covered by solid stone works, many of which gave flanking fire on the less precipitous parts of the slope; there were two guns in the centre of the position, in a redan looking down the ravine between the Lesser Rhune and the Mouiz height. Nevertheless, after minute study of the ground, from his eyrie on top of the Great Rhune, Wellington had come to the conclusion that the works might be 'rushed' by a surprise at early dawn, provided that the troops had been moved in the dark to the foot of the defences, and that the assault was sudden, simultaneous, and resolute. If the attacking force got through at one point, the French line would be broken,

---

[1] This path or pass is the Col d'Argaïneco of Clerc's excellent map of the Rhune positions.

and the garrisons of the forts would have to choose between prompt retreat and the prolonging of a resistance which would end in their being surrounded and captured *en masse*.

The plan of attack which General Alten had worked out with his brigadiers, Kempt and Colborne, was as follows. On the extreme right the 2/95th, the only battalion which was actually on the main block of the Great Rhune, was to pick its way down into the bottom, rush the outlying French 'strong-point' in the ravine, and then assail the gap above it, the 'Col de Argaïneco', as it is now called. It was not a promising point to attack, and if matters looked hopeless the advance was not to be pushed, the main object of the movement being to 'contain' the French troops opposite (the 1/34th) and to prevent them from lending help elsewhere.

A more serious attempt was to be made by Kempt, with the 43rd leading, and the 17th Portuguese in support, to storm the Lesser Rhune from the only front on which it was really vulnerable, its south-western slope. This involved the carrying in succession of all its three defences, the Place D'Armes, the Nid de Pie, and the Donjon, each a formidable line of stone walling. Moreover, to reach the foot of the lowest of them the assailants had to turn the moss or turf-bed which lay between their position at starting and the front which they had to assail. This involved a flank march round the south-eastern end of the Lesser Rhune, in full sight of the enemy, and under fire from his lower w rks, as also from the guns at the head of the ravine.

There remained the Mouiz works: against the front of these the 1/95th and 3/95th were to develop an attack, and drive as far forward as was possible. But the true blow was to be delivered by Colborne with the 52nd, who was to go, as fast as he could, leftward, behind the fighting screen of the two Rifle battalions, and, when he had got beyond the extreme western point of the French defences, to turn uphill and climb the slopes of the Mouiz, so as to take in flank the line of breastworks and 'strong-points' against which the 95th were operating, and—by clearing the enemy out of them—allow the whole line to go forward against the forts on top of the hill. The 1st and 3rd Caçadores were placed in support of the 52nd—a general reserve to the left wing of the Light Division as the 17th Portuguese were to the right wing[1]. Longa's Spaniards, detached far to the left, were intended to cover the flank of the Light Division against any possible—if unlikely—advance of the French from the side of Ascain. They were also to try to get in touch with their compatriots of the Army of Galicia, who were advancing against Ascain from the other direction. As Villatte never moved from his positions, Longa's little division had, all through the day, no more than 'containing' work to do.

The storm of the Lesser Rhune and the Mouiz heights was certainly one of the most astonishing achievements of the Light Division, both for rapidity of execution and for desperate daring. A brilliant passage in William Napier's famous book has made it also one of the best-known exploits of British soldiers; and in this case Napier was describing the most splendid day of his own military life, as it was his good fortune to lead the 43rd into action, and to storm at their head the craggy fastnesses of the 'Place d'Armes' and 'Magpie's Nest'. It is no wonder that the page which tells of that desperate climb stands out with special vividness among many chapters of stirring narrative.

The sequence of events, going from right to left, seems to have been as follows. The 2/95th clambered with some difficulty down into the northern end of the ravine between the two Rhunes, dislodged the company of the French 34th which was ensconced in the 'strong-point' among the boulders, and then pushed up the narrow approach to the Col d'Argaïneco, where they became engaged with the battalion holding it.[2] They could not get forward to the crest, and took shelter under such cover as was available, exchanging shots with the enemy above. Here there was a block in the operations, but neither side had many casualties. The French fire was somewhat kept down by shells from three mountain guns, which had been brought up with much difficulty to the lower slope of the Great Rhune.

[1] Snodgrass, commanding the 3rd Caçadores, begged Colborne to let him lead the assault, urging that if his men were beaten back the 52nd would still be there to renew the attempt. But if the 52nd stormed and were repulsed, he was sure that the Caçadores would never repeat the assault after seeing the British battalion defeated. Colborne would not consent. 'The 52nd *won't* give way', he answered, and led the brigade on. *Life of Lord Seaton*, p. 192.   [2] The 1/34 Ligne.

Meanwhile, the 43rd swung round the south end of the Little
Rhune at a run, exposed to heavy fire on their flank till they
reached the ground from which the assault was to be delivered.
This circling movement was covered by two companies in
skirmishing order, which struck right across the peat-bog at the
south end of the Little Rhune, while the rest of the regiment
turned it. The skirmishing line, driving in some French pickets
before it, arrived at the foot of the entrenchment of the 'Place
d'Armes', the lowest of the three works on the fastness. Here
the men threw themselves down among boulders, keeping up a
fire at the heads of the enemy, visible above the breastwork as
they stood up to shoot. Meanwhile the main body of the 43rd
reached its destined ground, and formed up, five companies
(with William Napier at their head), in line, three others in
column as reserve. The 17th Portuguese followed at a distance.
When the formation was complete, Napier's men charged uphill
at the stone wall of the 'Place d'Armes', passing over, and carrying with them, the two companies already lying down in front
of its line. The garrison of the work shot fast and furiously,
but the mass of stormers swept right up to and over the seven-
foot wall, an astonishing feat. Some got foothold between
projecting stones of the larger sort, others were hoisted on their
comrades' shoulders, others again clutched at the topmost layer
of the wall, and dragged themselves up. Scores of them leapt
down simultaneously among the garrison, who flinched and gave
way before the torrent of red coats. William Napier, it is
recorded, narrowly escaped being bayoneted as he clung to the
wall, unable to hoist himself completely over; two of his subalterns dragged him down, to his great wrath, and then helped
him over at an easier spot a few yards away [1].

The men were so exhausted by the 500 yards of running
followed by the scramble over the wall, that most of them threw
themselves down, panting hard, for a minute or two, disregarding a dropping fire from the 'Magpie's Nest' above. But after
a short rest their officers hustled them together, and the whole
crowd, in no order, dashed at the second line of defence, which
was accessible either by scrambling up rough slopes, or by

---

[1] See the letter of Lieutenant Maclean in Levinge's *Regimental History
of the* 43rd, p. 196.

following several zigzag paths which had been made by the
garrison. The 'Magpie's Nest' is described by a French officer
who inspected it, long years after, as a 'pâté de rochers amorcés
et reliés par des murs'[1], with the isolated rock which gave the
work its name standing out on one side, and affording a post
for a few marksmen on its summit. The face was irregular and
of various heights—partly natural rock, partly breastwork.
Along its front the 43rd scrambled up at various points, some
to find themselves hopelessly blocked, others to discover walls
not wholly inaccessible. The garrison seems to have been somewhat demoralized; no doubt the men of the companies which
had been hunted out of the Place d'Armes were in poor spirits
after their early experiences. We are told that the officers
showed distinguished courage—one was seen standing on the
wall and throwing stones down upon the stormers till he was
shot through the head, others were thrusting knots of unwilling
soldiers towards the danger points, others cutting at the British
bayonets as they came up over the wall-top. But they were not
well seconded by the rank and file—the first officer among the
stormers who got over the defences saw some of the French
already making off by the back-door of the work, before its
front had been forced by any large number of assailants. In
a very few minutes the 'Magpie's Nest' was in the hands of
the 43rd. They were now on the very crest of the Lesser
Rhune, for the last French redoubt, the 'Donjon', was but a
few feet above the 'Nest'. But it was separated from that work
by a cutting fifteen feet deep, round which there was no way
save by a side-path which would not bear two men abreast.
Napier would have liked to try this narrow access, but could
get no body of formed men together; the reserve (contrary to his
orders) had joined in with the main body in the second storm,
and the companies were all mixed up. There were long minutes
of delay, while order was being re-established, and meanwhile
the matter was being settled for the 43rd at another point of
the front of attack of the Light Division.

Standing on the 'Magpie's Nest', and looking down to their
left, the officers could see what was happening in the ravine
below them, and on the slopes of the Mouiz height beyond it.

[1] See Clerc's *Le Maréchal Soult dans des Pyrénées*, p. 160.

When Kempt, the brigadier to whom the 43rd belonged, saw the capture of the Place d'Armes and the commencement of the assault on the 'Magpie's Nest', he had led the 17th Portuguese, his reserve, up the gully between the Lesser Rhune and the Mouiz. Men from the rear companies of the 43rd joined in with them. They were already attacking the long wall at the head of the hollow by which the two groups of entrenchments were joined, and were making good progress, though Kempt had been wounded. For the wall was thinly manned, though there were two guns placed in its middle.

But the decisive blow was being delivered on the Mouiz heights. While the screen of riflemen of the 1/95th and 3/95th was engaged with the defenders of its lower works, the 52nd, with Colborne at its head, had passed, almost unperceived, along the dead ground of the ravine on the south side of the slope, and had actually got beyond the western end of the French defences. They emerged suddenly from their cover, and, climbing rapidly, appeared outflanking the whole line of entrenchments which the Rifles were attacking, and actually in the rear of some of them. This was accomplished with hardly a single casualty—no enemy had been met with save small pickets. On seeing themselves turned, and in grave danger of being cut off, the French on the Mouiz heights left their trenches and ran northward in haste, abandoning éven the star-fort at the north-east point of the position. The troops holding the cross-wall opposite the 17th Portuguese did the same, leaving their two guns behind them, and when these were seen absconding in disorder, the garrison of the 'Donjon' on the Lesser Rhune followed suit. Thus William Napier had no occasion to waste lives in the storming of that fastness. 'They are wavering', was the cry, and the 43rd crossed the deep cut in front of it, and occupied it, with little opposition or loss[1]. The enemy from the Rhune and the Mouiz works escaped for the most part northward, covered by the battalion on the Col d'Argaïneco, which did not join in the general stampede, and retreated steadily, shepherding the fugitives before it. Very few prisoners were

---

[1] See William Napier's letter in his *Life*, i. p. 132. A Lieutenant Steele detected the absconding of the French, and the Colonel led the nearest men, in no order, into the formidable work.

taken—not over 100—for the pursuers were exhausted by their climb. Barbot's brigade took some time to shake itself into order, but was ultimately rallied on the line of redoubts which formed the second French line. But it was a spent force, had suffered heavy losses in men and more in morale, and took little part in the subsequent operations.

Meanwhile Alten reformed the whole Light Division on the Mouiz height, and prepared to attack, when the operations of the troops to his right should permit it, the entrenchments now facing him, in the direction of the Signals and St. Ignace forts of the enemy's rear line. The division had suffered far less than might have been expected—the only serious losses being in the 43rd, where 11 officers and 67 men had been killed or hurt in storming the rocks of the Lesser Rhune. The other corps had not, as yet, lost much over a hundred casualties between them—but there was still some heavy fighting before Colborne's brigade in the afternoon hours.

While the Light Division had been storming the Lesser Rhune and the Mouiz slopes, the troops to the right of them had been breaking in the French centre in a no less effective style. The obstacles, though serious, were nothing to those on the left, and the attacking force, as Wellington had intended, was in over-powering strength. Four columns operated between the north end of the Great Rhune and the bridge of Amotz—Giron's Andalusians, the 4th Division on their right, the 7th Division in the centre, the 3rd next the Nivelle. To oppose them Clausel had in his first line Rouget's brigade of Maransin's division, at the works north of Sare—the other brigade was being dealt with by the Light Division. The redoubts in front of Sare (Ste. Barbe and Grenade) and the crenellated village above them were held by Rey's brigade of Conroux's division, those farther north, toward the Nivelle, by Baurot's brigade of that same division. Taupin's division was entirely in second line, holding the chain of redoubts and entrenchments, immediately above the Nivelle, on which Soult intended the main defence to be made, if the outlying positions should be forced. Beyond the Nivelle eastward D'Erlon's sector commenced—and the fighting in this direction was wholly disconnected from that in Clausel's front. It will be observed that the French centre was held by

three divisions—under 16,000 men—and that Wellington sent
five and a half divisions (Longa's 2,000 men cannot count as
a division) or 33,000 men to break it in. The elaborate fortifications of the French could not compensate for the terrible disproportion of numbers[1]. With such preponderance, the British
general could attack every point of his adversary's line, which
was not really continuous, in spite of the multiplication of
strong points. And in the first clash only two of Clausel's
divisions were engaged, while all of Wellington's were put in.
The disproportion at the commencement was even greater than
the total numbers would seem to show. For Taupin's division
only came into action when all Conroux's and most of Maransin's
battalions had been badly knocked about, and were in some
cases completely 'spent troops' incapable of serious resistance.
For this disproportion between the opposing forces Soult must
be held entirely responsible—he never put in his reserves from
the camp of Serres—still less did he think of counter-attacks.
There would apparently have been a good opportunity to distract his enemy by falling upon the weak force in Wellington's
centre—the two Galician divisions—with the considerable
accumulation of troops—Villatte, Daricau, &c.—which lay in
front of them.

The attack of the Allied divisions between the Rhunes and
the Nivelle was absolutely overwhelming; the two French
brigades (Rey and Baurot) were not only subjected to a fierce
frontal attack by double their own numbers, but completely
turned on their western flank, which was left exposed by the
capture of the Lesser Rhune and the works depending on it.
So violent was the assault that the front line of works did not
hold out for more than a very short space of time. For the Allies
came pouring in between the 'strong points', penetrating with
ease, in sectors where there were trenches held by *minimum*
garrisons, or no trenches at all.

The outlying redoubts of Ste. Barbe and Grenade were carried

[1] The figures, from returns of November 1, run to

French: Conroux, 5,300; Maransin, 5,500; Taupin, 4,800; Total, 15,600.
Allies: Picton, 7,000; Cole, 6,200; Le Cor, 5,700; Alten, 4,700; Giron,
7,000; Longa, 2,000; Total, 32,600.
Adding gunners and sappers Clausel's force must have counted over
16,000 in all—Beresford's over 33,000.

in the first rush, the former by Anson's brigade of the
4th Division, the latter by Inglis's brigade of the 7th. Against
these works artillery was used—almost the only guns that got to
the front on this day, owing to the roughness of the ground.
Before the infantry assault was delivered three batteries opened
with shrapnel against the parapet of Ste. Barbe. This apparently made the enemy keep their heads down, and when the
infantry advanced they suffered little. The French battalion in
Ste. Barbe evacuated it without staying to fight—probably
their departure was hastened by the sight of one of Giron's
Andalusian divisions coming over the hill-side well to their
right rear. For this column, moving along the lower slopes of
the Rhune, had found only one French battalion of the 50th Ligne
in its way, and had brushed away the trifling opposition[1].

The garrison of the Grenade redoubt held out a little longer,
but on being shelled by one of the British batteries from the
flank, while Inglis attacked its front, retired in time to avoid
being surrounded. The two evicted battalions fell back on their
brigade (Rey's) which was now called upon to defend the fortified
village of Sare, and the works on each side of it, where it was
joined by the stray battalion of the 50th from Barbot's brigade.
These seven battalions had now two whole divisions in front of
them, and could see that their comrades on the Lesser Rhune had
been forced back to the second line of defences, so that their
flank was completely exposed. After some bickering in Sare they
gave back in considerable disorder, and endeavoured to establish
themselves in the redoubts behind them. The time was now
about 8 o'clock in the morning.

But meanwhile the front of attack had been extending itself
eastward. The 3rd Division, advancing on the right of the 7th,
with its Caçadores and light companies in front, and Keane's
brigade deployed behind them, had come up in front of the
French works north-east of Sare, where the first and second
lines of defence joined, hard by the Nivelle. After crossing the
ravine of the Harane, a petty tributary of the Nivelle, Colville's
troops found themselves faced by the mile-long *abattis* with

---

[1] Maransin's report calls the loss of Ste. Barbe an 'évacuation', but says
that the Grenade was 'prise'. Clausel says that the garrison of Ste. Barbe
'l'abandonna, et bientôt celle de Grenade en fit autant'.

which Soult had blocked the lower ground by the river, and saw behind it the Madeleine and Louis XIV redoubts of the rear line of defence. Below the Madeleine was the bridge of Amotz, over which all communications between the French left and centre passed. It was guarded by breastworks on both sides. This sector of the line, as we have seen, was in charge of Conroux's division, of which one brigade (Baurot's) was manning the *abattis* and the neighbouring works, the other (Rey's) was already engaged with Cole and Le Cor in and about Sare. The 3rd Division had heavy work in forcing the *abattis*[1],—the French accounts speak of two repulses to the assailants,—but finally burst through, and the 94th running in on the bridge of Amotz stormed its works, and so cut the French line of defence in two. Meanwhile the other regiments of Keane's brigade turned up against the heights overhanging the bridge, and captured the Madeleine redoubt after a sharp struggle. Conroux was killed somewhere in the fight[2].

Thus the eastern end of Clausel's second or main position had already been turned, before the centre or western end of it had been attacked. Nevertheless the general resolved to hold on, being under the impression that he would be reinforced ere long by Villatte or Daricau from the camp of Serres—as indeed he should have been. But Soult did not move a man, and allowed Freire's Galicians to paralyse the strong force in his right-centre by feeble demonstrations. Clausel had now the wrecks of Conroux's division clustered to the left of the Louis XIV redoubt, with Maransin's two brigades in the works to the west of that redoubt and in the breastworks close by, which covered the Col de Mendionde, the depression by which all the local paths from north to south cross the hills. Taupin, hitherto unattacked, held the rest of the line from the Signals Redoubt to the two redoubts of St. Ignace, where the position ended in the precipitous under-features of the slopes of the Little Rhune.

The position was strong; it was entrenched from end to end, though some of the redoubts were unfinished, and it had a

---

[1] Power's report in *Supplementary Dispatches*, viii. p. 369, speaks of the difficulties of his Caçadores at the *abattis*.

[2] By Clausel's account the Amotz works fell by 9.30, well before the big attack, on his second line.

competent garrison—so far as numbers went—now that the
front of attack had been narrowed down from six miles to only
three. But the fatal point was that a good half of this garrison
consisted of 'spent troops'. The battalions which had been
hustled out of the crags of the Rhune, or which had found the
abattis and breastworks between Sare and Amotz no protection
to them, were not in a state to face a second general action. They
saw before them the thick double line of assailants formed up for
the assault of the heights, in numbers more than double their
own, and had no confidence in their power to hold them back.

The confused (and confusing) narratives of Clausel, Maransin,
and Taupin, as to the way in which the French main line was
forced, are so full of details as to futile movements of individual
battalions that 'one cannot see the wood for the trees'. What
really happened was this. Some time was occupied by Beresford
in getting his troops, much disordered by their victorious
advance, into good order. Each division formed up again with
its skirmishing line of light companies and Caçadores in front,
one brigade deployed behind them, and the other two brigades
in support. In each case the original attacking brigade was
retained in the front line, to save time, as is shown by the fact
that in every division the Portuguese and the second British
brigade had practically no losses that day[1].

At about 10 o'clock the assault was delivered, the 3rd Division
tackling the rallied troops of Conroux on the height to the east
of the Louis XIV redoubt, the 4th and 7th Divisions advancing
against that redoubt itself, and Maransin's two brigades at
the side of it, as far as the depression of the Col de Mendionde,
where Maransin's line joined that of Taupin. The Light Division,
arriving later and from a different direction, not in line with the
other three, had to attack the redoubts to the west of the Col,
that of the Signals (or Suhamendia as French dispatches name
it) and the two covering the Col de St. Ignace—which bore the
queer Basque names of Mondadibia and Hermitzebaita. All

---

[1] 3rd Division: Brisbane's brigade about 20 casualties; Power's Portuguese, 90. 4th Division: Ross's brigade, 24 casualties; Vasconcellos's Portuguese, 25. 7th Division: Barnes's brigade, 17 casualties outside the Brunswick light companies which were used as skirmishing line; Douglas's
Portuguese, 27.

these were in charge of Taupin's division, which had not yet been engaged. Giron's Andalusians were to come up between the Light and the 4th Divisions; Bradford's Portuguese independent brigade had arrived within supporting distance of the Light Division. Longa's three battalions had lost touch with this front of attack, having diverged westward, and came out opposite the French entrenchments in front of Ascain.

The first impression on the French line was undoubtedly made by the 3rd Division, who were already in possession of the works by the bridge of Amotz and the lower slopes of the hill-side above them. Working upward they won the crest of the main spur, and drove Conroux's already dispirited troops down into the ravines behind. Some of the battalions then pushed on to turn Maransin's flank on the ridge further west; others, among whom were Power's Caçadores, after driving off the enemy in their front, crossed the bridge of Amotz, to get into touch with Hill's troops, who had now converged on to the same point from the other side of the Nivelle, as will be presently related.

All this took much time, and meanwhile the 4th and 7th Divisions were hotly engaged on both sides of the Louis XIV redoubt, where some of the French resisted very stoutly. For Clausel had thrown into the redoubt itself an intact unit (1/59th Ligne) which had not been engaged in the previous fighting, and had also two battalions of the 130th (of Rouget's brigade) which had not yet been in action. He (unwisely as it turned out) also sent for help to Taupin, who obeyed by dispatching half his divisional battery and two battalions of his divisional reserve (1/31st and 2/31st Léger) along the crest of the heights. They were much missed later on, when the Light Division delivered its attack, which had been delayed by difficulties of ground from synchronizing with that of Cole's and Le Cor's troops. Meanwhile the 31st Léger reached the Col de Mendionde and got into touch with Maransin's flank. The Louis XIV redoubt had no guns of its own, being incomplete, but on its flank were nine (perhaps fifteen) field-guns, the divisional artillery of Clausel's corps[1]. Their enfilading salvoes

[1] Certainly the divisional battery of Maransin, close to the redoubt, and three guns of Taupin's farther west. Perhaps also that of Conroux, whose position and work I have not been able to trace.

of case-shot beat back more than one attack of Cole's and Le Cor's infantry, when they had pressed close up to the entrenchments. It was only after some time that they were answered, and their attention distracted, by Ross's R.H.A. troop, which had been got to the front across the ravines with great difficulty. This was the only British battery which succeeded in surmounting the inequalities of the ground, and co-operating in the main attack.

The French artillery-fire growing less destructive, the higher slopes of the range were at last reached, and there was hard fighting in and about the Louis XIV redoubt, which was finally carried by the 4th Division despite of the efforts of Maransin, who had placed himself there in person, and was for a moment a prisoner, when the work was stormed. He escaped in the confusion, and tried to retake the work with his reserve, the two battalions of the 130th Ligne, but failed and was driven westward along the top of the heights.

The fight about the Louis XIV redoubt was nearing its end when the Light Division got to close grips with Taupin, along the right sector of the French position. The defence here was feeble; the division was very weak in old soldiers, having suffered terribly on the day of the crossing of the Bidassoa. It had since then received a draft of 1,300 conscript recruits from the Bayonne general reserve. But Taupin, with very doubtful policy, had not incorporated them in the old battalions, but had formed out of them two new units, with old cadres, which he was using to hold the parts of his line which he considered unlikely to be attacked[1]. This left the old battalions very low in numbers, some with no more than 400 bayonets. Taupin's fighting line was composed of the 88th in the Suhamendia or Signals Redoubt, of the three battalions of the 9th Léger and 26th Ligne in the breastworks along the main front, of the 70th in the two St. Ignace redoubts, and of the 47th prolonging the line towards Ascain. There was no proper reserve, since Clausel had requisitioned the two old battalions of the 31st Léger to hold the Col de Mendionde. Later, when he saw Maransin's men beginning to give way, he sent for more troops. Taupin obeyed by sending

[1] These battalions were known as the 2/47th and 3/9th Léger. See Vidal de la Blache, i. p. 574.

him the 47th from the extreme right of his position[1], opposite which he could see no enemy nearer than the Spaniards who were facing Ascain. This regiment also, like the 31st Léger, got involved in the fighting about the Col de Mendionde.

Thus when the Light Division attacked—rather late—it had in front of it only five French battalions, plus the new units—for what they were worth[2]. The descent of Alten's troops from the Rhune slopes and the plateau of the Mouiz was necessarily slow; the ground being in many places absolutely precipitous. Colborne's brigade was in front, the 52nd had the right, the Rifle battalions and the Caçadores the left. Kempt's brigade followed in support. On reaching the ravine at the foot of Taupin's position the line spread out very much, on account of the limited number of points at which it was passable. The 52nd had to utilize a small stone bridge, which was the only spot in its front which was not precipitous, and found that three guns in the French position had been trained upon it. They were forced to cross it by sudden dashes of platoons, choosing as far as possible the moments just after the enemy's guns had fired. As each group had passed, it took shelter under a high bank on the opposite slope, to wait till the whole battalion was over.

This took some time, and meanwhile the Rifles and Caçadores were crossing at various points lower down the ravine. When all were more or less formed up in a very rough line, the 52nd sprang up and charged at the breastworks above them[3]. To their surprise the enemy gave way without delivering more than a few hasty volleys. 'We could only account for it', writes a rifleman, 'by supposing that the works were defended by the same troops who fought on the outposts in the morning, and that they did not choose to sustain *two* hard beatings on one day. The attack succeeded on every point[4].' As a matter of fact it was a different French brigade, and the causes of its discomfiture require explanation. Taupin says in his report that the matter started with a *défaillance* on the part of the 70th Ligne, his right battalion. They had seen the 47th, the regiment

[1] This is Taupin's excuse for the disaster on his right, see below.
[2] viz. 9th Léger (2 batts.), 26th Ligne, 70th Ligne, 88th Ligne.
[3] I rather fancy that the 95th got off before the 52nd.
[4] Kincaid, p. 272.

covering their right, marched off eastward to the Col, and realized
that their flank was 'in the air'. When the Rifles and Caçadores
came up against the first St. Ignace redoubt, and overlapped it,
the commanding officer considered that they were 'turned' and
'cut off', and that retreat was the only course. The evacuation
of the St. Ignace redoubts left the breastworks parallel with
them exposed to flank attack, and the troops holding them
flinched and retired. Clausel and Taupin at this moment were
both in the Signals Redoubt, at the east end of the line. 'I told
General Taupin', writes the former, 'that he must retake the
works, since I saw no more than a skirmishing line of the enemy
in possession of them, and I said that I was going to hold on,
even though the Louis XIV redoubt and the Amotz works had
been lost.' Taupin in his counter-report defends himself by
saying that he went off to rally his right wing, but that the
troops had seen the Louis XIV redoubt fall, had observed
retreat all around them, and thought themselves turned;
Longa's Spaniards opposite Ascain were actually in their rear.
They could not be induced to make a counter-attack; indeed the
70th disappeared so completely that their general only discovered
what had become of them twenty-four hours later. They had
gone off north-west, while the rest had given back north-eastward.

Clausel, for his part, told the commander of the 88th in the
Signals Redoubt to hold on, while he went off himself to rally
the remains of Maransin's division upon the 31st Léger, who
were still holding out on the Col de Mendionde. It was high
time, for the Portuguese brigade of the 7th Division had come
up laterally from the Allied second line, to outflank the Col, and
Giron's Spaniards were also swarming up it in front. While the
corps-commander was doing his best to re-form a line at the
crucial point, Taupin came up to him, to report that it was
hopeless to think of retaking the St. Ignace: its garrison had
disappeared from the field. Clausel himself rode up to Taupin's
nearest battalions, now retreating before the 52nd, and told
them to turn, but 'ils s'en allaient sans vouloir rien entendre'.
A general retreat had become inevitable[1].

Meanwhile Clausel's order to the commander of the 88th in the

[1] See Clausel to Soult, November 11, and Taupin to Clausel of November 15, in the Archives de la Guerre. Both are very interesting.

Signals Redoubt to hold on at all costs led to the ruin of that regiment. Giron's Andalusians had penetrated between it and the rest of the division, while on the other side Colborne and the 52nd were close upon it. There was no way of escape left, and the work and its garrison were obviously doomed to surrender. At this moment Colborne received, from an officer of Alten's staff[1], a vaguely worded message which he could only interpret as an order to storm the redoubt. It was a closed work, and unlike many of the French fortifications, complete, with a glacis, a deep ditch, and a 'fraise' along its parapet. In supposed obedience to orders, the 52nd was set to storm it, and ran in, to find itself checked by the impassable ditch some twenty feet deep, which there was no means of crossing. Meanwhile the fire of the garrison beat heavily upon the assailants who, after losing many lives, fell back into the dead ground of a ravine below the brow of the hill. Colborne led them round, under the cover of the slope, to seek for a point where the ditch might be passable. But twice, when the leading company crossed the sky-line, it received a deadly volley, and found the defences as complete as at the first point that had been tried.

Meanwhile half an hour had elapsed, and the routed French divisions were now two miles away. Colborne, taking with him his bugler to sound a parley, and holding his white handkerchief on his sword, rode round to the gorge of the redoubt, and (risking shots) presented himself before the gate. His signalling was recognized, and the French *chef de bataillon*—his name was Gilles—came round to meet him. Colborne pointed out his position, his friends had fled, and several thousand Spaniards were between him and safety. Cursing his luck, the French veteran acknowledged that he must yield, but asked that he might not be given over to the Spaniards. On these terms, written on a scrap of paper, the garrison surrendered, and marched out with the honours of war before the 52nd drawn up in line. A company escorted them down to Sare, and turned

---

[1] Harry Smith says that it was Major Charles Beckwith, the divisional A.Q.M.G., and that the message was simply to push on at once. Its bearer refused to explain its meaning and rode off. Alten always denied that he had meant that the redoubt should be attacked, as it was already surrounded. See Harry Smith's *Autobiography*, i. pp. 147–8.

them over to Victor Alten's Hussars. Of the 32 killed and 208 wounded whom the 52nd lost that day, four-fifths were hit in this unfortunate and unnecessary affair. Napier is wrong in saying that the garrison were so well covered that they lost only one man killed. The regimental report of the 88th Ligne shows that it had one officer killed, seven wounded, and many scores of casualties in 'other ranks'. Only 350 unhurt men laid down their arms[1].

Clausel, when his last efforts to hold the debouches of the Col de Mendionde had failed, drew off his shattered divisions towards the Nivelle. Around the redoubt of Arostegui, half a mile above the river, he made one final attempt to halt his troops, and at least to reconstitute a rear-guard with the least shaken battalions. The attempt was foiled by a vigorous attack of the Light Division, in which Barnard, the much-loved commander of the 1/95th, was severely wounded. '*Les régiments continuèrent de s'en aller.*' Taupin's men crossed the river at the bridge of Arostegui, and at fords below it, Maransin's found the bridge of St. Pée already beset by Power's Portuguese, who had crossed at the bridge of Amotz. They had to turn downstream, and passed at Ibarren. The bulk of Conroux's fugitives, who had gone off at an earlier hour, had collected at Habancen farther to the east. The time was now 2 o'clock in the afternoon.

[1] The regimental number disappears from Soult's muster rolls; but the existence of the corps was continued by the 3rd battalion, serving in Ney's corps in Germany.

THE BATTLE OF THE NIVELLE. THE RIGHT WING. THE END OF THE DAY

THE fight, or rather the two separate fights, one great and one small, on the eastern bank of the Nivelle had so little influence on the main battle on the heights above Sare that we have had no occasion to mention them hitherto. Moreover they commenced at a much later hour, for the four divisions of Hill had a much longer march before them at dawn than the troops of Alten, Cole, or Le Cor on the other side of the river. Though the divisions moved off from their respective camps at 6.30, it was not till 9 o'clock or so, when Clausel had already lost all his front-line positions, that Hill got to close grips with D'Erlon.

The French general, as we have already seen, had only two divisions under his hand, though a third, that of Foy, was close enough to have come in to his support, if its commander had so chosen. But Foy preferred to play his own game—which turned out to be a very futile one. Of the two divisions actually on the spot, one brigade, Maucomble's of Abbé's division, held the works along the lofty Ereby and Mondarrain heights on the extreme left of the whole French position, not far from the Nive. They had four closed redoubts and a long line of trenches in front. The flank-guard was the work on the Mondarrain—over 2,000 feet above sea-level—a ruined castle surrounded by stone breast-works, and held by a battalion. This sector of the line was so formidably steep that Wellington only demonstrated against it, with Morillo's five Spanish battalions. Separated from the Mondarrain mountain-group by a pass called the Col de Finodetta was D'Erlon's main position, along a range of heights much less imposing than those on their left, running down from the Finodetta redoubt, 700 feet above sea-level, close to the pass, to the Harismendia redoubt on the hill immediately above the bridge of Amotz, which is no more than 400 feet high. Along this line were five closed redoubts, several of them furnished with artillery, with a number of trenches below and between them. The three eastern redoubts were held by Abbé's second brigade,

BATTLE OF THE NIVELLE, NOV. 10TH 1813

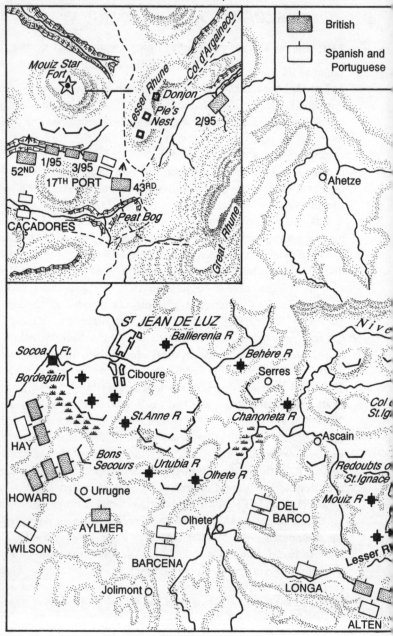

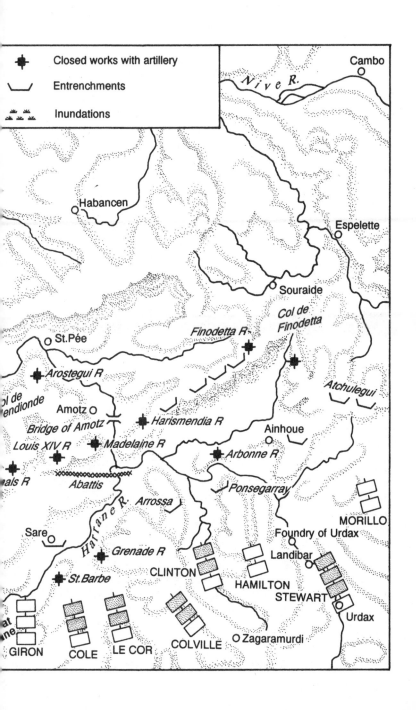

that of Boivin[1]: the two western ones by Gruardet's brigade of
Darmagnac's division. The other brigade of this division, that
of Chassé, was out in front of the range of hills, with its main
body on a hill behind the village of Ainhoue, but having advanced
detachments thrown out to strong points in its front on both
sides of the Nivelle—the crenellated Foundry of Urdax, Ritou,
Arbonne (where there was a battery), and the Maison Ponsegaray.
As this disposition shows, Chassé's brigade was evidently intended to be a detaining force, which would impede the hostile
advance against the main position, and was not to stand for
serious resistance.

Hill's divisions advanced in échelon, the left leading the right
much refused. Clinton with the 6th Division and Hamilton's
Portuguese were on the west bank of the Upper Nivelle, the
2nd Division under William Stewart—long recovered from his
wound at Maya—and Morillo's Spaniards on the east bank.
Clinton's designated objective was the same that had been given
to Colville in the central sector of the battle—the bridge of
Amotz. To reach it, he would have to storm the Harismendia
redoubt, and the other works that protected it on the east side.
Hamilton was to make for the second redoubt, on the next ridge
to his right. The 2nd Division was to march on the Col de Finodetta, and to capture the redoubt of the same name, which commanded it. Morillo was to demonstrate against the Ereby–
Mondarrain positions, but by no means to assail them, unless he
should see the garrison commence to move off, in consequence
of events elsewhere. In case the enemy troops in this sector
should counter-attack against Stewart's flank, Walker's brigade
of the 2nd Division was to be dropped at the bridge of Landi-
bar, in Morillo's rear, where it would be able to support him if
necessary.

D'Erlon, standing in the Harismendia redoubt, had a good
view of the whole plain from Urdax to Sare, and could count
each unit of the approaching army, as it crossed the treeless open
upland in four serpent-like columns of immense length. The
force shown terrified him—it was certainly more than double his
own, and he had a long front to defend, and practically no

[1] Boivin himself had just been invalided, and no successor had been
appointed, but General Abbé himself was with this brigade.

reserves, for nearly all his battalions were locked up in the
redoubts and trenches. Nor did the beginning of the battle
please him—he saw Conroux's troops, away on his right, swept
out of the Ste. Barbe and Grenade redoubts and the works at
Sare, in a short space and with little resistance, long ere the tide
of battle washed up to his own front. The driving in of Clausel's
outlying posts seemed to him to leave his own in a dangerous
salient, whereupon he sent orders to Chassé not to stand, but
to let his detachments in front be driven in, and to retire himself,
when they should have been rallied, on to the main ridge,
abandoning Ainhoue, the battery at Arbonne, and all the rest.
When, therefore, the head of Clinton's column reached the
Maison Ponsegaray, and that of Hamilton's the Foundry of
Urdax, the French retired before them after firing a few shots,
and later Chassé's brigade left Ainhoue and went up on to the
main position, taking post between Gruardet's and Boivin's
brigades. Here therefore three-quarters of D'Erlon's force stood
in line, well entrenched, with five closed redoubts as 'strong
points', and a considerable artillery, to receive the attack of
Clinton, Hamilton, and William Stewart. There was absolutely
no reserve in the rear; all the thirteen French battalions were in
a single line, a formidable one indeed, but no stronger than its
weakest link.

Before reaching the Nivelle, which he had to cross as best as
he could, Clinton drew up his division in fighting order: there
was a thick skirmishing line composed of Brown's Caçadores
(the 9th) and the light companies of Lambert's brigade. Behind
these Lambert's brigade and the 12th Portuguese line were
deployed as the striking force: Pack's brigade and the 8th
Portuguese followed in support. On reaching the south bank of
the Nivelle, which Clinton in his report calls a mere rivulet, the
Caçadores discovered two fords, practically hidden from the
enemy above by a copse on the other side. The French hill
indeed was (unlike most parts of the field) much studded with
brushwood and small trees, which even in November made it
hard for the enemy to detect movements below them. Clinton
crossed with little difficulty or loss, and formed his two lines
again on the north bank. But he would not attack till Hamilton
had come up on his flank, as he had been directed to keep touch

with his neighbours. The Portuguese division had more difficulty in passing the Nivelle than the 6th, partly because it was
on more exposed ground, partly because some of Chassé's
skirmishers were still lying out on the farther bank, and offering
opposition, but most of all because a distant battery of heavy
guns, on the part of the French heights held by Abbé's troops,
was sending an enfilading fire from the right which beat upon
this sector of the river bank. Clinton, after waiting for a short
space, sent a detachment out from his right wing, which cleared
away the skirmishers, and Hamilton's men then crossed and
formed up in two lines to Clinton's right rear—10th Caçadores
and four grenadier companies in skirmishing line, A. Campbell's
brigade deployed, and Buchan's in support. He got some relief
from the French artillery fire when Tulloh's Portuguese battery
came up, and began to answer and distract the attention of the
enemy's guns.

The assault was then delivered by both divisions: Clinton's
leading, as it was at the very foot of the heights, while Hamilton's
had still half a mile of open to cross. The skirmishing line and
Lambert's battalions had a stiff climb up a slope covered with
brushwood, with occasional breastworks covering the bare spots,
but won their way to the top without excessive loss[1], and found
themselves facing the Harismendia redoubt and the trenches
above the bridge of Amotz. To their amazement the French
then flinched and retired, abandoning all the works.

D'Erlon explains this surprising action on the part of
Gruardet's brigade by the fact that by this time the head of the
3rd Division had got possession of the bridge of Amotz, and that
Allied troops—Power's Caçadores and others—were pouring
across it in his rear, and showing on the back slopes of his position
at the same moment that Lambert's brigade was climbing its
front. And this would appear to be perfectly true: the hour was
now 10 o'clock: the 3rd Division had captured the Madeleine
redoubt and won the bridge at least half an hour earlier[2].

Meanwhile Hamilton's front line had climbed the hill half a
mile to the east of Clinton's flank, with much less resistance than

[1] Under 200 men in Lambert's brigade, under 60 among the Caçadores
and the 12th Portuguese Line.

[2] See above, p. 187.

had been expected—the division had only 120 casualties in all, and many of these had been caused by artillery fire during the passage of the Nivelle. When the crest was reached, the Portuguese found themselves between the Harismendia redoubt and that next to its right, but directly in front of the winter hutments of Gruardet's brigade—long rows of wooden shanties with straw roofs. The French were already running off along the crest, pressed by two battalions of the 6th Division: as they passed the huts were set on fire—with intent to delay Hamilton's advance. This did indeed result—the volume of flame and smoke swept into the faces of the advancing line and caused it to halt. But the Caçador battalion on the right, and some companies more, were to windward of the conflagration, and could push on. Coming against the flank of the second redoubt they attacked its gorge and saw the garrison leap down over the parapets and follow the other fugitives. Six guns, unspiked, were found in it, so hasty had the evacuation been.

D'Erlon in fact had ordered Darmagnac's division to make off at once, and the whole was retiring northward towards Habancen, abandoning everything. That no serious resistance was made is shown by the fact that the whole division of 5,000 bayonets only lost 400 men, of whom no more than 30 were prisoners, i. e. very few of them had ever got into close contact with the attacking force. Clinton and Hamilton had lost just about as many[1].

Meanwhile Stewart, with the 2nd Division, had reached the foot of the more lofty eastern heights, and was facing the redoubts to the west side of the Col de Finodetta, held by Abbé's first brigade. He waited, as he had been ordered to wait, till he saw Clinton and Hamilton well on top of the westward hills, and then delivered his attack, Byng's brigade making for the culminating height above the pass, with the strong Finodetta redoubt on its summit, while Ashworth's Portuguese were directed against the redoubt on the next and lower hill-top. Both, as in all these operations on the Nivelle, had a very strong skirmishing line to screen them—the four light companies of the brigade were in front of Byng, the 6th Caçadores in front of Ashworth.

The fighting here was much more serious than that on the

[1] viz. 6th Division, in all three brigades 262, Hamilton's division, 122.

heights to the west. Abbé, who was present in person, made no
such hurry to draw off his troops as had Darmagnac, and the
garrison of the lofty Finodetta redoubt offered a strong defence,
held off the light companies, and was only evicted by the general
assault of Byng's brigade. The 1st Provisional battalion (2/31st
and 2/66th) was the force which actually stormed the redoubt.
Opposite Ashworth the resistance was not nearly so resolute—
the enemy gave way suddenly, perhaps when he saw the
stronger Finodetta redoubt fall—and the Portuguese brigade
reached its objective with the loss of a dozen men only, while
Byng had 130 casualties. Abbé took off his brigade not by the
route that Darmagnac had taken, but due eastward by Espelette
towards the Nive and the bridge of Cambo. This he did in order
to pick up his other brigade, which had been holding the
Mondarrain position, observed but not attacked by Morillo. He
had lost about 200 men in the fight. At dark his division was
concentrated at Cambo. There had been no pursuit, as Morillo
was distracted by another affair—of which more in its due place
—the diversion by Foy.

Wellington's scheme of battle had not been limited to the
forcing of the French lines, and the cutting of the enemy's army
in twain, by the capture of the bridge of Amotz and the works
on each side of it. His intention had been to push through the
gap made, and to fall upon the rear of Soult's right wing, in the
camp of Serres and the works before St. Jean de Luz. If the
time permitted, he had hoped to close in rapidly on the enemy
with the force which had made the break, and so encircle him
that not only his works but great part of their garrisons would
be surrounded and taken. Two facts rendered this idea, as it
turned out, impracticable. The first was the shortness of a
November day: the second was that it took much time to collect
the victorious troops on both sides of the Nivelle, who had been
fighting broadcast over a long and hilly front. In the end Giron,
Longa, and the 4th and Light Divisions were drawn up opposite
the camp of Serres, where they had joined their flank to that of
the Army of Galicia. The 3rd and 7th Divisions crossed the
bridge of St. Pée, save that fraction of the 3rd (Power's Portuguese) which had already passed by the bridge of Amotz. On
the other bank the 6th Division came up, and formed on the

right of the 3rd. An attempt of Clausel to make head again on the hills north of St. Pée, with the rallied wrecks of Taupin and Maransin, naturally failed, though it caused some casualties in the 7th Division. But, by the time that he had been driven away, the early November dusk was falling, the troops were desperately tired—they had been fighting and marching on rough ground for ten continuous hours—and Wellington reluctantly concluded that further operations in an unknown country-side must be put off till the morrow. This allowed Soult time to evacuate all his redoubts seaward, and to abscond under cover of the darkness. He made no delay, bidding his right wing abandon everything, spike the guns of position, and get off without losing a moment on the road to Bayonne. 'Soult had a very narrow escape', wrote Wellington to Graham. 'If I had had an hour or two more of daylight, or two fresh divisions in reserve, I could have caught his right before they could have got back into the entrenched camp at Bayonne[1].' The plan failed mainly, it is clear, from Clausel's desperate if fruitless attempts to continue resistance, first after the bridge of Amotz fell, then after the Louis XIV redoubt was lost, then again in front of the Arostegui works, and lastly above St. Pée. For this the French general deserves all credit—he got his divisions completely knocked to pieces, but he practically saved Soult from envelopment and complete disaster. It was no thanks to the Marshal himself that his army got away: he and his reserves were in the wrong place all day, leaving Clausel to be destroyed.

It only remains to speak of the petty fighting that was going on, in the passes far to the east, during the hours of noon. Foy, as we have had already mentioned, had been called forward from St.-Jean-Pied-du-Port to Bidarray, when Soult got clear intelligence of Hill's departure from Roncesvalles. At Bidarray, ten miles south-east from Cambo, he was in a good position for joining D'Erlon on the one side, or for launching a flank attack against the Allied right rear on the other. He himself had made up his mind that the latter was the right policy. As early as November 5th he wrote in his diary:

'The main attack will not come my way, nor against the extreme right [St. Jean de Luz]. It will be between the Rhune

---

[1] *Wellington Dispatches*, xi. p. 298, November 11.

and the Mondarrain, from Clausel's front to D'Erlon's. . . . If
I am not attacked myself I shall move against the enemy's
flank and rear, to draw off troops against me. If the centre
gives, it will be difficult to hold on to St.-Jean-Pied-du-Port[1].'

The Marshal's original directions had left Foy the choice
between joining D'Erlon or operating as a detached force against
Hill's flank[2]. But on November 9th he sent Foy orders placing
him under D'Erlon's command, which cannot have failed to
reach him. And at 12 p.m. on the night of the 9th D'Erlon
notified to him that he was to close in, sending one of his two
brigades at once to Espelette, in the rear of Abbé's position.
The aide-de-camp bearing this dispatch lost his way in the dark,
but reached Foy at 7 o'clock on the morning of the 10th, just as
the noise of battle was beginning to be heard from the direction
of the Rhunes. He found the division already starting out for
a long sweep through the hills to attack the pass of Maya, where
on the previous day the presence of Clinton's division had been
discovered. Foy's intention was to distract Wellington's offensive by this irruption.

D'Erlon's commands met blank disobedience. 'Judging',
wrote Foy, 'that by reason of the distances to be covered, the
execution of such an order could only be harmful, and seeing
that it meant the breaking up of my division to no profit, and
the risk of seeing part of it never getting into action anywhere,
I resolved to keep it together[3].' And, putting D'Erlon's dispatch
into his pocket, he started off on the route that he had chosen,
the Gorospil track, the *Chemin des Anglais* of which we heard
during the battles of the Pyrenees. He had gone some miles,
when he ran at 11.30 a.m. into a battalion of Mina's Navarrese,
holding the defile of Ausamendi. This was a surprise, as no
troops had been there on the previous day—Hill had been taking

---

[1] Foy's *Diary* in Girod de l'Ain, p. 226.

[2] Soult to the Minister of War, November 9, says that Foy was told 'to
manœuvre on the enemy's right flank, and compromise him, if he attacked
D'Erlon, or else to come and join D'Erlon between Espelette and Ainhoue,
if the enemy's attack took another direction'. 'But', he adds, 'I have
authorized D'Erlon to send his orders to Foy, in accordance with the
situation that may arise.' And again in his dispatch of the 10th, 'je l'avais
mis à la disposition d'Erlon : il devait venir le rejoindre en avant d'Espelette'.

[3] Foy to Soult, night of the 10th.

precautions to guard all possible issues on his flank. Foy had to deploy the head of his column to brush away this resistance. The Navarrese retired, and fell back on to the point where the track debouches on to the plateau above Maya—near the spot where the 50th and 92nd had fought so bitterly against Darmagnac's division during the battles of the Pyrenees. Here the brigadier Andrade had brought up to their aid the rest of the force which Morillo had left behind him, when he marched off in the morning—another of Mina's battalions (the 3rd Volunteers of Navarre), the regiment of Jaen, and a stray company of La Union which had been detailed as camp-guard. With these 2,000 men Andrade held the exit of the pass, and made a most creditable defence for two hours, against 5,000 bayonets. Foy remarks in his dispatch that 'they fought as well as the best troops in Europe could have done[1]'. He had to deploy the whole of his front brigade against them before their line broke; then they were pushed past the Aretesque knoll, and Hill's old entrenchments, and had to drop down into the vale of the Bastan. Near its first village, Maya, Foy captured the impedimenta of some of the regiments of the 6th Division, left behind when they marched off in the previous night. The alarm spread down to Errazu, where, from the main camps of the 2nd and 6th Divisions, 'hospital orderlies, convalescents and stragglers in the uniforms of a dozen corps turned out in something like military order, weak as they were, to show a fight[2]'. But Foy halted at Maya. It was now afternoon; he had discovered that he was delivering his blow into an empty space—there was nothing but a few Spaniards in front of him—the troops that he was aiming at had gone to the front long ago. The noise of a receding battle was audible from the north, and it would seem from his report that he actually got news that the general action on the Nivelle was going badly.

At any rate Foy halted at Maya, and then hastily returned by the way that he had come, having to show as the profits of his diversion 100 Spanish prisoners, 20 British stragglers, and 150 horses and mules laden with plunder. His own casualty list was 28 killed and 192 wounded—among the former the colonel of the

[1] Foy to Soult, printed in Girod de l'Ain, Appendix, No. 77.
[2] Memoirs of Anton of the 42nd, p. 75.

69th Ligne. Disobedience to the orders of a superior may be
morally, if not technically, excused if that disobedience has had
brilliant results[1]. Foy's 'partisan raid', as a critical contemporary called it[2], had none; and he was fortunate in that Soult
did not immediately send him before a court-martial, when he
reported his return to Bidarray[3]. It is curious to note that this
was the fourth time on which this capable officer got separated
from the main army, and failed to take part in a general action.
The first was at Vittoria where he had the chance of joining
Jourdan, the second after Sorauren, when he went off on a line
of retreat of his own, the third at San Marcial, when he spent
the day countermarching between two fields of combat.

It should be noted that if Foy had delivered his attack farther
north, against Hill's flank instead of far in his rear, he would
have found Morillo's five battalions, with Walker's British
brigade in immediate support, waiting for him, so that it is
unlikely that he would have effected much. Hill had been expecting trouble from this direction, and this was the reason why
he left a strong flank-guard, and in addition kept the rear
brigades of three divisions practically at his disposition. The
general scheme would hardly have been disturbed. Whether the
result would have been more satisfactory had Foy obeyed
D'Erlon's orders is a doubtful point. As he himself pleaded in
his exculpatory letter to Soult, it is a long way by a bad road
from Bidarray to Espelette via Cambo, and whether D'Erlon
would have accomplished more if he had possessed another
brigade in the afternoon, or even a whole division, is problemati-

---

[1] Foy alleges in his dispatch to Soult that he fought 5,000 Spaniards on
the Gorospil path. But the very full report of the brigadier, José Andrade,
to Morillo, printed in Morillo's life, ii. pp. 309–11, shows that the precise
force opposite him was three battalions and one company. Andrade says
that he faced about for the third time at Maya, and was ready to stand once
more, when the enemy suddenly made off. If this is so, Foy cannot even
have occupied the village, but only have plundered camps outside it.

[2] Report of Colonel Michaux in the Paris Archives.

[3] That Morillo was not engaged with Foy, as that general and countless
French writers have alleged, is sufficiently proved by his detailed report
of his doings on the 10th to Freire, his army commander, dated at Espelette
on November 11th. He spent the battle-day before the Mondarrain positions, and pursued Abbé in the evening. His dispatch in full is printed in
his life by Rodriguez Villa, vol. ii. pp. 307–9.

cal. But anything would have been better than the erratic excursion to Maya, to plunder the empty camps of one of Clinton's brigades.

By dawn on the 11th Soult's army was in a state of complete dispersion. Daricau had marched off first, though his division had never been engaged at all, and reached Bidart, on the road to Bayonne, leaving Villatte to follow him from the camp of Serres. The latter had evacuated Ascain in the evening, and, abandoning Serres also a few hours later, followed Daricau before sunrise. Reille was busily engaged in hurrying his two divisions out of the works around St. Jean de Luz—he had abandoned all the guns in the Bordagain, Ciboure, and Socoa batteries, and was destroying the bridges of the Nivelle—they were not completely wrecked when the British came up in the morning. Clausel, with the bulk of the division of Maransin and part of Taupin's troops, was at Ahetze north of St. Pée, Conroux's remnants were at Habancen. All these three divisions were still in disorder: some battalions had not yet turned up, and stragglers were wandering broadcast. D'Erlon, with Darmagnac's division practically intact, was at Ustaritz on the Nive: he had got into touch with Abbé, who was—also in good condition—at the bridge-head of Cambo, a few miles up-stream. Foy was on the march from Bidarray to Cambo, and was due there in the course of the morning. It is clear that if Wellington had chosen to start an offensive movement soon after daylight he could have cut the French army in two—four divisions must have got beyond the Nive to save themselves, while the other five must have retreated straight into the lines of Bayonne. But the orders which George Murray drew up under his commander's direction during the night of the 10th–11th do not contain such a plan. They presuppose rather a general advance in order of battle, with the right wing—Hill's corps—refused. Hill was to face towards Ustaritz and Cambo, and contain D'Erlon. The rest, Beresford's corps in the centre, Hope and Freire on the left, were to move forward in parallel columns, and attack the French wherever found. If Reille lingered overlong in St. Jean de Luz, there was some chance of cutting him off from Soult. But as Hope did not succeed in getting his vanguard across the repaired bridges of St. Jean de Luz till 11.30 in the morning, and the centre advanced slowly, waiting for him to come up into line, Soult had the whole day before him, in which to organize some sort of a front from the Ocean to the Nive. Wellington's tactics seem cautious, even allowing for the fatigue of his troops, when we consider the state into which half the divisions opposite him had been battered overnight. But he refused to push forward with his victorious centre, into the gap that lay before him, till his left wing could co-operate. And while Hope was coming up, the opportunity slipped away. There was no attempt to divide and smash up, by an irruption into their midst, the much de-moralized enemy. For that Soult's troops were demoralized there can be no doubt, after they had been hustled out of a position of such strength, so elaborately fortified. The officers had just received the report of the battle of Leipzig [October 19],—suffici-ently discouraging news, even when toned down in the Emperor's Erfurt bulletin. There is a curious side-light on their feelings in one of Wellington's private letters. 'On the 11th', he writes to Hope, 'the colonel who was taken yesterday dined with me. He was at first very melancholy, and would not talk: but he afterwards became more communicative. Having been asked where the Emperor's Head-Quarters now were, he answered *Nulle part: il n'y a point de Quartier General, et point d'Armée*[1].' And he was not so very far out.

French generals were heard conversing among themselves to the effect that the next step would be a retreat beyond the Garonne. A number of officers were court-martialled for cowardice[2]. The most striking testimony to Soult's feelings was given by his disbanding Taupin's division, which had indeed behaved very feebly at the St. Ignace redoubts and before the Light Division. The general himself was clear of all blame; he had risked his life freely while trying to bring up shaken battalions. He was given the command of the division belonging to Conroux, who had fallen in the battle. But the 26th and 70th with the conscript battalions of the 9th Léger and 47th were taken out of the line, and transferred to the sedentary garrison of Bayonne, while the 31st Léger, which had behaved well, and the veteran

---

[1] Wellington to Hope. *Dispatches*, xi. p. 275.
[2] See the interesting details as to demoralization collected by Vidal de la Blache, in his vol. i. pp. 574–5.

battalions of the 9th Léger and 47th were transferred to other divisions. The remaining unit of the division, the 1/88th, had been captured whole in the Signals Redoubt, as we have already seen.

The total loss of the French Army at the Nivelle had been 4,351[1]—of which 2,900 casualties belonged to Clausel's three unlucky divisions, just 600 to D'Erlon, 220 to Foy, and only 493 to the four strong divisions[2] which had held Soult's line from Ascain to the sea. Of the prisoners numbering about 1,200, almost all (30 officers and 1,125 men) came from Clausel's corps. In the redoubts 59 cannon were taken, mostly guns of position from the arsenal of Bayonne, but including some pieces from divisional batteries. There were some useful magazines captured in St. Jean de Luz, which the enemy had not been granted time to destroy. The little port, too, was full of fishing boats and luggers, which were found to have their uses later on.

The Anglo-Portuguese loss was under 2,450, among whom 2,000 were British: but to this has to be added an estimate for Spanish casualties, for which no figures are available—Morillo's and Freire's reports survive, but not the tables of losses which must have accompanied them. The total must have been about 800, allowing 400 for Andrade's gallant defence against Foy on the Gorospil track. The other Spanish corps were not seriously engaged—we may grant that Longa and the Galicians suffered about the same loss as Villatte and Daricau, against whom they skirmished all day with no serious intentions. Morillo, standing opposite the Mondarrain, had practically no fighting, and Giron's Andalusians in the centre were generally acting in second line.

It will be noted in the casualty tables at the end of the volume that just as Clausel's divisions bore three-fourths of the losses of Soult's army, so Beresford's units which attacked them had 1,569 killed and wounded out of the whole 2,400 in the Anglo-Portuguese ranks. On both sides the high proportion of officers to other ranks killed is quite surprising—32 to 372 in Wellington's army, 37 to 414 in Soult's. The ratio of 1 to 11 is wholly exceptional—probably it must be attributed in both cases to

---

[1] See tables at end of volume.

[2] Leval, Boyer, Daricau, Villatte, and some 25,000 men.

gallant leading of troops storming or defending forts. The British officers, as we know from several personal diaries, took wild risks in storming such fastnesses as the Lesser Rhune, and the French officers sacrificed themselves in the most desperate fashion while holding together troops who were inclined to flinch[1].

The British casualty list shows four officers and 69 men missing, only about a score of these were prisoners—the rest were individuals whose bodies had not been discovered when the rolls were drawn up, because they were lost in thickets or lying among inaccessible rocks. It is believed that the stragglers whom Foy captured at Maya were the only 'missing' who were not dead.

N.B. It is vexatious that while we have excellent personal narratives of the Nivelle from the Light Division, and some interesting notes from the 2nd and 3rd, there are none from the 4th and 7th. And while we have the official reports of Clinton, Alten, Hamilton, and W. Stewart, Beresford never sent to Wellington those of Cole, Colville, and Le Cor, but only extracts from them.

SECTION XLII

THE BATTLES OF THE NIVE

CHAPTER I

WELLINGTON'S PROBLEMS
NOVEMBER 11–DECEMBER 9, 1813

FINDING that he was not attacked by Wellington at dawn on November 11th, and driven helter-skelter into the works of Bayonne, as he had feared might be the case, Soult had some hours in which to review his position. Three courses were open to him:

(1) He might form a new line of resistance from Bidart on the sea, by Arbonne and Arcangues, to the Nive at Ustaritz, and stand to fight upon it. The line would be much shorter—only eight miles—if much less steep and well-fortified than that which he had just lost upon the Nivelle. But this course would have been madness, considering the morale of the army on the day after a disaster—though that is not the reason which Soult gives for rejecting it in his first report to the Minister of War at Paris.

(2) Or he might, after strengthening the garrison of Bayonne, take the bulk of his army across the Nive, and form it on a line from the outskirts of Bayonne to Ustaritz or Cambo, so as to place himself on the flank of Wellington, if the latter should press forward to invest Bayonne on the narrow front between the sea and the Nive. He had several bridges, and a fortified *tête-de-pont* at Cambo, which would make it possible for him to threaten, or actually attack, the Allied army, if it advanced into the cul-de-sac whose exit is blocked by Bayonne.

(3) But on reflection the Marshal thought it quite likely that Wellington would not confine himself to such a narrow front of attack, but would try to throw part of his army across the Nive, so as to invest not only the southern but the eastern side of Bayonne, the sector covered by the newly built entrenched camp of Mousserolles. If Wellington should divide his army

in two by the formidable stream of the Nive, now swollen by
winter rains, the French forces, concentrated in and about
Bayonne and using its bridges, might possibly be able to pounce
upon one half or the other, before it could be succoured by its
friends. And a partial defeat either on the eastern or the
western bank of the Nive would send the Allies back to the
Nivelle, if not to the Bidassoa.

In the letter which he sent to the Minister of War at Paris
on the night of November 10th–11th Soult declared himself in
favour of the second plan—that of retiring across the Nive,
placing himself on Wellington's flank, and defying him to invest
Bayonne, when 50,000 men were ready to fall upon him from
the side or the rear. And he began to execute this plan: on the
12th he ordered the divisions of Darmagnac, Daricau, and Abbé
to cross the Nive, and put themselves in touch with Foy, who
was to remain at Cambo. D'Erlon was to take charge of the
whole. The rest of the field army was to follow, the Bayonne
garrison being first strengthened by drafts such as the wrecks
of Taupin's old division, and then left to its own devices[1].
To cover Foy's flank at Cambo the isolated brigade of Paris—the
old garrison of Saragossa—was brought into Bidarray from
St.-Jean-Pied-du-Port—there was no danger to that fortress
from the Roncesvalles passes, now that winter was set in. And
Foy was also strengthened with Pierre Soult's division of light
cavalry, which was placed at Hasparren and Urcarray, linking
him up with Paris[2].

The transference of the whole field army beyond the Nive
would probably have followed, if Wellington had carried out
the plan which Soult originally attributed to him, that of
pressing forward between the sea and the Nive, and investing
the south front of Bayonne. But within three or four days it
became evident that no such advance was taking place—the
Allied divisions moved up to a line parallel to that which Soult's
outposts were holding, many miles south of Bayonne, and there
established themselves. Hope lay in St. Jean de Luz with outposts

[1] Taupin's old division being suppressed, there now remained with Soult
at Bayonne the divisions of Leval and Boyer, Maransin, Taupin (late
Conroux), and Villatte's reserve.

[2] Soult to Minister of War, Bayonne, November 12. Paris Archives.

towards Bidart and Arbonne, Beresford's divisions at Arbonne, Arcangues, and Arrauntz, Hill at Espelette and Suraide, with a strong flank-guard, watching Foy at Cambo. No signs were to be seen of a design to push on farther toward Bayonne. This was puzzling, and it was some days before Soult grasped the idea that Wellington had, for the present, no intention of advancing farther, and was putting his army into winter quarters. The weather had been abominable since the 11th, and the British general, seeing that the opportunity of turning the victory of the Nivelle to greater account had passed by, had made up his mind, for political no less than for military reasons, to call a halt. On November 12th he issued orders for all the Spanish troops, save Morillo's division, to recross the frontier and establish themselves in cantonments in their own country[1]. But the Anglo-Portuguese divisions had winter quarters along the north bank of the Nivelle duly assigned to them. There was only one point on which he intended to take action. The large fortified *tête-de-pont* on the Nive at Cambo, now held by Foy, gave the enemy an opportunity of making dangerous diversions against his flank. He wrote on the 14th to Hope[2] that 'we must deprive them of it, or we shall have no peace during the winter; we must wait for a fair day or two. I am besides desirous of keeping the troops together for a little longer, in order to learn from England how the Allies in Germany propose to spend the winter.'

Before proceeding to explain all that Wellington meant by sending the Spaniards across the Bidassoa, and by declaring his intention of making no general movement till he knew the results of the battle of Leipzig, we must dismiss the small affair of the bridge of Cambo. On the first available day, as had been intended, Hill moved up opposite to it with a couple of brigades, and showed obvious interest in it; indeed a reconnaissance in force against the *tête-de-pont* led to some slight skirmishing on November 12th. Soult, not yet realizing his adversary's resolve to go into winter quarters, thought that this

[1] See dispatches of November 12 to Giron, Wimpfen (chief of the Spanish General Staff), and of November 14 to Freire, *Wellington Dispatches*, xi. pp. 277–87.

[2] *Wellington Dispatches*, xi. p. 286.

movement opposite Cambo was the preparation for a general
attempt to force the line of the Nive, and to extend the Allied
line beyond it, as a preliminary to a close investment of Bayonne.
He had already four divisions—nearly half his army—ready to
resist such an attack, but thought that he must examine localities
for himself before committing the entire force to the defence
of the line Bayonne–Cambo. On November 14th he rode with
D'Erlon along the whole front, though the weather was still
very bad, and carefully studied all the possible points of passage.
As a result of this exploration he decided that it would be
impossible to rely on the Nive as a sound fighting line; there
were many reaches where the ground on the western bank
completely commanded that on the eastern, so that the Allies
could certainly get across if they chose. And there were other
reaches where, despite of the recent rains, frequent fords were
still available. 'If I formed a line of battle in front of the
English general, I conceive that, with troops twice as numerous
as mine, he could carry out his plan[1], turn my flank, or crush
the section of my army on which he thought fit to throw his
main force. And so, from position to position, he might drive
me far back, with new losses and new dangers every day;
I should not be able to retard his plans, and I should have com-
promised the safety both of Bayonne and of St. Jean-Pied-du-
Port, the only fortresses of our frontier[2].' Therefore as a battle
to defend the line of the Nive would involve, if lost, a retreat
eastward, and far away from Bayonne, he resolved to make no
more than a first line of resistance upon that river, and to draw

[1] Soult formed his conception of Wellington's plan on false information.
The officer [a Captain Pomade] bearing from Cassan, governor of Pampeluna, the report of the surrender of that place, had been detained at
Wellington's Head-quarters for ten days, in order that he might not
notify to Soult the preparation (obvious behind the British lines) for the
advance of November 10th. He was released on the 12th, and reported to
Soult that the whole talk at British Head-quarters was of instant advance
and pushing forward to the Garonne. 'Their project is to break through
between Bayonne and St.-Jean-Pied-du-Port, leaving only their worst
troops to besiege these places.' The Marshal thought this a very likely
project, and took it as the basis of his decision. Soult to the Minister of
War, Bayonne, November 14. For Pomade dining at Head-quarters, see
Larpent, p. 296.

[2] Soult to the Minister, Bayonne, November 14.

all the troops along it back toward Bayonne, when it should be passed at any point by the enemy. Massed under the protection of the fortress, they could then sally out, along with the remainder of the army, either to fall on any investing force which Wellington might have left before Bayonne, or to attack his flank and rear if he showed signs of moving off eastward with his main body, bent on a general invasion of Gascony.

So Bayonne was to be the rallying point and *place d'armes* of the French army, which must not on any account allow itself to be cut off from such a splendid '*point d'appui*'. Thus within three days Soult moved completely round from the second to the third of the three courses which, as we have seen, were presented to him. Meanwhile, if he were not going to hold on to the line of the Nive, the bridge-head at Cambo was useless to him. He directed Foy to withdraw the guns in the works, to leave only one battalion in them, to mine the bridge, and to take off the troops, and fire the mine, the moment that a serious attack was made upon him. The evacuation took place even earlier than Soult had intended; while it was in progress during the night of the 15th, a cannon was discharged accidentally, whereupon Hill, seeing that something abnormal was going on, put a brigade under arms and ordered it to press in upon the works at dawn. Foy, seeing signs of an attack, withdrew the garrison, and blew up the works and the bridge. Thus Wellington got what he wanted, without having to waste any lives in storming the *tête-de-pont*. He was at once able to place his divisions in their projected winter quarters. It was not till the 17th that Soult realized that 'le mauvais temps qu'il fait à présent pourrait faire supposer que l'ennemi cherche à mettre ses troupes à couvert[1]'. Even on the 23rd he was not sure that a general attack on Cambo and the Upper Nive might not be imminent[2]. And on the same day an affair of pickets, caused by the Light Division trying to throw forward its advanced lines on the plateau of Bassussary, caused a general alert[3].

[1] Soult to the Minister, Bayonne, November 17.

[2] Same to same, Bayonne, November 23.

[3] This was an unfortunate affair—apparently misconceiving orders of their brigadier Kempt, the Light Division pickets pushed right against the French line of resistance, and got a severe repulse, losing some 80 men, including an officer of the 43rd and 15 men prisoners.

Wellington's resolve to take up winter quarters was not so much the result of the military fact that the weather continued to be very bad, and that the troops were suffering from exposure, as of political considerations of two sorts. The first was that, as always, he was somewhat suspicious of the general policy of the Allies in Germany. Napoleon was known to have retired beyond the Rhine, and it was certain that his army had been terribly reduced by the disaster of Leipzig and the disorderly retreat that followed. But would the Allies follow him up without delay at midwinter, pass the Rhine in pursuit, and prevent him from rallying his forces and defending the line of the great river? If they did, it would be the duty of Wellington to push on into France and to distract the enemy by a vigorous assault upon his rear. But if the Allies were almost as exhausted as the emperor, went into winter quarters, and allowed time for the enemy to rally, matters would not be so simple. To defend the prestige of the 'sacred soil' Napoleon might find troops to help Soult—in particular he might order Suchet to evacuate Catalonia, and bring 40,000 veterans to the western Pyrenees. In such a case a vigorous offensive towards the Adour and the Garonne would have its dangers. It would be satisfactory to know precisely what plans Tsar Alexander and Prince Metternich had in their heads. A lapse into negotiations with Napoleon, such as those which had prevailed in the midsummer months, would much affect the situation. If Wellington had but known it, most dangerous *pourparlers* were going on at Frankfurt at the very moment when he was winning the battle of the Nivelle, and if Napoleon had only been wise enough to accept what terms he could get, he might have remained on his throne, and kept the limits of France as she was in 1797, including Belgium, Savoy, and all the Rhine Provinces from Cleves to Landau.

While these negotiations were proceeding, the Allies did not cross the Rhine. It was only when the Emperor refused to sign anything, and made dilatory proposals for a European Congress, that their armies moved forward again, and in December crossed the boundary stream and flooded into Switzerland, Alsace, and the valleys of the Moselle and Meuse. Wellington, therefore, was even better justified than he could know, when he waited anxiously, day by day, for dispatches from

London giving the last news from Germany. The Allies wasted many weeks after Leipzig; that battle was over on October 19th —it was not till December 22nd that their leading corps passed the Rhine, and in two months Napoleon could do much in the way of reorganization.

These were the considerations of higher politics which discouraged Wellington from immediate action. Next in importance came a question of national psychology. What would be the moral effect on the French people of a bold advance into France? There were those who maintained—and they were right—that the country was so sick of constant disasters, interminable conscriptions, and the crushing taxation of the *droits réunis*, that it would fail to respond to the Emperor's appeal for a final effort. Others went so far as to assert—but they were wrong—that Napoleon was now so much hated that a rising in the name of the Bourbons would provoke general support. And this theory was continuously presented to Wellington by *émigré* emissaries from London, who began to appear in his camp in November, with letters of credence from the half-forgotten Louis XVIII. On the other hand there were pessimists who declared that the national spirit was still so strong in France that an invasion would provoke a general rush to arms, and that the country on each side of the Allied army would soon swarm with partisan raiders, the French equivalent for *guerrilleros*. They pointed to the active resistance that the *chasseurs des montagnes* and the national guards of the Pyrenean valleys had offered against the raiding bands of Mina during the past autumn.

Wellington was only certain of one thing; it was quite possible that the French people were by now tired of the Napoleonic régime and unwilling to do anything to support it. But if an invading army carried fire and sword into Béarn and Gascony, and treated French departments as Spanish provinces had been treated during the last five years, self-preservation might inspire the energy which loyalty to Napoleon had failed to produce. Wherefore the invasion must be accompanied with the most meticulous care for the safety of the civil population, who must be conciliated at all costs. If it were true, as the *émigrés* kept asserting, that there was a latent affection for the Bourbons in many quarters, good treatment of the country-side would bring it out, while devastation and pillage would kill it effectually.

But there was a large section of Wellington's army which would certainly spread ruin all over the face of France, if only it got the chance. The Spanish divisions were not only half-starved at the moment, owing to the neglect of their own government, so that they must plunder or die, but also inspired by bitter resentment at the treatment which their own land had been suffering at the hands of the French for so many years. If ever there were troops to whom revenge was a natural and permissible impulse, it was Longa's Cantabrians, and Morillo's Estremadurans, and Giron's Andalusians, in whose ranks every man had seen his native village burnt and plundered—perhaps his relatives massacred. Despite of the British subsidies—which never seemed to get to the front—the Spanish divisions were absolutely starving. Wellington had only got the Galicians to the Nivelle by advancing huge quantities of food from his own stores—under protest and with bitter reproaches[1]. The sick-lists of every corps were appalling—3,200 in hospital to 7,100 with the colours in Giron's divisions, 4,100 to 10,600 in the Galician units which fought on November 10th. It was natural that troops in such condition should take food by force, wherever they could find it—and not surprising that plunder was often accompanied by outrage. Wellington made up his mind that if he had to choose between invading France with a small army which could be kept within the bounds of discipline, or a large army which would pillage right and left and rouse the country-side, he must sacrifice his numerical superiority rather than run the risk of general insurrection.

'I am in despair about the Spaniards,' wrote Wellington to Bathurst on November 21st. 'They are in so miserable a state that it is hardly fair to expect that they will refrain from plundering a beautiful country, into which they are entering as conquerors—particularly adverting to the misery which their own country has suffered. I cannot, therefore, venture to bring them into France, unless I can feed them and pay them. If I

[1] See Wellington to Freire, November 3. *Wellington Dispatches*, xi. pp. 250–1.

could now bring forward 20,000 good Spaniards, paid and fed,
I should have Bayonne. If I could bring forward 40,000, I do
not know where I should stop. Now I have both the 20,000 and
the 40,000 at my command on this frontier, yet I cannot venture
to bring forward any, for want of means to support and pay
them. Without food or pay they must plunder; and if they
plunder they will ruin us all[1].'

Some days before he wrote thus to the Secretary of State,
Wellington had actually taken the extraordinary step of sending
back all his Spanish troops, save Morillo's small division, to
their own country. Longa was in the worst disgrace; his troops
had sacked Ascain with every circumstance of atrocity on the
night of the 10th–11th, after the French left that little town.
He and his corps were therefore sent back as far as Medina
Pomar in Old Castile. Giron was told to quarter his four brigades
in Errazu, Elizondo, Ariscun, and Irrurita, the four chief villages
of the Bastan, and given the whole of Navarre to draw upon for
requisitions. The Galician divisions were sent back to Irun,
Fuenterabia, Vera, and St. Sebastian, with directions to try to
get food from Guipuscoa and Biscay. Their commander,
Freire, received, along with his orders to march, one of the most
mordant letters that Wellington's pen ever indited.

'Indiscipline is general in your corps. Undoubtedly it was
guilty of grave disorders on the evening of the 10th and the
morning of the 11th—the soldiers of all three nations mis-
behaved. Now I do not enter France in order to plunder: I have
not had so many thousands of officers and men killed and
wounded merely in order that the survivors should be able to
rob the French. On the contrary, it is my duty, and the duty
of us all, to stop pillage, especially if we intend to make our
army live on the resources of the country. The only way to stop
pillage is to keep the troops under arms. Individual punishments
are no good; for one man punished there are a hundred who
escape detection. If you keep the troops under arms, pillage is
prevented. I have tried this device with my own troops frequently, so I must beg you to explain to your officers that I have
no intention of insulting any one. If you want your army to do

[1] Wellington to Bathurst, November 23. *Wellington Dispatches*, xi.
p. 306.

great things, it must submit to discipline, without which nothing can be accomplished[1].'

It seems from Wellington's correspondence with Morillo[2], whose division was the only unit not sent back to Spain, that this tiresome punishment of keeping the men under arms all day was applied to his troops as well as to Freire's. The latter's corps was only subjected to it for two days, as it was back beyond the Bidassoa by November 14th.

It was a serious matter to send away from the front 20,000 troops who had been fighting creditably in the recent campaign. And it must be remembered that there were another 20,000 who had never crossed the frontier, but were close enough to it to have been utilized, if only Wellington could have relied on their being properly fed and kept under strict discipline—viz. Carlos de España's corps which had recently been besieging Pampeluna, Mina's 8,000 Navarrese volunteers, and the two divisions of the Galician army which had never yet crossed the Bidassoa. Moreover, the Duke del Parque's 'Third Army' had now come up from the lower Ebro, and was lying about Miranda, Haro, and Tudela. It required an iron will to refrain from using all these resources, on the ground that 'plunder in France would ruin us all'.

This self-denial made the military problem twice as hard for Wellington, but it did not prevent him from solving it in a satisfactory fashion. And it is certainly true that no army of invasion was ever received with such equanimity by the people of the invaded country as were the British in South France; it was a reward for consistent good behaviour. Those who read the diaries of the officers and men of Wellington's army for the months November 1813 to April 1814 are irresistibly reminded of the position of the British army of occupation on the Rhine during the winter and spring of 1918–19. After some little experience, the invaders found themselves actually popular. Soult's dispatches are full of complaints that he could get far less out of the country-side than his enemy could, and that the

[1] *Wellington Dispatches*, xi. pp. 288–9 and 296.
[2] See correspondence in vol. ii of Morillo's life by Rodriguez Villa, vol. ii. pp. 131–2, and Wellington to Morillo, December 22. *Wellington Dispatches*, x. p. 390.

inhabitants showed undisguised relief whenever the French troops[1] were withdrawn from a town. Much pinched for money though Wellington was, he contrived to find cash to pay for all requisitions, even though his own troops were still months in arrears for their pay. And his camps, in which regular markets were held, and payment made on the nail, proved irresistibly attractive to the peasantry. Similar phenomena were to be seen at St. Jean de Luz, where the owners of boats and small vessels were all to be found after a few days in the service of the army, transhipping goods from the depots at Fuenterabia, Passages, or San Sebastian, and bringing them up the tidal water of the Nivelle to Ascain, which became a centre of distribution for food and other necessaries to the troops cantoned in front of it at Arbonne, Arcangues, Arrauntz, and Cambo.

During the six nights for which Wellington had his headquarters at St. Pée [November 11–17] before settling down in more permanent lodgings at St. Jean de Luz, he had many conversations with Frenchmen of all sorts[2]. But he used to say in after times that the most illuminating summary of the state of mind of Napoleon's subjects was that which he got from the old parish priest, in whose house he had billeted himself[3], 'a very clever and well informed man, who took not only *right* but *large* views of things. He gave me such valuable intelligence as to the state and spirit of the South of France, that I repeated it in a dispatch to the government at home. . . . My meeting with him in that remote and muddy village had perhaps some influence on the destinies of the House of Bourbon.' This dispatch is the long one of November 21st[4], in which Wellington sums up the situation; he says that the French have an earnest desire to get rid of their ruler, from a conviction that so long as he governs them they will never have peace. But who would replace him? 'I have not myself heard any opinions in favour of the House of Bourbon. Twenty years have elapsed since the princes quitted France; they are equally (or more) unknown to France

[1] See Vidal de la Blache, ii. p. 130.
[2] See *Wellington Dispatches*, xi. p. 304.
[3] See Croker's *Diary*, iii. pp. 340–1, for a recent interesting conversation with the Duke in 1826.
[4] *Wellington Dispatches*, xi. pp. 304–7.

than the princes of other European royal houses. But the Allies ought to agree on a sovereign for France instead of Napoleon, if it is intended that Europe should ever enjoy peace. It is not material whether it be one of the House of Bourbon, or of any other royal family.'

Nevertheless, Wellington thought it conceivable that, if the Emperor were to consent to give up all that could be reasonably demanded from him, it might be well to grant him peace. 'Possibly all the powers of Europe require peace even more than France. If Buonaparte became moderate, he would probably be as good a sovereign as we could desire in France. If he did not, we should have a new war in a few years. But, if my speculations are well founded, he would have all France against him: his diminished resources would have decreased his means of corruption, and he would find himself engaged single-handed against an insurgent France as well as all Europe.'

But it was absolutely necessary to know what the Allies intended to do. Were they for dethroning Napoleon, or for imposing an advantageous peace upon him? Further sounding of French public opinion was necessary, before Wellington could make up his own mind as to whether the right move would be to favour the intrigues of the Royalists. But, he concludes—

'I can only tell you that if I were a prince of the House of Bourbon, nothing should prevent me from now coming forward, not in a good house in London, but in the field in France. If Great Britain would stand by him, I think that he would succeed. And his success would be much more certain in a month or two, when Napoleon is carrying out the oppressive measures which he must adopt in order to try to retrieve his fortunes.'

Unable, without a knowledge of the intentions of the Allies, to say whether Napoleon was to be deposed or not, Wellington had to play the difficult game of endeavouring to conciliate the French provinces, without offering them freedom from the imperial régime, and without recommending to them any alternative to it. A hideous moral responsibility would have fallen on him if he had encouraged a number of enthusiasts to raise the flag of the Lilies, and had then learnt that the Emperor was to keep his crown. He would have had to leave them to the vengeance of Napoleon, or to miserable exile. This was the shame that fell on the Tory government of Great Britain just a hundred years before, when the unfortunate Catalans, who had been encouraged to rise in the name of the Archduke Charles, were handed back to Philip V as King of Spain, at the Peace of Utrecht. That desertion had not been forgotten even in 1813, and was a rankling memory. Wherefore Wellington had to write non-committal proclamations to the people of the occupied districts[1], and to tell the Royalist emissaries to do what they could, on their own responsibility. It did not look, on the face of it, a very high-minded policy; but till the Allies had made up their minds as to the future of the French crown, none other was possible.

Meanwhile every British officer who came in contact with educated Frenchmen was beginning to see the problem[2]. The French were surprisingly friendly, had no good word to say for the Emperor, desired peace without delay—but could not make any definite suggestion as to the constitutional future of their own country. The enthusiastic Royalists were few and far between—no one talked of a republic—the memories of 1794 were too bitter. But as to what should be done, if Napoleon were to be evicted, few could offer any practical suggestion. A typical expression of French public opinion in November 1813 is the curious address presented to Wellington by the mayor and notables of St. Jean de Luz[3].

'Une guerre affreuse fait gémir en secret toute la France, qui n'a d'autre désir, d'autre besoin, que de paix. Nous savons, Monseigneur, que tous vos soins ne tendent qu'à atteindre ce but. Puissiez vous réussir dans un si noble projet! Vous aurez mérité des droits à la reconnaissance de l'univers, et nous ne cesserons d'adresser des vœux au ciel pour bénir un héros aussi grand que sage.'

Wellington then had to adapt his military policy to the political future, and concerning that future he had as yet no clear indications from London. He was in no hurry to begin a great campaign of invasion, and was not altogether sorry that

---

[1] See, e.g., *Wellington Dispatches*, xi. p. 307.

[2] See, for example, Hennel's amusing talk with the owner of the Chateau of Arcangues, reprinted in Levinge's *History of the 43rd*, p. 203.

[3] *Wellington Dispatches*, xi. p. 304.

the vile weather of mid-November imposed on him delays, since
decisive political directions from Downing Street might reach
him at any moment. Meanwhile, if 'grand strategy' could wait,
there was no reason why he should not manœuvre for a better
situation round Bayonne, where at present his army faced a
cul-de-sac. It would be profitable to extend his front beyond
the Nive, if his strength permitted[1]. And he was under the
impression that, if he brought his right wing up to the Adour,
and shut in Bayonne on two sides, Soult would have to cut
himself loose from it, and retire into the interior. This would
not be the result of fear on the Marshal's part lest he should be
shut up and surrounded in Bayonne, as Blake had been in
Valencia. It would result from the impossibility of keeping
a large army supplied, when all roads except that northward
into the desolate Landes had been intercepted. And in particular
the closing of the Adour to navigation would be decisive, for
a great part of the food and munitions of the French army was
water-borne[2]. There remained, of course, the question whether
the army was strong enough, when the Spaniards had gone
home, to hold its own on both banks of the Nive, supposing that
Soult should mass his whole force against the half of it on one
side of the river, and strike hard, before the troops on the other
side could get back to reinforce the front that was attacked.
This danger Wellington had taken into consideration, and he was
prepared to accept the risk. Perhaps he underrated a little the
enterprise of Soult and the fighting power of the French army,
and overrated the demoralization of both the Marshal and his
troops in consequence of the battle of the Nivelle. At any rate,
though he achieved his purpose, he had some very anxious
moments before him, ere he succeeded in manœuvring Soult
out of the Bayonne defences, and forcing him to take his
departure eastward.

---

[1] See Wellington to Bathurst. *Wellington Dispatches*, xi. p. 353.
[2] Wellington to Bathurst. Ibid., pp. 365-6.

SECTION XLII: CHAPTER II

THE CROSSING OF THE NIVE. DECEMBER 9

As early as November 15th, as we have already seen, Soult had explained to the Minister of War that he could not hope to defend the whole line of the Nive from Cambo to Bayonne[1]. His intention was to leave only a detaining force along the river, which would inevitably be driven off, but to concentrate all his disposable divisions close in to Bayonne, and to fall upon the enemy, when he had divided his army, on the one bank or the other, as the occasion might offer. And this is precisely what he did: he waited till Wellington had forced the line of the Nive, without much difficulty, on December 9th and when half of the Allied army was on the east bank of the river, fell furiously with eight divisions upon the four British divisions which were observing Bayonne on the west bank. Contrary to his expectation, he was completely checked in the fighting on December 10th–12th, which is generally called the first battle of the Nive. The line held, till Wellington had brought back to its relief two of the divisions from the other bank. Then, after a short delay, Soult crossed the Bayonne bridges in the dark with six divisions on December 13th, and fell upon the two under Hill which were still left on the eastern bank. In the second engagement, often called the second battle of the Nive, but more properly that of St. Pierre, Hill held out heroically against an enemy double his strength till the afternoon. When he was almost exhausted, three British divisions, returning across the river, appeared to succour him. Before they had got into action, Soult gave up the game and retired into Bayonne. He had carried out his well-planned scheme, and it had failed entirely. Historians have an interesting field of debate when they try to decide whether Wellington was a little rash, or whether he was perfectly justified in trusting to the solidity of his army. And

[1] See above, p. 213. The phrases are quite clear, 'tenir l'armée prête à se réunir à Bayonne, en cas de nouvelle attaque de l'énnemi, et si le passage de la Nive était forcé, afin de marcher à l'ennemi sur l'une ou l'autre rive, suivant qu'il serait engagé'.

similarly discussion may arise on the question whether Soult
had a feasible plan, and only failed in it by reason of his mal-
adroit handling of troops in action, which we have already noted
at Albuera and Sorauren, or, on the other hand, whether this
elaborate plan was faulty from the first, because it did not allow
for the detaining power of good troops fighting to gain time,
with the knowledge that they will be succoured, if they can hold
out long enough. On the whole Wellington could plead that
he knew Soult's limitations well, that he was aware that much
of the French army was not in good fighting order, and that
the risk was not over great.

Since Wellington had chosen to send the Spaniards back
beyond the Bidassoa, only retaining Morillo's 4,500 men—who
were moreover employed only on a side issue—he had deliberately sacrificed his numerical superiority. Setting aside the
cavalry, of which three brigades had been brought up to or near
the front, but took no effective part in the fighting, he operated
on December 9th–13th with about 36,000 British, 23,000 Portuguese, and 4,500 Spanish infantry[1]—some 63,500 bayonets in
all. Soult, as his 'morning state' of December 1st shows, had
in his eight fighting divisions[2] and in Villatte's reserve, which
also went into the battle, 51,000 bayonets. Paris's detached
brigade, which paired off against Morillo, had 3,500 more. This
gives about 54,500 infantry available against Wellington's
63,500, so that it was clear that if Soult could force an action
with his whole army against that position of Wellington's which
was on one side of the Nive, he would possess the superiority
which ought to secure success. We do not reckon into his force
either his cavalry—which like Wellington's was hardly used—
or the 8,800 men of the sedentary garrison of Bayonne.

Wellington's orders for the crossing of the Nive were as
follows. Hill, with the infantry divisions which had so long been
with him, the 2nd under William Stewart, the Portuguese
formerly under Hamilton but now commanded by Le Cor, and
Morillo's Spaniards, was to cross the river at Cambo, using all

---

[1] See Tables in Appendix of the army on November 10th, with deduction
allowed for Nivelle losses.

[2] No longer nine, since the abolition of Taupin's old division, see above,
p. 206.

the fords which had been found. When over the Nive he was
to re-establish the broken bridge, and to leave Morillo up-stream
opposite Itzassou to act as a flank-guard. With the rest of his
troops he was to push up the Bayonne road to his left, coming
in upon the flank and rear of any French units which might be
found watching the line of the river. As the country here was
comparatively open, he was given two brigades of light cavalry,
Vivian's and V. Alten's, who were to push out in all directions,
particularly towards Hasparren, to find the position of the
enemy. Hill, seeing the importance of Morillo's function of
flank-guard, gave him Vivian's hussars for reconnoitring purposes.

This was only part of the scheme. Beresford with two
divisions, the 3rd and 6th, was to come down to the Nive at
Ustaritz, throw an advanced guard across the river by the ford,
and there build a pontoon bridge, on which his whole force was
to cross. After driving off any French whom he might discover,
he would strike into the Bayonne *chaussée*, where he would find
himself in touch with Hill, who would be already advancing
up it. To replace the 3rd and 6th Divisions in their late position
between Ustaritz and Arrauntz, the 7th and 4th Divisions would
come up from the cantonments in the rear, and close the gap,
getting into touch with the Light Division on their left. Finally,
to distract the enemy, and to cause him to feel uncertain of the
main point of attack, Sir John Hope was to bring up the whole
of his corps, and push forward on a broad front in the wooded
country between Biarritz and Bassussary, driving in all French
outposts till he should run against the main line of defence—
the fortified camps outside Bayonne[1]. Hope, it will be remembered, had under him the 1st and 5th Divisions, with the
unattached brigades of Lord Aylmer and of Bradford and
A. Campbell. He was to keep in touch on his right with the Light
Division, which would also join in his reconnaissance, false
attack, or demonstration, whatever it may be called. He was
not to attempt the French line, when he should have discovered
it. The country being wooded on the right Wellington was not
sure of its exact position[2].

---

[1] For these orders in detail see *Wellington Supplementary Dispatches*, viii.
pp. 410–11.

[2] There had been in the British, as in the French, Army some changes of

Thus five divisions were to cross the Nive, two to remain in a 'refused' position in the centre, and the equivalent of four[1] to demonstrate on the side of the Ocean. All communications between the troops beyond the Nive and the main body depended on fords about Ustaritz and Cambo, which might possibly become impassable if heavy rain came on, and upon the bridges which Hill and Beresford were to build—their construction might take longer than was expected. If both fords and bridges failed, there would be a dangerous breach of continuity between the right and the left wings. On the other hand Wellington had by now a well-founded confidence in the staying-power of his troops. Either half of the army, if attacked by superior numbers, might be relied upon to make a stout resistance, sufficient to allow of its reinforcement from the unattacked front, unless, indeed, some wholly incalculable combination of cataclysmic weather and misunderstood orders should supervene. In Hill there could be every confidence placed; he had never got himself into a mess. Hope was a more doubtful factor in the problem. He was brave and able—but he knew little of the Peninsula, and had never before been in charge of a battle.

To observe the passages of the Nive from Cambo to Villefranque, D'Erlon had placed in succession the divisions of Foy, Daricau, and Darmagnac, while that of Abbé was in reserve at Mouguerre only a couple of miles outside Bayonne. Foy had the section on each side of Cambo, Darmagnac that on each side of Ustaritz, Daricau that on each side of Villefranque. Paris's detached brigade was at Louhossoa, far to the left, and out of touch with the rest; he had no good road by which he could retreat on Bayonne, if the enemy passed the river at Cambo. The force with which Wellington proposed to effect the crossing was, therefore, not much greater than that opposed to him. But,

command of late, which make the continuity of divisional history hard to follow. Le Cor, who had commanded the 7th Division at the Nivelle, had been transferred to the Portuguese division, where he replaced Hamilton, now invalided. The 7th was under Walker, its senior brigadier. A. Campbell had replaced Wilson, wounded on November 18th, in command of the 1st Portuguese independent brigade, so long under Pack in earlier years.

[1] Counting the three independent brigades together as equivalent to a weak division.

as Napoleon once observed[1], nothing is more dangerous than to attempt to defend a river by picketing its whole course. There is always some point where an enemy will get across in force, and will find but a thin line of defenders to oppose him. The only way to deal with the problem is to mass the defending force, and to fall on the head of the enemy's column when it has half completed its passage—or on the head of one of his columns if he has crossed at several places. A typical example of this treatment of the problem had been seen at the Katzbach only a few months before, when Blücher allowed some of Macdonald's troops to pass the river, and then fell on them with all his strength, while half of the French army was still on the other bank. The only thing to be urged in defence of the way in which Soult and D'Erlon had placed their men, is to remember that the Marshal hoped that Wellington would divide his army, and that he had no intention of risking much in the defence of the Nive line. But he was, as a matter of fact, in grave danger of losing some of his troops, or of seeing them driven away in excentric directions, because of the faulty placing of the line.

At daybreak on December 9th the kindling of a great beacon-fire on the hill before Cambo gave the signal for all Hill's troops to plunge at the fords. The 2nd Division made for two fords below and one above the broken bridge. Le Cor's Portuguese division followed. Pringle's brigade, leading at the northern ford, waded across with some difficulty—the stream was swollen—and had a slight engagement with the pickets of Foy's line, which gave way with unexpected facility. This was the result of their general's perceiving that Clinton and the 6th Division were already over the fords at Ustaritz, and would, if he were to hang on too long, cut the high road to Bayonne by which he had to retreat. But the cessation of all opposition enabled Pringle to reach the high road, and there he lay in the way of the retirement of the southern part of Foy's line, which had been opposing Barnes's brigade, on the other side of the village, at the upper ford. Berlier, the brigadier here in command, only saved his five battalions by striking straight to his rear, abandoning all attempts to utilize the *chaussee*, and plunging into a network of

[1] The letter was written to Eugène Beauharnais, then commanding in Italy. *Correspondence of Napoleon*, no. 19721.

country roads in the direction of Hasparren. Not being pursued,
he ultimately succeeded in rejoining his division in the afternoon.

At Ustaritz, four miles down-stream from Cambo, the 6th
Division had got across even more easily than the 2nd—the river
here had two channels divided by an island. In the dark the
western channel had been secretly bridged with pontoons, and
the smaller eastern branch of the Nive was forded very rapidly,
the pickets of Darmagnac being driven in without difficulty.
When a brigade was across, pontoons were laid over the second
channel, and the rest of the division passed by them—followed
in due course by the 3rd Division. The latter remained close
to the river, in charge of the now completed bridge. The old
wooden bridge which Soult had destroyed was also repaired.
But Clinton advanced, pushing before him Gruardet's brigade of
Darmagnac's division, the troops which had been in charge of
this sector of the Nive. The French retired towards Villefranque,
where Daricau was in position, and to which Darmagnac's
other brigade had already retreated.

The farther bank of the Nive was found to be country in which
advance was not easy. The minor roads leading into the
Bayonne *chaussée* were ruined, ankle-deep in mud, and there was
no help to be got by turning off into the fields on each side of
them, which were absolutely rain-sodden. It was long after noon
before Clinton, pushing along a very bad road close to the Nive,
arrived in front of the position of Villefranque, and got into
touch on his right with two of Hill's British brigades and with
Le Cor's Portuguese, who had advanced along the *chaussée* in
the wake of Foy's retreating troops. Hill had dropped his third
British brigade (Byng's) at Urcarray to cover his flank and rear.
This he did because he had seen Berlier's retreat away from the
chaussée, and feared that either he, or Paris, or both of them, might
turn on to Cambo when the main column had passed by. But
Foy was really at Lorminthoa, where he was awaiting with
anxiety the arrival of Berlier's brigade, which was trying to rejoin
him by its long detour.

On hearing of the advance of Hill along the *chaussée*, and of
the isolated position of Foy, D'Erlon had sent out his reserve,
Abbé's division, from Mouguerre, to pick up Foy, bring him in
if necessary, or to make a stand at Lorminthoa if the enemy

seemed weak and unenterprising. There was a gap of three miles between these two divisions and those of Daricau and Darmagnac at Villefranque, and when Hill advanced in force along the high road, D'Erlon brought back Abbé and Foy—who had been joined at 2 o'clock by Berlier's wandering brigade—to a position parallel with the other two divisions and in touch with them, placing them across the high road, on the ridge which four days later was to be Hill's fighting ground at the battle of St. Pierre.

The British forces did not come up in front of D'Erlon's new line till the afternoon was far spent, and Hill, seeing the strength of the enemy, made no general attack. Indeed D'Erlon had in hand a force rather larger than his enemy's, since the 3rd Division was waiting by the pontoon-bridge of Ustaritz, and Byng and Morillo had been left far behind. But noting that the village of Villefranque was much in advance of the French position on the heights behind it, Hill resolved to take possession of it. Douglas's Portuguese brigade of the 6th Division was sent out to seize it, and evicted two of Darmagnac's battalions, which were holding it. D'Erlon thereupon sent down reinforcements, and the Portuguese in their turn were expelled. But Hill ordered them to repeat their attack, supporting them this time with Pringle's brigade of the 2nd Division. This renewed assault was successful, and dusk being now at hand, D'Erlon made no further attempt to recover the village.

So ended the day—the losses on both sides had been trifling. Hill had under 80 casualties in the 2nd Division, under 120 in Douglas's Portuguese of the 6th Division, under 90 in its two British brigades—in all less than 300. The troops of Foy and Darmagnac cannot have had any heavier casualty-list; unfortunately we have no details, these figures having been recorded in one table along with those of the 10th, 11th, and 12th of December.

Criticisms of various kinds are possible on the manœuvres on both sides on this miserable rainy day. D'Erlon, or Soult rather since he approved of D'Erlon's arrangements, tried to defend ten miles of river bank in linear fashion, and his front was naturally pierced at the two points where the enemy struck in force. Supposing, instead, that he had left a mere line of vedettes

south of Villefranque, had massed all his four divisions in front of
that place, and had fallen on Clinton when only half his division
was across the river, and before any of the 3rd Division had
begun to file over the pontoons or wade through the fords, it is
hard to see how he could have failed to administer an unpleasant
check to Wellington's move. For Hill, whose divisions were
slowly and with difficulty threading their way across the dangerous fords of Cambo, was too far off to be of much use to
Clinton in the first hours after he had begun his passage. It is
probable that Wellington under-estimated the proportion of
Soult's army that was on the east bank of the Nive that morning,
and thought that his simultaneous demonstration against the
south side of Bayonne would be containing more than five of the
nine French divisions. As a matter of fact he was sending four
divisions (Morillo does not count, since he was dispatched in
an excentric direction) to attack four, and the French had good
defensive positions. Soult, on the other side, seems also to have
been misled as to the strength of Hill's corps, and estimated it
at two divisions over its real force, having erroneous information
that all Beresford's divisions—i. e. the 7th and 4th as well as the
3rd and 6th—had crossed at Ustaritz. This, in his conception,
was all for the best, since he was about to fall with his whole
strength not upon Hill, but upon Hope and the left wing of
Wellington's army, whose numbers he was underrating, just
as his adversary was underrating those of D'Erlon.

And so, as we shall see, it came to pass that at dawn on the
following morning Hill found nothing in front of him on the
hill-sides of Horlopo and Mouguerre, and was able to push his
exploring parties right up to the outworks built in front of the
old south-eastern front of the fortress of Bayonne.

While the tedious manœuvres of Hill's and D'Erlon's divisions
were dragging on, over the rain-sodden roads on the east side of
the Nive, Morillo and his 4,500 Spaniards, with Vivian's light
cavalry in front, was pushing out from Itzassou eastward—
the hussars searching the country as far as Mendionde and
Hasparren. They fell in, upon the St.-Jean-Pied-du-Port
chaussée, with the troops of Paris, who had been sent a regiment
of Pierre Soult's chasseurs, and was expecting further cavalry
assistance from the north. The exploring parties on either side

succeeded in locating the enemy's infantry, whereupon Paris retreated eastward to Helette without offering resistance; he had given up any idea of keeping touch with Foy, when he heard that the passage of the Nive had been forced at Cambo. Morillo followed cautiously, having no orders to fight at all costs, but only to find and contain the French detachment, which was known to be lying in this direction. For the next three days these two small detached forces paired off against each other, without affecting in any way the general situation.

SECTION XLII: CHAPTER III

THE BATTLES OF THE NIVE. DECEMBER 9-10

I. COMBATS OF ANGLET (9TH) AND ARCANGUES (10TH)

A LITTLE later than the moment at which Hill's and Beresford's divisions stepped into the swirling fords of the upper Nive, the forces which Wellington had entrusted to Sir John Hope started on widely spread demonstrations against the main French positions in front of Bayonne.

The ground on which the advance was made was difficult, blind, and tiresome to a degree. The town of Bayonne is built along the south bank of the Adour at about three miles from its mouth. It lies in a hole; its seventeenth-century fortifications are so much above the level of the place that only the roof of the Cathedral is visible to those approaching from the south, and the Cathedral itself is high above the narrow arcaded streets below. The Nive flows to join the Adour right through the town, cutting it into two halves joined by several bridges. The bastions and curtains on the west bank are called the *Front d'Espagne*, those on the east bank the *Front de Mousserolles*. On the opposite side of the broad sandy tidal Adour is a small suburb, St. Esprit, completely dominated by a very strong and lofty citadel, whose guns command the whole of the low-lying town opposite.

If Bayonne had been in November 1813 the same old-fashioned fortress that it was at the time of the commencement of the Peninsular War, it could only have been called a weak and faulty stronghold, for its old *enceinte*, dating back to Vauban's time, was narrow and destitute of outer works. No Spanish army had ever crossed the Bidassoa to test its strength since the days of Charles V, so that it had never been brought up to date. And as the ground outside the *enceinte* continues to rise slightly, the place had no command over it, and is indeed somewhat overlooked itself by a low ridge about a mile away. But after the battle of Vittoria the prospect of an invasion of France had become imminent, and from August onward Soult had been throwing out in front of the old line of defence a series of vast entrenched camps on both sides of the Nive, which trebled the perimeter of the place, and put the old walls out of any danger of insult. On the side of the lower Adour he had dammed up the mouth of a brook called the Aritzague, and flooded the ground near the river, thus narrowing the possible front of attack. On each side of the point where the high road from Spain enters the walls, there were two big redoubts, connected by trenches. Outside them, and beyond the Aritzague brook already mentioned, was a long irregular entrenchment called the *Camp de Beyris*, with ditch and palisades. Further to the east and on the other bank of the brook lay another entrenchment, the *Camp de Marrac*, so called because it lay around the Imperial Palace of that name, where the shocking scenes of the 'complot de Bayonne' had taken place in May 1808, where Napoleon had exposed King Ferdinand to the villainous taunts of his mother, and had threatened him with death if he did not abdicate[1]. Was it some memory of these infamies which made him write on Nov. 15, 'if the English burst in, burn Marrac to the ground; no one shall sleep in my bed[2].'

Finally east of the Camp of Marrac, and on the other side of the Nive, was the *Camp de Mousserolles*, extending over the whole space between the Nive and the Adour, and taking in the suburb of St. Pierre d'Irrube. It had two heavy redoubts in its front, and was connected with the Marrac works by a newly constructed bridge, outside the old *enceinte*. The exact condition and extent of all the three camps was not well known to Wellington, more especially that of the Beyris sector, which was much screened by woods and plantations lying out in front of it. Hence Hope's advance was a reconnaissance no less than a demonstration.

The ground between Soult's lines and the British outposts in front of Bidart and Arcangues might be described as a rolling plateau, if that word did not imply a certain breadth and level. But the plateau, if so it could be called, has no continuous breadth—its outlines are as irregular as those of a piece from a child's jig-saw puzzle. It has length in some places and breadth

[1] See vol. i. pp. 53–4.
[2] Napoleon to Caulaincourt, Nov. 15. *Correspondence* No. 20895.

in others, but the higher ground is cut into, on both east and west, by a great number of small ravines, some running east to join the Aritzague and the Urdains brooks, others west to join the Mouriscot and Ourhabia brooks. There is, of course, a watershed on the plateau separating these small watercourses, but it is very narrow at two points. One, less than a mile broad, is across the great *chaussée* between the lake of Mouriscot, near the headwater of the brook of the same name, and the slightly smaller Étang de Brindos, from which the Aritzague brook flows. The second, farther south, is where the ravines whose water feeds the Urdains brook on the east are only separated by half a mile from those which combine to form the Ourhabia brook, which falls into the ocean just south of the village of Bidart. These two narrowings of the plateau had an immense importance in the fighting which was coming, because troops moving either south or north were irresistibly led to stick to the watershed, and not to drop down into the ravines on either side, which were in December water-sodden to a desperate degree, as well as in many cases decidedly steep to climb. For though their depth is never great, their slope is often very sharp.

At the northern narrowing of the plateau, just where the *chaussée* passes above the Lake of Mouriscot[1], was a considerable block of buildings, the abode of the Mayor of the then insignificant village of Biarritz, something between a chateau and a very large farm, and surrounded by walled and hedged gardens and orchards. Its proper name was Barrouillet, but contemporary writers generally call it 'the Mayor's House'. This place, blocking the issue from the narrow part of the plateau, attracted the troops of both sides in the battles of December 10th–12th, all the more so because there were dense woods to the east of it which looked rather impassable. So Barrouillet became the gage for which many successive combats were fought. Almost as notable was the position at the southern narrowing of the plateau, a mile and a half to the right rear of Barrouillet, where the watershed was crowned by the church and Chateau of Arcangues, one of the few points which stand out on the horizon,

---

[1] In summer the Lake of Mouriscot is a lovely little woodland tarn, surrounded on all sides by foliage, and harbouring the canoes of Biarritz holiday-makers. But in December it is said to have looked grim.

and from which a better view toward the flat country along
the Nive can be got than from any other spot. This point
of vantage was also destined to be much fought over on
December 10th.

The east flank of the plateau is separated from the Nive by
swampy meadows, through which a secondary road, in no very
good order, ran from Bayonne and the Palace of Marrac to
Ustaritz. Its main drawback was the lower course of the
Urdains brook, only easily crossable in a wet winter by the
bridge of the same name. A third of a mile south of this defile
was the chateau of Urdains[1], on a knoll projecting from the
central plateau. A mile and a half south of the chateau lies the
highest point of the whole neighbourhood, the hill of Sainte Barbe
400 feet above sea-level, looking down on the fords at Ustaritz
and Villefranque. Like Arcangues this point of view commands
the whole valley of the lower Nive. As a position for defence
the chateau of Urdains and the slopes beside and behind it are
admirable, all the more so because they are covered with woods,
in which any amount of troops can be placed without betraying
their strength. From the north side of the bridge of Urdains
there is a diverging cross-road to Bassussary and Arcangues,
climbing on to the plateau near the former village. But it goes
up through a narrow front: there are only 1,000 yards between
the Nive and the Urdains brook on the east, and the course of
the Aritzague brook on the west. The last-named watercourse
shows several big pools, and swampy low ground hard to cross,
in this section of its very devious course. The ridge of Bassussary therefore is very well protected on its front, but more or
less accessible either from the Barrouillet side, or from the bridge
of Urdains.

At seven o'clock on the morning of December 9th Sir John
Hope started out from Bidart and Guéthary with the force
which Wellington had allotted to him for his reconnaissance—
the 1st and 5th Divisions and the 'unattached' Portuguese
Brigades of A. Campbell and Bradford. He had also been lent
the 12th Light Dragoons for purposes of general exploration—
the ground was not suitable for cavalry acting in mass. In
collaboration with Hope's force, Alten was told to bring the

---

[1] Usually called in diaries of 1813 'Garat's House'.

Light Division forward from Arcangues, and sweep the plateau of Bassussary in front of him, as far as the depression of the Aritzague brook. In the rear of the reconnoitring forces Lord Aylmer's brigade was brought up to Bidart, and the 4th Division from Ascain to the north edge of the woods of St. Pée, in rear of Arbonne. The 7th Division was placed on the hill of Ste. Barbe, with an advanced guard holding the chateau of Urdains.

Hope advanced on a broad front—the 5th Division west of the *chaussée* between the Lake of Mouriscot and the sea, along the rolling ground where the suburbs of Biarritz now lie. The two Guards brigades of the 1st Division took the high road; the light battalions of the King's German Legion brigade diverged eastward from it, when the defile beyond Barrouillet had been passed, and spread out towards Pucho and Bellevue—where the modern Tour de Lannes lies, on rather high ground. The French outposts were found in front of the village of Anglet, and were driven in on their supports, who held that place for some time. They were a brigade from each of the divisions of Boyer and Leval, who were in charge of this sector of Soult's front. There was considerable fighting in and about Anglet, which had to be evacuated when the German Legion Light battalions turned its eastern side. The enemy then retired into the fortified Camp of Beyris, whose whole bastioned front was discovered and reconnoitred. But, as he had been ordered, Hope made no attempt to break into it. On his left he sent out patrols of the Light Dragoons, and intelligence officers, to inspect the country north of Biarritz as far as the mouth of the Adour, which is covered by the long pine wood, the *Grand Pignadar*, which reaches to the sea. The engineer Burgoyne, whose diaries are so often useful, surveyed on this morning the ground along the Adour where Wellington's wonderful bridge of boats was about to be constructed after the New Year[1].

Meanwhile the Light Division, to cover more or less Hope's right flank, advanced from Arcangues, occupied the ridge of Bassussary, and pushed out an advanced line of pickets into the low ground in front of it, on a long front from the bridge of Urdains to the mill by the Étang de Brindos.

[1] For his report as to the state and character of the Camp of Beyris, see his *Life and Letters*, i. pp. 288-9.

At nightfall Hope sent back his troops to their cantonments, the 1st Division and Lord Aylmer's brigade even as far as St. Jean de Luz—a weary tramp—the 5th Division to Bidart and Guéthary. Only A. Campbell's and Bradford's Portuguese brigades remained at Barrouillet, in support of the line of pickets, which had been left on the ground conquered in the morning. The Light Division returned to Arcangues, in similar fashion, leaving its pickets on Bassussary ridge.

The losses on December 9th had been trifling, under 40 in the two Guards brigades, 70 in the King's German Legion, about 150 in the 5th Division[1], 37 in the Light Division—about 350 casualties in all. A curious point in the statistics is that not one officer was killed, and that the dead were to the wounded only in the proportion of 1 to 7, much lower than the average in Peninsular fighting. It is probable that the losses of the French were much about the same, but Soult compiled the casualties of all the days December 9th–13th in one list, so that the separate figures for the 9th are unavailable.

Hope's dispersion of his troops after this very provocative action was decidedly dangerous. Supposing that the enemy considered the lost ground in his front worth recovering, he would find it held by a picket line thrown very far forward, with only two Portuguese brigades in immediate support—the 5th Division three miles to the rear, the 1st Division ten miles. The first line might be rushed before the 5th Division could get up, and it would take three or four hours before the 1st Division and Lord Aylmer's brigade could come upon the scene. Evidently Hope never dreamed that a counter-attack might be impending.

But Soult was planning not mere recovery of the ground lost on the previous day, but a general assault with his whole nine mobile divisions upon Hope's wing. The conditions on which he hoped to fight were exactly those which he had sketched out in his letter to the Paris War Office on November 15th[2]. The enemy had divided his army into halves, and he himself, owing to the Bayonne bridges, could fall on whichever half he might please to select with every disposable man, many hours before the

---

[1] The only corps with appreciable casualty-lists were the 2/59th and 1/38th of the 5th Division, which lost respectively 47 and 50 killed and wounded. [2] See above, p. 210.

part of the Allied force on the other bank of the Nive could come
into action. It looks on the map as if his plan had every chance
of success: the Allied divisions in Hope's sector were separated
by wide gaps, and arranged as if they were in perfect security.
Of those on the farther bank only the 3rd Division would be
available till the day was far spent.

Fortunately for Wellington the Marshal had failed to reckon
with three all-important factors, which made his scheme very
different in practice from what it was in theory. The first was
time, the second the details of the terrain over which he intended
to operate, the third the difficulty of getting satisfactory work
out of over-tired troops.

Soult started the battle with four-ninths of his army desperately fatigued by a night march in pouring rain: his whole plan
rested on bringing over D'Erlon's four divisions to fall upon
Hope's right. Of these four divisions one—Foy's—had been
marching and fighting all day on the 9th: the others had been
under arms and partially engaged, on the hill-sides about Villefranque. At midnight all four were ordered to build up their
watch-fires, so as to keep Hill unaware of their departure, and
then to file down to the boat-bridge over the Nive, just outside
the fortifications of Bayonne. On the time required to file
20,000 men, two abreast, over a narrow bridge in pouring rain
and blank darkness we need not insist. When across the bridge
they had to be got into position—still in the dark—on the ground
outside the 'Camp of Marrac' from which it was intended that
they should deploy and make their advance. It is not surprising
that, when day broke, one division was still not across the bridge,
and that every man was soaked through and tired out by six
or seven hours of marching, or standing about, in December rain.
Meanwhile the ground on which they had stood on the previous
day was evacuated, the outer fortifications of the camp of
Mousserolles being handed over to four battalions of the sedentary
garrison and some conscript units. To keep Hill away from the
abandoned front Soult had also directed some gunboats from
the small Bayonne flotilla to moor themselves on the Adour
opposite the Mousserolles works, so as to be able to shell any
hostile force which might approach them.

The Marshal's first plan, as he describes it himself, was as follows. The main attack on Hope's front was to be delivered from the Camp of Marrac; Clausel's two divisions [Taupin and Maransin], which were already in position, were to lead it, while D'Erlon's four [Foy, Darmagnac, Abbé, Daricau] were to follow in support. They would have to debouch by the Bayonne–Ustaritz road, and when clear of the narrow defile between the Nive and the Aritzague brook, to deploy and attack the ridge of Bassussary and the bridge of Urdains. Meanwhile on the other side of Bayonne, Reille's two divisions [Boyer and Leval] would advance down the great *chaussée*, sweep away the hostile pickets, and break, by Barrouillet, into the middle of Hope's left wing. Villatte's reserve, equivalent to a ninth division, was to support Reille or Clausel as might be found necessary. The whole of the works behind were to be handed over to the sedentary garrison, every mobile unit being employed for the two strokes.

This is not at all how the battle was actually fought: the attack of Clausel and D'Erlon—the original main effort—petered out into a very feeble assault on the Arcangues position. The attack of Reille on the *chaussée*, strengthened ultimately by some of D'Erlon's troops, had considerable success at first, put Hope in a desperate position for some hours, and ended in a very bloody drawn game, when the British reserves came up in the afternoon from St. Jean de Luz. For the morning hours saw only the Light Division, the 5th Division, and the two Portuguese unattached brigades holding back Soult's attack with triple forces. That they succeeded in doing so was due not only to their own steadfastness but to the peculiarities of the ground about Arcangues and Barrouillet, of which we have already spoken.

The rain had ceased at six o'clock, and the dawn of the 10th showed a pale grey sky, with a north-east wind, and good visibility in all directions. The French advance had been intended to start with the earliest light on both fronts of attack, though in the rear of each of them there was an enormous accumulation of troops out of their due position, who had placed themselves wrongly in the dark, and were trying to find their designated places. But the heads of the columns, the units which were already on the ground on the preceding night, had been brought up to the line of their advanced pickets, and were ready to start the game early. The supports, however, were so misplaced that Soult had to wait till 9 o'clock before he thought himself able to give the order to advance.

On the eastern attack Taupin's division had worked up to the foot of the Bassussary plateau, its *voltigeur* companies sheltering behind hedges and cottages, the formed battalions in cover behind some knolls, over which the road passes. Maransin's division was behind, just emerging from the narrow strip between the Nive and the Aritzague brook, where there is only a frontage of 300 yards. Three of D'Erlon's divisions were massed uncomfortably in front of the Camp of Marrac, with the narrow passage still in front of them. The fourth was crossing the bridge of boats in the rear.

The pickets of the Light Division, as we have said before, were in a long line along the Bassussary ridge, from near the bridge of Urdains as far as the Croix d'Olhar, a knoll half-way toward Barrouillet, overlooking the Étang de Brindos and the swampy upper valley of the Aritzague. It shows how little any attack was expected, that Alten had just sent orders to withdraw the pickets across the dip that separates the Bassussary ridge from the Arcangues ridge, a mile in its rear, and had ordered the second brigade of the Light Division to move back to Arbonne, and take up its quarters there.

These orders were in process of execution, and part of the second brigade had already gone off to the rear, when Alten was warned that there was a probability of trouble in front of him. The officers commanding the pickets on the east end of Bassussary ridge had noticed suspicious movements of French parties among the hedges below them, and had caught glimpses of bayonets behind the knolls farther back. Kempt, the commander of the first brigade, chanced at the moment to be superintending the proposed withdrawal of the picket line—his attention was drawn to the shifting of small groups of enemy skirmishers in his front, and, though at first incredulous, he was convinced when it was pointed out to him that a group of French staff officers had been seen on one of the nearer knolls, and that a glimpse of a mountain-gun on mule-back had been caught at a gap in a hedge not far below. Kempt had hardly been convinced that trouble was coming, and had not long sent off a warning to Alten, when the whole French skirmishing line broke out from its hiding places, and charged uphill. There was a very thick chain of *tirailleurs* in front, with formed battalions in support, at least a brigade deployed[1]. The Light Division pickets had of course to make off at top speed, in order to fall back on their fighting position at Arcangues. The irruption of the French along the hill-side was so rapid, and in such irresistible force, that the pickets lost a certain amount of men, sentries and small parties in advanced posts, who were cut off from their line of retreat. An officer (of the Rifle Brigade) and about two score men from the 43rd and 1/95th were made prisoners, as were more than a dozen of the Light Division Portuguese. One company of the 43rd was in great danger of being captured whole in the village of Bassussary, and only escaped by a desperate charge right through a line of French skirmishers, who had got in between them and Arcangues, for which they were making[2].

Always extending to their right along the plateau, the assailants had soon two brigades deployed, facing the whole front of the Light Division, with heavy supports behind. They then worked forward, across the slight dip which separates Bassussary from Arcangues, and developed an attack upon that village. Here the advance became very slow, as the Light Division had got into order, and its skirmishing line made an obstinate defence of the hedges and isolated houses, which lay on the slope below the main position. It took an hour to drive the riflemen and Caçadores back, and to penetrate into the small and scattered village. The main problem then became evident to Clausel. On the culminating point of the ridge was the

---

[1] There is a full and interesting account of all this in the *Memoirs* of Captain Cooke of the 43rd, who commanded the outlying picket of his regiment, vol. ii. pp. 60–4. The author himself was the first man who noticed anything; William Napier thought there was something impending. Beckwith was the man who advised Kempt to take precautions at once.

[2] The company was led by Lieutenant Duncan *Campbell*, not Duncan *Cameron*, as erroneously in Levinge's *History of the 43rd*, p. 207, where the incident is described otherwise in good style. Napier calls him 'an ensign barely 18 years of age', but he had been a lieutenant more than two years, and as he had been four years in the regiment, and had served in Spain since 1811, I should doubt if he was not somewhat over 18. He fell at New Orleans.

carefully selected fighting ground of the defence—not more than 1,000 yards of front, with the large chateau of Arcangues and its outbuildings on the right next the road, a thickly hedged avenue leading out from it, and the solid Gothic church at the left end of the position, on higher ground than the chateau, in a walled churchyard. A little beyond the church is a steep ravine which sends a branch of the Ourhabia brook towards the ocean. Beyond the chateau, at the other end of the ridge, is another steep ravine down which a small affluent of the Urdains brook flows towards the Nive. Both the chateau and the church had already received some slight extemporized fortification of *abattis* blocking their accesses, while Arcangues had been the advanced point of Wellington's central line during the previous month, and the chateau's outlying dependencies had been loopholed. The position was so short that it could be easily held by 4,000 men, and to turn it the enemy would have had to descend into deep water-logged ravines, from which exit would be very difficult. Clausel never tried to utilize them, but only essayed the frontal push. The chateau and its outbuildings were held by the 1/95th, the hedge between it and the church by the 3/95th and the Caçadores. The 43rd were in the church and churchyard, the 52nd on the west end of the position, close to the flanking ravine beyond the church. The 17th Portuguese and 2/95th were available as reserve, and there were two mountain-guns, placed to command the road, hard by the chateau.

Clausel made one attempt to break into the centre of the position, between church and chateau; it was made by only a single battalion, and met by such a storm of musketry that the assailants gave back at once. Evidently he misliked the situation, for instead of attacking frankly and with all his force, he held back, and ordered up two batteries from the rear to shell the British out of their defences. This wasted time, and time was all-important, since it was clear that the Light Division, at present isolated, might be reinforced, if noon was allowed to go by. The guns were brought up with difficulty and set to shell the church and churchyard of Arcangues, the crucial point of the defensive position. They were placed about 400 yards from the church, on somewhat lower ground. The moment that they opened, they were met with three tiers of volley-firing by the

43rd. Though the distance at which accurate shooting was possible with the weapon of those days was much less than this, yet high trajectory firing would carry the missile much farther[1]. The volume of balls poured on to the site of the batteries was so great that the gunners began to fall fast, and finally flinched from their pieces. It must be remembered that three lines of fire were bearing on them—one from men behind the churchyard wall, a second from men firing through the church windows on the ground floor, and a third from men in the women's galleries, which at Arcangues, as in all Basque churches, are high above the nave, with clerestory-windows of their own. This unaimed but directed volley-firing proved devastating, and the few shots which the guns got in, before they were silenced, failed to breach the walls of the solid church—they only did harm if they went through a window. The French artillery commander finally had his guns man-handled backward below the sky-line. Such shots as they fired without seeing their mark were practically harmless. After an interval another attempt to bring forward the batteries was made, but they were met with such a hail of balls that they were driven back again out of sight. Hereafter they continued to fire intermittently and innocuously, for direction by 'observation officers' in front was unknown in 1813. Early in the afternoon Alten saw the 4th Division arrive at Arbonne, and draw up to support him: he now felt quite safe.

Clausel never delivered a general infantry attack on the Arcangues position, though he had now got up a third division —that of Daricau from D'Erlon's column—on to the Bassussary plateau, to support Taupin and Maransin. The second division of this belated reserve—that of Abbé—had been turned aside to block the bridge of Urdains, because the discovery had been made that there were British troops in the chateau and the woods on the other side—part of Walker's 7th Division as we have already seen. Clausel had a suspicion that the enemy might be there in force, about to sally out upon his rear, and so detailed Abbé as a flank-guard. Darmagnac, with D'Erlon's third division, was halted still in the narrow passage between the Nive and the Aritzague, ready to support Abbé, or to follow

[1] For judicious remarks on this, see Dumas's *Neuf mois à la suite du Maréchal Soult*, p. 275.

Daricau on to the Bassussary plateau. Foy, with D'Erlon's rear division, had been turned off by Soult on another tack, as we shall see, and had passed out of Clausel's sphere of action.

By this time the afternoon was far spent, and Clausel got sight of new British forces approaching. These were the 3rd and the 6th Divisions coming from Ustaritz, across the bridge of boats, and the 7th Division—relieved by them at Urdains— marching towards Arbonne. Wellington had started them off to Hope's assistance as soon as the noise of battle on the farther side of the Nive had reached him. When he saw the ground opposite Hill unoccupied, he knew exactly what had happened. But it took long hours before Colville and Clinton reached the site of the danger, and meanwhile Clausel had his opportunity —and failed to use it. Yet at 9 in the morning he seemed to have everything in his favour. At 3 o'clock he gave up the game.

As this general was usually full of enterprise—which he had shown at Salamanca and Sorauren—his extremely feeble conduct on December 10th seems surprising. He had been ordered to deliver the main attack, and had originally six divisions under him—opposite these was only Alten and the brigade of the 7th Division that lay behind the bridge of Urdains. It seems necessary to attribute his entire failure first to the narrow front from which he had to debouch, secondly to the rain-sodden ground, but probably in a very large degree to his want of confidence in his troóps. All D'Erlon's divisions were tired out by the night march, long before the fighting began. Taupin's and Maransin's divisions were the two which had been smashed on the Nivelle a month before—where each had lost over a thousand men and a disproportionate number of its officers. Their ranks had been filled up again with con- scripts—but the morale cannot have been good. The Light Division could never understand why the attack on Arcangues was not pressed.

The best commentary on the combat of Arcangues is that Taupin's division only reported 197 casualties and Maransin's 299: each had 5,000 men present under arms. Moreover some of Maransin's reported losses belong to the 13th and not to the 10th of December. Daricau and Abbé were practically not engaged[1], and Darmagnac never got near the scene of the fight. Probably the real total of the day was about 400 in the two divisions which fought. On the other side the Light Division had 224 casualties, 138 British, 86 Portuguese, of whom 73 were prisoners captured at the driving in of the pickets when the action began. The 7th Division reported one man wounded in the Caçador battalion of its Portuguese brigade, skirmishing near the bridge of Urdains. The reinforcements that appeared at the end of the day, the 4th, 3rd, and 6th Divisions, had of course no losses.

[1] Two officers in Daricau's division were wounded on the 10th, and no doubt a few 'other ranks'.

NOTE

I walked all over this ground on August 22nd, 1926—Bassussary and Arcangues ridges from end to end. The ravine of the Aritzague with its bushy bottom and frequent pools, in front of the Bassussary ridge, must have been almost impossible to cross in December. But Bassussary is quite accessible from east or west, though not from north.

Arcangues church is a fine large building, with the typical galleried interior of Basque churches, and a nice memorial chapel dated 1516 of Augier d'Arcangues, *écuyer, seigneur d'Arcangues*, and a little British monument in the churchyard. It is the highest ground of all this country-side, which is mainly furzy open ground, with much brushwood. The ravine to west of the church is very steep—quite a definite military obstacle. There are good views toward the Pyrenees and the Nive, but Bayonne is quite invisible.

SECTION XLII: CHAPTER IV

THE COMBATS OF BARROUILLET. DECEMBER 10–11–12

WHILE Clausel's attack on Arcangues, which Soult had intended to be his main effort on December 10th, was dwindling down into a petty skirmish and an ineffectual cannonade, his secondary attack, on the British positions near the sea, swelled up into a fierce battle, and came near to breaking Sir John Hope's left wing. As we have seen, the arrangement of the Allied troops, on the morning after the reconnaissance of the 9th, was a very bad one. There was a widely extended picket line, reaching far out towards Anglet, with nothing close behind it, but in ultimate support A. Campbell's and Bradford's Portuguese independent brigades, billeted, the former in the mansion and out-buildings of Barrouillet, the latter in the scattered cottages, on the east side of the great *chaussée*, just beyond the Lake of Mouriscot. The 5th Division was three miles behind Bárrouillet, quartered in the village of Guéthary. The 1st Division and Lord Aylmer's brigade had marched ten miles to the rear, to their usual lodgements in St. Jean de Luz and Ciboure, and could not be brought up for many hours. Hope had never considered the possibility of a heavy French counter-stroke, when he drove in a couple of hostile brigades on to the entrenchments of Beyris on the previous afternoon.

Soult was probably contemplating at first nothing more than a demonstration on this side, in order to hold the enemy to his ground, and to allow Clausel's great advance to sweep on to Arcangues and Arbonne, and possibly to cut off the Allied troops in and about Barrouillet and Guéthary from their line of retreat on St. Jean de Luz. If he had meant more, he would have started with a greater force in this direction, but he only designated for the enterprise the two divisions of Reille—Boyer and Leval—which were already in the Beyris entrenchments, though Villatte's Reserve was placed in a position from which it could support Reille or Clausel, according as tactics might dictate when the first move was over. Sparre's brigade of dragoons, the only cavalry used on this day, had also been sent up to the Beyris front.

Accordingly Boyer's and Leval's divisions were brought out of their entrenchments before dawn, and pushed along the *chaussée* till they came on the hostile pickets. They had to debouch out of a very narrow front, for the ground on each side of the *chaussée* is limited by the large Étang de Brindos, with a turf-bog at its head, on the east of the road, and the small Étang de Marion on the west side. Only one brigade of Leval's could be deployed across the *chaussée* for the first attack. The pickets facing it, supplied from the British brigade of Robinson, of the 5th Division, and from the Portuguese independent brigade of A. Campbell, were—as it seems—taken completely by surprise, when the French attack was delivered at about 9.30. Reille had waited till he heard the noise of Clausel's attack on Bassussary rolling over from the hills from the east. When the attack came, it broke through the centre of the line at once, and all the flanking pickets had to run hard, in order to reach their supports a full mile behind. Many of them were cut off and captured before they could reach safety—Campbell's brigade shows in its casualty list 6 officers and 137 men missing, Robinson's 4 officers and 78 men. An officer of Caçadores[1], standing in front of Barrouillet, describes the scene as a wild scramble—only an hour after the first shot had been heard on the far right a perfect rabble, composed of men of many regiments, Portuguese and English, came pouring down the high road, their officers storming at them, and trying in vain to get them to face about. Fortunately there had been time to get Campbell's brigade into formation, the 4th Caçadores in a coppice on the right of the road, the line regiments between the road and the Lake of Mouriscot. The first rush of the French was stopped here; but Reille now deployed Boyer's division to the left of Leval's, and brought up some squadrons of Sparre's dragoons. The latter, coming up unexpectedly, got among the 1st Portuguese Line, and did dreadful damage to them[2]. Campbell had to fall back on Barrouillet, where his men manned the garden walls of the chateau, and the plantations immediately around it, and were

---

[1] See Bunbury, *Reminiscences of a Veteran*, vol. i. p. 221.
[2] 15 officers and over 120 men killed and wounded.

presently joined both by Bradford's Portuguese and by the
leading British brigade of the 5th Division, that of Robinson,
which had gained time to hurry up from Bidart. The other two
brigades, those of Greville and De Regoa, had been quartered
farther back, in and about Guéthary, and had not yet appeared.

The hour that followed was almost the most dangerous of the
day, for when the frontal attack down the *chaussée* was held up,
Reille sent Boyer's division into the woods to the east of
Barrouillet, and tried to turn the position and cut off the troops
in the chateau from their retreat. There was much confused
wood-fighting, as both sides kept extending their line eastward
farther into the bush; Bradford's Caçadores and other units
were thrust into the copses to cover the flank. On both sides
small clumps of men were continually getting isolated, surrounded, and captured.

Nothing decisive had happened, though the Allies were hard
pressed, when Foy and his division, rather unexpectedly, turned
up and reported for duty to Reille. Soult had been watching
Clausel's attack on Arcangues, judged that it was blocked and
held up, and had suddenly resolved to strengthen his right
attack, which looked more promising. Accordingly Foy, with the
rear division of D'Erlon's four, was hurried across from the
Marrac front, and put at Reille's disposition, and Villatte's
Reserve was also told to join him. This doubled the French
force engaged on the western front, and led to the most critical
fighting of the action. Foy was put into line to the east of
Boyer's front, driving through the woods, and succeeded in
turning the flank of Hope's line, and thrusting it back toward
Barrouillet, though Greville's brigade, which had now come up,
was thrown in to stop him[1]. Boyer, meanwhile, was attacking
the front of the chateau buildings, and Leval trying to push down
the high road. The fighting was most severe, and Robinson's
brigade in the chateau stood in great danger of being surrounded, for the line to the right of it had given way.

---

[1] The 1/9th of Greville's brigade was in great danger at this time, having
held its ground in the copses, while French troops in small parties passed
round its flanks. It had to escape by facing to the rear and charging through
the intercepting body—just as the company of the 43rd had done some
hours earlier at Bassussary. See above, p. 241.

At the critical moment Foy's right brigade [Berlier] was actually under the eastern wall of the chateau, and Boyer's left brigade [Gautier] against the northern, both in a confused mass, trying to break in, and only just failing, when the day was saved by the tardy arrival of Hope's reserves—the 1st Division and Lord Aylmer's brigade—which had just marched up from St. Jean de Luz. They had been pounding along the muddy *chaussée* for four hours, past long strings of wounded 5th Division men, who kept gasping to them 'push on—or it's all over—there are only 2,000 of us left down there'[1]. As they came up they saw Barrouillet beset on all sides, from the main road to the woods. But the French were already almost exhausted, and when they descried the head of a long column coming down the Bidart road, observers saw them slacken, 'not that they fell into confusion, or showed symptoms of dismay, but confidence was gone'. Lord Aylmer's brigade, which led the column, deployed itself and, leaving the *chaussée* to one side, struck at the copses from which Foy's attack was emerging, catching it in flank. The enemy gave back at once, Barrouillet was cleared from assailants, and the fighting rolled back into the woods[2]. To keep his line unbroken Reille had to throw in the German brigade from Villatte's Reserve, which covered the retreat. Villatte himself was wounded by a chance long-distance shot at the moment. It was some time after 3 o'clock when the action dwindled down into a skirmish in the woods. Hope did not put in his last reserves—neither the Guards nor the German Legion brigades lost a man this day—and was well content to have kept his position. The enemy had given back less than a mile from Barrouillet, and his rear-guards held the ground from which Hope's pickets had been evicted in the morning.

It is clear that if the 1st Division and Lord Aylmer's brigade had come an hour later, the line would have been broken—with

---

[1] Gleig, p. 172.

[2] French accounts make the last blow to be inflicted on Foy by the 4th Division [Vidal de la Blache, ii. p. 170; Dumas, p. 277]. They seem to have been misled by some lines in Napier, vi. p. 401. But the 4th Division was not engaged, and did not lose a man this day. The turning movement was made by Lord Aylmer's people: that the resistance was not very great is shown by the brigade's modest casualty-list of 1 officer and 30 men. Neither the Guards nor the Germans were employed.

obviously disastrous results to the 5th Division and the Portuguese unattached brigades. And equally clear is it that if Hope
had kept his reserves at Bidart instead of at St. Jean de Luz,
Soult's attack—originally planned on quite a modest scale—
would never have had the least chance of success. French critics
remark that Soult and Reille acted this day just as at Waterloo—
throwing every man against a well-defended chateau, instead of
turning it by a wide movement[1]. But in the dense copses east
of Barrouillet direction was less easy than in the wheat-fields
east of Hougoumont. It must be confessed that Hope's and
Soult's reports of the action are equally unsatisfactory. Soult's
version is so deceptive as to be worth quoting—it conceals both
his intentions and the results.

'Reille, having under his orders the divisions Leval and Boyer,
whom I afterwards reinforced with the division Foy, and supported with Villatte's Reserve, attacked the woods of Barrouillet,
where the 1st and 5th English divisions were entrenched. The
ground made it impossible for him to put in more than two
brigades, which were repulsed. I was about to recommence the
attack when Clausel reported to me that heavy hostile columns,
apparently coming from the other side of the Nive, were forming
up on the heights of Urdains. So I suspended the movements of
my right wing[2].'

Every fact here is wrong: the British 1st Division was not
entrenched at Barrouillet: Reille put in, during the action, seven
brigades, not two. The cessation of the attack was not due to
Clausel's reports but to a complete repulse.

Hope's dispatch gives no hint of the facts that his reserves
were ten miles to the rear, and that the day was wellnigh lost
in consequence; and the course of the fighting cannot be reconstructed from his narrative. Indeed the whole mentality of this
gallant officer during the battle makes us ponder on what would
have happened if Wellington had fallen sick, and the command
of the whole Allied forces had devolved on him. He seems to
have held that the proper position of an army-corps commander
was in the skirmishing line. He was conspicuous everywhere,
leading troops into position, and once, when Barrouillet seemed

[1] Vidal de la Blache, ii. p. 169.
[2] Soult to the Minister of War, Bassussary, night of December 10th.

about to fall, and he was forced to leave it, he was seen to gallop from its side door under the fire of many hundred French skirmishers. His horse was shot, and he had three musket balls through his hat. Wellington wrote, in his dry style, to the Horse Guards[1]. 'We shall lose him if he continues to expose himself to fire as he did in those last three days: indeed his escape has been wonderful. He places himself among the sharp-shooters, without (as they do) sheltering himself from the enemy's fire. This will not answer; and I hope that his friends will give him a hint on the subject. But it is a *delicate* subject.' It will be remembered that Sir John closed his military career four months later, by being wounded and taken prisoner in the confusion of a night skirmish in the suburbs of Bayonne.

The losses of December 10th in Hope's corps appear to have been 3 officers and 58 men killed, 18 officers and 339 men wounded, 5 officers and 92 men missing in the two British brigades of the 5th Division, and in the three Portuguese brigades engaged [Bradford, A. Campbell, De Regoa] 11 officers with 142 men killed, 39 officers and 418 men wounded, and 8 officers and 329 men missing[2]. Adding 1 officer and 30 men from Lord Aylmer's brigade, the total comes to about 1,496 casualties. Soult reported in his usual vague style that his losses had been 'about 1,000 in all', probably an understatement[3], but they may have been slightly less than those of Hope's troops, who had been surprised, and had lost many prisoners in the first moments of the attack.

The night of December 10th closed with a most unexpected and unparalleled incident. Three German battalions walked over from the French lines and entered the British. This was one of the results of Leipzig. When Napoleon had been driven out of Germany, and all the petty princes of the 'Rheinbund' hastened to make their peace with the victorious Allies, the Duke of Nassau was one of the not-unwilling converts to the cause of the 'liberty of Europe'. He had one regiment serving with Soult, another

---

[1] Wellington to Torrens. *Wellington Dispatches,* xi. pp. 371–2.

[2] In the whole Peninsular War Wellington's army never lost so many prisoners as it did this day—over 500 in all—73 on the Arcangues front, 434 on the Barrouillet front. About 150 were British, rather over 350 Portuguese. Nearly all came from the smashed lines of pickets.

[3] So the very judicious Dumas, p. 280.

with Suchet in Catalonia. He sent secret agents overland to explain the situation to his colonels. Kruse, commanding the 2nd Nassau regiment, in Villatte's reserve division, received his message, and contrived to get into communication with an old friend in Wellington's camp, Bäring of the King's German Legion. Already in October the British Commander-in-Chief knew that the Rheinbund troops were ready to come over, and waiting their opportunity[1]. He had promised that they should not be treated as prisoners of war, and should be sent at once to Germany. Kruse settled matters with the officers commanding the Baden and Frankfurt battalions, which were brigaded with his own regiment. On the night of December 10th, Villatte's Reserve being on rear-guard duty, the chance came. But when Kruse was managing his manœuvre, he found his way blocked by a French regiment of another brigade—this little difficulty he got over by persuading the colonel of the 34th Léger to take a side-path, as he himself had found the road before him encumbered with other troops. The way being clear, the Nassau and Frankfurt battalions marched into Barrouillet. The Baden battalion failed to follow, from a chance cause—its commander Major Hennig, who had been wounded that afternoon, was in the secret, the second in command was not, and, failing to understand the eccentric direction in which his comrades were marching, kept on and followed the 34th Léger.

The three battalions which had escaped marched through St. Jean de Luz on the following day with trumpets sounding, and colours flying, about 1,400 strong, showing every sign of enthusiasm, and were at once embarked at Passages and sent home[2]. Kruse afterwards commanded the Nassau contingent at Waterloo, which contained the very regiment at whose head he had fought so long for Napoleon in Spain. Soult disarmed the Baden battalion next day, and sent warning to Suchet that the 1st Nassau regiment at Barcelona would probably follow the example of the 2nd if it got the chance. Even before this came to hand the problem had cropped up; Colonel Kruse had sent

---

[1] Cf. Bathurst to Wellington. *Supplementary Dispatches*, xi. p. 279. 'Dutch' here means 'German'.

[2] See Larpent's *Journal*, p. 320, with an interesting account of Kruse's explanation of his doings.

to his 'opposite number', Colonel Meder of the 1st Nassau, a propagandic letter, explaining his action and inviting his comrade to do likewise. Meder, more of a professional soldier than a German patriot, took the document to Suchet without a moment's hesitation. The Duke of Albufera thereupon disarmed the Nassau, Würzburg, and Westphalian units in Catalonia—about 2,400 strong. Meder asked and obtained leave to enter the French army, and was killed at the head of the 18th Léger two months later. Fourteen of his officers deserted to the Anglo-Sicilian camp, so it is clear that Kruse had sympathizers, and that Suchet was not acting unwisely[1].

It may be well to mention here, disregarding exact chronology, that Kruse's action caused Soult not only to disarm the Baden battalion, but to disband the wreck of King Joseph's Spanish army, the forlorn regiments of Casapalacios and Guy. The French officers and men of the Spanish Guards were formed into a new regiment, the 14th Voltigeurs of the French Imperial Guard, which went to Champagne, and perished whole at the bloody battle of Craonne on March 7th, 1814, where 32 of its officers fell[2]. The men of the Line corps, which contained all manner of Swiss, Poles, Italians, &c., besides the real *Afrancesados*, were sent to Toulouse or turned adrift. Their horses and arms were useful for the French regiments.

On the morning of December 11th the troops both of Wellington and of Soult found their opponents lying much where they had been at the cessation of the combats of the preceding day. Clausel was still holding the plateau of Bassussary, in front of the Light Division, Reille's divisions were across the high road a mile north-east of Barrouillet. Abbé and Darmagnac were still watching the bridge of Urdains, where they now had the 3rd British Division opposite them, not the 7th, since the latter had moved eastward to support Wellington's centre.

---

[1] There is a good account of all this in Vidal de la Blache, ii. pp. 106–10, and in Sauzey's 'Les Allemands sous les aigles', vi. p. 245–53.

[2] See Martinien, p. 90. Vidal de la Blache—whom one seldom catches in a slip—says wrongly on p. 104 of his second volume that the Spanish guardsmen were drafted into Soult's Army. The only other serious mistake that I find in this excellent author is that he always treats the Light Division as consisting of two British and one Portuguese brigades, instead of two composite Anglo-Portuguese brigades.

Each of the two adversaries seems on this day to have credited the other with offensive designs, and waited for them to develop —Soult seeing the movements of British troops (4th, 6th, 7th Divisions) towards the west, expected to see Reille or Clausel attacked in force. Wellington, looking two days forward into the future, thought rather that Soult might take the bulk of his men back across the Nive, and fall upon Hill, now left alone on the right bank with his own division and Le Cor's Portuguese. And indeed the Marshal had already that design in his head, but put off executing it, because he was not sure that Wellington did not intend to make a general assault on his line, if he should see troops moving off eastward in daylight. To be sure of easy communication with Hill, Beresford was ordered to throw one or more bridges across the Nive at Villefranque—a matter which turned out a more tiresome business than had been expected, owing to a freshet on the river, caused by the heavy rains that had fallen on the night of the 9th–10th in the mountains upstream. To guard against an attack from Arcangues on Clausel's position Soult ordered a long redoubt, pierced for no less than thirty guns, to be erected on the point of the dip between the Bassussary and the Arcangues ridges. But, though it much intrigued the Light Division, this work was never armed.

The 11th of December was not, however, destined to pass by without some fighting—rather objectless as it turned out. About 10 on this foggy morning Wellington came to the conclusion that Reille's outposts were closer to Barrouillet than was comfortable. He directed Greville's brigade of the 5th Division to drive them in: this was done without much trouble. But by the error of a staff-officer[1] the 9th regiment was not stopped at the point that had been marked out for it, and pushed right into the hamlet of Pucho, in the middle of Leval's main fighting position. Here it was attacked on both flanks, and cast back with the loss of over 100 men, including some prisoners. But the line of pickets was re-established where Wellington had intended, and he departed, thinking that matters had settled down.

This, however, was not the case. Soult had resented the advance and meditated a counter-attack. He brought over

[1] According to Napier, vi. p. 402, it was Colonel Delancy, who afterwards fell at Waterloo, who committed the error.

another division—Daricau's—from Clausel's wing, and at 2
o'clock in the afternoon delivered a serious attack with this, and
Boyer's divisions, upon the whole line of Hope's outposts from
the *chaussée* eastward, including the high ground in the woods[1].
For the second time there seems to have been something wrong
with the staff-work of Hope's corps, for, just as on the previous
day, the supports for the pickets were caught unprepared, and
none of the brigades behind was ready to get under arms. The
men, worn out with yesterday's work, were very much off duty—
many, it is said, gathering wood for their camp-fires in the
copses: others far afield on fatigue-parties. This was in spite of
the fact that the outposts had reported that the French were
cutting outlets in the hedges in their front, and lying very thick
behind their pickets.

The same thing then happened as had occurred on the 10th—
a sudden swarm of *tirailleurs* on a long front burst out of the
French lines, with formed battalions behind them, and swept in
Hope's pickets and their supports, both on the open ground
along the *chaussée* and in the woods to its eastern side. For a
second time there was a stampede down the road, and a hasty
turning out of scattered men to form up across the fields and
copses, and to man the loopholes of the Chateau of Barrouillet.
Some of the farm buildings—never lost on the preceding day—
were actually in the hands of the enemy for a short time.
De Regoa's Portuguese and several of the British regiments of
the 5th Division were completely broken up, and it was some
time before a line of resistance was formed between the Lake of
Mouriscot and the woods, with the Chateau—still intact—in its
centre. Sir John Hope was seen everywhere—as on the 10th—
bustling together broken companies, and leading his reserves
into position as they came up. This time he was not bullet-
proof and was wounded—though not seriously—in the leg. Fortunately there were plenty of troops on the spot this day—the odds
were not so desperate as they had been on the preceding morning. Flanking fire from the remnant of the much-tried 9th
regiment on the left stopped the French on the main road—
Aylmer's brigade plunged into the woods and held back

---

[1] Sir John Fortescue (ix. p. 461) says Foy's division: but, as Soult's report
shows, it was Daricau's that attacked.

Daricau, and the Guards and Germans formed a second line in the rear.

Then the French attack died out as suddenly as it had begun —very probably the troops had outrun their mark, like the British 9th Foot in the morning, and had been tempted forward by the disorder in front of them. Soult in his dispatch treats the matter as 'an affair of outposts', not as a serious attempt to break through, such as the action of the 10th had been. And it is obvious that having now five divisions on this front (Boyer, Leval, Foy, Villatte, and Daricau) he would not have made a serious stroke with two only, and, when it was rather successful, have refrained from putting in the rest, if he had really meant mischief.

The skirmish cost the British 320 casualties, all in the 5th Division, in which the 1/9th and 1/4th each lost 100 men, and De Regoa's Portuguese brigade nearly as many. It is improbable that the French losses were so heavy, as they stopped and turned back when the first check brought their initial success to an end. It is not impossible that they may have been as few as 200, as only 10 officers were killed or wounded in Boyer's and Daricau's divisions[1] on December 11th.

When the fighting died down, Sir John Hope withdrew the 5th Division from the front line, and replaced it by the 1st Division. It was high time for the change to be made, for in the three days of December 9th–10th–11th, it had lost 1,200 men, being already the smallest division in Wellington's army. Neither its English nor its Portuguese brigades had yet replaced the awful gaps in their ranks made at the storm of St. Sebastian. On December 1st it had only 4,300 of all ranks present, all the rest having nearer 6,000 save, of course, the Light Division with its specially small establishment of only 5 British and 4 Portuguese battalions[2]. On the last day, therefore, of the fighting on the Barrouillet front—December 12th—it was the 1st Division which got the responsibilities and the hard knocks, and not the much-tried 5th.

Soult had, as early as the morning of December 11th, written

---

[1] Six officer-casualties in Daricau's and four only in Boyer's are recorded by Martinien.

[2] The 2/59th, with under 500 of all ranks, had lost over 200; the 1/9th with 600, 214; the 2/47th with only 350 as many as 118.

to the Minister of War at Paris, to explain that when he had
attracted the greater part of Wellington's forces back to the
western bank of the Nive, he intended to countermarch the
bulk of his army to the eastern bank and fall upon Hill's depleted
corps[1]. This would have to be done at night, lest the enemy,
having sighted it, should make the corresponding move, and
reinforce Hill before the attack upon him was delivered. That
Soult did not carry out his plan on the night of the 11th was due
to two causes—the first was that the weather was bad, the second
was that the fighting about Barrouillet had dragged on so late
into the afternoon of the 11th that the movement after dark of
any troops there engaged, for a long night march, would have
been too exhausting for them. For Foy's and Daricau's divisions
were earmarked, in the Marshal's scheme, as part of the force
which was to recross the Nive and fall upon Hill. The night
march, therefore, had to be put off till after dusk on the 12th;
this had the additional convenience of allowing the whole army
another day's rest, of which it was much in need.

Wellington, for his part, had guessed the Marshal's intentions
on the night of the 10th, as his letter to Beresford written after
the action clearly shows[2]. He had directed Beresford to build
another pontoon-bridge lower down the Nive, facing Villefranque, so as to make communication with Hill far more rapid
than could be the case when the Ustaritz bridge was the only
available passage for reinforcing troops. And he had designated
the 6th and 7th Divisions as the units which must be ready to
cross the Nive, by the new bridge, at the first warning. He might,
of course, have stopped Soult's game by attacking himself, since
he could accumulate superior forces against either the enemy
before Barrouillet or the enemy before Arcangues, by throwing
his disposable reserve divisions—the 3rd, 4th, 6th, 7th—on to
either of those points. But there would be little profit in the
mere driving Soult back into his fortified camps outside Bayonne.
It would be a costly business, and the enemy had a safe retreat.
Moreover, Wellington usually preferred to be attacked rather

---

[1] Soult to the Minister, Bayonne, December 11. But 'J'ai jugé à propos de
différer encore pour voir les dispositions de l'ennemi. . . . Je serais porté à croire
que dans la nuit ou demain d'autres troupes encore passeront la Nive.'

[2] To Beresford, 9.40, December 10. *Dispatches*, xi. p. 357.

than to attack himself, on general principles—unless the advantage of taking the initiative was very great. So he waited for Soult's move—rather surprised to find that the morning of the 12th did not show the enemy in front of him vanished, or at least much diminished in numbers. It is probable that he thrust forward the 5th Division pickets on the morning of the 11th with an expectation that the enemy would be found to have gone already; but the move had only provoked a strong counter-attack, and proved that the French were still in great force in front of Barrouillet.

The morning of the 12th found the adversaries still waiting each for the other to move. In front of Urdains bridge Abbé was paired off against Colville. At Arcangues the Light Division, having had two quiet days, had made their position practically impregnable with trenches and *abattis*. They could see in front of them the fieldwork, with embrasures for guns, which Clausel had thrown up—but it was never armed, nor did it ever speak. At Barrouillet both parties were very much on the *qui vive* after their experiences of attack and counter-attack on the previous day. This state of strained attention finally brought on a skirmish, not deliberately sought by either party. At about ten in the morning the French reinforced their outpost line: this is said to have been done because Reille had observed new troops in front of him—the 1st Division had replaced the 5th, and all the Portuguese were gone. A shifting of the French picket-line caused a suspicious British artillery officer to shell the sector of the enemy's posts where he had seen movement. This was at once answered by a French battery, the infantry followed suit, and a vigorous *tiraillade* went on for some time, which each party suspected to be the preliminary to an attack by the other. So noisy did it grow that Wellington moved the 7th Division from near the hill of Sainte Barbe toward Arbonne, where it would be better placed for supporting Barrouillet or Arcangues. As it chanced, Soult noted this movement and took it for the arrival of another division from across the Nive, a theory which made him more anxious than ever to get his troops westward, and to fall upon Hill. Since neither party made any attempt to attack, the firing along the front line finally died down—it cost the British about 180 casualties, all in the two Guards brigades of the 1st Division. The French cannot have lost more, and may have lost a few less. In the whole four days December 9th–12th it seems likely that Soult lost about 2,300 men on this front— Hope something more like 2,500.

Before dusk, satisfied that Wellington was not about to attack, as he had suspected at noon, Soult gave his orders for the night march back to the east bank of the Nive, which he had so long meditated. It was to be made by all Clausel's and D'Erlon's divisions—Abbé, Darmagnac, Daricau, Foy, Taupin, and Maransin. Boyer, Leval, and Villatte's Reserve alone were left on the left bank, with orders to get back into the lines of Beyris and Marrac when they were pressed, but not till then.

Meanwhile a few words are necessary to describe what had been going on upon the 10th–11th–12th of December on the farther bank of the Nive. When Hill, on the morning of the 10th, found that he had no enemy left opposite him, he occupied the heights which they had evacuated, and then felt his way forward cautiously to reconnoitre the outworks of Bayonne. The fortified camp of Mousserolles and its two redoubts were only too visible from the heights facing them. Here a good blockading position, reaching from the Adour to the Nive, about two miles outside the French works, was taken up. Pringle's brigade occupied the Chateau of Larralde, on a knoll in front of Ville-franque, near the Nive. Byng's brigade took post on a corre-sponding height next the Adour, the hill of Mouguerre, with quarters in the village of the same name, but with one battalion pushed forward to the ridge of Partouhiria, which actually looks down on the great river and a broad section of its opposite banks. Ashworth's and Barnes's battalions lay, some in the village of Petit Mouguerre, others across the high road, in a series of farms and small houses along the way, which were then known as Haut-St.-Pierre, though the name has now disappeared—no doubt because of perpetual confusion between it and that of St. Pierre d'Irrube, the suburban village outside Bayonne, which lies along the *chaussée* a mile and a half in front. Le Cor's Portuguese division was left a little to the rear, by the high hill called Horlopo, the loftiest point on the road, quartered in hamlets and cottages along the *chaussée*, or scattered along the side-roads from several directions which come in here.

BATTLE OF THE NIVE, DECEMBER 10TH 1813

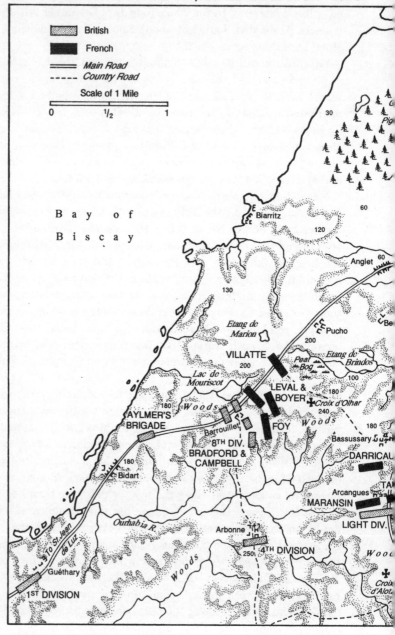

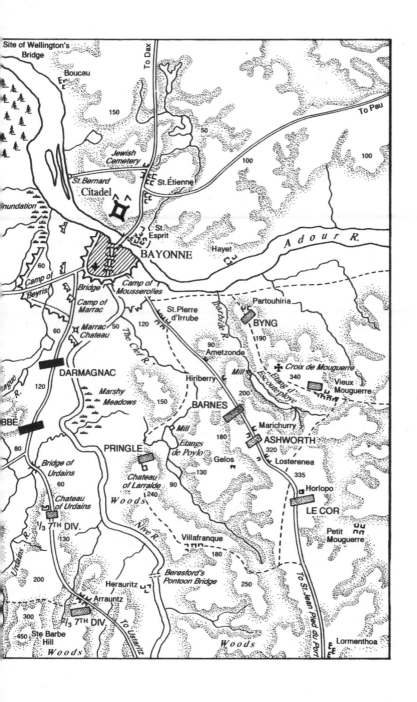

On the 11th, when Hill had settled into position, Sparre's brigade of Dragoons, sent back by Soult from Barrouillet, came out of Bayonne, with a small body of infantry in support, and felt for Hill's outposts—they did not press, when they had found out what they wanted to see. Meanwhile urgent messages had been received from Wellington, to warn Hill that the enemy might be expected to recross the Nive and to fall upon him in force on any morning. But the early hours of the 12th passed by without any such trouble developing.

Such distractions as Hill endured on this day were from quite another direction. It has been already mentioned[1] that to cover his rear from possible interference from the east, Hill had been given Morillo's small Spanish division and Vivian's cavalry brigade, who were pushed out to look for Paris and his detached force, which was known to be on the road from St.-Jean-Pied-du-Port. On the 9th Paris had retired eastward, when the British crossed the Nive: but he had now been reinforced by the whole of Pierre Soult's cavalry division—coming in from its cantonments in the direction of Oloron and Pau. This made him more adventurous, and he was detected on the 11th pushing forward a broad cavalry screen on both sides of Morillo's force. On the 12th Pierre Soult and Paris pressed in with some 5,000 men on to the line of Vivian's vedettes, and drove his brigade back for some distance, till they came on Morillo's infantry in battle order on the heights of Chouya, in front of Urcarray. After some skirmishing Pierre Soult—never an enterprising person—retired past Hasparren as far as Bonloc. This diversion's only tangible effect was to induce Hill to send back one of his British brigades [that of Barnes[2]] to support Morillo if necessary. Barnes's men trudged over a vile road for many miles, only to be turned back, when near Urcarray, by the report that Paris had retired, and that they were not wanted. They returned to Petit Mouguerre that same night, tired out, but in time for the great battle of the succeeding day[3].

[1] See above, p. 230–1.

[2] Sir John Fortescue, ix. p. 464, calls it Cameron's brigade. But Cameron was not in command till Barnes was wounded at the battle of St. Pierre.

[3] For those interested in minute points of regimental history, there is a rich treat in the controversy in the *United Service Journal* for 1846, on the skirmish in front of Hasparren on the 12th between Pierre Soult's

cavalry and Vivian's brigade—or rather the 14th Light Dragoons, for the other regiment of the brigade was not present. The matter started with William Napier's statement that Vivian's mismanagement caused the capture of Major Brotherton and Lieutenant Southwell, sent on a mad venture to charge across a narrow bridge. Vivian resented this, and put the blame on the quixotic pugnacity of Brotherton. Brotherton and Southwell both wrote at length on the subject. The odd thing is that none of them could know that a French officer, Lemonnier-Delafosse, Pierre Soult's aide-de-camp, had left an elaborate account of the incident in his diary, which was not·published till 1850. His view is that Brotherton was led into a trap by a stratagem of the major commanding the 13th *Chasseurs à cheval*; certainly he seems to support Vivian rather than Napier.

NOTE

While the combat of Arcangues is well described by six or eight Light Division authors, there is great obscurity about the details of the fighting of December 10th at Barrouillet. There are no useful personal narratives from the 5th Division, which had the thick of the battle, though we have good details from Bunbury of the 5th Caçadores, Gleig in Lord Aylmer's brigade, and Batty of the Grenadier Guards. The thing which puzzles the observer of to-day, when going over the ground, is to discover why the French made no attempt to turn the Barrouillet position by passing troops between the pretty little Lake of Mouriscot and the sea. There is a front of over half a mile between them, and to-day a road to Biarritz goes through it. I can only conjecture that in December 1813 the ravine, by which the water of the lake falls into the sea, must have been water-logged and practically impassable. And the woods still existing round the lake may have extended farther, and have been more tangled. No writer, contemporary or modern, says a word on this problem.

SECTION XLII: CHAPTER V

THE BATTLE OF ST. PIERRE. DECEMBER 13, 1813

THERE had never, from the first, been any chance that Soult would surprise Hill, as he had hoped; for Wellington (as we have already seen) had warned his lieutenant, as early as the night of the 10th, that he considered it very likely that he might be attacked by the whole French army on any of the succeeding mornings. And to guard against this probability he had ordered the building of the extra bridge opposite Villefranque, and always left several divisions near it, ready to cross and reinforce Hill at the first alarm. On the 11th the 6th and 7th Divisions were ready: on the 12th Walker had been ordered westward to near Arbonne, but to replace him Colville and the 3rd Division had been brought up from Ustaritz, where the 6th Division still remained. But there was one contingency against which Wellington could not guard himself—danger to the bridges, both at Ustaritz and at Villefranque, from a sudden rise in the Nive, swollen by Pyrenean rains near its source. And this contingency did arise, and gave Soult a chance on which he could not have counted—we know indeed that he had not taken it into consideration.

Beresford had been ordered to build the new Villefranque bridge as early as the night of the 10th. His engineers got to work on it next morning, but found it a difficult task, for the river was running strongly. By the late afternoon of the 11th it was completed, and Wellington considered Hill's position pretty safe, whatever might happen. The only danger that occurred to him was that Soult might send some of his gunboats on the Adour into the lower course of the Nive, which is more or less navigable for small craft even up to Ustaritz, and might use them against the lower bridge. This did not happen—but a greater power than Soult intervened: a freshet came down the river from heavy rain up-stream, and the Villefranque bridge was broken late on the afternoon of the 12th. Fortunately the upper bridge at Ustaritz held firm—this was an old structure, now repaired, and put in tolerable order with woodwork since the 10th, while the lower bridge was only made with pontoons. The serious thing was that, while the 3rd Division would have had only four miles to march if the Villefranque bridge had been standing, the 6th Division had nine or ten to go in order to pass the Nive at Ustaritz, get into the *chaussée*, and come up to the Horlopo heights in Hill's rear. Naturally, when the battle of the 13th commenced, Beresford's engineers made heroic efforts to relay the pontoons, and succeeded before noon; but the troops which crossed over them arrived later than the division which had the long trudge from Ustaritz[1]. It is of course wrong to say, as many narrators of this campaign have done, that by the temporary destruction of the Villefranque bridge Hill was 'cut off' or 'completely isolated': this was not the fact: but the disaster trebled the time which it would take to reinforce him, if he were attacked at dawn. The problem which lay before him, when he heard the news that the pontoons had been sunk, was whether he could hold his chosen position for four hours—the time which would elapse before succour could reach him. This he thought that he could manage to do, considering the strength of his ground, and the quality of his troops—the two old Albuera divisions.

Hill had obeyed Wellington's orders, and pushed his northern wing right up to the heights which overhang the Adour, whose navigation it was intended to impede. The position was over three miles long when the curve of its concave centre is allowed for, a considerable front for 14,000 men to hold, but it was stayed on both flanks by impassable obstacles—the Adour and the Nive—it was all on commanding ground, and considerable sectors of it were practically unassailable[2].

The long line of heights which forms the watershed between

---

[1] Writers on the Battle of St. Pierre often speak of the 6th Division as having crossed the repaired pontoon bridge. But the two 42nd diaries of this time, Anton's and that of the anonymous 'Scottish Soldier', show that Ustaritz was the starting-point of the 6th Division. Even Napier (vi. p. 410) has got things wrong, and makes the division cross at Villefranque. One French commentator, Colonel Dumas (pp. 287–8), is the only person who has put things straight.

[2] The three British brigades of the 2nd Division were about 5,700 strong —the three Portuguese brigades of Ashworth, Da Costa, and Buchan about 7,500; there were two batteries—one British (Ross), one Portuguese (Tulloh).

the Nive and the Adour ends, opposite Bayonne, in three projecting eminences. Next the Nive is a wooded summit, about 240 feet above sea-level, on which lies the Chateau of Larralde: next the Adour is a much loftier ridge, the heights of Mouguerre, whose highest point rises to 360 feet and is crowned to-day by the obelisk erected by modern piety to the memory of Soult's army. From the 'Croix de Mouguerre' may be had the finest view in all this part of France, ranging from the ocean to the Rhune and the distant Pyrenees. Between the Croix de Mouguerre and the Larralde Chateau is the central ridge; the Horlopo hill, 350 feet high, is its culminating point, but this lies far back, and if a line is drawn from the Croix to the Chateau, the central slopes are somewhat lower than the flanks. Up them runs, rather steeply, the main *chaussée* from Bayonne to St.-Jean-Pied-du-Port: it rises 200 feet in the mile. Along it on either side are small farms and isolated cottages, with stone-walled or thorn-hedged enclosures round each. On the sky-line of the ridge are the groups of houses then called Haut-St.-Pierre, but now better known as the hamlets of Marichurry and Losterenea: the old name has vanished. Hill's head-quarters were on the Horlopo, from whence a good view can be obtained. The fighting ground of his centre was on the slopes below Marichurry, two-thirds of a mile in front, with the skirmishing line above the farm called Hiriberry, toward the foot of the heights.

The peculiar feature in Hill's position was that the line of three separate heights, of which it was composed, was cut into in the most perplexing fashion by two deep gullies, each with water at the bottom, which made direct communication between the two wings and the centre impossible, save by cross-roads starting from the Horlopo knoll, nearly a mile behind the fighting ground of the centre, more than a mile from that of either of the two wings. These gullies were the beds of the Ibarbide stream, between the Croix de Mouguerre and Marichurry, and of the Clef stream between the latter hamlet and the Chateau of Larralde. Each of these streams had been dammed up at the point where it nears the low ground, so as to make a large marshy mill-pond, to drive the machinery of a water-mill. The narrow Étang d'Escouteplouye, which served (and still serves) the mill of the same name, is a good half-mile long, sunk in a veritable ravine only 150 yards broad. The steep slope of the hill of Mouguerre towers above it in an almost precipitous fashion[1]. The other gully, on the west of the high road, is not so narrow or so steep; it has at its bottom a marshy tract in which a sheet of water, sometimes divided into two separate ponds, sometimes continuous[2], is held up by the mill-dam of Poylo. The *Étangs de Poylo* extend more or less up-stream according to the state of the weather: in a particularly wet December they were at their largest. There were therefore two complete gaps between the centre and the flanks of Hill's position, but they were gaps of which an enemy could take no advantage. The forthcoming battle had, from the nature of the ground, to be fought on three separate fronts, and neither the defender nor the assailant could move troops from one to the other, without an interminable countermarch to the rear. Both parties had to keep their eventual reserves very far back, Hill on the Horlopo, Soult on the hill of St. Pierre d'Irrube, only just outside the fortifications of Bayonne. These were the only points from which all the three fighting fronts could be fed.

Hill had disposed his six brigades so as to cover all the three possible routes of access to his position. Pringle's brigade was on the Larralde hill, where it had barricaded and loopholed the chateau; Byng's was on the Mouguerre hill, where one battalion, the Buffs, was pushed far forward to hold the ridge near the Adour [Partouhiria] which watches the opposite heights of St. Pierre d'Irrube across a narrow gap—the mouth of the Ibarbide brook. Here the uphill road from Bayonne to Vieux Mouguerre crossed the brook by a little bridge—this defile was the only way on to the heights. The other two battalions [57th and 1st Provisional] of Byng's brigade were far back, at the head of the Escouteplouye ravine, near the picturesque village of Vieux Mouguerre with its little romanesque church and its chateau with two pepper-box turrets. From this point they could, if needful, reinforce the centre, which would have been impossible had they been placed on the projecting slope of

---

[1] The modern high road, Bayonne–Oloron, which coasts along the south side of the Escouteplouye water had not been built in 1813. It does not appear in Wilde's map of the country outside Bayonne.

[2] The 1926 Survey of Bayonne only gives one pond: older maps two.

Partouhiria. The centre of Hill's position was held by Ashworth's Portuguese, deployed across the *chaussée*: the 6th Line to the north of it, the 18th to the south, above the farm of Hiriberry, two-thirds of the way down the slope. The Caçador battalion of the brigade (No. 6) was in the copse to the right of Hiriberry, well covered by hedges. On the sky-line at the top of the slope of the *chaussée*, in front of Marichurry, were established ten guns looking down the road and all the slopes on each side of it. These were Tulloh's Portuguese field-battery, and four guns of Ross's British Horse Battery. Barnes's brigade—very tired after its fruitless march toward Urcarray—was in reserve behind the guns. Le Cor's Portuguese division was two-thirds of a mile farther back, waiting at the foot of the Horlopo knoll, with the two remaining guns of Ross's battery. This was the only spot from which Hill could send it to feed any one of the three fronts which the enemy might attack.

On the night of December 12th–13th reports were made to Hill from the outposts, of sights and sounds which made it probable that the enemy was massing in his front. There was a vast group of bivouac fires in front of the Camp of Mousserolles, and a continuous sound of distant rumbling, as of wagons or artillery, had been noted[1]. It is even said that glimpses had been caught of columns crossing the Nive bridge—there was a frost and bright moonlight, so this is possible. But the dawn of the 13th was foggy—as so often happens after a cold night—and for some time nothing was visible in the lowland, though suspicious noises could be heard. It was not till after 7 o'clock that the mist began to grow patchy, and the French columns, already in order and advancing, became visible. The first shot was fired before 8, and for the next five hours the din was incessant.

Soult's main difficulty was to deploy a whole army from the narrow front of less than a mile between the Clef and Ibarbide brooks, by which it had to issue from its positions of the night. He had four divisions packed close on the plateau of St. Pierre d'Irrube, and two more were still to come up from the Camp of

---

[1] This from the pickets of Byng's brigade on the Partouhiria ridge—see the narrative of L'Estrange of the 31st, then in charge of the foremost advance picket. *Recollections*, p. 144.

Marrac, and had not crossed the bridge. As the movement developed, it was seen that there was a division coming up the *chaussée*—that of Abbé; then a second division—Daricau—was seen making for the country-road that diverges along the low-lying valley of the Clef towards Larralde and Villefranque. A third column was visible close to the Adour, on the bypath that crosses the bridge of the Ibarbide and turns up on to the heights of Mouguerre—this was Chassé's brigade of Darmagnac's division. The plateau behind was still crowded with more troops—Gruardet's brigade of Darmagnac—which ultimately followed Abbé down the main road—Foy's whole division, which afterwards went up after Chassé on to the northern heights. When Foy had cleared off, Maransin came up from Marrac, and replaced him; the last division to be used—that of Taupin—was only brought over the Nive at the very end of the day, to cover a retreat. Sparre's brigade of dragoons—quite useless as it turned out—was also in the rear. But very much in front were four batteries of divisional artillery[1], drawn up in a long line on the lower slope of St. Pierre d'Irrube, which was less than 800 yards from Hill's advanced troops by Partouhiria and Hiriberry. They opened—almost immediately—a long-distance fire on Ashworth's Portuguese. Very soon after, Ross and Tulloh began to reply on Abbé's division, as it advanced along the *chaussée* towards the foot of the British position.

It was past 8 o'clock before serious fighting began—Soult had lost an hour and more since dawn, owing to the necessity for debouching from such a narrow front. He had now a time-problem before him: if he could not win his battle in four hours Hill's reserves would have arrived, and a stalemate would be the best that he could hope for. But the Marshal had under-estimated the number of men that Wellington had got close to the Nive, and (what is strange) had never learnt of Beresford's pontoon-bridge, which was to be re-established before midday. He did not understand that he must win early—or not at all.

To the modern historian—wise after the event—it looks as if Soult's best chance would have been to send out a few battalions

---

[1] But apparently only 22 guns, not 24. One was the H.A. battery attached to Sparre's cavalry; the other three belonged to Abbé, Daricau, and Darmagnac.

to 'contain' Byng and Pringle—who could bring no help to the British centre—and to have plunged in mass, division after division, against Hill's troops ranged across the *chaussée*. It would have been brutal tactics, but the Marshal could have put in three men to one, even when Hill should have brought up his two Portuguese reserve brigades. And matters might certainly have been settled, one way or the other, before Hill's reserves could have come up. It must be granted that the experiment would have been costly—the enemy had a good position, and two batteries well established in his centre. But if—as we shall see—Soult nearly broke through, when he used only one and a half divisions for his central attack, what might not have happened if he had used four? The ground between the Poylo ravine and the Escouteplouye ravine was a bare mile broad, but, in the columnar formation which French commanders invariably used, a good deal more than Abbé's single division could have been placed upon it. Napoleon at Waterloo attacked with the four divisions of D'Erlon's corps, elbow to elbow, on a front of little more than half a mile. And he was attacking a whole army—not like Soult at St. Pierre a front held by one Portuguese brigade in front line, a British brigade in support, and two more Portuguese brigades as last and only reserve.

Abbé's frontal attack on Hill's centre started off long before Daricau had got near the hill of Larralde, or Chassé had climbed far on Partouhiria. His was the finest division in Soult's army, a veteran unit of the Army of Andalusia which had suffered less in the battles of the Pyrenees than any other French division, and by the chance of war had been out of the main game alike at San Marcial, at the crossing of the Bidassoa, and at the Nivelle. The battalions were still over 800 strong, and there had been no need to dilute them with conscripts. The division had not been seriously engaged since Vittoria[1]. This, no doubt, was the reason

[1] This division had been that commanded for so many years by Villatte when it was in the Army of Andalusia. Abbé took it over when Soult reorganized the forces in July. It lost only 700 men in the Pyrenean fighting in August, being in D'Erlon's column and the least used of his three divisions. On the day of San Marcial it had about 300 casualties, on the day of the crossing of the Bidassoa only 20, at the Nivelle under 200. Unlike all the other divisions of the army of Spain, it had never yet suffered a disaster, or experienced a serious casualty-list. It had well over 6,000

why Soult had chosen it for the central blow, on the day when he hoped to obtain his long-deferred revenge on Wellington. Nor was he wrong: Abbé's men fought splendidly—but why were they not supported in time? While they were being used up, brigade on brigade of reserves stood idle on the slopes of St. Pierre d'Irrube waiting for the order to march. The only possible solution would seem to be that Soult intended to win his battle by means of his two flank movements, and was using his central attack to detain in position Hill's main body, rather than to break through it. Yet here, as we shall see, lay his real chance of success.

Deploying in the low ground below the hill of St. Pierre d'Irrube, Abbé's division advanced on each side of the *chaussée*, and on beginning to mount the opposite hill became engaged with Ashworth's Portuguese. Both sides had a thick skirmishing line in front, and the ground was suited for light troops, rather than for formed battalions, being cut up into small crofts belonging to scattered farms and cottages. The neighbourhood of the *chaussée* was 'unhealthy'—each side had a powerful battery bearing upon it—on the other hand the ground on each side gave ample cover. The game started with a steady but slow advance on the part of Abbé's men, who drove the Portuguese uphill on many points, though at others the defence held its own. But sectors on which troops in position find themselves turned on one or both flanks have ultimately to be abandoned, for fear of envelopment—as every one knows who has studied the tactics of the Great War of 1914–18. The defence in the centre was in charge of William Stewart, the divisional commander, who had taken up his position on the high road near the guns. His policy was to continue feeding the Portuguese line with reinforcements from his local reserve, Barnes's brigade, which lay under his hand. First its three light companies were put in—next the 71st whole, to the west of the *chaussée* on the slope where lie the farms of Bidegain and Gelos—then two companies of the 92nd on the high road in front of the hamlet of Marichurry. All these made local counter-attacks, which stopped the French at the particular point where they were pressing for the moment, but had no

bayonets, when nearly all the other divisions in Soult's army had no more than 5,000 and those largely conscripts. Hence its high morale and splendid fighting on December 13th.

permanent effect. Ashworth's Caçadores had lost the farmstead
of Hiriberry on the north side of the road, looking toward the
Étang d'Escouteplouye—a wing of the 50th was sent to help,
and with its aid the copse above Hiriberry, but not the farm
itself, was recovered—an important point, for it was the stay
of the right wing of Stewart's position. Barnes's brigade was
now almost used up—there remained at the top of the hill only
four companies of the 50th and seven of the 92nd.

At this moment things began to look serious, and Abbé's
skirmishers were creeping forward to the southern side of the
chaussée quite far up the hill, for a disaster had happened on the
left. It will be remembered that Stewart had sent forward the
71st to help Ashworth's 18th Portuguese. Unfortunately this
good old regiment was commanded that day by a new colonel,
who had come out to replace the much-loved Cadogan. Sir
Nathaniel Peacock had since his arrival caused some dismay to
his officers in minor affairs, by displaying caution of an exaggerated sort, combined with an absurd magniloquence of language[1].
This morning he showed the white feather in unmistakable style,
not only ordering his regiment to retire, but galloping off himself
to the rear, where Sir Rowland Hill was astonished to find him
beating Portuguese ammunition-carriers, whom he pretended to
be urging to the front—curious work for a colonel. The drawing
back of the 71st caused a nasty gap in the left centre of the line,
through which the French began to press forward, at the same
time that, nearer the road, other bodies of them were well up
the slope, pushing back the wrecks of the Portuguese regiment
next to the 71st, and the remaining wing of the 50th, which
Barnes had sent out to relieve the pressure.

Matters looked unpleasant at 11.30: the centre seemed to be
giving way, and at the same time there came an alarm from the
right. Sir John Byng had posted the Buffs on the Partouhiria

---

[1] 'A coward in action but a tyrant in quarters', says Gavin of the 71st.
He had acted very oddly at the crossing of the Nive, sending his major
with a wing of the regiment to do a job which would naturally have fallen
to himself 'declaring that it was to serve the major that he put him in
the way of danger and distinction'. He got himself returned as wounded
at St. Pierre, having had a ball through the skirts of his coat, 'a wound
which a tailor could cure'. Yet he kept boasting that he would be a major-
general in six months.

ridge, with orders to dispute the passage of the defile below, where the French of Chassé's brigade had to cross the bridge over the Ibarbide brook. Though strengthened by the three light companies of the brigade, the Buffs were pushed back by the very superior numbers of the advancing enemy. Thereupon Colonel Bunbury, in command of the regiment, lost his head[1] and drew back with unnecessary haste, abandoning Vieux Mouguerre to the French, who worked along the ridge till they were brought up by the 57th and the 1st Provisional battalion, standing above the east end of the Escouteplouye ravine. Chassé was almost in the rear of Marichurry and Losterenea, and there was a heavy force coming up behind him—the whole of Foy's division, which Soult had sent on in support of his left attack, bringing forward Maransin's division to the high ground in front of St. Pierre d'Irrube, when Foy had gone forward. Barnes thereupon threw his last reserve, seven companies of the 92nd, into the fight, Colonel Cameron charging down the high road, with one wing, while the surplus companies ran out to oppose the French skirmishers to the left. Again this local counter-attack was successful, and the enemy gave way and fell back for some distance down the slope.

But the crisis was not yet over. Soult sent down a horse-artillery battery from the heights of St. Pierre d'Irrube to the knoll of Ametzonde—the isolated 90-foot hump at the foot of the British position—and under cover of its fire, which ranged all up the slope, Abbé rallied his centre battalions, put in his last reserve, and advanced again. Undoubtedly this was the moment at which the Marshal should have provided heavy infantry supports for the attack; but he only sent down Gruardet's brigade to the low ground behind Abbé, and brought Maransin's division to the brow of the heights, where his main battery was in action. Probably he also sent for Taupin's division from the Marrac camp, but the moment of its crossing the Nive cannot be ascertained. Apparently he was hoping that the decisive blow would be administered by Chassé and Foy, who were now well forward on Stewart's right flank, and contained with great difficulty by Byng's brigade.

[1] Byng had already put a bad mark against him for shirking responsibility, see Henry's *Memoirs*, vol. i. p. 182.

It was certain that he would get no great help from his other flank attack, for Daricau had been completely held up in front of the Chateau of Larralde by Pringle's brigade. The course of the fighting here is somewhat of a puzzle. When Daricau had once extricated himself from the narrow approach round the Étang de Poylo, he had a plain objective before him, and some elbow-room to deploy. But he displayed a great caution, which had nothing to justify it, for he had more than two men to Pringle's one—seven battalions to three, 5,000 bayonets against 1,900—and though to attack a wooded front is tiresome, yet, when battle has been joined, numbers and the power to outflank are all-important. All that he did, according to British witnesses on the spot, was to keep up a long skirmish in the woods, by which he gained half a mile of ground in two or three hours, and to make one serious attack about noon, which failed in front of the chateau. The weakness of his operations is best shown by the fact that Pringle's reserve battalion had only 5 casualties—i. e. cannot have been engaged to any extent, though the other two (1/28th and 1/39th) had 120 between them. Daricau's own loss was not excessive, apparently about 400 or 500 men, so that it is clear that his effort was rather a half-hearted one[1]. Possibly the fact that the division had been somewhat heavily engaged at Barrouillet on the 11th may have had something to do with its conduct on the 13th. At any rate Soult had good reason to be discontented with its collaboration at the battle of St. Pierre.

But though Hill had no reason to fear for his left wing, at noon on the 13th, his centre and right were in a very serious condition—of the three brigades hitherto engaged every unit had been wellnigh used up—some had been in action for four hours—and the casualties had been very heavy. There only remained intact the reserve, Le Cor's two Portuguese brigades, still halted in front of the hill of Horlopo. On the other hand Hill had news that the 6th Division was now closing in on his rear, after its long march from Ustaritz, and that the pontoon-

---

[1] The total losses of Daricau's division in the whole of the Nive battles was 869, but we have to deduct casualties on the 11th, when Daricau's was one of the two divisions used for Soult's afternoon raid on Barrouillet—in which it lost 9 officers and presumably about two hundred of other ranks. I fancy that its losses on the 13th were largely during its retreat, when Pringle came out of his position and attacked its rear fiercely.

bridge opposite Villefranque had just been restored, so that the
3rd Division was beginning to cross. If he could hold out for
half an hour more the game might yet be saved.

Abbé's battalions were now as exhausted as those of the British
2nd Division, and their general must have been maddened by
the non-appearance of the infantry supports for which he had
repeatedly been asking. But for the third time he renewed his
frontal assault, and it reached to the very brow of the hill. Ross's
and Tulloh's gunners, whose fire alone kept the *chaussée* clear,
were now being picked off by the skirmishers on the flanks, so
that the officer in command (Colonel Tulloh had been wounded)
was about to order the batteries to limber up and retire. Barnes,
the brigadier of the 2nd brigade, rode up and forbade retreat—
the guns must keep back the enemy to the last moment, at
imminent risk of capture, for minutes were now precious. Very
soon after Barnes himself was wounded, and Ashworth took over
the command of the troops about the *chaussée*.

A counter-attack was obviously the only method for saving
the day, and Hill put in his last reserve, riding forward himself
at the head of Da Costa's brigade on the left of the *chaussée*,
while Buchan's took the right. But even before they came up
a desperate last push was made with the exhausted troops of the
front line. William Stewart charged south of the road with the
rallied 71st—leading it himself, for its disgraceful colonel had
gone to the rear a second time, with an alleged wound, and its
major had been killed. Da Costa's brigade came up in time to
give good support. Though Byng's position was very dangerous,
Hill told him to leave the Buffs and the light companies alone
opposite Chassé, and to charge with his other two battalions
along the south side of the Escouteplouye ravine. In the centre
the remnants of the 92nd, rallied by its colonel, Cameron of
Fassifern, behind the houses of Losterenea, made a last effort—
there were only a few hundred men left; Cameron, whose horse
had been killed, led them on foot, with the one surviving piper
playing 'Cogag na shee' just behind him, and the tattered
colours flying in the front rank.

The general counter-attack was made by tired men upon tired
men, but the gesture of taking the initiative was once more
successful. All along the line the French gave way, without

356.7   T

allowing the assailants to close—Cameron saw the officer commanding the battalion opposite him on the *chaussée* turn in his
saddle, look back at his shaken following, and give the order to
retreat. Abbé's whole division fell back down the slope, not in
panic flight but sullenly, many men turning back to fire a last
shot uphill. One of these last shots disabled Ashworth, who had
been leading the remnants of his brigade not far from the point
where the 71st charged. It is impossible not to pity Abbé, who
had made such a gallant series of attacks with his own unaided
division, left unsupported by Soult, though the Marshal had
ample reserves in hand. He had lost one of his brigadiers—
Maucomble—59 officers and 1,276 men. No other French division fought that day with anything like the pertinacity of
this unit—indeed the conduct of some of them was extremely
feeble.

It was only when Abbé's line was recoiling down the hill that
Soult ordered Gruardet's brigade of Darmagnac's division, which
had already been brought forward to the foot of the heights, to
resume the attack. The order had no effect—the men refused
to move—the task being an obviously hopeless one when every
one could see the two Portuguese reserve brigades up in line,
and the guns on the *chaussée* pouring salvoes down the slope[1].
D'Erlon's report to Soult glozes matters over, by saying that
the reflux of wounded men and stragglers down the road was
so great that Gruardet's battalions were thrown into disorder
and could not get forward. They must have suffered somewhat from the cannonade, as they had twelve officers and a good
many scores of men killed and wounded.

At this moment Wellington came upon the field, having
crossed the now-repaired pontoon-bridge, for whose completion

---

[1] A similar phenomenon was seen in 1864 in General Grant's army at
the battle of Cold Harbour in Virginia—a number of desperate assaults
on the Confederate trenches having failed to break in, the units detailed for
the last attack grounded arms and refused to budge. 'Though the order
to advance had been given, not a man stirred. The troops stood silent but
immovable, presenting the verdict of the rank and file against the murderous work decided upon by their commander.' Long's *Life of Robert E.
Lee*, p. 348. Cf. Swinton's *Army of the Potomac*, p. 487 ; and Wilkeson's
Life in the Ranks of the Army of the Potomac, p. 109. 'Not a man stirred
from his place—I heard the order given, and I saw it disobeyed.'

he had been waiting for some time. He was not far ahead of two brigades of the 3rd Division—the Portuguese brigade had been left behind to guard the bridge,—and he was able to assure Hill that the 4th Division from near Arbonne, and two brigades of the 7th Division would be with him ere very long. The 6th Division was already up; it had just reached the Horlopo knoll as Abbé's last attack was repelled, having come up from Ustaritz as hard as it could march. 'The battle is all your own', said Wellington to Hill, and he very handsomely directed his lieutenant to finish it for himself, and to take the credit. Sir Rowland, with his usual competence and coolness, resolved to end the game with his own forces, and not to wait till the reinforcements came up.

In the centre matters were clearly finished. On the left Daricau had abandoned his half-hearted attempts on the Larralde height, and was drawing back by the road along which he had come, through the flats. Pringle detached his light companies to follow in pursuit, and, when relieved by a 3rd Division brigade, followed with all his force, not intending of course to close, but to harass the rear-guard, and to pick up stragglers, which he did with some effect. At the end of the day, it is recorded, his foremost skirmishers had got within 800 yards of the fortification of the Camp of Mousserolles.

But on the right Chassé's brigade, supported by Foy, was still in possession of Vieux Mouguerre and of all the heights behind it, as far as the Adour. Hill resolved to drive them off, calculating that they would probably make no great stand, when they saw the central assault completely foiled. The attack was made by Byng's brigade—which had suffered not nearly so much as that of Barnes in the battle of the morning—supported by the five fresh battalions of Buchan's Portuguese. Byng came back with the two battalions which had just taken part in the central advance, picked up the Buffs and the light companies, and started round the head of the Escouteplouye ravine to retake Vieux Mouguerre. This was done with no great loss—and I should gather against no very firm resistance—Chassé's brigade showed that day a casualty-list of only 8 officers and 150 men, though it had been engaged since the early morning. But there was much tougher work on the hill-top behind Vieux Mouguerre,

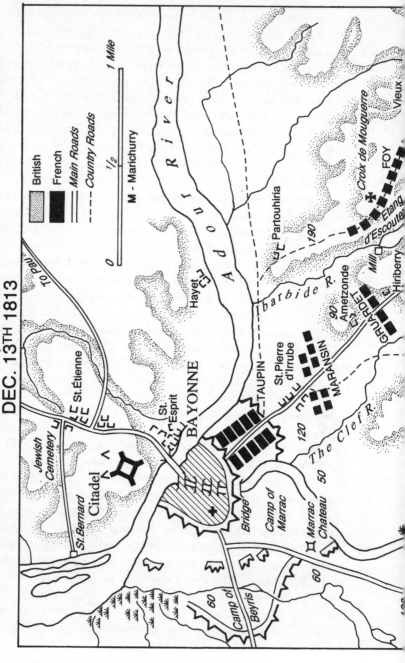

BATTLE OF ST. PIERRE, at the Moment of Hill's Counterstroke
DEC. 13TH 1813

British
French
Main Roads
Country Roads

0 ½ 1 Mile

M - Marichurry

To Paul
St. Étienne
Jewish Cemetery
St. Bernard
Citadel
St. Esprit
BAYONNE
Bridge
Camp of Marrac
Marrac Chateau
Camp of Beyris
60
60
Hayet
Adour River
Partouhiria
190
Ibarbide R.
TAUPIN
St. Pierre d'Irrube
Ametzonde
90
GRUARDET
MARANSIN
120
50
The Clef R.
Croix de Mouguerre
FOY
Vieux
Etang d'Escouter
Mill
Hiriberry

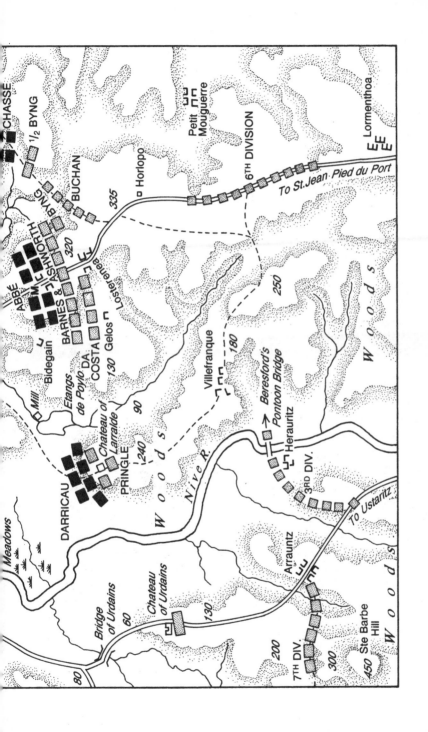

CHASSE

½ BYNG

BYNG

BUCHAN

335

ABBÉ

BIDEGAIN

M°CLORTH
ASHWORTH

320

BARNES &

DA
COSTA

130 Gelos

Losterenea

Horlopo

Petit
Mouguerre

6TH DIVISION

To St.Jean-Pied du Port

250

Lormenthoa

Woods

180

Villefranque

Berestord's
Pontoon Bridge

Herauritz

Etangs
de Poylo

Mill

Chateau of
Larralde

90

PRINGLE

240

DARRICAU

Niver R.

Woods

3RD DIV.

To Ustaritz

Meadows

Bridge
of Urdains

60

Chateau
of Urdains

130

Arraunz

200

7TH DIV.

300

Ste Barbe
Hill

450

Woods

80

where Foy's division was in position, with apparently some
horse-artillery guns, which are specially mentioned in Hill's
dispatch. Foy refused to give way, and the Croix de Mouguerre
summit had to be stormed—Byng, it is recorded, led the assault,
riding in front of his central battalion, the 1st Provisional, with
the King's colour of the 31st in his hand—not a job for a general
in the estimation of the junior ensign from whom he had
snatched it[1]. This was the prelude to a running fight, in which
the French were driven along the heights and ultimately down
to the Adour. Buchan's Portuguese finished the game very
successfully—losing 14 officers and 180 men before it was over,
and capturing a gun.

Soult seems to have considered this advance along the Mouguerre heights as a threat to turn his flank, and threw forward
Maransin's division to cover Foy's and Chassé's retreating
battalions. Hill then sent out, to reinforce Byng, the only troops
not belonging to his own corps which he employed that day—
the 9th Caçadores[2] from the 6th Division—they had a few
casualties, but the greatest part in repulsing this move of Soult's
—which Hill called 'an ill-planned attempt to retake his position'—was played by the artillery, Ross's guns brought forward
to a favourable point bearing on the French left, and perhaps the
6th Division battery also[3]. Maransin's troops had appreciable
losses, 9 officers and presumably well over 100 men, in this last
stage of the fight, and even Taupin's division appears to have
been brought up, as it shows a few casualties on this day, though
Soult says in his report 'that it was not necessary to put the
sixth of my divisions into the line'. The Marshal ends up with
'l'ennemi était arrêté, et le combat traîna sur place', as if he
had repulsed an attack. Hill concludes with the summary that
the enemy had been driven back to his original position. There
can, of course, never have been any intention of attacking the
heights of St. Pierre d'Irrube, for the redoubts and glacis of the
'Camp of Mousserolles' were only half a mile behind the French

[1] According to L'Estrange of the 31st, Ensign Elwyn took the matter
bitterly to heart and would not be comforted by his comrades, maintaining
that it was a slur on his personal honour. L'Estrange, pp. 145–6.

[2] Mentioned as giving aid to Byng on the Mouguerre front in W. Stewart's
Dispatch.

[3] This I am inclined to infer but cannot verify.

fighting line—it would have been useless as well as costly to drive them into those impregnable works.

So ended, at about 3 o'clock in the afternoon, a very hard day's work for Stewart's and Abbé's divisions, which—it cannot be denied—did the best part of the fighting. For on the British side Le Cor's reserve was only used in the last phase of the action, and the 6th Division had an almost bloodless day—while on the French side Daricau's, Darmagnac's, and Foy's divisions never pressed hard, Maransin's made as tardy an appearance as did the British 6th Division, and Taupin cannot be said to have been engaged at all. Hill's losses—1,775 in all—can be accurately calculated. As shown in the tables in the appendix the total came to 17 officers and 340 men killed, 88 officers and 1,276 men wounded, and 2 officers and 52 men missing. Of these 903 belonged to the British brigades of the 2nd Division, 839 to the three Portuguese brigades of Hill's corps, and the trifling balance of 33 to staff, artillery, and the Caçadores of the 6th Division, who made a short appearance at the end of the day. The casualties had been very heavy among the staff—all of whom had exposed themselves recklessly at the critical moments. Le Cor, Barnes, Ashworth, among the generals, were hit, as also Tulloh, commanding the artillery, and three lieutenant-colonels of Portuguese regiments. Stewart remarks that every single one of the aides-de-camp of himself and Barnes and Byng had been disabled—seven in all.

The French losses are more difficult to determine, because Soult's casualty list, as we have remarked before, gives together all losses from the 9th to the 13th of December. But it is possible to get fairly close to their total, which must have been about 3,300. For Abbé and Darmagnac were not engaged on any other day of the Nive fighting, so that their losses of 1,276 and 778 men respectively must certainly belong to St. Pierre; while a good estimate of the casualties of Foy and Daricau—who had fought at Barrouillet—and of Maransin—who had fought at Arcangues—can be arrived at in the following fashion. We have the list of their officer-casualties[1] in the earlier days of battle, the 10th–12th, and separately those of the 13th of December. On the 10th–12th they lost between them 38 officers, on the 13th

---

[1] From Martinien's invaluable tables of course.

69 officers. Applying the same ratio to their total casualties in other ranks, which were in all 2,071, during the whole five days of battle, it would seem logical to deduce that about 800 men of these three divisions fell at Barrouillet or Arcangues, and nearly 1,300 at St. Pierre. This cannot be far wrong; so in all probability Soult's total loss on this field, whose tactics he so wofully mismanaged, must have been about 3,300. Among them were three brigadier-generals wounded—Maucomble of Abbé's division and Mocquery and St. Pol of Daricau's.

We have already commented on Soult's plan and its execution. The strategy of it was excellent—he saw Wellington's danger from an army divided by the Nive, and fell in succession and suddenly on the two divided halves of the enemy's force, with every man that he could gather. But the tactics were deplorable —on the 10th he arranged to attack the Arcangues front with six divisions—and then suddenly threw up his plan, and attacked on the Barrouillet front with four—halting between two opinions, and sacrificing the advantage of the local numerical superiority secured by a tiring night march. Rapid action was all-important, and an unhesitating use of the reserves in which lay his temporary advantage. If he dallied overlong the enemy would have the time to bring up his reinforcements. Full allowance must of course be made for the narrowness of the fronts from which Soult's divisions had to debouch, and for the sodden condition of slopes and ravines after long and continuous rain. But this does not account for all the Marshal's tardiness. When he had succeeded—even if rather late—in closing with the enemy, he refused to put in all his strength, and kept whole divisions in reserve, while his front line was being used up. This was particularly evident in front of Arcangues on the 10th, where (as the table of Taupin's and Maransin's losses shows) no really determined attempt was made to drive in the Light Division. It was still more obvious on the 13th at St. Pierre, when, after Abbé had twice reached the crest of Hill's position, he was refused any reinforcement till it was too late, and the impetus of the attack of the first line had died down. At noon on the 13th Soult had still in reserve, behind Abbé, two and a half divisions of fresh troops—Hill had put in his last man. All this bears out Wellington's standing criticism on his opponent that he was a splendid mover of troops, but that in directing a battle he did not shine. This was as true at Albuera as at St. Pierre. And at Sorauren, in a similar fashion, he lost all the advantage of rapid concentration, by delaying until his adversary had time to call up his distant reserves. When asked which of the Marshals that he had faced was the more dangerous enemy, Wellington gave his vote for Masséna—'Soult never seemed to know how to handle his troops after a battle had begun[1].'

Wellington's strategy in these five days looks, perhaps, a little more risky at first sight than on mature consideration. Undoubtedly his army—after he had left all the Spaniards behind save Morillo's small division—had no such numerical superiority over the enemy as would enable one half of it to face the whole of Soult's concentrated force. And the existence of the Bayonne bridges gave the Marshal a much more easy means of bringing his whole force to one side or other of the Nive, than Wellington possessed. He seems to have felt this lack of numbers himself on the last day of the campaign, when he ordered Freire to send a Galician division to St. Jean de Luz, and O'Donnell (who had just returned convalescent, and superseded Giron in command of the Andalusian Reserves) to push two brigades forward to Itzassou. This he did with extreme reluctance, and only after making elaborate arrangements for feeding these troops from British magazines—he still held that they would plunder if left to their own resources, and that a moderate amount of plundering would rouse the French civil population, and spoil his own game.

But in justification of Wellington it must be remembered that he knew Soult thoroughly, and judged—quite rightly—that the Marshal's conduct of a battle would be feeble, and that he could be contained by the front-line divisions till the reserves had time to come up. He paid great attention to the Nive bridges, and always kept two—sometimes three—divisions close to them, ready to be transferred from one bank to the other at short notice. And, as it turned out, these reserves did arrive as had been intended, even though the swollen river had destroyed one of the bridges on December 12th. Moreover, Wellington was

---

[1] Wellington to Croker. *Croker Papers*, iii. p. 275.

not wrong in considering that some of Soult's troops were no longer up to their old standard in morale—those which fought well were the ones which had escaped lightly in the slaughter of the last four months. Abbé's, Foy's, and Boyer's divisions had none of them been in the thick of the engagement either at the battles of the Pyrenees, the passage of the Bidassoa, or the Nivelle. Those of Soult's units which had been half destroyed, and made up by huge drafts of conscripts, did not distinguish themselves in December, and were not used for any crucial shock by the Marshal, for the best of reasons.

Against bad luck and the mistakes of lieutenants even the best of generals is not immune. All that he can do is to foresee possibilities of danger, and make provision for them. Wellington was not well served by all his subordinates during these five days. Hope allowed himself to be surprised twice, on the 10th and the 11th, by bad disposition of his outposts—and this want of caution was the explanation of the considerable loss of prisoners on each of those days. One cannot imagine anything of the kind happening to Robert Craufurd. And not only was Hope surprised, but he had kept his supports so far from his fighting line that there was serious danger of a break-through at Barrouillet, before they could come up. The flood from the Pyrenees which broke the Villefranque bridge was a chance which might have been foreseen as a possibility—but so long as the Ustaritz bridge stood firm it was vexatious rather than ruinous. If St. Pierre looked like a disaster for one short midday hour, the main cause was an exceptional circumstance, such as had never occurred before—the cowardice of a battalion-commander who withdrew his men in panic, and opened a gap in the line of defence. It is satisfactory to know that Peacock was cashiered: Bunbury, whose conduct on the Mouguerre ridge was considered feeble to the verge of criminality, was allowed to resign his commission, and not publicly disgraced. It will be remembered that the ever-genial Rowland Hill, the most placid as well as the most competent of generals, was only twice heard to swear during his long career in the Peninsula[1]. The first occasion was during the confusion of the night-attack at

[1] See vol. ii. p. 524.

Talavera[1]—the second was at the moment when he met Peacock beating Portuguese munition-carriers half a mile in the rear of the regiment which he had deserted.

[1] These punishments came late—it was only after Orthez that the two colonels disappeared—reference to the War Office having been necessary. There was a third colonel removed at that time—unjustly linked in disgrace with the others, as many thought—an officer whose battalion was a day late for Orthez, owing, as was generally held, to a mere stupid misinterpretation of orders given him.

SECTION XLIII

WELLINGTON ON THE ADOUR

CHAPTER I

WINTER QUARTERS. DECEMBER 1813–JANUARY 1814

THE result of the prolonged fighting south and east of Bayonne on December 9th–12th had been to show that Soult must give up any idea of further offensive operations. He had, as he hoped to do, caught Wellington's army divided by the Nive, and had thrown his whole force first against the section between the Nive and the sea, then against that between the Nive and the Adour. Both attacks, though temporary numerical superiority had been secured in each case, had failed lamentably. If the whole French army could not beat one half of Wellington's, there was no more to be hoped from assaults on the adversary's line. Soult's men had not only suffered heavily in casualties, but were discouraged in spirit. And the British were now strengthening their front by covering the weaker points with *abattis* and crenellating the advanced houses of the hamlets in their line. If the weather had not been so abominable, the Marshal would have thought that Wellington might be contemplating a formal siege of Bayonne on the south side. But of this there was no sign: the Allied troops did not move forward to take up the positions on the plateau facing the camps of Beyris and Marrac, which would have been the necessary preliminary for bringing pressure to bear on the fortress. The other possible design which Soult might attribute to his enemy was that of forcing the passage of the Adour above Bayonne: he did not yet dream that Wellington might force it *below* that fortress, on the side of the sea. The reason why this possible danger hovered before Soult's mind was that at this moment by far the larger portion of his supplies and munitions were reaching him by water. The Adour was his main line of communication with the resources of France. In weather like that of the past month, the direct road to Bordeaux through the pine forests and sandy wastes of the Landes was of comparatively little consequence. It did not pass through a single town of importance, and it was in bad order. The true line of supply was that along the north bank of the Adour running inland to Dax, a considerable road-centre, from which branched out the routes to all the chief towns of Gascony and Languedoc—Mont de Marsan, Montauban, Auch, Pau, Tarbes, Toulouse, as well as the inland route to Bordeaux which was infinitely preferable to the direct line close to the ocean. All land transport being at a discount during this exceptionally rainy winter, Soult was victualling Bayonne and his army mainly by barges which ran down from Port de Lanne, the river-side town at the junction of the Adour and its main tributary the Gave de Pau, under convoy of the twenty-four gunboats which formed the naval equipment of Bayonne. Should Wellington force the line of the Adour anywhere between Port de Lanne and Bayonne, Soult felt that he could no longer feed both fortress and army by the inferior land route, which would then be his only resource, and would be obliged to remove himself inland, leaving Bayonne to its own resources. It would be almost as dangerous if the enemy should establish batteries on the south bank of the Adour, which would command the stream, and compel every passing convoy to run the gauntlet by night. There was one point, the village of Urt, which lies on rising ground, where the south bank so much overlooks the river and the north bank that the Marshal thought that it must be occupied as a *tête-de-pont*, in order that it might be kept out of the enemy's hands.

Accordingly Soult arrayed his army, when the disastrous fighting on the Nive was over, with the purpose of defending the line of the lower Adour. Four divisions—Leval, Abbé, Taupin, and Maransin remained in Bayonne, under the charge of Reille, but were to be ready to move up-stream, if Wellington should approach the Adour anywhere in their neighbourhood. Foy's division was spread out along the river, immediately to the east of Bayonne, with head-quarters at St.-Martin-de-Seignans. In and about Port de Lanne were the divisions of Boyer and Darmagnac. The Marshal established his own head-quarters at Peyrehorade, south of the Adour, which from Port de Lanne up-stream is flowing south and not west—the direction of its lower course, however, is prolonged by its largest tributary the

Gave de Pau, on which Peyrehorade lies. The Marshal was thus at the junction-point of his centre and his left wing, now under Clausel, which lay south of the Adour. It consisted of the division of Daricau—head-quarters at Hastingues—of the whole of his cavalry, for Treillard's dragoons had been brought up to join P. Soult's *chasseurs à cheval*, and of a newly formed infantry division, to which he gave the number 8.[1] This had been constructed by adding to Paris's hitherto independent brigade, which had operated on this side of St.-Jean-Pied-du-Port, the French brigade of Villatte's recently dissolved 'Reserve', and several battalions of the National Guard of the department of the Basses-Pyrénées. The whole made a strong division of 7,000 men, which was placed under the command of General Harispe, a distinguished officer of Basque origin, who was sent round from Catalonia, where he had long served under Suchet. It was reckoned that he would know his native country-side better than any other commander, and could exercise an inspiring influence over the population.

Thus Soult stood to defend the line of the Adour from Bayonne to Port de Lanne with seven divisions, while two others and the cavalry were on Wellington's flank, south of the river, ready to attack him from the side, if he should move forward to force a passage, as the Marshal expected.

Such, however, was not at all the purpose of the British general. For the moment Wellington did not intend to cross the Adour: his first game was to draw Soult's whole army away from Bayonne eastward. And this he intended to do by threatening the divisions on the Marshal's left flank, south of the Adour, and so luring him to detach troops from the accumulation that lay in and about Bayonne. If (or when) Soult transferred the main bulk of his army far inland, and away from the neighbourhood of Bayonne, it would be time enough to think of crossing the river and investing the fortress. And the passage was to be made not between Bayonne and Port de Lanne, but down-stream between Bayonne and the sea.

Meanwhile Wellington made no forward move at all after his victories on the Nive. He remained practically quiescent for the best part of a month. The only movement which he made was a

[1] Vacant since Taupin's original division had been dissolved after the battle of the Nive.

very petty one—Hill was directed to turn Foy's half-battalion out of Urt, so as to leave the enemy no foothold south of the Adour. This was done with no trouble on December 16th. Hill placed some guns above the captured village, to molest the river convoys, and threw up another battery lower down the river's bank. These incommoded, but did not altogether stop, Soult's river transport, which was still carried on by night with some slight losses of boats. Wellington expressed his opinion that he would in the end stop this line of supply altogether, and that Soult would then be obliged to withdraw the heavy mass of troops still left in Bayonne, because he would be unable to feed both them and the large garrison of the place by land transport[1].

For his quiescence in his winter quarters in mid-December, Wellington gave the simplest of explanations to the War Minister at home. 'In military operations there are some things which *can not be done*: one of them is to move troops in this country during or immediately after a violent fall of rain. . . . I should be guilty of a useless waste of men if I were to attempt an operation here during these violent falls of rain. Our operations, then, must be slow: but they shall not be discontinued[2].' In this and other letters he set forth the reasons why, even when the weather should have improved, too much must not be expected from him—such as an instant march on Bordeaux, of which many people in London were talking.

The first was that, in the highest regions of politics and strategy, it was all-important for him to know whether the Allies intended to make peace with Napoleon, on such terms as they thought themselves able to dictate, or whether they were set on dethroning him altogether, as a neighbour who could never be trusted and whom no treaties would bind. There was, so far as he could see, good reason to think that the Continental Powers were still ready to treat with the Emperor. He heard of the Frankfurt negotiations of November, and he would have been still more confirmed in his opinion if he could have looked a couple of months into the future, and foreseen the Châtillon negotiations of February–March 1814. If the Allies were prepared

---

[1] Wellington to Bathurst. *Dispatches*, xi. p. 365, and to Castaños, ibid., p. 364.

[2] Wellington to Bathurst. *Dispatches*, xi. p. 384, December 21.

to leave Napoleon ruler of the old France of 1792, after taking from him Italy, the Rhine provinces, and Belgium as well as Holland, and if he were about to accept those terms, then a campaign with limited objectives was all that need now be contemplated. But he thought himself that the Emperor was so besotted with the idea of his own invincibility that he would refuse all reasonable terms, and fight on. In that case it would be a war *à l'outrance*, and a more drastic military policy would be advisable. In particular it would be quite worth while to think of utilizing the claims of the Bourbons, and of stirring up civil strife in France.

This was one of the most pressing problems presented to Wellington. He was being importuned more than ever both by *émigrés* coming from England, and by crypto-Royalists who slunk into his camp from various directions, to proclaim the restoration of the Bourbons, and to raise the White Banner. But, so far as his personal impressions went, he could see no district where the Royalists were in a majority, and able or willing to take arms in his aid. Discontent with the Napoleonic régime was almost universal: both the lower and the upper classes were prepared to receive the Allied troops with equanimity, so long as they were well treated. And anti-imperialist sentiment went even farther: not only was Wellington getting excellent information from many sources, but the peasants were eager to sell him their cattle, and the mercantile classes to procure him wine and brandy, corn and timber. Most astonishing of all, bankers, not only from St. Jean de Luz but from Bayonne, offered to find him French hard cash in napoleons and francs for British Treasury Bills, on certain conditions. Those which Batbedat, the leading banker in Bayonne, suggested were that he should be given leave to transport from St. Jean de Luz to Bordeaux or other ports, some of the great bulk of British goods which private ships were already bringing in as a commercial speculation[1]. Wellington licensed twenty vessels, on condition

---

[1] See Wellington to Bathurst. *Dispatches*, xi. p. 412. 'He came nominally to settle with me the accounts of various officers, prisoners in France, but really to offer his services to supply the army with articles which the troops might want, and held out hopes of supplying me with money for Bills upon the Treasury.'

that they should not carry colonial produce, but only English merchandise.

Such chances as this of obtaining French money were by no means to be despised. For, as so often before, Wellington found financial problems pressing hard upon him. His whole policy at present was to pay his way in France, and he rightly believed that hard cash was the best form of propaganda, when dealing with a population inclined to be friendly but still suspicious. But the military chest was unpleasantly near the bottom of its resources. It was true that the Home Government had made a special effort to find money for the Peninsular army in 1813. Wellington acknowledged that he had received with regularity over £100,000 in gold or dollars every month, and had got in £121,000 on December 23rd, 'yet it is still incontestable that the army and all its departments (as well as the Portuguese and Spanish armies) are at present paralysed for want of money'. When Marshal Beresford received from Lisbon 200,000 dollars for his Portuguese, Wellington had deducted 50,000 of them for the crying needs of the moment—in order to keep the Spaniards from actually perishing. 'I can scarcely stir out of my house', he wrote, 'on account of the public creditors waiting to demand what is due to them. Some of the muleteers are 26 months in arrears—I have been obliged to pay them in Treasury Bills for part of their demand. These bills, I know, they will sell at a depreciated rate of exchange to *sharks*, who are waiting at Passages and in this town to take advantage of the public distress.' The British infantry were six months in arrears. Although the total sum which had passed through the military chest between January 1st, 1813, and December 31st was £2,572,126—more than double the £100,000 a month of which Bathurst had spoken as the minimum that he could promise yet that was not enough. The size of the army was much greater than in any previous campaign, when all the additional Spanish troops were taken into account. Wellington ended up with the rather unhelpful remark that 'it did not form any part of his duty to suggest measures for relief, but that it was obvious that large and immediate future supplies of money from England were necessary'[1].

[1] Cf. Wellington to Bathurst, December 21, 1813, and January 8, 1814. *Dispatches*, xi. pp. 387 and 425-7.

The Home Government rose to the occasion—in addition to £100,000 sent as a second December instalment, the very large sum of £400,000 was shipped in a single mass in January, despite of the dreadful drain on the Treasury caused by the subsidies to the continental Allies, and a new call for money to support the insurrection which had broken out in Holland. Napier frequently insists on the neglect which was shown by the Liverpool ministry for Wellington's needs—we must rather wonder at the way in which they found guineas and dollars, when all England was living on five-pound and one-pound Bank of England notes, and gold was at a premium of 20 per cent.

Two curious monetary incidents of 1813 are worth noting—one, which has already been mentioned in an earlier chapter, was that the Mint was ordered to strike guineas purely for the army in Spain[1]. The 'military guinea', as it is called by numismatists, was mostly coined from mohurs and pagodas brought all the way from India, where alone in all the world there seemed to be an abundance of the precious metal, procurable at reasonable rates. The whole issue was sent straight to Passages for Wellington's needs. But silver was wanted for all small transactions, and the difficulty about silver was even greater than that about gold.

The other incident finds no place in official records, but may be found mentioned by Napier[2], and related by Wellington himself in one of his conversations with Lord Stanhope[3] in 1831. One of the main difficulties in dealing with the French peasantry was that though they would take gold readily in payment, they would not look at Spanish or Portuguese silver. Most of the cash in the military chest was in dollars. These the Basques and Gascons would not accept, professing to be wholly unacquainted with their real value. It was in vain that Wellington issued a proclamation[4] to the effect that the guinea was worth 25 francs 20 centimes, the dollar 5 francs 40 centimes, and that a franc meant 3 reals 24 maravedis. These were very fair valuations, but the peasantry would take French silver only, and serious difficulty was experienced in getting them to look at dollars and

[1] See above, p. 147.
[2] *Peninsular War*, vol. vi, chapter v.
[3] *Conversations with the Duke of Wellington*, p. 6.
[4] *Dispatches*, xi. p. 364.

reals. The strange solution which Wellington found for the problem was to set up a secret mint of his own at St. Jean de Luz for striking Napoleonic 5-franc pieces. He caused private information to be circulated among the colonels of regiments that there would be an indemnity, and good pay, for all professional coiners who would report themselves at a certain office near his head-quarters. Among the shady characters who had escaped from the dangers of civil life into the army there was a percentage of habitual makers of false money. Forty or fifty of them were found, and were set to work to melt dollars and cast their metal into 5-franc pieces. A strict, and very necessary, supervision was kept over them, to see that they did not fall into their old practice of mixing lead or pewter with good metal, an expert testing every coin. The dies were so well made that the pieces passed quite freely when mixed with genuine French money. Care was, I believe, taken to see that they were not dated 1813 or 1814, but reproduced coins of some years back of the Paris mint.

So silver, like gold, spoke for itself, and transactions became easy. Neither the peasantry nor the townsfolk had by this time any prejudices in favour of the existing government of France. No one knew this better than Soult, whose dispatches are full of complaints as to the impossibility of preventing the country-folk from driving their cattle into the English lines, rather than allowing them to be requisitioned by the French commissariat. The officers who had been sent out to 'galvanize' the frontier population, the prefects of the southern departments, finally the senators whom Napoleon sent down from Paris to play the role of the old Republican 'Representatives on Mission' had all the same report to make. Complete apathy prevailed, except indeed in one or two Pyrenean valleys, where the inhabitants suffered from the incursions of Mina's plundering bands. The people of the Val de Baygorry did take arms to defend their flocks and houses from plunder: but where the provocation did not appear the governmental invitation for a *levée en masse* and a national war fell flat. The word had been passed on from village to village that Wellington's army was behaving well, and that there was good money to be made by furnishing it with provisions.

The absolute failure of the arrangements for filling up Soult's depleted ranks, either by large drafts of conscripts, or by putting battalions of the National Guard into the field, was growing more evident each day. The Emperor, acknowledging the wastage that war was making in the Armies of Spain and of Catalonia, had ordered in November[1] the creation of 40 new battalions of the Line for their reinforcement. They were to be formed by ordering twenty of Soult's and Suchet's regiments, which had more than one battalion in the field, to detach one or two *cadres* of officers and sergeants, sufficient to incorporate and train conscripts from the levies of the southern departments. Ten battalions were to be formed at Bordeaux, ten at Toulouse, ten at Montpellier, and ten at Nîmes. Their establishment was to be very high—1,500 men in each unit. When they had received sufficient training, each was to draft 400 men into the field-battalions of the regiment from which its *cadre* had been drawn, while the remaining 1,100 were to form a reserve unit—suitable at least for line-of-communications or garrison duty. These forty battalions were given the pompous title of the 'Army of Reserve of the Pyrenees'. They never came to any practical use, though Soult complained that they thinned his veteran battalions of several hundred useful officers and non-commissioned officers, who were not easily to be spared. The Bordeaux division, so far from recruiting itself up to 15,000 men, could never reach the figure of 9,000; and in January the Emperor suddenly sent orders that the first six battalions which were formed should march for Orleans, and join the Grand Army. Of the incomplete units that remained, General L'Huillier, after throwing garrisons into Blaye and the other forts along the Gironde, could only collect for the field less than 3,000 ill-trained men, and got hopelessly beaten at the combat of Étauliers, when Wellington sent a detachment to occupy Bordeaux.

The Toulouse division was not quite so useless to Soult; formed by General Travot, it succeeded in putting about 8,000 men into the field by March, almost too late to be of any use. Four of its battalions reached Soult on the evening of the battle of Orthez—the rest were only collected for the battle of Toulouse, during which they were set to man the less assailable parts of the fortifications. The Nîmes division, like that of Bordeaux,

[1] Napoleon to the Minister of War, November 16. *Correspondance*, No. 20,898.

was requisitioned for service with the Grand Army; the Mont-pellier division gave Suchet some 6,000 recruits.

Obviously three months' training would have been inadequate, in any case, to turn absolutely untrained conscripts into troops fit for the battle line, even if they had good and sufficiently numerous *cadres*. But neither the Bordeaux nor the Toulouse battalions had a real three months' training, for an Imperial Decree could not create the muskets and uniforms for them. It was many weeks before any sufficient stock of firearms could be scraped together. All the magazines of France had been emptied to equip the *Grande Armée* of 1813, which perished at Leipzig. Right down to the end of the war in April both L'Huillier and Travot are found complaining that many of their men were still without muskets, and that hardly any had the full regula-tion uniform. Like the 'Marie Louise' conscripts of the Emperor's own army of 1814 they marched for the most part in *capotes* and forage-caps[1].

The fact that while Soult had been promised 20,000 men only something like 14,000 ever were under his orders, came from the revolt against the conscription which swept over the whole south of France. The lads whose turn had come drifted off in parties out of their own districts; some took refuge with the smugglers of the foot-hills of the Pyrenees, some within the English lines, others in the sandy woods of the Landes. The *gendarmerie* tried to hunt them down, and for the most part failed. In some districts the 'refractories', as they were called, formed themselves into bands, lived on the country-side, got arms of sorts, and openly resisted the gendarmes. They mobbed mayors, and terrorized *sous-préfets*. The *émigrés*, who haunted Wellington's head-quarters, pointed out, not without some plausibility, that these rebels against imperialism would furnish the nucleus for an insurgent army, when once the White Banner was raised. This was a doubtful thesis—the 'refractories' did

---

[1] I have searched unfruitfully in the Paris War Office Archives for figures giving the numbers of the battalions actually raised. I can only find that Travot had formed '6th battalions' for the 4th, 9th, and 12th Léger, and 32nd, 47th, 50th, 64th, 81st of the Line, making 3,760 men, besides others incomplete, and that among L'Huillier's '6th battalions' were those of the 102nd, 120th, 66th, and 27th. I imagine that fragments were made into 'provisional battalions'.

not want to fight for any cause at all. They simply constituted 'fermentations séditieuses' as Soult phrases it, in one of his letters to the War Minister[1].

As to the National Guards, of whose service the Emperor had directed Soult to make all possible use, they were with a few exceptions an almost negligible quantity. The only region where they showed any willingness to serve was the mountainous frontier of the Basses-Pyrénées, and here their sole incentive was the determination to keep off Mina's plundering bands. Elsewhere the only battalions that could be kept together in full force were those which were shut up in company with regular troops inside the walls of a fortress. Such was the case with three or four units in St.-Jean-Pied-du-Port, and two more in Bayonne. But when trusted by themselves they disappeared, with or without their muskets. The records in the angry reports of their commanding officers are often ludicrous. When General Harispe called on the National Guards of the Hautes-Pyrénées to concentrate at Oloron, during Wellington's February advance, of 3,300 men under arms only 500 turned up. 'I do not need any munitions for the National Guards', wrote Harispe, 'a panic has seized them, and all have gone home, some taking their arms with them, some throwing them away. In the 3rd Legion, ordered to work at making the fords at Artix impassable, the desertion has been so complete, that the colonel alone remained: and he, seeing no utility in stopping there alone, finally went home also. The Mauléon battalion has gone off to Tarbes, under the pretext that resistance might compromise its native town[2].' The battalion left in Dax, to cover a considerable accumulation of stores, escaladed the ramparts in the rear of the town, when the first of Wellington's cavalry scouts appeared before the gate at its other end. A more absurd case was that of a commandant who, suspecting his men of a wish to abscond, carefully barred the gates of the fort that he was told to defend, but found next morning that he and his sentries at the gate were alone, his flock having spent the night in descending by ropes from embrasures on a steep side of the place[3]. The fact was that

---

[1] So Soult to the Minister of War, Archives de la Guerre, January 28, 1814.
[2] All these incidents, and many others, are cited by Vidal de la Blache, vol. ii. pp. 133–42.   [3] Vidal de la Blache, ii. p. 446.

the whole civil population of the South was determined to make
no attempt to prop up the falling fabric of the Napoleonic
régime. When once assured that Wellington's army would not
behave like cossacks or guerrilleros, they faced its arrival with
complacency—sometimes with polite addresses of welcome and
free drinks[1]. Nothing can illustrate better the tendency of
Napoleon to 'se faire des tableaux'—the fault that he was
always denouncing in his subordinates—than his idea that it
would be possible to raise *levées en masse* in Guienne or Languedoc by appeals to the loyalty of his people. One cannot turn
to account that which does not exist.

The sole element on whose support the Emperor could count
was the old regular army, all the more perhaps because the
soldier was beginning to feel and to resent the attitude of the
civil population. When requisitions were not attended to with
a good grace, and when wholesale trafficking with the enemy was
discovered to exist, both among peasants and among townsfolk,
it was natural that generals should grow ruthless, and that the
private soldier should help himself to the food and wine that
was grudged him by the country-folk. The plundering habits of
Spanish warfare still persisted among the veterans of Soult's old
Army of the South; the Marshal had at first tried to restrain
them by punishments and even executions[2], but the undisguised
ill will which was shown by the civil population in almost every
region tended to make him less careful for its welfare. And if
some effort continued to be made to keep the rank and file under
control, it was more for the benefit of military discipline than
for the protection of the disloyal inhabitants. The soldier and
the peasant were at odds; and, when Wellington's offensive commenced in February, his advanced guards were welcomed almost
everywhere, as guests far preferable to Soult's troops whom they
were displacing. The same thing had been seen in Normandy in
1418, when the French chroniclers confess that the passage of the
well-disciplined army of Henry V was much less burdensome to
the country-side than that of the plundering Armagnacs and
Dauphinois who represented the national cause.

[1] See the case of the refreshments offered to the English cavalry at
Mauléon, to Soult's high wrath, quoted by Vidal de la Blache, ii. p. 135.
[2] See above, p. 141.

It is a curious psychological fact that during these last months of the Peninsular War the French soldiery were far more friendly to the English army than to their own civilian compatriots. It is to this period that there belong most of the extraordinary cases of 'fraternization' recorded by Kincaid, Woodberry, Gleig, Bell, and other English diarists. Not only the old soldiers but the subordinate officers on each side had arrived at a system of signals and warnings, intended to spare unnecessary waste of life in petty outpost bickering. Remembering the sniping and the trench-raids of 1914–18, it is astonishing to read of the way in which English and French dealt with each other in 1813–14, when 'no man's land' did not exist, and sentry-shooting was held to be not only unsportsmanlike but morally disgusting. When a permanent line of outposts had been laid out, no one on either side dreamed of molesting the individual sentry. The two strings of pickets were often within twenty yards of each other, separated sometimes by a stream, sometimes only by a dip in the ground, or a hedge. Individuals at the two opposite sides of a ford or a barricaded bridge grew colloquial—generally in imperfect 'pidgin-Spanish'. Not only would a lieutenant suggest to his French 'opposite number' that his sentry was ten yards too forward this morning, and get him moved back[1], but more responsible officers made bargains on a larger scale. The colonels of the 18th Hussars and the 21st *Chasseurs à cheval* arranged that their men should water their horses in the Joyeuse at alternate hours[2]. A bullock issued as rations to a company of the 26th Ligne having escaped from the butcher and galloped into the English lines, Captain Grignon sent a corporal and a drummer across to the pickets of the 3rd Division with a pathetic petition that his men had not had a meat ration for a week. The British major opposite returned the two hind-quarters of the beast, with a basket of loaves as compensation for the rest, 'beef being not too common in our quarters'[3]. At Arcangues the French officer in charge of the pickets in front of Bassussary sent two bottles of brandy to the subaltern commanding the out-lying party of the 95th with a request for half a pound of tea in return—which was duly pro-

[1] Gleig, p. 201.   [2] Woodberry, p. 144.
[3] Doisy de Villargennes, p. 30.

cured for him[1]. The same British officer once found his own
sentry and the French sentry duly placed, but the rest of the
two pickets seated in a ruined house between the lines, amicably
discussing a find of wine-bottles, which had been discovered in
its cellar. On his arrival both parties saluted him and returned
to their proper posts. On Christmas Eve 1813 the privates of
a company of the 95th holding the line in front of the Chateau of
Urdains 'clubbed half a dollar each' and sent a man into the
French lines to purchase brandy. The messenger succeeded in
buying it in plenty, but sampled it so freely that the French
sentry on the high road had to shout to the English sentry
opposite to send a party to carry him in, as he was lying drunk
and incapable by the wayside[2]. George Bell of the 34th succeeded in procuring from Bayonne[3] a roll of grey cloth to make him
a new pair of regimental breeches. I can, however, hardly credit
the tale told by this same officer of the Irish sentry who was
found with a French and an English musket on his two shoulders,
guarding a bridge over a brook on behalf of both armies. For he
explained to the officer going the rounds that his French neighbour had gone off on his behalf, with his last precious half-dollar,
to buy brandy for both, and had left his musket in pledge till
his return. The French officer going his rounds on the other side
of the brook then turned up, and explained that he had caught
his sentry, without arms and carrying two bottles, a long way to
the rear. If either of them reported what had happened to their
colonels, both sentries would be court-martialled and shot.
Wherefore both subalterns agreed to hush up the matter
altogether[4]!

Stagnation continued all along the front till the new year of
1814 came round. It was shortly after that date that Wellington received news which made it possible for him to prepare for
future movement, though for the present the weather and the
state of the roads forbade an advance. By January 10th he was
aware that the Austrian, Prussian, and Russian armies had
crossed the Rhine on December 22nd, and that a general invasion of France was in progress[5]. He did not particularly

---

[1] Costello, p. 263.   [2] Harry Smith, i. p. 285.
[3] *Memoirs of Sir George Bell*, i. p. 141.
[4] Ibid., p. 133.   [5] *Wellington Dispatches*, xi. p. 435.

approve of the scheme of operations which was reported to him,
being of opinion that the Allies should have marched in mass
upon Paris on a comparatively short front, and not have made
large detachments for flanking operations through Switzerland,
aimed at Lyons, or thrown so many Austrian troops into Italy.
However the die was apparently cast, and it had become possible
to think of utilizing the Bourbons for stirring up civil war in
France. 'I agree with you about Louis XVIII in the existing
situation of affairs. But if you cannot make peace with Bonaparte this winter, we must *run at him*, in the spring, and it would
be advisable to put forward one of the Bourbons in that case.'
Wellington added that he was certain that the Emperor had no
intention of making peace. But what if the French people forced
him to offer peace, and the Allies accepted his terms of submission? The position of any partisans of the old régime who had
taken arms by the permission of the Allies would then be deplorable, and the Allies would be responsible for them. So it was
to be hoped that Bonaparte would fight on to the end, and be
crushed.

Meanwhile, however, at this particular moment it was not the
head of the elder branch of the Bourbons, at Hartwell House,
Buckinghamshire, who was engrossing Wellington's attention,
so much as Ferdinand of Spain, the prisoner of Valençay, who
had suddenly become, after five years, an important political
personage. For Napoleon's last vain attempt to get out of his
Spanish entanglements was now in progress.

SECTION XLIII: CHAPTER II

THE 'TREATY OF VALENÇAY'.
NOVEMBER 1913–JANUARY 1914

WE have seen in an earlier chapter that Napoleon's dream of a dependent kingdom of Spain ruled by his brother had vanished perforce, after the news of the battle of Vittoria reached him at Dresden in July. Joseph and Jourdan had been disgraced, and the 'intrusive king' had been stripped of his guards and his title, arrested, and finally consigned, under a strict sentence of boycotting, to the solitudes of Mortefontaine[1].

Between July and November the Emperor had not much attention to spare for the Iberian Peninsula; he had given Soult *carte blanche*, and directed him to protect the French frontier by taking a vigorous offensive. The results of that policy had been seen at Sorauren and San Marcial. When the Emperor could find a moment of leisure from the problems of his own disastrous campaign in Saxony, he could only write to the Duke of Dalmatia that with such a splendid army at his disposition, he ought to have done better. But, even now, the order was 'attaquez toujours'—and so Soult did, with small success, at Arcangues and Barrouillet and St. Pierre d'Irrube.

But after getting back to Paris in November, with the surviving wrecks of his army left to guard the Rhine, Napoleon had time to develop a most infelicitous political scheme, which displayed a singular want of appreciation both of the mentality of Ferdinand VII and of that of the Spanish nation.

The prisoner of Valençay he regarded as a mere worm. He had not seen him since the treachery at Bayonne in 1808, and had then formed the impression that he was a creature destitute of any instincts save that of self-preservation. And it must be confessed that the captive's conduct had seemed to justify such a conception of him—his frequent complimentary letters to his oppressor, and his refusal to escape when the trap of the false Baron Kolli was set for him[2], seemed to mark

---

[1] See vol. vi. p. 552.   [2] See vol. i. p. 18.

him as a hopeless being, destitute alike of self-respect and of initiative.

This was to misjudge Ferdinand. He had his private feelings, though he had been so careful to conceal them, alike when he was an oppressed and persecuted heir-apparent in 1806–8, and when he was a prisoner under guard in 1808–13. Ferdinand was quite capable of hatred; he had a long memory, and he could feel as strong a passion for revenge as other men. The Spanish Liberals of his later years painted him as a Machiavelli, with an occasional dash of Nero in his composition. This was a gross exaggeration; but he was undoubtedly unscrupulous, hard-hearted, selfish to a degree unusual even among Bourbon princes, and revengeful when he got a chance. Those who were to know him, during his kingship in Spain, came to understand that he would sign anything in the way of treaties or constitutions, without the slightest intention of abiding by his signature or his oath. Also that he had a long memory for slights and insults.

When Napoleon in November 1813 took up the idea of offering Ferdinand freedom and a restoration to the throne of his fathers, on condition that he would sign a treaty advantageous to France, he did not understand either that the captive was perfectly prepared to sign anything, with no intention of abiding by his signature, or that he had a very justifiable personal hatred for his Imperial gaoler, which would lead him to take every opportunity of harming him, cheating him, or ruining him. If some queer chance had thrown Napoleon into Ferdinand's power after Waterloo, I do not think that his lot would have been an enviable one. There would have been five years of degrading hypocrisy and hateful servility to be expiated. For Ferdinand, though he grovelled when he thought it necessary, did not like grovelling.

And if the Emperor misjudged Ferdinand's character, much more did he misjudge the general mentality of the Spanish patriot party. He knew them to be factious, short-sighted, and obstinately suspicious of their British allies. But he failed to recognize that no bargains which he might offer them would cause them to forget the treachery of Bayonne, the *Dos Mayo*, and the five years of devastation and slaughter that followed.

In this case, as in many others, he did not realize how much he was hated. Nor did he recognize the fact that with many people revenge is a stronger motive than gain or personal interest.

To Napoleon's mind the situation that presented itself in November 1813 was that he had still two veteran armies in the south, numbering over 100,000 men, even after all their recent losses. And these were now the only veteran troops that he possessed anywhere; they would not melt under his hands, like the conscripts whom he had been using in Saxony and Silesia. They would be invaluable to stem the oncoming flood of the armies of Schwarzenberg and Blücher. And to redeem them he had certain pledges still in his hands—he could offer Spain firstly her captive king—a gift whose worthlessness he well appreciated—and secondly all the fortresses of the East Coast from Saguntum to Figueras, which Suchet's garrisons were still occupying, not to speak of the isolated Santoña on the Bay of Biscay, where Lameth was holding out successfully against the unskilful attacks of Mendizabal's engineers. Ferdinand must undoubtedly be desirous of his liberty, and the Spaniards were as certainly desirous of recovering him. What price would they pay for him, and for the evacuation of the Valencian and Catalan fortresses? The Emperor resolved to ask for no less than the withdrawal of Spain from the war, to be accompanied by the removal of all British and Portuguese troops now on Spanish soil, viz. Clinton's army in Catalonia, and the detachments still left at Cadiz and Cartagena. But these were trifles—the main point was that Spain was to deny itself as a base of operations to Wellington; he would lose his ports of supply at Passages, St. Sebastian, and Santander, and would be left in occupation only of his recent conquests in France between the Bidassóa and the Adour, with the single small harbour of St. Jean de Luz as his sole point of communication with the fleet and the resources of England.

It is a proof of Napoleon's incurable optimism, when his own interests were concerned, and his incredible underrating of the pride and rancour of his adversaries, that he believed for some weeks that the bargain could be carried out, and began to send Soult and Suchet elaborate instructions, as to what they were to do when they saw the Spanish armies retiring from their front and deserting the British. A perusal of his orders shows that he was not merely sending hypothetical directions for a possible change, which might never occur, but laying down plans for a certainty. The Spaniards were to withdraw, and then Soult and Suchet were to dispatch the bulk of their troops to join the Grand Army in the north.

The Emperor's intrigue commenced, of course, at Valençay, for Ferdinand was, in his opinion, an easy person to browbeat and deceive. Having been fed on the stories of the *Moniteur* for five years, and sedulously kept from all communication with patriot Spain, he would probably sign any terms that were offered him, in return for liberty and the restoration of his stolen crown.

Accordingly La Forest, formerly ambassador at Madrid, came to Valençay on November 17th and opened up his master's proposals to the captive. It was a marvellous break in the daily life of the place, where Ferdinand had been so long engaged in the dullest of routine—interminable church services, a little ecclesiastical embroidery (in which he had become an expert), some experiments in chemistry, some shooting in the park, and limited rides in its avenues, with the occasional composition of adulatory letters to the Emperor as intellectual diversion. His uncle Don Antonio had found a more interesting employment in censoring the large library of Talleyrand. While the latter was in disgrace with his master, in 1809–12, the old prince had gone through the whole of the books, and inked out all lascivious and obscene passages in the Latin, French, and Italian literature, occasionally removing whole pages with a pen-knife. He had also torn out a number of lewd engravings and consigned them to the fire.

La Forest laid before Ferdinand, who received him seated between Don Carlos and Don Antonio, a short letter of Napoleon;
'My Cousin,
'The present political condition of my empire makes me desirous to put an end to the problems of Spain. England is fomenting in that country anarchy, Jacobinism, the annihilation of the monarchy and of the nobility, with the object of setting up a republic. I cannot be indifferent to the ruin of a nation so

near my own border, and with which I have so many maritime interests in common. I am therefore desirous to remove all pretexts for the English intervention, and to re-establish those bonds of friendship and neighbourly affection which long united our two nations. I send Count La Forest as my envoy: your royal highness may put confidence in all that he says.'

The captive king retired to his apartment, read the letter, and returned to say that he must talk over its contents with his two relatives. La Forest might return next morning for a discussion of the subject. On the 18th, therefore, the count was again received, and set forth the arguments with which his master had primed him. No more preposterous farrago of lies was ever put forward by a diplomatist. Ferdinand was invited to believe that the British Government—George Prince Regent, Lord Castlereagh, Wellesley the ambassador, and Wellington the Generalissimo—had planned the setting up of a Jacobin republic in Spain. If this wicked plan should miscarry, they had a scheme for giving the crown to Carlotta of Portugal, the wife of John of Braganza Prince of the Brazils, to the detriment of her three brothers Ferdinand, Carlos, and Francisco d'Assis ! These nefarious designs must be foiled. Apparently Napoleon and his mouthpiece La Forest thought it conceivable that the captive of Valençay had been so thoroughly cut off from all knowledge of the outer world that he would swallow all this stuff, being ignorant of the fact that the British Government had spent untold pains in checking the Liberal party in the Cortes, and putting off the claims of Carlotta. Ferdinand was not so wholly destitute of external information as his gaoler conceived, and he prepared to play a most skilful, if unscrupulous, game[1].

After La Forest had finished what was apparently a very long harangue, to which no interruption was given by his three auditors, Ferdinand made the cautious reply that an answer to such a serious proposition required mature consideration. On the following day (November 19) La Forest made the definite proposal that the Emperor was ready to recognize his captive as

[1] For all this see Toreno, iii. pp. 307–8 ; Escoiquiz, *Idea Sencilla*, pp. 95–6 ; Vidal de la Blache, ii. pp. 12–16.

King of Spain, if he were given guarantees that the English
should be removed from his realm. Ferdinand replied that his
personal pledge would be of no value, without the formal
approval of the Regency and the Spanish nation. 'But', asked
La Forest, 'if he were restored to Spain, would he undertake that
it would be as the friend and not the enemy of the Emperor?'
To which the cautious reply was that if the Emperor wished for
the friendship of Spain, he had better open negotiations with
the Regency, and allow its envoys to come to Valençay, where
they could concert in common a joint answer from the king and
the nation of Spain. This would not have suited Napoleon's
intentions, since he was well aware that the Cortes had declared
all acts or documents of the king, while he was in France, to be
null and void.

Finally Ferdinand presented to the French envoy a formal
answer, dated November 21st, to the Emperor's letter, in which
he set forth his satisfaction at being honoured with the interesting propositions laid before him. But being kept from all
knowledge of the actual condition of Spain, he was unable to
make a suitable reply. He would only be in a position to enter
into the subject if he were allowed to take counsel with the
Cortes and the nation. His duty was to consult the interests of
Spain, not those of France or of England. Meanwhile he had
spent five years in Valençay, but was prepared to spend his
whole life there if it were necessary.

This was a sort of *non possumus* reply, intended to show the
Emperor that he could not hope to get any profit out of the
mere attempt to screw a signature to a dictated treaty out of
a king still in captivity. Ferdinand wanted to get back to
Madrid—he did not really suppose that Napoleon would allow
a deputation from the Cortes to come to Valençay, or that the
Regency would have the least intention of sending one thither.
The proposition was of course wholly useless to La Forest, who
replied with another, for which he had already received authorization from Maret, the Minister for Foreign Affairs at Paris,
and presumably from Napoleon himself. Ferdinand might be
allowed to take counsel not with emissaries of the Regency, but
with Spanish notables of his own party, now in exile with him
in France. The most prominent of them was José Carvajal, Duke

of San Carlos, Ferdinand's old confidant in his intrigues of 1807[1], who arrived at Valençay with suspicious promptitude on the day after Ferdinand had given his formal letter to La Forest. He had been interviewed by Maret at Paris and afterwards by the Emperor himself, and had been indoctrinated (as the French minister thought) with the idea that he, his master, and all their imprisoned friends could get home only by accepting Napoleon's terms. The Canon Escoiquiz, who had acted as Ferdinand's secret secretary in the old days of Godoy's domination, turned up a little later[2]. Also José Palafox, released unexpectedly from a long and dreary captivity in the donjon of Vincennes, and somewhat later General Zayas, one of the captives of Suchet's Valencian campaign of 1812.

San Carlos duly laid before Ferdinand Napoleon's confidences to him—the Spanish crown should be restored, the French alliance secured by the marriage of the captive king to Zenaïde, the eldest daughter of the *Rey Intruso* Joseph[3], the 100,000 Spanish soldiers prisoners in France should be restored to liberty, the Catalan fortresses evacuated, all in return for the king's pledge to break the British alliance, to see the British troops removed from Catalonia, Cadiz, Cartagena, and other points where they were to be found. Moreover, complete pardon and amnesty should be granted to all the *Afrancesados*. On the following day (November 22) La Forest produced the draft of the famous Treaty of Valençay, in which all these points were formulated.

There followed nearly a fortnight of haggling—Ferdinand suggesting all sorts of difficulties. Would the Regency and the Cortes consent to the formal repudiation of their treaty of alliance with England? Only, he thought, if the personal influence of a king present in Madrid were brought to bear upon them. The marriage with Zenaïde Bonaparte would be offensive to Spanish public opinion. It would be necessary to communicate to the British Government—and also to those of Russia and Sweden, with whom treaties had been made by the Regency—the formal repudiation of those engagements. Would

---

[1] See vol. i, p. 22.
[2] Ibid., pp. 19–20.
[3] The poor child was only 14 years of age.

the Cortes tolerate such a sudden *volte-face*? And what would be the consequent action of the British Government, and of the Spanish Liberal party? With feigned reluctance Ferdinand let himself be talked over by La Forest, and persuaded to take the political risks. Only he must be allowed to go to Madrid in person, to impose the necessity of the agreement on his subjects. La Forest suggested that, if Ferdinand himself were permitted to depart, his brother Carlos should remain behind as a hostage. The king caught his brother in his arms, and sobbed, with tears in his eyes, that they should never be separated. Whereupon the French envoy gave way—the histrionics on both sides assuming the most pathetic aspect[1].

On December 10th La Forest produced, and Ferdinand assented to, the formal revised version of the Treaty of Valençay, and San Carlos was given his passport for Madrid—he was to go by way of Gerona, where Suchet would pass him on to Copons, a well-known royalist and no friend to liberal ideas. A few days later José Palafox was sent off with a second copy of the Treaty, in case San Carlos should miscarry on the road.

There cannot be the slightest doubt that Ferdinand signed the Treaty with every intention of repudiating it, the moment that he should have escaped through the French lines. For several of the stipulations were personally offensive to him in the highest degree. Of the fifteen clauses the important ones were: (A) No. VI, which obliged Ferdinand to evict, from all points of Spanish soil where they were at present stationed, all British troops. (B) No. VII, which stated that the French garrisons should only evacuate the Catalan and Valencian fortresses when the British had departed. (C) clause VIII, whereby Spain undertook to support the 'Freedom of the Seas', i. e. to repudiate the existing British 'Orders in Council' relating to the Continental Blockade. (D) clause IX, whereby Ferdinand promised to all the late supporters of King Joseph not only personal pardon and immunity, but the retention of all honours, rights, and properties which had been conferred upon them in Joseph's time. (E) clause XIII secured to the old King Charles IV and his Queen the monstrous pension of 30,000,000 reals *per annum*, i.e. no less

---

[1] For details of the negotiation, see Vidal de la Blache, ii. pp. 20–1.

than £320,000 a year. They were at present living at Rome, still accompanied by the now somewhat bloated and battered Godoy[1].

On hearing of the Treaty, King Joseph wrote to his brother, offering to make things easy by a formal abdication of his claim to the Spanish throne. The Emperor replied in brutal terms— 'I do not require any abdication of yours: you are no longer King of Spain. I have given up the country altogether, and only want to get it off my hands, and to be able to utilize my armies[2].'

San Carlos started from Valençay on December 11th, 1813—in the middle day of the battles of the Nive—but having to go by the circuitous route Perpignan–Gerona–Saragossa, he only reached Madrid on January 4th. He took with him not only the actual Treaty of Valençay, but private instructions which were, in reality, far more important. 'If the Regency and the Cortes were loyal and well-disposed, and not so inclined to Jacobinism, as His Majesty recently supposed, he might tell the Regents that it was his royal will that the Treaty should be ratified, but only so far as was consistent with the relations existing between Spain and the Allied Powers leagued against Napoleon, and in no other fashion. If the Regency, without compromises, ratified the Treaty, they might inform the British Government that His Majesty was intending to declare the instrument null and void the moment that he got back to Spain, because of the evils which his confirmation of it would bring on the nation. But if the Duke should find the Regency and the Cortes dominated by a Jacobin spirit, he was not to make the above private communication to the Regents, and was simply to urge the ratification of the Treaty—His Majesty reserving to himself the right to continue the war with France or not, according as the interest and good faith of the nation might dictate[3].'

It is evident, therefore, that Ferdinand had no intention whatever of carrying out his pledge to Napoleon, and intended to repudiate the Treaty the moment that he had got out of the

---

[1] He had received permanent injuries—especially to one eye, during the tumult of Aranjuez, and had grown enormously stout.

[2] Lecestre's *Correspondance inédite de Napoleon*, under January 7, 1814.

[3] See Toreno, iii. p. 312, and Appendix, p. 391.

power of his gaoler. But its reception by the Regency was of such a nature that neither of the alternative orders given to San Carlos could be put into operation. On January 8th the duke was given a formal document, signed by the old Cardinal Bourbon, president of the Regency, and by Lujando, the Foreign Minister, setting forth the joy which the sight of His Majesty's signature had given to all his loyal subjects, and the satisfaction caused by the prospect of his possible return, but citing the decree of the Cortes dated on January 1st, 1811, which stated that no treaty, convention, or proclamation signed by His Majesty while in captivity should have any validity, as the nation considered that he would be acting under duresse, and would regard such documents as null and void. A similar response was given to José Palafox when he turned up with the second copy of the Treaty on January 28th.

Meanwhile the Regency intended to lay the Treaty before the Cortes; San Carlos remained in Madrid for a few days, explaining (no doubt) to prominent members of the *Serviles* faction that his master did not intend to abide by his promises. But he was accused by the Liberals of being the bearer of a disgraceful offer of peace, suffered much unpopularity, and thought it well to return to France, which he reached before January was ended.

On February 2nd the Regency laid the Treaty before the Cortes, and a debate of two days followed. By a practically unanimous vote the assembly declared the Treaty destitute of any validity, and contrary to the pledges given by Spain to Great Britain and the other Allied Powers. The Liberal majority then added a declaration of a very unwise sort, certain to offend the King if ever he should gain his liberty. It stated that if and when Ferdinand should appear in Spain, he should be required to sign the Constitution of 1811 before being permitted to resume his royal rights, and that the Regency should send orders to this effect to the generals of the armies on the frontier, and should lay down an itinerary for His Majesty to observe on his journey to Madrid. These provisions roused an opposition among the *Serviles* which was ominous of future trouble. Juan Lopez Reina, deputy for Seville, rose to tell his colleagues that Charles IV had been absolute king in Spain, that his son inherited all his rights, and that on reaching Spanish soil Ferdinand became *de jure* an absolute king also. To impose conditions on him would be unconstitutional, and offensive. Reina was shouted down, and not more than twenty of the *Serviles* voted against the clause. But his speech should have been a warning to the Liberal party of approaching civil strife. Ferdinand would be sure of supporters, if he refused to swear to the Constitution.

All through the months of December and January Napoleon —strange as it may seem—had been under the expectation that the Spanish Government would ratify the Treaty of Valençay. He thought that the Cortes was so discontented with the British alliance, and so desirous of peace, that it would welcome the agreement, and he imagined that Ferdinand would not only promise anything to obtain his liberty, but would keep his promise when released. He judged him anxious above all things to destroy the Liberal party in the Cortes, and to shake off the British yoke. No allowance was made for the fact that the Valençay Treaty contained things abhorrent to every member of the Cortes, *Servile* or Liberal. The proposal to restore the *Afrancesados* to all their offices and their properties—many of them got by the confiscation of the lands, goods, and employ-ments of good patriots—provoked wild indignation. So did the monstrous pension allotted to King Charles IV, i. e. to his wife and Godoy. But these, after all, were minor considerations com-pared with the deep-rooted hatred of Napoleon himself. Why should matters be settled for his convenience, when his power was at last broken, and when Spanish armies had penetrated into France? As to Ferdinand, he was as rancorous in his hatred of the *Afrancesados* as were his subjects: and this he showed by his conduct after his restoration. It was long years before one of them was allowed to return to Spain. But though he hated the 'Constitutionalists', he hated Napoleon more. He thought, from what he could learn of the politics of his kingdom, that he would be able to crush the Liberals, without accepting the odious bargain with the Emperor, on whom he was determined to avenge himself. And events showed that his views were correct.

Meanwhile Napoleon had actually been making preparations for drawing off the greater part of the armies of Soult and Suchet

to the main theatre of war, on the vain hypothesis that the
Spanish Government would ratify and carry out the Treaty, and
that Wellington, with his English and Portuguese troops alone
remaining, and with his base in Spain taken from him, would be
unable to prosecute the war in France. He thought it likely that
the British Government would move the whole army round to
Holland—a project which had actually occurred to Lord
Bathurst and Lord Liverpool when the Dutch insurrection broke
out[1]. On December 25th we find the Emperor writing to his
minister in Italy, Melzi, Duke of Lodi, 'I have made an arrangement with the Spaniards which gives me the free use of my troops
in Aragon, Catalonia, and Bayonne. Do not let this out: it is
at present news for you alone[2].' On January 10th, believing
San Carlos to have reached Madrid by this time, he dictated to
his Minister of War orders for Soult to send half of his cavalry
and of his horse artillery to Orleans without delay. And a
satisfactory treaty having been concluded with 'Prince Ferdinand', 10,000 men of infantry were to be got ready to start for
Paris 'by post' the moment that the retreat of the Spanish
armies across their own frontier should be confirmed. When
their disappearance should be certainly ascertained, the other
half of the cavalry and another large force of infantry should
be directed on Orleans[3].

Soult replied that though he was making every endeavour to
get news, he could see no sign of the withdrawal of the Spaniards.
If the Cortes and the Regency accepted the Treaty of Valençay,
the English would no doubt be reduced to impotence. But
what if they did not, and the French army in front of Wellington
was reduced before his eyes in the fashion directed by these
orders? There would not be left a sufficient force to contain
him—he could march on Bordeaux, and do anything he might
please. The Emperor, no doubt, must have taken into consideration this possibility[4].

[1] See Bathurst to Wellington, December 10. *Supplementary Dispatches*,
viii. pp. 414–15.
[2] Napoleon *Correspondance*, No. 21,039.
[3] Clarke to Soult, January 10, 1814. And orders dictated by Napoleon
(in Lecestre's *Correspondance inédite* under the same date).
[4] Soult to Clarke, January 14.

Nevertheless Soult obeyed the first section of the imperial command. He sent off on the Orleans road half his cavalry—the three heavy dragoon brigades of Sparre, Ismert, and Ormancy, under General Treilhard, with their three horse batteries—over 3,000 sabres with 18 guns. They began their march on January 16th, 1814. He reported to Clarke that he had also collected a column of 10,000 infantry, composed of the divisions of Boyer and Leval[1], which was ready to march when the retirement of the Spaniards should be reported: at present they showed no signs of moving.

Three days later Soult received from the War Minister the order to start off the infantry column, without waiting for the confirmation of the news of the ratification of the Treaty of Valençay. The divisions marched accordingly on January 21st by way of Peyrehorade and Montauban, taking with them their two divisional batteries of field artillery. The force made 17 battalions in all—11,005 bayonets. The War Minister directed Soult to draw in, as some compensation, all the reserve battalions under Travot which were in formation at Toulouse. None of them reached him before February, when about 3,700 raw troops came up, as he was retreating during the battle of Orthez.

Thus Soult was deprived, by January 21st, of 14,000 veteran soldiers. His army had already been enfeebled not only by the losses in the battles of the Nive, but by the disbanding of his Spanish brigade, by the desertion of the Nassau and Frankfurt German battalions, by the departure of the Italian brigade to join the Viceroy on the Adige, and by the drafting off of the twenty *cadres* on which the reserve divisions of Bordeaux and Toulouse were to be built up. Soult had now only seven infantry divisions instead of nine, one cavalry division instead of two, and 77 field-guns instead of 112, disposable for active operations. Adding the 8,000 men of the garrison of Bayonne, and three regular battalions in St.-Jean-Pied-du-Port—the National Guards need not be taken into consideration—the gross total of his troops was now only 60,000 men instead of 87,000, at which it

---

[1] In Boyer's division there was a change of units—it left behind Menne's brigade [118th and 120th Ligne] and took away instead Chassé's brigade of Darmagnac's division [16th Léger and 8th and 28th Ligne].

had stood on December 1st. And of these 10,000 were locked up
in the garrisons, and only counted as useful in that Wellington
would have to tell off a considerable force in order to contain,
i.e. blockade or besiege them[1].

Thus the French Army of the Pyrenees was, because of the
Emperor's absurdly optimistic reliance on the Treaty of Valençay,
reduced to a force somewhat smaller than Wellington's own
Anglo-Portuguese divisions, leaving the whole of his Spaniards
as a surplus. Obviously the latter could be used, if Wellington
chose to take the risk, for the siege of Bayonne, leaving all his
own troops free for field operations. He had in January some
67,000 men of all ranks, of whom 44,000 were British and 23,000
Portuguese[2]. Of the Spaniards only Morillo's and Carlos de
España's men were at this time at the front—two much de-

[1] The figures appear to have stood as follows, deducting sick and
detached:

	Dec. 1, 1813.	Jan. 20, 1814,
1st Division, Foy	5,600	4,600
2nd Division, Darmagnac . .	5,900	5,500
3rd Division, Abbé . . .	6,300	5,300
4th Division, Taupin . . .	6,000	5,600
5th Division, Maransin . . .	5,200	5,000
6th Division, Daricau . . .	5,500	5,200
7th Division, Leval . . .	4,700	— gone north
8th Division, Harispe . . .	non-existent	6,600
9th Division, Boyer . . .	6,400	— gone north
Paris's detached Brigade . .	3,800	— absorbed
Reserve of Villatte . . .	5,400	non-existent
Heavy Cavalry, Treilhard . .	3,200	— gone north
Cavalry of P. Soult . . .	5,300	3,800 one brigade gone north
Garrison of Bayonne . . .	7,000	8,800
Garrison of St.-Jean-Pied-du-Port .	1,600	2,400
Artillery, sappers, train, &c. . .	10,000	7,300
	81,900	60,100

[2] Vidal de la Blache, usually so accurate, has fallen into an error in his
vol. ii. p. 212, by understating Wellington's army at only 38,000 British
and 20,000 Portuguese, from not seeing that the return of January 16th
which he quotes from *Supplementary Dispatches*, xi. p. 513, includes only
'effective rank and file'. It does not include officers, sergeants, drummers,
nor any artillery. For these an allowance of over 9,000 must be made.
A few days later a return of January 28th (*Supplementary Dispatches*,
xi. p. 546) shows that 3,000 officers, 4,000 sergeants, and 1,500 drummers
were present with the army, who do not appear in the 'effective rank and
file' return of January 16th.

pleted divisions down to 4,000 men apiece. The Army of Reserve of Andalusia whose two divisions had shrunk to 9,000 bayonets was just leaving the Bastan, and some of Freire's Galicians were still beyond the Bidassoa. It will be remembered that Longa's troops had been sent back to Castile in disgrace, while Mendizabal's division was blockading the French garrison of Santoña. Freire had with him therefore only the divisions of Del Barco, Espeleta, and Marcilla, all in a sad condition for want of food and winter clothing. At the end of the year they had between them only 13,000 men under arms, and 6,500 in hospital—these last were dying, like flies in autumn, from lack of vitality and warmth. For operations in the field it would not have done to take forward Mina's Navarrese irregulars, who were employed in blockading Jaca and making occasional threatening movements against St.-Jean-Pied-du-Port and the French Pyrenean valleys. They were in all 8,000 strong. The '3rd Army', long under Del Parque but now commanded by the Prince of Anglona, had its quarters by Wellington's orders in Tudela, Logroño, and other billets along the Ebro. It was destitute of cavalry, and almost destitute of artillery and transport, and the Generalissimo had no intention of using it—at any rate for operations in the winter —though it had nominally 15,000 or 16,000 men on the rolls. The total of the Spaniards in close contact with Wellington's main army—Morillo, España, the Reserve of Andalusia, and Freire's Galicians—was about 30,000 bayonets, available at short notice for a crisis, but for the most part inutilizable for a serious winter campaign. Mina and the Prince of Anglona would have added 24,000 more if they could have been moved forward, which Wellington did not think possible. But if he should resolve to take the offensive against Soult with his own Anglo-Portuguese, he had close to his hand 30,000 Spaniards who could be used to block Bayonne, if they could be fed and kept supplied with other necessaries, and restrained from plundering.

While Soult's army was being depleted on the strength of the Treaty of Valençay, Suchet's army in Catalonia was being treated in the same fashion. A dispatch of January 10th, exactly corresponding to that sent to Soult on the same day, ordered the Duke of Albufera to draw back all his cavalry to the Pyrenees, and the moment that the results of the mission of

San Carlos should be known, to start it for Lyons, as also half his infantry[1]. The rest of the army was to follow, when news should have come that the Treaty of Valençay had been ratified at Madrid. And precisely as Soult, a few days later, was told to send off Leval, Boyer, and Treilhard, though nothing had yet been heard from Madrid, so on January 15th Berthier wrote from Napoleon's head-quarters[2] to direct that an infantry division of at least 8,000 men and three of Suchet's five cavalry regiments should march for Lyons without waiting any longer. On January 24th Suchet wrote back that they were starting— 8,000 infantry, over 2,000 cavalry, and 12 guns. Their departure took away from him the power to hold back Clinton and Copons, which he had hitherto possessed[3].

It will be remembered that the total force of the Armies of Aragon and Catalonia still looked very formidable on paper in the autumn[4]. But copying the example of his master in the Leipzig campaign, Suchet had left an enormous proportion of it shut up in garrisons, with which all communication had been lost. And several thousand more were locked up in the Catalan fortresses, and could not be used in the field without risking the loss of those places. With an army amounting on paper to 52,000 men, Suchet had in January only 28,000 disposable for field service, and of these a good third were keeping open his communication with Northern Catalonia and France. In front of Barcelona, along the Llobregat, his main army was only some 18,000 strong. It was therefore a severe blow when the orders of January 14th arrived from Paris, and he was directed to detach 10,000 men without delay toward Lyons. The results of this deduction from his army will be dealt with in its proper place.

It is strange to find that Wellington was almost as much deceived about the possible results of the Treaty of Valençay as Napoleon. He wrote to Bathurst that he had long suspected some such a move on the Emperor's part, and that he was not at all sure that the Spaniards might not accept the bargain[5]. He was harassed by the fact that Copons had not sent him any notice of the passage of San Carlos through his lines[6]. And he

---

[1] Clarke to Suchet, January 10.   [2] Berthier to Suchet, January 14.
[3] Suchet to Clarke, January 24.   [4] See above, p. 88.
[5] *Dispatches*, xi. p. 433.   [6] Ibid., p. 445.

had heard that *Afrancesado* agents had been seen in the camps of Giron and Freire. This last fact was true, but they had been duly arrested, and their designs reported to the Regency, which ordered that 'they should receive exemplary castigation[1]'. It was therefore a great relief to Wellington to learn the peremptory reply which the Regency and the Cortes had given to San Carlos. 'They have conducted themselves with great candour and frankness', he wrote—but, 'he could not admire the delicacy of their mode of proposing to receive the king—what is to be done if he refuses to swear to the Constitution on the frontier? Is he then to be sent back[2]?' However, sufficient for the day was the evil thereof: a great peril had been avoided.

[1] See Toreno, iii. pp. 313–14, and *Wellington Dispatches*, xi. p. 444.
[2] Wellington to Henry Wellesley. Ibid., p. 500.

SECTION XLIII: CHAPTER III

WELLINGTON'S OFFENSIVE. THE FIRST DAYS.
FEBRUARY 14–18, 1814

SOULT's whole position was changed when his master had, after so many other deductions from his army, taken from him in January the three divisions of Leval, Boyer, and Treilhard, and so placed him in a numerical inferiority to his enemy such as he had never known before. This would have mattered little if the Treaty of Valençay had been ratified; for, if the Spanish armies had retired from the war, the numerical inferiority would have disappeared. But they never did retire, and the Marshal kept repeating to the Emperor that he could detect no sign whatever of their withdrawal: indeed he seems from the first to have been very doubtful of the practical effect of the Treaty on the progress of the campaign. On January 17th he wrote to the Minister of War that the Army of Spain would now be so enfeebled that, after the departure of Boyer and Leval, it would no longer be able to make an effective resistance to Wellington. He proposed to the Minister that Clausel should be left in command, and that he himself with the bulk of his force should be recalled to serve with the Grand Army. Regular fighting with Wellington on a scientific scale might be abandoned. 'If the Spaniards refuse to recognize the arrangement made with Prince Ferdinand, and still the situation becomes so pressing that the Emperor has to recall from the Army of Spain the second corps of 10,000 infantry and the rest of the cavalry—as was suggested in the dispatch of January 10th—we must obviously change the whole system on this frontier, and make war with corps of partisans, rather than with a skeleton army, which has lost its cohesion and its self-confidence, and which might be completely destroyed if asked to face new battles.' He then asks the Minister to formulate definite orders for him on the three possible situations that might arise—viz. (1) If the Spaniards repudiate the Treaty and their troops remain with Wellington. (2) If the Spaniards withdraw, but Wellington persists in attacking with his Anglo-Portuguese alone. (3) If the Spaniards withdraw, and Wellington sees himself forced to take his army home[1].

Before there was time to consult the Emperor on this matter of high strategy, it became evident that case no. 1 was that which had arisen. No demand was made for the departure of the additional reinforcements for the Grand Army. Soult was told to make the best of the situation, and to fight on with the force that remained to him. It was some weeks before the Emperor found leisure to dictate a strategic plan for him; when it arrived the Marshal found it not very helpful. 'Write to the Duke of Dalmatia', said Napoleon to his Minister of War, 'to leave a minimum garrison in Bayonne—a fortress is not of much use when the enemy has his communication with the sea, and can bring up all the shot, shell, and powder that he needs. He had better keep in close touch with Bayonne, but resume the offensive at once, falling on one of the enemy's wings even if it is only with 20,000 men. Let him seize his opportunity boldly, and he should be able to gain the advantage over the English: he has talent enough to understand what I mean[2].' Unfortunately, before this belated programme came to hand, Soult had thrown an immense garrison of 15,000 men into Bayonne, and had just been forced to drop all communication with the place, owing to Wellington's victory of Orthez.

The operations which took place in the Bayonne area before Wellington commenced his offensive on February 13th were of no importance, and need only the slightest mention. On December 16th and again on January 10th, Mina raided the French frontier valleys in the direction of St.-Jean-Pied-du-Port, and on each occasion was repulsed by the local levies aided by the garrison of the fortress. These forays were made without Wellington's permission, and gave him great displeasure, as he was specially anxious not to provoke the civil population by gratuitous plundering[3]. On December 18th Morillo, on Wellington's extreme inland flank, made an excursion against Mendionde and Hellette, equally without leave, and for much the same purpose. He had borrowed two squadrons of the 18th Hussars

[1] Soult to Clarke, Bayonne, January 17.
[2] Napoleon to Clarke, Troyes, February 25.
[3] See Wellington to Bathurst, January 16. *Dispatches*, xi. p. 455.

from Victor Alten, who had not been authorized to lend them. After driving in the French outposts, and pillaging the country-side as far as the Joyeuse river, Morillo found himself beset by all Pierre Soult's cavalry, and turned back in haste. The British Hussars, covering his retreat, were badly mauled and lost some prisoners[1]. Both Morillo and Alten received vigorous reprimands from Wellington[2]. As a punishment for plundering, the whole Spanish division was ordered to be kept under arms for five days in bitter weather. 'If the measures which I am obliged to adopt', wrote Wellington to the angry general, 'to enforce obedience and good order occasion the loss of men, and the reduction of my force, it is totally indifferent to me. I prefer to have a small army that will preserve discipline, to a larger one that is dis-obedient and undisciplined.'

There was some more serious bickering on January 3rd–6th, when Soult tried to molest Wellington's right flank beyond the Nive, which lay along the lower course of the Joyeuse, with an advanced post at La Bastide-Clarence. He reinforced his own left flank beyond the Adour by bringing the division of Taupin out of Bayonne, and ordered Clausel, with that division and Daricau's, to drive in the Allied line opposite him, of which Buchan's brigade of Le Cor's Portuguese division was the out-lying unit. Harispe and Pierre Soult's cavalry were to co-operate. Under this pressure Buchan was driven out of La Bastide-Clarence and back on to Briscous. This provoked Wellington, who brought up at once the 3rd and 7th Divisions from the Nive valley, and the remainder of Le Cor's Portuguese, while he shifted the 4th and 6th Divisions into a position from which they could support Picton and Walker if necessary. He intended to thrust back the French on the morning of the 4th, but two days of desperate rain prevented all movement, and it was only on the 6th that a concentrated advance of the 3rd and 4th Divisions and Le Cor drove back the French to their former position beyond the Joyeuse. Only one brigade of Taupin and one of Daricau seem to have been engaged. The losses on both sides

---

[1] Woodberry, the diarist of the 18th Hussars, was one of four officers wounded.

[2] See Wellington to Morillo, December 23. *Dispatches*, xi. pp. 391–2, and an explanatory letter to Freire of December 24. Ibid., p. 395.

were trifling—Soult thought it possible that his adversary was
about to begin a general advance, and ordered a concentration
towards his left. But satisfied with having cleared his flank and
shown that he was not to be meddled with, Wellington sent his
troops back to their old positions between the Nive and the
Adour. It is difficult to see what object Soult had intended to
secure by this isolated and purposeless thrust. Wellington in
his dispatch does not hazard any explanation of it[1]. Soult's
statement that he was wanting to make his line of communication between Bayonne and St.-Jean-Pied-du-Port more secure
seems unconvincing[2].

All this had happened before the Emperor requisitioned from
Soult the 14,000 sabres and bayonets of Treilhard, Leval, and
Boyer. When they had departed, Soult had to rearrange the
balance of his army. Leval's division had been taken from the
heavy force which Reille still held massed in and about Bayonne.
Boyer had been in the centre of the line, close to Port de Lanne.
Treilhard's dragoons, after the skirmishing on the Joyeuse river
in early January, had been sent to the rear, leaving only Pierre
Soult's light cavalry to hold the front opposite Wellington's
right wing.

The new arrangement of the seven infantry divisions still remaining to Soult was that Reille still stopped in and about
Bayonne, with Abbé's division in the fortress (in addition to its
usual garrison of 8,000 men) and Maransin's disposed along the
Adour just outside Bayonne, replacing Foy, who had been holding this stretch of the river in December. To the left of Maransin
Darmagnac's division lay along the river as far as Port de
Lanne. Eastward, and south of the Adour, lay Foy, Taupin, and
the division lately commanded by Daricau, all in front of Soult's
head-quarters at Peyrehorade. Daricau, it must be explained,
had just been detached to the department of the Landes, of
which he was a native, to stir up the deplorably backward
organization of the National Guard, and to stimulate the population generally—a hopeless task as it turned out. His old division
was now under Villatte, who had been without a command since

---

[1] Wellington to Bathurst. *Dispatches*, xi. pp. 428–9. It is very short and
shows that he considered the whole affair very unimportant.

[2] Soult to Clarke, January 5.

the old 'Reserve' had been broken up in December. Harispe
lay at some distance south of the position of Foy, Taupin, and
Villatte, near Hellette, with Pierre Soult's cavalry connecting
him with them. He had in front of him Morillo's Spaniards on
Wellington's extreme left flank at Itzassou. It will be seen
therefore that Soult had strengthened his left wing, south of the
Adour, to a force of four divisions, leaving only three to guard
the lower Adour, though he thought that Wellington's next
move would be an attempt to cross that river. His notion was to
strike at his adversary's flank with the larger half of his army,
when the latter should be attempting to force the passage somewhere between Bayonne and Port de Lanne. But Wellington
never had any such intention: and as his real plan was to cross
the river near its mouth, below Bayonne, he was rejoiced to see
the enemy moving more and more troops eastward, where they
would not be available to resist such an enterprise.

His scheme may be described as a design on a modest scale,
having as its main object the investment of Bayonne. He intended to start by attacking Soult's left wing, south of the
Adour, with the larger part of the Allied army, and driving it
eastward and away from Bayonne—a movement which would
probably induce the Marshal to strengthen it with every man
that he could bring up—and then to throw a bridge across the
Adour near its mouth and pass over it the smaller section of his
army, which would invest Bayonne on its northern side. There
was, of course, a fundamental objection to dividing the army in
face of an enemy who might throw his whole force against one
half or the other. But this Wellington intended to render impossible, by driving the inland divisions of Soult's host so far
to the east that it would be impracticable for them to return to
Bayonne and aid its garrison, within any reasonable space of
time. Only when they should have been pushed a long way off
any road by which they could return to the lower Adour, would
the bridge-project be carried out. The whole plan turned on the
fact that Wellington was now so much superior in total numbers
to the French as would enable him to find a field-force sufficient
to deal with Soult's main body, and at the same time a separate
detachment strong enough to invest Bayonne on all its three
fronts.

The division which Wellington made of his whole army was that he would march against Soult with the 2nd, 3rd, 4th, 6th, 7th and Light Divisions, with Le Cor's Portuguese and Morillo's Spaniards, and with three[1] of the four light cavalry brigades present with the army. The four heavy brigades[2] were still cantoned in Spain for the winter, but came up while the campaign was in progress, joining only in March. A number of infantry battalions were at this time absent from their brigades[3], having been sent back to Passages or St. Jean de Luz, to pick up their new clothing, which was arriving very tardily, when winter was nearing its end. The whole made up about 43,000 bayonets and 2,500 sabres from the Light Brigades.

Wellington left behind him under Sir John Hope, in the circle of fortified positions round Bayonne, the 1st and 5th Divisions, Aylmer's British and Bradford's and Campbell's Portuguese unattached brigades, with Vandeleur's cavalry. This was the force with which he intended to seize the passage of the Adour: it amounted to 18,000 men. But, seeing that if Hope should succeed in crossing, and investing Bayonne on all sides, he would require to have a very heavy force to cover three separate fronts divided from each other by the Adour and the Nive, he made arrangements for utilizing not only Carlos de España's Spaniards but also Freire's three divisions from Irun and Fuenterabia, though in order to move them he had to undertake to feed them—a considerable drain on his magazines at Passages and St. Jean de Luz. The reason why so many troops—18,000 Anglo-Portuguese and 16,000 Spaniards were heaped upon Bayonne was that it was absolutely necessary to keep the army's maritime bases safe. For if Wellington went off inland with his main body, he would still be dependent for his supply of munitions on his ports, and partly for his food-supplies also, since he had no intention of living on the country-side by requisitions, as a

---

[1] Fane's, Vivian's, and Somerset's brigades, all light cavalry.

[2] O'Loghlin's, Manners's, Clifton's, and Arentschildt's heavy dragoons of the K.G.L. Boch, so long in command of the legionary heavy brigade, had sailed for Germany in January, and was drowned on his way, off the coast of Brittany.

[3] This was the case with the 34th, 43rd, 79th, 1/95th and other battalions who show no casualties in the list of killed and wounded, at the battle of Orthez.

French army would have done. His whole policy was to conciliate the civil population by scrupulous respect for property.

The movement began on February 12th, when a week of fine
weather had made the roads comparatively firm. Even so the
country was not favourable for an advance on a broad front.
The rolling plateau east of the Nive is cut up by a series of rivers
fed by Pyrenean rainfall: they were very full at the moment, they
all flow in deep ravines worn in a soil of shale or hard clay, and
all save the Joyeuse had few fords that could be utilized in
winter. There were in succession the Joyeuse, the Bidouze, the
Saison, the Gave d'Oloron (which joins the Saison at Sauveterre),
and the Gave de Pau. All run from south to north, and all fall
into the Adour: the Saison and the Gave de Pau, the largest
of the series, unite near Peyrehorade—Soult's head-quarters—
just before they mingle their joint waters with the Adour. It
would have to be Wellington's object to push Soult from river
to river, till he should be driven so far eastward that it would
be impossible for him to get back to the Adour anywhere near
Bayonne, so as to interfere with the separate operations which
Hope's corps was to carry out near the sea.

Wellington's manœuvre—to put things shortly—consisted in
the turning of Soult's left wing by the persistent advance of
a large flanking column under Hill, which got well south of
Harispe's division, and by dislodging it in succession from the
lines of the Joyeuse, the Bidouze, and the Saison, forced the
other three French divisions, which lay north of Harispe, to con-
form to his retreat, and abandon those river-lines, under pain
of being taken in flank and rear by the turning column[1]. But
lest Soult should take the offensive with these divisions, when
Harispe began to fall back, the English general kept three
divisions in front of them, so as to contain them. And these
three divisions were reinforced up to five, when Soult began (as
Wellington had hoped) to draw in the rest of his field-force from

[1] As my friend Atkinson suggests, there was a similarity between the
way in which Wellington used Graham and his left wing in the Victoria
campaign, and the way in which Hill was employed on the right wing
in the Orthez campaign. In each case the extreme outer flank of the
enemy was turned, and all the rest of the line had to go back, stage after
stage, in consequence.

the neighbourhood of Bayonne. There was no moment at which
the Marshal would have been able to take Wellington's advancing
line in flank—a sufficient containing force was always opposite
him. Hence Soult was driven to successive retreats from river-
line to river-line, till, when he had been drawn to a very great
distance from Bayonne, and had lost his communication with
that fortress, he finally massed six of his seven divisions, and
stood to fight at Orthez, behind the Gave de Pau, in what he
considered an almost inexpugnable position. He failed once
again in face of Wellington—as he always did in battle,—and the
campaign took a new turn.

It is proverbially difficult to hold a long river-line against an
equal or superior enemy, since the general who has taken up
a passive defensive has to guard every point, while his adversary
can strike in full force at one or two weak places in the front,
while making demonstrations with trifling detachments against
the other fords or bridges. And Soult's front was too long to be
held by four divisions, when it was 'turned' by Hill, and 'contained' by the rest of Wellington's operating force.

But to come to details. On February 12th, after several days
of fine weather, Hill was told to pick up from their cantonments,
facing the Mousserolles front of the Bayonne works, his old
familiar divisions, the 2nd and Le Cor's (once Hamilton's)
Portuguese. In addition he was given his old Spanish auxiliaries
—Morillo's division—which had been operating with him ever
since 1811. For cavalry he had at first only Fane's light brigade.
And to act as a flank-guard to the north of him, on which side
danger lay, Picton with the 3rd Division was to move forward
in echelon with him, always keeping touch with the rest of the
army, which was 'containing' Soult's main body. This force,
of which Beresford was in charge, originally consisted of the
4th and 7th Divisions, with Vivian's and Somerset's light cavalry
watching their front, but was strengthened on the fourth day of
the campaign by the bringing up from the Nive of the Light
Division and on the ninth day by that of the 6th Division. It
was not till the movement had been well developed, that in the
last days of February and the first of March, the heavy cavalry
brigades of O'Loghlin, Manners, Clifton, and Arentschildt came
up from south of the Pyrenees and joined Wellington's left wing

—giving him an immense superiority over Soult in the mounted arm. When the advance began he had only seven cavalry regiments with him.

On February 14th Hill marched against Harispe in two columns from Urcarray, while Morillo, starting from his old quarters of Itzassou, moved farther south, to find the flank of the French division. Harispe was caught in evil case, for he had detached one of his brigades to make a forced march for the relief of the isolated French garrison of Jaca, which had been beset for long months by Mina, and had sent word that it would be starved out if not relieved in a few days. And so indeed it was, for it surrendered on February 17th, when the relieving force had been called back by Harispe's urgent summons. But on the 13th Harispe had, in and about his head-quarters at Hellette, only seven battalions and a cavalry regiment. Seeing Hill advancing against him with two divisions, and Morillo likely to get behind his flank, he abandoned the line of the Joyeuse after some skirmishing, and had retreated by nightfall to Méharin half-way towards the Bidouze river, the next possible line of defence. Hill followed along the high road to St. Palais, while Morillo continued his flanking movement toward the south.

Meanwhile Picton, with the 3rd Division, had covered Hill's flank by advancing on Bonloc against Villatte's division, which was holding the stretch of the Joyeuse river north of Harispe's position. On hearing that his colleague had given way before Hill, and that the latter was across the river, and able to attack him in flank, Villatte abandoned his position at once, and retreated to Oregne, half-way between the Joyeuse and the Bidouze, so preserving his relative position with regard to Harispe. Picton followed, keeping touch with Hill.

But Clausel, in command of this wing of Soult's army, saw that if Villatte and Harispe had retired, the division north of them—that of Taupin—must go back also. For though Beresford had not yet attacked the position on the lower Joyeuse, he was in front of it and demonstrating with the 4th and 7th Divisions, while Picton was now across the river and able to get behind Taupin. Accordingly the line along the Joyeuse was evacuated, and on the 15th both Villatte and Taupin had taken up positions behind the Bidouze, the former at Ilharre, the latter at Bergoney, without any fighting.

Harispe, however, on this same day was involved in a serious affair. When he had reached Garris, four miles on the near side of the Bidouze, he picked up his missing brigade, which had returned in all haste from the Jaca road, and three cavalry regiments under Berton, and resolved to fight a rear-guard action on the Motte de Garris, a good position on a long hill covered by a ravine. This was rash, as he had only 7,000 men, and had 12,000 in front of him, with Morillo's division in addition working far out on his flank. The day was far spent, and the 2nd Division and Le Cor's Portuguese were forming in a leisurely way in front of the French, vexing them with long-range artillery-fire and rather expecting them to retire, when Wellington arrived suddenly from the rear, and riding to the front of the leading brigade, that of Pringle, surveyed the position and told the brigadier 'You must take the hill before dark'. Accordingly Pringle with his brigade in echelon, the 39th leading, the 28th a little to the side and rear[1], crossed the ravine and stormed the northern crest of the Motte de Garris, while Le Cor's Portuguese attacked along the high road and south of the hill. Morillo was in march to turn the whole position, and cut off Harispe's retreat on St. Palais and the bridge of the Bidouze.

This turned out a very stiff affair—Pringle had to deal with troops of Paris's brigade, which had belonged to the Army of Aragon and had never met British infantry before, as it had been operating on the St.-Jean-Pied-du-Port front ever since it fell under Soult's command. The attacking force had to cross the ravine, and then to mount a stiff slope under heavy musketry-fire which brought down the gallant brigadier—who led his foremost battalion in person—and the horses of every mounted officer present. On reaching the crest, the 39th was twice charged by the French 81st, which came on in column and actually closed, so that some fighting with the bayonet took place. On being once repulsed, this old Aragonese regiment rallied and charged again; the losses on both sides were heavy and the fighting hand to hand. But the 28th having now reached the hill-top on the

[1] The 34th, the other battalion of the brigade, was absent, refitting at St. Jean de Luz.

flank of the 39th, its fire began to tell on the defenders, who
sullenly gave back[1]. Harispe then ordered a general retreat,
having at last realized his danger, for Morillo was circling round
his flank, Le Cor was already engaged with his centre, and three
more brigades of the 2nd Division were moving up in support of
the 39th and 28th. But the French troops were now so closely
engaged all along their front, that it was impossible to extricate
them without severe loss: many parties were cut off, and the
whole division poured back in disorder along the high road and
across the bridge of St. Palais, where they were nearly intercepted by Morillo's leading troops. So complete was the rout
that Harispe failed to rally his men for the defence of St. Palais
and the line of the Bidouze, which he had intended to hold. It
was now black night, and, unable to dispose his forces for the
protection of the town and bridge, the French general hurried
them on for ten miles and only halted them half-way to the
Saison river. The bridge was blown up at the last moment, but
rather ineffectually; and Hill's engineers, starting work at dawn,
got it repaired and fit for the passage of all arms by noon on
the 16th. The whole corps crossed during the course of the day,
and Fane's cavalry resumed the pursuit of Harispe. The latter,
conscious at last of the very heavy force opposite him, and of
the danger that he had run at Garris, by his rash rear-guard
action, fell back on the night of the 16th to Arriverayte behind
the Saison river. He had lost 500 men in the combat of Garris,
200 of them prisoners; Hill's casualties were about 170, one
quarter of them Portuguese. The gallant 39th, which alone had
been closely engaged, lost one officer and 42 rank and file, a
surprisingly small casualty-list.

Harispe's rout and the loss of the bridge of St. Palais completely wrecked Soult's plan for holding the line of the Bidouze.
He had written to the Minister of War on the morning of the
16th that the course of that river would be good to defend, if he
could keep Harispe at St. Palais and also guard the passage
higher up at Mauléon. '*Mais je suis déjà trop étendu*', and it might
be necessary to get the divisions closer together and to find a

---

[1] There is an excellent account of Garris in Maxwell's *Peninsular
Sketches*, ii. p. 153, which Napier evidently used, before it got to Maxwell's
hands.

still better defensive front[1]. This would be behind the Gave d'Oloron and the lower Saison, with the left flank resting on the walls of Navarrenx and the right on the fortified bridge-head at Peyrehorade on the Gave de Pau. Navarrenx, it may be mentioned, was a little old-fashioned frontier fortress, where the Gave d'Oloron comes out of the foot-hills of the Pyrenees. It was held at this time by one regular battalion and another of National Guards. It may be noted that from Navarrenx to Peyrehorade is a front of over 30 miles. Obviously this could not be held securely by the four divisions of Foy, Taupin, Villatte, and Harispe, if Wellington attacked with the eight divisions which he was now setting in motion.

On the 16th, in consequence of Harispe's retreat, the other French divisions retired beyond the Saison, abandoning the line of the Bidouze. Villatte was not followed by Picton; Taupin reports that only cavalry was in touch with him. Farther north Beresford was at last set in motion by Wellington, part of the 7th Division crossing the Joyeuse at La Bastide-Clarence, and occupying the heights east of it. But the important thing on this part of the front was that Beresford received the news that the Light and 6th Divisions were now coming up in his rear, both having been given orders to move up from their billets along the Nive. The former was up to the front by the 16th—the latter not till the 21st. However, Foy, though in no wise molested as yet, drew back his advanced posts from Bardos, crossed the Bidouze at Came, and, not lingering behind that river, for the upper reaches of it had been lost, retired to Hastingues, in front of the fortified bridge-head of Peyrehorade on the Saison. Thus all the four divisions of Soult's left wing had got back to the line of the latter river.

But this was not all. On this same day, February 16th, Soult took up the policy which Wellington had hoped to see, by ordering two of the three divisions which he had hitherto retained in the neighbourhood of Bayonne, and north of the Adour, to quit their positions and move off eastward. Darmagnac was directed to cross the Adour by the bridge at Port de Lanne and to draw in towards Foy at Peyrehorade: the second division,

[1] Soult to Clarke, from Bastide de Béarn. Morning of February 16. Results of Garris apparently not yet known.

which had been at St. Étienne, the transpontine suburb of Bayonne, was ordered to march off on the Dax road. This was the unit hitherto commanded by Maransin: but that general had just been drafted off to Tarbes, to stir up and organize the National Guards of the Hautes-Pyrénées, of which he was a native—the same sort of unhappy duty on which Daricau had been sent off a few days before[1]. His division had been taken over by Rouget, its senior general of brigade. This left at Bayonne only the single division of Abbé, over and above its usual sedentary garrison—and so the task for which Hope was destined became much more easy, as Wellington had intended.

General Reille, it will be remembered, had originally been left at Bayonne with four divisions: of these one had been drawn away to the north by Napoleon, and two others had been successively withdrawn from his control and taken eastward. He chafed greatly against this arrangement, and began an angry correspondence with Soult as early as January 17th, declaring that he did not wish to be shut up in Bayonne along with Thouvenot, who, as the governor of the place by imperial patent, though much his junior in standing, would dispute his authority, and would be in charge of great part of the troops[2]. A double command in a fortress would be ruinous, and his own position would be undignified. Stripped at last of all his original divisions save that of Abbé, he wrote an insubordinate letter to the Marshal, announced his resignation of the command on the lower Adour, turned over his remaining battalions to Thouvenot and departed for Dax as a private person on February 15th, after sending a letter of complaints to Paris. The War Minister, it is surprising to find, decided in favour of Reille, informing Soult that as Thouvenot was the governor of Bayonne by imperial warrant, he had no right to put a senior general over his head, and that he must keep Reille with the field-army. Soult had to submit to this snubbing, and by February 27th Reille was at head-quarters again, and had been put in command of the two divisions of Rouget and Taupin. Naturally the relations between him and the Marshal remained extremely unpleasant.

Meanwhile, on February 16th, Beresford received his orders to

[1] See above, p. 317.
[2] For all this see the detailed account in Vidal de la Blache, ii. pp. 204–8.

push his advance beyond the Bidouze, with Somerset's and Vivian's hussar brigades well in his front. The 4th Division was to occupy Bidache—the 7th, near the Adour, might stand still for a day, and the Light Division, coming up from beyond the Nive, would get no further than La Bastide-Clarence. Somerset's exploring parties found Foy across the Bidouze with his divisions in bivouac in front of Hastingues[1] and Peyrehorade, while Taupin —farther south—was located behind the Saison at Caresse, half-way between Peyrehorade and Sauveterre. At the latter place Vivian's vedettes discovered Villatte's division, in close touch with Harispe, who had taken up his position behind the Saison at Arriverayte. But there was a gap between Foy and Taupin, and another between Taupin and Villatte.

Hill's columns, which had rested in and about St. Palais on the 16th, had orders to start at dawn on the 17th to place themselves in front of the French line on the Saison, the 2nd Division and Le Cor had Arriverayte as their point of direction—Morillo's goal was Nabas, farther up-stream, on the road St. Palais–Navarrenx. Picton, who had found the roads near the central Bidouze almost impassable, was brought down to St. Palais, and so fell in to the rear of Hill's main column, to which he could act as a reserve. In the afternoon, after a fatiguing march, the 2nd Division arrived in front of Harispe's position behind the Saison, at Arriverayte where the bridge leading to Sauveterre lay, and along the banks south of that passage. Having Wellington's orders to push the enemy as far as they could be driven, Hill did not hesitate to attack the force that lay in his way, despite of the fact that the bridge of Arriverayte was blocked and entrenched, and that the fords above and below it were deep and dangerous. And he was justified in his daring, for though the bridge was held against him for some time, two of the fords were seized with no great hindrance from the enemy—though much from the swirling ice-cold water. The decisive blow was given by the 92nd, which found an unguarded ford a little above the bridge, at a corner with steep banks and wood on both sides. Plunging in, the regiment crossed, hardly opposed—its total

---

[1] Hastingues and Bastide-Clarence appear to be names recalling the old English domination in Gascony, when many new towns were laid out by the early Edwards.

loss was one killed and two wounded—and forming on the eastern
bank came in upon the rear of the French, who were defending
the bridge against a frontal attack. Seeing themselves likely to
be surrounded and captured, the enemy (25th Léger) decamped
in haste[1]. As another ford at Osserain had also been passed,
Harispe drew back his division behind the line of the Gave
d'Oloron, crossing at Sauveterre, but leaving some trifling rear-
guards on the left or western bank. At Sauveterre he found
himself in touch with Villatte's troops arriving from another
direction. The bridge of Arriverayte[2], almost uninjured, fell
into Hill's hands and was invaluable for the passage of guns and
wheeled traffic. The line of the Saison had thus been won, with
incredibly small loss—under twenty casualties[3]. But that of the
Gave d'Oloron still remained to be passed, the combat of Arriverayte having put Hill in possession of no more than the narrow
tongue of land between the two rivers. On the 18th Harispe and
Villatte expected to be attacked in their new positions behind
the Gave, but rather to their surprise Hill did no more than feel
their front along the river with small reconnaissances—a few
cannon-shot were fired in front of Sauveterre, where Villatte was
fortifying the bridge, and mounting masked guns on its flank.
But having located the enemy the British reconnoitring parties
retired.

On this same day (February 18) Picton's division was drawn
down to Garris and St. Palais in Hill's rear. The Light Division
remained stationary at La Bastide-Clarence in Beresford's rear:
the 6th Division had not yet come up from its cantonments on
the Nive, but was starting for Hasparren. Evidently Wellington
was not intending to make his second series of blows against
Soult's left flank until he was sure that Beresford was in no
danger from the French divisions in the direction of Peyrehorade
and Port de Lanne. It was not till he ascertained that not only
Foy but Darmagnac also had moved eastward, behind the line

---

[1] For an account of this from the ranks, see Sergeant Robertson, pp. 127–8.
He says that Wellington himself was present, and started the regiment for
the attack, sitting on the bank near Bean's horse-artillery battery.

[2] No two people seem to be able to spell the name of this place in
the same way. Soult calls it Riveyrete, Napier Arriveriete, Lapène
Arriverette, Wellington Arriverete. I follow modern maps.

[3] To be exact, 3 killed and 15 wounded.

of the Gave de Pau, that he drew off the Light and 6th Divisions from Beresford's area of operations to that of Hill.

There was now to be a four days' interval on the Gave d'Oloron before the great game of turning Soult's left wing was resumed. Wellington, as we shall see, having succeeded in his initial manœuvre, the drawing off of the greater part of his adversary's army far to the east and the inland, was now about to direct in person the second act—the investment of Bayonne by the crossing of the Adour at its mouth, for which he had left the corps of Hope behind him. If Soult had tried any offensive scheme in this period of four days—February 19th–23rd—he would have run against Beresford with four divisions that could be easily concentrated in the north, or against Hill, also with four divisions, in the south. The two British generals were in good communication with each other by means of their cavalry. But the Marshal, who had written to Clarke that he was being attacked by an army of 100,000 men including 10,000 horse, was at this time very far from intending to take the offensive, and defined his present purpose as being the holding of the line of the Gave d'Oloron. His orders contain directions for breaking of bridges and the removal of magazines to the rear, and he was already informing the Minister that if he were forced from the Gave d'Oloron he should fall back on Orthez, and defend the line of the Gave de Pau, after having called in Foy and Darmagnac from Peyrehorade[1]. The cessation for several days of Hill's hitherto rapid advance puzzled rather than reassured him. And he began constructing hypotheses as to Wellington's intentions, which had very little relation to the actual facts.

[1] Soult to Clarke, evenings of February 17th, and of the 18th also, from Sauveterre.

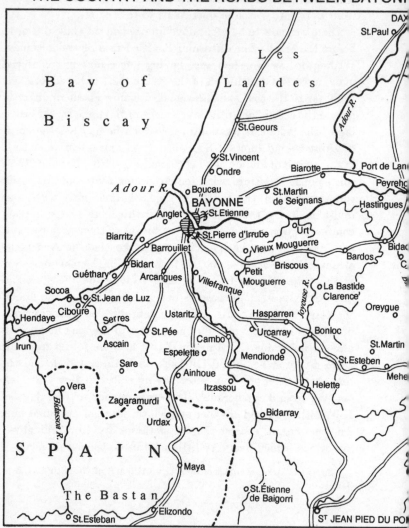

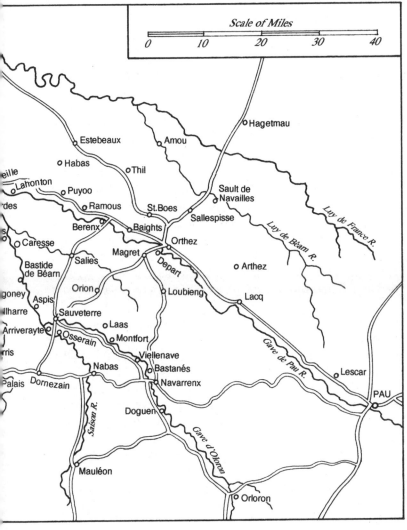

Scale of Miles

0   10   20   30   40

Hagetmau

Estebeaux   Amou

Habas   Thil

eille
Lahonton   Puyoo
des   Ramous   St.Boes
Berenx   Baights   Sallespisse
Caresse   Magret   Orthez
Bastide   Salies   Depart
de Béarn
goney   Aspis   Orion   Loubieng   Lacq
Ilharre   Sauveterre
Arriverayte   Osserain   Laas   Montfort
rris   Nabas   Bastanés
Palais   Dornezain   Navarrenx   Lescar

Sault de
Navailles

Arthez

Viellenave

PAU

Doguen

Saison R.

Gave d'Oloron

Gave de Pau R.

Luy de Béarn R.

Luy de France R.

Mauléon

Orloron

SECTION XLIII: CHAPTER IV

THE PASSAGE OF THE ADOUR. FEBRUARY 19–24

At 4 o'clock on the afternoon of February 19th Wellington turned up at St. Jean de Luz, after a long cold ride over the country-side from Garris—more than thirty miles—and before dismounting from his horse called on Admiral Penrose, in charge of naval co-operation, and Colonel Elphinstone his chief engineer, to summon them to give him their report as to the preparations for bridging the Adour at its mouth, which he expected to find in a state of completion[1]. But even the greatest generals cannot command the weather, and at this moment it was abominable. The arrangements were complete, in so far that the place of crossing had been chosen and surveyed, and a masked battery prepared in the pine-wood at the mouth of the river to cover the crossing. Over fifty *chasse-marées*—the local form of lugger—had been collected and were lying anchored in the small harbours of St. Jean de Luz and the neighbouring Socoa. An immense store of cables had been got together, and an equally good provision of planks and beams—which had been made in rather an expensive fashion, by sawing up wood prepared for artillery platforms. Each *chasse-marée* had a proportion of the wood and cordage stocked on board. Also there was a pontoon-train ready, with attendant companies of British and Portuguese sappers. But to bridge the estuary of the Adour it was necessary to get the vessels into it, and the weather made it absolutely impossible for them to move. The wind was due west, and furious, the Biscay rollers were crashing in with even more than their usual ferocity—on the 14th the storm had been so high that a spit of gravel had been thrown up, almost closing the narrow entrance to the harbour of St. Jean—there was a dry bank a hundred feet long, which had to be shovelled away at low tide by fatigue parties of the 1st Division[2]. And at the mouth of the Adour, the bar, always a nasty obstacle, was marked by a churning line of surf, in which no small vessel could possibly live, and where

---

[1] Larpent's *Journal*, p. 398.　　　　　[2] Ibid., p. 390.

a large vessel would certainly touch ground and be driven ashore or slowly battered to pieces.

On the morning of the 20th things still looked very bad—Wellington stood on the sea-wall of St. Jean de Luz with Admiral Penrose beside him, listening to the wind that still blew straight into the bay, and surveying the lines of *chasse-marées*, anchored bow and stern, and tugging at their cables. But at any moment a shift in the wind might come, and the sea calm down: Wellington spent the day in revising court-martial reports, and writing necessary dispatches to Bathurst at home—accounts of the doings on the Bidouze and the Saison—and to Freire on the Bidassoa, bidding him be ready to march and replace Hope's troops on the south side of Bayonne at an hour's notice—he had been given his orders to have his baggage packed, and to draw his rations from the British magazines, several days before. The staff settled with Hope the exact details of the way in which the blockading force was to be redistributed, when the move should begin. And then Wellington saw that he could wait no longer to superintend the matter himself—Soult might be inspired to take liberties, if the pressure on him was relaxed for too many days. So at night he was forced to write to Bathurst 'the weather is so unfavourable that it is impossible to attempt this operation at the present moment. I therefore return to Sir Rowland Hill's corps to-morrow morning (February 21) and I leave it to Sir John Hope to cross the Adour when the weather will permit[1].'

By the night of the 21st Wellington was at Garris, giving Hill directions for the resumption of his forward movement against the Gave d'Oloron. The details of that very risky business the passage of the Adour fell entirely under Hope's responsibility. It was, as we shall see, a complete success: but it might very well have ended in a disaster. Obstinate determination sometimes wins a merited victory, though it would not have been expected by any dispassionate looker-on.

When the 6th Division marched for Hasparren, to join Beresford's column, the troops round Bayonne had been redistributed. The 5th Division took over for a short time the fortified line in front of the Mousserolles defences, where the 6th

[1] Wellington to Bathurst. *Dispatches*, xi. p. 523.

had been lying. Lord Aylmer's independent brigade, Carlos de España's Spaniards, and Campbell's Portuguese were distributed along the south front, from Urdains through Bassussary to near Barrouillet. The 1st Division, which was to lead the advance towards the Adour, was massed opposite Anglet, in the villages of Bidart and Biarritz, and the pine-wood north of them extending to the river. Bradford's Portuguese were behind the 1st Division. The pontoon-train and engineers were hidden in the north end of that same long wood, close to the river, and the emplacement for a masked battery for heavy guns was prepared, from which the 18-pounders of the reserve artillery were to open against the opposite bank, where, near the hamlet of Le Boucau, the French had a small post, a two-gun battery, and the corvette *Sapho* and some gunboats lying up-stream.

On the afternoon of the 22nd the wind fell, and the whole of the lines of *chasse-marées* lying at St. Jean de Luz and Socoa received orders to put out to sea, and try to make the mouth of the Adour. After midnight of the 22nd–23rd the 1st Division marched off to the designated point of crossing, coasting along the French outposts in Anglet and to the north of it. The paths were deep sand, and the pontoon-train and artillery accompanying the division found going very difficult—one 18-pounder got off the road and stuck tight till hauled out by the infantry, so did many of the pontoons. At dawn the head of the 1st Division —Stopford's brigade—was at the destined starting-point, with the other troops behind. But there were no signs of the *chasse-marées* that were to form the bridge, nor of the small ships of war which were to escort them. They had all been blown out to sea by a change of the wind, and not one of them was visible. Sir John Hope's problem was difficult. Must he wait till the flotilla came in sight—which might be a very long time—or should he attempt the passage without them, having no better means than his pontoons, and five small boats, belonging to the pontoon-train, which had been lugged up in company with it? Every moment of delay was dangerous, for the French might detect the troops in the wood, and hurry out a considerable force from the north side of Bayonne to occupy the sand-hills about Le Boucau.

After waiting all the morning hours for some signs of the

flotilla, Sir John took the very risky step of attempting to cross by means of his pontoons and boats only, while the French still seemed unconscious of the situation. To distract them from the real point of danger he ordered the blockading troops all round the south front to simulate a concentric attack on the French entrenched camps. Lord Aylmer's brigade, Campbell's Portuguese, and Carlos de España's Spaniards all pressed in the enemy's outlying pickets, and showed formed battalions behind their skirmishing lines: the German Light Infantry brigade of the 1st Division came out of the pine-wood, and stormed Anglet, where the French had a heavy picket. There was a noisy *tiraillade* on a front of three or four miles, and the guns in the entrenched camps began to try long shots at the formed troops visible in the distance[1]. Moreover, the masked battery in the pine-wood opened upon the French corvette and gunboats lying in the Lower Adour, near the destined crossing point: red-hot shot was tried—also rockets. The corvette, badly injured, ran up-stream and took refuge near Bayonne bridge: some of the gunboats were sunk, the others followed the corvette away from the important stretch of shore.

Hope's demonstrations completely fulfilled their object. General Thouvenot made up his mind that the enemy was about to attempt to storm his lines on the Beyris and Marrac fronts, and brought up his reserves to support the troops that were holding the earthworks. As, including Abbé's division, he had 14,000 men at his disposal, behind a most formidable and well-gunned line of redoubts, he might have welcomed any assault with confidence. That danger on the north bank of the Adour might be impending does not seem to have struck him. Though Soult had made a slight mention of the possibility of a crossing in that direction[2], and had heard of the accumulation of fishing-boats at St. Jean de Luz[3], neither he nor Thouvenot seems to have taken any serious heed of possible enterprise in that quarter[4]. And indeed the appearance of the majority of Welling-

---

[1] For a good description of the demonstration, see Gleig's *Subaltern*, pp. 293–6.   [2] Soult to Clarke, February 12.

[3] Ibid., February 12. 'On sait de St. Jean de Luz que tout ce qu'il a d'embarcations est mis en mouvement.'

[4] See letters quoted in Vidal de la Blache, ii. p. 260.

ton's divisions on the Bidouze and the Saison had persuaded the Marshal that no attempt on Bayonne was likely at present. Thouvenot was so convinced that there was no danger at the estuary of the Adour, that on February 17th he had removed the two guns in the small battery at Le Boucau, and on the 22nd withdrew the two companies hitherto watching that place—as if for the express purpose of facilitating Hope's task[1]. He explained, in a letter to the War Minister, the accumulation of shipping at St. Jean de Luz, by suggesting that the English had in mind a disembarkation somewhere on the coast of the Landes —where the population was disloyal and no French troops were on guard[2]. Moreover, naval experts had assured him that the estuary of the Adour was unapproachable during such weather as was now prevailing. If the French generals had not been utterly blind to their danger, it is possible that Hope's adventure would have ended in disaster.

For, having set his noisy demonstration on the south front to work, and having driven away the *Sapho* and the gunboats, Hope resolved to send troops across the Adour, though he was almost without means for moving them. At 11 a.m., the hour between falling and rising tide, he launched the five small boats which had been brought up along with the pontoon-train. They could only hold eight or ten men apiece[3], but, since there was no opposition, this small party got across the Adour in safety. They had with them a long hawser, which was secured to the opposite bank, and made fast there. Along this hawser rafts, made from the small number of pontoons which had got to the shore, were worked—they had been lashed together into small rafts, which would each hold fifty men. After 2 p.m. slack water had ceased, and it became very difficult and slow work to pass the rafts, for the tide had begun to run again at the rate of seven miles an hour, and the hawser sagged wofully. By 5 o'clock only five companies of the Guards and two of the 5/60th had reached the north bank. As each raft-load came across, the men were dis-

[1] Thouvenot to Clarke, February 16.

[2] As late as February 23rd Soult wrote to the Minister that only one English division was left in front of Bayonne, and that it would probably march to join Wellington.

[3] So Hope in his report to Wellington on the 25th.

posed by General Stopford, who passed early, in position among the sand-hills, covering the point of passage[1].

It is obvious that if Thouvenot had not withdrawn his post of two companies from Le Boucau on the preceding day, the original landing in boats would have ended in a petty disaster. The men would have been driven into the water, or captured. 'The first party I would rather not accompany', wrote Larpent, before the crossing had taken place[2]. But even when 500 men had straggled across in the course of the afternoon, the position was most perilous. For the enemy had 2,700 men under General Maucomble in the Citadel and other transpontine fortifications of Bayonne, only two miles away, and could reinforce them from the south bank to any extent, now that it was clear that the noise in front of the entrenched camps was only a demonstration. It seems an incredible error of judgement that Thouvenot made no serious attempt to destroy the seven companies established among the Boucau sand-hills before dark. But the orders which he sent to Maucomble were merely 'to reconnoitre the troops which had got across, to act according as their number made it possible to act, without compromising his troops destined for the defence of the Citadel, and not to get separated from them'. This is his own account of the lamentable directions which he issued. Maucomble, also missing all insight into the situation, drew out from his works only two incomplete battalions of the 5th Léger and 62nd Ligne, certainly under 1,000 bayonets[3], and dispatched them against Le Boucau. They came against a hidden enemy of unknown force, and were received with a telling fire from the long line of occupied sand-hills. But what settled the matter, according to all the English accounts, was a flight of Congreve rockets, let off by a party of 'rocketeers' who had crossed with the Guards. These missiles, new to the enemy, happened to burst correctly in the head of the approaching column, and threw it into such disorder that the commanding officer ordered instant retreat to the Citadel, though he had lost

---

[1] Most of these details are from the good technical description by Colonel Jones, R.E., in his *Peninsular Sieges*, vol. ii, pp. 114–18.

[2] Larpent, p. 396.

[3] Maucomble in his report to Thouvenot calls them *parties de bataillons*. Clerc (p. 370) guesses them at 600 bayonets—probably too low. Larpent, who watched the affair, estimates them at 700 or so.

only thirty or forty men. Maucomble reported that 'the enemy's skirmishers had been driven back, but that the fall of night prevented any further damage being done to them'. But what might have happened if Thouvenot had sent to Maucomble not timid orders but a couple of thousand men from his reserve, or if the brigadier had sallied out from the Citadel not with a third of his force, but with 1,500 or 1,800 men? The main blame certainly rests on the governor—the brigadier might defend himself as being fettered by the tenor of the orders sent him.

The night of the 23rd–24th was brilliant moonlight, frosty, and calm—contrasting extraordinarily with the rough weather of the preceding day—and at slack tide many more raft-loads were conveyed across the river to support Stopford in case of his being attacked on the following morning[1]. The loading and disembarking of the men was done by the light of large bonfires erected on the bank on either side, where the cables were fixed. The dawn revealed a welcome sight, the whole flotilla was discovered lying off the mouth of the Adour, and only waiting for daylight and high tide to cross the dangerous bar. There were over forty *chasse-marées* and six or seven war-vessels in sight. The difficulty was to hit the comparatively narrow navigable channel: it was prone to shift after a heavy gale, and the French had of course removed the signal-staffs by which the local coasters had been wont to steer their course. The Admiral, waiting for high tide, sent some large ships' boats to try for the presumed channel, where the surf was not flying so high as along most of the length of the bar. The first boat, on which were Captain O'Reilly of the *Lyra* and a local pilot, got over the bar, but was swept aside and upset by the swirl immediately after its passage. The captain and crew were nearly all fished out of the surf by men of the Guards, and hardly a life was lost. The second boat found a better point of passage and came through without mishap: a third, with Cheyne of the *Woodlark*, hit the central channel still more accurately, and passed without any difficulty. The way had now been shown, but the tide had turned and the depth of water was decreasing every minute—the fall of the tide here is no less than nineteen feet—so the Admiral resolved not to set the *chasse-marées* at the now-discovered

[1] Batty's *Campaign of the Pyrenees*, p. 122.

channel till the water had again reached a high level. This meant a six hours' delay—a thing most exasperating to Sir John Hope, who had thought that the flotilla might be got through, and the bridging work begun, in the course of the morning.

The passage of the troops therefore had to be continued by the row-boats and rafts: more pontoons presumably were launched and worked with oars, and all through the morning men continued to pour across. Even a few of Vandeleur's light dragoons were got over—their horses swimming behind, held by the reins. Matters were still a little dangerous at noon, for though three thousand men had crossed, Thouvenot might easily have spared 5,000 for a sortie. But he remained perfectly quiescent, his attention apparently distracted by a false attack made by Hope's orders on the Mousserolles front by two brigades of the 5th Division. By the evening, however, three brigades of the 1st Division had got safely over, and some of Campbell's Portuguese, with two guns and a troop of horse, some 8,000 in all. This force, dug in on the sand-hills, was strong enough to face any sally which the garrison could have afforded to make.

Towards the end of the afternoon, the tide being now favourable, and the channel known, Admiral Penrose directed the *chasse-marées* to enter the estuary and round the end of the bar. The man-of-war boat steered by Bloye of the *Lyra*, which guided the procession, was wrecked, with the loss of all hands, but the vessels came through, for the most part, without too much difficulty—the Basque and Spanish crews stimulated by the British engineer and naval officers who were in charge. Thirty-four passed the bar successfully, one grounded on the bar and was battered to pieces with loss of life, another ran ashore outside the entry, and twelve returned to St. Jean de Luz, having failed to make the passage before the tide began to fall. The casualties were far less numerous than the admiral had expected—two man-of-war boats were upset, with the loss of Captain Elliott of the *Martial*, master's mate Bloye of the *Lyra*, a surgeon, and twelve men, also three country boats—a Spanish *chasse-marée* and two small craft, with some twenty lives more.

As the vessels had each got their provision of planks and cordage aboard, it was not very long before the preparations for bridging could begin. The exact spot selected was one where the estuary was abnormally narrow, not over 300 yards wide, though there were points both below and above where it measured 500 or 600. It was found that the space could be filled with 26 *chasse-marées* moored side by side with their heads up-stream: all were anchored stern and bow, and lashed together so as to allow a certain power to rise and fall according as the tide was running. The main connexion was by five strong cables stretched by capstans from deck to deck of the whole row. On the cables stout planks were laid transversely, each bound at either end to the two outermost cables. The ends of the cables on the west bank were fastened to some of the heavy French guns of position taken in the lines of the Nivelle three months before, those on the east bank to capstans fixed in the sand and secured with large stakes and wedges. The whole rose and fell without disruption as the tide varied: the only criticism made on the construction was that at low water there was some sagging between boat and boat in the platform: but it never gave way, nor did the planks get out of touch with each other[1]. This was a very fine piece of military engineering, and reflected equal credit on the naval officer who got the ships into line—a Lieutenant Collins—and on the military engineers who bound them together —the chief of these were Colonel Sturgeon and Major Todd, the men who had already constructed the famous temporary bridge at Alcantara[2].

The bridge-building, begun on the 25th, was finished by the afternoon of the 26th. While it was in progress Hope continued to pour men across by means of his boats and rafts, a slow but continuous business. On the 25th not only the remainder of the 1st Division and of Campbell's Portuguese were got over, but Bradford's brigade also, and two squadrons of Vandeleur's Light Dragoons. On the 26th, the bridge being completed, Carlôs de España's Spaniards and the bulk of the cavalry and artillery followed. This caused a rearrangement of the blockading force left on the south side of Bayonne—Freire's divisions, which had now come up from the Bidassoa, replaced Carlos de España;

---

[1] All this detail is from Batty, pp. 125-7, and Jones, *Peninsular Sieges*, ii. pp. 116-20.

[2] See above, vol. v, p. 333.

the 5th Division sent one brigade across to the west bank of the
Nive, leaving two only in face of the works on the Mousserolles
front. Lord Aylmer's unattached British brigade was moved
back from Urdains to Anglet: thus the investing force had some
15,000 men on the north side and 16,000 on the south of
Bayonne.

The investment was completed on the 27th, when Hope, who
had been extending his foothold on the north bank of the Adour
as each brigade came up, advanced against the transpontine
works of the fortress, and stormed all the minor fortifications
up to the base of the Citadel hill—a series of fortified houses and
earthworks which surrounded the suburbs of St. Étienne. This
was a costly business, mainly street-fighting, in which the enemy
had to be evicted from loopholed houses and barricades. It was
completely successful, but cost Hope many more men than the
French lost. Their casualties were 55 killed and 103 wounded,
with some 30 or 40 prisoners. The German Legion brigades,
which stormed St. Étienne, had no less than 328 casualties, in the
1st and 5th line and 2nd Light battalions, and their senior officer
General Hinüber was wounded. As the Guards and Portuguese,
who supported the K.G.L., also had some small losses, the total
came to nearly double the French list[1]. But the occupation of
St. Étienne was absolutely necessary if the north side of Bayonne
was to be shut in—all the more so because it was intended that
the formal siege of the fortress, by batteries and trenches, was to
be carried out on this front, against the Citadel works, which
dominated the whole of the town from the opposite side of the
river, much as San Cristobal dominated Badajoz.

The French having been driven within their inner works, the
blockading line was established completely surrounding them,
starting from the convent and glass-works of St. Bernard, a
mile down-stream from the bridge, circling round the Citadel
hill, embracing the whole suburb of St. Étienne, and descending
to the small group of houses called Hayet, on the Adour half

---

[1] The fact that Wellington made no mention of the K.G.L. in his official
account of the investment of Bayonne provoked much grumbling, and
General Hinüber protested, in a letter which got a very formal and dry
answer from Pakenham, the Adjutant-General, writing on Wellington's
behalf. See Beamish, *History of the K.G.L.*, ii. pp. 443–6.

a mile above the bridge. Where houses existed in the line they were loopholed, and the roads coming out of the town, especially the two *chaussées* leading to Daxand Peyrehorade, were barricaded with earthworks.

The Governor remained on the complete defensive all through the crucial days after the crossing, save for a feeble sortie against the line held by the K.G.L. on March 1st. As the enemy was shut up tight in Bayonne, Hope was able to finish the work on the bridge undisturbed: the last touch was the construction of a barrier of floating spars and chains above that structure, intended to catch fire-ships or fire-rafts, which the enemy might send down-stream against it. But no such molestation was tried. One serious disappointment, discovered ere very long, was that the Adour mouth, which Wellington intended to use as a port of supply supplementary to St. Jean de Luz, could not be used for war-ships or merchant-vessels of any size, because of its shallowness at the bar. Only small craft could be sure of entering, and those only at high tide and in favourable weather.

Meanwhile Vandeleur's cavalry was sent out on all sides, to look for traces of the enemy. It explored on February 25th as far as St. Vincent on the Landes road, and up to St. Paul, opposite Dax on the 26th. A post of National Guards at Dax bridge was all that could be found. Similarly, going east, the 16th Light Dragoons discovered no signs of the French on the road to Port de Lanne, and when they crossed the Adour near the broken bridge of that place—long Soult's central magazine of supplies—they explored as far as Peyrehorade on February 27th, meeting there a patrol of Somerset's hussars, belonging to the main army. Thus Hope got into direct touch with Wellington, and the only thing wanting to make a secure line of communication was the restoration of the bridge of Port de Lanne. Soult had withdrawn far eastward, for the battle of Orthez had been fought on February 27th, the day after the great bridge of boats was completed.

SECTION XLIII: CHAPTER V

FROM SAUVETERRE TO ORTHEZ. FEBRUARY 21-6, 1814

WELLINGTON had spent the greater part of February 21st in a long ride from St. Jean de Luz to Garris, through the same blustering weather that had prevented him from letting loose his flotilla. Next day he picked up the threads of his main campaign; but it is a sign of his many-sided activity that this morning, before he started on his ride to the front, he wrote a well-considered memorandum on the defence of Canada. This was in reply to a demand for advice which he had just received from Lord Bathurst—a token of the way in which the ministry had come to regard him as a source of valuable suggestions on all possible problems. Discovering from Hill, and from the report sent in from Beresford, that the positions of all, or nearly all, the French divisions had now been located, that troops from Bayonne and the other side of the Adour had recently joined Foy, and that Soult showed no signs of offensive inclinations on the side of Peyrehorade, he could now issue his orders for the second great turning movement.

Once more Soult's line of defence was to be outflanked by Hill, and rolled up from the south. But as the French were now much more concentrated than they had been on the 14th, the turning column was to be larger than ever. The enemy had no solid force south of Harispe's division, which now held the line of the Gave d'Oloron south of Sauveterre. Between him and Navarrenx nothing had been seen but cavalry pickets watching the fords. On the other hand Villatte had closed in on Harispe, and about Sauveterre northward and southward the enemy was in some force. But there was a gap between Villatte's northern-most infantry and Taupin's division, which had been located in and about Caresse, and another between Taupin and the force under Foy and Darmagnac in front of Peyrehorade.

The plan now selected by Wellington was to reinforce Hill's column up to a strength which would make it irresistible, to force with it the fords of the Gave d'Oloron south of Harispe's position, and to demonstrate meanwhile, both against Sauveterre and against Peyrehorade, with sufficient vigour to make the enemy uncertain whether he was not about to receive a general attack all along the line. The really important part of the orders of February 22nd was that they suddenly brought down the Light and 6th Divisions, which had hitherto been placed as a sort of reserve for Beresford's column, to join the other flank and co-operate with Hill[1]. The former was marched from La Bastide-Clarence to St. Palais—a long day's tramp—the latter from Hasparren to the same place. Both were now directly behind Hill, and ready to join in his next movement on the 24th. Meanwhile Beresford with the 4th and 7th Divisions began to get into position for demonstrating against Foy and Darmagnac, on the lower course of the Saison. He drove in Foy's detachments from Hastingues, and appeared in front of the bridge-head of Peyrehorade.

Soult was puzzled by the situation. It seemed clear at last that Wellington was not set on crossing the Adour about Urt, with Beresford's force, which was the first operation that Soult had attributed to him. But could he possibly be intending to strike far south, and to march by Pau and Tarbes on Toulouse, imperilling his communications with the sea? 'That would be a very rash movement', and would give a fine opportunity for falling on his rear, as he marched past, however great the disproportion of numbers[2]. Two days later, just as Wellington concentrated to deliver his blow, Soult was writing 'all my reports attribute to him the project of moving by Oloron on Pau and Tarbes: I am astonished at the idea. Whatever happens I have made arrangements to mass my troops, and attack him if a favourable opportunity offers[3]'. But of course Wellington's objective was not Pau or Toulouse but the hostile army, and he was about to complete his plan for outflanking it, and rolling it up from the south. His final end was not an invasion of France, but the thrusting away of Soult's army to such a distance from Bayonne that the siege of that fortress might proceed with

---

[1] The 6th Division detached its 'Provisional battalion' (2nd and 53rd) to Bidache, to keep up touch with Beresford, and this battalion, therefore, was not at Orthez. [Rogerson's *History of the 53rd*, p. 88.]

[2] Soult to Clarke, February 20.   [3] Same to same, February 23.

security. This was all that he contemplated at present, though larger schemes might supervene, if the Allies determined to make no peace with Napoleon but to 'run in upon him[1]' as Wellington hoped that they might.

On February 24th the heads of Wellington's columns appeared before the fords of the Gave d'Oloron at more than half a dozen different points, on a front of fifteen miles. The only advance that was not meant seriously was that of Picton upon Sauveterre: the 3rd Division was to menace Harispe with frontal attacks upon his strong position, but not to commit itself to serious fighting. Only Harispe, and Villatte his neighbour, must be kept fixed to their ground, and prevented from detaching troops to the south. This scheme was quite successful; though Picton disobeyed orders by pressing on too far, and losing some men. All the other columns found themselves practically unopposed —five divisions of infantry launched against the upper fords had opposite to them only one brigade of French light cavalry, and two isolated battalions, and walked across the Gave with practically no loss.

The scheme was as follows. In the extreme south Morillo kept the garrison of Navarrenx quiet, by threatening the ford of Doguen, above that fortress, and then crossing much lower down the river at Bastanès. Hill laid his pontoon-train at Viellenave and passed over it the 2nd Division and Le Cor's Portuguese; the Light Division, coming from Nabas, crossed by a ford north of Viellenave, the 6th Division a little farther down-stream at Montfort. Most of these troops saw no more than a squadron or two of Berton's *chasseurs à cheval*, who sheered off when fired upon. The total loss of Hill's central column was two rank and file drowned. By the evening over 20,000 men were across the Gave d'Oloron, but the crossing had taken much time, and even the leading brigades did not get far enough in Harispe's rear to cut him off from the road to Orthez and surround him, as had been intended.

Meanwhile, in front of Sauveterre, Picton, coming from Arriverayte, developed a demonstration against the bridge of the Gave d'Oloron and opened with his artillery against its defences, spreading infantry also along the banks to the east of

[1] See above, p. 296.

it, while Somerset's Hussars put themselves in evidence along
the river-front north of Sauveterre, opposite Villatte. They had
been intended to do no more, but Picton having discovered a
very bad ford about 1,000 yards from the bridge, which seemed
unguarded, sent a party of the 7th Hussars across it, and when
they found it passable, drew them back, and ordered the four
light companies of Keane's brigade to cross. This they did, and
found themselves obliged to mount on to the plateau above by
a steep path between stone walls. When they had reached its
top, they were suddenly charged by a battalion of the 119th of
Villatte's division, and driven down to the ford in disorder and
with much loss. Some missed their footing in the river and were
drowned, about thirty were taken prisoners. The whole loss was
80 out of perhaps 250 who had crossed[1]. This was an example of
Picton's not infrequent headlong disobedience of orders, which
had been shown at Vittoria[2], and was to appear again with more
tiresome results at Toulouse. The survivors of the unlucky light
companies owed their safety to the rapid arrival of a British
battery, which shelled the pursuing enemy away from the
opposite bank[3]. Later in the day Harispe got news of Hill's
having forced the Gave far up-stream[4], and, seeing that he was
in great danger, marched off to Orion; whereupon Villatte, uncovered by Harispe's departure, blew up the bridge of Sauveterre
and his works around it, and followed Harispe in rapid retreat
towards Orthez. Picton could then repair the bridge, and follow
in pursuit next morning. If he had not risked Keane's light

[1] According to Vivian (p. 198) there were high words between Picton
and Stapleton Cotton, commanding the cavalry, as to responsibility for
the move. Picton apparently thought that the Hussars had guaranteed the
ford unprotected. The exact loss was 1 officer and 13 men killed, 4 officers
and 32 men wounded, and 1 officer and 28 men prisoners. The company
of the 5th Fusiliers suffered most—34 casualties.

[2] See above, vol. vi. p. 419.

[3] Soult in his dispatch says that this fighting occurred at the ford by
the Mill of Mussein, 1,000 metres *above* the bridge, and I suppose he must
be right, but many speak of a ford down-stream, e. g. Lapène (p. 243), a
contemporary: and Dumas (p. 361) calls it the ford of Aspis, which is
several miles below the bridge. Napier merely says that the ford was *near*
the bridge (vi. p. 197). Mr. Fortescue follows Dumas and says *below* the
bridge (ix. p. 497).

[4] See above, p. 343.

companies, there would have been practically no casualties at all in the passage of the Gave d'Oloron.

Down-stream from Sauveterre there was no fighting. Vivian's Hussars demonstrated against many fords in the neighbourhood of Taupin's position. Cole with the 4th Division had been sent by Beresford in this direction, while Walker with the 7th threatened Peyrehorade, where Foy and Darmagnac lay. In one or two places Vivian's reconnoitring parties got across the river—not without having men drowned, for the water was high. So did the 4th Division by missing a ford at St. Dos. Beresford therefore brought it farther down-stream to Sordes, where it ultimately succeeded in negotiating a passage very late in the day. Walker, facing Foy's bridge-head at Peyrehorade, was well satisfied to see the enemy keeping strictly on the defensive. This was the point where Soult might possibly have meditated a counterstroke, as he had two divisions on the ground, and another approaching. The last-named was that of Rouget (late Maransin) which had been drawn out of Bayonne on the 17th and sent on the Dax road. What it did between that date and the 24th does not appear from any document—but it was recalled and came down by Port de Lanne to join Foy. At any rate it was in touch with him on the 25th, probably after a circuitous journey from Bayonne to Dax and from Dax to Peyrehorade[1].

On finding that he had been completely turned by Hill's big column, Soult gave instant orders for all his divisions to concentrate on Orthez, and to be ready to defend the line of the Gave de Pau—as he had told the Minister of War that he would do, if the line of the Gave d'Oloron were lost. But it would take a long march to bring in Foy, Darmagnac, and Rouget from Peyrehorade, and meanwhile Hill would be pressing on Harispe and Villatte. The concentration, however, was completed without any trouble by the afternoon of the 25th. Harispe, marching all night, reached Orthez by dawn. Villatte who had halted till 5 a.m. on the heights before Orion, to cover his colleague's movement if Hill should press hard, followed, and reached Orthez by 8 a.m. Taupin, who had retired from the banks of the Saison in the evening as far as Saillies, crossed the bridge of Berenx, four

---

[1] This I deduce from one battalion of this division, the 1/34th, having been at Dax on February 28th, evidently left as garrison.

miles west of Orthez, and blew it up behind him, as he had
been directed. The three divisions from the lower course of
the Saison and the entrenchments of Peyrehorade had a much
longer march, along the high road north of the Gave de
Pau. They were kept travelling for many of the hours of a
frosty night, and far on into the following morning, till they
reached Baights, some four miles on the west side of Orthez.
Foy left a battalion behind to watch the bridge of Berenx, which
Taupin had blown up, and the 15th *chasseurs à cheval* remained
out beyond Berenx, watching the road by which the three
divisions had come. Thus Soult by noon on the 25th had
concentrated his whole field-army, save Abbé's division, which he
had rather unaccountably left inside Bayonne. There were
some 32,000 foot and 3,000 horse. It remained to be seen
whether he would carry out the plan of which he had written
to Clarke—to mass every man, and attack any isolated column
of Wellington's army which exposed itself to him.

Wellington, having failed to envelop Harispe on the 24th–
25th, owing to the fatigue of Hill's divisions after their crossing
the Gave d'Oloron, was concentrating also, intending to push
Soult one more stage away from Bayonne. He does not seem
to have considered it likely that the Marshal would at last risk
a battle, though the massing of the French army at Orthez
obviously made this a possible contingency. He resumed his
plan of showing a large force in the enemy's front, but turning
his position unexpectedly on one flank. Only Hill on the right
wing was not this time to be the turning force, but Beresford on
the left, reinforced from Hill's column on this occasion, just as
Hill had been reinforced by Beresford's reserves on the 24th[1].
The orders for the 26th were for the left-wing divisions, the 4th
and 7th with Somerset's cavalry, to follow the route that Foy
had taken along the Peyrehorade–Orthez road, crossing the
Gave de Pau near its junction with the Adour, so as to have
made their passage on to its north bank far outside the enemy's
flank. When they had reached the broken bridge of Berenx, and
could cover it securely, they were to be joined by three divisions
(3rd, 6th, Light) and Vivian's cavalry from Hill's column, who
would cross by Hill's pontoon-train, laid to replace the vanished

[1] See orders for the 26th in *Supplementary Dispatches*, xi. p. 599.

bridge. Thus five divisions and two cavalry brigades would be
north of the river and on the flank of Soult's newly-assumed
position. Meanwhile Hill with the 2nd Division, Le Cor's Portuguese, and Fane's light cavalry would appear before Orthez, and
menace it from the front. The river was impassable there, as
it runs in a narrow course between rocky banks on each side of
Orthez bridge; and this handsome medieval structure had been
partly blown up, but more effectively blocked by the building
up with large stones of the tower which stands upon its central
arch. This tower, a reproduction on a smaller scale of the great
bridge-towers of Cahors, constitutes a gate in itself, only wide
enough to allow a single wagon to pass. There was no chance
of forcing it, but at the right moment, when Beresford's columns
were nearing the enemy's flank, Hill was to turn his demonstration at the bridge into a real attempt to cross the Gave at the
fords of Souars, a mile up-stream from Orthez, where the banks
are less steep and the river broader and shallower.

Morillo's division had been left behind to invest the little
fortress of Navarrenx, and the general and three of his battalions
lay there during the short remainder of the war. They were lost
to Wellington as an operating force. To look after the larger and
more heavily garrisoned St.-Jean-Pied-du-Port, now far behind
Wellington's theatre of operations, and entirely isolated, Mina
had been ordered to collect as many of his battalions as possible
—Jaca had now surrendered and set free several of them—and
to invest St. Jean, where General Blondeau had a considerable
garrison of three regular battalions and some National Guards.
Like Morillo, Mina was immobilized till the end of the war, for
the fortress never fell: but his Navarrese had never been part of
Wellington's field-army, while Morillo had been playing a part
in the great game ever since Vittoria, and was a net loss to the
commander-in-chief, being a stout fighter. On February 26th
Wellington resolved to make up for the loss of Morillo by drawing
on Freire for a couple of his best divisions now before Bayonne[1],
while these were to be replaced by bringing across the Pyrenees,
from the Bastan, Giron's 'Army of Andalusia' which had been
mouldering in winter quarters ever since the battle of the Nivelle,

[1] *Dispatches*, xi. p. 529, to Hope, and February 26 to Freire, ibid.,
p. 531.

very short of supplies and reduced to a strength of 8,000 men in
its two divisions. To utilize it Wellington found that he would
have to feed and pay it[1]. At this he murmured, for he was unwilling to use Spanish troops in France, for fear that they might
plunder, and rouse an insurrection in the country-side: and if
unpaid and unfed it was certain that they would do so. Wherefore he grudgingly took them on his own responsibility for
sustenance, and once more issued the most stringent orders to
their commanders as to the maintenance of discipline[2]. But
Giron did not cross the frontier for some time yet, while
Freire obeyed orders at once, and came in person to the front
with two weak divisions by March 4th. Wellington had
directed him to bring up the 3rd (Del Barco) and the 4th
(Espeleta), but Freire substituted for the former a 'provisional
division' picked from the battalions which were in best order[3].
The two units together only made up 7,500 bayonets, and did
not reach the front till long after Orthez had been fought. The
remaining part of the Army of Galicia, left in front of Bayonne,
passed under the command of Carlos de España.

When Hill's column arrived in front of Orthez and the course
of the Gave de Pau, on the afternoon of the 25th, he drove in the
outposts which Soult had left on the south side of the river, and
occupied the transpontine suburb of Départ with the Caçadores
of the Light Division, who kept up a noisy skirmishing fire all
day against Villatte's *voltigeurs* in the fortified bridge and the
outer houses of the town stretching down to the water. Nothing
of course could be done in the way of crossing, nor did Wellington
intend it. Neither was a shelling of Villatte's supports by Bean's
horse-artillery battery meant for anything but annoyance. Meanwhile the rest of the Allied forces were moving into position.
Picton had gone forward to Salies, while the exploring parties
of Somerset's hussars in front of him, surveying the broken
bridge of Berenx, discovered a passable ford in its vicinity.
Beresford had crossed the Saison at Sordes and other passages in

---

[1] *Dispatches*, xi. p. 531.

[2] Wellington to Freire, March 4. *Dispatches*, xi. p. 546, and same to
same, much more stringent, of March 5th. *Dispatches*, xi. p. 551.

[3] Three of these were drawn from Porlier's division, then besieging Santoña, others being made over to Porlier as substitutes.

its neighbourhood, and had seen that Peyrehorade had been evacuated by the enemy. He had now to seek for fords on the Gave de Pau, which still had to be crossed in order to turn Soult's new position farther up that river. The exploring officers from Vivian's hussar brigade discovered difficult but practicable passages at Cauneille and Lahonton, by which the whole of Beresford's infantry passed on the following day[1]. So completely had this part of the country been evacuated by the French, that Soult got no news of the position of this turning column: he had plenty of occupation in watching the threatening movements of Hill's force, in the immediate front of his own army at Orthez.

Owing to the distance which Beresford had to cover, the whole of the 26th was occupied in getting the Allied army into the position from which it was to deliver its stroke against Soult on the following day. Beresford, leaving the 51st regiment to hold the important point of Peyrehorade, forded the Gave de Pau at Cauneille and Lahonton—the way for the infantry being shown by Vivian's hussars, who crossed first. The water was icy cold, and almost waist-deep, so the passage took a long time. But about midday Vivian, riding himself with the 18th Hussars far in front of the column, came on the first French whom the turning force had yet seen—a squadron of the 15th Chasseurs blocking the high road at Puyoo. He charged them in person at the head of Burke's squadron of the 18th, and chased them as far as Ramous, where the French found their supports, who counter-attacked, and tumbled back the pursuing squadron for some distance. But the rest of the 18th coming up, the tables were turned, the beaten squadron rallied, and Vivian drove the chasseurs back some miles, past the point where the road from the broken bridge of Berenx comes into the Peyrehorade–Orthez *chaussée*[2].

This skirmish secured the junction of Beresford's column with that of Picton, whose hussars had already crossed the ford below

---

[1] For this ford-hunting, see Woodberry, pp. 164–5.

[2] There is an interesting account of this in Vivian's letter on p. 200 of his *Life* by Claude Vivian. Incidentally one may remark that a brigadier in charge of a covering screen of cavalry, in front of an army corps, had no business to charge at the head of the leading squadron.

the broken bridge: the 3rd Division, following, had driven away
the single battalion which Foy had left to watch the passage.
Thus the two columns met, and between 3 and 4 in the afternoon
Picton joined Beresford's column. When he got news that this
junction had been made, Wellington sent up from Hill's block
of troops, opposite Orthez, both the Light and the 6th Divisions,
who, approaching Berenx by side roads, were able to cross in
Picton's rear at dawn next day. Their passage was facilitated by
Hill's pontoon-bridge, which they had brought along with them.
Thus five divisions and two cavalry brigades were concentrated
on the French side of the Gave de Pau, on the early morning of
the 27th, and Soult's project for holding the line of that river
had been frustrated.

The Marshal, looking for scapegoats after the battle which
followed, found one in Colonel Faverot of the 15th Chasseurs,
who having been attacked by Vivian at Puyoo, and engaged in
some lively fighting, committed a fault of omission in failing
to send to his chief the news that there was a heavy column of
all arms coming down the Peyrehorade *chaussée* against his
flank. He reported in person, late in the day, at Orthez. Soult
was furious, loaded him with abuse, and sent him before a court-
martial some days after the battle, though he was an officer
of good reputation, who had distinguished himself in 1812 at
the combat of Villadrigo[1]. Disregarding chronology, we may
mention that the court-martial acquitted Faverot. It is in his
report written after the battle that the Marshal discharges vials
of wrath on the colonel. 'I had resolved', he wrote to Clarke,
'to march straight at the first hostile corps which should present
itself, and to attack it when it was passing the river. Colonel
Faverot's fault deprived me of this chance. I found myself faced
by a whole army, and had at a moment's notice to make arrangements for receiving battle[2].' There is, as the best French critic
of this campaign remarks[3], a good deal of humbug in Soult's
denunciations of Faverot. He had not (though he often wrote
to Clarke of his intention of falling upon the first hostile column
that approached him) any real inclination to take the offensive.

[1] Soult to Clarke, February 28.
[2] Dumas, *Neuf Mois de Campagne*, pp. 373–83.
[3] Foy's *Memoirs*, ed. Girod de l'Ain, p. 238.

This seems settled by Foy's journal of the campaign. That general writes that he was present at a sort of council of war on the 26th, held in front of his own position on the heights above Orthez, at which Soult called together D'Erlon and Clausel and four generals of division, himself included. 'Only Clausel, who was always inclined to a bold, not to say a rash policy, advocated instant action. All the rest were against it. Soult finally ordered his whole army to change its positions during the night, and make a front westwards, from Orthez along the heights up the Dax road. Even so, he had not decided to offer battle, hoping that the sight of his whole army united on a strong position would impose upon the English.' And this, undoubtedly, was the true mentality of the Marshal on February 26th. Since the battle of St. Pierre he had no real inclination to take the offensive, and he had found at Orthez a very fine defensive position, short, steep, and very difficult to turn.

The Marshal had undoubtedly for the last two days allowed his attention to be fixed on Hill's column, with which he knew that Wellington was present—the English head-quarters staff had been seen surveying Orthez from the heights of Magret, at such a close distance that a French battery had tried some shots at it. And each of the previous turning movements on the Joyeuse, the Bidouze, and the Gave d'Oloron had been made up-stream. Soult had sent all his cavalry, save the one regiment which Faverot commanded, to watch the fords between Orthez and Pau. His preparations had been made for resisting another flank attack from this side, not from the west. But there was an admirable position facing west, which he now made haste to occupy. Possibly it might be strong enough to stop Wellington, if he risked a frontal attack.

Orthez is a well-built place, containing many pleasant seventeenth-century houses; it slopes up from the river and the bridge to the castle of Moncade, an old stronghold of the counts of Béarn, which lies at the head of the town. It is a centre of roads—first-rate *chaussées* to St. Palais, Pau, St. Sever, Dax, and Peyrehorade forking out from it. While very defensible from the south or east, it is particularly so from the west, where Beresford was now showing himself. The Dax road, mounting steeply out of the town, runs along the narrow plateau of a well-

marked ridge with an average height of 500 feet, overlooking
all the country-side westward, till it reaches the village of
St. Boes, where it quits the sky-line and falls northward into
lower ground. There the ridge turns north-westward and is
continued for some miles, with a secondary road to St. Girons
on its crest. The line of the Dax *chaussée* along the heights is
very commanding, and the slopes up to it are completely exposed, and made uninviting by three brooks in sunken muddy
channels, which run down from the sky-line along which the road
passes, and fall into the Gave de Pau. The slopes between them
are open ground covered by coarse grass and a few stunted
shrubs. The track of the road along the heights is of an up-and-
down description: thrice it goes over rising ground much loftier
than its average course, the knolls by Lafaurie (558 feet), Luc,
and Plassotte (595 feet) farms. These were famous positions for
artillery facing down the western slopes, and were utilized as
such. Just after the Plassotte knoll the road dips down suddenly,
through what was then the village street of St. Boes, with a ravine
on either side, one running south, the other north[1]. When this
dip is crossed, it rises again to pass the isolated church of St. Boes[2]
on a knoll of its own (560 feet), the last dominating point on the
sky-line, and very visible from all the low ground by the river.
Facing Plassotte and St. Boes, on the farther side of the southern
ravine, was a wooded hill crowned by an old Roman Camp,
whose quadrangular outline is still visible. It lies on a separate
ridge, which descends to the Gave de Pau with a muddy brook
on each side of it. The only lines of access to the high-lying
position along the Dax *chaussée* are, on its northern end, the
track of the St. Girons road along the crest west of St. Boes,
and farther south two spurs running down steeply from the
main ridge toward the Gave, between the three brooks above
mentioned—the right-hand spur rises from the river near the
village of Castetarbe, the left-hand from above the west side of
the village of Cason[3]. Between them the brooks make marshy

[1] Being entirely destroyed in the battle, the village was rebuilt on a new
site, rather eastward, and its present situation does not correspond to that
of 1814. See Dumas, pp. 402–3.

[2] Called by Napier and others the 'high church of Baights', which is
confusing.

[3] Right and left when looking from the *French* position.

ground, almost impassable for horse or foot. Any force approaching from the west is almost compelled to select the comparatively dry ascent up the two narrow spurs, where it can advance only on short fronts, and is completely exposed to artillery-fire from the knolls above, along the Dax road.

At the back, or east side, of the whole French position there is a slow but well-marked drop into a high-lying plateau, which rolls downward toward the Luy de Béarn and the bridge of Sault de Navailles, six miles to the rear. This plateau is broken up into slight ridges, is commanded from the Dax road, and offers no such good positions as the ridge along that *chaussée*. The high road from Orthez to Sault runs across it at its lowest slope, about 300 feet above sea-level, along its southern edge. Rising above this road eastward is a separate line of heights, running up from the Gave, into one lofty knoll, the Motte de Tury (or de Turenne in old maps), which reaches 600 feet. This is also a good position against an attack from the west, but has two disadvantages, which no doubt prevented Soult from choosing it as his fighting ground—it has no bridge in its rear, as the Dax *chaussée* position has, and to have held it would have involved giving up the town of Orthez, which was an invaluable flank-guard to the line which the Marshal actually defended.

Soult's detailed arrangements for the manning of the battle-ground have been preserved. They ran as follows. Reille— restored to command despite of his insubordination on February 17th—was to hold the northern part of the position with the divisions of Taupin and Rouget. He was also given Paris's brigade (deducted from Harispe's three-brigade division) as a reserve. His task was to defend the line of the Dax *chaussée* from St. Boes for a mile southward. He placed only one regiment[1] in the outlying knoll on which stands the isolated church of St. Boes, but established himself in force on the strong position, south of the well-marked dip, which separates the church from its village. Taupin's division was mainly on the Plassotte knoll, with its divisional battery: Rouget's on Taupin's left, extending the line south, with his divisional guns, and a reserve battery also, on the Luc and Berge knolls, looking down into the lower

---

[1] 12th Léger of Taupin.

ground westward[1]. Paris's brigade was placed on the back of the position out of sight, as a reserve should be[2]. Rouget's left approached the right of the French central corps, commanded by D'Erlon, which consisted on this day of the divisions of Darmagnac and Foy. The former was in the very centre of the position, looking down into the hollows of the marshy brooks below. His artillery was on the rising ground on the *chaussée*, on the knoll of Lafaurie[3]. Foy prolonged Darmagnac's line southward along the descending slope of the high road towards Orthez. His left-hand battalion occupied the convent of the Bernardines, just outside the north-western end of the town. The defence of the town itself, and of the fords of Souars—a mile to the east upstream—was left to Clausel's corps—which consisted of the divisions of Harispe (less one brigade) and Villatte. The former had only a couple of battalions occupying the bridge and the houses near it, a couple more[4] above the fords of Souars, with a cavalry regiment[5]. As two battalions (25th Line) had been left to guard the fords of Lescar, many miles up-stream, and were quite out of the battle, this left five battalions for Harispe's reserve, which was placed outside the town on the high road, under the old castle of Moncade, with orders to support either the troops in the town or those holding the fords of Souars as events might dictate. Clausel's other division, that of Villatte, formed the general reserve of the army: it was placed on the lower slopes above Orthez west of the village of Rontun, with orders to be ready either to support Harispe, if Hill's corps—clearly visible on the south bank of the Gave de Pau—should push forward from the side of the river, or on the other hand to march uphill to reinforce Reille, if Wellington's attack should turn out to be an attempt to envelop the French right wing near St. Boes.

Of Pierre Soult's seven regiments of cavalry two were 'off the map'—the 22nd Chasseurs in front of Pau, the 2nd Hussars at Lescar, half-way to Pau, along with the two battalions of the 25th Line already mentioned. The 21st Chasseurs were attached

---

[1] Rouget was short of one battalion, the 1/34th, left at Dax.

[2] Four battalions, 2 each of the 10th and 81st Line.

[3] Defined by Soult as the fork of the Dax road and the path to Sallespisse.

[4] Of the 115th Ligne. [5] 15th Chasseurs.

to Reille, the 15th to D'Erlon, for reconnaissance work, the 18th was with Harispe's battalions watching the fords of Souars, the remaining two regiments, the 5th and 10th, we are a little surprised to find under orders to retire to the rear of the army, to Sallespisse in front of the bridge of Sault de Navailles, 'in case the troops should be obliged to make a retrograde movement'. It is clear from this and other details in his orders that the Marshal, who much overvalued Wellington's disposable force, was contemplating retreat as a likely possibility.

The force on the field, deducting the three battalions and two cavalry regiments which were detached at a distance, amounted to about 36,000 men, with 48 guns[1]. There were also due to arrive this day the first-formed brigade of the conscript 'division of reserve of Toulouse', 3,750 strong. And as a matter of fact the head of their column did appear in the late afternoon—an asset of doubtful value, half-trained troops, short of uniforms and cartridges too.

[1] viz. infantry in the six divisions (after deducting 3 battalions absent) about 33,000; cavalry, five regiments, 2,000; artillery, sappers, &c., 1,500. The artillery-train and some reserve batteries had been sent back to Sallespisse, along with P. Soult's two cavalry regiments mentioned above.

SECTION XLIII: CHAPTER VI

THE BATTLE OF ORTHEZ. FEBRUARY 27, 1814

EVEN on the night before the battle Wellington had not been quite sure that the enemy would not evacuate his positions under cover of the darkness, as he had done at the passages of the Saison and the Gave d'Oloron. It was not till he received Beresford's report at dawn that he discovered that Soult was ready to fight, having now got his whole army concentrated. The plan which the British general first put in play was to turn the French right with Beresford's two divisions in the direction of St. Boes, and the French left with Hill's corps crossing the fords of Souars above the town. While Beresford executed a laborious flank march from Baights, up muddy roads, to establish himself on the St. Girons road, and so to get beyond the enemy's flank at St. Boes, Picton and the 3rd Division, with Somerset's cavalry brigade, deployed themselves opposite the French centre and left, the cavalry on the Peyrehorade–Orthez *chaussée*, the infantry on the lower slopes of the two spurs which have already been mentioned as leading up from the river towards the heights of the enemy's main position. Picton's deployment was to cover the passage over the pontoon-bridge near Berenx of the two divisions which had been borrowed from Hill's column—the 6th and Light—of which the former, crossing first, took post behind Picton, while the latter followed Beresford's marching columns up the country roads leading towards St. Boes[1]. The movements of all these three divisions were screened from Soult by the minor hills north of Baights. Hill meanwhile was to make a noisy demonstration against Orthez town and bridge, with one of Le Cor's Portuguese brigades, but to be ready to make a dash for the fords of Souars with his main body, so soon as he should receive the news that Beresford's attack had begun, and that the French right was being turned.

The 6th and Light Divisions began to file over the bridge

---

[1] But it is not quite clear which of several bad roads north from Baights the Light Division followed.

at dawn; the former had but a short way to go before it fell
in behind Picton's covering force. The latter had a much longer
journey before it, and did not reach its destination till after the
fighting had begun in the north. It was placed by Wellington
behind the Roman Camp, on the ridge which faces the right of
the French position, and kept out of sight. The commander-in-
chief himself took his stand for the greater part of the day on
the front wall of the camp, from which every section of the hostile
line was well under his view.

Wellington, it will be remembered, had seven cavalry regiments with him this day. Two, Fane's brigade, were with Hill
south of the Gave; two more, Vivian's brigade, had sent out
vedettes in front of Beresford's marching column, and accompanied it all day. The three remaining, Somerset's hussars, were
with Picton, and formed a screen on the flanks of his infantry,
sending a squadron or two to explore down the Peyrehorade–
Orthez road, as near to the town as they could venture.

Deducting the five battalions which were absent from their
divisions this day[1], Wellington had with him in his seven
divisions and three cavalry brigades 38,000 bayonets and 3,300
sabres, as also 54 guns and about 1,500 more of 'other arms',
artillery, sappers, &c. His force, therefore, was about 7,000
greater than Soult's, a superiority which does not justify the
excuses made by French writers, from the Marshal down to some
serious military historians of modern times, as to the enormous
superiority in numbers of the Allied army[2]. Indeed it was rather
a bold venture to attack an almost equal enemy, placed in
a very strong position, when Hill's two divisions were divided
from the rest of the army by a river only passable by one bridge
at the west end of the theatre of operations.

As soon as the 7th Division was seen coming up behind the
4th, and the 6th Division behind the 3rd, but before the Light
Division had reached its appointed destination, the battle began,
at about 8.30 on a clear morning of slight frost, which had not,
however, made the ground hard to the foot. When Cole had

---

[1] 1/43rd, 1/95th of Light Division, 51st of 7th Division, 79th of 6th
Division, 2nd Provisional of 4th Division.

[2] Clerc, for example, gives Wellington 44,000 men; but the contemporaries, Pellot and Lapène, 70,000 !

established himself on the heights along the St. Girons road, he opened his attack on the French flank by sending Ross's brigade to turn the enemy out of the church of St. Boes, the last point held by him on his right. The church on its prominent knoll was carried without much difficulty, the 12th Léger falling back to join the rest of Taupin's division. But the serious work was yet to come; when Ross, having re-formed his battalions, started along the crest of the heights to dislodge the enemy from the village of St. Boes and the Plassotte knoll above it, he was soon checked. Taupin's battery had been placed so as to sweep the narrow front between the two ravines, and the dip in the road along which ran the scattered cottages of the street. Ross's brigade penetrated into the open space beyond the houses, but could get no farther, and fell back with loss, taking what cover it could among the buildings. Cole then brought up his divisional battery, that of Sympher of the K.G.L., on to the church knoll, and tried to silence Taupin's guns; but it was under fire before it could open, Sympher was killed early and a couple of his pieces dismounted; the battery could make no head, being engaged frontally with Taupin's artillery and raked by other pieces belonging to Rouget's line of guns on the Luc knoll to the left of the road. Ross's brigade, being rallied, was then sent forward by Cole to repeat its attempt, being strengthened by Vasconcellos's Portuguese, who tried to advance on the steep slope to the right of the crest, so as to avoid the fire that swept the road above. This attempt was no more successful than the first: the assailing troops could never reach the foot of the French knoll. Ross was wounded, and his men fell back and again took cover. After this the fighting died down into an infantry *tiraillade*, punctuated by cannon-balls when the French could find a formed body at which to fire. Cole refused to put in his reserve brigade, Anson's, for fear of a French counter-attack, and such indeed did come, for Taupin's infantry tried to recover the village, and cleared many of its houses before they could be stopped. After this there was only intermittent skirmishing; the best account that we have of the fight of Ross's brigade, that of a sergeant of the 7th Fusiliers, tells of his company 'firing in rapid bo-peep fashion from behind the corners of a large building[1] 'and occasion-

[1] Cooper's *Rough Notes of Seven Campaigns*, pp. 110–11.

ally making a sortie to drive off French skirmishers, who came skulking up behind hedges by the ravine on the left. Finding wine in some of the houses, the men alternately plied bottle and musket 'drink and fire—fire and drink'. There was no getting forward, and presently there was some getting back, for Vasconcellos's Portuguese, who had no shelter from houses and little from hedges, began to waver.

Wellington, who had been watching all this from the Roman Camp, ordered the Light Division, which had now come up behind him, to detach the 1st Caçadores to cover Vasconcellos's flank. But, just as they arrived, the line gave way, and both the Allied brigades retired on to their own side of the dip below the church, losing all that had been gained. The 1st Caçadores got mixed with them, and never rejoined their division during the battle; it was only after two days that their brigadier discovered what had become of his 'lost battalion'[1].

Altogether the attempt to turn Taupin's division out of its position on the neck with two brigades had been a costly failure. There was no danger, since the 7th Division was now closed up behind the 4th, and Anson's brigade was practically intact. But the original plan for turning the French right had failed.

Meanwhile, in the centre Picton's attack on the troops of D'Erlon, which was never intended for much more than a demonstration, had also been held up. The general had divided his division into two columns, each of which was to ascend one of the spurs which trend down from the French position toward the Gave de Pau. Keane's brigade, followed by Power's Portuguese—nine battalions in all—went up the northern spur, opposite Darmagnac's line, Brisbane's brigade—three battalions —up the Castetarbe spur, which brought them opposite to Foy. The 6th Division, which was in close supporting distance, came up behind Brisbane, but was held back as a reserve. The advance had to be in column up the narrow crests of the two spurs, as on each side there were muddy brooks which rendered it impossible to deploy on a broad front. Each column was preceded by its light companies as a screen. The outlying skirmishers of the French, thrown forward some distance down the two spurs,

[1] Harry Smith's *Autobiography*, i. p. 165.

were easily driven in on to the main position. But when the heads of the columns began to come under fire from the French batteries about Lafaurie on the one side, and about Escorial on the other, Picton halted them and ordered his powerful skirmishing line[1] only to advance farther uphill. It had not been intended that he should strike hard, till Cole had made some way on the French right. The light troops pushed on till they came in contact with formed battalions, and were then checked: the enemy gave no signs of recoiling. Meanwhile the heads of the two columns on the spurs were suffering from distant artillery-fire, but not seriously[2], the distance being great. This state of affairs went on for some two hours, the order for a general advance being delayed till Cole's division should have turned the French right, which (as we have seen) it never succeeded in doing.

The fighting at St. Boes had begun before 9 o'clock, and had become heavy between 10 and 11 a.m. It was only after witnessing from his post on the Roman Camp Cole's final repulse that Wellington, as he explains in his dispatch to Bathurst, 'so far altered my plan of the action as to order the immediate advance of the 3rd and 6th Divisions, and to move forward Colonel Barnard's brigade of the Light Division to attack the left of the heights on which the enemy's right stood'[3]. That is to say, instead of relying on the turning movement, he threw in the mass of his army against the French right and centre. He does not mention (oddly enough) in this dispatch that the advance of the troops whom he cites was aided by an attack on the St. Boes front by the 7th Division, brought forward to replace the two much-mauled brigades of the 4th. But certainly about 11.30 he attacked with every disposable man, leaving only as reserve on the Roman Camp a remnant of the Light Division, the second and third battalions of the 95th, and three Portuguese battalions[4].

The advance seems to have been fairly simultaneous along

---

[1] Light companies of seven British regiments, three companies of the 5/60th rifles, and all Power's Caçador battalion—fourteen companies in all.

[2] Picton in his letter to Colonel Pleydell exaggerates its damage. *Life*, p. 274.   [3] *Dispatches*, xi. p. 536.

[4] 3rd Caçadores and two battalions of the 17th Line.

the whole front, and as the attacks were completely successful
on three separate points, at which different sections of the
French line were pierced and broken in, it is difficult to follow
Napier in calling that of his own Light Division the decisive one.

What happened in the two hours of bitter fighting between
11.30 and 1.30 was apparently as follows,—starting from the
south end of the line. Brisbane's brigade of the 3rd Division on
the Castetarbe—the southern spur—attacked Fririon's brigade
of Foy's division, and gradually drove it uphill, till, as Foy
explains in his memoirs, they had got up on a level with him[1],
i. e. had won up to the edge of the plateau, with the divisional
battery behind, and the 6th Division following. A good account
of this advance happens to have been preserved in the memoirs
of a man of the 45th, and as this is the only detailed narrative
of this part of the fight it is worth giving:

'Our brigade had to pass along a narrow path directly in
front of the enemy's centre, from which they kept up a heavy
cannonade, by which we were sorely annoyed, and had many
killed and wounded. We dashed on, however, at double quick
time, and soon got under cover of the height on which the
enemy was placed. Being then secure from the destructive fire
of their cannon, our general halted, and, after drawing us up in
close column by regiments, he seemed to get into a kind of
quandary, and not to know what to do. Meantime the enemy's
skirmishers advanced to the brow of the hill, and began to fire
into us, until the Adjutant-General [Pakenham], a most gallant
officer, came galloping from the left exclaiming, "Good God!
General Brisbane, why stand here while the brigade gets cut
up? Form line, and send out the 45th skirmishing." Two
companies being left with the colours, the rest of us ascended
the hill, to be received in such a manner as I had never before
experienced. We were but a skirmishing line opposed to a dense
column supported by artillery and cavalry. The bullets flew
thick as hail, thirteen men of my company alone fell within a
few yards of me on the brow of the hill. Notwithstanding we
pressed on, and the enemy after dreadful carnage gave way,
and left us in possession of a ditch, which we held till the brigade

[1] Foy, ed. Girod de l'Ain, p. 240. 'Voilà la 3ᵐᵉ division Anglaise établie
de plein-pied avec la mienne.'

came up in line. We then gave three cheers, charged the enemy's
light troops, and drove them from another ditch parallel with
the one we had just taken. Having repeatedly charged, and
been charged in turn, we got on the height, from which we had
a complete view of the dark masses of the enemy in column,
one of which was moving against us, the officers hat in hand
waving on the men in advance. By this time we were greatly
diminished—nearly a half down or disabled—and might have
given way, if a staff-officer had not come up at the critical
moment and encouraged us to hold our ground, as we should
be relieved in a minute. Two brigades of the 6th Division,
which had hitherto been in reserve, formed immediately in our
rear, and we retired through their line, which advanced and
encountered the French on the summit of the heights, where
a most desperate conflict ensued. Our troops fired a volley
at a distance of a very few yards from the enemy, and instantly
closed and pushed on with the bayonet. Their adversaries
rolled downhill in the greatest haste and consternation[1].'

From the 88th, which must have been the left regiment of the
brigade formed in line, we have another account, as it chances,
of happenings in their front. They had reached the line of the
chaussée on the top of the plateau when the divisional battery,
which had followed them closely, drew up and came into action,
the two leading companies of the regiment acting as its escort.
The fire of the guns was proving most effective, when quite
suddenly a squadron of French chasseurs charged down the
road from the north, rode down these companies with severe loss,
and fell upon the guns. But the other companies of the 88th,
lining the bank of the *chaussée*, gave such a well-directed dis-
charge that the horsemen were nearly all destroyed. This incident
is borne out by several French sources. Apparently Soult, close
by at the moment, saw that the intervention of the guns would
be decisive, and ordered Leclerc's squadron of the 21st Chasseurs
to silence them at all costs. The three contemporary French

[1] Narrative of a soldier, William Brown, 45th regiment, pp. 259–60.
Kilmarnock, 1828. By a curious slip of the pen Brown writes that the
brigade was relieved by two brigades of the *Light* division. He *must* mean
6th Division, which was close by, while the Light Division was away on
the left.

narrators of the charge, Lapène, Pellot, and Lemonnier, all state
that the squadron rode down a regiment of British infantry,
and would have forced it to surrender, if the fire from the banks
had not annihilated it in the moment of victory. The losses of
this daring band of horsemen may be estimated from the fact
that in the muster rolls of Pierre Soult's division the 21st
appears before the battle with 401 sabres, and after it with
236 on March 10th[1].

From the French side we have to depend for the narrative
of this part of the battle mainly on Foy's autobiography, which
only covers the earlier stages of it, as he was wounded before
the critical moment when the line broke. He says that he was
conducting the defence of the part of the position covered by
Fririon's brigade, which lay behind an undulation in the plateau,
two hundred yards in front of the *chaussée*, with its divisional
battery on the summit of a knoll. When Picton's guns were
brought up high on the slope, the French line began to be badly
annoyed by them. Foy himself, while walking on foot behind
the infantry firing-line, was struck by a shrapnel-bullet, from
a shell which exploded six feet above his head. He was badly
wounded in the left shoulder, and had to be helped back to the
chaussée, where he received first aid, and was carried to the
rear[2]. All the French accounts say that the general's wound and
departure affected the morale of his troops, who began to give
way at once. Their retreat uncovered the flank of Berlier's
brigade to their left, on the lower slopes, who retired before
the leading battalions of the 6th Division, just at the moment
when the already mentioned cavalry charge was delivered down
the high road. Apparently the 42nd, Clinton's leading battalion,
was partly involved in it. The other regiments of that division
suffered practically no losses in their pursuit of Foy's routed
troops[3].

---

[1] Several French sources say that General Pierre Soult ordered this
charge. But Lemonnier-Delafosse, his aide-de-camp, distinctly asserts that
the Marshal and not his brother directed its execution. And he was at
P. Soult's elbow all day.

[2] Foy's little monument, beside the highway, marks the place where
he was bandaged, not where he was hit, I imagine.

[3] There were only 19 casualties in the other five British regiments of
Clinton's division, and 24 in its Portuguese brigade, that of Douglas.

When Foy's division went to the rear in disorder, it was obvious that Harispe's two battalions in Orthez town would be cut off, if they lingered there. They retired in haste, leaving the bridge undefended. Meanwhile the main body of Picton's division—Keane's British and Power's Portuguese brigades—had been forcing their way up the northern spur, which brought them in face of Darmagnac's line, in the very centre of Soult's position. We have no good account of the fighting here, but it was evidently severe, and the line of the *chaussée* does not seem to have been reached till Foy's troops gave way farther down the road. The 2/87th, a weak battalion of only 350 bayonets, suffered a check high up the slope, and had 109 casualties[1], including 23 prisoners—almost the only British soldiers captured by the enemy that day[2]. The brigade lost in all 220 men, and Power's Portuguese, supporting it, 100 more. No doubt Darmagnac's losses also were heavy—they totalled more than those of Foy[3], but it seems likely that many of them were suffered during his retreat, in the subsequent phase of the action. It would appear that it was the breaking of the line farther south which forced Darmagnac to disentangle himself from the strife with Keane's and Power's men, and to withdraw downhill toward the solid reserve formed by Villatte's division, on the next ridge of the plateau. This unit had been brought up to the rear of the French centre, and now stood in the middle front of a new line of battle, Darmagnac's troops forming up on its right, and Harispe's—after the evacuation of Orthez—on its left.

The re-formed line came under a destructive artillery-fire from Picton's and Clinton's batteries, now aligned along the *chaussée*, in a very commanding position. Under cover of this cannonade the 6th Division, supported by the much-tried 3rd Division, made ready for a new advance.

In the northern sector of his general attack on the French line

[1] This is evidently the incident to which Napier alludes (vi. p. 105) speaking of a small detachment which Picton pushed to his left to gain the smaller tongue jutting out from the central hill, which was charged and driven back in confusion, losing prisoners.

[2] They were only 41 in all—not including 16 men of the *Chasseurs Britanniques* and Brunswick Oels, who were certainly deserters who absconded, not captives.

[3] 566, including 116 prisoners, as against 340.

Wellington had plenty of fresh troops to employ against Reille. Anson's brigade of the 4th Division had not yet been engaged; behind it were the whole of Walker's three brigades of the 7th Division, and to the right of these there was the Light Division—very weak, it is true, from the absence of the 43rd and the 1/95th, but intact save for the 1st Caçadores, who had been drawn off to the St. Boes fighting, and had never returned.

The attack on Taupin's division, still holding its positions in which it had fought Cole's men, and the street of St. Boes in front of them, was delivered by a very heavy force—Walker's whole division plus Anson's still fresh brigade of the 4th, with a most effective side intervention from the Light Division. Walker, as his very full report to Wellington shows, made great preparation for covering his flanks, before he struck with his main body at the track along the crest and between the houses of St. Boes, which was still strewn with the dead and wounded of Ross's and Vasconcellos's battalions. The flanking fire, both of artillery and of infantry, on this much-disputed neck of ground, had been a very large factor in Cole's repulses. Care was therefore taken to distract it as far as possible; two British batteries on the church knoll were employed against the French guns, the Portuguese brigade under Doyle took up its position on the slopes below the south side of the neck—where Vasconcellos's battalions had been placed during the earlier fighting, with orders to engage the French infantry on the opposite side of the combe in long-distance fire. On the other flank two battalions—the 3rd Provisional and Brunswick Oels— were similarly detached to the north of the crest, to deal with the French infantry in and about the ravine on that side—one party of them is said to have advanced beyond it. The remainder of the division, the 6th Foot leading in deployed formation, the other three battalions (68th, 82nd, and *Chasseurs Britanniques*) following in succession, charged across the narrow front on the road, down the dip, and up the steep slope on the other side of it, where the previous fruitless advance had been made[1].

Taupin's division had been fighting for four hours, had suffered

[1] For Walker's very full account of his proceedings, see *Supplementary Dispatches*, viii. pp. 612–13.

heavy losses—one of its brigadiers had been killed—and must obviously have been exhausted by this moment. It is certain, at any rate, that this time the attack was completely successful. Walker's four battalions crossed the contested neck, and charged right up the French slope—only the leading regiment, the 6th, suffering any very serious loss[1]. The enemy gave way, but rallied behind the Plassotte knoll and the crossing-point of the Dax and the St. Girons roads. This gave the 7th Division battalions space to deploy, and they found themselves steadily advancing. It is surprising to find that no aid seems to have been given to Taupin either by Paris's reserve brigade, which was lying behind his position, or by Rouget's division, which was holding the line of the *chaussée* on the south flank of his front. It seems likely that both these units were already retiring when Walker's attack was made, having been drawn back when Darmagnac lost his section of the heights farther south to the 3rd Division.

Simultaneous with Walker's frontal attack came the famous and oft-described charge of the 52nd Light Infantry from the Roman Camp, across the marshy ground below, and into the gap behind Taupin's flank. Wellington had obviously noted that such an interval existed, and thought that it might be utilized. Fortunately we have an excellent account of the work of the 52nd on this afternoon from the pen of Colborne, who led it to victory.

'Lord Wellington was standing dismounted on the knoll, with Fitzroy Somerset. When I rode below him he called out, "Hallo! Colborne, ride on and see if artillery can pass there." (The marshy ground was in general impassable.) I galloped on, and back, as fast as I could, and said, "Yes—anything can pass." "Well then, make haste, take your regiment on and deploy into the plain, I leave it to your disposition."

'So we moved in column from the Roman Camp up the road toward St. Boes. There we met, at the ridge, Sir Lowry Cole coming back with his division. He was much excited, and said, "Well, Colborne, what's to be done? Here we are [the 4th

---

[1] Apparently the detached elements of the 7th Division, to right and left, crossed the ravines, and closed in, when the main body charged the centre, for Lapène, commanding Taupin's artillery, complains that the position was turned by encircling Allied flank detachments.

Division] coming back as fast as we can". I was rather provoked, and said, "Only have patience and we shall see what's to be done." Then I saw Picton's division scattering to the left[1]. My adjutant came up and asked what we were to do now. I said, "Deploy into the low ground as fast as you can." They did it beautifully. While all the rest [4th Division of course] were in confusion, the 52nd marched down as evenly and regularly as on parade, accelerating their march as we approached the hill. The French were keeping up a heavy fire, but fortunately all the balls passed over our heads. I rode to the top of the hill and waved my cap, and though the men were over their knees in mud in the marsh, they trotted up in the finest order. As soon as they got to the top I ordered them to halt and open fire. We were soon supported by the other divisions [7th and 4th] and the French were dispersed. Fitzroy Somerset rode up to me with an order from Lord Wellington, that we should not on any account advance farther, but remain in line. The French then began to retreat and we moved on to the position which had been occupied by Foy[2]. Lord Wellington and his staff were riding behind me, and saw it all. He said in his dispatch that the attack led by the 52nd regiment dislodged the enemy from the heights and gave us the victory[3].'

It will be seen from this narrative that the 52nd marched, not straight from the Roman Camp to the hill opposite, but from the Camp to the side of the St. Boes heights, where Colborne met Cole and conversed with him, and then from that point across the head of the marshy combe to a point of the French front some where about the Luc knoll and farm. Here the 52nd got in on Taupin's left, and between his position and that which Rouget had been holding farther along the road.

The narrative of the one eyewitness, Lapène—who was with Taupin's division, and commanded his divisional battery—takes up the tale. He states that D'Erlon's divisions (Foy's and Darmagnac's) had been driven off their position for some time,

[1] As Picton was far on Colborne's right, what he means is that Picton's men were moving in a somewhat disordered way to their own left, i. e. coming along the heights leftward, not of course breaking or retiring. If he had meant that, Colborne would have said 'scattering on the right'.

[2] Evidently a mistake for Taupin.

[3] Colborne's narrative in his *Life*, pp. 201–2.

and that Rouget was already retiring, when Taupin, while deeply engaged in front, found British troops behind him on the Dax *chaussée*. This must have been the appearance of the 52nd upon the heights. 'The cry "we are cut off, the enemy is across the road," began to be heard in our ranks. The regiments, their flank turned, without any hopé of safety if they held on to their position and prolonged a useless defence, ended by abandoning the ground they had so gloriously defended for nearly eight hours, and plunged to their right down a deep ravine, the only line of exit still left open[1].' This was the hollow road which leads to the farm of La Porte, at the back of the heights along the *chaussée*. Apparently Taupin brought off most of his guns, which is surprising; it is said that only two were captured. But the division never rallied, and went off in disorder, along the slopes from La Porte, across the plateau behind, which trends down to the bridge of Sault de Navailles. It is clear that Taupin's expulsion from his position was some time after the retreat of Foy and Darmagnac farther south.

The movements of Rouget's division are more puzzling. According to Lapène it had retired to the lower plateau behind some time before Taupin was evicted. And we are told that it fell back on Paris's reserve brigade, and there fought a hard battle. 'General Rouget withdrew, without any hurry, by a path which runs at right angles to the Dax *chaussée*, and which had been pointed out as his proper line of retreat[2]. The enemy was master of the whole line of the Dax road from this moment.'

The battle, therefore, had been settled in Wellington's favour on two separate points by 2.30 in the afternoon. But there was also a third point where he had obtained a decisive advantage, almost without any fighting. When Soult had ranged Villatte's and Rouget's divisions and Paris's brigade along the lower heights below the Dax *chaussée*, to protect the routed troops of Foy, Darmagnac, and Taupin, he rode to the left end of his new line, to see how matters were going with Harispe's division on the banks of the Gave de Pau. What he saw compelled him to give hasty orders for a general retreat from his new position. Hill was across the Gave, and driving in Harispe's scattered division with very superior forces—two to one or more—and

[1] Lapène, pp. 263–4.   [2] Ibid.

was already getting round the flank of the Marshal's second position.

Hill, it will be remembered, had been told to demonstrate against Orthez and its bridge with one of the two brigades of Le Cor's Portuguese, but to hold all the rest of his corps hidden behind the hills of Magret, ready to strike at the fords of Souars, when the enemy was being attacked in his positions north of the river. Accordingly Buchan's brigade bickered across the river with Harispe's detachment in Orthez all the morning; as its total loss was three killed and nine wounded, the demonstration was obviously not pressed home. At or about 11 o'clock Hill got his orders to march for the Souars fords[1], only a mile away on his right. Harispe, as has been already mentioned, had a cavalry regiment and two battalions of the 115th Ligne watching them. But such a force was hopelessly inadequate when the four brigades of the 2nd Division, followed by Da Costa's Portuguese, appeared in their front, and Hill's horse artillery opened upon them effectively across the river. The French detachment gave way at once, and the long defilade of five brigades of infantry and one of cavalry—12,000 men— across the rather deep fords, was entirely undisturbed by opposition. Hill had then to turn the French left, by reaching the Orthez–Sault de Navailles road, and pushing along it so as to get into the rear of Soult's newly assumed second line of positions. Deploying in several columns along the slopes above the Souars fords, he marched for Sallespisse, the village on the high road in Soult's left rear. He had first to drive off Harispe, who united all his scattered detachments, drawing out the force which had been holding Orthez town and bridge[2]; but even so he had only two brigades against five, and no hope of help from anywhere, since Villatte's division, the general reserve of the army, had been drawn off elsewhere, and already engaged.

Accordingly when Soult took a glance, from the heights above the old castle, along his left wing, he saw it retreating before

---

[1] In all this I agree with General Beatson's conclusion in his *Orthez Campaign*, pp. 230–1.

[2] Whereupon Buchan's brigade, finding the enemy gone, pulled down the obstructions on Orthez bridge, crossed the Gave, and marched up the Sault road, joining in the pursuit of Harispe.

Hill's advance, and obviously unable to hold it back, though Harispe did his best, and halted several times to make a stand. About the level of the village of Routun he ranged himself across the road, and placed on the lofty Motte de Tury, above his left, an unexpected reinforcement—two battalions of the 'Toulouse Reserve Division' which had just arrived from the rear. These conscript battalions of the new levy were, however, not serious fighting stuff, and Hill's next push sent Harispe's line back in disorder, with the loss of three guns. Soult could see that he had not a moment to spare, if he was to escape from the danger of having his retreat to the bridge of Sault de Navailles intercepted by Hill, and gave orders for a general retreat of his main body, which was being cannonaded by four or five British batteries on the Dax road heights, while the 6th Division on its left, and the 7th Division and Light Division on its right, were developing flank attacks, with the somewhat exhausted 3rd and 4th Divisions supporting them.

The troops of Villatte, Darmagnac, Rouget, and Paris, covering the other broken divisions, had to execute a very difficult manœuvre—a continuous retreat by successive lines of battalions, harassed all the way across the plateau by gun-fire —for the British horse artillery followed them close—and pressed by infantry whenever they stayed too long in a position. Wellington remarks, 'the enemy retreated at first in admirable order, taking advantage of the many good positions which the country offered him. The losses, however, which he sustained in the continued attacks of our troops, and the danger with which he was threatened by General Hill's movement, soon accelerated his pace, and the retreat at last became a flight, with his troops in the utmost confusion[1].' This is well borne out by French narrators, 'Before reaching the high road the troops, obliged to use narrow muddy by-paths, or to strike across country, with all arms mixed up, and the enemy's guns thundering in their rear, experienced a crisis of disorder. The confusion was augmented when it became known that Hill's corps was pressing up the high road. The moment was critical, the hurry grew more urgent, and the army experienced a long period of disunion and disorder which nothing could prevent[2].' In this

---

[1] *Dispatches*, xi. p. 537.   [2] Lapène, p. 266.

condition it poured across the plateau and down the high road, towards the all-important bridge behind it at Sault de Navailles. Harispe and Villatte brought up the rear, making intermittent stands; the van was led by the disbanded battalions of Foy and Taupin, which had never been properly rallied since their defeat on the Dax *chaussée*. The only serious fighting was at the village of Sallespisse, when the disordered French troops coming down from the plateau passed into the high road. Some of Villatte's men made an obstinate attempt to hold the village, and had to be evicted by the Black Watch, who were leading the advance of the 6th Division, not without considerable loss to the attacking party[1].

For the last three miles towards the bridge of Sault, the French army had become a mere hurrying crowd. That it suffered no greater damage than it did from the British cavalry was due to the character of the country—cultivated fields surrounded by walls, and cut across by ditches. Though Vivian's, Fane's, and Somerset's brigades were all to the front, they got few opportunities of dealing effective blows[2]. The only success of note was to the credit of the 7th Hussars in Somerset's brigade, who entering fields to the left of the high road, cut off, charged, and captured great part of two of Harispe's units— one battalion of the 115th and one of the unsteady National Guards attached to this division. The French returns show 600 men 'missing' from Harispe—half of them National Guards. But many other prisoners were taken in small bodies, and the total of Soult's losses in the 'missing' column was 20 officers and 1,346 other ranks.

Some order was restored at the bridge of Sault de Navailles, where General Tirlet, in charge of the artillery, had placed twelve guns commanding the bridge, backed by the massed sapper companies of the army, and by two battalions of the conscripts of the Toulouse Division of Reserve, which had come up, following those which had joined Harispe earlier in the day. According to one French narrative these battalions were found to have no cartridges in their pouches, but were put in position

---

[1] Accounts of this fight may be found in the narratives of Anton and of the anonymous soldier who chronicles the doings of the 42nd.

[2] Vivian bewails this in his letter home—see his *Life*, p. 203.

BATTLE OF ORTHEZ, FEBRUARY 27TH 1814

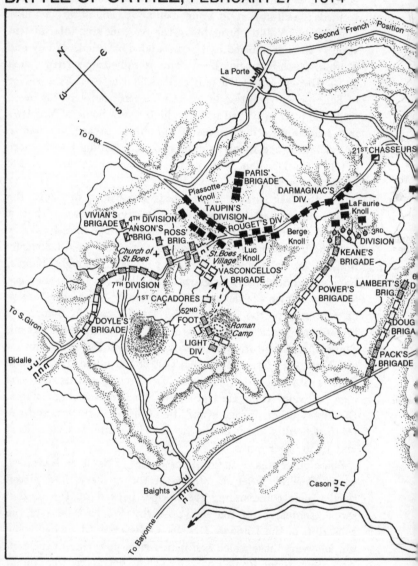

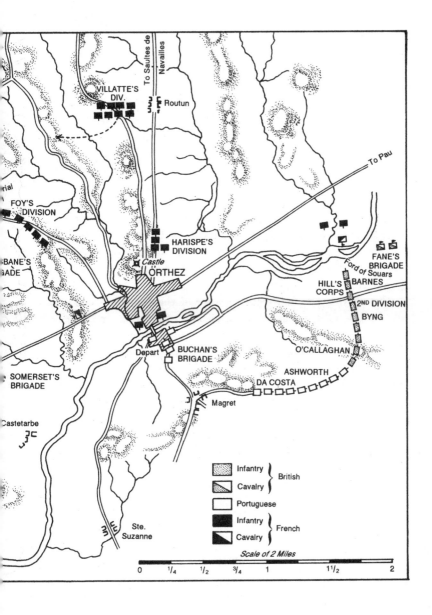

Infantry } British
Cavalry }
Portuguese
Infantry } French
Cavalry }

Scale of 2 Miles

nevertheless, and endured some shelling from the British horse-artillery guns accompanying Fane's brigade[1]. 'One saw these conscripts, who heard the cannon for the first time, standing with grounded arms, like old soldiers, under heavy fire and without a cartridge, while a mass of veterans in panic fled past them with pouches full, so closely pressed together that they looked like troops manœuvring in order.' The bulk of the infantry passed the bridge in a crowd, the cavalry crossed the Luy de Béarn by fords hastily discovered[2], as did also some of Reille's scattered units. After this the disordered army pressed on, and did not stop till it had reached Hagetmau, sixteen miles behind the battle-field. Pierre Soult's cavalry, Villatte, and Harispe, in the rear, remained to cover the bridge till 10 o'clock at night, and then blew it up, and followed the rest[3]. The British cavalry made no attempt to press them, and bivouacked on the south side of the Luy; the infantry does not seem to have gone farther than Sallespisse that evening.

Considering the desperate disorder of the French at the end of the day, it looks as if more might have been done in the way of smashing in and capturing the whole of their rear-guard, instead of two battalions only. The want of guidance shown may be attributed to the fact that Wellington had been almost disabled during the final advance, and had dropped back. While he was riding near the 3rd Caçadores of the Light Division[4] during the movement against the second French position, a bullet struck his sword-hilt and forced it against his thigh with such violence that the muscles were injured and the skin broken. Though he did not dismount, he was in great pain, and could not follow the advance to its end. For some days he was seriously incommoded by stiffness, and found mounting and dismounting very trying matters[5].

Soult's total loss had been just over 4,000 men, of whom

---

[1] So Lemonnier, p. 269, but Lapène says nothing about this curious instance of maladministration.

[2] Lemonnier-Delafosse, Pierre Soult's aide-de-camp, gives the best account of this chaos, with personal adventures (and a ducking) experienced in discovering an extemporized ford for the cavalry, pp. 268-9.

[3] Villatte nearly ruined Harispe, by blowing up the bridge before the latter's men had finished crossing.

[4] Blakiston, ii. p. 329.   [5] Larpent, p. 422.

1,350 were prisoners[1]. It is interesting to note that the large majority of these last (1,060 of all ranks) were in the units which covered the retreat, those of Villatte, Harispe, and Paris. Foy's, Taupin's, and Darmagnac's troops, who did the hardest of the fighting in the first stages of the battle, had comparatively few 'missing', though heavy lists of killed and wounded. Taupin and Darmagnac show far the heaviest figures in this line. Of general officers, besides Béchaud (of Taupin's division) killed, Foy and two brigadiers, Barbot and Gruardet, were wounded.

Wellington's casualty list amounted to 2,164 of all ranks, including 80 missing[2]; of these 519 were Portuguese. The large majority of the losses were in the 3rd, 4th, and 7th Divisions, as might have been guessed from the course of the battle. Brisbane's brigade in the first named, and Ross's and Vasconcellos's brigades in the others, had very serious casualties. In the 6th Division only the 42nd of Pack's brigade had any heavy losses, and in Walker's division only the 6th, which led the final charge against Taupin's position. In the Light Division the 52nd had 89 killed and wounded in its brilliant advance, and the 1st Caçadores 47, when it shared in the rout of Vasconcellos's brigade—the other battalions were hardly touched. Hill's corps was almost without casualties, some brigades in it entirely so; those which did the important work in driving Harispe away paid a very slight price for their success[3]—33 British and 15 Portuguese in all.

[1] See tables in Appendix.

[2] These last mainly from Vasconcellos's Portuguese and the 2/87th. Twelve *Chasseurs Britannique* were probably deserters.

[3] See tables in the Appendix. Barnes's brigade had 29 casualties, Byng's 4, O'Callaghan's and Harding's Portuguese none at all.

NOTE

I walked carefully round the field of Orthez on August 15th, 1926, inspecting the ground, and found myself obliged to differ in my reading of the battle not only from Napier but from Sir John Fortescue and General Beatson. The lower slopes of the spurs on which Picton attacked are now largely covered with brushwood. The Roman Camp dominates Rouget's position opposite it. The dip which separates the St. Boes church, on its knoll, from the position of Taupin opposite is very steep; there is now hardly a building save the church and the *presbytère* on this site—the village has entirely migrated in the direction of the Plassotte knoll opposite.

This battle was an example of the fact that, with fairly equal numbers in the field, passive defence is very helpless against an active offensive concentrated on certain limited points, unless the defender uses adequate reserves for counter-attacks. Soult had his reserves—Villatte and Paris—but instead of employing them to crush the heads of Wellington's advanced columns, treated them rather as 'échelons de recul', designed to cover a routed first line. He had in his favour the fact that Wellington had to strike on very limited fronts, since Picton's division was forced to move up two narrow spurs, and Cole's division along a sort of isthmus between ravines. In neither case could the full effective force of a British advance in line be brought to bear—there was not space to deploy. Indeed it was only after reaching the crest that the assailants were able to develop into their normal formation. It looks as if Soult had been planning a mere rear-guard action, in which he could force the enemy to deploy, and then, after inflicting some loss, could retire himself. And this he might, perhaps, have done after Cole's repulse and Picton's long halt. But if he intended to fight a real battle, he should have counter-attacked with energy—which he entirely failed to do. Nor does he even appear to have helped one part of his fighting line from another. Rouget's division does not seem to have assisted either Darmagnac or Taupin. And Foy's left-hand brigade (Berlier) rather covered the retreat of his right-hand brigade (Fririon) than aided, by counter-attacking the head of Keane's column when it mounted off the spur on to the heights. What would have happened to Wellington at Bussaco, if he had not moved troops along his line, to counter-attack Reynier's assaulting columns on the heights of St. Antonio de Cantaro? It cannot be denied that

---

⁶ I make the total Allied loss 2,164 by the tables shown in the Appendix. This exceeds Sir John Fortescue's estimate by more than 150. He says [*British Army*, ix. p. 514] that he calculates it out to be just short of 2,000, which does not seem to coincide with the official report. He also observes that Picton claimed to have lost 825 men, but really could not show more than 700 casualties. But Picton was quite right, as the total of his two British brigades only (699) seems to have been taken by Sir John Fortescue, while we have to add the figure for Power's Portuguese brigade, 109 casualties, plus some gunners from the divisional battery, of which Picton remembers that he saw all the men serving one piece killed or wounded. The total of 825, therefore, must be accurate to within a man or two.

Wellington took a considerable risk at Orthez when he made his final general attack. He was assailing five divisions in a very strong position with an exactly equal force—five divisions of his own. Hill and Harispe may be counted out, as occupying each other. And the attack had to be made on very narrow fronts, and under heavy artillery-fire. It was not a fair fight between line and column, as at Talavera, Salamanca, or Albuera. In his defence it may be pleaded that he had always ample reserves—the casualty lists show that Anson's brigade of the 4th Division, the whole Light Division save the 52nd and the 1st Caçadores, six British battalions of the 7th Division, five of the 6th Division, and the Portuguese brigades of Doyle and Douglas were practically intact, and quite available, if Soult had counter-attacked. They would have been needed if he had done so. But this, as Wellington had discovered, was not Soult's method. At the Nivelle and the Bidassoa he had allowed himself to be assailed in a fortified position, without coming out of it for any retaliatory counterstroke. And no doubt the British general relied on Hill's flanking move having an earlier effect than it actually produced. Soult stopped so long fighting that he was nearly cut off from his line of retreat. He should have retired at an earlier hour to save himself.

SECTION XLIII: CHAPTER VII

SOULT'S RETREAT EASTWARD. COMBAT OF AIRE

THE victorious army after the battle of Orthez bivouacked for the most part on the heights above Sallespisse. The infantry was tired out—the men would not even pitch their tents when they were brought up, built large fires on which they frizzled their ration beef, and sank into heavy sleep early. The night was frosty, and next morning it was a very stiff and rheumatic army which fell slowly into its ranks, after the uncovenanted · mercy of a tot of rum, served out by a thoughtful order from head-quarters[1]. Head-quarters was late in rising itself—the commander-in-chief was abominably stiff from his contusion of the previous evening, and suffered considerable pain for several days; he found riding difficult. The French were quite out of touch—they had only rested for a few hours at Hagetmau, and then started down the high road again for St. Sever, twenty-five miles from the battle-field—which they reached in disorder on the forenoon of the 28th. Soult then began to sort his army, and to estimate its losses and its position. In addition to the 4,000 men killed, wounded, or prisoners in the battle of Orthez, he found that there had been a terrible amount of desertion. The remnant of Harispe's National Guards had disappeared, so had nearly half of the four battalions of the 'Toulouse Division of Reserve' which had appeared late on the ground. 'The conscripts of the new levy had behaved themselves like old soldiers during the battle, but afterwards, during the retreat, the spirit of desertion seized them; each started for his own home, as if peace had been declared. The Marshal sent orders in all directions to have them brought back to the colours, which they had defended with courage on the day of Orthez. But it was much more difficult to get them back to their battalions than to get them to fight[2].' English observers began, during this advance, to note for the first time young men in the

[1] Interesting notes on this frosty morning are to be found in Brown of the 45th, pp. 271–2.
[2] Pellot, pp. 114–15.

villages. Some were nonchalant and rather cheerful—these were the 'refractories', who had bolted from the conscription and now reappeared at home. Others were sheepish and shirked observation; their close-cropped hair showed that they were recent deserters[1].

Soult had now two days, before he found himself pressed in front of St. Sever, in which to make up his mind between the only two strategical alternatives which were open to him. The first was to continue to retreat straight to his rear, covering Bordeaux, the capital of the south, and the third city of France, from the attack which Wellington was certain to deliver upon it. The other was to risk the loss of Bordeaux, and to endeavour to keep Wellington employed, as far from it as possible, by drawing back the French army eastward instead of northward, i.e. making Toulouse its base instead of Bordeaux. It is well known that an invader can be checked quite as well by placing oneself upon his flank as upon his front. He cannot neglect an enemy who may fall upon his rear, and his line of communications, if he marches past toward the goal which for political reasons he wishes to reach. Many sound considerations bid him to smash the army upon his flank at all costs, before proceeding with his main scheme. So the Marshal hoped to draw Wellington after himself, and thus to distract him from Bordeaux. At the worst his adversary might seize Bordeaux, but this could only be by detaching a very considerable corps from his army— perhaps one large enough to reduce its force to a strength with which he himself might be able to cope. For Soult was aware that Wellington's numbers were not so overpowering as he persisted in representing them to be, whenever he wrote to the Minister of War at Paris. It was irritating to receive at St. Sever, three days after the battle, the Emperor's last orders, written as he was mounting his horse near Troyes, about to throw himself upon the army of Schwarzenberg, 'Tell the Duke of Dalmatia that I order him to resume the offensive at once, and to fall upon

---

[1] Larpent (p. 421), on March 1, writes 'All the conscripts are running home as fast as they can. About 20 have come back to Peyrehorade. One gentlemanlike young man said he was now a convalescent conscript, and such he would remain till things took their next turn. Three days later deserters along the road all day—conscripts going home', and p. 425, 'You may know the new levy by their close-cropped heads.'

one of the wings of the enemy; even if he has but 20,000 men, by seizing his opportunity boldly, he ought to be able to get the advantage over the English. And he has talent enough to understand what I mean[1].' This was an explosion in a moment of irritation, perfectly insane orders under the circumstances. But we shall see that a few days later Napoleon had come to a better appreciation of things, and practically approved of the Marshal's next move.

Soult's own plan is ably set forth in a dispatch of the 28th sent to Clarke. 'Saint Sever could be defended, but behind it there are the worst defiles possible—the line of retreat completely commanded from the enemy's side of the Adour. . . . Unless I get positive orders to the contrary, I shall not manœuvre in the direction of Bordeaux, where I should have much trouble in passing the Garonne, and should leave the whole of the south of France exposed to the enemy. I shall base myself upon Toulouse, and take my first positions at Aire and Barcelonne, where I shall be able to prevent the enemy from moving on Bordeaux, no less than upon Toulouse. If the enemy does not attack me for several days, I shall be in a state to fight again. But I have only 30,000 infantry, 3,000 sabres, and 40 guns— a force terribly disproportionate in all arms to that of the enemy[2].'

Another fact which influenced Soult's determination to leave the straight road to Bordeaux open to Wellington, was that after passing Mont-de-Marsan, the large town and road-centre behind St. Sever, the *chaussée* passes for sixty miles through a barren and thinly peopled country, the main bulk of the sandy pine-forest of the Landes. At Mont-de-Marsan, it was true, he had large depots of all sorts, but they were non-transportable; he had no means of carrying them off; hitherto the stuff had been sent down to Bayonne by water-carriage on the Adour. If turned out of Mont-de-Marsan, as he certainly would be in a few days, he would be thrown into the Landes, where his army could not possibly feed itself, and the nearest resources would be in the very distant Bordeaux. It was far better, from the point of view of sustenance, to fall back on the fertile country east-

---

[1] Troyes, February 25. *Correspondance de Napoléon*, No. 21 365
[2] Soult to Clarke, February 28.

ward, where there were minor depots in several places, and good communication with Toulouse and Montauban.

The retreat eastward from St. Sever involved the abandonment of all the county down the Adour, as far as Bayonne—especially that of Dax, which had hitherto been the advanced centre of distribution for the wants of the army. Soult had hoped to hold the place, and had ordered Daricau to fortify it, and to gather there, round the one regular battalion left him, all the National Guards of the department of the Landes. But these local troops had turned out as hopeless as those of the other departments. The moment that Daricau scraped together a 'cohort' it deserted. On March 1st Vandeleur's dragoons from Hope's army having shown themselves in front of the place, and news coming that there was British infantry at St. Geours, Daricau realized that Dax was untenable, whereupon the last 450 National Guards in the place deserted, by escalading the ramparts at the rear of the town, and the General started off with his one weak battalion of regulars to rejoin Soult through the Landes. Only the *sous-préfet* followed him—the rest of the authorities remained behind to welcome the English. Only part of the great mass of stores was destroyed[1].

Now Aire and Barcelonne, to which Soult was moving, are due east of St. Sever, and by going off in that direction the Marshal left the high road St. Sever–Mont-de-Marsan–Bordeaux completely open to Wellington. What he hoped was that if he took this position the enemy would not dare to move past him and march on Bordeaux, but would be compelled to turn upon him, and so be drawn eastward. As a matter of fact the Marshal was partly right and partly wrong. Wellington did turn upon him, and was distracted in the Toulouse direction. But Soult entirely failed to save Bordeaux, because Wellington, calling up such help as he could from the rear, improvised a force sufficiently strong to seize that great city, while retaining enough troops under his own hand to drive his enemy before him, whenever he tried to make a stand.

But the Bordeaux expedition was not one which Wellington would have undertaken on purely military grounds. It was

[1] For interesting details about Dax, see Dumas, pp. 437–8, containing much official matter.

a political move, destined to shatter the morale of the whole of southern France, and to break the prestige of the Emperor. And it would not have been tried, but for the fact that there was at last evidence leading to the conclusion that the public opinion of the country was such, that it was possible to play the card which had hitherto never been brought out—that of favouring insurrection in favour of the Bourbons. Wellington had at last got evidence that there were people of importance who were ready to hoist the White Banner, and risk their necks in open rebellion. But of Count Lynch and the Bordeaux conspiracy we must not speak, till the armies have assumed the relative positions which made the expedition to the Gironde a feasible venture.

Wellington's cavalry appeared in front of St. Sever on the afternoon of February 28th; that night he slept himself at Hagetmau. That same evening Soult evacuated St. Sever, and moved eastward to Grenade on the way to Aire and Barcelonne, after blowing up the bridge of St. Sever. Wellington entered the place on March 1st, and remained there for eight days, making it his head-quarters. He had now to revise his whole scheme of strategy, owing to Soult's unexpected withdrawal eastward. This long halt suited him personally, in that it permitted him to lie up, and allow his injured leg to grow supple again, but this was the least of the causes of what looks like a curious break in the continuity of the campaign.

The first reason for the halt was the necessity for reorganizing the army in face of the problem of a large-scale invasion of France, which was now presented to him. His object, till Soult had been driven away, had been no more than to make it possible to isolate and besiege Bayonne. This task had been completed. What was to be the next step? With about 40,000 men, all that he now had about him, he could hardly hope to occupy the whole of south-western France. The question of *étapes* and communications presented itself. Could he leave behind him whole departments ungarrisoned, while he struck inland from his distant base at St. Jean de Luz? There were French fortresses left behind him. Morillo had been told off to blockade Navarrenx, Mina to blockade St.-Jean-Pied-du-Port; they might be considered as cancelled, with no very great deduction from the force of his own operating army. But the problem of Bayonne was a very serious one; he had discovered that Thouvenot had 14,000 regular troops in the town—not to speak of some National Guards and naval detachments. And the place was most difficult to besiege, because the investing army was cut up by the Adour and the Nive into three separate sections, connected only by bridges of boats. Thouvenot had shown himself hitherto a very unenterprising person, but his resources were so considerable that it would be unsafe to leave him lightly watched. The obvious thing would have been to hand over the entire siege to the Spaniards, to bring up O'Donnell's Reserve of Andalusia from the Bastan, and the 3rd Army from Navarre, and then to carry off the 1st and 5th Divisions, with Aylmer's, Bradford's, and Campbell's brigades, to join the field-army. This would have added nearly 20,000 good Anglo-Portuguese troops to the operating force. But Wellington could not make up his mind to take this step. The first reason was that he wished to preserve a complete control over the whole of the operations of the troops at his disposal. And if he gathered 30,000 Spanish troops round Bayonne, he must have left Freire, or else Henry O'Donnell, the latter most untrustworthy, in command. As he had written to Bathurst a year back, he was determined never again to trust a crucial part of a campaign to a Spanish general. 'Have I any reason to suppose that the game would be *well* played? Certainly not. I have never known the Spaniards do anything *well*[1].' This being so, he had to leave a large part of his own army behind, in order to justify his putting an English general in charge of the siege. He could not have continued Hope in command before Bayonne if no British and Portuguese troops had been entrusted to him. It must be remembered that the line of communication of the army now passed over the Adour bridge, within two miles of Bayonne, and that all stores, munitions, and reinforcements had to go over that ingenious structure. For, now that it was built, Wellington had ordered that nothing should be sent over the bad cross-roads on the Gaves, but everything by the good roads north of the Adour by Port de Lanne (where the bridge was now restored) and then either by Dax–St. Sever or by Peyrehorade–Orthez–St. Sever.

[1] See Wellington to Bathurst, quoted in vol. vi, p. 300.

All that he borrowed from the blockading army before Bayonne was two of Freire's divisions, which were to be replaced by bringing up the 'Army of Reserve of Andalusia' from the Bastan. As Freire brought his two best divisions, this would be a very appreciable help.

But there was another useful reinforcement coming—the whole of the Heavy Cavalry, which had so long been relegated to winter quarters beyond the Pyrenees. So the Household Brigade of O'Loghlin, Bock's Heavy Germans[1], and Ponsonby's and Clifton's dragoons started off from their cantonments at various dates between February 24th and March 2nd, and were getting in touch with the army by March 10–11th. With them came the five weak regiments of Portuguese light horse under Barbaçena and Campbell, which had also been hibernating in the south. These accretions more than doubled Wellington's cavalry force—he had 8,000 sabres now instead of 3,500. And though the country in which they were to operate was not at all good cavalry ground, being nearly all enclosed and tilled, yet he had now sufficient mounted men not only to dominate the enemy completely, but to scour the country for miles on every side. They were largely used for communication purposes, to keep roads open, and as convoy escorts. The farther the distance grew from the base, the more useful was a preponderant cavalry.

On March 1st Beresford was pushed forward to Mont-de-Marsan with the Light Division. A very considerable accumulation of food-stuffs was captured, which Soult had neither found transport, to remove, nor time to destroy. Hill, with his normal following—the 2nd Division and Le Cor's Portuguese—was sent out eastward to locate Soult's army, which was reported to have retreated entirely in that direction. He moved south of the Adour; a parallel column, the 3rd and 6th Divisions, marched on the main road north of that river by Grenade, with the same destination. Hill found no opposition till he had almost reached Aire, but the other column came upon D'Erlon's two divisions (Foy's and Darmagnac's) at Cazères, and had to use some force to push them back. They

---

[1] But Bock himself, going away by sea to serve in Germany, was drowned off the coast of Brittany in February.

halted on heights which on the other side of the Adour faced
Aire. Here they joined the whole of the rest of the French army
—Clausel's two divisions (Harispe and Villatte) were south of
the river, Reille's (Taupin and Rouget) north of it. Soult, being
under the impression that he had the whole of Wellington's
army in front of him, was not intending to risk a general action,
and proposed to give way, after fighting a cautious rear-guard
combat for so long as it might be prudent to remain in position.
His purpose was shown by orders given to Reille to retire up-
stream to Barcelonne, and to be ready to cross the Adour southward by its bridge, while D'Erlon and Clausel were detaining
the enemy. This meant that he had resolved to move south-
eastward towards Tarbes, if pressed, and to throw up all chances
of keeping his communication with Bordeaux. For, the moment
that Barcelonne was passed, the last road leading towards the
lower Garonne would be abandoned. But Soult was let in for
some sharper fighting than he had expected. D'Erlon, on the
north bank of the Adour, gave way when pressed, and followed
Reille toward Barcelonne. But Clausel found himself tackled
and assaulted by Hill's column in an unexpected fashion.
Strange as it may appear, the Marshal had altogether failed to
discover Hill's force, and did not know that he was going to
be attacked on the south side of the river[1]. Clausel had been
placed on a line of steep eminences covering Aire, with his right
resting on the Adour, and his front protected by the small river
Grave. The position was extremely strong, but so close (only
2,000 yards) in front of the town that no retreat was possible
for the right wing save into that place, where there was no
bridge[2], and no exit save a road leading eastward parallel with
the river.

Hill, on discovering Clausel's position, did not wait to form
a regular line of battle, for he thought that the French would be
off, if he left them the time to do so. But he had misjudged the
situation, for Clausel was under orders to hold on until Reille

---

[1] This is shown by the statement in his dispatch that Hill must have
crossed the Adour about Grenade, a few miles below Aire. But Hill had
always been south of the river, and had no need to cross it.

[2] There had been one, but it had been carried away in a flood many
years back and never rebuilt.

had crossed to the south side of the Adour by the bridge at Barcelonne. He had five brigades in line, in a position masked by copses and thickets, for the hills above the Grave river were well wooded.

Hill, however, coming up at about 2 o'clock in the afternoon—in two columns, the 2nd Division near the river, Le Cor's a mile to the right—attacked with his three leading brigades, while the others were still far off. From the 2nd Division, Barnes's brigade, with Byng's in support, were directed against the extreme right of the enemy, above the Adour, where the hill was steepest, operating against Villatte's flank. Da Costa's Portuguese brigade, from Le Cor's division, moved against the French centre, i. e. Harispe's right wing, a mile farther from the river. Both attacking columns forded the Grave, and went up-hill among the copses. Their fates were completely different. Barnes's brigade, though on the steeper ground, won the crest with no great difficulty, and, even before Byng had come up in support, drove Villatte's division right down from the heights into the low-lying town of Aire. The resistance must have been very weak, for the French casualty lists show that Villatte's whole division lost on that day only one officer killed and four wounded—i. e. probably only 100 men in all.

But Da Costa with the Algarve brigade, attacking with the same headlong impetus, met with a complete repulse. When he neared the brow of the hill he was charged by Dauture's brigade of Harispe's division and cast down the slopes in great disorder and with considerable loss. The brigade rallied with difficulty along the stream at the foot of the heights. Noting Da Costa's rout, William Stewart, who was leading the two victorious brigades of the 2nd Division, detached Barnes with the 50th and 92nd, by the path along the summit of the heights, to take Dauture in flank, while the 71st and the light companies of the brigade kept touch with Villatte's retiring troops till Byng should come up. The reinforcements, operating against Harispe's exposed flank, restored the fight on this side, and presently Buchan's brigade, the belated unit of Le Cor's division, came up and commenced to bicker with the rest of Harispe's line. But the business on this wing was not settled till more troops were put in—when Harding's Portuguese brigade came

up behind Byng, Hill turned over the task of pursuing Villatte
to them and to the 71st, and sent off Byng's battalions to follow
the track already taken by Barnes's along the crest of the
heights. The arrival of this brigade settled the matter—Harispe
was thrown back on his reserve—Paris's four battalions stationed
in front of the village of Nauzeilles—and then thrust off eastward along the plateau. Thus the two French divisions were
completely separated and driven in different directions.

Harispe had a clear line of retreat, but Villatte had sought
a very dubious place of refuge in the town of Aire. The main
body of this place[1] is on a sort of island, enclosed between two
branches of the Adour, and though it was strong for immediate
defence, yet troops holding it had no way of retreat save by
a bridge at the farther side of the island, over which they would
have to defile. Pushing along the edge of the nearer branch of
the Adour, the British light troops were threatening to reach
the level of this bridge and intercept the enemy's only line of
retirement. Villatte, however, was saved from this danger by
the providence of Reille. Hearing the heavy firing at Aire, that
general, who was now lying on the south side of the bridge of
Barcelonne, sent out his two divisions to cover the retreat of
Clausel's corps. Rouget's division, marching towards the sound
of battle, took post at the head of the bridge over the minor
branch of the Adour, and the troops in Aire were able to escape
from the island under its cover. They had only to brush away
the advanced skirmishers of Harding's Caçadores. The main
body of that brigade and the 71st were occupied in street-
fighting within the town, into which they had penetrated by
its southern bridge, or by using fords and passages at mill-dams
of which there are several on this narrow stream. Villatte's
broken battalions made no very serious attempt to hold the place
—and acted wisely.

Indeed the French resistance at all points during the combat of
Aire seems to have been feeble—despite Napier's remarks to
the contrary. This is shown by the fact that the whole loss in
the British brigades this day was only 156 men—nearly all in
the 50th, 71st, and 92nd of Barnes's brigade. That general

---

[1] There is a high-lying suburb on the hill above, round a church and
seminary.

himself was wounded. Byng's brigade had only about 20 casualties—O'Callaghan's none—it never got near the fighting at all[1]. The losses of Harding's and Buchan's Portuguese were also negligible; Da Costa's unlucky battalions, which opened the combat so inauspiciously, had, of course, heavier losses—five officers and over 100 men, including a very few prisoners. Beresford sent the brigadier back to Lisbon in disgrace; his very severe report on the affair mentions that Da Costa did not even rally the troops himself—this was done by Colonel Avillez of the 14th Line—and showed complete incapacity. He was replaced in command of the brigade by Colonel João de Almeida[2].

The French casualties at Aire were probably no greater in killed and wounded than those of the Allies—the reports only show one brigadier-general (Dauture)[3] and about a dozen officers killed or wounded—which probably means a total loss of 250 or so, in addition to 100 prisoners. But many regiments straggled in the dark, and their conscripts took the opportunity of deserting—the 'morning states' of the two divisions engaged show on March 10th some battalions which had shrunk to 260 or 290 bayonets, and all their missing had certainly not been killed, wounded, or taken[4].

Forced to abandon his idea of making a stand at Aire and Barcelonne, Soult withdrew his troops south-eastwards, and was surprised not to find himself pursued. D'Erlon on the north bank of the Adour marched as far as Plaisance, where he turned south and found Reille and Clausel concentrated at Maubourget. The Marshal, who had calculated that Hill had three divisions at Aire, and that six more had marched from St. Sever on the track of D'Erlon's column, found himself

[1] According to Cadell of the 28th it went miles astray, misdirected by an orderly dragoon.

[2] For Beresford's report and comments, and dismissal of Da Costa in disgrace, see Chaby, iii. pp. 970-7. He imputes the disgrace mainly to the brigadier and the staff—the regiments having an old and good reputation.

[3] All narratives from Napier onward speak of *two* brigadiers *hors de combat*. But the second general, Gasquet, did not belong to the corps of Clausel, and must have been hit during the skirmishing on the other side of the river.

[4] On March 10th the 34th Léger, two battalions strong, of Harispe was down to 524 rank and file, and the 10th Line of Paris's brigade, also of two battalions, to 538.

unexpectedly free, and was able to call a halt, much to his satisfaction, and to take stock of his diminished army. The enemies were now completely out of touch with each other, for Wellington had fixed his head-quarters at St. Sever, and sent out nothing but cavalry reconnaissances beyond Aire and Barcelonne. The weather was abominable, and having driven Soult right away from the Bordeaux road, and put him out of action. for some time, the Allied commander-in-chief was about to try his great political experiment—the raid on Bordeaux in support of the Royalist rising which, as he was assured, was now ready to take place in that great city.

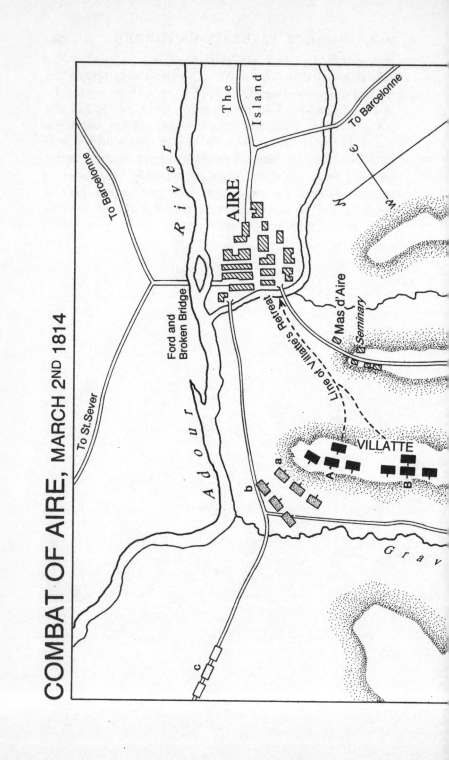

COMBAT OF AIRE, MARCH 2ND 1814

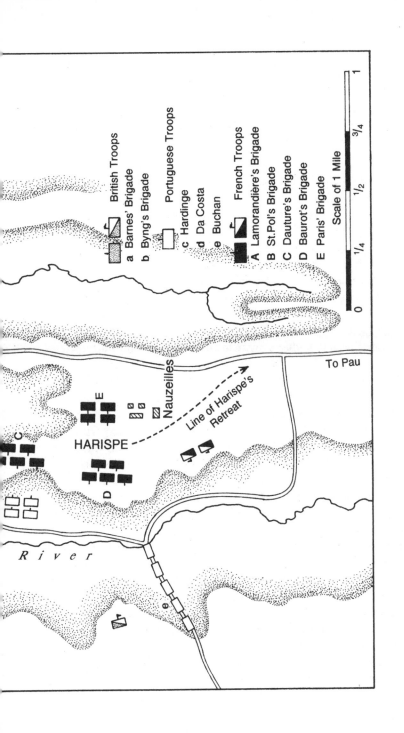

British Troops

a Barnes' Brigade
b Byng's Brigade

Portuguese Troops

c Hardinge
d Da Costa
e Buchan

French Troops

A Lamorandière's Brigade
B St.Pol's Brigade
C Dauture's Brigade
D Baurot's Brigade
E Paris' Brigade

Scale of 1 Mile

0   1/4   1/2   3/4   1

Nauzeilles

To Pau

Line of Harispe's Retreat

HARISPE

River

SECTION XLIII: CHAPTER VIII

CONCERNING COUNT LYNCH, THE DUKE OF ANGOULÊME,
AND LORD DALHOUSIE AT BORDEAUX. MARCH–
APRIL 1814

As we have already had to remark more than once, the policy
which Wellington had been forced to adopt with regard to the
French Royalists, whose pressure upon him had been increasing
from week to week, was entirely dependent on the general determination of the Allied Powers with regard to Napoleon. If the
Emperor was to be allowed to remain ruler of a humbled and
diminished France, it would be treacherous and immoral to
encourage Frenchmen to rise in revolt against him, and then to
hand them over to his vengeance. If on the other hand the
Allies made up their minds to dethrone Napoleon, and to impose some other monarch on France, then it would be not only
permissible but highly proper to utilize against him insurgents
of any sort. So long as the tedious negotiations which had opened
at Frankfurt, and were dragging on at Châtillon till March 11th,
were in progress, there was a chance that the Emperor would be
granted terms, and permitted to keep his crown. It is hard to
see why he refused to recognize the inevitable, and to take what
terms Caulaincourt could get for him: his petty successes at
Champaubert, Montmirail, and other partial engagements had
settled nothing, brilliant though his strategy had been. Beaten
at Laon (March 9th–10th) he was a ruined man—his forces were
too weak to face the masses directed against him. Probably the
explanation of his obstinacy was not megalomania—though he
was even yet boasting that he was 'the man of Austerlitz and
Wagram'—but the reasoned conclusion that a military usurper,
who had suffered complete disaster, could not hope to impose
himself any longer upon the nation whose blood and wealth he
had drained with such reckless extravagance. As he had confessed to Metternich at Dresden in 1813, 'Sovereigns born to
the throne may be beaten twenty times, and still go back to their
palaces. So cannot I—the child of Fortune. My reign will not
outlast the day when I have ceased to be omnipotent—and

therefore to be feared[1].' Hence his resolve to risk everything on the last throw of the dice. But why did the Allies not gauge his psychology better, and declare after Leipzig or the crossing of the Rhine, that there were no terms for him—but only for France?

So long as the deposition of Napoleon had not been decreed Wellington dared not incite French insurgents to take arms against him. He could at most give them their chance to make manifestations. The Duke of Angoulême had come to St. Jean de Luz as early as February 2nd, but in strict *incognito*. Wellington only knew him officially as the 'Comte de Pradel', a French gentleman on his travels, and no royal honours were granted him. He lived obscurely in the house of two old ladies of approved Royalist tendencies: numerous Frenchmen of doubtful importance visited him—so did certain British officers, with whom he was inclined to be courteous and confidential, for obvious propagandic reasons[2]. He was not an imposing personality—short, commonplace, fluent but not impressive in his talk, given to queer gestures and tricks of manner which provoked a smile. In fact he was not a very promising head for a projected rebellion. An acute and humorous observer remarked: 'He seems affable and good tempered; his talents appear not very great. Though seemingly not the being to *make* a kingdom, he may do to govern one when well established. Lord Wellington was in his manner droll towards them [the Duke and his companion Count Damas]. As we went out he put them first: they bowed and scraped right and left so oddly and so actively that he followed with a face much nearer a grin than a smile[3].'

Secret visits from local *hobereaux* and petty officials were almost all that the Duke could show, till the moment of the great advance in the end of February. His visitors reported a general detestation of the Napoleonic régime, but only a few fanatics dared to promise an armed rising. And all insisted that it would only follow an advance of the Allied army into the interior, and a bold statement that the Emperor was to be proscribed and dethroned. This promise Wellington could not give, so long as he was aware that the congress of Châtillon was still sitting. He

---

[1] Metternich's *Autobiography*, i. p. 186.
[2] See, for example, Larpent, pp. 384–5.   [3] Ibid., p. 385.

nourished the gravest doubts of the sincerity, or sanity, of emissaries like the schoolmaster Mailhos from Mont-de-Marşan, who spoke of ten thousand zealous partisans who would muster around the royal banner if it were ever raised[1]. The only personage of any standing who risked his neck, even after the battle of Orthez, was Maluquer, commanding the *gendarmerie* of the department of the Basses-Pyrénées, who entered Pau after its evacuation by the French, delivered some English prisoners, and tried to induce the town-council to declare for the king. Finding that, though they would not oppose him, they would not join him, he was constrained to take refuge in Wellington's camp, with a following of only two or three gendarmes. The Duke of Angoulême followed the track of the Allied army to Dax, Orthez, and St. Sever. He was received with ceremony by some of the clergy, and visited by many members of the local squirearchy, who protested their devotion to the old house, but their inability to collect men for a rising. Outside the limits of the old *noblesse*, and of the mercantile classes, who were being slowly ruined by the war, English observers could detect no Royalists, but only countless enemies of Napoleon. When sounded as to the wishes of the nation in the event of the Emperor's fall, they refused to give any practical suggestion. One commentator remarked that they would be perfectly satisfied to take Buddha as king, if the Allies nominated him[2]. Another said that he had always understood that Aquitaine was very prosperous in the old medieval days, when the King of England reigned at Bordeaux[3].

The most forlorn proposition was that made by Horace de Viel Castel, an *émigré* aide-de-camp of Bernadotte, the Prince Royal of Sweden. He was detected making secret propaganda in favour of his master, who was a Béarnais from Pau by origin. His suggestions came to naught, for it was found that the prince's name was practically forgotten in his own birth-place: his nearest relation, a respectable market-gardener, was found selling winter vegetables in the streets. Viel Castel had to turn Bourbonist, but was none the less imprisoned by the Duke of Angoulême, when the latter found himself in power a few weeks later. But

---

[1] *Wellington Dispatches*, xi. p. 441.
[2] *Wellington Supplementary Dispatches*, iv. p. 427.
[3] Cf. Larpent, p. 426.

though it was impossible to discover a royalist party in any district of Gascony, Wellington found it equally impossible to detect a Napoleonist party. Everywhere the magistrates remained at home, and consented to work under British authority—the peasantry flocked in to sell beasts and food-stuffs, and the *bourgeoisie* of the towns welcomed the arrival of the British with affability, sometimes even with enthusiasm.

After much waiting for the appearance of a royalist rising, Wellington was at last, to his surprise, confronted with the materialization of such a phenomenon. On the fourth day after his arrival at St. Sever, he received an offer from the Mayor of Bordeaux, who promised to raise the White Banner in that great city. Jean-Baptiste Lynch was not at all the kind of personage who is normally found at the head of an insurrection. He was neither an adventurer, nor a fanatic, nor an '*arriviste*' set on rising quickly to the top, nor a spendthrift, nor a man with a grievance. He was sixty-four years of age, wealthy, and occupying the highest position to which a civilian of his rank could aspire. His career had been entirely creditable; his grandfather had been an Irish Jacobite exile of 1688, of good family. Like so many others of his compatriots, he had settled in France, and had married a French woman. He became a prosperous wine-merchant in Bordeaux, and passed on his business and his vineyard to his son Thomas. Jean-Baptiste, his grandson, had taken to the law, was a member of the old 'Parliament of Bordeaux', and had distinguished himself while quite young by his defence of the rights of that ancient body against the crown. In 1775 he had married the daughter of the President Le Berthon, head of the Parliament, and when 1789 came round he had followed his father-in-law to Paris and the States General. Both developed into prominent 'Girondists', and both were in prison, and in danger of death, when they were liberated by the revolution of Thermidor. Returning home to Bordeaux, Lynch became under the Directory a member of the Council General of the Gironde, in which he sat for fifteen years as a respected and influential member. He distinguished himself by carrying out successful plans for the afforestation of the Landes, in 1808 was made Mayor of Bordeaux, and in the following year created a 'count of the Empire'. He was universally regarded as a 'safe man', his only weak point being a tendency to rhetorical and exaggerated praise of the 'powers that were'. His Irish fluency came out in effusive laudations of the glories of the Emperor and the imperial régime. He made many speeches, and was responsible for some actions which he would have liked to forget after March, 1814, but which his enemies never tired of recalling. As late as November 1813 he had been summoned with other dignitaries to Paris, and had been heard to declaim in pompous periods that, 'Napoleon has done everything for the French people: it is now time that the French people should do everything for Napoleon.' But what he saw and heard in Paris at the time of his visit had apparently brought him to the cold conclusion that the Emperor was ruined, and that France could only be saved by getting rid of him. A good many other of the magnates and officials drawn in to the capital had come to the same conclusion—which had been reached long before by the old intriguers like Fouché and Talleyrand. But comparatively honest men were now feeling that the only solution of the problem was the removal of the Emperor by any means possible, even rather unscrupulous ones.

On his return to the Gironde Lynch put himself in touch with a rather effete and very subterranean association, the 'Royalist Committee of Bordeaux', which he knew to have been in existence for many years. It had never done anything beyond holding secret meetings, and drawing up lists of persons who would be ready, at some time undesignated, to act as officers of the eight 'companies of Royal Volunteers' which they calculated that their party could raise at a crisis. Lynch breathed sudden life into this conspiracy, assuring its members that the crisis had come now, that the Allies would be over the Rhine before the winter was out, that Wellington would drive Soult from the southern frontier, and that, from all that he had seen in Paris, he judged that the crash was inevitable. His own share in the matter was to paralyse the imperialist organization in Bordeaux, which he did most effectively by criticizing and making ineffective every measure taken by Cornudet, the 'Commissioner Extraordinary', and L'Huillier, the military governor. He was specially active in raising legal and practical hindrances to the organization of the National Guard. The department of the Gironde ought to have

furnished eight cohorts—it never produced more than one, and
that under strength, and consisting entirely of hired substitutes,
not of solid householders. On February 27th, to gratify Cornudet
—and perhaps his own sense of humour— Lynch solemnly presented a regimental flag to these 500 scarecrows, with a pompous
address concerning their duties to their august sovereign, for
whom they were ready to shed their blood. Lynch had invaluable
tools in Tauzia, the commissary of police, and Mondenard, the
municipal secretary, both of them men whom he had chosen and
promoted some time back. The one used the police to suppress
all information which might have frightened the prefect or the
'Commissioner Extraordinary', the other sounded the municipal
councillors and enrolled most of them in the plot.

Napoleon had done his best to favour Lynch's plans, when he
stole from Soult all the best of the newly raised battalions of the
much-advertised 'Army of the Gironde', and drew them off to
join the Grand Army in Champagne. He left General L'Huillier
only five or six incomplete cadres, the units which were not ready
in December. In and about Bordeaux there were some 3,000 or
4,000 of these conscripts, many without arms, and nearly all without uniform. They were mostly placed in the forts down the
Gironde, which were always kept garrisoned for fear of English
naval descents—Pointe de Graves, Fort Médoc, Blaye, Fort
Pâté. In Bordeaux itself, as L'Huillier calculated on March 1st,
there were only 2,200 troops of all sorts—including gendarmes,
douaniers, and 1,100 men of the so-called 'Urban Guard', who
were pledged to local service alone, and did not live in barracks
nor keep under arms all day.

Even before the battle of Orthez Soult wrote to L'Huillier that
he was compelled to retreat eastward, and to uncover the direct
road to Bordeaux through the Landes. It was possible that
Wellington might direct a raid against the city: it must defend
itself. 'Que tout prenne une attitude militaire dans le départe-
ment de la Gironde! Que toute la population s'arme! Quand
on veut se défendre on en trouve le moyen.' Meanwhile he
suggested that the military hospitals, the powder-magazines, the
depots of arms, and the imperial treasury should all be discharged on to the farther bank of the Garonne, to Libourne or
even farther inland.

The unhappy L'Huillier realized, after the news of Orthez arrived, that, for all he knew, Wellington might be marching on Bordeaux with 50,000 men; but even if he were not, and only a column of 10,000 men was on the way, he could do nothing to stop it. Soult sent further dispatches suggesting that Bordeaux might be defended by a *levée en masse*, and recommending the proclamation of a state of siege. This, as L'Huillier knew, was impossible, considering the disposition of the inhabitants. He began to move the hospitals and depots of arms across the river, and would have done the same with the magazines of food at Podensac, but rioters, secretly set on by the mayor, prevented this from being accomplished. When news came to hand that the English had occupied Mont-de-Marsan on March 2nd[1], and had pushed cavalry out as far as Roquefort on the 5th[1], L'Huillier jumped to the conclusion that the invasion was actually coming. He moved his handful of conscripts and *douaniers* across the Gironde on March 10th, leaving in the city only the sedentary 'Urban Guard' who were not expected to fight. But as a matter of fact Beresford's march on Bordeaux had only started upon the 8th, and the French general was not aware of its actual commencement when he made his retreat. He was, however, cozened by the alarmist reports of the mayor, and appalled at the disloyal apathy displayed by most of the greater and many of the poorer inhabitants of Bordeaux. The 'Extraordinary Commissioner' Cornudet went off a few hours before the general.

It is clear that Wellington would never have delivered his stroke at Bordeaux, if it had not been for the very clear account of the state of affairs in that city which Lynch had sent him. On March 4th he had been visited at St. Sever by the mayor's confidential agents, Bontemps-Dubarry and Louis de Rochejaquelin (kinsman of the Vendéan leader of 1794), who gave the exact figures of the imaginary 'Army of the Gironde' which had once somewhat impressed Wellington's mind, delivered the mayor's written promise to hand over the city, and recounted the names of all the local notables—merchants and officials—who were pledged to back him. They asked that the English on arriving should proclaim Louis XVIII, but this Wellington refused to

[1] Vivian's *Memoirs*, p. 213.

promise, though he undertook that nothing should be done to prevent a spontaneous action by the Bordelais themselves.

On the 7th Beresford received his orders to march from Mont-de-Marsan with the 7th Division—now again under Lord Dalhousie, who had returned from his long winter holiday in England. The 4th Division was to follow him from St. Sever, a day's journey behind. Vivian's cavalry, already at Roquefort, rode ahead of the column. All these moved on the high road by Roquefort, Bazas, Langon, Podensac, avoiding the Landes by turning their eastern flank. Only two squadrons of Vandeleur's Light Dragoons, detached from the camp before Bayonne, took a separate route through those sandy wastes, and joined the main column in front of Bordeaux. On neither track did the advanced cavalry meet with any opposition: indeed the only enemy seen was a picket of gendarmes, which was dispersed on the road beyond Langon. The weather was abominable, and the first part of the road, as far as Bazas, rather ill-kept, but nevertheless the pace maintained was very good. Vivian's Hussars covered the 80 miles from Roquefort to Bordeaux in four days, and the leading infantry brigade of the 7th Division, which had the longer distance, Mont-de-Marsan–Bordeaux, to traverse, was only fifteen hours later. Beresford, continuing to receive constant information from Lynch as to the state of affairs on the Gironde, learned that he might be confident of meeting no opposition. He therefore left the 4th Division at Langon, from whence it might easily be drawn back to rejoin Wellington, and went on with the 7th Division only. Vivian with the 1st Hussars of the K.G.L. reached the outskirts of Bordeaux on the morning of March 12th, the three brigades of Dalhousie's infantry following him at short intervals. The 18th Hussars were left out on the right flank, to watch the various passages on the Garonne, by which hostile forces coming from the east might possibly appear. As a matter of fact none such existed—beyond the garrisons of the forts down the Gironde at Blaye, Fort Médoc, Pointe de Graves, Fort Pâté, &c., and the 1,000 or 1,500 men with whom L'Huillier had withdrawn to Libourne, the only organized unit in the neighbourhood was a conscript battalion at La Réole, which withdrew eastward to Marmande on Beresford's approach.

At 8 o'clock on the morning of March 12th a troop of the
German Hussars rode into the suburbs of Bordeaux, and halted
at the barrier. They were received by a sympathetic crowd,
and handed laurel sprays to wear in their caps by two enthusiastic gentlemen. When Vivian came up, with the main body of
his regiment, and heard that the mayor was preparing to come
out in state, to combine his formal reception of the British Army
with a declaration that Louis XVIII now reigned in France with
the goodwill of the Allies, he hurried back to Beresford, who was
a few miles behind, to warn him of this intention on Lynch's
part. The Marshal, carrying out the orders which Wellington
had given him, to the effect that the occupation of Bordeaux
was to have a military not a political aspect, sent Vivian back
to meet the mayor, and to warn him that, while England wished
well to the royalist cause, he was not authorized either to urge
or to disapprove the proclamation of Louis XVIII, and that
whatever happened must be considered as an act of the
Bordelais themselves, and not directed, still less dictated,
by the English[1]. The brigadier caught the mayor approaching
in his carriage, preceded by twelve gendarmes, and followed by
about 150 young men on horseback who represented the
'Chevaux légers de la garde royale de Bordeaux' with 'an
enormous mass of respectable people' following on foot. Vivian
gave the message to Lynch, who replied that he was much
obliged for the Marshal's warning, and would himself explain his
feelings when they met.

Outside the Place St. Julien (now the Place d'Aquitaine) the
mayor descended from his carriage and mounted a horse, and
so met the Marshal, who was also mounted. After making his
salute, he declaimed his celebrated speech—The Allied troops
were about to enter a loyal town which yearned for the return
of its legitimate sovereign. 'A bas les aigles, vivent les Bourbons,'
shouted the chevaux légers. Lynch then tore the Legion of
Honour from his coat, and the tricoloured scarf from his waist,
and fixed in his hat a large white cockade. Among cheers of
Vive le Roi! his horsemen did the same, casting down their
imperial cockades and mounting white ones. Their gesture was
copied by thousands in the crowd, who had come prepared with

[1] Vivian's *Memoirs*, p. 216.

the royalist badge in their pockets. At the same moment Lynch
pointed to the white flag running up on the towers of St. Michel
and the Cathedral—trusty friends had been ready with them
since dawn. Beresford replied, keeping strictly to the orders
that he had received, that he took possession of the town in the
name of Lord Wellington, not (as Lynch had hoped) in the name
of Louis XVIII. He complimented the mayor on the enthusiasm
of his citizens, expressed hopes that peace was at hand, and
promised that his troops would remember that they were among
friends, 'we have made war not on Frenchmen but only on the
French Government'.

Lynch, a little disappointed, finished the scene with effect,
inviting the Marshal to visit the town hall, and to receive the
greetings of the municipal council. The majority of it was indeed
present (a few Bonapartists had emigrated, others had shut
themselves up in their houses) and cheered the mayor as he
declaimed his sentiments of loyalty. Beresford and his staff
were escorted to the empty abode of the absconded prefect.

All this was over by noon—at 2 o'clock another ceremony
took place, for which Beresford had not been prepared. On
hearing that the Allied troops had reached Langon, the Duke of
Angoulême, without getting any authorization from Wellington,
had ridden up from St. Sever at furious speed, picking up La
Roche Jacquelin, the Duc de Guiche, and a number of other
zealous Bourbonists on the way. As he had arranged with Lynch,
he was received at the barriers of Bordeaux by that magistrate,
his *chevaux légers*, and an enthusiastic crowd. The mayor and his
horsemen escorted the duke to the Cathedral, where the old
Archbishop Dubois de Sanzay, who was deep in the plot, intoned
a *Te Deum* in honour of the restoration of Louis XVIII, and
offered the Prince the·hospitality of his palace. The prefecture
was already in the occupation of Beresford. So far so good—
Wellington had instructed Beresford that he was not to hinder
any spontaneous outburst of royalist enthusiasm.

But Lynch and the Prince then proceeded, on that same evening, to draw up a proclamation, which made Beresford sulky and
Wellington furious. It was an address to the Bordelais to the
effect that the Duke of Angoulême had taken over the administration of their city in the name of the king, and with the

approval of the Allies, who were united in their desire to dethrone Bonaparte and to replace him by the legitimate sovereign[1]. Now this was precisely what Wellington had not authorized the duke to state; since, until he should be aware that the conference at Châtillon had ended in a rupture, it was impossible to pronounce openly in favour of the Bourbons. Beresford had to warn the mayor that he had no authority to hand over the government of the occupied regions to the civil authorities[2], and said that he would have issued a formal notice to that effect, if it had not been that he did not want to discourage the Royalists. Wellington was still more drastic; having received a letter from the duke announcing his (unauthorized) assumption of power, and requesting that Beresford should be ordered to assist him, and that he should have leave to embody troops, and to take over the whole administration of the country-side[3], he replied in very stiff terms. It was not true, as the proclamation of March 12th stated, that the English, Spanish, and Portuguese armies were only present in the south of France in order to restore the 'paternal monarch', nor that 'the Bourbons have returned conducted by their generous allies'. He was carrying out military operations under the directions of the British Government, and he had no orders from Whitehall to restore the old régime, nor to put British troops at the disposition of claimants to the French throne, in order to force submission to them on the French people. He had no objection to the proclamation of Louis XVIII, nor to the raising of royalist troops, and arms could be found for them. But the Duke would have to raise money to pay them, from the resources of Bordeaux, of which he had taken over charge. It would not be furnished from the British military chest. The main thing was that the Duke must realize that not a British soldier would be moved except for military objects—dynastic objects did not concern him[4].

There can be no doubt that Wellington's caution was justified.

[1] Beresford to Wellington, March 16. *Supplementary Dispatches*, viii. p. 653.

[2] Text in *Wellington Dispatches*, xi. p. 579.

[3] Angoulême to Wellington. *Supplementary Dispatches*, viii. p. 640, and ibid., p. 651, March 13.

[4] Wellington to Angoulême. *Wellington Dispatches*, xi. pp. 584–5, March 15. Cf. that of March 14 also.

What would have been his position if news had come from Châtillon that peace had been concluded with Bonaparte? Fortunately, during the four weeks for which the war had yet to run, nothing untoward happened on the Bordeaux side. It was true that Angoulême proved absolutely unable to raise a royalist army—plenty of officers presented themselves, but no recruits for the rank and file. In the country-side the peasantry hunted away the tax-collectors and the *sous-préfets*, but showed no wish to indulge in anything better than taxless anarchy. When Beresford sent a squadron to summon the coast-fort at the Teste de Buch, where the single cohort of National Guards which Bordeaux had raised was in garrison, the commandant surrendered and mounted the white cockade, but the rank and file mostly dispersed: 200 of them were the only body of armed men whom the royalists succeeded in rallying to their banners. The mayor and the duke soon got uneasy at the small show of troops which Beresford displayed—one brigade of infantry and Vivian's Hussars were alone visible. The rest of the 7th Division was écheloned up the Garonne, at Castres and Podensac—the 4th Division had never moved farther than Langon. And their spirits sank still lower when Beresford received orders to rejoin the main army, because Soult was showing unexpected signs of activity in the south. On the 15th Vivian's brigade—all save one squadron—marched for Aire, escorting Beresford, who picked up the 4th Division at Bazas, and hurried, through dreadful weather, to report himself to Wellington.

This left only 5,000 men on the Gironde—the three brigades of the 7th Division, the two squadrons which Vandeleur had detached across the Landes, and one extra squadron left behind by Vivian. With them was one single battery. This would have formed an admirable nucleus for a royalist army—but the royalist army consisted of the 150 gentleman-troopers of the *Garde Royale*, a hundred officers of sorts—largely civilians—and about 600 recruits of the lowest class—generally to be found drinking in wine-shops. Dalhousie, left in command by Beresford, finding no signs of hostile troops up the Garonne, finally brought Doyle's Portuguese to join Gardiner's British brigade in Bordeaux. Inglis's brigade was sent to Langon. Everything remained perfectly quiet till the end of the month—the only excitement was the cutting up on March 18th of a company of the *Chasseurs Britanniques*, which had been exploring across the river at St. Macaire. They were surprised, owing to the careless-ness of their captain, by a party from the conscript-battalion at Marmande, which had now moved forward to La Réole, and 2 officers and 50 men were 'missing[1]'. But this was an isolated incident—L'Huillier had no idea of any general molestation of Dalhousie's outposts.

When Wellington had made up his mind to risk the stroke at Bordeaux, he had realized the fact that if it succeeded he might secure for himself a much better base for all his future operations than St. Jean de Luz, which was growing more inconveniently remote on each day that he advanced farther into the interior. But Bordeaux is so far up the long estuary of the Gironde, that ships making for it have to face several successive dangers from land fortifications. For the water is not so wide but that guns on either bank might make their passage dangerous, or even impracticable. It was therefore in order to clear away these hindrances that he desired Admiral Penrose on March 17th to collect a sufficient naval force to destroy the shore-batteries all up the river, as well as the French squadron—consisting of one 80-gun ship, the *Regulus*, three brigs, and some thirty gunboats —which was lying in the Gironde[2]. This Penrose proceeded, though in a somewhat leisurely way, to effect: the usual excuse of contrary winds was given. But on the 27th he ran into the mouth of the Gironde with a 74 and four frigates, and found the fort at Pointe de Graves on the west side evacuated: a distant fire from the batteries by Royan and Coubres on the other bank did no harm. The French 80-gun ship refused to fight—its captain ran it on shore, under the protection of two old batteries by Meschers, which he manned with gunners disembarked from his vessel. The three brigs took shelter beside the *Regulus*. Penrose did not attack—being apparently afraid of the shore-batteries—but detached light vessels up the Gironde, which re-ported the rest of the French naval force moored under the cover of the citadel of Blaye—an old *chef-d'œuvre* of Vauban—which lies high and commands the whole breadth of the estuary. On

---

[1] Dalhousie to Wellington. *Supplementary Dispatches*, viii. p. 668, March 19.   [2] Wellington to Penrose. *Dispatches*, xi. p. 588.

April 2nd these gunboats loosed from their safe position, and ran down the Gironde—apparently with the intention of joining the *Regulus* at Meschers. They were intercepted half-way by Penrose's light vessels, forced to run on shore, and there destroyed, mainly by rocket-fire. Eight were sunk or burnt, a few others dragged off by landing parties—the whole loss to the British Navy was only six men. Four days later Penrose, having been joined by a second ship of the line, resolved to push inshore and capture and destroy the *Regulus* and her smaller consorts— but was disappointed, for the French set fire to the vessels early on the night chosen for the enterprise [April 6]. On the next morning they evacuated all the shore-batteries along both sides of the Gironde, leaving only Blaye and Fort Pâté occupied. But Blaye still blocked the passage up-stream to Bordeaux, since it commanded the whole navigable channel, and Penrose was not yet in military touch with Dalhousie, though they exchanged communications by land on the west bank of the Gironde[1]. If the war had continued a few days longer, it is obvious that a joint attack by sea and land on Blaye would have been the necessary move. But—as we shall see—external events intervened to make this unnecessary.

During the last ten days of March Dalhousie, informed by royalist agents of the hopeless situation of L'Huillier on the other side of the Gironde, began to think that, even with his modest force of three brigades, he might aim at something more ambitious than the passive occupation of Bordeaux. The Duke of Angoulême and Lynch were strongly of opinion that if he crossed the Garonne and the Dordogne, all Périgord, Saintonge, and La Vendée would rally to the White Banner. This they did not do—but on the other hand the country beyond the Garonne lapsed into complete disobedience to the imperial authorities; Dalhousie found willing guides everywhere, plentiful supplies, and all the information that he could desire. In some places the inhabitants brought boats to ferry him over rivers, and suggested how outlying parties of L'Huillier's men could be cut off.

Dalhousie made what he calls his first 'little show'[2] on March

---

[1] Dalhousie to Murray. *Supplementary Dispatches*, viii. p. 709.

[2] Dalhousie to Wellington, April 2. *Supplementary Dispatches*, viii. p. 709.

24th, when, leaving in Bordeaux only Elder's 7th Portuguese Line, he sent Doyle and the other three Portuguese battalions to menace Blaye, and marched through Libourne as far as St. André de Cubsac on the Dordogne with Gardiner's brigade, one squadron of the 12th Light Dragoons, and four guns[1]. Inglis at Langon was ordered to seize La Réole and St. Macaire, on the other side of the Garonne. The advance was stopped at the Dordogne, which Dalhousie considered rather a formidable obstacle, even when he found in his front an enemy who gave way at once, with every sign of precipitation. Accordingly he withdrew again to Bordeaux, after a short circular tour. On April 2nd, however, having got into touch with the fleet at last, he resolved that he might make a serious advance to attack Blaye, whose fall was necessary, if communication with Penrose was to be free, and the port of Bordeaux to be opened.

Accordingly he started out again with much the same force that he had used in the preceding week, save that he left the 19th Portuguese to garrison Bordeaux instead of the 7th. The whole was under 2,500 men, as the battalions were all very weak. On hearing of his approach L'Huillier with his small field-force retired to get under cover of the fortification of Blaye. But he soon received orders to quit this shelter, from a new commander who had come upon the scene.

On March 20th Napoleon, having received with great rage the news of the surrender of Bordeaux, was constrained to take new measures, to prevent what looked like the general revolt of the south-western departments. He sent to Périgueux General Decaen, late in command of the Army of Catalonia, with orders to collect all possible bodies of troops, however small, and to demonstrate against Lord Dalhousie, till he should receive an addition of force which would give him a marked superiority over the English division at Bordeaux. This reinforcement, whose origin will be spoken of in its proper place, consisted of 6,000 men under General Beurmann, the second detachment which Suchet had been ordered to send away from his Catalan army, when affairs were growing desperate on the eastern frontier

[1] The third squadron of the 12th Light Dragoons having come up from Bayonne, the squadron of Vivian's Hussars hitherto left at Bordeaux went south.

of France[1]. This force, originally destined to strengthen Augereau's army at Lyons, was ordered to turn off westward and move
en poste—i. e. on requisitioned vehicles—right across country
from the Rhone to the Dordogne. Beurmann received these
orders on April 2nd when already engaged with the Austrians,
but, duly obeying them, turned off by Clermont Ferrand, and
reached Périgueux on April 9th with a force reduced to 3,500
men by desertion and straggling, for the news of the fall of Paris
had reached the column on its way, and the troops showed signs
of mutiny, and began to disperse.

They were, at any rate, too late to be of any use to Decaen or
L'Huillier. The latter, receiving his new chief's orders to avoid
being shut up in Blaye, and to fall back to join him, had marched
on the morning of April 6th with three or four of his raw
battalions[2]—those which were at least armed and clothed—two
guns, and three provisional squadrons of cavalry, which had just
reached him from the central cavalry depot at Niort. Marching
northward out of Blaye, with perhaps some 2,000 men, he ran
into the advance of Dalhousie's column, which was circling round
that fortress with the intention of investing it. The two forces
met on the heath of Étauliers, five miles outside of Blaye,
Dalhousie having a clear superiority in numbers as well as in
quality. L'Huillier formed something like a line of battle along
thickets at the edge of the heath, but when Gardiner's brigade
charged, the whole broke up, and fled in disorder. Three
hundred men and twenty officers were captured, the majority
of the rest dispersed, and L'Huillier reached Saintes with
no more than 500 men—mostly from the cavalry, who got
away easily. The unfortunate field-force was practically annihilated. Dalhousie had only about twenty casualties[3].

Leaving Gardiner's brigade on the battle-ground, Dalhousie
sent his three Portuguese battalions against Blaye. He had
received information—which was quite correct—that the

[1] See below, p. 424.

[2] There were certainly present battalions of the 27th, 105th, 120th, as
officer-casualties in Martinien's lists indicate. Beer, the officer commanding the 105th, was killed.

[3] The only personal narrative of the Combat of Étauliers which I have
discovered is that of Hay of the 12th Light Dragoons, *Reminiscences*,
pp. 140–2.

garrison was demoralized, and half of it without arms. But
Admiral Jacob, who had taken refuge in Blaye after the destruction of the Gironde flotilla, and was in command, refused to treat,
and when the 2nd Caçadores (without having any orders) tried
to rush the outworks, he fired on them and drove them off with
a loss of 3 officers and 20 men (April 7). Dalhousie then resolved
that he and Admiral Penrose must combine to invest the place,
and the fleet came up that same evening. But no siege was
actually begun—the Admiral reported that the news from Paris,
combined with L'Huillier's disaster on the preceding day, had
converted the whole country-side to Bourbonism. The White
Banner was flying from every spire and mast along the river, and
the inhabitants were putting out in boats to greet the squadron
with loyal protestations and useful supplies of provisions. There
would probably be no difficulty in dealing with the garrison of
Blaye, when once the news got round, even though the Admiral
in command might be a staunch Bonapartist.

And this proved indeed to be the case. The news of the rupture
of the congress of Châtillon, of the entry of the Allies into Paris,
and of the decree of the Senate declaring Napoleon deposed,
suddenly converted hundreds of thousands of those who had
hitherto been 'sitting on the fence': they descended on the
legitimist side. Most of the imperial officials hastened to Paris
to make their peace with the new government—the more enterprising of them came to Bordeaux to offer their homage to the
Duke of Angoulême. The late prefect of the Gironde, Valsuzenay,
was one of the first to appear—he was followed a little later by
General Decaen himself, who as early as April 11th sent in his
adhesion to the new government at Paris. The tricolour floated
for a few days longer on the citadel of Blaye, but the mayor of
the town came out to explain to Dalhousie that it would come
down the moment that Admiral Jacob was convinced that the
revolution had taken place. And this was indeed the case: after
Decaen's repudiation of the imperial régime, Blaye hoisted the
White Banner like every other place in the South, and English
vessels ran in safety up to the quays of Bordeaux. Government
transports presently brought a brigade of English militia which
had volunteered for foreign service, under the Marquis of Bucking-
ham—the first experiment of the kind. Dalhousie would have

welcomed them on April 1st, but they only appeared after the war was over. More welcome were the merchantmen bringing colonial wares for southern France, which had so long been deprived of them. Bordeaux showed for the next month a scene of continuous festivity—merchants, shipmasters, lawyers, and the long-submerged or exiled *noblesse* fraternized in the crowded ante-room of the Duke of Angoulême, and united to make life pleasant for the English garrison. Every diary of a Peninsular officer who passed through the city in the spring of 1814 is full of tales of good cheer and friendly acquaintances. Dalhousie, who had found his troops surprisingly well-behaved[1], could send to Wellington assurances that all was well in the best of all possible worlds. He was immensely popular in the city, and when he quitted it, two months later, was presented with a sword of honour by the municipality.

[1] He expresses his surprise in his letter to Wellington, *Supplementary Dispatches*, viii. p. 696. 'Their excellent conduct astonishes the city and even myself. I assure your Lordship that I am not merely paying them compliments when I say so.'

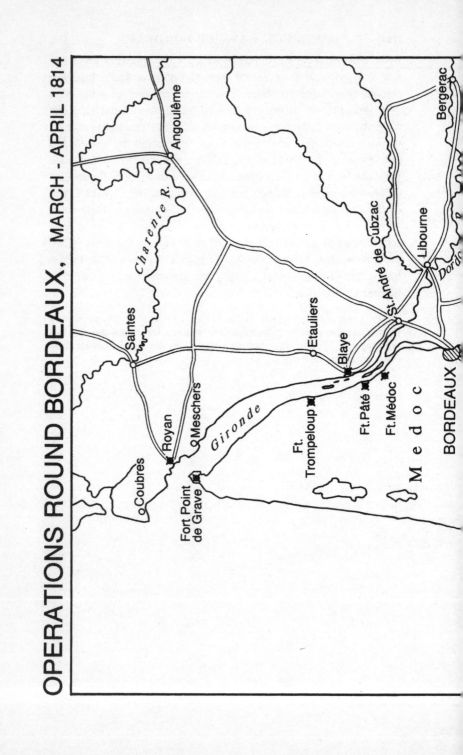

OPERATIONS ROUND BORDEAUX. MARCH - APRIL 1814

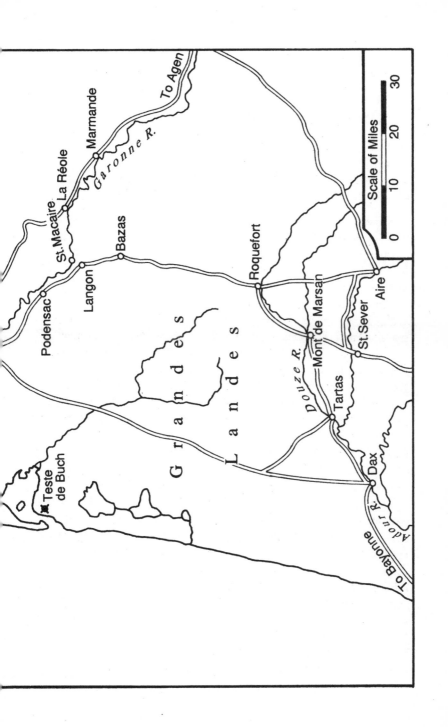

SECTION XLIV

END OF THE WAR ON THE EAST COAST

CHAPTER I

THE WINTER ON THE EAST COAST. THE TREACHERY OF JUAN VAN HALEN. SUCHET AND KING FERDINAND

NOTHING from the point of view of military narrative can be less interesting than the last six months of the war on the Catalan side. After the combat of Ordal and Bentinck's retreat to Tarragona in September, active operations languished altogether. Bentinck had been replaced by the diffident William Clinton, whose guiding principle was that, in obedience to Wellington's orders of the preceding spring, he was not to risk the destruction of his very miscellaneous corps by any rash manœuvring. A very large Spanish force could have been collected to join him, but Wellington deprecated any such plan. He had called off the Duke del Parque's '3rd Army' to the upper Ebro, and allowed Elio's '2nd Army' to settle down to the interminable sieges, or rather blockades, of Saguntum, Tortosa, Lerida, and the smaller French garrisons of the East. Of Elio's five divisions four were thus absorbed—only one, that of Sarsfield, had come up into central Catalonia, and put itself in touch with Clinton and with Copons's little '1st Army'.

Suchet, in addition to the 24,000 men locked up in the garrisons from Denia in the extreme south to Barcelona, had still a field-army of 28,000 men, which was far more than was required to deal with Clinton and Copons, whose total force was little, if at all, greater than his. But he had no intention of taking the offensive, and when reporting the situation to Paris often spoke of the 70,000 enemies by whom he was surrounded —a figure arrived at by crediting them with the whole of Del Parque's and Elio's distant divisions, and by overestimating every unit in their force[1]. He was well aware of the unhappy situation that had arisen from his resolve in the summer to

[1] Suchet to Clarke, November 23.

leave such large garrisons in Tortosa and Lerida, and sometimes thought of relieving them by a sudden raid, and carrying them off. This would have been a practicable scheme all through the autumn, for Copons and Clinton were divided from each other by long distances, and, even if they had united, all their strength would probably have been unable to foil the plan. But Suchet feared to offend his master by giving up all the keys of eastern Spain, and excused himself to Paris by saying that the garrisons, after all, were detaining very large hostile forces in front of them, and that, if he succeeded in carrying them off, the Allied field-army would become immense, and even capable of invading France. This was an insincere plea, for the Marshal must have known that Elio and Del Parque's armies were incapable of joining in an invasion, being destitute of transport and supplies, while Copons and Clinton were in not very much better case.

All through September and early October Suchet had been keeping up his fruitless correspondence with Soult concerning a projected union of their forces in Aragon, for the purpose of taking Wellington in flank and rear—as has been already explained[1]. Any such scheme became impossible when Wellington assumed the offensive on October 7th, forced the passage of the Bidassoa, and pinned Soult down to the lines of the Nivelle, where his whole army was absorbed in entrenchments. An equally cogent hindrance was the closing of the Pyrenean passes by the first snows of autumn.

Meanwhile, a month after Leipzig and all too late, the Emperor suddenly resolved to evacuate the Ebro fortresses, and wrote on November 25th that he authorized Suchet to march on Lerida, to pick up its garrison and that of Mequinenza, and then to turn south, release Robert's division from Tortosa, and so raise his army to a force sufficient to drive off all enemies[2]. The fortresses were to be blown up on evacuation. The Marshal accordingly got on the move, for the first time for three months. But before taking away his whole field-army from the neighbourhood of Barcelona, and exposing his central base of operation to Clinton and Copons, who might close in upon it the moment that he started off for the distant Lerida, Suchet thought it necessary

---

[1] See above, pp. 90–3.
[2] Napoleon to Clarke, November 25. *Correspondance*, No. 20,942.

to dispose of the Anglo-Sicilians. Accordingly he collected on December 2nd the whole of Habert's and Musnier's divisions, part of Pannetier's, with a brigade from the garrison of Barcelona, and three of his four cavalry regiments, and marched on Clinton's head-quarters at Villafranca, by the two roads through San Sadurni and Ordal which he had used in September in his similar assault on Bentinck. Warned in time[1], Clinton drew back from Villafranca, and offered battle south of it, on a strong position in front of Arbos, with his whole force and Whittingham's and Sarsfield's Spanish divisions. Suchet looked at the battle-line, refused to attack—no doubt he had Castalla in his mind—and returned to his cantonments on the Llobregat round Barcelona. He was wanted there, for Copons, hearing of the concentration against Clinton, had closed in toward the northern side of the fortress. He had to turn back, however, when he found that the French field-force had returned from its ineffectual march to Villafranca, and resumed its old positions. Suchet says nothing in his memoirs of this operation, no doubt (as Napier remarks) because of its entire futility[2]. Clinton returned to Villafranca when the enemy had retired.

This feeble demonstration was all that came of the Emperor's tardy order to Suchet to carry off the garrisons of Lerida and Tortosa. The Marshal explained his quiescence during the rest of the winter by the sudden diminution of his forces. He received from Paris orders to disarm and send away his three German battalions and two German regiments of cavalry[3]—this was due to the desertion of the Nassau and Frankfurt infantry from Soult's army during the battle of the Nive. The Emperor feared that the Westphalian and Nassau troops in Catalonia would follow their example. And indeed Kruse, the colonel who had led the defection at Bayonne, had sent letters to the officer commanding the sister regiment to his own at Barcelona, inciting him to follow suit. Colonel Meder of the 1st Nassau handed over the letter to Suchet—but that all of these Germans were not of

---

[1] The pass of Ordal this time, remarks Napier, was *not* watched by Adam, who had shown such deplorable blindness in September (vi. p. 51).

[2] Napier, vi. p. 51.

[3] Two battalions of 1st Nassau, one of 4th Westphalians, the regiment of Nassau light horse, two squadrons Westphalian light horse.

the same way of thinking was shown by the fact that many scores
of them deserted to Clinton's outposts in December[1]. This disarmament deprived Suchet of some 2,500 old soldiers, but was
not such a blow to the strength of the Catalan Army as the order
to detach a cadre of 120 men from each of its regiments to form
the nucleus for the organization of a new battalion at Mont-
pellier or Nîmes. Soult had received similar orders dated Nov. 16,
and was equally discontented, as will be remembered[2]. And, like
Soult, Suchet was ultimately defrauded by his master, for the
'reserve division' formed at Nîmes was sent off to join Augereau's
army at Lyons, while the Montpellier division, never quite
complete, was utilized to form garrisons for Perpignan, Montlouis,
and other fortresses of the eastern Pyrenean frontier. The
formation of the two reserve-divisions did not give Suchet a
single extra man for his field-force, in the last months of the war.
Moreover, the Catalan Army was thinned at the same time by a
draft of 800 old soldiers to recruit the wasted Imperial Guard.
Yet these various deductions from Suchet's force, amounting
to 6,000 men at least, were a trifle compared with the appalling
requisition which was about to be made on him in January.

But the Marshal's quiescence in the last weeks of the year 1813
was due not so much to the falling numbers of his army as to
the negotiations which followed on the hollow and abortive
Treaty of Valençay. It will be remembered that Napoleon had
started his preposterous scheme, for producing a breach between
Spain and England by the release of Ferdinand VII, as early as
November 18th, and that on December 10th[3] the king had given
his acceptance of the Emperor's terms, without any intention
of keeping his word. On the following day the Duke of San Carlos
had been started off to Suchet's head-quarters with a copy of the
treaty, and the Marshal was directed to send him under a flag
of truce to the outposts of General Copons, who was known to
be one of the faction of the 'Serviles', and no particular friend
of the Regency or the Cortes. Copons received the duke and
sent him on to Madrid, which he reached on January 4th—there

---

[1] For a full account of this intrigue see Sauzey's 'Les Allemands sous les
Aigles', vi, pp. 229–30. Meder was given a French commission, and was
killed in Habert's April sortie.
[2] Wellington Dispatches, xi. p. 433.   [3] See above, p. 304.

(as we have already seen)[1] to find the treaty repudiated, and to be dismissed in some disgrace. Copons did not send word of San Carlos's passage through his lines to Wellington—as he undoubtedly should have done—and this caused the latter to entertain some suspicions that the general was acting treacherously, and favouring a secret peace between France and Spain[2]. But the whole of Copons's subsequent conduct sufficiently showed that he was no friend of France, and that he was prepared to cheat and deceive Suchet to the best of his power. It is probable that San Carlos revealed to him Ferdinand's secret intentions—his resolve to get out of France by making any promises required of him, and then to repudiate those promises the moment that he was among his own people. But this could not be known to the British general.

Wellington, however, was suspicious that Copons and Elio (also a noted *Servile*) might be tempted into buying back the king by permitting the French garrisons to depart—which would be convenient for themselves, and a great relief to the provinces of Valencia and Catalonia. He therefore repeated to them in January a warning which he had already sent some time before —that no capitulation should be made with any French garrison, save on the terms that the troops should surrender as prisoners of war. For he was strongly of opinion that the blockaded force would be of more use to Suchet than the corresponding blockading force would be to the cause of Spain[3]. However, all these suspicions died down when the Cortes published its drastic repudiation of the treaty, and when Copons, early in February, played off on the French the unscrupulous trick of the forged 'Convention of Tarrasa', which led to the capture of the garrisons of Lerida, Monzon, and Mequinenza, and might also, but for a chance, have involved that of Tortosa in the snare.

We have already told how Soult's position in January was influenced by Napoleon's absurdly optimistic idea that the Spaniards would be so completely dominated by a desire to get back their king, that they would at once accept the Treaty of Valençay, withdraw Freire's and Mina's divisions from France, desire the British troops to evacuate Spain, and allow the

---

[1] See above, p. 306.
[2] *Wellington Dispatches*, xi. pp. 445 and 480.   [3] See above, p. 312.

numérous garrisons of the East, from Denia to Tortosa, to join
Suchet's army, which would then amount to a field-force of
43,000 men. When withdrawn from Catalonia such an army
could either turn the tide of war in eastern France, or, if sent to
join Soult, could make Wellington's position perilous. For when
deprived of their Spanish auxiliaries the Anglo-Portuguese had
not more than 63,000 men in all, and would have been terribly
outnumbered, if Soult had been reinforced by the whole Army
of Catalonia.

But Napoleon's actual project was, as explained elsewhere, not
to attack Wellington, but to carry off the greater part of both
Soult's and Suchet's armies northward and eastward, leaving
only a screen in front of the Anglo-Portuguese. He had come to
the conclusion that the British Government would probably
withdraw the army now on the Nive and the Adour, and send it
to Holland, rather than pursue an active policy in southern
France after the loss of the Spanish base[1]. The orders sent to
Suchet in December and January presuppose the complete
success of the Treaty of Valençay, and the withdrawal of Spain
from the War. On January 4th the Marshal received an elaborate scheme from the Paris War Office[2], warning him to prepare
to withdraw his army from Spain, and to be ready to evacuate
fortress after fortress, and region after region in succession, as
each of the blockaded garrisons was released and came in to join
him. On January 10th came a definite order. Suchet was to
concentrate all his cavalry and horse artillery at once at the foot
of the Pyrenees, and the moment that the news of the ratification
of the Treaty of Valençay should come to hand, to send off this
force and half of the infantry of his field-army on the road to
Lyons. These preparations were to be made, even if the negotiations at Madrid should hang fire. The Marshal was to get ready
to start himself with the other half of his infantry, the moment
that news of the ratification of the treaty should arrive from
the Spanish capital. Presumably the Emperor imagined that
Clinton's Anglo-Sicilians would be taken off by sea the moment
that Spain retired from the war.

[1] Clarke to Suchet, January 15.
[2] Dated November 15, it seems to have taken a preposterous time to
get to Barcelona.

Suchet replied that there was nothing that he desired more than to bring back the whole Army of Catalonia for the Emperor's service. He suggested that he might march with 25,000 men for France, if he were allowed to evacuate the town of Barcelona and to leave 2,500 men only in its citadel of Montjuich. All the rest of Catalonia he would abandon, leaving only a garrison of 2,000 men in Figueras—this fortress and Montjuich should be given over to the Spaniards the moment that the garrisons of Tortosa, Lerida, and Saguntum, &c., should arrive on the frontier. He suggested that it might have a good effect on the Cortes and the Regency, and hasten the conclusion of affairs, if King Ferdinand were brought down to Barcelona. 'They would be forced to recognize him, and to place their power in the hands of the prince in whose name they have been governing so long[1].' The people of Spain were so pervaded with a sincere desire for peace —and the army shared the feeling—that this move would defeat all English intrigues for the continuance of the war[2].

The Marshal was bitterly disappointed when he received, a few days after writing this letter, a dispatch from Clarke dated January 14th informing him that matters had now become so desperate in France, that he must send off at once two-thirds of his cavalry and a division of 8,000 or 10,000 infantry, even if no news had come to hand of the ratification of the treaty[3]. This was the order corresponding to that which robbed Soult of Treilhard's dragoons and the divisions of Boyer and Leval. But he was given no leave to abandon Barcelona, which required a garrison of 7,500 men. The Marshal obeyed, and sent off on February 1st a composite division of six regiments of infantry under General Pannetier[4], and three of his five cavalry regiments, 2,132 sabres and 8,051 bayonets. This brought down the strength of his field-army to less than 18,000 men, including all those scattered about in northern Catalonia. But what was worst was that he was forced to abandon his position outside Barcelona, and to leave that great city, with its enormous garrison, to be

[1] Suchet to Clarke, January 16.
[2] Suchet to Clarke, Barcelona, January 16.
[3] Clarke to Suchet, January 14, in Suchet's *Memoirs*, ii. p. 497.
[4] Brigades Ordonneau, Estéve, Gudin, 7th, 16th, 20th, 67th Line, and 1st and 23rd Léger with the 13th Cuirassiers and 4th and 12th Hussars.

invested by Copons and the Anglo-Sicilians. For, deducting the troops in the north, and the immovable garrison of Barcelona, he was left with only 7,000 or 8,000 men on the Llobregat, to maintain the old line which he had been holding since October. He withdrew unwillingly to Gerona, after putting Habert in command at Barcelona, with provisions for the best part of a year. And in and about Gerona he reconcentrated such a field-army as he could, adding to the troops which he had brought back from the Llobregat those which he found disposable in the north, mainly the division of Maximilien Lamarque.

Before making this retreat Suchet had become fully aware of the fact that the Treaty of Valençay was not working, and that the Spanish Army of Catalonia had not become a friendly or even a neutral force. For on January 16th, just as he was preparing to make up the first draft of regiments to be sent north-ward, his lines along the Llobregat were attacked by the Anglo-Sicilians and the army of Copons in combination. Fortunately for himself he was still in full strength, the troops ear-marked for removal not having moved from their positions. Clinton had received reports which exaggerated the thinning out of Suchet's army—the disarmament of the Germans had been reported to him by deserters, along with the dispatch of the *cadres* for the new battalions to France, and the deduction of men for the Imperial Guard. Underrating the force still in position opposite to him, he offered to Copons to attack frontally the seaward end of Suchet's lines, on each side of the *tête-de-pont* of Molins de Rey, if the Spaniards would demonstrate against the enemy's lines of communication between Barcelona and Gerona. Copons replied that if he took the part allotted to him, he might find himself overwhelmed by the whole French army marching out of Barcelona in retreat. He suggested instead that while Clinton should attack the positions about Molins de Rey, he would send two brigades under Manso to take those lines in flank and rear, at the same moment that the Anglo-Sicilians appeared in front of them. Clinton consented, remarking, however, that Manso would have a very long flank-march to make, and that he must start early, in order to be punctual on the morning of January 16th, the chosen day[1].

[1] Clinton to Wellington. *Supplementary Dispatches*, viii. pp. 521–2.

The combination failed—as such operations by forces coming from remote bases often do. Clinton duly approached the French positions at daybreak on the 16th, with Sarsfield's Spaniards in front line, and British brigades in reserve. The operation was intended to be of the nature of a surprise, but the stroke was only to be delivered when it was certain that Manso's troops had arrived. After waiting for three hours, Clinton's advanced line got into bickering with the French posts in front of them, and the general, seeing that he was discovered, ordered an attack all along the line. The French retired and the battalions of Sarsfield forded the river at several points in pursuit. Just at this time the musketry of Manso's brigades began to be heard on the French flank, and Mesclop—whose troops had been in charge of this section of the French line—drew back hastily to the villages of St. Julian and St. Justo close to Barcelona. Here he was reinforced by the whole of Suchet's army, which had been warned early of Clinton's presence, and came in from many cantonments, offering battle. Clinton refused it, and withdrew: 'Circumstances', he said, 'would not have admitted of the combined forces pushing on, had even the enemy not been able to assemble in such force as he appeared to be[1].' He excused himself to Wellington with the remark that 'the operation though not attended with the success that might have been reasonably expected, had not been attended by any disgrace'. This was cold comfort! The general added that, though Manso's late arrival had wrecked the idea of a surprise, he could not blame that officer, considering the difficulty of a night march at mid-winter over bad cross-roads.

This inglorious affair was the last operation undertaken by the Anglo-Sicilian Army. No British troops had been engaged in it, save one battery of artillery, all the fighting having been done by Sarsfield's division. The loss was trifling—Clinton reported only 64 casualties. Mesclop had nearer 200[2]. The sole importance of the combat was that it showed Suchet that, however devoted to King Ferdinand General Copons might be, he was not going to betray the cause of Spain for the personal interests of his monarch[3]. That he was, indeed, ready to employ

---

[1] *Supplementary Dispatches*, viii. p. 522.

[2] Suchet (ii. p. 365) says 30 killed and 150 wounded.

[3] Napier, a consistent detractor of Copons, calls his action in January

every means of annoying the French, was sufficiently proved in the next month, by the piece of ingenious treachery of which the governors of Lerida, Mequinenza, and Monzon were the victims.

Meanwhile Suchet, abandoning Barcelona to the fate of Tortosa and the other blockaded fortresses, had fixed himself at Gerona, and had reorganized his depleted army, calling in some flying columns and evacuating some small posts. He formed two divisions under Maximilien Lamarque and Beurmann, and a reserve brigade. The figure of 15,000 sabres and bayonets given for them does not include the garrisons of Figueras, Puigcerda, and other fortresses of northern Catalonia. Altogether the Marshal had still 25,000 men under him, even after sending off the column of Pannetier to Lyons, and leaving behind him the garrison of Barcelona. As might have been foreseen, Copons and Clinton proceeded to close around that great city, and blockaded it at a distance and in a cautious fashion. As Habert had abundant provisions in store, and the Allies no siege-train, it was not likely that anything very exciting would occur in this direction.

The great event of February in Catalonia was not any clash of arms, but the astounding and partly successful plot of the traitor Juan Van Halen for the deception of Suchet's outlying garrisons. This sinister personage, a Fleming by birth, but long holding a commission in the Spanish service, had been one of those officers who had adhered to King Joseph after the breakdown of the Spanish defence in 1809. He had served for four years on the staff of the 'Juramentado' division of the Army of the Centre, and was one of the numerous people turned adrift after Vittoria, when the old organization of the French forces into separate armies was abolished. Going to Paris in search of a new berth, he found the Ministry of War short of trained staff-officers, and obtained without much difficulty a transfer to the Army of Catalonia, which he joined on November 1st, 1813. He was placed by Suchet on the staff, and served for more than two months with every appearance of zeal and efficiency. A typical cosmopolitan military adventurer, with neither national

'misconduct' and hints at treachery (vi. p. 54). I cannot see any justification for this view. Copons, looking at his whole command in Catalonia, seems quite above the average of the Spanish generals.

feeling nor personal loyalty, he had taken service in Catalonia for the mere purpose of quitting a losing cause with profit. As soon as he had settled down to work at Suchet's head-quarters, he opened up secret communications with the Baron Eroles, commanding the 1st Division of Copons's army. Schemes of treachery had been common in this region—as witness the betrayal of Figueras in April 1811[1] and the abortive attempt to enter Barcelona with the connivance of a supposedly friendly French officer in the preceding January[2]. But this was on a grander scale—Van Halen proposed to issue forged orders with Suchet's name and seal to the governors of all the outlying French garrisons, bidding them evacuate their fortresses.

The negotiations following on the Treaty of Valençay were now known everywhere, and Van Halen's scheme was to inform the governors of Tortosa, Lerida, Mequinenza, and Monzon that they had been brought to a successful issue, by an imaginary convention signed at Tarrasa on January 30th between Suchet and Copons. The governors were to quit their fortresses with all the honours of war, with their arms and baggage and field-guns, and to march to Barcelona, where they would join the Marshal and return with his army to France—peace having been concluded with Spain.

On the day after the combat of Molins de Rey, January 17th, 1814, Van Halen came over to Eroles's camp, bringing with him a seal belonging to the État-Major, the key of the military cipher, and a quantity of blank paper with official headings. He apparently tried to signalize his evasion by an act of very mean treachery. At the French outposts he announced that he was being sent to the Spanish lines as a *parlementaire*, and asked for a cavalry escort. This being granted, he led the troopers into a defile far to the front, and bade them wait for him there. The officer of the escort, misliking the position, and seeing traces of Spaniards all around, suddenly retreated without long waiting —otherwise he would have been surrounded and captured. Van Halen handed over the trumpeter and flag-bearer who had accompanied him as prisoners to Eroles.

With the active assistance of Eroles, and with the full know-ledge of Copons—who sent word to Wellington that he had in

[1] See vol. iv. p. 591.   [2] See vol. iv. p. 215.

hand a plan for capturing four French garrisons[1]—Van Halen worked out his ingenious scheme. His first attempt was on Tortosa. He sent in, by a supposed spy, a letter in the official cipher, to the effect that negotiations for peace were nearly complete, and that in a few days General Robert might expect orders to evacuate his fortress, and march on Barcelona with his whole division and its artillery. This was followed a few days later by the arrival of a *parlementaire* from General Sanz, commanding Elio's two divisions now lying before Tortosa, with a letter desiring Robert to be ready to give over the place to him when Suchet's orders for evacuation should arrive. Made suspicious, as he explained afterwards, by some curious turns of expression in the cipher letter, the governor prepared a reply to it, also in cipher, which he gave to a trusty emissary, who was ordered to get himself captured by the Spanish outposts, and not to go to Barcelona. The trick succeeded: for answers came to this epistle, which as Robert knew could not have reached the Marshal, first from Major Deschallard, one of the general staff, and then from Suchet himself, saying that the convention had been signed, and that the *chef d'escadron* Van Halen was bearing a copy of it, and the order for the garrison to march. These forgeries were well made, on official paper, and in handwriting much like that of Deschallard and Suchet. But Robert knew that they could not be genuine. Van Halen arrived on February 5th, accompanied by three orderlies in French uniforms, and sent in to the governor a specious-looking document in twenty clauses, purporting to be the 'Convention of Tarrasa', with the Marshal's covering letter ordering immediate evacuation. The governor invited him to enter the town, and also notified General Sanz that one of the gates should be given over to a Spanish battalion, as the pledge of the fulfilment of the Convention. But Van Halen, either losing his nerve, or suspecting that he had been found out, made frivolous excuses for not entering Tortosa, and Sanz did not send up a battalion to take over the gate. And so the plot fell through—Van Halen

[1] *Wellington Dispatches*, February 7, xi. p. 503. Wellington remarked that he had no hopes whatever that any French general would be taken in by the methods proposed by Baron Eroles. He underrated Van Halen's ingenuity and overvalued Lamarque's intelligence.

escaped a military execution, and Sanz the cutting up of one
of his battalions by concentrated artillery-fire from the walls.
This is Robert's version of the story—it appears therefore that
Napier's statement that the plan was spoiled by the inopportune
arrival of a real dispatch from Suchet on February 4th, alluding
to anything rather than the 'Convention of Tarrasa', is not
correct[1].

Van Halen and Eroles then transferred their energies to
Lerida, where (despite of Wellington's doubts as to the gullibility
of French generals) they had a complete success. The preliminary preparation was first made: on February 9th a false
messenger brought in to General Isidore Lamarque, there commanding, a very plausible cipher-dispatch, saying that Suchet
and his whole army were on the march to carry off the garrison,
preparatory to a retreat on France, made possible by the
negotiations with the Spanish generals, and the approaching
consummation of peace. It purported to be signed by St. Clair-
Nugues, Suchet's chief of the staff. On February '12th the
Baron Eroles appeared before Lerida, and had an interview
under flag of truce with Lamarque: he informed the governor
that a convention had been concluded, with an armistice of
twelve days, during which all the outlying French garrisons
might fall back unmolested on Barcelona. On February 13th
Lamarque summoned together his superior officers, and laid
before them a letter purporting to be signed by Major Deschallard
—the same staff-officer whose name and signature had been
forged at Tortosa—it was accompanied by a copy of the
apocryphal 'Convention of Tarrasa'. Some of the officers
present expressed doubts as to the genuineness of the letter
of Deschallard—of which some paragraphs looked more like
Castilian translated into French than the phraseology of an
educated Frenchman. They asked the governor whether he had
seen the French officer who had brought the copy of the Convention to Eroles, and why this aide-de-camp of Suchet was not
now present. Lamarque, a veteran of the campaigns of Egypt

---

[1] For the whole story see Vidal de la Blache, ii. pp. 34–5, and Napier,
vi. pp. 56–7. Several of the details given by the latter do not seem to be
borne out by the French narrative, and Robert was not for a moment
deceived, as Napier states him to have been. Cf. Toreno, iii. p. 524.

and Austerlitz, was apparently vexed at criticism—he answered that he had seen this officer—Van Halen, of course—and that the reason for his not having come into Lerida was that he had hastened on, to deliver another copy of the Convention to the governor of the neighbouring fortress of Mequinenza. On the 14th. the garrison, 1,800 strong, marched out with bag and baggage, and was joined a day later by the battalion from Mequinenza. There the governor, General Bourgeois, had allowed himself to be completely deceived by Van Halen's statement that Lerida was already being evacuated, and having verified the fact, had started off to join Lamarque's column, and caught it up near Cervera on the Barcelona road. The French were preceded and followed by Catalan troops. Eroles explained that this was necessary, as the unruly miqueletes of the mountains would cut off all stragglers, and snipe at detachments, unless they saw a Spanish escort.

On the 16th Lamarque reached Igualada, on the 17th Esparraguera—only 25 miles from Barcelona. On the 18th he ran, near Martorel, into British outposts from Clinton's army. Eroles had conducted him into the middle of the cantonments of the Anglo-Sicilians. The officer leading the French advance-guard informed the captain commanding the English picket that the column had a free pass into Barcelona, by virtue of the Convention of Tarrasa. He was told that the English had never heard of any such convention, and that he could not proceed. Superior officers on both sides came up, Lamarque exhibited his copy of the Convention, but Clinton's representative denied all knowledge of it, and referred the French general to Copons—an English brigade drew up across the road and denied all passage.

A Spanish aide-de-camp then came up, and invited Lamarque to visit his general who was close by, and would explain the whole matter. While he was on his way, the hills on both sides and in the rear were suddenly crowned by Catalan troops, Eroles had closed in, and Manso's brigade also. Copons was found waiting by the roadside; while Lamarque was still some distance off, he shouted to the French general that he and his troops were prisoners, and that he had been deceived by a forgery and a *ruse de guerre*. The unfortunate governor burst out into bitter language about treason and dishonour, to which Copons replied that the French had seized Barcelona and Pampeluna in 1808 by disgusting exhibitions of treason and dishonour[1], and that they were being paid in their own coin.

Copons promised the French generals that their troops, on laying down their arms, and waiting till they were exchanged for an equivalent number of Spanish prisoners, should be allowed to return to France. But he withdrew his first conditions (the so-called 'Convention of Martorel') on the pretext that the French had hidden in their ranks a number of *Afrancesados* whom he was desirous of arresting, and had not surrendered all their horses and baggage. But he allowed the French civilians and the women and children accompanying the column to be sent into Barcelona. One would have preferred that Clinton's troops should not have played any part—even a passive one— in this treacherous business.

Among the minor victims of Van Halen were the French garrison of Monzon. They were a mere handful, holding an old citadel on a rock above the Cinca against the rather unscientific attacks of Duran's men. Only 4 officers and 95 men, reduced by February to only 47 capable of bearing arms, they had held out for nearly eight months, foiling many attempts to reduce them by mining as well as by escalade. The hero of the defence had been a non-commissioned officer of engineers, named St. Jacques; the record of his resourceful ingenuity fills many pages of Belmas's big *Sièges de la Guerre d'Espagne*[2]. Von Halen offered the captain commanding the relics of the garrison free permission to send an officer to Lerida, so as to verify his statement that Lamarque had already evacuated the place under the 'Convention of Tarrasa'. This was done, and the garrison marched out in state, with a solitary drum beating in front, and dragging a field-gun behind. On reaching Lerida they found themselves surrounded by a Spanish battalion, were told to consider themselves prisoners of war, and were sent off to join Lamarque's men.

The after-career of the detestable Van Halen is curious. Received into the Spanish army, he displayed his talent for conspiracy at every possible turn of politics. For reasons best known to himself he became a Liberal, and intrigued against

---

[1] See vol. i. pp. 31–7, for the incidents alluded to by Copons.
[2] Vol. iv. pp. 831–64.

the autocratic government of Ferdinand at the earliest opportunity. Implicated in the abortive rising of Porlier in 1815, he
was thrown into the dungeons of the Inquisition, but escaped,
and getting somehow a commission in the Russian Army fought
in the Caucasus in 1819–20. When the Liberals under Riego
and Quiroga overthrew absolutism in 1820 he returned to Spain,
and served in 1823 on the staff of Mina, when the great guerrillero
tried in vain to defend the Pyrenees against the army of the
Duke of Angoulême. On the triumph of the Reaction and
Absolutists, Van Halen fled, first to the United States, and then
to Belgium. Here he was found in 1830 as one of the leaders of
the insurrectionary mob which chased the Dutch out of Brussels.
He was for a moment a Belgian general—but was deposed ere
long on the accusation of secret intriguing with the Orange
party. He is next heard of in 1835, once more in Spain: on
the outbreak of the Carlist War he put his somewhat tarnished
sword at the disposition of Queen Cristina. During that civil
strife, and the struggle between the Queen and Espartero which
followed, Van Halen suffered all manner of vicissitudes—at
least once he was in prison as a traitor—at another time he was
Captain-General of Catalonia and bombarded Barcelona. Finally,
he was hunted out of Spain on the fall of Espartero in 1843, and
lived long years in exile, returning only in 1851, at a general
amnesty, to end in obscurity. It is astonishing that he came
through so many years of turbulence to die in his bed, when so
many better men faced a firing-squad, or died by the assassin's
hand—like Porlier and Elio, Carlos de España, and Lacy.

SECTION XLIV: CHAPTER II

FERDINAND'S RETURN TO MADRID. FALL OF THE REGENCY AND THE CORTES. LAST DAYS OF THE WAR IN CATALONIA

THE month of March was nearing its end when the tardily released Ferdinand neared the frontier, and came under the care of the commander of the armies of Aragon and Catalonia—now a much harassed man, who saw ruin impending, and had little hope of being able to stave it off.

After Copons had displayed his true mentality over the matter of the Lerida garrison, it is strange that Suchet should have believed that there could be anything gained from negotiations with him, or appeals to his loyalty to Ferdinand VII. But the Marshal was disposed to attach a very ill-founded importance to the king's signature attached to the Treaty of Valençay, and to his intention of carrying out its provisions. If he had known that, in his secret instructions to San Carlos[1], Ferdinand had stated his intention of repudiating the whole agreement on obtaining his liberty, his action would no doubt have been different. About February 18th the failure of San Carlos's mission to Madrid was known to Suchet, but he still held it to be possible that if Ferdinand were brought down to the frontier and exhibited to the Spaniards close at hand, the bargain of exchanging his person for the garrisons of the fortresses (including now that of Barcelona) could be carried out. The idea of making this desperate experiment was now shared by Napoleon himself[2], who found time to write, during his retreat after the defeat of La Rothière, a hasty note to his Minister of War, 'Give the Marshal *carte blanche*: he may demolish Barcelona or keep it as best suits him. As to King Ferdinand, we hear no more of what has happened about the treaty. San Carlos is apparently

---

[1] See above, p. 305.

[2] Napier's hypothesis (vol. vi, pp. 20–1) that Napoleon's resolve to release Ferdinand and make a separate peace with Spain was conceived early, and foiled by treacherous counsellors, is unfounded. It was his pride that was in question; he hated to confess himself foiled, and only gave way when things grew absolutely desperate.

detained somewhere. Things being so, if King Ferdinand wants
to go to Barcelona let him go there *incognito*. We would hand
over the fortresses to him in return for the recovery of their
garrisons[1].'

The reception of these orders, transmitted by Clarke, was very
irritating to Suchet, for he had now abandoned Barcelona, so
that he could not send the King thither. If he had been given
the *carte blanche* a few weeks earlier, he could have conducted
Ferdinand to the city, and made a good show of his strength
to impress the Spanish generals. Or, if they had refused to
negotiate, he could have evacuated Barcelona and have massed
a very respectable force of 23,000 men at Gerona. Neither course
was now possible, and he had betrayed his weakness by his
retreat to the north.

And even now that the Emperor had resolved to send Ferdinand to Catalonia, and to try the hazardous experiment of
trusting to his goodwill and observance of a bargain, matters
were allowed to drag on with great slowness. Ferdinand only
received his passport to leave Valençay, with his brother and
uncle, on March 1st, and did not depart till the 13th. He reached
Perpignan, and placed himself at the disposition of Suchet on
the 21st. Before allowing him to cross the French lines the
Marshal exacted from him a written pledge, that he would at
once send back the captive garrisons of Lerida and Mequinenza,
and allow that of Barcelona to join the French army. The King
signed the document with cheerful facility, having no intention
whatever of observing its conditions[2], and crossed the Fluvia in
presence of a, division of the Army of Copons drawn up on the
other side and a crowd of cheering peasants, on March 24th.
Suchet had accompanied him to the water's edge, and the parting was ceremonious and even cordial[3]. Two days later the
Marshal sent the king's brother Don Carlos to join him—he had
for a moment contemplated holding the prince as a hostage for
the delivery of the garrisons, but gave up the idea, partly because

[1] Napoleon to Clarke, February 8.
[2] Suchet to Clarke, March 24.
[3] I have a fine Spanish engraving of the time, showing Ferdinand embracing General Copons in the midst of a throng of enthusiastic Catalans,
while French and Spanish troops line the two banks of the narrow but deep
Fluvia.

it implied a doubt of the king's good faith, but more because he reflected that when Ferdinand had been released the Spaniards would attach little importance to his brother's whereabouts.

Suchet's condition at this moment was most forlorn. For he had received orders from Paris to send off a second division from his depleted army on the road to Lyons, whatever might happen about Ferdinand and the fortresses. On March 1st the War Minister had written to him, 'The Emperor's orders are that you send off, on receipt of this dispatch, a second column of 10,000 infantry *en poste* in the direction of Lyons. I know that by the departure of these troops the frontier on the Eastern Pyrenees will be left exposed, but the Emperor says nothing about this —his silence will show you that he holds that, when the heart of the empire is menaced, one must not hesitate about the momentary abandonment of outlying parts. The general situation is such that you are left to trace for yourself whatever system of operation you please. If, gathering together all that remains of your army, and getting what help you can from the frontier departments, you can keep the enemy in your front occupied for a time, you will have done all that His Majesty expects of you[1].'

Suchet obeyed and on March 7th Beurmann's division of 9,661 bayonets marched for Perpignan, Narbonne, and Lyons—which last, as we have already seen[2], they were never destined to reach[3]. This move necessitated the abandonment of all the Catalan fortresses except Figueras, which Suchet regarded as absolutely necessary for the protection of the frontier. Gerona, Puigcerda, Rosas, and a dozen smaller posts were evacuated, after their walls had been blown up. It is a notable comment on Suchet's strategy that by these evacuations he once more succeeded in scraping together a field-army—in April he could report that he had got 14,000 men concentrated in front of Figueras— though when it was a matter of corresponding with Soult for common action, he was able to demonstrate to his own satis-

[1] Clarke to Suchet, March 1, received March 4. Suchet's *Memoirs*, ii. p. 490.

[2] See above, p. 403.

[3] The regiments were the 79th, 102nd, 115th, 116th Line, and 32nd Léger, 12 battalions, with 2 batteries.

faction that he had not more than 3,000 or 4,000 available. And at that moment 13,000 men were still shut up in Barcelona, Tortosa, Saguntum, &c.—in pursuance of the fatal policy that had prevailed ever since the preceding autumn. King Ferdinand and Copons were fully aware of these facts, and well understood that Suchet had no power to revenge himself for broken oaths.

Once free, Ferdinand consigned his obligations under the Treaty of Valençay to oblivion, and set himself to the more interesting problem of recovering political authority from the hands of the Regency and the Cortes. He had made his arrangements with Copons, by means of San Carlos, long before he crossed the frontier. The commander of the 1st Army ought, according to the decree of the Cortes, to have required the king to take the oath to the Constitution immediately on his arrival, and then to have forwarded him to Madrid by the itinerary, via Tarragona and Valencia, prescribed in that rather unwise document. He did neither—Ferdinand went through the Catalan towns in triumphant procession, and then turned aside to Saragossa, on the invitation of José Palafox, who came to greet him at the head of an Aragonese deputation. This visit was made partly to compliment the Saragossans on their splendid deeds of 1808, partly to please Palafox, who, after six years in a French dungeon, was received 'like Lazarus risen from the tomb' by his ancient followers. But its main object was to test the temper of a large military force there assembled—all the cavalry of the 2nd and 3rd Armies, and the infantry division lately engaged in the sieges of Lerida and Mequinenza. To the king's high satisfaction no signs of Liberalism were discovered. All the officers of the 2nd Army, from its commander Elio downward, were avowed *Serviles*.

A typical incident of the time is recorded in the memoirs of Samford Whittingham, whose cavalry lay at Saragossa, and furnished the escort for the royal equipage (an English-built landau!) through the long plains of Aragon.

'I always rode at the side of the carriage—witnessing the wild expressions of joy to which the Spaniards universally gave way on seeing their king returned from his infamous captivity. His Majesty during his long drive was constantly occupied in studying the Constitution, which he was required to swear to. As I

rode by the side of his carriage he repeatedly entered into conversation with me. "Santiago[1], You will hardly imagine what
book this is that I am reading. It is the new Constitution framed
by the Cortes during my absence. I find much that is good in
it: but also many things absolutely inadmissible. Yet if my
refusal to swear would cost Spanish blood, I would swear it
to-morrow." A few days later Whittingham was visited by
General Zayas (of Albuera and Saguntum memory), one of the
most violent *Serviles* in Spain, who came to sound him on his
views. Whittingham says that he replied that, while the Constitution had many good points, it was not in His Majesty's power to
swear to it in its present form. Especially absurd was the clause
which required him to swear that no alteration or modification
of any section of it should take place for seven years. So he
advised that the King should go to Madrid, thank the Cortes in
person for their good services, and then dissolve them, and express
his intention to convoke the ancient Cortes of Spain for their
opinion and advice[2].'

This was, in a moderate form, much the same counsel that was
being given to the king from all military quarters. Whittingham
was told to return to Saragossa, and to get ready his cavalry
there for a ride to Madrid within a few days. Ferdinand reached
Valencia on April 16th, and found there General Elio backed by
the greater part of the divisions that had been besieging Saguntum and Peniscola, which he had concentrated for his own
purposes. On the day after the king's arrival, the Captain-
General carried out the first of the long series of military 'pro-
nunciamientos' which makes such an unhappy record in the
history of Spain. He came to the palace, bringing with him his
staff and many scores more of officers. After presenting them to
Ferdinand, he cried in a loud voice, 'Gentlemen, do you swear
to maintain the king in the plenitude of all his rights?' And
when the cries of 'We swear' had died away, he adjured the king
to exercise his absolute sovereignty in Valencia, and to declare
null and void all the decrees of the Cortes. Then, handing over

---

[1] The Spaniards could not get hold of Whittingham's Christian names,
Samuel Ford, and had universally shortened them into Santiago. He
himself used to sign 'Samford'.

[2] *Memoirs of Whittingham*, pp. 243–4.

his baton of office as captain-general to Ferdinand, he bade him take with it military authority, and the power to punish the enemies of the Crown, the Army, and the Church. From that night the king acted as an absolute monarch—he treated with great coldness his cousin the Cardinal Bourbon—head of the Regency—who came to Valencia to salute him, and to receive his oath to the Constitution. The old prelate was recommended to retire to his archiepiscopal palace at Toledo. Lujando, Minister of Foreign Affairs, who had accompanied the Cardinal, was directed to betake himself to Cartagena, where he had been in charge of the navy yard. When Ferdinand started for Madrid and was met near Ciudad Real by a complimentary deputation from the Cortes, he refused to receive them—they represented a body whose validity he did not recognize.

As the news of these incidents came to Madrid in succession, the Regency and the Liberal majority in the Cortes were struck with progressive spasms of dismay, but felt themselves helpless. They had no troops at their disposition, and the populace of Madrid was displaying no feeling save joy at the approach of the much-desired king—absolute or no. In the remoter armies there were several generals, appointed by the Liberal party, who might sympathize with the Cortes, but they were far off, and surrounded by subordinates who were resolute *Serviles*, and ready to depose their chiefs if necessary. Such were Freire and the Prince of Anglona, commanding the 4th and 3rd Armies, Porlier, and Lacy, Captain-General of Galicia and head of the 'Army of Reserve' of that province. But the great guerrillero Mina was probably the only 'Liberal' commander who could have got his men to follow him, if he had declared against the king. Henry O'Donnell who had resumed his command of the Andalusian Reserves, now on the Nive, is said to have deputed one of his aides-de-camp to go to Madrid with two alternative letters in his sabretache—one congratulating the Cortes on the taking of the oath by Ferdinand, the other congratulating Ferdinand on having got rid of the Cortes—the latter was actually delivered[1].

Though the king's approach was awaited with anxiety by the politicians in Madrid, no one foresaw the violence with which his resumption of power was about to be attended. While he

[1] Toreno, iii. p. 363.

himself, escorted by 5,000 Valencian troops, was approaching on the main road, and Whittingham's cavalry from Saragossa had closed in on the by-road from Aragon, a *coup d'état* was carried out three days before his arrival. General Eguia[1], appointed Captain-General of New Castile, rode into Madrid on the night of May 10th–11th, with a cavalry regiment, and arrested in their beds all the leading members of the Liberal party, the Regents Agar and Cisgar, and of the deputies Argüelles, Martinez de la Rosa, Oliveros, Larrazabal, Calatrava, and a score of others. Toreno the historian escaped, by getting an early warning. The president of the Cortes, Antonio Perez, who was personally a *Servile*, received a royal letter, informing him that the members should retire to their homes, as they formed part of an illegal gathering. Not the least resistance was met in any direction: the populace amused themselves by hacking to pieces the 'Stone of the Constitution' which had been set up in the Plaza Mayor, and when Ferdinand made his state entry on May 18th he was received with universal acclamation. Whittingham, who rode near him, says that he heard the cry, 'God's blessing on Ferdinand. May he be absolute king, and do whatever may be his royal pleasure[2].'

So fell the Regency, the Cortes, the Constitution, and the Liberal party. Ferdinand published on his arrival in the capital a decree dated May 4th and signed at Valencia. It was a lengthy document which, opening with some rancorous but well-justified remarks on the infamy of Napoleon and the treason of the *Afrancesados*, passed on to declare that things had reverted to the status of 1808. The Constitution and all the legislation of the Cortes were null and void. But the king would be no tyrant— indeed he abhorred despotism, and the legitimate kings of Spain had never really been despots, though from time to time they had been guilty of abuses of power. He intended to summon the ancient and legitimate Cortes of the realm, and to establish with their counsel ordinances which would make his people contented and prosperous—and so forth for innumerable paragraphs.

[1] The man with whom Wellington quarrelled after Talavera, see vol. ii. p. 606.

[2] *Whittingham's Memoirs*, p. 246.

With these hollow words the people seemed for the moment satisfied—it took five years of freakish misgovernment to exhaust Ferdinand's ill-deserved popularity, and to lead to the Liberal reaction of 1820, which sent Elio to the scaffold in that same Valencia where he had issued his 'pronunciamiento', and which compelled Ferdinand to swear to the Constitution over and over again, with the ribald popular song of '*Tragala, perro!*' —'Swallow it, dog!' ringing in his ears.

King Ferdinand had forded the Fluvia on March 24th—Paris fell on March 31st, the news of the abdication of Napoleon reached Suchet on April 13th. There were therefore twenty days of war still to run when the Marshal took stock of the situation, and realized ere long that Ferdinand's promises about the garrisons were vain words, never intended to be fulfilled. Of military operations of importance none took place on the East Coast in this interval. Clinton settled down to the blockade of Barcelona, indifferently aided by Copons, who was much more interested in Ferdinand's approaching *coup d'état*, and followed him all the way to Saragossa. The English general wanted the Catalan army either to take over the blockade, or to push Suchet —whose surviving force was underrated—over the Fluvia and across the Pyrenees into France.

On March 10th Clinton had received a dispatch from Wellington, to the effect that since Suchet's force had been reduced to a shadow, the Anglo-Sicilians were no longer needed in Catalonia. He was ordered to break up his corps, and to march with six of his British and German Legion battalions to join his chief's army on the Adour[1]. The Sicilians and a few other units might be returned to Lord William Bentinck, to aid in his invasion of Italy. Sarsfield's and Whittingham's Spaniards might be made over to Copons and Elio. The six battalions ear-marked for France would have given Wellington the numbers sufficient for him to constitute a new division for his own field-army, if one of the unattached Portuguese brigades were added to them, and

[1] He was to bring the 1st and 2nd battalion of the 27th, the 44th, 58th, 81st, and 4th Line K.G.L. with three field-batteries. The 10th, De Roll's, the Anglo-Italian battalions, the Calabrians, and the Sicilian 'Estero' regiment were to go back to Sicily, Dillon's and the 2/67th to strengthen the garrison of Gibraltar, then much depleted. Wellington to Clinton, March 4. *Dispatches*, xi. p. 544.

this would have been most useful aid, the troops being all veterans with several years' experience of Spain. Clinton, however, ventured to raise objections: he made arrangements for the breaking up of the army, but did not execute them. In two long letters of March he urged that Copons had left only one Spanish brigade before Barcelona: even with the addition of Sarsfield's and Whittingham's divisions, a total force of 10,000 men would not be strong enough to hold the immensely long lines of investment. The governor Habert, with his 8,000 men, could break out, if he chose, at some point of the thinly held circle. Moreover, Suchet's army on the Fluvia was not so negligible as had been supposed—by calling in the garrisons he had collected at least 10,000 men—and Copons's troops in the northern parts of the principality, only 6,000 strong, could not cope with such a force. That general wrote that he could not possibly spare another brigade to strengthen the Barcelona investment-line, if the Anglo-Sicilians were to depart[1]. So Clinton stated that he should not move, unless peremptory orders were sent him, till either he were certain that Suchet had no more than 5,000 men left, or else that more Spanish troops were ready to reinforce the divisions left before Barcelona[2].

Neither of these contingencies occurred, and since Wellington did not press for the dissolution of Clinton's army, things settled down in Catalonia in the most uninteresting fashion. The only incident had been that Habert, on a false rumour that the Anglo-Sicilians had departed, made a furious sally on February 23rd against the front of the investment-lines held by Sarsfield. It was not, apparently, an attempt to break out, but an experiment to see whether it would be possible to break out hereafter, if Suchet should order the evacuation of Barcelona. Sarsfield's men fought well, and the sortie was beaten off with some loss.

On April 6th Clinton received from Eroles, on the side of Gerona, the perfectly incorrect news that Suchet had departed for Lyons with 8,000 men, and that the remainder of the Army of Catalonia was crossing the Pyrenees, with orders to join Soult[3]. He therefore determined that the condition of affairs was such

---

[1] Clinton to Wellington, March 18. *Supplementary Dispatches*, viii. p. 663, and March 24. Ibid., p. 684.

[2] Ibid., p. 696.   [3] Ibid., pp. 719–20.

that his promise of March 24th could be redeemed, and that it was safe to break up the army, and direct the march of its most efficient part to join Wellington on the Garonne. The premisses on which this conclusion was reached were false, but no particular harm resulted. A great part of the troops were already on the march—some for Tarragona to embark, others for Lerida, to join Wellington's army by way of Saragossa and Tolosa—when Habert executed a second sortie, even more violent than the last, on April 16th. It was again directed against Sarsfield's front, and again failed—the French being repulsed with a loss of over 300 men. This sortie, as it chanced, was wholly purposeless, like Thouvenot's similar sally from Bayonne, since by April 16th Napoleon had abdicated and the war was over. But the news only reached Barcelona two days after the second sortie.

Suchet, after the departure of Beurmann's column, lay for the whole of the remaining weeks of the war with his field-force concentrated on a short front near Figueras to the number of some 14,000 men. His mind was occupied partly by fears as to what might happen in his rear, should Soult be driven beyond Toulouse by Wellington[1], partly by schemes, which never took definite shape, for a desperate attempt to save the garrisons of Barcelona and Tortosa. On March 31st he got false news from German deserters that Clinton was already marching off to join Wellington—which was wholly premature—and suggested to Habert that, if guarded by Spaniards alone, he might break out and join the garrison of Tortosa, which should also have orders to sally forth. If they could unite 12,000 men in the rear of Copons, and the Anglo-Sicilians had gone off, they would be able to force their way to join him on the Fluvia[2]. It was probably this suggestion which caused Habert's sally of April 16th— which would seem to have been an attempt to test the accuracy of the Marshal's hypothesis, and to see whether a break in the lines of the investing army round Barcelona could be made. The same suggestion had been sent to Robert at Tortosa, but led to no action, for that general had a comparatively small force with him, was beset by a larger proportion of Spaniards,

---

[1] Suchet to Clarke, March 28, in his *Memoirs*, ii. p. 499.
[2] Suchet to Habert, in Suchet's *Memoirs*, ii. p. 501, on March 31.

and was in a much more remote situation than was Habert in Barcelona.

And so matters dragged on in Catalonia, till the news of Napoleon's abdication came to hand in mid-April. For the first fortnight of that month Suchet was—as will presently be shown —engaged in an angry controversy with Soult, who kept suggesting to him that he might abandon Catalonia altogether, and fall with a not inconsiderable force on Wellington's flank or rear, via Quillan and the line of the Ariège[1]. Suchet demonstrated, to his own satisfaction, that the suggested line of march was impossible, and that, if he did make this move, he would appear with a negligible force of 3,000 or 4,000 men, without any artillery. Of this more in its proper place. There can be little doubt that a personal dislike for Soult, and a determination not to come under his orders, were far more potent than strategical reasons in the mind of the Duke of Albufera. But he succeeded in formulating a very plausible *non possumus*, which convinced the Minister of War, though it may not have convinced the Duke of Dalmatia!

[1] Suchet to Clarke, April 2, and to Soult, April 6, in his *Memoirs*, ii. pp. 505–7.

SECTION XLV

THE CAMPAIGN OF TOULOUSE

CHAPTER I

FROM THE ADOUR TO THE GARONNE. MARCH 13–26, 1814. COMBATS OF VIC-BIGORRE (MARCH 19) AND TARBES (MARCH 20)

WHILE the war in Catalonia had reached a stage of stagnation, a vigorous campaign had recommenced on the upper Adour. Wellington, it will be remembered, had halted for twelve days after the combat of Aire, partly to give his troops rest, but partly to avoid critical operations while Beresford's expedition against Bordeaux was in progress. Having deprived himself for a time of the 4th and 7th Divisions, he wished to draw in whatever reinforcements were available, to make up, so far as was possible, for the absence of this invaluable infantry. The troops on the move, and due to join in a few days, were the four heavy cavalry brigades and the Portuguese horse, ordered up from their winter quarters on the Ebro, with the two Spanish divisions which Freire was bringing up from Bayonne. But infantry was still so much needed that Wellington ordered Morillo to send him half of the old Estremaduran division with which he was blockading the fortress of Navarrenx. The Spanish general duly detached three of his six battalions[1]—the other brigade sufficed for the blockade. They made up 2,100 bayonets, and were attached to the corps of Hill, with which they had been wont to operate ever since 1811. Beresford had gone off with 12,000 men, including only two cavalry regiments. The force that came up to replace him consisted of 4,000 sabres and (counting Freire and Morillo together) 10,000 Spanish infantry. The change in the composition of his main army gave Wellington an enormous preponderance in the cavalry arm—in which he had hitherto possessed only a slight advantage over Soult—but left him decidedly weaker in

[1] Leon, Vittoria, and Doyle, while Morillo himself remained in front of Navarrenx with 2nd of Jaen, Union, and the Legion Estremena.

infantry than he had been at the time of Orthez. Of his own old
units he had only at hand for the moment the 2nd, 3rd, 6th and
Light Divisions, and Le Cor's Portuguese. Three cavalry brigades
joined the field-army in succession between March 11th and
18th, Freire's divisions had reached St. Sever on the 18th,
Morillo's brigade reported to Hill on the 15th. But, as has been
shown in another chapter, Wellington had a notion that he
was in need of still more reinforcements, for news had come to
him from Catalonia of the march of Pannetier's column across
the Pyrenees, accompanied by the false addition that it was
intended to reinforce Soult, not (as was really the case) to join
Augereau at Lyons[1]. If 10,000 veteran French troops were to
unite with the force already on the Adour, at the moment when
the Allied army was at its weakest, the situation would be serious.
This accounts for the orders which Wellington dispatched to
Clinton on March 8th, bidding him send off six of his British
battalions, and three batteries, to join him by the circuitous
route Saragossa–Tolosa, Irun. As Pannetier had really moved
on Lyons, Clinton's neglect to obey this order was harmless.
But all through mid-March Wellington was expecting to detect
Suchet's troops in his front. It was this surmise which caused
him to recall Beresford and the 4th Division from the lower
Garonne on March 14th[2], leaving Dalhousie in a rather isolated
position at Bordeaux.

After the combat of Aire, Soult, as we have already seen[3], had
drawn back his way-worn and war-worn army to cantonments
round his head-quarters at Rabastens, between the upper Adour
and the Larros. D'Erlon's two divisions were about Marciac,
Clausel's at Vic de Bigorre, Reille's at Maubourget. He did not
expect to be left long unmolested, and had made up his mind that
he would retreat, if pressed, upon Tarbes due south, with the
intention as he said, of drawing Wellington after him toward the
Pyrenees, and off the direct road to Toulouse. But, contrary to
expectation, he found himself unpursued, Hill hanging back at

---

[1] Wellington to Clinton. *Dispatches*, xi. p. 566, and to Henry O'Donnell,
ibid.

[2] Wellington to Beresford, March 14. *Dispatches*, xi. p. 578. He was
quite aware of the risk to which he was exposing Dalhousie.

[3] See above, p. 387.

Aire, and the rest of the Allied army in the neighbourhood of Barcelonne. At first the Marshal was rather surprised to be left alone—and it was not till March 8th that he began to guess that Wellington might have made a large detachment on the side of Bordeaux[1]: as late as the 11th he was still doubtful whether this was the case[2]. Meanwhile a rest of ten days was an 'uncovenanted mercy', and he utilized it for the reorganization of his much disordered army. Paris's brigade was abolished as a unit, and distributed among the more battered divisions: the cavalry was recruited, in numbers if not in efficiency, by having drafted into it men, and above all horses, from the artillery-train—of which there was a superfluity considering the size of the army. The *gendarmerie* were sent out to sweep in stragglers and deserting conscripts, of whom Soult calculated that at least 3,000 were missing since the combat of Aire. Travot's conscript brigade, which had made such an ineffective appearance at the battle of Orthez, had dwindled down to 600 men for the five battalions. Their wrecks were sent back straight to Toulouse, to be re-formed. Exaggerating somewhat, Soult wrote to Clarke that he could not count on more than 25,000 infantry, and that of his 2,500 cavalry only 1,000 had horses fit for active service. The minister replied, demonstrating from Soult's own figures of morning states, that he must have something more like 39,000 men than 26,000. And he was apparently not far out, as the 'morning state' for March 10th, after the reorganization, shows 36,600 of all arms—this (it is true) including artillery, sappers, and train, which Soult had omitted in his rough calculation. It adds somewhat to the difficulties of keeping the organization of the army in mind, that on March 13 Maransin returned from his ineffective campaign of propaganda among the Basques, and resumed command of his old division, which Rouget had been leading for the last six weeks. And similarly Daricau, who had equally failed to galvanize the people of the Landes, also returned, and displaced Fririon, the interim commander of Foy's old division. But the unit which Daricau had been accustomed

---

[1] Soult to Clarke, March 8.

[2] Same to same, March 11, 'les ennemis ont ajourné leur projet de marcher sur Bordeaux, ils nous croient trop forts, et surtout trop rapprochés pour se livrer à cette entreprise'.

to lead on the Pyrenees and the Nive was now under Villatte.
It is curious to note how the names of the generals in the latter
stages of the campaigns of 1813–14 give deceptive impressions
as to the identity of the troops which they were leading: for
of all the six divisions operating in March 1814 but one was
commanded by the same officer who led it at Sorauren or the
Bidassoa[1]. Yet of the six divisional generals five had been
present at those earlier fights in command of other units.

After ten days of rest Soult had recovered his confidence, and
wrote to the Minister of War that, being somewhat hurt in spirit
by the Emperor's letter of March 2nd[2], which reproached him
for being destitute of initiative, and bade him attack at all costs
rather than allow himself to be attacked, he was about to take
the offensive[3]. It being at last certain that Wellington had made
a large detachment for the seizure of Bordeaux, the opportunity
was favourable. He did not, as a matter of fact, carry out the
Emperor's policy or his own expressed purpose, but he made a
showy demonstration against that part of the Allied front which
was held by Hill's two divisions, advancing with his entire force
against Aire. The whole of Soult's army took part in the movement on March 13th. Clausel on the one flank, D'Erlon on the
other, moved up against the line held by Fane's cavalry along
the Leéz river, with Reille in reserve. If Soult had risked a down-
right attack on Hill on the 14th, it would appear that the latter
would have been in some danger. But he acted with the greatest
caution, and spent the day in thrusting back the cavalry screen
in front of him. Fane was driven in on the left, Campbell's Portuguese horse in the centre, with some loss[4]. The latter had only

---

[1] The succession was:

1st Division: Foy [till Orthez], Fririon, Paris, Daricau.

2nd Division: Darmagnac—the units much changed; only three battalions of the old 2nd Division of 1813 remained in April 1814.

4th Division: Conroux, Taupin.

5th Division: Vandermaesen, Maransin, Rouget, Maransin.

6th Division: Daricau, Villatte.

8th Division: Taupin, Harispe. [Nos. 7 and 9 had gone to join Napoleon.]

[2] See above, pp. 377–8.

[3] Soult to Clarke, March 10.

[4] They made a good resistance before being driven in by superior numbers, and earned Wellington's commendation; see his remarks to Bathurst,
Dispatches, xi. p. 597.

just arrived from Spain—their presence made Soult doubtful
whether other new troops were not now in his front. In the
evening the French head-quarters were no farther forward
than Conchez, the infantry a few miles in front, facing the
position behind the little river Leéz, where Hill was visible
in a line reaching from the village of Garlin to the heights
above Aire.

Wellington had been somewhat surprised by Soult's offensive
movement, and knowing the dilapidated state in which his
adversary's army had retired from St. Sever and Aire, could only
conclude that he had received the reinforcement from Catalonia
of which so much had been heard of late. He therefore resolved
for the moment to stand on the defensive in front of Aire, and
ordered the 3rd and 6th Divisions from Barcelonne to cross the
Adour and join Hill, followed by Freire's Spaniards, who had
reached St. Sever on the morning of the 13th, and were now
disposable. This left on the north side of the Adour only the
Light Division and Somerset's hussars, kept as a flank-guard in
front of Barcelonne. Two brigades of heavy dragoons—Bülow's
German Legion regiments and Clifton's—arrived in time to join
the line at Garlin; the other two, Manners's[1], and O'Loghlin's
Household Cavalry, had not come up.

On the morning of the 15th Wellington offered battle in the
position in front of Aire, having with him four Anglo-Portuguese
divisions, Freire's Spaniards, and four brigades of cavalry—
about 32,000 men in all—very much the same force that Soult
had opposite him. But this was not his whole tactical plan. He
had made up his mind to turn the enemy's right flank with a
detached force, which would not be available for a day or two.
This was to be composed of the Light Division and Somerset's
hussars, who began to move eastward from Barcelonne toward
Plaisance on the 16th, and were to be joined there on the 18th
by the 4th Division and Vivian's cavalry, hastily recalled from
the Bordeaux road. Beresford was to return with them, and to
take command of this turning column. The Light Division was
not to press in upon the enemy till Beresford should have
appeared, and several days would have to pass before he could

---

[1] Lord C. Manners had taken over Ponsonby's brigade, when the latter
went on leave in February.

arrive. The hussars at the front had insignificant skirmishes with Soult's flank cavalry at Tarsac, and inflicted some loss on the 13th Chasseurs.

This involved very heavy forced marches for Cole and the 4th Division, who were at and about Bazas and Langon on the Garonne, more than half-way to Bordeaux and over 70 miles from Plaisance, where they were to pick up the Light Division. And those of Vivian's hussars who had gone on to Bordeaux had a still longer stretch to cover—but cavalry at the worst can travel faster than infantry. The 4th Division marched from Langon and Bazas on the 14th, and reached Plaisance on the 19th. Vivian, with so much more ground to cover, was at Barcelonne on the 18th, and Plaisance on the 19th. Both Cole and Vivian found very bad weather and bad roads: the stages Bazas–Roquefort and Roquefort–Barcelonne were specially remembered as terrible marches of eight and seven leagues respectively, which knocked up all the baggage-horses and mules—mud was up to the horses' fetlocks and the men's ankles[1]. Till Beresford had assembled the two divisions and two cavalry brigades at Plaisance, Wellington had no intention of pressing on Soult; indeed on the 14th–15th he had considered it likely that he would be attacked himself, since he believed that the troops from Catalonia were now opposite him.

But Soult, though he had informed the War Minister that he was about to carry out the Emperor's instructions, and to fall upon one of the enemy's flanks, executed no more than a very half-hearted demonstration. On the 15th he made no further advance—according to his own story he was waiting for information from his cavalry on the wings. His brother, Pierre Soult, had been directed to feel for the enemy in the direction of Pau: on the other flank the 13th Chasseurs had to explore in the direction of Barcelonne and the Adour. But he complains that his feeble cavalry could get him no information—it was everywhere 'contained'. On the 16th he began a slight movement of retreat, apparently on the rumour that Wellington was receiving reinforcements from the north[2], and his orders to his generals

---

[1] See Vivian's *Memoirs*, p. 226.

[2] He wrote to Clarke that Wellington was reported to have 50,000 men in position at Aire and Garlin!

begin to speak of precautions to be taken, in the case that they might find themselves attacked. Head-quarters drew back to Simacourbe near Lembeye, seven miles behind their previous position at Conchez. Soult's explanation to the War Minister was that he was set on luring Wellington toward the Pyrenees, and drawing him off from the short road to Toulouse, and that when the enemy should follow, he intended to fall unexpectedly upon his most advanced and isolated column[1]. This was all vain talk—he had shown on the 13th–14th that he had no heart to fight. On the 17th the Marshal issued definite orders for a general retreat on Tarbes, if the enemy should attack in force, but not otherwise. Wellington had hitherto shown no signs of taking the offensive: only his cavalry screen had advanced cautiously and crossed the Léez as the French vedettes withdrew from its front. He was waiting for the news of the arrival of Beresford and the troops from the Bordeaux road at Barcelonne, where they were not due till the 18th.

On the 17th Soult made the one effective move—on an infinitesimal scale—of his whole campaign. A reconnaissance party of 100 picked men on picked horses, from his left-wing cavalry, made a wide sweep round Wellington's extreme southern flank, and created considerable alarm in his rear. This raid was headed by a Captain Daunia of the 5th Chasseurs. He crossed the Pau road by night, and appeared on the 18th at Hagetmau near St. Sever, where he rushed the town at dawn, and captured six medical officers, a small convoy, and two drafts of convalescents who were on their way to the front—nearly a hundred prisoners in all. He made off without a moment's delay, and rejoined Pierre Soult that same night, having covered 84 kilometres in thirty hours. Wellington, unable to believe that this raid had been executed by regular cavalry at such a distance from the enemy's front, concluded that it was the work of a partisan corps of local irregulars. On this hypothesis he arrested the mayor and *adjoints* of Hagetmau, and issued a drastic proclamation, to the effect that all civilians taken in arms would be hanged or shot. There was some excuse for this belief, for Soult had been issuing proclamations inciting the country-side to rise, and one band of irregular horse had actually appeared on the

[1] Soult to Clarke, March 17, from Simacourbe.

Bordeaux road, headed by Florian, a celebrated Franco-Spanish partisan, who had served King Joseph. This party had run across some of Beresford's convoys, and taken some plunder[1]. But this was an isolated phenomenon, and Florian soon disappeared. His men, and those of one or two other bands, according to French sources, were mere highway robbers, and more dangerous to the peasantry than to English stragglers. Complaints as to their doings led Wellington to authorize the local *maires* to form 'urban guards' to defend themselves: this order was carried out, and proved quite effective, the 'partisans' were considered as public enemies in Gascony, and the British as friends!

The news of Daunia's exploit at Hagetmau came too late to have any effect on Wellington's plans for the 18th March. He had now heard of Beresford's arrival at Barcelonne, and had issued orders for a general advance. Looked at on the largest scale, the plan was to cut off Soult from his lines of retreat eastward, by turning his right or eastern flank, and to thrust him back against the Pyrenees to the west of Tarbes, where there were no roads or line of escape. It was a scheme for annihilation, if only the turning column could cut in succession Soult's three possible routes eastward, Rabastens–Auch–Toulouse, Tarbes–Trie–Castelnau–Lombes–Toulouse, and Tarbes–Tournay–St. Gaudens–Toulouse. As we shall see, Wellington succeeded in blocking the first two of these bolt-holes, but not the third and most remote. For Soult, by fighting the two delaying actions of Vic-Bigorre and Tarbes, just succeeded in gaining time to scramble past the front of Beresford's turning column, at no great expense of lives and material.

On the 18th the general advance of the Allied army began. Hill with the western column starting from Garlin about 13,000 strong[2]: Wellington himself with the central column, 25,000 strong, starting from in front of Aire[3], and Beresford marching on Plaisance with the Light Division and Somerset's Hussars,

---

[1] Woodberry of the 18th Hussars notes that his baggage was captured by Florian's men, and saw two of them, who had been captured, hanging on gallows at Roquefort. *Journal*, pp. 174 and 177. Cf. Pellot, p. 122, for the bad character of these 'partisans'.

[2] With the 2nd Division, Le Cor, Morillo's brigade, and Fane's light cavalry.

[3] With the 3rd and 6th Divisions, Freire's Spaniards, and Manners's, Bülow's, Campbell's, and Clifton's cavalry.

followed closely by the 4th Division and Vivian's horse, just arrived from their forced march. After reaching Plaisance Beresford was to turn south, and move with all possible speed on Maubourget and Rabastens, turning (as was hoped) Soult's right wing. He had in all about 12,000 men.

The Marshal had written to the Minister of War that if the Allied army took the offensive against him, he intended to fall upon any section of it which was advanced and isolated. But he had no chance of doing this, as Wellington moved with his columns closely linked and on a level front, taking care to get into touch with Beresford's wing the moment that it neared the front. Indeed he avoided hurrying on his right and central columns, till his left column should have got in line with them. Soult was in a dangerous position, for facing Beresford's turning force he had only a single regiment of Chasseurs, which was hustled back, and could only report that it had superior cavalry (Somerset's brigade) in front of it, and could make no guess as to what was behind. Not fully realizing the situation, nor seeing that he was threatened with a frontal attack combined with a wide turning movement on his right, the Marshal did no more on the 18th than draw in his front, and somewhat concentrate his divisions in an easterly direction. Meanwhile the enemy was on the move.

On the morning of the 19th Wellington delivered his blow. In cavalry skirmishes soon after dawn Somerset's Hussars from the left drove the French flank-guard of cavalry out of Rabastens, while Bülow's heavy dragoons of the K.G.L., from the centre column, came in toward Vic-Bigorre, the important junction of roads by which Soult had been intending to retreat upon Tarbes, if he should find no opportunity of molesting any isolated column from Wellington's army. Bülow's Hanoverians had a sharp skirmish with Berton's cavalry brigade, which they found opposite them. Their leading squadron was repulsed with some loss, but on the coming up of the main body the French had to retire up the Tarbes road. This news alarmed Soult: he ordered D'Erlon to hurry with his two divisions to Vic-Bigorre and to endeavour to cover the line of the road, while the other four divisions, under Clausel and Reille, cut across country towards Tarbes on bypaths across the plateau of Gers, abandoning any attempt to get off by the great *chaussée*.

This led to a rear-guard action—D'Erlon arrived only just in time to take up a position above Vic-Bigorre with his leading division, that of Paris[1], when Picton's infantry, at the head of Wellington's centre column, came up and attacked him.. When the combat was well engaged—Power's Portuguese were pressing in heavily—D'Erlon detected a column on his right marching hard along the Adour to turn his flank. This was the Light Division, at the head of Beresford's wing of the Allied army. He accordingly gave back, and took up a second position behind Vic, where he was joined by his other division, that of Darmagnac, and was involved in another partial action against Picton and Clinton's 6th Division, which had come up to Picton's support. But seeing the cavalry at the head of Beresford's column still pointing for his flank and rear, he retired again at dark up the Tarbes road. His manœuvring had been good and correct, as he had covered the retreat of the rest of the army at no very great expense of men. His total loss cannot have been much over 300 men[2], and that of the British was about 250. But though he had fought intelligently, and carried out his orders, yet at dusk Beresford's column was out upon his right, with nothing in front to hold it back. There was considerable danger in store for the morrow. One of Soult's three possible lines of retreat on Toulouse had been blocked, and the second was imperilled—for to defile across the front of Wellington's advance on the road Tarbes–Trie–Castelnau was obviously dangerous, though Soult was still hoping to make this manœuvre[3]. There remained only the southern and more hilly road by Tournay and St. Gaudens which was not yet menaced.

Soult's main body had trailed across bad by-ways all through the day of the 19th, and was lucky not to have been molested in its retreat, for there was now an overpowering cavalry force in front of Hill's column—his old mounted regiments, Fane's British and Campbell's Portuguese, had just been reinforced by the coming up of Clifton's heavy dragoon brigade fresh from

---

[1] Late Fririon's division, and before that, Foy's division. Daricau took it over a few days later.

[2] Martinien's list shows 15 officers killed and wounded in Paris's and Darmagnac's divisions. Soult called his loss 'sensible'. Soult to Clarke, March 20.   [3] Ibid.

Spain. There were only two *Chasseur* regiments with Reille's and Clausel's retreating force. Apparently their movement was made under cover of successive deployments of an infantry rear-guard, placed in a favourable position, which the pursuing cavalry dared not attack. And when the head of William Stewart's division came up, the enemy on each occasion retired behind a second rear-guard, placed a few miles back. Hence if the retreat was slow and difficult, the pursuit was always checked till the leading infantry had arrived and begun to deploy—when the enemy absconded. The only incident recorded from this fatiguing series of operations is the story given by Napier of the daring ride of Captain William Light[1]. At nightfall Reille's and Clausel's divisions bivouacked about Ibos and other villages just to the west of Tarbes, Hill's a few miles behind them. All the forces on both sides were now converging on Tarbes, where there was a defile to be passed—first the narrow streets of the town and then the bridge of the Adour behind it, from which fork the two roads to Trie–Castelnau and to Tournay–St. Gaudens.

Early on March 20th, therefore, Soult made his dispositions, putting out two covering forces which were to detain the advance of Wellington's army, while the main body, following the train, should take the Tournay–St. Gaudens road. Tarbes and its bridge lie close below the first foot-hills of the Pyrenean chain, and the routes chosen for the line of retreat mount across the nearest of them, the Mont de Piétat.

Soult was set on fighting one more rear-guard action at Tarbes—mainly with the object of getting a good start for his train and artillery on the St. Gaudens road. A pitched battle

---

[1] This ingenious dragoon, on one of the occasions when Hill's cavalry advance was brought to a stand by deployed infantry, on a wooded hill-side, where nothing could be made out save the French skirmishing line, tried a most daring device. He turned the flank of the French by passing through a wood, and then rode all along the back of the skirmishing line as if wounded, with his reins dropped, and hanging half off his saddle like a trick-rider. Hardly any shots were fired at him, as he appeared mortally wounded, and likely to fall off his horse at any moment. Having cantered wildly along the front of the French supporting line, and counted just five battalions, he sat up suddenly, and broke through the skirmishing line from the rear, passing unhurt, though fired at by many startled *tirailleurs.* See Napier, vol. vi. p. 146.

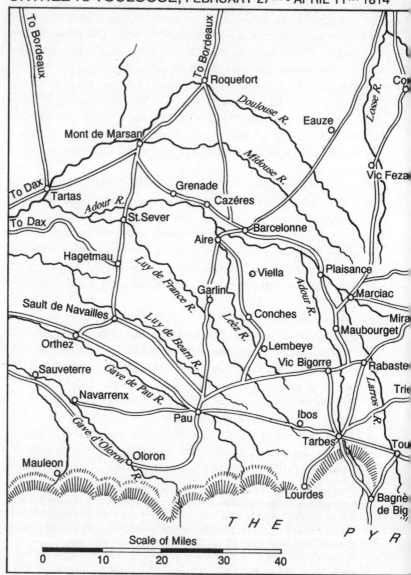

ORTHEZ TO TOULOUSE, FEBRUARY 27TH - APRIL 11TH 1814

To Bordeaux

To Bordeaux

To Bordeaux

Roquefort

Doulouse R.

Eauze

Losse R.

Co

Mont de Marsan

Midouse R.

Vic Feza

Grenade

Cazéres

Adour R.

St.Sever

Barcelonne

To Dax

Tartas

Aire

To Dax

Hagetmau

Luy de France R.

Viella

Plaisance

Garlin

Adour R.

Marciac

Sault de Navailles

Luy de Bearn R.

Conches

Léez R.

Mira

Maubourget

Orthez

Gave de Pau R.

Lembeye

Vic Bigorre

Rabaste

Sauveterre

Navarrenx

Larros R.

Trie

Pau

Ibos

Gave d'Oloron

Tarbes

Tou

Mauleon

Oloron

Lourdes

Bagnè
de Big

THE

PYR

Scale of Miles

0   10   20   30   40

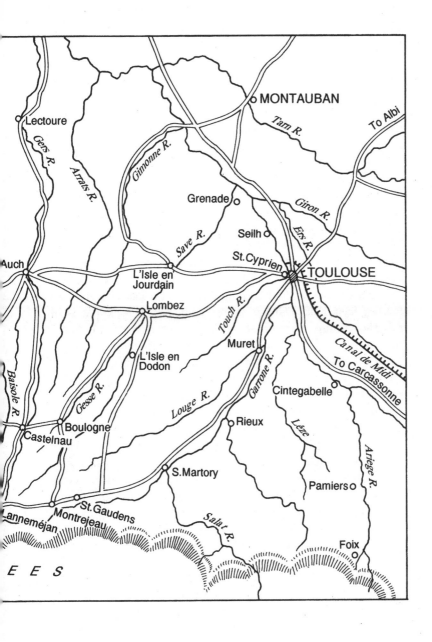

was far from his thoughts, but he imagined that he could gain a day without over-much risk. And he was still under the impression that he could use the Trie–Castelnau road for his right-hand column, though the main body would have to take the longer St. Gaudens road. The object of this partition of forces was to get a solid force into Toulouse by the shorter road, though the main body, forced to take the longer and steeper route, might arrive there somewhat later.

The detaining forces consisted on the right of Clausel's two divisions (Harispe and Villatte) which were placed on the heights of Oleac above the village of Orleix, covering the Trie–Toulouse road, with Pierre Soult's cavalry out on their flank, and on the left of Taupin's division of Reille's corps, which was left in Tarbes, with orders to make a show of defending the town, and then to fall back over the bridge, and make a more real stand on the low hills beyond the Adour. Clausel would be opposed to Beresford's column, the turning force, while Taupin would be holding back Hill's column, as long as he could. As a matter of fact the turning column now consisted of nearly half of Wellington's army, for the 6th Division, Freire's Spaniards, and the cavalry brigades of Somerset and Manners had all swung across country into the wake of the Light Division, and had joined it on the Rabastens–Tarbes road: Cole and the 4th Division, which had never fully caught up Beresford's leading troops, were now at the tail of the long line of march, with Vivian's Hussars as their flank-guard.

Having detached three of his divisions to act as containing forces, Soult sent on the other three to take a position some miles behind Tarbes, in front of Tournay, on the heights which overhang the Larros river, with the Larret stream in front of them. D'Erlon's two divisions, which had fought at Vic-Bigorre on the previous day, and one of Reille's were thus sent on.

The morning was far advanced when the heads of the two British columns drew near Soult's two rear-guards, and discovered their position. Clausel's troops were not drawn up across the Rabastens–Tarbes road, which keeps to the flat ground near the Adour, but on heights flanking it. Wellington did not, of course, intend to march past them, but began to detach units from the head of his long column to turn their flank. First the Light Division swerved off the high road, and deployed to attack the right-hand part of Clausel's front, and later the 6th Division started to make a wider turn, and to get round Clausel's flank. Somerset's Hussars were detached to push out still farther to the north, and to contain Pierre Soult's horsemen, whose flanking position had been discovered.

On the other side of the Adour, Hill's column[1] was longer in getting into serious action, since after driving Taupin out of Tarbes, where no serious opposition was offered, it had then to thread the tortuous streets of the town, and debouch from the narrow bridge—which had rather unaccountably been left undestroyed when the French retired. An attempt to pursue Taupin's rear-guard across country with the advanced cavalry failed entirely—the ground beyond the bridge, though flat, was cut up by three successive narrow watercourses, and Fane's light dragoons, stopped again and again by impassable cuts, had finally to come back to the main road, where alone progress was possible.

The only serious fighting this day took place on Clausel's front, where the Light Division opened the game by attacking the hill crowned by the windmill of Oleac, held by one of Harispe's brigades. This was a steep wooded slope; Alten therefore attacked it not with troops in line, but with the whole three battalions of the 95th dispersed in a thick cloud of skirmishers. When the riflemen had won their way to the top of the slope, they were charged by the French battalions opposite them, and a severe clash took place. Napier asserts, and the fact seems probable, that the enemy was encouraged to take a bold offensive because he mistook these dark-coated troops in front of him for Portuguese. It was only after a close and well-sustained fight that Harispe's men gave way. French authors say that they held their own, and only retreated when they saw their flank being turned by Clinton's division farther to their right. Several of the numerous diarists of the 95th state that they consider that this was the toughest fight in which they were engaged during the whole Peninsular War. Costello, Surtees, Kincaid, Harry Smith, and Simmons all testify to this effect, and their

[1] Now joined by the 3rd Division and Bülow's K.G.L. dragoons.

evidence is well borne out by Cooke of the 43rd and Blakiston of the Caçadores, who watched the affair from the supporting line of the Light Division. One proof of the desperate nature of the fighting is the wholly disproportionate loss of officers as compared with rank and file in the three rifle battalions—11 were killed or wounded to only 80 of other ranks.

By the time that the struggle round the windmill of Oleac was over, the 6th Division had got far forward on its long turning movement; passing through the village of Dours it began to show behind Harispe's flank. The French were then set upon the run, and both Harispe's and Villatte's men began a hasty retreat eastward, along the crests of the line of heights which they had been defending. They were driven ere long across the Trie road, and Pierre Soult's cavalry, which had been watching it, was cut off from the infantry and had to escape by a separate line of retreat.

The whole British turning column then pressed southward— Charles Manners's[1] dragoons on the high road, the Light and 6th Divisions on the heights. Wellington sent up Freire's Spaniards to support the Light Division, but their aid was not required, as the French never made another stand. For a moment the troops on the hills thought they had a chance of cutting off Taupin's division, which, opposing Hill's advance, had lingered too long on the position above the bridge of Tarbes. But these troops, recognizing their danger a little late, went off in a hurry along the Tournay road and over the slopes of the Mont de Piétat.

Hill's column, having its front now free, could deploy beyond the Adour, a lengthy business, since ten brigades[2] in succession had to cross a bridge which would only take four men abreast. The cavalry, pushing along the high road, and over some by-roads also, went as far east as Barbazon, and its main body discovered D'Erlon's divisions drawn up behind the Larret stream, and drew some shots from their artillery. The infantry, following slowly, was facing the French by 4 o'clock.

[1] It is confusing that Wellington (*Disp.* xi. p. 597) persists in calling this 'Ponsonby's brigade' though that officer had gone on leave some weeks back.

[2] Four of the 2nd Division, three of the 3rd Division, two of Le Cor's Portuguese, one of Morillo's Spaniards.

Meanwhile the Light and 6th Divisions, with Freire's Spaniards following them, were engaged in a long scrambling pursuit of Harispe's and Villatte's men across the hills and bottoms south of the Trie road. The French, in considerable disorder, were driven down during the afternoon into the lower ground near the Larret stream—apparently cut off by its ravine from D'Erlon's divisions farther south. At any rate they made their retreat, as did Pierre Soult's cavalry, not on Tournay but on Galan. It was now nearly 5 o'clock, and in March evening was coming on. Many of the British officers expected that the commander-in-chief would order a general attack[1] on the enemy drawn up on the heights above the Larret, and drive them against the Larros river, which lay close in their rear, with no passage save the single bridge of Tournay. It looks as if a decisive push by the 6th Division, on the extreme left, would have turned Soult's flank, and jammed the whole French army against the bridge. In such a case the Marshal would have been in a very desperate position, with no way open for so much of his army as he could save except toward Bagnères de Bigorre, a perfect *cul-de-sac* in the Pyrenees. But Wellington, seeing that the hour was late, the French position bristling with guns, and his own line unformed, while the men had been marching or fighting for twelve continuous hours, called for a halt. The divisions bivouacked, each where it stood, on the lower slopes of the Mont de Piétat, facing the French position. In the night Soult slipped away, crossed the Larros and marched hard along the St. Gaudens road with Reille's and D'Erlon's divisions. Clausel and Pierre Soult's cavalry, being cut off from the main body, made a separate retreat, and fell into the high road at Montrejeau, some miles to the east.

So ended a long day of much marching and little fighting, for save when the 95th stormed the windmill-crest of Oleac there had been no close combat. This is best shown by the fact that of 125 British casualties that day no less than 91 were in the three battalions of the Rifle Brigade. Only 15 were in Hill's column. Nor do the French losses seem to have been serious— they probably did not exceed 200—almost all in Harispe's

---

[1] So Surtees (p. 288) who says that he heard Pakenham, the Adjutant-General, giving vent to his annoyance.

COMBAT OF TARBES, MARCH 20ᵀᴴ 1814

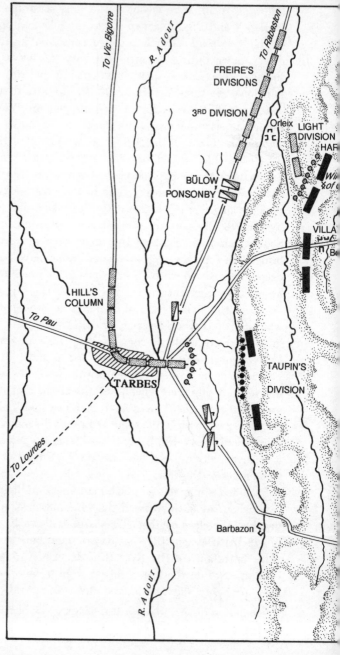

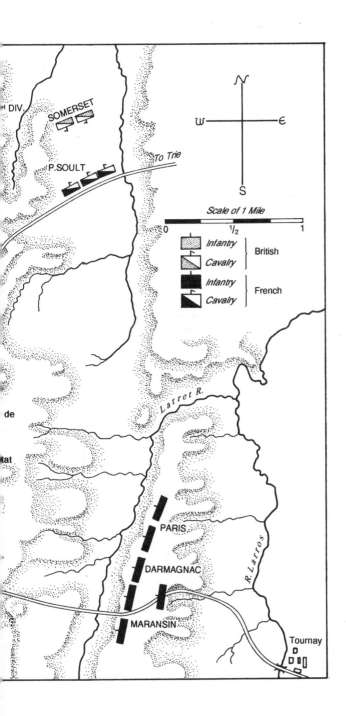

division[1]. The net results of the combat were more satisfactory, on the whole, to Soult than to Wellington. If the Marshal had lost his chance of using the Trie road, the shortest route to Toulouse, he had on the other hand got off with his army intact, and with little loss. Wellington had failed in his project for crushing Soult against the Pyrenees and cutting him off from his communications. Though he had turned the French out of every position that they had taken on March 18th–19th–20th by his great flanking movement, he had been just too late to entrap them on the last day. Soult owed his escape at Tarbes to the wise precaution which he had taken in leaving three divisions behind him as a detaining or covering force. They entirely fulfilled their purpose, suffered no great loss, and so wasted time for Wellington that he arrived at the decisive point only at nightfall, when he judged it too late to deliver the intended blow. It is true that he had secured the short road to Toulouse by Trie–Castelnau, but he was to find that progress along it was extremely difficult in such weather as he was destined to meet. It was on soft ground all the way, and badly engineered, close to the banks of the Gesse river in a flat and water-logged country. The economy in mere mileage was more than balanced by the slow travelling that was found necessary.

On the morning of the 21st, when it was found that Soult had slipped away under cover of the darkness, and was far advanced on the St. Gaudens road, Wellington made up his mind that an attempt to pursue him closely would be useless, and that it would be preferable to strike at Toulouse with his main body, using the Trie–Castelnau road, whose badness he was far from appreciating. Accordingly he detached Hill with his right-hand column to follow the Marshal, and threw the rest of his army upon the Trie road, to march directly upon Toulouse. Hill had with him—as before—Stewart's and Le Cor's divisions, Morillo's Spanish brigade, and the horsemen of Fane and Clifton. He was directed to follow Soult cautiously, and not to accept a general action if the French should halt and offer battle. For,

---

[1] I can only trace in Martinien's invaluable lists 10 officer-casualties for Tarbes—which might imply 200 in all—but looking at the record of the 95th (with its 11 officers hurt to 80 men) might possibly give a much less total.

with some 13,000 of all arms, he would not be strong enough to face an army which, though in a dilapidated condition, outnumbered him by much more than two to one[1].

Wellington himself took the main body on to the Castelnau road. As the whole was now wheeling to the left, the rear division, at the tail of Beresford's column, now became the head of the marching force, i. e. the 4th Division, with Vivian's Hussars which had been acting as its flank-guard. The other units, which had been engaged in the combat of Tarbes, fell in behind the 4th Division as their relative situations required. The 6th Division, from the left of the battle-field, followed Cole immediately: with it went Beresford, now once more in command of this wing. The 3rd and Light Divisions, from the right of the field, struck across country from Galan to fall into the Trie–Castelnau road behind Beresford's force. They were preceded as before by Bülow's, Somerset's, and Manners's cavalry, and followed by Freire's Spanish divisions, who brought up the rear in charge of the pontoon-train and the reserve artillery[2].

The complete marching directions for the army for the next week chance to have been preserved[3]—a thing rather rare with Wellington's staff papers. They show a most careful and elaborate cavalry screen established all round the infantry columns— Bülow's dragoons kept south of the road and were in daily contact with the flanking cavalry of Hill's column. Somerset's and Vivian's Hussars, on the other flank, sent out squadrons all over the country as far as Auch and Gimont, while Manners's dragoons kept ahead of the main body, searching in vain for any trace of French troops in front of them. It was not indeed till March 26th that any hostile force was discovered in face of Wellington's column, and then, when the river Touch, quite close to the outskirts of Toulouse, was reached, the French outposts were found to be held by troops belonging to familiar units. For the Marshal had made such haste that his whole army was concentrated in and about Toulouse two days before Wellington's vanguard approached the city, and this though he had fifty miles more of road to cover.

---

[1] *Supplementary Dispatches*, xiv. p. 431.
[2] For all this see *Supplementary Dispatches*, xiv. pp. 429–30.
[3] See *Supplementary Dispatches*, xiv, under the days March 21–8.

Wellington's march, indeed, from Tarbes to the Touch, through Castelnau, Lombes, and l'Isle en Jourdain, was rather slow, partly because of the badness of the roads along the Gesse river, but partly because the commander-in-chief was cautious in plunging into a new district, very remote from his base, in which he was not sure of the attitude of the population. In this matter, however, everything turned out as satisfactory as could have been hoped. The mayors hastened to put themselves at Wellington's disposition, the peasantry eagerly sold cattle and corn. An enraged *sous-préfet* wrote to Soult that the whole population 'had ceased to have any national spirit'. Royalist emissaries from Toulouse crept into the British camp to whisper that the whole city was ready to revolt at the first sight of the Allied colours, and that Soult's starving army was behaving abominably, and was regarded with loathing by the whole population. Nevertheless Wellington felt that he must not leave his rear unguarded. Very unwillingly he ordered the Prince of Anglona to bring up the 3rd Army, and to occupy Pau and Orthez.

Hill's column, which followed Soult's retreat along the Garonne by St. Gaudens and Martres, as far as Muret, lost touch with the enemy's main body quite early in the advance, and only came into contact with the cavalry of his extreme rear-guard. On the 21st the French infantry executed a forced march of 30 miles, and were never seen again. On the 22nd Fane's horse discovered the last unit of the enemy, Berton's Chasseurs, near St. Gaudens. The 13th Light Dragoons charged headlong at the regiment—the 10th Chasseurs—which was bringing up the rear, caught it unprepared, and routed it with a loss of 100 prisoners. But nothing was discovered of Soult's main body, which was already a full day's march ahead. On the 24th the French army poured into Toulouse, in terrible condition. The Marshal wrote to Paris that 8,000 men were without shoes, and that his cavalry was mainly occupied in hunting forward 5,000 stragglers who strewed the roads behind him. Fortunately for him Toulouse was the main depot of military stores of Southern France, its arsenal was full of artillery and munitions, food was once more procurable without marauding, and missing equipment could be replaced. Moreover—for what they were worth—strong reinforcements were available. Travot had three brigades of conscript-battalions, reorganized since Orthez, in the city. And even after detaching one of them to Montauban, to cover his flank and rear, Soult had over 7,000 more men at his disposition —not battle-troops indeed, but available to man walls and entrenchments such as surrounded Toulouse.

On the day (March 24) that Soult entered Toulouse, Hill was forty miles away, near St. Martory, Beresford at Lombes, almost as far off. The enemy was about to gain not two days of respite, but much more, before Wellington had his army reunited and concentrated in front of the ancient capital of Languedoc.

SECTION XLV: CHAPTER II

THE OPERATIONS PRECEDING THE BATTLE OF TOULOUSE
MARCH 26–APRIL 9, 1814

WHEN Wellington, after his slow march along the rain-sodden valley of the Gesse, found himself once more in face of the old enemy, whose line of cavalry vedettes was discovered ten miles outside Toulouse, he had to take stock of his position. He had failed to drive Soult into the pathless Pyrenees at Tarbes, by his outflanking movement, and the Marshal had escaped, with an army in evil condition but still capable of resistance.

Wellington had not been at all certain, when he lost sight of the French, that Soult would not cross the Garonne and make off eastward to join Suchet[1]. More than one report had come to hand that the French from Catalonia were moving up to unite with the old 'Army of Spain'[2]. Hill had been requested to make all endeavours to ascertain whether there were any signs that Soult was turning his troops toward Carcassonne rather than toward Toulouse. He was able to reply that he saw no trace of such a movement: the Duke of Dalmatia, indeed, had been urging Suchet to come to meet him on the Garonne, and had no intention of retiring himself toward the Mediterranean coast. And advices from Catalonia showed that Suchet's field-force was still in the neighbourhood of Figueras. There remained a doubt as to what had become of Beurmann's column, which was reported to have marched for Lyons, but might conceivably have been directed to Toulouse. As a matter of fact, we have already seen that it had been turned off on to the Bordeaux road—but this Wellington could not know.

Things being as they were, it would appear that the British general now made up his mind to drive Soult out of Toulouse, and this mainly for political rather than for strategical reasons,

---

[1] 'I shall be glad to hear from you whether any of the enemy's force has gone to the right bank of the Garonne.' *Supplementary Dispatches*, xiv. p. 480.

[2] e.g. Wellington to Bathurst, March 20. *Dispatches*, xi. pp. 592–3, and later, ibid., pp. 626–7. Cf. Larpent, p. 455.

for many emissaries had come to head-quarters to assure him
that Toulouse was eager to follow the example of Bordeaux.
And this was perfectly true: as after-events showed, the capital
of Languedoc was a focus of Royalist sentiment, and the partisans
of the Bourbons were only awaiting their opportunity. Wellington was told that if he could drive Soult's army away, the whole
country-side would be ready to hoist the White Banner of the
old monarchy.

Toulouse, unfortunately, was on the wrong side of the broad
Garonne: on the front accessible to the British army there was
only the well-fortified bridge-head of St. Cyprien: the city was
across the water, and was a place almost as difficult to tackle as
Bayonne. For though its solid walls were of medieval and not
of modern date, and though they were in some places masked
by the houses of extra-mural suburbs of recent growth, they had
for three-fourths of their circumference one of the largest wet-
ditches in Europe. This was formed by the celebrated 'Royal
Canal', the *Canal des deux mers*, a hundred yards broad, which
linked the Mediterranean and the Bay of Biscay—it could carry
vessels of some size. From Bordeaux to Toulouse the Garonne
had been made navigable—from Toulouse to Carcassonne the
canal cut across country till it got into the valley of the Aude
river, down which it was carried to the sea near Agde. The *Canal
Royal* enclosed Toulouse on its northern and eastern sides, the
Garonne covered its western side: only the narrow south front
was not shielded by a broad water defence. And it must be added
that outside the canal, at a distance ranging from five miles to
a mile and a half, ran the Ers river, a large tributary of the
Garonne, which falls into the greater stream some twelve miles
north of Toulouse. Running parallel to the Garonne for mile
after mile, it constitutes an advanced line of defence, outside
that formed by the Royal Canal. Immediately above the east
front of Toulouse, between the canal and the Ers, lies a ridge
three miles long, the Mont Rave, which rises to a height of 300
feet and looks down into the city. This is the only high ground
in the neighbourhood: it completely commands Toulouse at a
distance of only half a mile at its northern end, and three-
quarters of a mile at the southern. When the medieval walls of
Toulouse were built, before the invention of artillery, this long

ridge had no importance. But under modern conditions any enemy in possession of it could blow the place to pieces at his leisure. Soult, therefore, was compelled to hold the Mont Rave as an integral part of his defences, though it was beyond the canal which hugs the east front of the city. The moment that he had made up his mind to retreat on Toulouse, he had sent back orders to fortify all critical points about the city: not only was a broad line of outer entrenchments thrown out in front of the bridge-head on the west side of the place, but a little later additional plans were made to strengthen the eastern face, and to include Mont Rave in the scheme. Civilian labour was utilized as well as military. In the fortnight which elapsed between March 26th and the battle of April 10th Mont Rave had been turned into a sort of entrenched camp, with five redoubts connected by long lines of trenches.

The only front of Toulouse not covered by water defence is its southern one, out of which the road to Carcassonne runs, between the Garonne on its left side, and the Royal Canal on its right. And this was the front which Wellington would have liked to attack. To get to it he would have to cross the Garonne above the city, forcing a passage somewhere up-stream. It was obvious that, to do so, he would probably have to fight Soult, who could come out of Toulouse with all his available strength and establish himself opposite the chosen point of passage. The nearer the point selected might be to the city, the quicker would the enemy be in getting into position to defend the eastern bank. This would be a dangerous business—no general welcomes the prospect of crossing a broad and flooded stream on improvised bridges, in face of the artillery of a competent defence. And Wellington had not on the Garonne the advantage which Napoleon possessed when faced by the similar problem of crossing the Danube at Essling and Wagram. There were no convenient islands, or cover of woods on the west bank south of Toulouse, to facilitate preparations for an attack by surprise[1], though on other reaches of the Garonne such are to be found not unfrequently.

[1] Though there are islands down-stream, e.g. at Toulouse itself, which divide the channel; but it was not in this direction that Wellington originally intended to cross.

Wellington, nevertheless, had made up his mind to take the risk, and to force the passage at Portet, a bare five miles south of Toulouse, hoping to throw his pontoon-bridge across in the night, and to pass sufficient troops across it before the enemy should be alarmed in the morning, and come down in force to resist him. Meanwhile he endeavoured to distract Soult's attention from the point which he had selected, by pressing in closely to the west front of Toulouse itself, as if he were about to attack the bridge-head. On the afternoon of March 27th the 4th, 6th, and Light Divisions, with cavalry in front of them, marched against the positions outside the bridge-head, which were occupied on this day by D'Erlon's two divisions—those of Daricau and Darmagnac. After a trifling skirmish at the bridge of Tournefeuille on the Touch stream, the French withdrew to a line half a mile outside the bridge-head, where entrenching had already been begun[1], and stood to fight. They were not pressed, for this was only a demonstration.

It had the effect that Wellington desired, for Soult had made up his mind that his enemy's attempt to pass the Garonne would be made down-stream from Toulouse, and not up-stream. Seeing a heavy force in front of the bridge-head, he guessed that his attention was being drawn in this direction, not to distract him from schemes to the south, but from schemes to the north. He sent four of his seven regiments of cavalry to patrol the Garonne down-stream, and left its banks up-stream practically un-watched. There was actually only one picket on the whole stretch for ten miles south of Toulouse, where the British army was about to attempt a passage.

From this it resulted, strange as it may seem, that Wellington's abortive attempt to pass the Garonne at Portet on the night of the 27th–28th was never discovered by Soult! But the occurrences of the dark hours were most desperately disappointing. The pontoon-train was duly brought down to the bank, and Hill's divisions at Muret were warned to be ready to pass the moment that the bridge should be laid. But on launching the pontoons it

---

[1] The outer works here had started by the 25th, and were being rapidly pressed on, but it is doubtful whether they could have stood an assault on the 27th. See Larpent, pp. 452–3. A few days later they were getting quite formidable.

was discovered that there were not nearly enough of them to span the swollen river. The bridge was eighty feet too short, and there was no possibility of laying *chevalets* or trestles at the water's edge, to eke out the deficiency. Colonel Elphinstone, the senior officer of engineers, declared that he had explained to Wellington at St. Jean de Luz that the number of pontoons for which transport had been allotted to him was insufficient for a really large river: but his objection had been overruled. His defence had to be accepted, but the commander-in-chief was in no good temper that night[1].

Foiled at Portet, Wellington still held to his idea of passing the Garonne above Toulouse. But his second scheme was destined to no better fortune than his first. He ordered the pontoons to be moved, and relaid three miles farther to the south, above the junction of the Garonne and its large tributary the Ariège. The volume of water brought down by the latter was so great that the Garonne above the junction was only two-thirds as wide as below it. Hence the pontoon-bridge was thrown over, with some difficulty, on the night of the 30th at Pinsaguel near Muret, and on the following morning Hill's whole corps crossed unopposed and with great swiftness—Stewart's and Le Cor's divisions, Fane's four cavalry regiments, and the Spanish brigade belonging to Morillo—in all 13,000 men. Soult had not a single cavalry vedette watching the Garonne at this point—his nearest post was at Vieille Toulouse, a village on the Carcassonne road, many miles behind the Ariège. A day elapsed before the cavalry officer there placed discovered Hill's move.

But the crossing of the Garonne at Pinsaguel turned out to be a useless move. Hill reported that he could not get across the lower Ariège—the pontoons were all in use on the Garonne, and there was no bridge on that river nearer than Cintegabelle fifteen miles up-stream. Moreover, there was no road that would carry anything on wheels between the reaches of the lower Ariège and Toulouse. The whole country was rain-sodden. He

---

[1] 'It will be a triumph for Elphinstone—though I am sure he will not feel it as such. Lord W. has for once suffered for not attending to the counsel of a regularly-bred scientific observer.' Larpent, p. 458. George Napier (p. 254) says that 'Lord Wellington was furious: I never saw him in such a rage—and no wonder!'

had passed some dragoons across the river at a place called Venerque, by means of a boat, the only one to be discovered. They had found no roads at all between the eastern bank of the Ariège and the Royal Canal. Another party rode as far as the bridge of Cintegabelle, crossed it unopposed, and explored as far as Villefranche on the Royal Canal, but reported that they could find no roads leading towards Toulouse, and that the whole region was practically water-logged. The head of the infantry column therefore halted short of the bridge of Cintegabelle.

Much irritated at this news, Wellington ordered Hill to countermarch and return to Pinsaguel. These directions were promptly carried out on the night of April 1st, and the pontoon-bridge was taken up and packed on its travelling carriages. The days between March 28th and April 2nd had been completely wasted. It would appear that Hill's second expedition was planned with wholly inadequate local information—the staff had supposed that roads existed where there chanced to be none.

Soult, informed somewhat tardily of Hill's second passage, had ordered out Clausel's two divisions from Toulouse on the morning of April 1st as far as Vieille Toulouse, directing him to fall on the head of the British column when it should try to cross the Ariège, and promising him the support of D'Erlon's two divisions if matters should grow serious. But as Hill made no attempt to pass the river, and as Clausel reported that he could not approach it, on account of the same want of practicable roads which had foiled the British advance, no collision took place. The Marshal himself, taking a long-distance view over the flooded country from a mound at Vieille Toulouse, on the morning of the 1st, and seeing Hill's column come to a standstill, concluded that the whole movement had been no more than a diversion to induce him to send troops away from Toulouse southward. He guessed that Wellington was about either to make an assault on the bridge-head at St. Cyprien, or else to throw the rest of his army across the Garonne below Toulouse. He was confirmed in this view by a false report that a second bridge-equipage had been sighted opposite Blagnac a few miles north of Toulouse.

Although Soult's hypothesis was erroneous, for the turning move had been intended to be no mere demonstration, it received apparent confirmation by the disappearance of Hill's column on the night of April 1st, and its return to Pinsaguel. French light cavalry, following in its track, discovered that it was recrossing the Garonne, and took a few stragglers from its rear-guard—Spaniards of Morillo's brigade, who had dropped behind for purposes of plunder. Congratulating himself on not having been lured into sending troops far out from Toulouse southward, the Marshal prepared to be attacked on the other flank, and turned his energy to perfecting the local defences of the city. Expecting to see the enemy cross somewhere in the long stretch of the Garonne northward, he made up his mind to concentrate every man in the Toulouse positions, and to make all sides of the city impregnable. Hence redoubled exertions were made to improve the newly begun entrenchments on Mont Rave, and to strengthen the points of danger along the front of the Canal Royal—the bridges by which six separate roads crossed it on the east and north sides of Toulouse. The arsenal was full of guns of position: a number of these were brought forward and placed some in the new works, some on the old city-wall, whose bastions were broad enough to bear the heaviest pieces. About forty guns in all were mounted; they were served by the officers and men of the permanent staff of the arsenal, aided by drafts from the artillery-train of the field-army. The second line of the bridge-head of St. Cyprien was defended entirely by these heavy guns, so that the batteries belonging to the infantry there stationed were available for use on other fronts. In the battle which followed it must be remembered that the artillery of the defence was not only double in the mere number of guns of that of the attack, but was for half its strength composed of pieces of the heaviest calibre and longest range. And they were lodged in solid works, not used in the open as the batteries of the Allied army had to be.

On April 2nd Wellington, quite contrary to his original intentions, made up his mind that he must cross the Garonne below Toulouse, as Soult had always expected that he would. Staff-officers were occupied all day in looking for suitable points of passage: by the evening it was decided that the best available spot was at the hamlet of La Capellette near Grenade, some eleven miles north of Toulouse, where the west bank completely commands the east bank of the Garonne, and was covered by woods, which conveniently masked the accumulation of troops behind them.

The decisive orders were given on the afternoon of April 3rd. The pontoon-train from Pinsaguel marched by the cross-roads on the west bank of the Garonne after dark. It was escorted by a brigade of the 4th Division. Moving all night it was to reach La Capellette at dawn and to be laid there. The main body of the army was to get in motion as soon as the pontoons were well on their way, and to follow them. The order of march was headed by the 4th Division, then came Vivian's horse, the 6th Division, Somerset's Hussar brigade, the 3rd Division, and lastly Charles Manners's British and F. v. Arentschildt's German dragoons[1]. Freire's Spanish divisions were to take a parallel route a little farther from the river, accompanied by the 10 Portuguese guns of the artillery reserve. The Light Division was to remain in front of the bridge-head of St. Cyprien, till it should be relieved by the arrival of the whole of Hill's corps from Muret and Portet, when it would hand over the outpost position to Hill's troops and follow the rest—but only half-way to La Capellette.

In case of the departure of the main army northward being discovered by Soult, and of a heavy sally being made from the bridge-head of St. Cyprien, Hill was authorized to call back the Light Division and also Arentschildt's heavy dragoons to join him, and recommended to take a defensive position behind the stream of the Touch. With the 18,000 men thus at his disposition, Wellington judged that he was strong enough to defend himself till succour should come. But supposing that Soult made no sally from St. Cyprien, but marched out with his main force to resist the passage at La Capellette, Hill was ordered to assail the outer *enceinte* of St. Cyprien. Such an attack would either be successful, if the enemy had gone off in full strength, or at least would compel the French to send back a heavy force to defend Toulouse. Neither of these possible contingencies was destined to occur.

[1] Friedrich v. Arentschildt had Bock's old brigade from March 25th onward, *vice* Bülow who had been in temporary command. He must be carefully distinguished from Victor v. Arentschildt the artillery colonel.

The pontoons reached La Capellette with praiseworthy punctuality, and a bridge was thrown across the Garonne in four hours, no opposition being met. The troops commenced to pour over at once, and by dusk on April 4th, the three leading infantry divisions with Vivian's, Manners's, and Somerset's cavalry, and three divisional field-batteries were across the water. They took up a semicircular position, covering the bridge, with the Ers river on their left flank and the Garonne on their right—a front of less than two miles for a force of 19,000 men. The hussars pushed forward both across the Ers and up the bank of the Garonne, and established a cavalry screen well in front of the main position.

Now came a vexatious interlude. The weather again proved hostile to Wellington: rain began in the afternoon, the Garonne swelled ominously, and the bridge swayed, so that the later-crossing cavalry had to dismount and lead their horses across in single file. After dark the bridge-moorings broke, one pontoon was lost and went bobbing down-stream, and the rest were with difficulty drawn back to the west bank. Freire's Spaniards, the German Legion dragoons, the reserve artillery, and the Light Division were left on the wrong side of the water. For four days, from the evening of the 4th to the morning of the 7th, it was impossible to lay the bridge again—though the missing pontoon was tracked and retrieved, having been found uninjured on a sand-bank a few miles down-stream.

Beresford was in command across the water, but Wellington repeatedly went across in a rowing-boat to confer with him. He held that the situation was tiresome rather than dangerous, for the troops on the farther bank had an admirable position, with a narrow front and a deep river on either flank. Moreover all the artillery which had not crossed was brought up to the high bank on the western side, and trained on to the flat ground over which an enemy, advancing to attack Beresford's front, would have to deploy[1]. If Soult, after leaving behind him sufficient troops to maintain Toulouse against Hill, should come up the narrow path between the Ers and the Garonne to assail the three isolated divisions, Wellington did not think that he could break

[1] Apparently 22 guns—Victor v. Arentschildt's 10 Portuguese pieces and the batteries attached to the Light Division and the Cavalry Division.

them. The position was much sounder than Hill's at St. Pierre
had been on December 13th of the preceding year. Indeed
the British troops hoped to be attacked[1].

But Soult never had any intention of coming out of Toulouse
to fall upon Beresford's force. Military historians have often
accused him of lacking enterprise and self-confidence—the
opportunity being most tempting when Wellington's forces were
divided into three separate corps—Hill's force in front of
St. Cyprien, Beresford's three divisions on the right bank of the
Garonne, and the troops on the west bank which were waiting
to pass. But the Marshal made no move, and only put on still
more energy for the local fortification of Toulouse. The explanation, so far as can be gathered, was mainly that he did not know
how few of the enemy were across the Garonne, and credited
Wellington with having his whole army in hand, save the force
blocking the bridge-head of St. Cyprien. And this he believed
to consist of Freire's Spaniards alone, holding that Hill (who had
disappeared from Muret and Portet) was with the main army.
This error came from the chance fact that Morillo's brigade was
holding the outposts before St. Cyprien on April 4th, no British
troops being visible. Soult took Morillo's men for Freire's corps,
and opined (it would seem) that a sally and the driving off of
the Spaniards would be of no use to him, if Wellington were
across the Garonne with the whole of the rest of his army. He
made no effort to molest the enemy, save by floating trees, barges
loaded with stones, and logs set with sword-blades, down the
rapid Garonne, in the hope that they would break the bridge,
which (as a matter of fact) was drawn in at the moment. The
floating missiles nearly all ran ashore before reaching the
neighbourhood of Grenade. Soult's elaborate orders issued on
April 4th–5th–6th–7th are all devoted to the perfection of his
defences round the city. He wrote to the Minister of War that
he should accept battle in position, if he were attacked, but that
he thought that the bad weather would lead Wellington to defer
his advance. He would find it a costly business if he persisted
in pressing on. Meanwhile rumours of a disturbing sort were

---

[1] Vivian writes on April 7th: 'Here we are still, and much to our surprise
in peace! It is now 4 p.m. and Soult has not attacked us. I only wish he
had. He would have caught it properly,' p. 239.

coming in from the direction of Paris and the Emperor's army;
it was to be hoped that they would soon be contradicted[1].
Never for one moment, as is clear, did the Marshal dream
of marching out to attack the Allied troops which were across
the Garonne. He attributed their stationary position on the
4th–5th–6th–7th to the bad weather, not to the breaking of
their bridge.

During the period of stagnation Wellington's light cavalry
passed the Ers and cut the main road Toulouse–Montauban. The
French vedettes in this quarter were driven away, and reconnaissances pushed far afield. A captured dispatch from General
Leverdo, commanding at Montauban, gave the satisfactory intelligence that the garrison there was weak, and the public spirit
abominable. There was obviously little danger to be feared from
this quarter.

On the night of the 7th the flood of the Garonne abated, and
on the morning of the 8th the pontoon-bridge at La Capellette
was replaced, and Freire's Spaniards, the Portuguese artillery,
and Arentschildt's K.G.L. dragoons passed over it and joined
the troops of Beresford. But the Light Division, still halted a
few miles up-stream to the south, was ordered to wait at Seilh,
till the bridge should have been taken to pieces and relaid there:
for Wellington was anxious to have his communication with
Hill's corps shortened; so long as the pontoons were at La
Capellette there were more than twelve miles between the two
sections of the army, and for every mile that the main body
advanced southward, the longer would be the detour to be made
across the bridge.

Wellington had intended to spend the 8th in marching against
Toulouse, along the high road between Garonne and Ers, and to
fight upon the 9th. But this plan failed, owing to the removal and
relaying of the pontoon-bridge taking a far longer time than had
been calculated. Instead of being ready on the night of the 8th,
it was not refixed at Seilh till 3 o'clock on the afternoon of the
9th—an hour so late that by the time that the Light Division had
crossed, the commander-in-chief decided that it was impossible
to begin a battle that day.

[1] Soult's very interesting dispatches and orders of April 3rd–8th are all
printed in the *Wellington Supplementary Dispatches*, xiv. pp. 454–64.

The 8th indeed was mainly spent in getting the troops forward toward the outer defences of Toulouse. There was no fighting save at one point. Soult's *chasseurs à cheval* kept falling back before Wellington's advance on both sides of the Ers, breaking each bridge as they passed by southward: Berton's brigade was on the western bank of the Ers, Vial's on the eastern. No bridge was saved till that of Croix d'Orade, which was captured by a bold stroke of Vivian and the 18th Hussars. Vial had two regiments in position—the 5th and 22nd Chasseurs—and had made preparations for destroying the bridge and retiring at leisure, but was charged unexpectedly by Vivian, who caught the 22nd unawares, broke it, and chased it across the bridge—despite of a flanking fire from dismounted men of the 5th Chasseurs on the other side of the water. Vivian was disabled by a carbine-shot in the arm just as he gave the order to charge—but must surely be given the credit for this success, though Napier goes out of his way to transfer it to Major Hughes, the officer commanding the 18th, who simply obeyed orders. The French lost 120 prisoners, and the pursuit was only checked when the Hussars came under artillery-fire and had to retire[1]. Meanwhile Ross's brigade of the 4th Division had taken firm possession of the bridge. The 18th Hussars had only 15 casualties, their supporting regiment, the 1st Hussars K.G.L., was hardly engaged and suffered no losses[2]. Soult had to lay the blame for this check on his own brother Pierre, who was present with Vial's brigade at the moment, and narrowly escaped capture. He had been offered two companies of infantry to support him at the bridge, and had not accepted them, and he had distinctly been surprised[3].

On April 9th Soult expected to be attacked—but was not. Wellington, vexed at the failure to relay his pontoon-bridge in the morning, contented himself with bringing up all his troops

[1] There is a good account of this skirmish in the diary of Woodberry of the 18th, pp. 191–2. Cf. Vivian's *Life* by his son, pp. 240–1.

[2] Though a sergeant and 8 men are commended in its regimental record for a bold attack on the French flank. Schwertfeger's *K.G.L.*, i. p. 460.

[3] Cf. Soult to P. Soult in *Wellington Supplementary Dispatches*, xiv. pp. 464–5. Lemonnier-Delafosse, P. Soult's aide-de-camp, slurs the matter over as surprise caused by treachery! p. 286.

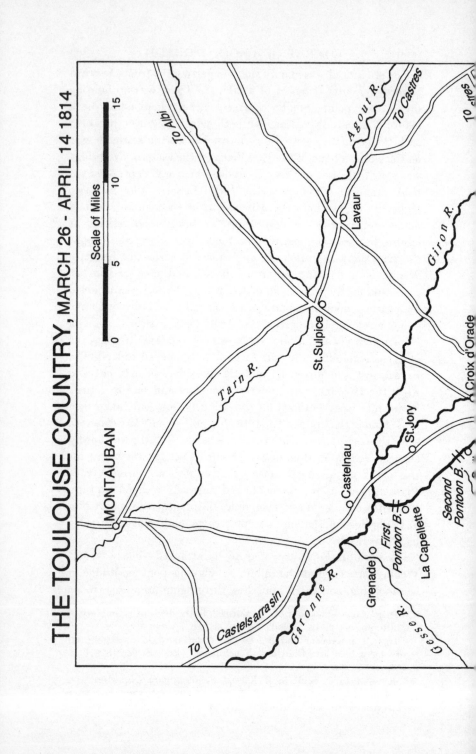

THE TOULOUSE COUNTRY, MARCH 26 - APRIL 14 1814

Scale of Miles

0   5   10   15

To Albi

Agout R.

To Castres

To tres

Lavaur

Giron R.

St.Sulpice

Croix d'Orade

Tarn R.

MONTAUBAN

St.Jory

Castelnau

Second Pontoon B. To

First Pontoon B.

La Capellette

Grenade

Garonne R.

Gesse R.

To Castelsarrasin

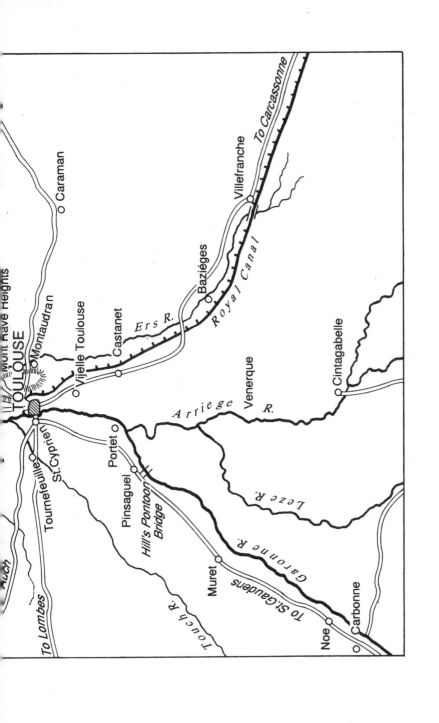

to the neighbourhood of Croix d'Orade—save the Light Division which only crossed the bridge at Seilh at dawn on the next day. The elaborate directions issued by the British commander-in-chief for the conduct of each of his corps were only issued at 8 in the morning of April 10th, from his head-quarters at St. Jory, between the Garonne and the Ers, some seven miles north of Croix d'Orade.

SECTION XLV: CHAPTER III

THE BATTLE OF TOULOUSE. APRIL 10, 1814

UNLIKE all the rest of Wellington's victories, the battle of Toulouse was not a fight—offensive or defensive—upon a long front, but the storming of an entrenched position, part of the works of a great fortress. For Toulouse, with its bastioned medieval wall and its almost complete circle of water-defences, was undoubtedly a fortress—though not one of modern type. It was safe against escalade, though it could not have stood many days' battering by a regular siege-train. Two-thirds of its front had before them the broad ditch of the Royal Canal: and the ramparts, within easy musketry-range of the canal, commanded the few passages at the locks and bridges of that water-way. Guns of position from the arsenal had been mounted on the bastions overlooking those points, and entrenched and palisaded *têtes-de-pont* on a small scale had been erected at each of them. Against all this western and northern side of the Toulouse works only demonstrations were possible—and necessary in order to compel the enemy to keep them manned. No real attack could be made. As to the St. Cyprien front across the river, the outer line—constructed during the last fortnight—was comparatively weak, being improvised by the fortification of suburban houses, and the throwing up of one large earthwork to cover the 'Patte d'Oie', the meeting-place of the three great roads which come into Toulouse from the west, those from Auch, Lombes, and St. Gaudens. But behind this outer and rather sketchy line was the old wall of the St. Cyprien suburb, only 600 yards long, solid masonry, with two bastions and a walled-up gate-work, now covered by a palisaded and ditched battery. There were fifteen guns of position from the arsenal placed in the St. Cyprien works. This line was as unassailable as the east front of the city itself, and Wellington gave Hill orders to overrun the outer entrenchments, if he could, but to leave the inner wall alone.

There remained the works on Mont Rave, which, though outside the broad ditch of the Royal Canal, were an essential part of the fortifications of Toulouse, because they overlooked from a commanding height both the canal and the city walls beyond it. With modern artillery any besieger in possession of Mont Rave had the whole of Toulouse at his mercy, and this was the reason why Soult had from the first devoted much attention to these heights, and had redoubled his energies during the days that followed April 4th and Wellington's passage of the Garonne at La Capellette. His chief engineer, Colonel Michaux, had sketched out five groups of redoubts on the more commanding points of the heights, with lines of trench between them. The range is loftiest at its northern and southern ends[1]—between them is a slight dip, over which pass the two roads which lead out of Toulouse eastward, those to Lavaur and Caraman, each of which crosses the crest in a cutting, contrived to make the gradient of ascent and descent less steep for vehicles. At the extreme northern and southern ends of the ridge are two other road-cuttings on a smaller scale, on the lower slopes of the ridge, the southern one leading to the village and bridge of Montaudran, the northern one containing the road which serves the suburban hamlets of Les Argoulets and Peyriolle: this last was to prove a dreadful trap to Wellington's Spanish troops during the battle.

Michaux's scheme of works on Mont Rave fell into five sections. (1) At the northern and highest summit of the ridge was a group of earthworks generally called by one name, as the 'Great Redoubt', but really consisting of five separate structures. The largest was a sort of two-fronted hornwork looking north-west and north; it was revetted with casks requisitioned in the city, and ditched. In it were heavy guns from the arsenal—brought up the slope with difficulty: the ground was so steep and slippery that 'duckboards' had to be laid in order to haul them up. Slightly to the south of the hornwork was a two-gun battery facing due east, and beyond this again two earthworks not furnished with artillery, destined to cover the flank of the more important parts of the group. While behind all, facing north-east, was a triangular work intended to support the whole system.

(2) After an interval of about 1,000 yards, covered by infantry trenches along the crest, were two closed redoubts overlooking the Lavaur road, distant from each other only about 100 yards.

---

[1] The Sypière height is 600 feet above sea-level, the Great Redoubt 610. But both are only 250 feet above the Ers valley.

The one on the actual head of the slope was a quadrangular work, containing in its middle an old two-storied manor-house formerly belonging to the Austin Friars of Toulouse[1]. The house had been barricaded and crenellated: the outer defence was a rampart of earth heaped up against the garden walls of the enclosure, and furnished with a banquette. To the west of this work, called the Mas des Augustins[2], was a second very similar structure, also constructed round a stone house, called the Colombette or sometimes the Calvinet redoubt, though the name Calvinet seems rather to belong to the whole of this section of the Mont Rave, and the two works together are called the Calvinet redoubts by some historians of the battle. They were connected by a short trench for infantry.

(3) Distant about as far from the Augustins as the latter was from the Great Redoubt, was a pentagonal work with a trench in front of it, half-way between the Lavaur and the Caraman roads: it seems to have had no proper name, and is only alluded to as 'the work south of the Lavaur road' by those who mention it. It was intended for infantry alone[3].

(4) At the highest southern point of Mont Rave, overlooking the Caraman road, was a square redoubt, which (like the Mas des Augustins) had a stone house in its centre. It was called the Sypière redoubt, and was intended for artillery, but was not yet armed. According to Soult it was not completed. This was the southernmost of the French defences.

(5) The rear slope of Mont Rave descends steeply toward the canal and the suburb of St. Étienne; about three-quarters of the way down to the canal there is a long knoll on each side of the Caraman road, in 1814 sparsely covered with residential houses of some importance. As a last protection, or a rallying point if the heights above should be lost, these houses had been barricaded and connected by trenches. The narratives of contemporaries name the chief dwellings from their owners—Saccarin, Cambon, and Bataille. Two bridges across the canal were

---

[1] There is a good description of this work in the account of Toulouse of Anton of the Black Watch, who was one of its stormers, and then of the defenders, of the Mas des Augustins.

[2] 'Mas' is Languedocian for Maison.

[3] Napier makes special note of this anonymity, vi. p. 160.

immediately below their backs. All this region of Toulouse is to-day built over with uninteresting houses, trending up-hill in steep streets towards Mont Rave—it is impossible to make out the topography of 1814. Even in that year the city wall was less well defined in this front than in any other, as many of the houses of the St. Étienne suburb had been built close into it—even encroaching on its ditch—while others abutted directly on the canal.

Wellington's orders issued from St. Jory to each of the corps for their movements on April 10th were very precise. When the Light Division got into its place—it crossed the pontoons at Seilh as early as 3 a.m.—the army was to make a concentric advance against the western, northern, and eastern fronts of Soult's position. But half the force employed was to be used for demonstrations only, the actual blow being entrusted to the other half.

(1) On the west bank of the Garonne, Hill was merely directed to threaten the St. Cyprien defences in such a way as to detain as many French beyond the Garonne as possible. He was given *carte blanche* to 'regulate his operations in accordance with what was going on east of the river[1]'. The demonstrations might be made more or less incisive as he deemed best.

(2) Picton and Alten were to draw up the 3rd and Light Divisions opposite the west side of the outer defences, from the Garonne as far as the Albi road. 'The attacks of these two divisions were meant more as a means of diversion, to draw as much as possible of the attention of the enemy to that quarter, than as real attacks, it not being expected that the divisions will be able to force any of the passages of the canal which covers Toulouse.' The line of the canal should be threatened chiefly at the bridges and locks. A 'considerable part' of each division must be kept strictly in reserve[2]. Arentschildt's heavy dragoons of the K.G.L. followed the Light Division, and were more or less attached to it. The 3rd Division was next the Garonne, the Light Division near to the Albi road.

The remaining troops on the east bank of the Garonne were to execute the real attack. Contrary to Wellington's practice in

---

[1] *Supplementary Dispatches*, viii. p. 728, night of April 9.
[2] Ibid., xiv. p. 493, 3 a.m., April 10.

all his earlier battles he allotted an important and responsible part of the work to his Spanish contingent.

(3) General Freire with the two Galician divisions was directed to take as his objective the northern end of the Mont Rave heights, including the Great Redoubt. As a preliminary operation he would seize the knoll of La Pujade, which lies above the village of the same name in front of the main French position on Mont Rave. The Spaniards would have Beresford with the 4th and 6th Divisions on their left. 'General Freire will direct his troops at first in the direction of the village of La Pujade, throwing out a skirmishing line to cover his march. After reaching this village the troops will form in two columns—the right one will move on La Pujade, keeping to the right side of the great road (the Albi *chaussée*) toward the great avenue of cypress trees. The left-hand one will follow the *chaussée* and advance so as to combine its operations with those of the other column. To the left of the *chaussée*, near where the great cypress avenue ends, there is a height (knoll of La Pujade): the Spanish troops should take possession of it: it will probably furnish an advantageous emplacement for the Portuguese artillery, when the attack begins. The troops should be formed in two lines, with a reserve. The attack will commence at the moment when General Freire sees the 4th and 6th Divisions advancing to deliver their attack. The Light Division, facing towards Toulouse, will always be in touch with the Spanish right. There will be cavalry (C. Manners's brigade) on the left of the Spanish troops, linking their advance with that of the 6th Division, and there will be a cavalry reserve (Arentschildt's brigade) in the directic of Croix d'Orade[1].'

(4) The most important task was allotted to Beresford and the 4th and 6th Divisions. After passing the village of Croix d'Orade they were to swerve to the left, and 'after proceeding for some time in that direction to form two lines and attack the right of the enemy's positions along the heights'. Somerset's Hussar brigade was attached to the column, with orders to take care to cover the left (i.e. the advanced) flank of the 4th Division, which led the march. Manners's brigade was to keep touch with

---

[1] These orders, written in French, can be found in *Supplementary Dispatches*, viii. pp. 735–6.

Beresford, but also with the Spaniards 'to be at all times near them to give immediate support[1]'.

(5) Vivian's two hussar regiments, commanded this day by von Grüben of the 1st K.G.L. Hussars, since Vivian had been wounded on the 8th, had a separate task. Keeping on the east side of the Ers, they were to proceed along the banks of that river southward, and to try to seize a bridge by which they could communicate with Beresford, and if possible fall in ahead of his line of march as an advanced guard. There were four such bridges—those of Peyriolle, Balma, Les Bordes, and Montaudran. But as the French cavalry (some of Berton's *chasseurs*) were in force to the east of the Ers, it was possible that any or all of these bridges might be found broken, or hotly disputed.

It will be noted that a good deal of discretion was given to Beresford, as to Hill. Being told to march 'for a certain time' parallel to the Mont Rave, and then to form his lines and attack the 'right of the enemy's position', he had to settle how long he would continue his flank-march between the Ers and the heights, and where precisely the French right might be considered to begin, or end.

It is interesting to follow the counter-arrangements of Soult, to face an attack which he had been expecting for two days.

(1) In the St. Cyprien bridge-head he left only Maransin's division to hold the two lines of defence, and to 'contain' Hill's corps. The general was told not to risk anything in defending the outer lines, but to fall back on the impregnable second line if attacked seriously. His divisional battery was taken from him to be used on the east bank, and he was to rely for artillery defence on the 15 heavy guns from the arsenal allotted to this front.

(2) On the long stretch of the Canal Royal, from the Garonne to the Albi road—over a mile—only Daricau's division was placed. It had to defend the two bridges and two locks which are the only points in this mile where the passage of the canal was possible. They had not been broken, but had been fortified in the most intensive fashion, with palisaded bridge-heads furnished with artillery, both at the Ponts Jumeaux, the double bridge where the Blagnac road crosses the canal, and at the Minimes

---

[1] *Supplementary Dispatches*, viii. pp. 735-6.

bridge, where the Montauban road passes. At the latter the prominent convent of the Minimes Brothers, just beyond the canal, had been crenellated and entrenched as one outwork. It was garrisoned by a regiment (31st Léger) lent by Darmagnac's division. Behind the canal Daricau had a second line to fall back upon, in the unlikely event of the enemy forcing a passage over the water—viz. the old city wall, on which some guns of position had been mounted, and part of Travot's conscript battalions posted.

(3) From the Montauban road northward, i. e. from the bridge of the Minimes, by which that road crosses the Royal Canal, Darmagnac's division took up the French line, which presently ceased to have the canal in front of it, as it stretched out to join the Mont Rave position, which is beyond that waterway. One of Darmagnac's brigades held the Matabiau bridge and the works constructed in front of it, as also some plantations and enclosures between the bridge and the foot of Mont Rave. The other brigade was in reserve behind the canal, and could support Villatte if necessary.

(4) Continuing the line northward from Darmagnac's front, Villatte's division held the Great Redoubt on Mont Rave and all the northern end of that ridge. At the moment when the action began one of its brigades, that of St. Pol, was on the Pujade knoll, with two guns. But this was only an outpost, destined to be withdrawn so soon as the serious fighting should begin, for Soult's engineer officers had decided that the Pujade was too advanced and too isolated to be held as part of the main position. St. Pol withdrew, to join Lamorandière's brigade in the redoubts, at the first threat of attack by Freire's Spaniards.

(5) The long range of Mont Rave, with the exception of the redoubts at its northern end, was held by Harispe's strong division of 13 battalions. Dauture's brigade was ensconced in the Sypière redoubt and the central lines of entrenchments, Baurot's brigade had charge of the Mas des Augustins and Colombette redoubts, and of the trenches linking them to Villatte's position.

(6) Soult's main mobile reserve was constituted by Taupin's division: this had originally been in St. Cyprien, along with Maransin. But when the entrenchments in the suburb across the water had been completed, Taupin was brought over to the

east bank. When the action commenced his troops were in column behind the centre of Mont Rave, near the Cambon–Saccarin houses, available for support either of Villatte or Harispe.

(7) Travot's conscript battalions were posted at various points on the old city wall, ready to act as supports to the old divisions in front of them.

(8) Of the cavalry much of Berton's brigade was still across the Ers river, facing Vivian's Hussars: it had orders, if driven in, to retire southward, destroying every bridge as it passed. Two regiments, however, were still on the west bank, opposite Somerset's Hussars. Vial's brigade had vedettes out in front of Mont Rave, between the heights and the Ers, but its main body was on the south end of the range, in support of Harispe.

Each infantry division had its usual battery with it, save that Maransin's, being provided with guns of position in St. Cyprien, had sent its field-battery to Mont Rave, where it was in reserve beside the Great Redoubt. The heavy guns from the arsenal were distributed partly in the frontal works along the north side, partly among the bastions of the old city wall.

The main clash of battle was long in coming, since Wellington's divisions had to move up some way before they were in touch with the French positions. The game seems to have commenced opposite St. Cyprien, where Hill, starting at 5 a.m., sent O'Callaghan's brigade to attack the weakest point of the outer lines. This was the mill of Bourassol, on the bank of the Garonne. It was stormed by the 28th and 34th without much trouble, whereupon O'Callaghan's people worked down the back of the French entrenchments as far as the redoubt covering the 'Patte d'Oie' junction of roads: this turning movement caused the evacuation of work after work. Maransin's battalions retreated hastily within the heavily fortified second line; they succeeded in carrying off all their guns save one. Hill sent in Barnes's brigade to support O'Callaghan's and formed a line with them facing the walls and bastions behind which the French had retired. The light companies spent the rest of the day in bickering with the French, from behind the shelter of houses in the outer suburb[1]. No attempt was made to storm—which would

---

[1] There is a good account of this sharpshooting in Sir George Bell's *Memoirs*, i. pp. 165–7.

indeed have been insane. Michael's Portuguese battery, having found good cover, exchanged a slow cannonade with the even better covered French guns. Maxwell's British battery was turned on to a side-issue: being sent down to the Garonne bank, it shelled across the river the flank of Daricau's entrenchments at the Ponts Jumeaux—quite effectively according to French accounts: but Picton's men complained that misdirected shells sometimes fell among them during their assault on that position.

Byng's and Harding's brigades, Le Cor's division, and the Spanish brigade, were all kept in reserve, and suffered no losses. Seeing that Hill did not intend to attack the second line, Soült, before midday, drew off one of Maransin's brigades (Rouget's, about 1,700 bayonets) and sent it over the Garonne to help in the defence of Mont Rave. Only the 2,000 men of Barbot's brigade continued to hold the short line of the inner defences. It looks as if Wellington might equally well have drawn troops from the St. Cyprien front, by bringing them round by the bridge at Seilh. They would have arrived late on the field, but not too late to be useful in the afternoon. Byng and one Portuguese brigade (or even two) could well have been spared from St. Cyprien.

The casualties on Hill's front were almost negligible—50 men in O'Callaghan's brigade, 28 in Barnes's, and 4 Portuguese gunners. Maransin's losses were little if at all greater: there were 12 officer-casualties in the division—probably representing 200 of all ranks—but half of these belonged to Rouget's brigade, which got involved in the fighting on Mont Rave late in the day.

On the east side of the Garonne Picton partly carried out the orders of Wellington that he was to make no attempt with the greater part of his division to press in upon the almost impregnable front of the Royal Canal. Power's Portuguese halted at a discreet distance from the Écluse du Béarnais, the lock in the centre of Daricau's line: Keane's brigade similarly placed itself opposite the convent and bridge of the Minimes: both sent out their light companies, which drove the French outlying pickets over the canal, but did not draw up closer. Turner's battery shelled the bridge-works. But at the right end of his line Picton was tempted to do something more than demonstrate. In front of the Ponts Jumeaux was a large farm with

orchards and outbuildings, called Petit Granague, which the
enemy was holding. Brisbane's brigade was ordered at 7 a.m.
to storm these enclosures; it deployed and did so with some
loss. Having secured cover close in to the bridge-head of Ponts
Jumeaux Picton was seized with the evil inspiration of making
a dash at the main works, the palisaded bridge-head and some
fortified buildings just outside it—the central offices of the canal
administration. The four companies of the 5/60th and the light
companies of the other regiments emerged from their cover and
tried to storm them—naturally to no effect. Brisbane's brigade
then lay down in the farm and enclosures of Petit Granague and
continued for a long time to interchange a dropping fire with the
French in their entrenchments. It would have been well if
Picton had been contented with this first failure—but some
hours later he was to make a second hopeless attempt against
the same position[1].

Alten strictly obeyed Wellington's orders for the Light
Division. It was drawn up half a mile or more outside the
Matabiau bridge-head and sent out its Caçadores to skirmish with
the French outlying pickets, but did no more. Bean's battery,
attached to the division, kept shelling the French works opposite.

The all-important section of the front was of course that
entrusted to Freire and Beresford. Here all went according to
plan for the first hour. After passing Croix d'Orade village the
Spanish general, as ordered, deployed his two rather weak
divisions, 7,300 bayonets in all, in two lines with one brigade
of Marcilla's in reserve. On approaching the Pujade knoll they
were fired on for a few minutes by St. Pol's French brigade,
which gave way, however, without offering serious resistance, and
retreated to join the rest of Villatte's division on Mont Rave.

The Spanish divisions halted to allow of Arentschildt's Portuguese guns[2] being brought up on to the Pujade, in accordance
with Wellington's directions, and then got into position, for the
assault on Mont Rave.

[1] I make out from the diary of Brown of the 45th that there were two
separate assaults, divided by some hours of time. Lapène bears this out
(p. 371), giving 7 a.m. as the hour at which Petit Granague was stormed.
He speaks of *three* attacks.

[2] Preto's six-gun field-battery, and Arriaga's 18-pound heavy guns of
the 'Reserve'—four of them.

Freire set the Portuguese guns playing on the Great Redoubt, and awaited the moment indicated to him for attack—when he should see the 4th and 6th Divisions deploy and ascend the slopes of Mont Rave farther south.

Meanwhile Beresford executed the flank march that had been prescribed; he moved in three parallel columns across the open ground between Mont Rave and the Ers: the advance had to be across rain-sodden ploughed fields, as there is no road running alongside of the river: the only tracks in this region are those going from Toulouse towards the five bridges of the Ers, precisely at right angles to Beresford's prescribed route. The 4th Division led, the 6th followed, in front were Somerset's Hussars, who drove before them small outlying pickets of Berton's and Vial's cavalry, which had been watching the bridges—each of which was blown up before the head of Beresford's column approached it. Somerset's advanced parties were never able to get in touch with Vivian's brigade on the other side of the river, as each bridge went up to the sky before either British force reached it. For the first mile of their march the infantry were quite outside the range of the French guns on Mont Rave, but after they had passed the farm of Falguière the right-hand column—Anson's brigade of the 4th Division, Lambert's of the 6th Division—began to be annoyed by the battery belonging to Harispe's division, which was in or near the Mas des Augustins redoubt[1]. The other two columns, those nearer the Ers, were still out of range but much incommoded by the state of the ground—the fields by the river being very wet, more so even than those along the foot of Mont Rave. The two divisional batteries were particularly slow in progress—the wheels often up to the axles in mud. Beresford finally ordered them to abandon the attempt to keep up with the infantry: they turned off on to a knoll half a mile south of the farm of Montblanc, and opened from thence an uphill fire at the flank of the Great Redoubt above them.

We shall never know whether General Freire took the appear-

---

[1] As far as I can make out the 4th Division marched with Anson's brigade on the right, Vasconcellos's Portuguese in the centre and Ross near the Ers; the 6th Division with Lambert on the right, Douglas's Portuguese in the centre, and Pack next the river.

ance of the British batteries in action beyond Montblanc as a sign that Beresford had reached his appointed position, or whether he had merely grown nervous and impatient at the long delay, and resolved to act for himself. But though two minutes' careful observation would have shown him that the 4th and 6th Divisions were still moving south, and had not wheeled into line, he ordered his troops to deliver their attack in the manner prescribed by Wellington. He therefore left one brigade of Marcilla's division as a reserve on the lower slopes of the Pujade, and formed a fighting front with his other three brigades, two in front line, one in second line[1]. The advance was intended to envelop the whole hill-side about the Great Redoubt, the right-hand battalions being somewhat held back, in order to guard against any counter-attack from the side of the bridge of Matabiau. The Spanish line advanced rapidly and in very good order 'looking as if they intended to do the thing handsomely', as an English onlooker observed. They soon came under very heavy artillery-fire, not only from the redoubts but from more distant guns on the right in the Matabiau positions, but swept on in perfect style, driving in a French skirmishing line. They mounted on the slope of Mont Rave and began to come under infantry fire from the trenches also, but pushed steadily on, though suffering heavy loss, till they came to the cutting of the Peyriolle road, only fifty yards in front of the Great Redoubt. Into this they plunged—it was 20 feet deep in some places—and found for a moment complete shelter both from artillery and from infantry-fire. In a thousand battles attacks have failed when the line of the assailants has found good cover and halted before reaching its objective. This was a clear case of the kind: though many officers tried to hustle their men up the opposite bank and to continue the advance, the bulk of the Spaniards hung back, some climbing the opposite bank and firing over it, but the majority keeping their heads low. The result was fatal: not only did Villatte's infantry come out of their trenches and begin firing down into the mass in the sunken road, but presently the guns by Matabiau started to enfilade the long cutting, on which they had been trained. And finally

[1] All this from Toreno, iii. p. 548, the only comprehensible Spanish narrative.

Darmagnac sallied out from the enclosures near that same bridge, and attacked the flank and rear of the Spanish right with three battalions of the 51st and 75th Line. This was the end of the matter: the three Spanish brigades extricated themselves in confusion from the hollow road, and fled back to the slopes of the Pujade. One regiment of Marcilla's division, Tiradores de Cantabria, held out on the extreme left when all the rest were gone, and had to be recalled by Wellington's own order. He mentions its creditable obstinacy in his dispatch, and the name of its colonel, Leonardo de Sicilia, who was killed—a rare honour from his pen.

The defeat of the Spaniards had no fatal consequences—V. Arentschildt's guns turned their fire against Darmagnac's advance: Manners's heavy dragoons formed up level with the Pujade, the brigades of the Light Division shifted leftward, so as to be on the flank of any counter-attack that Soult might launch. But the Marshal made none. Meanwhile the Spaniards rallied on their own reserve brigade, though it took their officers two hours to hunt them together, and re-form their line.

This was a most regrettable incident—delivered in isolation Freire's attack was bound to fail: he was actually outnumbered by the troops opposed to him, having attacked with eight battalions a similar number of Villatte's entrenched up to the eyes, and helped by three of Darmagnac's[1]. And the ten guns of Arentschildt had to compete with a decidedly larger number, all under cover. It had been intended that the assault on the Great Redoubt should synchronize with Beresford's attack farther up the line. Freire's unhappy error of advancing before the British divisions on his left were ready entailed inevitable defeat. The troops could not be blamed in any way—their task was impossible. John Colborne, who was looking on, said that to tackle that job he would have liked to have two Light Divisions[2]. It is highly to the credit of the Galicians that, at the end of two hours, they had the spirit to deliver another assault, which was pushed farther home than the first, and came within measurable

[1] Total of the Spaniards—Espeleta's division 3,476, one brigade of Marcilla 1,978 = 5,454. Villatte's whole division 4,609, 51st and 75th of Darmagnac 1,519 = 6,128.

[2] *Life of Lord Seaton*, p. 205.

distance of success. But at this second attack they were facing
an enemy whose attention was being drawn off by Beresford's
simultaneous battering on his flank.

While Freire's unhappy venture was in progress Beresford
was still moving southward, looking for the point on which he
had decided to deliver his attack. It would seem from his report
to Wellington[1] that when the Spanish advance was failing, the
commander-in-chief sent him the suggestion to stop his march
and attack uphill at once. He refused. 'I need not apologize to
your lordship for having put in practice your first scheme: the
enemy being posted as he was, I followed the spirit of your
orders in reverting to the first arrangement.' While, therefore,
Freire was suffering his disaster, Beresford's three columns continued to push on, in the continually decreasing space between
the Ers and the heights, till they had reached a position level
with the extreme right of the French entrenchments, the
Sypière redoubt. It was only then that Beresford gave the orders
for both divisions to wheel into line—which produced an order
of battle three lines deep, each consisting of two brigades, the
front and rear lines of British battalions, the central line of
Portuguese. The 4th Division deployed a little quicker than the
6th, so that a sort of advance *en échelon* was produced. Where
Somerset's Hussars were at the moment of the deployment is not
easy to make out—they *ought* according to Wellington's orders
to have been on the left of Cole, protecting his flank. But, so
far as can be made out, they only got into that position some
little time after the line of battle was formed. Possibly they
were merely late from the bad state of the ground—the deep
mud by the Ers was worse even for horses than for men. Possibly
they had been distracted by bickering for the bridges—but this
should not have accounted for all of them.

Soult had, during Freire's attack, called up Taupin's division
from his reserve to the rear of the Great Redoubt, and its
divisional battery also[2]. When the Spaniards had been beaten
off, and Beresford's column was seen still pushing along the
low ground by the Ers, the Marshal directed Taupin to march
along, behind the crest of the heights, till he got level with

---

[1] *Supplementary Dispatches*, viii. p. 740.

[2] Commanded by Lapène, by far the best French narrator of the battle.

Beresford, and then to cross the sky-line and charge downhill against the flank of the long column. Maransin's borrowed battery, hitherto near the Great Redoubt, was also sent south. Oddly enough Taupin's own battery got, in error, no orders to move, but Maransin's was a substitute for it. Taupin was told that Darmagnac's reserve brigade (that lying by the canal) would follow him and act as support, while half Harispe's division (Dauture's brigade) was already in the redoubts against which Beresford was moving[1]. And Vial's cavalry, with that part of Berton's which was east of the Ers, were to push in against the flanks of the advancing British. To replace Taupin's and Darmagnac's troops in general reserve, the Marshal sent to St. Cyprien, and ordered Maransin, who was safe behind his fortified second line, to dispatch one of his two brigades (Rouget's) to take post behind Mont Rave. This small reinforcement of 1,700 bayonets, of course, did not come up for some time.

Taupin's division pushed along the crest of Mont Rave for about a mile, finding (we are told) the ground unpleasantly slippery, and the crossing of the two sunken roads leading to the bridges of Les Bordes and Balma a tiresome hindrance. But it reached the position to the right of the Sypière redoubt, from which it was to operate, with half an hour to spare[2]. The cavalry also got up in good time, but not (apparently) the brigade belonging to Darmagnac, which was to support Taupin's downhill charge.

Cole's division was some way up the slope below the Sypière redoubt, and Clinton's a little in echelon to Cole's right, when Taupin delivered his attack. This courageous but hot-headed general gave the last example during the Peninsular War of the

---

[1] Soult is quite clear in his dispatch as to the fact that he told Taupin 'de se porter au pas de charge sur l'ennemi, de couper sa ligne, et d'enlever tout qui s'était ainsi imprudemment engagé'. And Lapène corroborates as to an offensive downhill being the Marshal's plan (p. 381). It is useless, therefore, for Lemonnier-Delafosse, who wants to exculpate Soult, and to heap all blame on Taupin (p. 295), to say that he personally heard the Marshal tell the general 'se former en bataille en crête du coteau Sypière, d'y attendre l'ennemi, de ne faire feu qu'à dix pas, et croiser la baïonnette pour le reçevoir'—i. e. to adopt a defensive position on the crest, not to charge downhill. Lemonnier actually says that Soult used the words *pas de charge* only for the rate at which Taupin was to march to his destined ground!   [2] Lapène, p. 380.

old French mistake of charging lines with columns, seen already at Maida, Vimiero, Albuera, and other fights, and destined to have its last and most disastrous exhibition at Waterloo. He came over the crest with his two brigades each massed in column of battalions, Rey's on the right, six battalions deep, with the 1/12th Léger in front, Gasquet's on the left, four battalions deep, with the 1/47th Line leading. At the same moment Harispe's troops in the Sypière and Caraman road redoubts opened their musketry-fire, and Maransin's battery began to play against Clinton. These were the only French guns on the spot, as the two redoubts had none, and Taupin's own battery had been forgotten and still lay a mile northward. Meanwhile a regiment of Vial's chasseurs (the 21st) came forward on Gasquet's flank, and six squadrons of Berton's horse on Rey's outer flank.

This looked like a very formidable assault to Lambert's and Anson's brigades, now toiling half-way up the slope. 'Darkening the whole hill, flanked by clouds of cavalry, and covered by the fire of their redoubts, the enemy came down upon us like a torrent, their generals and field-officers riding in front and waving their hats amidst the shouts of multitudes, resembling the roar of the sea[1].' The cavalry attacks looked so dangerous that Pack threw the 79th—on his right flank—into square[2]. On the opposite flank, that of the 4th Division, Berton did not close, for Somerset's Hussars came up just in time, if a little late, and deployed in force on the outer flank of Anson's brigade[3]. Berton naturally held back. Vial's regiment on the other flank apparently got blocked by the deep cutting of the Lavaur road. The whole matter was settled by the infantry, and mainly by Anson's right-hand battalion, the 2nd Provisional, and Lambert's left-hand unit, the 61st Foot.

Far the best account of the clash is given by Lapène of Taupin's division:

'By one of those deplorable errors of which our late campaigns gave too many examples, Taupin, carried away by his

[1] Malcolm's account of Toulouse in Constable's *Memorials*, i. p. 293.

[2] The brigade, as it chanced, was marching left in front, so the 79th was on the right, not the 42nd.

[3] Note by Cooper of the 7th Fusiliers in Ross's brigade, see his Memoir, p. 117.

ardour and the hope of a brilliant success, instead of deploying his brigade on the crest near the Sypière redoubt, advanced with his whole force still in column, the 12th Léger leading, and pushed in that order across the front of the redoubt, whose fire he thus masked. The English, instead of giving the French time to deploy, took up a brusque offensive, and commenced a vigorous fire. Among our massed ranks no ball could fail to find a mark, and we opposed to his front of fire only the insufficient reply of the 1/12th Léger. The men in the rear ranks, seeing comrades fall on every side without being able to retaliate, fell into discouragement. General Taupin, trying to keep up his soldiers' confidence, and to animate them by his personal example, was seen in the forefront of his leading battalion; soon— expiatory victim of his own error—he fell mortally wounded. Rey's brigade wavered—the English continued to advance, and the troops broke and poured back into the Sypière redoubt. Its garrison (9th Léger), seized with an inexplicable panic, abandoned the redoubt the moment that Taupin's troops came pouring past it. The enemy hastened to seize it, and crowned this important position after making but a very small sacrifice of men[1].'

Gasquet's brigade, a little to the left of Rey's, was engaged with Lambert's right-hand battalions while Taupin had been finding disaster and death opposite Anson's right and Lambert's left. It was hardly in serious action when Rey's column broke, whereupon it followed the example, and poured backwards in disorder down the rear slope of Mont Rave towards the secondary position along the canal. Apparently the rout of this unit was partly caused by a shower of Congreve rockets. I do not know how a rocket-party came to be attached to the 6th Division, but as three or four diarists from that unit mention them, there can be no doubt of their presence.

Soult, appalled at the disaster on his right caused by what he calls the 'irresolution' of Taupin's division[2], formed a new line

---

[1] Lapène, p. 385. Lemonnier-Delafosse (p. 298) has a ridiculous story that Taupin, seized with madness, ordered his men to retire and take up another position, and that when he called for 'l'arrière en bataille' the whole ran backwards *ad infinitum*.

[2] Soult to Clarke, printed in *Supplementary Dispatches*, xiv. p. 466.

along the unfinished field-works on the back-slope of Mont Rave, with Menne's brigade (of Darmagnac), which had been intended to join in the late abortive advance, and the rallied remnants of the routed troops from above. To these were soon added Rouget's weak brigade from St. Cyprien, which arrived after a cross-march through the streets of Toulouse, and two batteries, that of Maransin descending from the heights, and Taupin's battery which its commander, left without orders, had brought round from the Great Redoubt on his own initiative[1]. The Marshal expected to see Beresford descend from the crest and attack this position, the Saccarin–Cambon–Bataille entrenchments, which was completely dominated from above.

But no attack developed[2]. Beresford's commanding position was largely impaired by the fact that he had no guns with him —it was artillery which could have made the low-lying French works untenable. He sent back for his two batteries, ordering that they must be brought up at all costs, and reported to Wellington that he could only attack again when the Spaniards were ready for a second advance, and when he had got up his guns. Meanwhile he deployed his troops along the upper slopes of Mont Rave, the 4th Division below the Sypière redoubt, with Somerset's Hussars on its flank, reaching as far as the Corriége farm, facing the upper bridges of the Royal Canal. The 6th Division, formed at an angle *en potence* to the 4th, had its front covered by the deep cutting of the Lavaur road, where it was completely covered from the fire of the French batteries about the Mas des Augustins redoubt. This front was formed by Douglas's Portuguese on the left and Pack on the right: Lambert's brigade was now in reserve.

While Beresford was waiting for his guns, his left wing received a reinforcement. Von Grüben with the 18th Hussars and the K.G.L. Hussars had been making dashes on the other side of the Ers against four bridges in succession. He had been foiled at those of Peyriolle, Balma, and Les Bordes by Berton's rear-guard exploding a mine on each occasion. At the Balma bridge

---

[1] This was Lapène, the chronicler of the battle.

[2] The ingenious Choumara invents one, however, making the 4th Division attack the Bataille works, and be heavily repulsed. Its casualty list shows that this is impossible.

the passage was almost forced; some French squadrons covering it were driven in, and succeeded in retreating over it, but the mine failed, and the Hussars were galloping in, when a desperate French sergeant rode back and refired the fuse just before the first Hanoverians reached the barricade at the bridge-end. But persevering for several miles more, Von Grüben made a final attempt on the bridge of Montaudran, and there succeeded. The bridge, like the rest, was mined, but there was a strong body of French cavalry out in front of it: charging this force, the leading squadron of the K.G.L. regiment not only routed it, but pursued so closely that it passed the bridge by the gap in its barricade of casks, which had been left for the retreating horsemen, and swept away the bridge-guard before it could fire the mine. After this the whole of the brigade crossed the Ers and appeared far out on Beresford's left. Closing in to the battle-field it took position above the Pont des Demoiselles far up the canal, which was guarded by a detachment of Travot's conscript division only. This made Soult anxious for the extreme right of his new position, and was not without effect on his mentality.

There was a clear gap of two hours between Beresford's capture of the Sypière redoubt and his next move forward, which only came when he had received his guns, and had news that Freire was ready to make a new attempt on the north end of the French entrenchments. The only incident which occurred in this interval was an unlucky one. Picton had seen the first defeat of the Spaniards, and drew a wrong deduction from the cessation of the French fire at the south end of Mont Rave. He guessed that it might mean that Beresford also had been repulsed, and determined to distract the enemy by a serious attack on the Ponts Jumeaux. This was absolutely contrary to his orders—Wellington had told him that there was no hope of breaking the enemy's line on the lower end of the canal. Nevertheless soon after 2 o'clock he made three separate assaults on the bridge-head and the fortified buildings beside it, putting in successively all the regiments of Brisbane's brigade, except one wing of the 88th. The attacks were delivered with the old fury of the stormers of Badajoz: some of the men grappled vainly with the palisades of the bridge-head and tried to pull them down by main force. Others, wading into the canal, pushed under the first arch of the nearer bridge. A line of men quite without cover on the bank answered the fire of the well-sheltered French shot for shot. But all was hopeless—the defences could not have been breached save by heavy artillery, and though Picton brought up two field-guns they proved ineffective. The brigade lost in all 354 officers and men, including Forbes, colonel of the 45th, a very distinguished officer, killed, and Brisbane himself wounded. French narratives, and many English ones following them[1], say that Daricau's division lost only about 50 men while repulsing these desperate assaults. This is a complete mistake—the French casualty rolls show 23 officers killed and wounded in Daricau's regiments, including Berlier the brigadier in command at the Ponts Jumeaux. The enfilading fire[2] from Maxwell's battery in St. Cyprien did a good deal of damage, and the troops skirmishing along the canal lost heavily, though those under cover did not. Twenty-three officer-casualties among the French must at least imply not less than 350 casualties of all ranks.

The perversity of Picton's conduct may be judged from the fact that his other two brigades, demonstrating against the lock and bridge farther north, lost respectively 43 men and 37 men, yet were quite as effective in detaining enemies opposite them as Brisbane's unfortunate regiments.

Beresford's artillery only reached him about 2.30 o'clock, having had immense difficulty in climbing the sodden slippery slopes: Daniel's K.G.L. battery had to lend horses to Brandreth's battery for the final tug uphill, and then to wait till all the guns were again together[3]. Beresford planted them below the Sypière, and began to shell the Cambon–Saccarin entrenchments, in order to keep down any idea of a counter-attack from that quarter. It was not very likely to occur, as the intact 4th Division was waiting, high up the slope, ready to take any sally in flank. His own plan was to clear the north end of Mont Rave by an advance of the 6th Division along the crest, synchronizing

---

[1] It was a surprise to me when, working out the Toulouse casualties in Martinien's invaluable work, I found Daricau's division so hard hit. The most curious thing is that the battalion most thinned, the 65th Line, was not at the Ponts Jumeaux.

[2] Lapène, p. 90, says that the enfilading caused 'pertes considérables'.

[3] See Alex. Dickson's report for the Artillery on April 10.

with an attack by the Spaniards on the same objective from the east. For Freire's rallied divisions had been moved to the east side of the Pujade, and were to assail the Great Redoubt and the neighbouring works not frontally, as in the first assault, but laterally.

Before dealing with Beresford's storming of the Mas des Augustins and Colombette redoubts, it is well to dispose of Freire's part of the venture. His second attack was much better managed than the first. Napier slurs it over[1] but other British witnesses testify to its serious nature. 'It was a most gallant heavy and persevering attack', says Harry Smith[2], 'if my dear old Light Division had supported, it would have been successful.' Freire, in desperate earnest, for he had petitioned Wellington to allow his troops to take their full share in the battle that day, was seen leading his front line in person, with a group of mounted officers behind him[3], and the same was the case all down the line. Half the senior officers present were killed or wounded, including the division-commander Espeleta, the two brigadiers Vigo and Carillo, Colonel Ortega the chief staff-officer, and General Mendizabal who had come over the frontier on a visit to Freire, leaving his duties in Biscay, and rode at the side of the corps-commander all day. Freire even made his personal escort, a half-squadron of Hussars of Cantabria, join in the charge. The attack actually got into the French outworks, but could push no farther, and after long bickering in the front trenches the Spaniards recoiled, and came back in great disorder, flooding over the slopes of the Pujade and into the lines of Manners's dragoons and the nearest brigade of the Light Division. They were a spent force for the rest of the day, and only a remnant was properly rallied and in line at evening. But this long, if unlucky, assault had kept Villatte's division fully employed for the afternoon hours, while Beresford was winning the battle half a mile farther south.

Having got up his artillery, and arranged the 4th Division

---

[1] Napier, vi. p. 169. 'They once more attacked partially, and were once more put to flight.'

[2] *Autobiography*, i. p. 176.

[3] This was noticed by Cooke of the 43rd (ii. p. 130). Cf. Toreno, iii. p. 549.

in a position from which it would take in flank any attempt of
the French to counter-attack from the entrenchments along the
canal, Beresford made his final move, which was destined to
sweep along the crest of Mont Rave northward with the whole
6th Division, taking in flank the remaining French redoubts,
which were designed to resist assaults from the north and the
east, but not from the south. The main attack was delivered by
Pack's brigade, with the 42nd and 79th in front line, and the
91st supporting. The brigade had hitherto been in almost complete shelter, under the deep cutting of the Lavaur road, but
came under fire the moment that it went over the top of this
improvised entrenchment. Douglas's Portuguese advanced a
little to the left-rear of Pack's line, so as to cover it from any
attack from the flank. Lambert's brigade was in support of both
Pack and Douglas, well to the rear.

Harispe had got his second brigade (Baurot's)—seven battalions—in hand for the defence of the redoubts. The greater part
of the other brigade (Dauture's) had rolled down the slopes into
the Cambon–Saccarin works, when Taupin's disaster had taken
place. The French general had to make front at right angles to
his original position, owing to the unexpected direction of Beresford's attack. He caused the guns to be drawn out of the Mas
des Augustins redoubt, and placed in the open to its right,
because they no longer faced in the proper direction. He had no
hope of succour from Villatte, who was heavily engaged with the
Spaniards, but apparently relied for assistance on the troops to
the northern end of the Saccarin works—Darmagnac's reserve
brigade, perhaps also on the rest of that division, which lay
hard by, in the direction of the Matabiau defences.

We chance to have three good narratives—sometimes a little
contradictory to each other—of what occurred in the storming
of Harispe's redoubts from soldiers of Pack's brigade, none unfortunately from the ranks of Douglas's Portuguese, and only
one of any value from the French side[1]. The progress of events
seems to have been as follows:

The two Highland regiments stormed the Mas des Augustins

---

[1] Lapène was with Taupin's division, down by the canal: Lemonnier-
Delafosse gives only vague rhetoric. The other narrators were not eyewitnesses.

and Colombette redoubts in one strenuous charge. They had only 800 yards to go, but losses were heavy, particularly in the 42nd, whose colonel wasted some precious moments under fire, in getting his right and left wings into their proper relation to each other—they chanced to have been in reversed order while sheltering in the hollow road[1]. They broke into the redoubts, partly from the trench which connected them, and which had exits into both, partly from the rear of the Colombette, which was not quite closed. The two French battalions holding the works are accused of unsteadiness—they were 'troupes de nouvelle levée' according to Lapène[2]. These, though their names are not given, must have been the 4/116th and 7/117th, which (as their high numbers show) had not belonged to the old Army of Spain[3]. They made little attempt to hold the works. The two Highland regiments then pushed on, clearing the trenches which ran along the hill toward the Great Redoubt. But they had not gone far—they were under heavy artillery-fire—when they were counter-attacked by the 34th, 81st, and 115th of the Line, Harispe's reserve. Being caught in great disorder with a very broken front, the Black Watch were driven back to, and actually through, the Augustins redoubt, whereupon the 79th, in danger of being surrounded in the twin redoubt, retired also. Both regiments had suffered terrible losses—nearing or exceeding 50 per cent. of their total strength[4].

The French effort seemed to have been spent in recovering the redoubts: they made no attempt to pursue, and were themselves soon counter-attacked by the 91st, Pack's reserve battalion, and the 12th Portuguese from Douglas's brigade. Both redoubts were recovered, but not for long, for the French made one last effort with fresh troops[5] and once more got

[1] So Anton, p. 128.

[2] See Lapène, *Toulouse*, p. 92; of 64 officer-casualties in the division, these two battalions had only 3.

[3] So at least says Soult, extenuating the poor resistance.

[4] The Black Watch had 414 casualties out of 750 present, the 79th 214 casualties from a strength of 484.

[5] I am strongly of the opinion that these troops came from Darmagnac's division by the canal. No French source mentions their being in action; but when I note that the division had 41 officer-casualties out of 184 present, I am led to believe that it must have been on Mount Rave. For otherwise the division was hardly engaged. It sent three battalions to aid

possession of them. Beresford then put in the reserve brigade
of the 6th Division, that of Lambert, and after a struggle, which
cost very many casualties, the French broke. The bulk of them
ran down the back-slope of the Mont Rave, to take shelter with
the troops and batteries in the Saccarin–Cambon works. A
fraction, however, fell back on to Villatte's rear in the Great
Redoubt.

This had been a bloody business for both sides—Harispe had
his foot carried away by a cannon-ball about 3.30, Baurot, who
succeeded him in command, was severely wounded a little later.
Of 214 officers in Harispe's division 64 were dead or disabled.
On the other side Pack had been wounded, though he kept on
his horse to the end of the battle, the 6th Division had 1,500
casualties—735 in Pack's brigade, 465 in Lambert's, 315 among
Douglas's Portuguese. This represented a loss of about 33 per cent.
in all[1].

The final departure of the French from in front of the 6th
Division left Villatte's troops in the Great Redoubt in considerable danger of being surrounded. Though they had beaten off
Freire's last attack, they were still nailed to their position by the
fire of the Portuguese guns on the Pujade, which forced them to
keep under cover. And they were now threatened in their rear,
for though the mass of the 6th Division had halted on the line
of the captured redoubts, the skirmishers pushed forward, taking
advantage of dips in the ground. They came up quite close to the
rear of the Great Redoubt, shot nearly all the horses of the
artillery, which were parked behind that work, and killed many
gunners also[2]. To this was added, very soon, a tiresome enfilading

in Freire's first rout, and was then moved, save the 31st Léger, to the
Saccarin position (see Choumara, ii. p. 34). Here it *cannot* have suffered
a loss of nearly one-fourth of its officers, and presumably of over 600 men,
by being merely shelled, while under cover, by Beresford's tardily arriving
guns. I am constrained to believe that Clausel sent up at least one of its
brigades, perhaps part of both, to assist Harispe. In this way only could
such a loss have been incurred.

The two regiments of Baurot's brigade which were not concerned in the
Mas des Augustins fighting, the 10th and 45th Line, were presumably
engaged with Douglas's Portuguese; they suffered as heavily as the rest,
losing 20 officers between them.

[1] One of Lambert's battalions, the 1/32nd, being absent, the division's
total strength was just 5,000.   [2] Lapène, pp. 401–2.

artillery-fire, for Wellington had sent up to Beresford a new
battery—Gardiner's H. A. troop—which unlimbered beside the
Colombette redoubt, and sprayed all the French trenches from
the rear. The Spaniards were visible on the Pujade once more
advancing, though in sadly diminished numbers, and (what was
more serious) one of the brigades of the Light Division was
supporting them.

At about 4.30 or perhaps 5 p.m. Soult sent orders to Villatte
to evacuate his group of works and retire behind the canal,
bringing off his artillery, without awaiting a further attack.
This movement was carried out without much molestation, all
the guns being safely brought away, though most of them had
to be manhandled down the hill, for want of horses. Only when
the enemy had cleared off did Freire's Spaniards climb the slope
and occupy the position, at whose foot their own dead lay so
thick. Villatte's division had got off very cheaply, with only
350 or 400 casualties[1]—the unlucky Spaniards who had been
opposed to them had lost five times as many—so great is the
advantage of cover.

There was still an hour of daylight, and some of the French
officers expected to see an attack developing against the
Bataille–Cambon–Saccarin works, and the bridges of the Royal
Canal[2]. Nothing of the kind happened—for a simple reason.
Artillery preparation would be necessary, and very nearly all
Wellington's batteries on his victorious wing had got to the
bottom of their resources. The Portuguese guns had been firing
since 11 in the morning; Beresford's two divisional batteries had
first kept up a long engagement with the Great Redoubt, from
near Montblanc, and then exhausted the rest of their shot and
shell in the final clash between 2.30 and 5. Their fire began to
slacken even before the Great Redoubt was evacuated—not (as
the French gunners thought)[3] because they had been put out of
action by the counter-fire, but because their limbers were
empty. After 5 o'clock the infantry-fire between the skirmishing
line of the 4th Division and the French in and about the
Bataille works died down also. It flared up again, however, at

---

[1] 21 officer-casualties among 125 present. The divisional losses were
probably almost entirely from artillery-fire.

[2] See Lapène, *Toulouse*, p. 70.   [3] Ibid., p. 97.

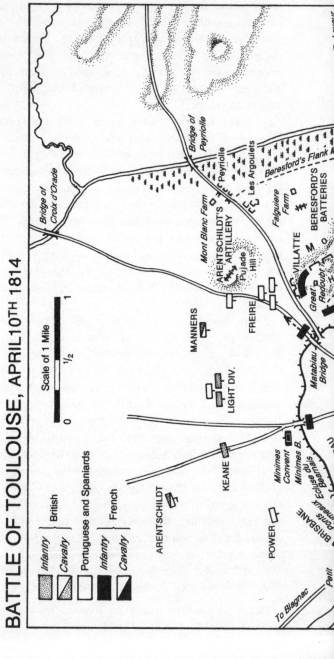

BATTLE OF TOULOUSE, APRIL 10TH 1814

Scale of 1 Mile

British
  Infantry
  Cavalry

Portuguese and Spaniards

French
  Infantry
  Cavalry

ARENTSCHILDT

POWER

KEANE

LIGHT DIV.

MANNERS

FREIRE

Minimes Convent
Minimes B.

BRISBANE

To Blagnac

Petit

Matabiau Bridge

Pont Jumeaux
Écluse du Béarnais

Minimes

Bridge of Croix d'Orade

Bridge of Peyriolle

Mont Blanc Farm

ARENTSCHILDT'S ARTILLERY

Pujade Hill

Peyriolle

Les Argoulets

Beresford's Flank M.

Falguiere Farm

VILLATTE

BERESFORD'S BATTERIES

Great Redoubt

To Lavaur

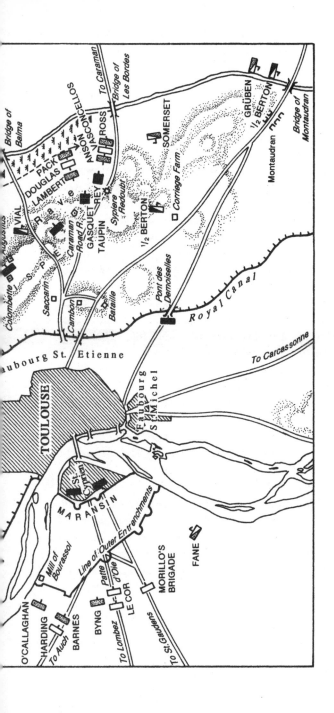

dusk, owing, it is said, to nervous firing on the part of some of Travot's conscript battalions along the canal, which provoked retaliation. But finally all quieted down before the night was far spent.

Both armies slept on their positions, the French behind the line of the canal, but with the Saccarin–Bataille works held as a *tête-de-pont* in front of it, Beresford's and Freire's divisions along the bloodstained heights of Mont Rave. It was generally expected that the struggle would recommence on the next morning. But nothing of the sort happened. To recommence at dawn, Wellington would have had to rearrange his whole front, for the divisions which were opposite the crucial point were precisely those which had suffered heavily in the battle. Of the 4,558 Allied casualties 3,847 belonged to Beresford's and Freire's troops. It would clearly be necessary to relieve them, by bringing up the Light Division, which was intact[1], and the 3rd Division which (despite of Picton's folly at the Ponts Jumeaux) had only lost 444 men out of 4,566. Still more obvious would it be to bring over the Garonne some of Hill's superfluous brigades—for only a small force was needful to block the inner *enceinte* of St. Cyprien.

But in addition to relieving the exhausted divisions on the Mont Rave, it was necessary to replenish the ammunition of the artillery, and this was a long business, the park being on Hill's side of the river. It was well past noon on the 11th before the needed shot and shell were served out. Any serious operations must be deferred to the next day. It is more than doubtful whether Wellington would have attacked frontally on the 12th, if the enemy had held to his position[2]. More probably he would have cut the Carcassonne road by means of his very superior cavalry, and compelled Soult either to allow himself to be besieged (with the memory of Blake at Valencia and similar incidents before him) or to cut his way out by force—always an

---

[1] It had 117 casualties out of 4,275 present under arms.

[2] The best indication of his intentions is his statement in his dispatch of April 12th to Bathurst, 'The army being thus established on three sides of Toulouse, I immediately detached our Light Cavalry to cut the only road practicable for the enemy, till I should be enabled to make arrangements to establish the troops between the Canal and the Garonne.'

expensive game. The Marshal had the same ideas in his head: on the night of the battle he called his chief of the staff Gazan and his three corps-commanders to a council of war, at which it was resolved to evacuate Toulouse after dusk on the 11th, but to hold on till the afternoon in the existing positions, in order to allow all preparations for retreat to be made. Next morning early Soult wrote to the Minister of War[1] that if attacked he would defend himself, but whether attacked or not he must get out of Toulouse that same night. To Suchet he had written on the night of the battle itself, while imploring his colleague to make arrangements for joining their armies, that he could not hope to make any long stay in Toulouse, and might even have to cut his way out. This letter is important as a token of the Marshal's mentality after the battle. He makes no claim to success: 'the fighting has been most bloody: Wellington has suffered great loss, but has won the position on the right side of Toulouse. If attacked again the army will defend itself, but it is impossible to hang on for long. If communications are still open on the 11th further news will be sent.' And the letter of next morning is to the effect that instant retreat is necessary, and that very possibly there will be fighting at the bridge of Baziège where Wellington may try to intercept the army[2].

To the infinite relief of the people of Toulouse, of whom the majority were Royalists and even those who were not Royalists were hoping that the honour of the army would not require their city to stand a bombardment, preparations for evacuation began on the morning of the 11th. And after dark Soult marched out on the Carcassonne road, which was still open, after having filled his soldiers' haversacks, and the caissons of his batteries, and taken off so many of the guns of position as could be horsed. A certain number of pieces, 1,600 non-transportable wounded including three generals[3], and a large store of provisions were abandoned.

---

[1] Soult to Clarke, printed in *Supplementary Dispatches*, xiv. p. 468.

[2] See Soult's two letters to Suchet of the night of the 10th and the morning of the 11th, printed in Choumara, i. p. 166.

[3] Wellington says 1,600—Soult 900. But the Marshal was always a very optimistic statistician—as witness his estimates for his losses at Albuera (iv. p. 395). He 'guessed' 2,000 as his total Toulouse losses.

Next morning at 6 o'clock messages came out from Toulouse from several sources, inviting Wellington to enter without delay, and promising that the city authorities would make their formal adhesion to the cause of Louis XVIII. Of the noisy and delirious jubilation that occurred at his formal entry—much to his surprise and not at all to his gratification—a word will be said in its proper place.

Meanwhile the moral of the battle must be discussed. It was the most difficult tactical problem—with the possible exception of Waterloo—that was ever set before Wellington. Storming an entrenched camp furnished with artillery of position is a very different thing from fighting a battle of manœuvre. Once before, at the battle of the Nive, Wellington had run over, with comparative ease, a strong hill position bristling with redoubts. But at the Nive the French line was fifteen miles long, and it was possible to choose weak points and to concentrate overwhelming forces upon them. At Toulouse the only vulnerable front was the two and a half miles of Mont Rave, and Soult (as was natural) had loaded it with defenders. Four and a half of his six veteran divisions[1] were, first and last, engaged upon its slopes. The attempt to distract the enemy by the demonstrations of Hill, Picton, and the Light Division had not been successful. Only one and a half divisions of the French army were left to hold St. Cyprien and the line of the canal from Matabiau to the Ponts Jumeaux. Beresford's turning movement was successful, but dangerous: a flank march of two miles along the front of an enemy's position had proved ruinous to the French at Salamanca. It was intended to synchronize with Freire's assault on the northern redoubts, but failed to do so, because the Spanish general made his first stroke too early, and before Beresford was in position. It remains a rather inexplicable problem why the storming of the most critical point of the enemy's works was entrusted to the Spaniards, even when we remember that Freire had asked for a responsible share in the venture, and that ever since San Marcial the Galician troops had been fighting very creditably. It would have been much more natural to use Picton

[1] viz. all Taupin's, Harispe's, and Villatte's divisions, all Darmagnac's except the 31st Léger, and Rouget's brigade of Maransin's—not to speak of a brigade of Travot's conscripts.

against the Mont Rave, and to have sent Freire to demonstrate in front of the Ponts Jumeaux, where he could certainly have dealt with the very unlikely chance of a French counter-attack. On the whole one is driven to conclude that Wellington over-estimated the demoralization of the French army, and under-estimated the destructive power of entrenched artillery. That he was not altogether wrong in his calculation as to moral weak-ness in the enemy was shown by the behaviour of Taupin's divi-sion, and of the battalions holding the Sypière and Colombettc redoubts on Mont Rave, which Soult kindly called 'irresolution' and might have called by a less colourless name[1]. One asks oneself why Hill was not made to spare a brigade or two from St. Cyprien. After its outer works had fallen, the enemy, pinched up in the narrow bridge-head, could not possibly have counter-attacked from it. So much did Soult feel this, that he took away before noon nearly half of its defenders, to serve on Mont Rave. It would have required a twelve-mile march by the bridge of Seilh to get troops from Hill's corps to Croix d'Orade— but British soldiers have often fought well after longer tramps than that, and the St. Cyprien outer works had been carried in the very early morning. If at 2.30 there had been three of Hill's brigades behind Wellington's centre, he could have spared the Light Division to assist Freire—in which case the Great Redoubt would have fallen at the same moment that Beresford stormed the Augustins and Colombette redoubts.

French authors have suggested that Wellington need not have attacked the Mont Rave at all[2], but might have marched the greater part of his army along the east bank of the Ers, have crossed that river at the bridge of Montaudran, and then have tackled the problem of the Royal Canal at points a long way out-side Soult's prepared positions, so as to cut the Carcassonne road far out. To this it may be answered that such strategy would have involved complete severance from Hill's corps, and that there is no available road parallel with the Ers till Baziège, twelve miles or more outside Toulouse. The high road Toulouse–Baziège is on the wrong side of the canal.

[1] Sir Lowry Cole told Lord Stanhope that the French fought twice as well at Orthez as at Toulouse.

[2] Especially Choumara, ii. p. 52.

Soult has been criticized for not following up the first rout of
Freire's Spaniards by an attack on the Pujade by Villatte's and
Darmagnac's divisions. This seems a proposition of doubtful
value—the heavy Portuguese batteries on the Pujade, the Light
Division, and the two dragoon brigades were ready for Freire to
rally upon. A more plausible suggestion is that when Beresford
climbed the Sypière slopes he might have been attacked not
merely by Taupin and Harispe, but by Darmagnac's division
from the canal side also. Soult *does* say that one brigade of
Darmagnac's was ordered to follow Taupin—but it was apparently too late. Why the whole division was not warned, and
why none of it was up in time does not appear. Undoubtedly
it would have made Beresford's position much more dangerous
if he had been contending with three divisions instead of two.

A glance at the casualty lists, which are given in full in
Appendix X, shows that the total loss of the Allies was 4,568,
that of the French 3,236. The whole of the difference is explained by the terrible losses of Freire's two divisions, 1,900
men out of 7,800 present—one in four, in causing which their
opponents of Villatte's division, well covered by their trenches
and redoubts, lost only 21 officers and perhaps some 350 men,
taking the proportion at which losses of commissioned to other
ranks stood that day. The only other unit in Wellington's army
which lost heavily was the 6th Division, with its 1,515 casualties
out of 5,600 present. Clinton's men won the day; their casualties
were terrible, but not unrevenged, for in fighting them Harispe's
division lost 64 officers and presumably 1,000 men, and Taupin's
and Darmagnac's divisions the great part of the 69 officers and
over 1,000 men whom they left behind on the hill. These three
divisions between them account for the larger half of the French
casualties—Villatte's and Daricau's had moderate losses—say
350 apiece, Maransin's and the cavalry almost negligible
quantities, perhaps 200 apiece. The casualties among superior
officers were very heavy: Taupin was killed, his brigadier
Gasquet wounded: Harispe lost a foot—his senior brigadier
Baurot a leg: his second brigadier Dauture was also wounded.
Two other brigadiers were hurt—Berlier at the Ponts Jumeaux,
Lamorandière in the Great Redoubt. Among other senior officers
disabled were Colonels Fontenay, chief of the staff of the artillery,

and Morlaincourt who commanded the batteries in the Great Redoubt. There were altogether 16 casualties in the *état-major général*[1].

In Wellington's army no officer of high rank was killed: but Pack, commanding the Scottish, and Douglas commanding the Portuguese brigades of the 6th Division were wounded. So were the Spanish Generals Mendizabal, Espeleta, Vigo, and Carillo. Of the divisions the 4th suffered comparatively moderate losses compared with their comrades of the 6th, only 400 out of 5,300 in the field. The 3rd had no more than 430 casualties, of which 354 were due to Picton's mad attempts on the Ponts Jumeaux. The Light Division lost 110 in all—mostly in skirmishing by the rifles and Caçadores along the canal: the 43rd and 52nd were not engaged. The cavalry with 50 casualties and the artillery with 35 got off easily. Hill's corps lost only 78 men in clearing the outer works of St. Cyprien.

---

[1] I cannot make out why my friend Sir J. Fortescue (*History of the Army*, x. p. 93) accepts Soult's figure of 2,000 for the French losses. They were really 3,236, including no less than 231 officers, whose names may be found in Martinien's lists.

SECTION XLV: CHAPTER IV

END OF THE WAR. APRIL 10-16, 1814

THE last shots in the Peninsular War were not fired till six days after the battle of Toulouse[1]. But the military interest of these final hours of the struggle was small—strategy was dominated by politics from the moment that the news of Napoleon's deposition reached the head-quarters of Soult and of Wellington. Neither of them was aware of the latest happenings at Paris and at Fontainebleau when they fought their last battle, though both had heard of the entry of the Allied troops into the French capital on March 31st. Napoleon's first tentative abdication was not signed till the night of April 4th—his final renunciation of the rights of himself and his whole family not till April 6th: the news had not reached the armies before Toulouse by April 10th. Soult fought the battle because he regarded himself as still responsible to the Emperor, and thought that he had made himself so strong in his entrenchments that he could not be evicted from the best strategical centre and base of operations in Southern France. Wellington attacked because he thought that it was his duty to continue hammering away at the army which was now the best card in Napoleon's hand. He had a notion that the Emperor was such a desperate gambler that he would struggle on as a great guerrilla chief, even after he had lost Paris, and would go down fighting to the last. 'In such a case Soult's army would be the *noyau* for the support of Napoleon's restoration[2].' He thought that he could evict Soult from Toulouse, and that the moral effect of his victory would be to precipitate the general Royalist rising which had been so long delayed, but which at last showed signs of materializing.

In this he was not mistaken. He compelled the Marshal to evacuate Toulouse, and the result was such an outburst of rampant enthusiasm for the cause of the Bourbons in that city that the whole Allied army from the commander-in-chief to the

[1] By Habert at Barcelona, as see p. 430-1.
[2] So Wellington explains things to Sir Charles Stewart, *Correspondence*, xi. p. 646.

youngest subaltern were astonished. The Prefect and the Mayor had fled with Soult, but the Deputy-Mayor Lanneluc, accompanied by practically the whole of the municipal council, was awaiting Wellington at the gates, with a band, the city keys on a velvet cushion, and the Urban Guard drawn up in rank, all with the white cockade, amid a vast assembly of citizens of all classes. Unfortunately Wellington, unaware of these arrangements, entered by another gate[1]—whereupon there was a general rush to the square in front of the 'Capitol', where the ceremony took place. The Deputy-Mayor offered the keys of the city to the victor, not as the conqueror of Toulouse but as the representative of the legitimate King of France, Louis, eighteenth of that name, whose twenty years of suffering in exile had endeared him to his people. And he made his compliments to the general whose justice and moderation during his recent campaigns were unexampled in history, and entitled him to the boundless gratitude of all Frenchmen. Wellington replied, as he had been replying in all cases during the last three months, that he rejoiced to see Toulouse following the example of Bordeaux in shaking off the yoke of a tyrant, and acclaiming its lawful king. The city should be treated as Allied territory, and every consideration paid to its inhabitants. But—and here came the usual note of discouragement—there was the chance that the Allies might make peace with the old government. He could not in that case guarantee immunity and protection after his army had departed. The declaration in favour of the Bourbons was the citizens' own voluntary act, not a policy dictated by himself.'

This would have been chilling comfort but for the fact that the Toulousans were well aware of the Allied entry into Paris, and from their knowledge of the state of public opinion all over Southern France had made up their minds that the Empire was doomed. They refused to be discouraged, declared that Wellington's warning was only another sign of his fairness of mind and scrupulous honesty, and multiplied their demonstrations of hatred for the fallen tyrant. As the Allied staff entered the Capitol the large statue of Napoleon was thrown off the roof and smashed to atoms. Willing hands with chisels or axes hacked off the capital N's from the public buildings, and the

[1] See for an amusing account of the day, Larpent, p. 485.

B's from the cornices. Wellington was escorted to the prefecture, where he was to lodge, by an immense mob of shouting
admirers wearing the white cockade.

At 5 o'clock Colonel Ponsonby rode in from Bordeaux, sent
on by Lord Dalhousie with the news of the abdication of the
Emperor on the 6th: he was to say that the officers bearing
the formal announcement of it would arrive in a few hours. This
brought the delirium of the day to a climax. At a hastily
organized dinner, to which the leading Royalists were invited,
Wellington stood up and drank to the health of Louis XVIII,
committing himself at last to the Royalist cause. General Alava
thereupon sprang up, and among a storm of cheers gave the toast
of 'Wellington—liberator of Spain—of France—of Europe'.
'The Liberator bowed, a little confused, and immediately called
for coffee'—a true instance of his dislike of compliments, noise,
and enthusiasm[1].

A further trial was before him, the magistrates invited him
to a gala performance at the theatre. After the opera of *Richard
Cœur de Lion*—produced at the shortest notice—had been got
through, the old air about Henri IV and his 'triple talent' was
sung in general chorus, and then the *prima donna* warbled a
hymn of triumph containing the following egregious stanzas,
which have survived because General Giron took them down in
his diary[2]. Napoleon was gone at last!

> Ce Corse abominable
> Qui a versé tant de sang,
> Portait le nom d'un diable[3]
> Et le cœur noir d'un tyran.
> Vive l'Europe entière
> Qui nous rend à jamais
> Les Lys—notre bannière—
> Les Bourbons, et LA PAIX.

There was sincerity in the last two words at any rate!

Late at night on the 12th arrived the two officers who were

---

[1] Larpent, p. 487.

[2] For the loan of which I am much obliged to General Dalton, R.A.

[3] This is not a sneer at the name Napoleon as foreign and grotesque, but
a record of the fact that a learned Abbé had discovered that Napoleon was
short for Νέος Ἀπολλύων—the Apollyon of the Book of Revelation!

bringing the news of the Emperor's abdication. Wellington sent them on at once to Soult, with a very laconic note, to the effect that the news which they brought seemed to show that peace was at hand, and that it was desirable that the Marshal should state his intentions, after reading all the documents forwarded.

Soult had evacuated Toulouse on the night of the 11th—the news of the abdication of Napoleon reached Wellington on the evening of the 12th—there was therefore only some twenty-four hours during which both armies moved without reference to the new political developments. On the 11th Wellington had done no more than throw out his light cavalry, Somerset's Hussars and the brigade recently led by Vivian[1], along both sides of the Ers, with orders to reconnoitre all the roads—those to Albi, Caraman, Revel, and Villefranche. No enemy was met, save an isolated party of 25 gèndarmes, which was captured whole by the 1st Hussars K.G.L. Apparently this exploring cavalry returned at evening, since Soult was able to march out by the Carcassonne road after dark. By dawn he was over the dangerous double defile across the bridges of the Royal Canal and the Ers near Bazière. He reports that ten squadrons of light cavalry came to inspect his line of retreat, but did not attempt to meddle with him as he marched on toward Villefranche. But in the afternoon he detected a long infantry column coming down the high road in pursuit of him. This was Hill's corps, which Wellington had pushed through Toulouse on the Carcassonne road, the moment that he learnt that the city was evacuated. Beresford's troops followed later, by another route north of the canal, with orders not to fight save in conjunction with Hill. But Soult was in no mood to stand, and continued his march till at night the head of his column was at Avignonet and the tail at Villefranche. No collision occurred, save that the K.G.L. Hussars cut off a patrol of P. Soult's 10th Chasseurs, and captured 25 men.

It was on the next morning (April 13), while on his march from Villefranche to Castelnaudary, that the Marshal was caught up by the two officers from Paris, whom Wellington had sent on

[1] It is tiresome to have to remember that this brigade, led by Von Grüben on the battle day, had now been given to F. Arentschildt, who was transferred from the K.G.L. heavy brigade.

after him. His only strategical design at this moment was to unite his army with that of Suchet, and he had sent a long and argumentative letter to the Duke of Albufera, inviting him to march with every available man of the Army of Catalonia by the route Perpignan–Quillan and to join him at Carcassonne: they might then get on Wellington's flank upon the upper Garonne, and stop his progress. His colleague, determined as always not to place himself under Soult's orders, replied in a rather sarcastic dispatch. There was no route for wheeled vehicles passing through Quillan, and he could not cut across country, without guns and transport, on mule-tracks. But why unite on the upper Garonne? If, as the Duke of Dalmatia had repeated to him on several occasions, Wellington had a numerical superiority of three to one in infantry, and seven to one in cavalry, their united armies would be so incapable of facing him that they would undoubtedly be driven up into the Pyrenees and starved. Meanwhile Wellington would be in possession of the whole of Languedoc, and would reach out to join the Austrians at Lyons. And the Spaniards from Catalonia, with no army left in front of them, would pour over the mountains and overrun the Mediterranean coast. In the present unhappy situation he could only adopt a strictly defensive policy. After completing the garrison of Perpignan, he would fall back on Narbonne, and then on Béziers. He advised his colleague, if he could not hold out at Carcassonne, to retire on St. Pons: but above all not to get on to the same line of communications as himself: the agglomeration of two independent corps on one route would be inconvenient to a degree[1].

So in 1814, as in 1813, Suchet found good reasons for not linking his fortunes with those of Soult. The fact was that he had a personal dislike for his senior, and was determined not to come under his command. It must be confessed that his objections and criticism, as always, were most plausible. This was by no means the last of the correspondence—the two Marshals continued to argue till the new royal government deposed Soult, and placed Suchet in command of their united armies.

Meanwhile, as has already been noted, two officers from Paris

---

[1] Suchet to Soult, April 12.

had reached Toulouse late on April 12th. These were Colonel Henry Cooke, a British officer attached to the Prussian staff, who had been selected by Charles Stewart as a man of 'weight and experience'[1], and Colonel St. Simon[2], aide-de-camp to Clarke the ex-War Minister, who had served long and well under Suchet down to 1813. They bore letters from Stewart on the one side, and Talleyrand on the other, authenticating their position as envoys, and were charged with copies of the decrees of the Senate deposing the Emperor, and of the Provisional Government assuming charge of affairs. Leaving Paris on the 7th they had heard of the Emperor's definite surrender on the 6th, but seem to have had no proof of it save the *Moniteur* of the day of their departure, which stated that Napoleon had resigned, but did not give the text of his abdication. They would possibly have reached Toulouse in time to prevent the battle if a gendarme officer at Blois had not arrested them, and taken them to Clarke, who was with the court of the Empress Marie Louise in that town. After some delay the ex-minister ordered their release, and wrote on the back of St. Simon's passport that he had no longer any authority to execute any official functions. The envoys had no trouble after Blois, the authorities were recognizing the Provisional Government in every department. But they only reached Toulouse after dinner-time on the 12th.

Wellington, as has been already said, sent them on to Soult that same night, and they were with the Marshal next morning. Quite unexpectedly they met with a rebuff—Soult declared himself not convinced of the authenticity of their credentials, and produced a letter which Clarke had sent him on April 3rd, before the Abdication, which declared that all orders emanating from Paris were to be ignored, the Provisional Government being an illegal assembly. He professed to disbelieve the detailed account of all that had happened since April 3rd, which St. Simon gave him, and was especially shocked by the fact that the acting War Minister of the new government was Dupont—of Baylen fame.

---

[1] Stewart to Wellington. *Supplementary Dispatches*, viii. p. 726.

[2] A descendant of the famous memoir-writer: after service in the Army of Catalonia, he had in 1813 been taken on by Clarke at the War Office. He became a fervent Royalist—as was natural with one who was to inherit the famous duchy.

He definitely refused to acknowledge the provisional régime, till he should have what he considered solid evidence of its legality —e. g. a warrant from the Empress-Regent, or from Berthier as Chief of the General Staff, announcing the Emperor's resignation.

Cooke was sent back to Wellington's head-quarters with the reply that the Duke of Dalmatia was prepared to sign an armistice, which should endure till indubitable evidence of the abdication of Napoleon should arrive, but that he was not ready to acknowledge the Provisional Government, as at present advised. St. Simon was not permitted to return along with Cooke —apparently Soult wished to detain him. But he contrived to get loose, and slipped away to seek Suchet at Perpignan[1]. The younger Marshal, who was well acquainted with him, accepted his evidence without hesitation[2], and declared that he placed himself at the disposition of the new government and of Louis XVIII. He wrote to Wellington asking for an armistice for his army, and to Paris for further orders.

This action of the Duke of Albufera put his senior colleague in an unpleasant position, as had (no doubt) been intended. On receiving Soult's refusal to acknowledge the Provisional Government, Wellington sent him on April 14th a reply to the effect that no armistice would be granted until he had made his submission. The events at Paris were perfectly well known, 'ils ne peuvent être mieux constatés,' and to avoid the danger of civil war it was necessary that the Marshal should make up his mind at once. In an explanatory letter, to Charles Stewart[3] at Paris, Wellington declared that he must take measures at once to bring pressure on Soult, who (as he suspected) wished to keep his army under his own hand for the support of Napoleonic intrigues. In another letter he declared that the Marshal might have to be treated as a rebel, and that he would march against him. And indeed on April 16th the troops of Hill, Beresford, and Freire, halted since the 14th, were ordered to advance again on the Carcassonne road[4].

---

[1] See Vidal de la Blache, ii. p. 505.
[2] Wellington to Soult. *Dispatches*, xi. p. 644.
[3] Wellington to Stewart, April 15. *Dispatches*, xi. p. 646.
[4] Arrangements for the Disposition of the Army. *Supplementary Dispatches*, ix. p. 22.

On April 17th, however, the tension was brought to an end. Soult at last received a dispatch from Berthier, dated at Fontainebleau on April 9th, which formally announced the Emperor's abdication, and the consequent cessation of hostilities in all quarters. There was nothing more to be done, and Gazan, the chief of the staff, went on the same day to Toulouse, and signed an armistice, in which the limits of the territory to be held by the Allied and French armies were defined, on the base of their actual occupation at the moment. The French fortresses besieged or blockaded by the Allies need not surrender, and were authorized to draw in provisions—these were Bayonne, St.-Jean-Pied-du-Port, Navarrenx, Lourdes, and Blaye on the Gironde. The Spanish fortresses still held by French garrisons were to be evacuated without delay, and made over to the Spanish authorities—these were Barcelona, Tortosa, Figueras, Rosas, Murviedro, Peniscola on the Mediterranean side, Venasque in the high Pyrenees, and Santoña on the Biscay coast. In the last-named the governor had been trying for some weeks to surrender, on the terms that his troops might have safe convoy to France—Wellington had always refused, and required that they should be treated as mere prisoners of war[1]. Of all Suchet's fortresses, which had swallowed up so much of his army, it will be noted that only the tiny Denia and Morella, each held by a single company, and Lerida, Monzon, and Mequinenza, captured by the treachery of Van Halen, had fallen into the hands of the Spaniards during the past winter. Copons and Elio, much more interested in the preliminaries of the restoration of Ferdinand VII than in mere military matters, had shown a surprising apathy.

The military chronicle of the Peninsular War should have ended with the arrival of Cooke and St. Simon at Wellington's head-quarters on April 12th, and at Soult's on the following day. Unfortunately it did not—two incidents of a similar sort, but of a very different importance, broke the record. Habert the governor of Barcelona, very loosely blockaded by the Catalans since Clinton's British battalions had been withdrawn, was given to sallies for foraging purposes. He made one on April 16th in the direction of Gracia, was stopped by the old division of Whitting-

[1] See *Wellington Dispatches*, xi. p. 621.

ham[1], and lost 200 men, of whom 30 were prisoners. This was
before the news of the deposition of Napoleon reached him: but
on April 19th secret agents brought him the story of Fontainebleau, and Copons sent to invite him to evacuate. Instead of
opening communication with the besieging force, Habert re-
viewed his troops and made them renew their oaths of military
fidelity to the Emperor. On the 24th he refused to admit into
his fortress the French Colonel Bertrand, who came, wearing
the white cockade, to deliver him a dispatch from General
Lamarque, giving the terms of the armistice of the 17th.
Bertrand came back on the 25th in company with a British
naval officer authorized to make arrangements for the evacuation. On this Habert burst out with such insane rage against
the 'traitor' that his aides-de-camp had to shut him up. It was
only on the 27th that his subordinates persuaded him to treat
with Copons, nor was it till May 28th that, after making all sorts
of difficulties, he marched for France[2].

All this was mere sound and fury, and led to no great loss of
French or Spanish life. But very different, and most bloody,
was the unfortunate sortie from Bayonne on the night of
April 14th, four days after the battle of Toulouse, and eight after
the Emperor's final abdication.

From the day of the departure of Wellington's army for the
Orthez campaign matters had been singularly quiet round
Bayonne, where Thouvenot's garrison of 14,000 men was being
closely blockaded by Sir John Hope and his large but miscellaneous force—the 1st and 5th Divisions, Lord Aylmer's, Campbell's, and Bradford's unattached brigades, and Carlos de España
with two divisions of the Army of Galicia. Wellington had intended that Bayonne should be formally besieged, and had indicated that the proper front of attack would be the citadel on
the north bank of the Adour[3], which, though strong in itself, was
rather isolated—standing just as San Cristobal had stood to

[1] But now no longer under Whittingham, who was commanding at
Saragossa.
[2] For details, see Vidal de la Blache, ii. pp. 58–60. One is naturally
prepared to find Habert commanding a division at Ligny next year.
[3] Wellington to Hope, February 24. *Dispatches*, xi. p. 528. Elaborate
directions as to parallel-digging are sent on March 5th. *Dispatches*, xi.
pp. 550–1, 564.

Badajoz. If the citadel fell the whole low-lying town on the other side of the water was commanded by it and exposed to its fire. Hope, though he prepared to execute Wellington's orders in a rather leisurely fashion, does not seem to have had any great enthusiasm for them. He had formed the conclusion that Thouvenot was very badly off for provisions, and would be starved into surrender at no very distant date[1]. This view—as it chanced —was entirely wrong: though the garrison and the inhabitants were decidedly pinched, and the latter very discontented, there was enough food in the place to last for weeks—or even months. Meanwhile, as so often happened during the last year of the Peninsular War, all was quiet at the outposts. The officers on both sides discouraged 'sniping', and came to a tacit agreement as to where sentinels might be placed. Men working on the outworks of the citadel were not molested, though well within rifle-range of the British trenches, and the French looked on placidly while reliefs took place in the chain of pickets along the front.

Hope's methods were so leisurely that though the battering train allotted to him was ready to move by April 1st, he reported to Wellington on April 10th that he did not intend to 'break ground' before the 27th[2]: no parallel had been dug or batteries begun when the war came to an end. A certain amount of stores had been brought up, and some gabions and fascines made, but that was all. Hope evidently persisted in his idea that Bayonne might be starved ere long. On April 10th he received from Bordeaux complete and detailed news not only of the entry of the Allies into Paris on March 21st, but of the decree of the Senate deposing the Emperor. He might have sent formal notice of these events to the governor, but thought that he had better obtain definite orders to do so from Wellington. The information, however, got into the town, both by private letters smuggled in by the Royalists to friends within, and by notice given at the outposts by several British officers to their 'opposite numbers'.

---

[1] *Supplementary Dispatches*, viii. p. 154. Hope to Wellington, 'I am of opinion that the reduction of Bayonne will be effected almost as soon by blockade as by siege.' Wellington replied, *Dispatches*, viii. p. 591, that he was sure that Hope was wrong.

[2] Hope to Wellington. *Supplementary Dispatches*, viii. p. 737.

The steady trickle of deserters to Hope's lines increased during the next few days—no doubt the news percolated.

Things political being in this position, Thouvenot's entirely passive and unenterprising defence of Bayonne came to an abrupt end on the night of April 14th, when he suddenly flung all the available troops of the garrison in a headlong raid upon the northern side of Hope's line of investment. There can be little doubt that the impelling cause was rage at the news from without—which the governor cannot really have disbelieved. He was in intermittent touch with friends outside, for the blockade was anything but effective, owing to the easy-going way in which both parties behaved at the outposts. And he must have been well aware that the latest news was only too consonant with that which had been arriving for some weeks.

Conviction as to the state of his mentality comes from a consideration of the military aspect of the situation. There was no possible justification for a sortie on the largest possible scale, which could not hope to secure any desirable end, and which might result in irreparable ruin to the garrison.

Sorties from a fortress closely invested may be made, with perfect justification, under four sets of circumstances:

(1) If a governor makes up his mind that his fortress is no longer tenable, but that he has a chance of cutting his way through the enemy's lines and saving all or part of his garrison. This was done successfully by Brennier at Almeida in 1811, and unsuccessfully by Blake at Valencia in January 1812.

(2) If a governor comes to the conclusion that the beleaguering force is so weak that he can hope not only to cut his way out, but to defeat and drive away the main body of the besiegers. Naturally this is not a common condition of affairs—but instances of it may be found: e. g. the great sortie from Gerona on August 16, 1808, which (aided by help from the outside) so broke Duhesme's force that the French general drew his men together and departed. A similar case was Sale's sally from Jelalabad on April 7th, 1842, when the Afghan beleaguering force was not only defeated but driven away entirely.

(3) When the besiegers have opened trenches and constructed batteries, which are beginning to endanger the defence of a fortress, the governor may very properly launch a sortie against

these advanced works, and try to fill in the trenches and spike or carry off the guns. Even if only partial success is gained, the besieger will have lost time, and will be compelled to do his work over again. To this class of sortie belong Philippon's attacks on the British advanced line at the siege of Badajoz, on March 24th, 1812, and Rey's sweeping of the trenches before St. Sebastian on July 26th, 1813.

(4) When a governor finds that he is in danger from the occupation of ground close to his defences, from which attacks may be made upon them with advantage, he is justified in endeavouring to seize this ground and occupy it permanently, taking it into the periphery of his works. This differs from the third class of sortie, because its object is not to get possession of the enemy's trenches for a few minutes and wreck them, but to take up new ground and hold it for tactical reasons. This is not a common case—but there were instances of it during Todleben's defence of Sebastopol, when new works were thrown up in front of the original line of defence.

Thouvenot's sally cannot be placed under any of these four heads. He did not want to escape into the inland with his whole garrison. Nor had he any hope of inflicting such loss on the besiegers that they would be forced to depart. Nor had the siege works begun to grow dangerous: they had not indeed even commenced: not a single gun had been brought up against the citadel, nor were approaches being dug in front of it. And certainly the governor had no intention of taking permanent possession of ground outside the old French lines, for the purpose of improving their contour.

The whole enterprise therefore seems to have been unjustifiable and objectless. It cost the French more men than the besiegers, and had not even the excuse of improving the *morale* of the garrison. One can only echo Colonel Clerc's exclamation, 'What a poor governor! What a pitiable defence! The sortie of April 14th was an affair of *amour propre*, conceived (one may say) on such a plan that it could have no result but the shedding of blood—the loss of a thousand good soldiers[1].'

While there is no reason to criticize Soult for fighting the battle of Toulouse, nor Habert for the Barcelona sally of April

[1] Clerc's *Campagne des Pyrénées*, p. 458.

16th, considering the information that they had at the moment, there is good cause for condemning Thouvenot's sortie. He had nothing to gain by it from the military point of view, while the information which he had received concerning the abdication of the Emperor and the cessation of hostilities elsewhere, might be false, but might be true. If the former were the case, he could have waited for further and more certain information—there was no desperate hurry. But if the news were true—as it was —he made himself responsible for 1,700 wholly unnecessary casualties. For, as Colonel Clerc observes, the sortie was so planned that it could have no beneficial result to the garrison. Wellington, justly indignant, called Thouvenot a blackguard: holding that he was really conscious that the war was ended, and tried to vent his rage by falling on an enemy who had relaxed his precautions because of the complete change in the general situation. It is impossible to know what was in the governor's mind: but it is certain that his futile sortie of April 14th was only of a piece with the rest of his doings. After the armistice he was very stiff: 'I will not have the English treated like demi-gods, as they have been at Bordeaux', he wrote, 'and I have put a stop to the foolish demonstrations which might have taken place here, as in other places: Frenchmen must not make themselves cheap[1].' But it is only fair to say that Colville considered him a 'well intentioned' man, and thought that he might have been egged on by fanatical subordinates[2].

Before dawn on April 14th Thouvenot assembled in and about the citadel Abbé's old division, the fine unit which Soult had left with him contrary to Napoleon's desire[3], and some picked battalions from the rest of the garrison[4]. The whole amounted to nearly 6,000 men out of the 12,000 to which his total strength had been reduced by sickness and desertion since the close investment began. The scheme consisted of a simultaneous advance by three columns, two starting respectively from the northern and north-eastern sides of the citadel works, the third from the suburb of St. Esprit at the bridge-head. The objective

[1] See Vidal de la Blache, ii. p. 510.
[2] Wellington, *Suppl. Disp.*, xix, p. 12.   [3] See above, p. 315.
[4] viz. a battalion each of the 26th, 66th, 70th, 82nd, and 119th Line.

point for all three was the village of St. Étienne, lying at the junction of the Toulouse and Bordeaux *chaussées*, which was the central and most advanced point in the line of investment, and barricaded. What particular profit was to come from the storming of St. Étienne does not appear—there is no sign that it was intended to take the scattered village into the circuit of the defences. Obviously the British could come back and re-establish themselves there at their leisure. Yet 6,000 men were being risked for this paltry advantage.

The investment line this night was held by Bradford's Portuguese on its extreme left, at Hayet on the Adour: the 1st Division continued the line, with the K.G.L. brigade on its left, Stopford's brigade of the Guards in the centre, and Maitland's to the west, facing the Adour below the town, near the hamlet of St. Bernard. But on this day it chanced that Sir John Hope had strengthened the line by bringing over Hay's brigade of the 5th Division from the other side of the water. This does not seem to have been the result of any previous warning as to a projected sortie—for though a French deserter came over that night with full notice of the approaching storm, Hay was already across the river when he arrived. He was the 'general officer of the day' and the pickets of his brigade were holding St. Étienne, with those of Stopford's Guards on their right, and those of Hinüber's Germans on their left. But the bulk of the brigade was left at Le Boucau. For Sir John Hope had an idea that, if a French sortie should occur, it would be aimed at the precious bridge of boats at Le Boucau, and this would have been a far more rational objective than the one which Thouvenot chose. Hence special care had been ordered, Hay's brigade was left near the bridge, and in advance of it the convent, glass-factory, and hamlet of St. Bernard were carefully crenellated and barricaded.

It cannot be said that the besiegers had received no warning, but they were certainly surprised by the strength and suddenness of the French assault. The distance which the enemy had to cover was very short, and he attacked in mass, and in the pitch darkness of a moonless night at 3 a.m.

The eastern column, which started from St. Esprit, completely overran the pickets of the 5th Division in St. Étienne, captured many of them, and stormed one after another most of the barricaded houses of the village. General Hay was killed early, at the village church which he was vainly trying to hold. The only points where the British succeeded in maintaining themselves were one fortified house defended by a party of the 38th, and the walled Jewish cemetery on the Bordeaux road. Some of the French penetrated right through the village, and had cut the investment line in two—though they may not have known it.

On the other flank things went at first quite as badly—the two columns which started from the citadel completely swamped the picket-line of Stopford's brigade—making 84 prisoners from the Coldstream and a good many from the 3rd Guards as well. The French swept right over the sunken road from Le Boucau to St. Étienne, which marked the investment line, and got into touch with their comrades of the eastern column. The bulk of Stopford's brigade, fighting confusedly, was driven in a northerly direction. The guns of the citadel meanwhile played—rather at random—over the roads from Le Boucau, and the flotilla of gunboats on the river dropped down-stream and shelled St. Bernard. But all this fire, though noisy, was not effective.

In the black darkness the French were not very certain what they had done, or what they had still to do—beyond the fact that their sappers started destroying the barricades and crenellated houses in St. Étienne.

The inevitable counter-attack was long in coming, for the British commander-in-chief had disappeared. Three months back Wellington had observed that if Sir John Hope persisted in managing affairs from the front skirmishing line he would get shot. This prediction now came true[1]—with the addition that Hope was taken prisoner also. Riding up furiously from Le Boucau with his staff, he dashed into the hollow road leading on to St. Étienne, from which Stopford's pickets had been driven at the first rush of the enemy. The French fired down from both banks on to the group of horsemen. Hope's charger was killed, he himself wounded in the shoulder and cast down. His two aides-de-camp, Herries and Moore[2], were both hit, while they were trying to disengage him, and all three were taken prisoners.

[1] See above, p. 251.
[2] A nephew of Sir John Moore of Corunna.

There was therefore no general direction during the rest of the fighting.

The responsibility for the counter-attack therefore fell on subordinates, who were out of touch with each other. But they rose to the occasion: on the eastern flank Hinüber of the K.G.L. had his five battalions already under arms, having been warned by the French deserter of whom mention has already been made. This veteran brigade, supported by two battalions of Bradford's Portuguese, came down upon St. Étienne from the flank, and cleared the French out of it as quickly as they had taken it an hour earlier.

On the other side General Howard, finding that Maitland's brigade in the St. Bernard positions had not been molested, drew it out, and, rallying what could still be collected of Stopford's brigade, attacked in flank the disordered French who were still bickering with the party ensconced in the Jewish cemetery. Disturbed by the victorious advance of the German Legion on their right, which was already making itself felt, these battalions gave way, and turned back up the steep paths to the citadel from which they had originally descended. The whole sallying force was now on the run, among obstructions, and in the dark. They were in many places completely jammed together, and suffered terribly from the musketry of the pursuers, before they could disengage themselves and get under cover. Thouvenot in his tardily written report of May 1st stated that the troops had returned in good order, after successfully accomplishing their task. The casualty list gives the best commentary on this—one man in six of the battalions engaged was lost—111 killed, 780 wounded, 16 captured, among them 53 officer-casualties. The British loss was slightly less, though it included 236 prisoners, lost in the first moments when Hay's and Stopford's pickets were cut up and for the most part captured. The rest of the casualty list consisted of 150 killed and 457 wounded, among them 42 officers. Included in this figure were Hope, wounded and captured, Hay killed, and Stopford wounded. The command of the troops before Bayonne fell to Colville of the 5th Division. In his laconic report of the proceedings Colville remarks, with truth, 'The injury done to the defences is as little as could well be supposed in an attack made in such force, and will (I hope) be mostly repaired in the course of one night[1].'

Thouvenot thanked his troops in the name of the Emperor for the courage shown in their successful enterprise, and refused to be shaken in his allegiance when Colville sent him the *Moniteur* and other Paris papers. He replied that only an official order from his superiors would authorize him to conclude a suspension of arms. This did not arrive till April 26th, when Gazan sent him Soult's copy of the armistice of the 17th, and notified his adhesion to the new government. Only then did the tricolour flag come down from the Citadel. The garrison still counted 11,800 men under arms—with several thousand sick and wounded.

Habert's sally from Barcelona, on April 16th, occurred two days after the Bayonne sortie of April 14th, so that Thouvenot did not actually fire the last shot in the war. But there was this difference in their cases that Habert could not have, and Thouvenot certainly did possess, information as to what had happened at Paris on March 31st and April 2nd. The governor of Bayonne made himself responsible for 1,700 casualties for a cause which he knew to be lost, in a sortie which had no military justification, and was the manifestation of mere useless rage.

[1] Colville to Wellington. *Dispatches*, xi. p. 661.

FINIS

THE PLACE OF THE PENINSULAR WAR IN HISTORY

THIS book, being a military history of the Peninsular War, and not a political history of Europe during the Napoleonic Era, comes naturally to an end with the complete execution of the armistice which Wellington concluded with Soult and Suchet on April 17th, 1814. It is not our task to tell of the details of the first Bourbon restoration—of the Duke of Angoulême's triumphal entry into Toulouse, of his reviews of the dejected and malcontent imperial regiments now wearing the white cockade[1], or of the prompt dismissal of Soult, and his super-session by his rival Suchet as commander of their united armies. Nor are we concerned with the pleasant and easy marches of the British to their great concentration camp of Blanquefort near Bordeaux, from which they were shipped off by degrees to England, or in many cases to North America. For there the war of 1812 was still in progress, though its ostensible causes had ceased to exist. The cavalry, by a special agreement with the new Royalist government, were allowed to avoid the long voyage over the Bay of Biscay by riding across the whole length of France, from Toulouse to Boulogne and Calais. This was a wonderful trek for those who took part in it—their memories are full of hospitable chateaux, and of inns where local cham-pagnes cost about a shilling a bottle. Nor need we tell at length of the breaking up of the old Peninsular divisions on their way to Bordeaux, when the faithful Portuguese brigades made their sorrowful adieux to their comrades of the last six years, not without tears and vain hopes of a future meeting[2]. Many in

---

[1] The Duke gave great offence by wearing a quasi-English uniform, and by having as his aides-de-camp émigré officers, like de Guiche, in full British hussar kit. The eagles had a queer appearance, from the imperial birds being muffled up in huge white satin cravats, provided by Suchet in a hurry.

[2] There were very harrowing scenes when Wellington's general order of April 26th directed that all Portuguese and Spanish women attached to soldiers but not married to them 'should be separated from those with

1815 hoped that the meeting would come, when Wellington applied for a Portuguese contingent for the Waterloo campaign. But all was over in Belgium before arrangements had been made in Lisbon.

The only task that remains for us is to estimate the place in the history of Europe, political and military, that belongs to this great struggle, which dragged over seven years from the *Dos Mayo* of 1808 to the Bayonne sortie of April 1814. Surveying the Napoleonic Era as a whole, there can be no doubt that the treachery at Bayonne, and the nomination of Joseph Bonaparte as King of Spain and the Indies was 'the beginning of the end'. It was the Emperor's first great mistake, or at least his first great mistake which the fates refused to pardon. When he began to conceive of himself as the successor of Charlemagne, and to plant out his numerous relatives as feudatory vassals all over Europe, he made the cardinal error of thinking that Spain could be dealt with like Naples, Lucca, or Berg. He argued that a nation sunk in spiritual decay, which had tolerated for twenty years the ignominious rule of Godoy and Queen Maria Luisa, might (when proper military precautions had been taken) receive with acquiescence, or at any rate with apathy, the removal of the decadent Bourbon house and the intrusion of a French dynasty. And herein he erred, not understanding that a proud and ancient nation might tolerate domestic misgovernment, but resent interference from outside. Moreover, that interference was begun with such cynical effrontery[1], and finished with an act of such unparalleled treachery at Bayonne, that a people much less proud and obstinate than the Spaniards must have

whom they have lived', and ordered to return to their homes, escort being provided by troops of their own nationality returning to Portugal or Spain. Colonels were allowed to select 'a few who have proved themselves useful and regular, with a view to their being married to the soldiers to whom they are attached'. But the 'unsettled habits of the majority would prevent them from being entitled to this privilege' [*Supplementary Dispatches*, xiv. pp. 515–16]. There were scores of these poor women, and the scenes at parting were heart-breaking [cf. Surtees, p. 316]. Costello [p. 277] says that some soldiers deserted and surreptitiously followed their girls—like José, in *Carmen*.

[1] I allude, of course, to the treacherous seizure of Pampeluna, Barcelona, and Figueras in February 1808, two months before the disgusting scenes at Bayonne. See vol. i. pp. 36–7.

been goaded into resistance. As the Emperor himself confessed years after, at St. Helena, 'the whole affair was too immoral.'

But once committed to this policy, and compelled for the sake of his prestige in Europe to persist in it to the end, Napoleon had loaded himself with a burden that proved in the end too heavy to be borne. To his high surprise and indignation the struggle began with two military disasters, such as the French arms had never known since he assumed the imperial title—the capitulation of Baylen, where a whole French corps surrendered to the extemporized host of Castaños, and the expulsion of Junot's force from Portugal under the Convention of Cintra. The effect all round Europe was so appalling that he had to take matters in hand himself, and to cut his way to Madrid at the head of the Grand Army. Having scattered the Spanish hosts, and chased Sir John Moore to the borders of Galicia, he left the work of the complete subjection of the Peninsula to his lieutenants. The causes of his departure from an unfinished task were indirectly due to his Spanish entanglements—conspiracy or at least intrigue at Paris, open preparation for war on the Danube—neither of which would have come to a head if Dupont had not been beaten at Baylen and Junot at Vimiero. The old prestige had been shaken.

Though victorious at Eckmühl and at Wagram the Emperor never came back to Spain[1], and without his personal presence in the Peninsula we may safely say that the Spanish war was doomed to drag on interminably. For this there were two causes: the first, and perhaps the more important, was the appearance in Portugal of that 'Sepoy General' whose iron endurance and perfect combination of caution and enterprise was to make the angry Emperor exclaim two years later that it was absurd that 40,000 British troops should spoil the whole affair in Spain[2]. It was not the mere presence of those 40,000 excellent soldiers, but the way in which they were used by their commander that

---

[1] Largely, as we have seen (vol. iii. pp. 198–9), owing to his preoccupation with his divorce and with the Austrian marriage. But partly, also, as he once observed, because Spain was 'too far off', and he disliked the idea of being drawn into a remote corner of Europe, when Russia might begin to give trouble.

[2] See above, vol. v. p. 314.

made the difference—though Napoleon would never confess it, and remarked on the morning of Waterloo that Wellington was a bad general, and the British infantry bad troops!

The second cause of the intolerable lingering on of the Spanish war came from the fact that the French were never able to turn against Wellington the whole of their Peninsular armies, owing to the stubborn tenacity of the Spanish nation. The resistance was ill managed, the politicians who obtained civil power were narrow-minded and factious, the generals with few exceptions were absolutely contemptible as strategists and tacticians, and led to almost unvarying defeat armies which they had failed to inspire with confidence. Yet, in spite of a score of lost battles, the strife dragged on, because the national pride was involved. After years of victorious fighting the armies of Napoleon only possessed in Spain the cities and regions which were held down by an adequate garrison. The moment that a province was left bare of French troops it lapsed into insurrection. Even at the high-water mark of conquest the guerrilleros were making the roads between the most important towns unsafe, and cutting off every detachment or convoy that was too weak to defend itself. It may be true, as Napier says, that without Wellington's army the struggle would some day have come to an end, with the subjection of the last Cantabrian or Catalan insurrectionary bands in the remotest mountain fastnesses. But Wellington was there and the struggle went on.

So the combination of two things—the inexhaustible endurance of Wellington and his army, and the perpetual worry and distraction caused to the French by the spasmodic efforts of the Spaniards—was fatal to the Emperor's scheme. He had 300,000 men in the Peninsula in 1810–11, but could only find 70,000 for Masséna's great invasion of Portugal, which was 'to drive the leopard into the sea'. The rest of his forces were dispersed, as troops of occupation, over provinces which would revolt the moment that their garrisons were concentrated for active service in the field.

After 1811 Napoleon ceased to pour new troops into the Peninsula, as he had been doing ever since Wagram[1]. Spain

---

[1] The last appreciable reinforcement of the army of Spain was by Reille's and Souham's divisions which came over the Pyrenees in the August of 1811.

had ceased to be his main political objective, and was about to become what he called 'the running sore'—the perpetual drain on his strength and energy when he was turning his main attention elsewhere, to the far north.

The final quarrel with Russia was in the main the result of the Emperor's obstinate determination to enforce the 'Continental System' on all Europe, though the eternal Polish question operated as a subsidiary cause. Napoleon was obviously straining too much the resources of his empire—great as they were—when he ventured to launch out on a second great war, while he had already the first one on his hands. The army that marched for Moscow was short of about half its veteran French regiments; they were tied up in Spain[1]. Their place was taken most inefficiently by masses of unwilling auxiliaries—of Rheinbund troops, Croats, and Neapolitans, of Austrians, and Prussians, ready to desert at the first chance, even unhappy Spanish and Portuguese battalions, stolen from their country before 1808, and filled up from prison camps.

It is interesting, but perhaps futile, to speculate as to what might have been the fate of the Russian campaigns of 1812, if Napoleon had been able to use 300,000 more of the best native French troops, instead of the polyglot horde that he had swept together for that great venture. But one thing· is certain—whatever was the case in 1812, it is obvious that the course of the Dresden–Leipzig campaign of 1813 would have been very different, if the 200,000 old French troops still left in the Peninsula had been present on the Elbe. Wellington had expected that Napoleon would evacuate Spain in the spring of 1813, and leave only a covering force on the Pyrenees. The Emperor preferred to maintain the now exploded fiction of his brother's royalty, and drew off to the North less than a third of his Spanish resources. The result of this option was that the Grand Army in Germany had an insufficient stiffening of veteran troops—especially in the cavalry arm—while the force left in Spain was just small enough and just so badly placed, as to justify Wellington's great offensive in the Vittoria campaign —the most brilliant strategical episode of his long career.

---

[1] There were only withdrawn from Spain for the Russian campaign the brigades of the 'Young Guard' and six or seven Polish regiments.

Undoubtedly, then, the Peninsular War was, as events worked out, the direct cause of the loss of Napoleon's prestige for invincibility, and the indirect cause of his downfall in 1813–14. And, if we are to seek for responsibilities, Wellington may well be granted that title of the liberator not only of Spain but of Europe, which was conferred on him by Alava at the celebrated banquet of April 12th at Toulouse, of which we had to tell in the last chapter. For without Wellington and his 40,000 British troops Spain would not have been liberated, nor Napoleon driven to fight his last campaign in Germany with a raw conscript army, which melted away under his hands, and his final campaign in France with forces so reduced that victory was impossible—even against the generalship of Schwarzenberg!

Of the strategical and tactical lessons of the Peninsular War a sufficient account will be found in Section II of Volume I, of this work, where the geography of Spain and Portugal and the tactical problem of line *versus* column, as dealt with by Wellington, are discussed. I have gone into the latter question in even greater detail elsewhere[1], and shown to what extent the general thesis that Wellington beat the column by the skilful use of the line is true, and to what extent it must be qualified by careful study of details. In the main it is true: and the astonishing fact remains that after six years of fighting in the Peninsula the French generals had failed to grasp the lesson. Taupin's charge at Toulouse—a headlong rush with an over-late attempt at deployment—was an exact repetition of the French tactics at Albuera. And at Waterloo D'Erlon, who should have known something about Wellington's methods, played the same game under Napoleon's own eye with a whole army corps of 18,000 men—the largest and most disastrous exhibition of columnar tactics ever seen. The only French officer who saw the psychological moral of such encounters was Bugeaud, whose illuminating paragraphs on the clash of column and line I have quoted at length elsewhere[2].

But Bugeaud was only a *chef de bataillon* in 1814: his superiors had apparently got no farther in drawing general deductions than Soult, who complained of the helplessness in fire-combat of

[1] See 'Column and Line in the Peninsular War', in *Studies of the Napoleonic Wars*, 1929.   [2] See *Wellington's Army*, pp. 90–3.

the French soldier as compared with the British riflemen[1], and
on the morning of Waterloo dared to tell Napoleon that 'l'in-
fanterie Anglaise en duel, c'est le diable', to which the Emperor
made only the brutal response, 'Parce que Wellington vous a
battu, vous le regardez comme un bon général: et, moi, je vous
dis que Wellington est un mauvais général, que les Anglais
sont de mauvaises troupes, et que ce sera l'affaire d'un déjeuner.'
Reille and Foy made, before Waterloo, remarks of much the same
tenor as Soult's, but each of them got no farther from his premisses than the conclusion that it was unwise to attack frontally
an English army settled down into the sort of position that
Wellington would choose for it[2].

Incidentally it is worth while remarking that an enormous
proportion of the French senior officers with whose names we
are familiar in Peninsular records appear in the Waterloo army.
Soult as chief of the staff to the Emperor, Ney commanding the
left wing of the advance, Reille and D'Erlon among the corps
commanders, Milhaud, Lefebvre-Desnouettes, and Pierre Soult,
all entrusted with large cavalry units, we know well. And
among the divisional commanders Marcognet, Girard, Foy,
Quiot, Habert, Barrois had held similar rank in the Peninsula,
while Berton, Vial, Pécheux, Lefol, Vichery, Vinot, had been
brigadiers in Spain. If the Waterloo army did not know how to
deal with the British tactics, it was not from want of experience.
Of the names with which we are most familiar in the campaigns
of 1809–14 Suchet, Masséna, Jourdan, Clausel, Harispe, Decaen,
Merle, Abbé, Maransin, Daricau, Darmagnac, are only missing,
because they were employed elsewhere than in Belgium. Of
all the more notable Peninsular commanders only Marmont
and Victor had retired to Ghent with Louis XVIII[3], Macdonald

---

[1] See Soult to Clarke of September 1813.

[2] Similar blindness is shown by many officers of lower rank, whose
memoirs serve us for studying the war from the French side, but are often
vitiated by reckless anti-British [or anti-Wellingtonian] prejudice, such as
Lemonnier-Delafosse, Lapène, the egregious Choumara, Pelet, Marbot, &c.
Foy's letters are often a useful corrective to this prejudice.

[3] With them the only other personage whom I have had occasion to
mention in these volumes, Donnadieu, the friend and co-conspirator with
Argenton at Oporto in 1809, who was a most furious royalist after three
years in prison under the empire.

and St. Cyr did not emigrate, but steadfastly refused to accept
any office under the restored empire. The great majority
of the others qualified for a place in the *Dictionnaire des
Girouettes*, by their rapid—sometimes shamelessly rapid—transference of allegiance. The fates of these officers who changed
their cockade once too often were varied and curious. To take
extreme examples, Ney ended before a firing-party, condemned
by a vote of the Chamber of Peers in which sat Marmont, Victor,
Kellermann, Latour-Maubourg, Dessolles, Dupont of Baylen
celebrity and other officers familiar in Peninsular annals. Only
a very few other generals shared his ill fortune, none of them (as
it chanced) men who had played any notable part in the Spanish
War[1].

At the other end of the scale Soult, who as Minister of War
for Louis XVIII, had issued bombastic proclamations against
'the usurper and adventurer Napoleon Bonaparte' had figured
three months later as the adventurer's chief of the staff at
Waterloo—a good parallel to Ney's case. Yet he had wriggled
back into favour by 1820, when he received a gift of 200,000
francs from the restored Bourbon, and was decorated with the
Grand Cordon of the Saint Esprit by Charles X in 1825. Under
Louis-Philippe he was to be minister and ambassador, and finally
to appear in state at the Court of St. James's, and to interchange
Peninsular reminiscences with Wellington in 1838. Between the
fate of Ney and the fate of Soult there were many intermediate
degrees of fortune. Some of the old Peninsular generals died in
exile before Louis XVIII had fully resumed the policy of
amnesty. More suffered no further ill than retirement into the
obscurity of private life. But the majority were pardoned after
a time, and resumed a military career. Several of them had the
curious experience of entering Spain in 1823, to restore Ferdinand
VII to liberty, under the command of Moncey, Oudinot, and the
Duke of Angoulême. The contrast to the purpose of their earlier
entry in 1808 is startling. Others took to politics like Foy, whom
Wellington considered more distinguished as a parliamentarian
than as a soldier. Others devoted their declining years to com-
posing memoirs—like St. Cyr and Macdonald. A small remnant

---

[1] Mouton-Duvernet, Chartran, the two Fouchers, Labédoyère—and some
others of less rank. Berton was executed for a later plot.

survived to see the Second Empire' of 1852—as did Jerome Bonaparte once King of Westphalia—and to be honoured as historic antiquities by the nephew of their old master—among them were Marshal Gérard, who had seen Fuentes de Oñoro, and General Flahaut, who had served on Murat's staff in Madrid during the unhappy times of the *Dos Mayo*.

It is a far more depressing record that has to be studied when we turn to the history of Spain after the end of the Peninsular War. The rising against Napoleon had been a generous effort—however ill conducted—and the obstinate perseverance in time of disaster a fine example of national spirit. The Spaniards were rightly proud of it—though their pride sometimes took the absurd form of asserting that they had freed themselves from the oppressor with no very great help from outside. The memory of the 'War of Independence' was very properly inspiring. But, as Toreno writes in the last page of his history, after a period rich in noble deeds, in constancy, and in unselfishness, what a change when we turn to the depressing years that follow! During the reign of the cowardly and unscrupulous Ferdinand VII the two political parties, which had contended with some degree of moderation as long as the war lasted, showed themselves at their worst. One would have felt inclined to sympathize with the Liberals when one reads of Ferdinand's first acts of freakish malevolence. But when they came to power they proved themselves quite as intolerant and unwise as the *Serviles*.

To trace the fortunes of the various Spanish generals with whose names we have grown familiar during the post-war period is a melancholy task. As early as September 1815 Porlier, the great Cantabrian guerrillero chief, led the first Liberal insurrection at Corunna, failed to get support, and was sent to the scaffold. Two years later Luis Lacy, sometime Captain-General of Galicia, put himself at the head of an ill-prepared Liberal rising in Catalonia, was captured by his old comrade Castaños, and sent to be shot in the ditch of the fortress of Palma in Majorca. But in 1820–2 the Liberals came to the top, forced the unwilling Ferdinand to swear fidelity to the Constitution of 1811, and had the pleasure of revenging Porlier and Lacy by executing Elio, the organizer of the royalist *coup d'état* of 1814 in Valencia. In this period of nightmares we find two famous guerrilleros, the Cura Merino (*Servile*) and the Empecinado (Liberal), fighting a battle with 1,000 irregulars a side at Salvatierra in 1821. The Empecinado won, but died on the scaffold a few years later, when the absolutist cause was again in the ascendant, after the Duke of Angoulême's army had crossed the Pyrenees to deliver the King from his ministers. It is astounding to find the bitterest enemies of France during the old war—Eroles, Carlos de España, Eguia, Merino—marching in the French ranks to attack Mina, Henry O'Donnell, and Ballasteros, who were now supposed to be defending the independence of Spain, and failed in their task, because of widespread disaffection among their officers. Only Mina made a good fight against the Bourbon army from beyond the Pyrenees. After the King's restoration Carlos de España earned himself an abominable reputation by wholesale executions in Catalonia: he paid for it long years after, when mutinous soldiers tied a millstone round his neck and threw him into the river Segre. The whole history of Spain from the restoration of Ferdinand to the end of the Carlist War in 1840 is a hideous chaos, depressing to the annalist not only for its wanton bloodshed—the Carlist wars were conducted with a ferocity far exceeding that of the Peninsular War—but from its endless vicissitudes of broken oaths, and of *coups d'état* by military adventurers, which have made the name *Pronunciamiento* odious. Fortunately we need not descant on this wretched period, which made old men sigh for the quiet corrupt days of Charles IV, before the Liberal virus got into the veins of fanatical reformers, or the words Liberty and Constitution had become familiar.

Portuguese civil wars stand to Spanish civil wars much as Portuguese stand to Spanish bull-fights—they are infinitely less distressing to the humanitarian observer. No lurid paragraphs need be written about the end of the régime set up in 1808, by the Lisbon revolution of 1820, and the expulsion of Lord Beresford —who had long outstayed his welcome, though he had re-created a national army. The wars of Miguel and Maria are as far outside our period as those of Carlos and Cristina.

Our story must end with a word as to things nearer home. Undoubtedly the Peninsular War placed Great Britain in a position of political dominance in Europe such as she never enjoyed before or after—neither at the end of the great war against Louis XIV nor at that of the greatest war of all against imperial Germany. Castlereagh and Wellington were more important figures at the Congress of Vienna than even Czar Alexander or Metternich—certainly more dominant than Mr. Lloyd George at Versailles in 1919. The abdication of Fontainebleau had marked the triumph of the policy which Great Britain had consistently pursued, ever since the rupture of the Peace of Amiens. As Pitt had prophesied in his last great public speech, when the news of Trafalgar was still fresh, 'England has saved herself by her exertions, and will (I trust) save Europe by her example.' This was literally true in 1814; not only had Britain served as the nucleus for coalition after coalition against the eternal enemy, but she had produced a general whose career of unbroken victory contrasted marvellously with the record of Austrian, Prussian, and Russian commanders, and an army which had marched in triumph from Torres Vedras to Toulouse. It will not be forgotten that the victory of Vittoria was the immediate cause of the Continental Allies' refusal to treat with Napoleon after the armistice of Plässwitz[1], and showed the way to Leipzig. It was the constancy of Britain, not the snows of Russia, which put an end to the long Napoleonic nightmare.

That Castlereagh and Wellington were happy in all their doings at Vienna no man will assert. They were committed by the alliance-treaties of 1812–13 to many unwise bargains. Their tolerance of the Allies' old-fashioned theory of 'territorial compensations', and blank disregard of national sentiment, proves that they could not read the signs of the times. They hindered some iniquities, but permitted others. Can Great Britain to-day assert that she is fully satisfied with certain things in the way of boundaries in which her statesmen acquiesced at Versailles in 1919? We have at least got rid of the old-world ideas of Legitimism, which had considerable influence at Vienna in 1814–15. But 'Natural Boundaries', so dear to certain continental minds, still survive as an almost equal source of danger far into the twentieth century. And is 'Self-determination' always a happy expedient?

[1] See vol. vi. p. 360.

Triumphant but exhausted, Great Britain had in 1814–15 to face the same problem of post-war economic difficulties that are still troubling her twelve years after the victory of 1918. The ministry which had overthrown Napoleon was destined to endure for many a year of domestic trouble and hard times, with an enormous army to disband, and industries over-stimulated by war-pressure drooping when the pressure was gone.

In this unhappy period Wellington was a dominating figure. If he had died in 1816 he would have been 'felix opportunitate mortis'. By 1830 it was a case of 'omnium consensu capax imperii nisi imperasset'. He turned from war and diplomacy to domestic politics, to become one of the unsuccessful prime ministers of the nineteenth century. In the short space of two years of premiership he proved that the eye which in war could always 'see what was going on upon the other side of the hill' was not able to read the signs of the times in peace. It was his lot to see his own political party break up, to bring England within measurable distance of a revolutionary outbreak, and then to find all the dangers that he had dreaded die away in the earlier years of Queen Victoria. Living to extreme old age, he survived his own unpopularity, and ended as a sort of national monument, a Nestor replete with strange tales of the old times for a worshipping younger generation.

Wellington's two chief lieutenants also died full of years and honours. Graham lived to be ninety-five, an even greater age than was reached by his chief. When the wars were over he relapsed into what he had been before he started on his crusade against the French Revolution in 1793—a Whig country gentleman of sporting tastes, much given to travel. He was a vigorous supporter of the Reform Bill which so much terrified Wellington —it was 'a redress by a liberal government and an enlightened king desirous of doing tardy justice to a loyal people. How can any man, however wedded to time-honoured institutions, stand forth as the advocate of acknowledged abuses?' At seventy-two years of age he was riding over the battle-field of Borodino—at eighty he was much enjoying the Ascot week! But he is mainly, perhaps, remembered as the founder of the Senior United Service Club, established by him (against the opposition of Lord Liverpool and Mr. Huskisson!) as the place where the veteran officer might meet his friends 'instead of being driven to expensive taverns and coffee-houses'.

Hill, unlike Graham, did not quit the service after 1815. He commanded the army of occupation in France for several years, and in 1828 was made commander-in-chief, when Wellington had to give up that office on becoming prime minister. He held the post till 1842, under Tories and Whigs alike, and only resigned it shortly before his death in 1843 at the age of eighty-one. To the last he kept up his old reputation of being the soldiers' friend —his dying words were that he had no enemy in the wide world. This was so even in politics—he voted neither for nor against the Great Reform Bill—though much solicited by the king on one side and Wellington on the other. I have never seen a hard word of 'Daddy Hill' in any of the hundred Peninsular diaries that I have read.

Beresford, whose name occurs so often in these volumes, survived Wellington and Hill, but did not attain to Graham's astounding record, reaching the age of eighty-six and dying in 1854. He stayed too long in Portugal after the war had ended, clinging to his post as commander-in-chief, and bickering continually with the Regency which represented that persistent absentee King John VI. The revolution of 1820 swept him out of power, and he returned to spend a long old age in England— many years of it were occupied in fierce pamphleteering controversy with William Napier, whose history of the Peninsular War had, as one of its minor purposes, the consistent depreciation of everything that Beresford had ever done[1]. The old Marshal was lured into controversy, and his pen was less skilful, if not less vitriolic, than that of the colonel. The result was that his reputation has been unfairly lessened: Wellington regarded him not only as a good organizer, but as a competent second in command[2], and such a verdict must outweigh much criticism.

[1] Napier's vicious feeling may be gathered from a letter of his brother George to Colborne in 1829. 'Beresford abuses William's book finely, and says that he has only two gods, Moore and Buonaparte. William says that he will see that he can have a *devil* as well as gods. The new volume will be ready by the end of spring.'

[2] See *Supplementary Dispatches*, vii. p. 484. Wellington to Bathurst. 'All that I can tell you is that the ablest man I have yet seen with the army, and the one having the largest views is Beresford. He wants decision

Picton, who fell at Waterloo just as his victorious brigades
were thrusting D'Erlon's men downhill—as they had done
before at Vittoria—died a disappointed man. He could never
forget his grievance that Sir John Hope and Stapleton Cotton
had been made peers at the end of the war, while he, whose
exploits was so far more brilliant, was not. 'If coronets were only
to be got on the crown of a breach, I should have as good a
chance as any', he remarked. That he died only a K.C.B. was
undoubtedly the result of the fact that (unlike Hill) he had many
enemies. Wellington did not love him: his rough tongue and his
frequent and flagrant disobedience of orders were the causes.

Of the other Peninsular Generals Pakenham and Ross died like
Picton, but not in the hour of victory—both were 'sniped' by
American riflemen, the one near New Orleans, the other near
Baltimore. Each had been an officer of high promise—but
neither seems to have learnt in Spain the style of fighting required on the other side of the Atlantic—though Ross before his
death had won the brilliant little battle of Bladensburg, and
Pakenham was the victim not so much of his own mistakes as
of those of the meddlesome Admiral Cochrane.

Many of the generals with whose names we are familiar spent
their remaining years of active life in colonial or Indian service.
Colville succeeded Cole as Governor of Mauritius, Leith died as
Governor of Barbados, Whittingham as commander-in-chief in
the Madras Presidency, Brisbane, in far-off Australia, left his
name to the capital city of the future colony of Queensland.
Colborne did most important work in Canada. Stapleton
Cotton—now Lord Combermere—had the satisfaction in his
decorative old age of capturing that formidable Bhurtpore
which had foiled Lord Lake a generation back.

It has often been said that Wellington bred no great school
of generals among his divisional and brigade commanders. This
statement needs modifying—Hill at least was a general of first-
rate merit in independent command. Of the rest he said himself
that they were heroes when under his eye, but children, capable
of terrible lapses into indecision, when he was not present. 'They
wanted this iron hand to guide them.' No doubt the Duke was

when I am not present, but he is the only person capable of conducting
a large concern.'

thinking of incidents such as Beresford at Albuera[1], of Cole and Picton on the Pampeluna road upon July 25th–26th, 1813[2], and of John Murray's six contradictory orders in one morning at Tarragona[3]. For this he was himself in no small degree to blame, since he was averse to the delegation of responsibility, habitually issued orders of a puzzling sort without giving reasons or explanations for them, and visited with the severest censure any unauthorized modification, even when it had turned out profitable. That he took upon himself much work which commanders-in-chief usually delegate to others was no doubt originally the result of his having many incapable subordinates. But it also prevented capable subordinates from displaying their best powers. The only persons whom he trusted with responsibility in important matters were Hill, and his Quarter-Master General Sir George Murray, who transacted some very critical business in 1813–14, and was not rebuked for doing so. It is easy to see the causes of Wellington's jealousy of initiative in his subordinates—when we remember Craufurd's wholly unnecessary combat of the Coa[4], or Picton's criminal disobedience of orders at Toulouse[5]. 'I knew', he said, 'that in my early years in the Peninsula if I were to lose 500 men without the clearest necessity, I should be recalled, and brought upon my knees to the bar of the House of Commons[6].' His system of concentration of command is easily explicable, but its results were not altogether happy. If he taught some of his followers to think and to act, it was the officers in the intermediate ranks, who caught some enthusiasm from his career, not those in higher command.

For the rest, the senior officers of Wellington's army had little opportunity for displaying their talents on a large scale after Waterloo; the long peace from 1815 onward prevented them from having their chance in European warfare. In India and the colonies several of his junior officers made brilliant careers for themselves, but in fighting very different from the old campaigns of 1808–14. When war on a great scale once more commenced, Peninsular training had much to do with the tactics of Chillianwallah, of the Alma, and (for the matter of that) of Colin Camp-

---

[1] See vol. iv. pp. 388–9.   [2] See vol. v. p. 652.
[3] See vol. vi. p. 510.   [4] See vol. iii. p. 258.   [5] See vol. vii. p. 474.
[6] *Wellington's Conversations with Lord Stanhope*, p. 31.

bell's operations in Oude—in all of which officers reared under Wellington had the responsibility of command. In each of these the advance of the long two-deep infantry line was the main inspiration—not always too happily applied. For though the Russian columns of Alma or Inkerman[1] were fair game for troops trained on the old Wellingtonian principles, the Sikhs of 1850 or the Sepoys of 1857–8 were wont to stockade themselves in jungle or in fortified villages, against which a linear array, with simultaneous attack all along a broad front, might not be the appropriate tactics. But the 'thin red line' was a glorious memory, and we cannot wonder that its glamour influenced to the end all those who had seen its ancient triumphs at Talavera, Bussaco, Salamanca, or Waterloo.

[1] Not, of course, that Inkerman was a linear battle, for it was a chaotic skirmish fought in a fog, but its tactical detail was always that of line attacking heavy columns, or disordered masses, of Russians.

THE END

APPENDICES

I

STATISTICS RELATING TO THE SIEGE AND STORM OF ST. SEBASTIAN, AUGUST 31, 1813

(A) STRENGTH OF THE GARRISON, JULY 1, AUGUST 15, AND SEPTEMBER 9, 1810

[From Belmas, iv. pp. 655 and 689.]

	Officers and Men.		
	July 1	August 15	Sept. 9
État-Major	8	10	7
1st Line	219	201	220
22nd Line	464	404	208
34th Line	434	399	224
62nd Line	812	608	308
119th Line	195	178	96
Chasseurs des Montagnes	255	204	74
Details of various regiments	244	220	
Gendarmes	9	8	no
Marines	22	21	return
Spanish Troops	19	18	
Artillery	166	153	75
Engineers and Sappers	252	195	68
Non-combatant services	68	74	97
	3,167	2,693	1,377

N.B.—On August 15, 296 wounded in hospital, on September 8, 481.

It is clear that drafts had been received during the siege on blockade-running vessels—see, e.g., the numbers of the 1st Line on the three days given above. It is known also that the artillery got several small reinforcements. But the figures cannot be ascertained.

(B) BRITISH LOSSES AT THE STORM: AUGUST 31, 1813

		Killed.		Wounded.		Missing.		
		Officers.	Men.	Officers.	Men.	Officers.	Men.	Total.
5th Division:								
Hay's Brigade	3/1st Foot	1	46	5	142	—	—	194
	1/9th Foot	4	47	7	102	—	6	166
	1/38th Foot	4	32	10	86	—	3	135
Robinson's Brigade	1/4th Foot	5	114	6	153	—	3	281
	2/47th Foot	7	88	10	127	—	—	232
	2/59th Foot	8	110	12	222	—	—	352
2 companies, Brunswick Oels		—	2	1	6	1	5	15
Spry's Portuguese Brigade	3rd Line	4	67	10	47	—	—	128
	15th Line	3	101	8	85	—	—	197
	8th Caçadores	1	31	1	49	—	1	83
Total 5th Division		37	638	70	1019	1	18	1,783

| | Killed. | | Wounded. | | Missing. | | |
	Officers.	Men.	Officers.	Men.	Officers.	Men.	Total.
1st Division Volunteers:							
Guards Brigades . .	—	23	3	73	—	23	122
K.G.L. Brigade . . .	—	16	2	35	—	—	53
4th Division Volunteers:							
Ross's Brigade . .	1	6	2	19	—	—	28
Anson's Brigade .	1	14	2	11	—	—	28
Stubbs's Portuguese .	—	13	3	16	—	—	32
Light Division Volunteers:							
Kempt's Brigade .	1	6	2	20	—	—	29
Skerrett's Brigade .	1	4	2	13	—	—	20
Caçadores . . .	—	2	—	5	—	—	7
Bradford's Portuguese { 13th Line .	2	24	4	43	—	—	73
24th Line .	2	45	3	32	—	2	84
5th Caçadores	—	21	1	7	—	—	29
General Staff . . .	—	—	3	—	—	—	3
Artillery	—	3	—	13	—	—	16
Engineers and Sappers .	3	4	3	10	—	—	20
General Total. . .	47	809	100	1,316	1	43	2,376

N.B.—Of whom British 106 officers and 1,590 men, Portuguese 41 officers and 536 men. Note the terrible proportion of killed to wounded.

II

ALLIED CASUALTIES OF AUGUST 31, 1813

BATTLE OF SAN MARCIAL, AND COMBATS OF SALAIN, VERA, AND ZAGARAMURDI

(1) BATTLE OF SAN MARCIAL

| | Killed. | | Wounded. | | Missing. | | |
	Officers.	Men.	Officers.	Men.	Officers.	Men.	Total.
SPANISH LOSS . . .	18	243	81	1,266	5	66	1,679
FRENCH LOSS:							
Lamartinière . . .	12	176	73	1,223	—	159	1,643
Maucune	2	35	11	224	—	43	315
Villatte's Reserve . .	7	69	23	335	1	18	453
Artillery	—	7	—	12	—	—	19
	21	287	107	1,794	1	220	2,430

(2) HEIGHTS OF SALAIN

	Killed. Officers.	Men.	Wounded. Officers.	Men.	Missing. Officers.	Men.	Total.
ALLIED LOSS:							
Inglis's Brigade, 7th Division:							
51st	1	6	11	74	—	—	92
68th	—	9	2	61	—	—	72
1/82nd	1	4	4	59	—	—	68
Chasseurs Britanniques .	—	15	6	23	—	28	72
Miller's Brigade, 4th Division:							
(11th and 23rd Portuguese Line, 7th Caçadores) . .	2	31	5	76	—	14	128
Anson's Brigade, 4th Division:							
3/27th Foot . . .	—	—	—	—	—	1	1
40th Foot . . .	—	1	—	3	—	1	5
2nd Provisional Battalion .	—	3	—	32	—	—	36
Total Allied Loss . .	4	69	28	328	—	44	474
FRENCH LOSS:							
Taupin's Division . .	2	23	9	254	—	128[1]	416
Darmagnac's Division .	2	40	17	344	—	3	406
Total French Loss . .	4	63	26	598	—	131	822

(3) FIGHTING ABOUT VERA

	Killed. Officers.	Men.	Wounded. Officers.	Men.	Missing. Officers.	Men.	Total.
BRITISH LOSS, LIGHT DIVISION:							
1/43rd	—	—	1	—	—	—	1
1/52nd	—	—	—	1	—	—	1
2/95th	1	16	3	39	—	2	61
3/95th	—	2	—	10	—	—	12
Portuguese . . .	—	6	2	12	—	2	22
	1	24	6	62	—	4	97
FRENCH LOSS:							
Vandermaesen's Division .	1	41	5	180	—	4	231

(4) COMBATS OF ZAGARAMURDI AND URDAX

	Killed. Officers.	Men.	Wounded. Officers.	Men.	Missing. Officers.	Men.	Total.
ALLIED LOSS:							
Le Cor's Portuguese of 7th Division . . .	4	15	2	45	—	4	70
Madden's Portuguese of 6th Division . . .	2	64	8	102	—	8	184
Total	6	79	10	147	—	12	254
FRENCH LOSS:							
Abbé's Division . .	3	47	9	265	—	1	325

[1] Believed to be mostly men drowned when recrossing the Bidassoa at night.

	Killed. Officers.	Men.	Wounded. Officers.	Men.	Missing. Officers.	Men.	Total.
GENERAL TOTALS. ALLIES:							
San Marcial	18	243	81	1,266	5	66	1,679
Heights of Salain	4	69	28	328	—	44	474
Combats about Vera	1	24	6	62	—	4	97
Zagaramurdi	6	79	10	147	—	12	254
Undistributable	2	1	1	15	—	—	19
Total	31	416	126	1,818	5	126	2,523
GENERAL TOTALS. FRENCH:							
San Marcial	21	287	107	1,794	1	220	2,430
Heights of Salain	4	63	26	598	—	131	822
Combats about Vera	1	41	5	180	—	4	231
Zagaramurdi	3	47	9	265	—	1	325
Total	29	438	147	2,837	1	536	3,808

III

BRITISH FORCE ON THE EAST COAST OF SPAIN IN THE AUTUMN, RETURN OF AUG. 25, 1813

[N.B.—This return only included corps on the British establishment, and not, therefore, the one Sicilian Infantry Regiment,* the two Sicilian Squadrons,* and the one Sicilian and one Portuguese batteries.* The figures for these are averaged from returns earlier and later than that of August 25, and must be nearly correct.]

		Officers.	Men.	Total.
Cavalry:				
Lord F. Bentinck's Brigade	20th Light Dragoons	15	254	269
	Brunswick Hussars	18	258	276
	Troop of Foreign Hussars	8	80	88
	*Sicilian Cavalry (2 Squadrons)	11	150	161
Total Cavalry		52	742	794
Infantry:				
Adam's 'Advance Guard'	2/27th Foot	23	721	744
	Rifle Company of De Roll	4	93	97
	Rifle Company of 4th K.G.L.	3	85	88
	Calabrese Free Corps	28	551	579
		58	1,450	1,508

		Officers.	Men.	Total.
W. Clinton's Division:				
Brigades of Haviland-Smith and Brooke[1]	1/44th Foot	27	589	616
	1/58th Foot	26	720	746
	2/67th Foot	24	417	441
	4th Line K.G.L. . . .	32	765	797
	1st Italian Levy . . .	35	954	989
	Sicilian* 'Estero' Regiment (2 battalions) . . .	50	1,100	1,150
		194	4,545	4,739
J. Mackenzie's Division:				
Brigades of G. Mackenzie and La Tour	1/10th Foot . . .	36	656	692
	1/27th Foot . . .	23	783	806
	1/81st Foot . . .	38	1,056	1,094
	De Roll-Dillon . . .	27	696	723
	2nd Italian Levy . .	36	921	957
		160	4,112	4,272
Artillery. British [4 batteries] and Siege-Train.		26	512	538
*Portuguese and Sicilian [2 batteries] . .		8	180	188
Engineers		14	106	120
Staff Corps		1	13	14
General Total		513	11,660	12,173

IV

ALLIED LOSSES.   COMBAT OF ORDAL, SEPTEMBER 12–13

	Killed.		Wounded.		Missing.		
	Officers.	Men.	Officers.	Men.	Officers.	Men.	Total.
Staff. . . .	—	—	2	0	—	—	2
2/27th Foot . .	1	31	8	76	1	247	364
Rifle Co., 4th K.G.L.	—	24	2	11	—	—	37
Rifle Co., De Roll's .	1	18	—	9	—	22	50
Calabrese Free Corps .	—	—	1	—	1	50	52
R.A. . . .	—	—	—	—	—	12	12
	2	73	13	96	2	331	517 ⎫ 975
Spaniards (all ranks) .	—	87	—	239	—	132	458 ⎭

N.B.—In the two Rifle companies, the 4th K.G.L. evidently put down their 'missing' as all *dead*, while De Roll did not. The Calabrese entered their dead and wounded as 'missing', all having fallen into the hands of the French, so did the R.A.

[1] Du Plat of 4th K.G.L. sometimes appears as an acting brigadier also. De Roll's and the 81st formed G. Mackenzie's brigade.

COMBAT OF VILLAFRANCA: SEPTEMBER 13

	Killed.		Wounded.		Missing.	
	Offi-cers.	Men.	Offi-cers.	Men.	Men only.	Total.
20th Light Dragoons .	1	6	—	23	6	36
Brunswick Hussars .	1	8	2	24	18	53
Sicilian Horse . .	—	6	—	4	2	12
Foreign Troop of Hussars .	—	1	—	4	—	5
1/10th Foot . . .	—	—	—	3	—	3
1/27th Foot . . .	—	—	—	3	2	5
1/81st Foot . . .	—	2	—	5	6	13
Artillery (Portuguese) .	—	—	1	—	6	7
	2	23	3	66	40	134

V

THE PASSAGE OF THE BIDASSOA, OCTOBER 7, 1813

BRITISH LOSSES

		Killed.		Wounded.		Missing.		
		Offi-cers.	Men.	Offi-cers.	Men.	Offi-cers.	Men.	Total.
1st Division:								
Howard's Brigade	1st Coldstream .	—	2	—	8	—	—	10
	1/3rd Guards .	—	—	—	9	—	2	11
Halkett's Brigade	1st K.G.L. Line.	—	—	—	8	—	—	8
	2nd K.G.L. Line	—	—	1	8	—	—	9
	5th K.G.L. Line.	—	1	—	3	—	—	4
	1st Light K.G.L.	1	6	4	63	—	—	74
	2nd Light K.G.L.	—	4	3	36	—	—	43
5th Division:								
Hay's Brigade	3/1st Foot .	—	1	—	19	—	—	20
	1/9th Foot .	—	8	10	64	—	—	82
	1/38th Foot .	—	1	—	19	—	—	20
Robinson's Brigade	1/4th Foot .	—	—	1	5	—	—	6
	2/47th Foot .	—	—	—	5	—	—	5
	2/59th Foot .	—	—	—	3	—	—	3
Light Division:								
1/43rd Foot . .	.	—	3	—	16	—	—	19
1/52nd Foot . .	.	—	12	6	62	—	—	80
1/95th Rifles . .	.	—	—	—	10	—	—	10
2/95th Rifles . .	.	2	30	6	72	—	1	111
3/95th Rifles . .	.	—	4	1	17	—	—	22
Carried forward	.	3	72	32	427	—	3	537

| | Killed. | | Wounded. | | Missing. | | |
	Offi- cers.	Men.	Offi- cers.	Men.	Offi- cers.	Men.	Total.
Brought forward .	3	72	82	427	—	8	537
Companies of Brunswick Oels attached to 4th Division and 1st Division . . .	—	7	7	18	—	—	32
Ditto, 5/60th . . .	—	—	—	1	—	2	3
Artillery	—	—	—	1	—	—	1
	3	79	39	447	—	5	573
Portuguese[1]	1	47	7	179	—	8	242
	4	126	46	626	—	13	815

SOULT'S ARMY AT THE PASSAGE OF THE BIDASSOA

[Morning State of Oct. 1, 1813.]

1st Division, Foy (8 battalions)	4,654	Detached at St. Jean-Pied-du-Port
2nd Division, Darmagnac (9 battalions)	4,447	In and about Ainhoue
3rd Division, Abbé (8 battalions)	6,051	Front to west of Ainhoue
4th Division, Conroux (9 battalions)	4,962	In and about Sare
5th Division, Maransin (9 battalions)	5,575	In and about Sare
6th Division, Daricau (7 battalions)	4,092	In reserve behind Ainhoue and Sare
7th Division, Maucune (8 battalions)	3,996	Lower Bidassoa as far as Biriatou
8th Division, Taupin (10 battalions)	4,778	Bayonnette and Commissari Works
9th Division, Boyer (12 battalions)	6,515	Urrogne and Bordagain
Villatte's Reserve (17 battalions)	8,018	Serres and Ascain

Total Infantry 53,088

Foy's division was far off the battle-field, and Daricau and Villatte were not engaged, and had no casualties. The cavalry were all in the rear, in the valleys of the Nive and Adour. Deducting Foy, but making an allowance for artillery (very numerous in the fortified works), sappers, train, &c., it would seem that Soult had about 50,000 men available.

[1] From the Light Division, Madden's brigade of the 6th Division, and Wilson's Independent brigade.

FRENCH LOSSES AT PASSAGE OF THE BIDASSOA

	Killed.		Wounded.		Missing.		
	Offi-cers.	Men.	Offi-cers.	Men.	Offi-cers.	Men.	Total.
Reille's Wing:							
Maucune's Division . .	7	40	20	229	1	60	357
Boyer [late Lamartinière] .	1	5	3	88	—	—	97
Foy [detached] . . .	—	—	—	—	—	—	—
Clausel's Centre:							
Conroux's Division . .	1	17	3	69	—	4	94
Maransin's Division [late							
Vandermaesen] . .	1	2	2	16	—	—	21
Taupin's[1] Division . .	3	50	10	287	21	512	883
D'Erlon's Wing:							
Darmagnac's Division .	3	29	4	167	—	—	203
Abbé's[2] Division . .	—	2	1	17	—	—	20
État-Major	—	—	1[3]	—	—	—	1
	16	145	44	873	22	576	1,676

N.B.—Martinien's lists give good cause to suppose that these official figures of Soult's are unsatisfactory. Instead of 1 officer killed and 3 wounded in Conroux's division they show 8, and I cannot conceive that this division, so long engaged against Giron's attack, can have lost only 4 officers and 90 men. If 8 officers were really lost, we may guess at 150 men. Similarly with Boyer's division: Martinien's lists name 8 officers against Soult's 4, and I should suspect that the total casualties should be doubled, as one brigade was well hustled between the Croix des Bouquets and Urrogne. In Maucune's and Taupin's divisions the discrepancies are not so great.

[1] Of the 34 officer-casualties 15 are from the 9th Léger, including many of the prisoners.

[2] 27th Léger alone engaged, it would seem.

[3] Béchaud, General of Brigade.

VI

BATTLE OF THE NIVELLE, NOVEMBER 10, 1813

WELLINGTON'S ARMY ENGAGED IN THE BATTLE OF THE NIVELLE

N.B.—The officers include the regimental paymasters and surgeons.

		Officers.	Men.
1st Division [HOWARD]:			
Maitland's Brigade	1st Guards, 1st Battalion . . .	37	848
	1st Guards, 3rd Battalion . . .	30	765
Stopford's Brigade	1st Coldstream Guards . . .	32	886
	1st 3rd Guards	31	1,093
Hinüber's Brigade	1st Line Battalion, K.G.L. . .	31	627
	2nd Battalion, K.G.L. . . .	25	585
	5th Battalion, K.G.L. . . .	33	549
	1st Light Battalion, K.G.L. . .	32	599
	2nd Light Battalion, K.G.L. . .	28	667
Total		279	6,619
2nd Division [W. STEWART]:			
Walker's Brigade	1/50th Foot	35	459
	1/71st Foot	38	583
	1/92nd Foot	36	495
Byng's Brigade	1/3rd Foot	44	750
	1/57th Foot	44	634
	1st Provisional Battalion[1] . .	53	659
Pringle's Brigade	1/28th Foot	47	686
	2/34th Foot	29	452
	1/39th Foot	38	685
Total		364	5,403
3rd Division [COLVILLE]:			
Brisbane's Brigade	1/45th Foot	40	549
	74th Foot	40	600
	1/88th Foot	38	771
	5/60th Foot[2]	31	615
Keane's Brigade	1/5th Foot	36	708
	2/83rd Foot	30	645
	2/87th Foot	34	466
	94th Foot	31	397
Total		280	4,751

[1] Consisting of four companies each of the 2/31st and 2/66th.

[2] Seven companies of the 5/60th were distributed among other brigades, but their losses are grouped with those of the battalion's head-quarters.

		Officers.	Men.
4th Division [Cole]:			
W. Anson's Brigade	3/27th Foot	44	587
	1/40th Foot	42	615
	1/48th Foot	32	480
	2nd Provisional Battalion [1] . . .	31	536
Ross's Brigade	1/7th Foot	37	663
	20th Foot	36	416
	1/23rd Foot	32	615
Total		254	3,912
5th Division [Hay]:			
Greville's Brigade	3/1st Foot	23	367
	1/9th Foot	35	588
	1/38th Foot	22	421
Robinson's Brigade	1/4th Foot	33	479
	2/47th Foot	31	314
	2/59th Foot	36	439
Total		180	2,608
6th Division [Clinton]:			
Pack's Brigade	1/42nd Foot	42	772
	1/79th Foot	49	662
	1/91st Foot	42	594
Lambert's Brigade	1/11th Foot	37	559
	1/32nd Foot	43	561
	1/39th Foot	37	675
	1/61st Foot	40	538
Total		290	4,361
7th Division [Le Cor]:			
Barnes's Brigade	1/6th Foot	44	838
	3rd Provisional Battalion [2] . . .	37	497
	Brunswick-Oels Chasseurs . . .	42	457
Inglis's Brigade	51st Foot	27	316
	68th Foot	33	398
	1/82nd Foot	32	604
	Chasseurs Britanniques . . .	46	371
Total		261	3,481
Aylmer's Independent Brigade	76th Foot	38	573
	2/84th Foot	36	718
	85th Foot	40	525
Total		114	1,816

[1] 2nd and 2/53rd.
[2] 2/24th and 2/58th.

		Officers.	Men.
Light Division [C. ALTEN]:			
Kempt's Brigade	1/43rd Foot	45	879
	1/95th Foot	31	532
	3/95th Foot	23	327
Colborne's Brigade	1/52nd Foot	42	886
	2/95th Foot	23	503
Total		164	3,127
Total British Infantry		2,186	36,078
Gunners of 5 batteries		28	600

PORTUGUESE

Ashworth's Brigade of 2nd Division (6th & 18th Line & 6th Caçadores)	2,713
Power's Brigade of 3rd Division (9th & 21st Line & 11th Caçadores)	2,303
Vasconcellos's Brigade of 4th Division (11th & 23rd Line & 7th Caçadores)	2,419
De Regoa's Brigade of 5th Division (3rd & 15th Line & 8th Caçadores)	1,765
Douglas's Brigade of 6th Division (8th & 12th Line & 9th Caçadores)	2,067
Doyle's Brigade of 7th Division (7th & 19th Line & 2nd Caçadores)	2,326
Wilson's Independent Brigade (1st & 16th Line & 4th Caçadores)	2,185
Bradford's Independent Brigade (13th & 24th Line & 5th Caçadores)	1,614
Hamilton's division:	
Da Costa's Brigade (4th & 10th Line & 10th Caçadores)	2,558
Buchan's Brigade (2nd & 14th Line)	2,391
Battalions attached to Light Division (17th Line & 1st & 3rd Caçadores)	1,679
Batteries of Arriaga, Cunha Preto, Judice	220
Portuguese Total	24,240

GENERAL TOTAL, ALL RANKS, BRITISH AND PORTUGUESE   .   63,140

Wellington also employed in the battle of the Nivelle Giron's 'Reserve of Andalusia', two divisions, viz.:

	Officers.	Men.	
Virues's Division	152	3,971	(6 battalions)
La Torre's Division	149	3,381	(6 battalions)
and of Freire's 4th Army:			
Morillo's Division	205	4,924	(6 battalions)
Longa's Division	112	2,495	(5 battalions)
Del Barco's Division	226	5,604	(8 battalions)
Barcena's Division	138	4,016	(6 battalions)
	982	24,391	

His total attacking force at the Nivelle was therefore about 88,513 of all three nations.

SOULT'S ARMY AT THE BATTLE OF THE NIVELLE
[Morning States of November 1, 1813.]

N.B. The regiments had one battalion each, save those marked with (2) or (3) after their number.

1st Division. FOY.

| Brigade Fririon: | 6th Léger, 69th (2), 76th Line | } 5,136 |
| Brigade Berlier: | 36th (2), 39th, 65th (2) Line | |

2nd Division. DARMAGNAC.

| Brigade Chassé: | 16th Léger, 8th, 28th (2) Line | } 4,705 |
| Brigade Gruardet: | 51st, 54th, 75th (2) Line | |

3rd Division. ABBÉ.

| Brigade Boivin: | 27th Léger, 63rd, 64th (2) Line | } 6,326 |
| Brigade Maucomble: | 5th Léger, 94th (2), 95th Line | |

4th Division. CONROUX.

| Brigade Rey: | 12th Léger (2), 32nd (2), 43rd (2) Line | } 5,399 |
| Brigade Baurot: | 45th, 55th, 58th Line | |

5th Division. MARANSIN.

| Brigade Barbot: | 4th Léger, 34th, 40th (2), 50th Line. | } 5,579 |
| Brigade Rouget: | 27th, 59th, 130th (2) Line | |

6th Division. DARICAU.

| Brigade St. Pol: | 21st Léger, 24th, 96th Line | } 5,782 |
| Brigade Mocquery: | 28th Léger, 100th, 103rd Line | |

7th Division. LEVAL.

| Brigade Pinoteau: | 17th Léger, 3rd, 15th Line | } 4,539 |
| Brigade Montfort: | 16th Léger (2), 101st, 105th (2) Line | |

8th Division. TAUPIN.

| Brigade Béchaud: | 9th Léger (2), 26th, 47th (2) Line | } 4,889 |
| Brigade Dein: | 31st Léger (3), 70th, 88th Line | |

9th Division. BOYER.

| Brigade Boyer: | 2nd Léger (2), 32nd (2), 43rd (2) Line | } 6,569 |
| Brigade Gauthier: | 120th (3), 122nd (2) Line | |

Reserve. VILLATTE.

Brigade Jamin: 34th Léger (2), 66th, 82nd, 115th (2) Line
Spanish Brigade (4), Italian Brigade (3), German Brigade (4)   } 8,319
Artillery, 97 guns, Sappers, État-Major, Gendarmérie and Train, say   4,200

TOTAL IN THE FIELD 61,443

Cavalry, all cantoned in the rear 6,788
Garrison of Bayonne 4,633

BRITISH AND PORTUGUESE LOSSES AT THE NIVELLE: NOVEMBER 10, 1813

	Killed.		Wounded.		Missing.		
	Offi-cers.	Men.	Offi-cers.	Men.	Offi-cers.	Men.	Total.
1st Division (HOWARD):							
Maitland's and Stopford's Brigades of the Guards . .	—	—	1	9	—	—	10
Hinüber's K.G.L. Brigade							
1st & 2nd Light Batts. .	—	17	3	89	—	—	109
1st, 2nd, 5th Line Batts. .	1	11	2	55	—	5	74
Total 1st Division . .	1	28	6	153	—	5	193
2nd Division (W. STEWART):							
Walker's Brigade							
1/50th, 1/71st, 1/92nd · .	—	—	—	—	—	—	—
Byng's Brigade							
1/3rd Foot . . .	—	3	1	8	—	—	12
1/57th Foot . . .	2	5	5	50	—	—	62
1st Provisional Batt. (2/31st, & 2/66th) . . .	—	6	3	45	—	—	54
Pringle's Brigade							
1/28th, 2/34th, 1/39th .	—	2	—	9	—	1	12
Ashworth's Portuguese							
6th Caçadores, 6th & 8th Line	—	2	1	8	—	—	11
Total 2nd Division . .	2	18	10	120	—	1	151
3rd Division (COLVILLE)							
Brisbane's Brigade							
1/45th, 5/60th, 74th, 88th .	1	7	3	58	—	2	71[1]
Keane's Brigade							
1/5th	—	15	2	109	1	3	130
2/83rd	—	7	4	36	—	—	47
2/87th	1	14	5	83	—	—	103
94th	1	10	2	60	—	2	75
Power's Portuguese							
11th Caçadores 9th & 21st Line	1	24	4	55	—	6	90
Total 3rd Division .	4	77	20	401	1	13	518

[1] Nearly all these casualties were from companies of the 5/60th detached to other divisions.

	Killed.		Wounded.		Missing.		
	Officers.	Men.	Officers.	Men.	Officers.	Men.	Total.
4th Division (COLE):							
Anson's Brigade							
3/27th Foot . . .	1	9	3	51	1	—	65
1/40th Foot . . .	1	15	6	80	—	—	102
1/48th Foot . . .	—	7	4	57	—	3	71
2nd Provisional Batt. (2nd & 53rd) . .	—	5	1	47	—	—	53
Ross's Brigade							
1/7th, 20th, 2/53rd . .	—	3	1	20	—	—	24
Vasconcellos's Portuguese							
7th Caçadores, 11th & 23rd Line	2	4	4	13	—	1	24
Total 4th Division . .	4	43	19	268	1	4	339
5th Division (HAY):							
Greville's Brigade							
3/1st, 1/9th, 1/38th, 2/47th .	—	3	3	10	—	—	16
Robinson's Brigade							
1/44th, 2/49th, 2/59th .	—	1	—	2	—	—	3
De Regoa's Portuguese							
8th Caçadores, 3rd & 15th Line	—	9	1	9	—	—	19
Total 5th Division . .	—	13	4	21	—	—	38
6th Division (CLINTON):							
Lambert's Brigade							
1/11th Foot . . .	—	3	1	8	—	—	12
1/32nd Foot . . .	1	5	1	43	—	—	50
1/36th Foot . . .	—	5	6	37	—	—	48
1/61st Foot . . .	2	5	5	37	—	—	49
Pack's Brigade							
1/42nd, 1/79th, 1/91st .	1	4	3	36	—	—	44
Douglas's Portuguese							
9th Caçadores, 9th & 12th Line	2	15	1	41	—	—	59
Total 6th Division . .	6	37	17	202	—	—	262
7th Division (LE COR):							
Inglis's Brigade							
51st Foot . . .	2	14	2	73	1	—	92
68th Foot . . .	2	6	6	34	—	—	48
1/82nd Foot . .	—	9	6	58	—	16	89
Chasseurs Britanniques .	—	2	1	13	—	3	19
Carried forward .	4	31	15	178	1	19	248

	Killed.		Wounded.		Missing.		
	Offi-cers.	Men.	Offi-cers.	Men.	Offi-cers.	Men.	Total.
Brought forward .	4	31	15	178	1	19	248
Barnes's Brigade							
1/6th, 3rd Provisional (2/24th, 2/58th) and Brunswick Oels	1	15	6	53	—	14	89
Doyle's Portuguese							
2nd Caçadores, 7th & 19th Line	1	6	1	16	—	2	26
Total 7th Division . .	6	52	22	247	1	35	363
Light Division							
Kempt's Brigade							
1/43rd Foot . . .	2	6	9	60	—	—	77
1/95th Foot . . .	—	6	4	42	—	—	52
3/95th Foot . . .	—	—	2	8	—	—	10
Colborne's Brigade							
1/52nd Foot . . .	—	32	6	202	—	—	240
2/95th Foot . . .	—	1	4	26	—	3	34
Portuguese Attached							
1st & 3rd Caçadores and 17th Line	3	7	3	23	—	2	38
Total Light Division .	5	52	28	361	—	5	451
Hamilton's Portuguese Division:							
R. Campbell's Brigade							
10th Caçadores, 4th & 10th Line	—	26	11	53	—	—	90
Buchan's Brigade							
2nd & 14th Line . .	2	11	2	12	—	6	33
Divisional Total . .	2	37	13	65	—	6	123
Lord Aylmer's Unattached Brigade							
76th, 2/84th, 85th . .	1	2	—	19	—	—	22
Bradford's Portuguese Brigade							
5th Caçadores, 13th & 24th Line	—	—	—	—	—	—	—
Wilson's Portuguese Brigade							
4th Caçadores, 1st & 16th Line	—	7	—	11	—	—	18
General Staff . . .	—	—	5	—	—	—	5
Royal Artillery . . .	—	6	1	34	—	—	41
Royal Engineers . . .	1	—	—	—	—	—	1
13th Light Dragoons . .	—	—	—	1	—	—	1

	Killed.		Wounded.		Missing.		
	Offi-cers.	Men.	Offi-cers.	Men.	Offi-cers.	Men.	Total.
General Totals.							
Hill's Corps:							
2nd Division . . .	2	18	10	120	—	1	151
6th Division	6	37	17	202	—	—	262
Hamilton's Division . .	2	37	13	65	—	6	123
	10	92	40	387	—	7	536
Beresford's Corps:							
3rd Division	4	77	20	401	1	13	518
4th Division	4	43	19	268	1	4	339
7th Division	6	52	22	247	1	35	363
Light Division . . .	5	52	28	361	—	5	451
Bradford's Portuguese . .	—	—	—	—	—	—	—
	19	224	89	1,277	3	57	1,669
Hope's Corps:							
1st Division	1	28	6	153	—	5	193
5th Division	—	13	4	21	—	—	38
Wilson's Portuguese . .	—	7	—	11	—	—	18
Lord Aylmer's Brigade . .	1	2	—	19	—	—	22
	2	50	10	204	—	5	271
Staff R.A. and R.E. . . .	1	6	6	35	—	—	48
GENERAL TOTAL . .	32	372	145	1,903	4	69	2,526

Spanish loss. No returns, but approximately Army of Galicia and Longa 200 (Daricau and Villatte who opposed them lost 190—neither side exposed itself). Giron, 200 [never seriously engaged]; Morillo, 20 [practically not engaged]; Andrade's Brigade at Maya 400 [double Foy's loss]. Total something like 820 all told.

FRENCH LOSSES AT THE NIVELLE: NOVEMBER 10, 1813

	Killed.		Wounded.		Missing.		
	Offi-cers.	Men.	Offi-cers.	Men.	Offi-cers.	Men.	Total.
État-Major . . .	2	—	6	—	—	—	8
Divisions:							
Conroux	8	63	19	510	7	390	997
Maransin . . .	14	143	32	568	7	253	1,017
Taupin	2	66	12	363	16	482	941
Darmagnac . . .	5	30	8	332	1	31	407
Abbé	1	5	7	149	3	34	199
Daricau	2	16	1	79	—	—	98
Boyer	1	25	7	156	—	—	189
Leval	—	21	7	86	—	—	114
Foy	1	27	9	183	—	—	220
Villatte's Reserve .	1	14	5	72	—	—	92
Artillery . . .	—	4	—	26	—	9	39
	37	414	113	2,524	34	1,199	4,321

The test by comparison of officer-casualties with the invaluable lists of Martinien suggests that these figures are not quite complete for the unlucky regiments of Clausel's command in the centre. Conroux has 40 officer-casualties in Martinien against 27 shown in the statistics above—Maransin 53 against 46, Taupin 21 against 14. It is certain, however, that some of the prisoners shown in the official table were also wounded—but we know that *all* were not: e. g., the 1/88th surrendered *en masse* at the Signals Redoubt with 14 officers and about 350 men intact. I should surmise, therefore, that the understatement in the table above is not more than 15 officers' names or so, and adding 'other ranks' casualties this would only mean a deficiency of 250 or 300 in the total loss. It seems incredible that Abbé's division should have had only *six* killed to 156 wounded. Perhaps its 'missing' include some dead men.

VII

BATTLES OF THE NIVE, DECEMBER 9–13

BRITISH AND PORTUGUESE LOSSES

DECEMBER 9

(1) Passage of the Nive by Hill's Corps.

	Killed.		Wounded.		Missing.		
	Offi-cers.	Men.	Offi-cers.	Men.	Offi-cers.	Men.	Total.
2nd Division:							
Pringle's Brigade . .	—	9	1	57	—	—	67
Barnes's Brigade . .	—	—	—	6	—	—	6
Attached Companies 5/60th	—	—	1	13	—	—	14
6th Division:							
Pack's Brigade . .	2	5	2	44	—	1	54
Lambert's Brigade .	—	3	3	28	—	2	36
Douglas's Portuguese .	1	15	10	87	—	4	117
	3	32	17	235	—	7	294

(2) Combats of Anglet and Bassussary. Hope's Corps and Light Division.

Staff	—	—	3	—	—	—	3
1st Division:							
Howard's Brigade . .	—	5	—	28	—	—	33
K.G.L. Brigade . .	—	5	4	61	—	—	70
5th Division :							
Greville's Brigade . .	—	7	3	64	—	4	78
Robinson's Brigade .	—	15	11	80	—	2	108
Light Division . . .	—	3	—	30	—	1	34
Detached Companies, Brunswick-Oels . . .	—	2	—	1	—	1	4
Artillery . . .	—	1	—	5	—	—	6
	—	38	21	269	—	8	336

DECEMBER 10

		Killed.		Wounded.		Missing.		
		Officers.	Men.	Officers.	Men.	Officers.	Men.	Total.

(3) Combat of Arcangues, Light Division.

		Off.	Men.	Off.	Men.	Off.	Men.	Total.
Kempt's Brigade	1/43rd . .	—	—	—	11	—	21	32
	1/95th . .	1	4	—	17	1	19	42
	3/95th . .	—	1	—	22	—	—	23
Colborne's Brigade	1/52nd . .	—	2	3	15	—	6	26
	2/95th . .	—	—	—	3	—	12	15
Portuguese	1st Caçadores	1	7	4	34	—	3	49
	3rd Caçadores	1	8	2	13	—	2	26
	17th Line .	—	—	—	2	—	9	11
		3	22	9	117	1	72	224

(4) First Combat of Barrouillet, Hope's Corps.

BRITISH:

		Off.	Men.	Off.	Men.	Off.	Men.	Total.
General Staff . .		—	—	3	—	—	—	3
5th Division.								
Greville's Brigade	3/1st Foot .	—	1	1	30	1	12	45
	1/9th Foot .	2	10	4	65	—	—	81
	1/38th Foot .	—	6	—	37	—	—	43
Robinson's Brigade	1/4th Foot .	—	6	3	45	—	2	56
	2/47th Foot .	—	12	2	50	1	50	115
	2/59th Foot .	—	6	2	56	—	10	74
	2/84th Foot .	1	16	2	54	3	18	94
Attached Companies, of Brunswick-Oels . .		—	—	1	2	—	—	3
Lord Aylmer's Brigade	2/62nd Foot .	—	—	—	1	—	—	1
	76th Foot .	—	1	—	15	—	—	16
	85th Foot .	—	1	1	11	—	—	13
Artillery . . .		—	—	—	6	—	—	6
Total British . .		3	59	19	372	5	92	550

PORTUGUESE (Including also losses on December 11).

		Off.	Men.	Off.	Men.	Off.	Men.	Total.
De Regoa's Brigade 5th Division	3rd Line .	2	26	6	70	—	—	104
	15th Line .	—	19	4	26	—	85	134
	8th Caçadores	—	4	3	16	1	10	34
A. Campbell's Brigade	1st Line .	2	6	13	93	1	25	140
	16th Line .	1	8	1	35	4	103	152
	4th Caçadores	1	17	5	9	1	9	42
Bradford's Brigade	13th Line .	—	21	1	32	—	46	100
	24th Line .	3	21	2	56	—	36	118
	5th Caçadores	2	20	4	81	1	15	123
Total Portuguese .		11	142	39	418	8	329	947
GENERAL TOTAL Barrouillet		14	201	58	790	13	421	1,497

DECEMBER 11

	Killed Offi-cers.	Killed Men.	Wounded Offi-cers.	Wounded Men.	Missing Offi-cers.	Missing Men.	Total.
(5) Second Combats of Barrouillet and Arcangues.							
Greville's Brigade . .	—	16	2	91	—	10	119
Robinson's Brigade . .	1	14	11	172	—	3	201
Brunswick-Oels . .	—	1	1	1	—	—	3
Light Division . . .	—	—	—	5	—	—	5
	1	31	14	269	—	13	328

DECEMBER 12

	Killed Offi-cers.	Killed Men.	Wounded Offi-cers.	Wounded Men.	Missing Offi-cers.	Missing Men.	Total.
(6) Third Combat of Barrouillet, and cavalry fight at Hasparren.							
Guards Brigades 1st Division	3	24	5	154	—	—	186
Artillery	—	1	—	7	—	—	8
5/60th	—	1	—	5	—	—	6
14th Light Dragoons (Hasparren) . . .	—	—	—	3	2	2	7
	3	26	5	169	2	2	207

DECEMBER 13

(7) Battle of St. Pierre (details in separate table).

	Killed Offi-cers.	Killed Men.	Wounded Offi-cers.	Wounded Men.	Missing Offi-cers.	Missing Men.	Total.
	17	340	88	1,276	2	52	1,775

Adding the seven separate items we get the total for December 9th–13th of

	Offi-cers.	Men.	Offi-cers.	Men.	Offi-cers.	Men.	Total.
Dec. 9. Crossing the Nive	3	32	17	235	—	7	294
Dec. 9. Anglet-Bassussary	—	38	21	269	—	8	336
Dec. 10. Barrouillet . .	14	201	58	790	13	421	1,497
Dec. 10. Arcangues . .	3	22	9	117	1	72	224
Dec. 11. Combats on .	1	31	14	269	—	13	328
Dec. 12. Combats on .	3	26	5	169	2	2	207
Dec. 13. St. Pierre . .	17	340	88	1,276	2	52	1,775
	41	690	212	3,125	18	575	4,662

This total does not, unfortunately, tally with Wellington's figures sent in with his Nive dispatch, which are

	32	618	233	3,674	17	473	5,047

Nor do the details tally—those which we have extracted above from regimental returns at the Record Office give:

BRITISH	19	261	126	2,038	10	197	2,651
PORTUGUESE . . .	22	429	86	1,085	8	378	2,009

While Wellington's figures are:

BRITISH	19	260	129	2,055	9	201	2,673
PORTUGUESE . . .	13	358	104	1,619	8	272	2,374

It certainly looks as if the Portuguese total for wounded was far too low in the figures which Beresford's staff drew up, some time after the battle.

In both the English and the French returns the proportion of killed to wounded was 7 or 8 to 1, instead of the 2½ to 1 which the Portuguese returns show. I am inclined to believe that in Beresford's return the lightly wounded who had got back to the ranks are omitted, while some 80 of the badly wounded had died, and got into the 'killed column'. There are also 100 more prisoners than Wellington's account allows for. These considerations may account for some of the deficit in Portuguese wounded, but apparently not for all. And I should guess that it would be safer to take 4,900 as the complete total, not the 4,660 arrived at from the figures of the regimental returns.

BRITISH LOSSES AT ST. PIERRE D'IRRUBE: DECEMBER 13, 1813

	Killed.		Wounded.		Missing.		
	Offi-cers.	Men.	Offi-cers.	Men.	Offi-cers.	Men.	Total.
2nd Division:							
Barnes's Brigade — 1/50th Foot .	—	20	11	91	—	8.	130
1/71st Foot .	3	7	6	96	—	10	122
1/92nd Foot .	3	28	10	143	—	1	185
Byng's Brigade — 1/3rd Foot .	—	3	10	73	—	—	86
1/57th Foot .	3	8	4	113	—	—	128
1st Provisional (1/31st & 2/66th)	—	10	3	94	1	—	108
Pringle's Brigade — 1/28th Foot .	—	6	4	91	—	—	101
2/34th Foot .	—	—	—	5	—	—	5
1/39th Foot .	—	1	1	15	—	1	18
Attached Companies of 5/60th	—	—	1	18	1	1	21
	9	83	50	739	2	21	904
Ashworth's 6th Line .	1	51	8	132	—	7	199
Portuguese 18th Line .	3	52	4	112	—	11	182
Brigade 8th Caçadores .	—	39	3	48	—	—	90
Le Cor's Division:							
Da Costa's 2nd Line .	—	19	—	29	—	6	54
Brigade 14th Line .	2	52	4	68	—	7	133
Buchan's 4th Line .	—	19	3	46	—	—	68
10th Line .	2	18	3	45	—	—	68
Brigade 10th Caçadores.	—	9	6	29	—	—	44
	8	259	31	519	—	31	838
General Staff . . .	—	—	7	—	—	—	7
British Artillery . . .	—	1	—	4	—	—	5
Portuguese Artillery . .	—	—	—	6	—	—	6
6th Division troops (9th Caça-dores)	—	2	1	12	—	—	15
	17	345	88	1,280	2	52	1,784

SOULT'S ARMY AT THE BATTLES OF THE NIVE
(DECEMBER 9-13, 1813)

[Morning State of December 1, 1813.]

1st Division Foy [composition exactly as at the Nivelle] . .	5,608
2nd Division DARMAGNAC [has received 2 batts. of 31st Léger from dissolved 8th Division]	5,914
3rd Division ABBÉ [Baurot had replaced Boivin as brigadier; composition exactly as at the Nivelle]	6,372
4th Division TAUPIN [vice Conroux killed]. Ditto . . .	6,098
5th Division MARANSIN [composition exactly as at the Nivelle] .	5,216
6th Division DARICAU [has exchanged 24th Line for 119th Line] .	5,519
7th Division LEVAL [vice Maucune] composition unchanged . .	4,704
8th Division. Dissolved after the Nivelle.	
9th Division BOYER [has received 24th Line, and 118th (3) Line, but surrendered 32nd and 43rd]	6,423
Reserve VILLATTE [has lost its Italian brigade, and 115th Line but has received the 9th Léger from the dissolved 8th Division] .	5,397
Brigade PARIS 10th (2), 81st (2), 114th, 117th, also 115th (2), taken from Villatte's Reserve	3,881
Garrison of Bayonne [increased by wrecks of dissolved 8th Division]	8,801
Artillery Sappers and train [90 guns], say	2,000
TOTAL	65,933
Cavalry all cantoned to the rear save 6 squadrons. (Sparre)	7,788

FRENCH LOSSES AT THE NIVE BATTLES
December 9-13, 1813, dated December 19.

Soult's official report to the Minister dated December 19th gives the following casualty list:

	Officers.	Other Ranks.	Total.
Killed . . .	31	482	513
Wounded . . .	222	4,613	4,835
Prisoners . . .	11	279	290
Missing . . .	—	276	276
	264	5,650	5,914

This does not quite tally with the list of divisional losses, which comes to a trifle more—viz.:

Foy's Division . . .	903		Daricau's Division . .	869
Leval's Division . .	395˙		Taupin's Division . .	197
Boyer's Division . .	1,149		Maransin's Division . .	299
Darmagnac's Division .	778		Villatte's Division . .	48
Abbé's Division . .	1,276		Artillery	33
			Total . .	5,947

Sir John Fortescue's estimate of the French total at 5,650 looks like Soult's first list with the officers omitted—the 'other ranks' there are just 5,650. And I note that both Clerc and Dumas quote the 5,914 figure, which is probably correct.

Martinien's *Liste des Officiers tués et blessés*, always useful and sometimes invaluable, seems a little incomplete for this period—e.g. he gives no casualties of the 95th Line, which was heavily engaged on December 13th. His figures are:

	December 9–12.		December 13.	
	Killed.	*Wounded.*	*Killed.*	*Wounded.*
Foy	5	22	1	22
Leval	4	11	—	—
Boyer	3	26	—	—
Darmagnac . . .	—	—	1	18
Abbé	—	—	3	56
Daricau	2	7	6	31
Taupin	—	5	—	2
Maransin	—	2	1	8
Villatte	—	5	—	—
Staff, Artillery, &c. . .	—	2	2	10
	14	80	14	147

Total for 9th–13th is 28 killed and 227 wounded, which agrees fairly well with Soult's 31 killed and 222 wounded.

VIII

TOTAL FORCE OF THE FRENCH EAST-COAST ARMIES AT THE END OF 1813

[After the departure of the Italian and the Disarmament of the German Troops.]

Field-Army:

1st Division, Musnier	3,561 of all ranks.	Head-quarters Granollers.
2nd Division, Harispe[1]	3,073 ,, ,,	Head-quarters Molins de Rey
3rd Division, Habert	3,975 ,, ,,	Head-quarters San Boy.
4th Division, M. Mathieu[2]	2,373 ,, ,,	Head-quarters San Celoni.
5th Division, Lamarque	4,205 ,, ,,	Head-quarters Gerona.
Cavalry, 5 regiments	2,501 ,, ,,	{ 3 regiments near Barcelona. { 2 in Northern Catalonia.
Artillery, sappers, train	3,000 ,, ,,	
	22,688	

[1] Pannetier got the division when Harispe went to join Soult's army.

[2] Maurice Mathieu's division, really over 5,000 strong, figures here for only 2,373, because some of its battalions were at the moment in Barcelona, where they are counted with the garrison, as given lower down.

Brought forward   22,688
Garrisons of Valencia
    and Aragon:
[Lerida, Tortosa, Sa-
    gunto, &c.] .   .   9,493
Garrisons of Catalonia:
    Barcelona   .   .   5,844
    Puigcerda   .   .   1,863 } Total in garrisons, 23,602.
    Figueras .   .   .   1,742
    Gerona .   .   .   1,605
    Smaller Fortresses .   3,055

GRAND TOTAL . 46,290 present under arms, not including sick,
                                    gendarmerie, ouvriers militaires, &c.

SUCHET'S FIELD-ARMY AT THE END OF THE WAR.
APRIL 16, 1813

Infantry:			
	3rd Léger . .	751	(1 battalion.)
	5th Line . .	1,834	(2 batts.)
Division Lamarque	14th Line . .	1,607	(2 batts.)
	60th Line . .	1,936	(3 batts.)
	121st Line . .	2,363	(3 batts.)
	11th Line . .	842	(2 batts.)
Brigade Mesclop	114th Line . .	2,059	(3 batts.)
	143rd Line 1 batt.	724	(1 batt.)
	86th Line 1 batt..	365	(1 batt.)

Cavalry : 24th Dragoons, 29th Chasseurs, gendarmes 1,449 (7 squadrons.)
Artillery, sappers, train, &c.   .   .   .   .   2,180 (4 batteries,
                                                                        3 comps.
                                                                        sappers.)

Total .   .   . 16,091 of all ranks.

IX

ORTHEZ, FEBRUARY 27, 1814

WELLINGTON'S ARMY AT ORTHEZ

[N.B. The figures include all ranks ; paymasters, surgeons, &c., are counted
    with the officers.]

2nd Division [W. STEWART]:		3rd Division [PICTON]:	
Barnes's Brigade . .	2,013	Brisbane's Brigade .	2,491
Byng's Brigade . . .	1,805	Keane's Brigade .	2,006
O'Callaghan's Brigade .	1,664	Power's Portuguese .	2,129
Harding's Portuguese[1] .	2,298		6,626
	7,780		

[1] Harding had replaced Ashworth as brigadier in February.

4th Division [COLE]:
Anson's Brigade[1] . . 1,814
Ross's Brigade . . . 1,753
Vasconcellos's Portuguese . 2,385
———
5,952

6th Division [CLINTON]:
Pack's Brigade[2] . . . 1,415
Lambert's Brigade . . 2,300
Douglas's Portuguese . . 1,856
———
5,571

7th Division [WALKER]:
Gardiner's Brigade . . 1,865
Inglis's Brigade[3] . . 1,420
Doyle's Portuguese . . 2,358
———
5,643

Light Division[4] [ALTEN]:
1/52nd, 2/95th, 3/95th . 1,777
Portuguese (9 batts.) . . 1,703
———
3,480

LE COR's Portuguese Division:
Da Costa's Brigade . . 2,109
Buchan's Brigade . . 2,356
———
4,465

Cavalry [STAPLETON COTTON]:
Fane's Brigade . . . 765
Vivian's Brigade . . 989
Somerset's Brigade . . 1,619
———
3,373

Artillery:
6 British and 1 K.G.L. batteries and train . . 1,052
1 Portuguese battery . . 110
———
1,162

Staff-corps, engineers, and
Wagon-train . . . 350
Total, all ranks . . 44,402
of whom British . . 26,798
Portuguese . 17,604

BRITISH CASUALTIES AT ORTHEZ. FEBRUARY 27, 1814

		Killed. Offi-cers.	Men.	Wounded. Offi-cers.	Men.	Missing. Offi-cers.	Men.	Total.
CAVALRY:								
Fane's Brigade	13th Light Dragoons . .	—	2	1	6	—	—	9
	14th Light Dragoons . .	—	—	—	2	—	—	2
Vivian's Brigade	18th Hussars and 1st Hussars K.G.L. . .	—	—	—	—	—	—	—
		—	—	—	—	—	—	—
Somerset's Brigade	7th Hussars .	—	4	3	9	—	—	16
	10th Hussars .	—	—	—	1	—	—	1
	15th Hussars .	—	—	—	9	—	—	9
	Total Cavalry . .	—	6	4	27	—	—	37

[1] Minus 2nd Provisional Battalion, absent.
[2] Minus 1/79th absent.
[3] Minus 51st absent.
[4] Minus 1/43rd and 1/95th absent.

		Killed. Offi-cers.	Men.	Wounded. Offi-cers.	Men.	Missing. Offi-cers.	Men.	Total.
2nd Division [W. Stewart]:								
Barnes's Brigade	1/50th Foot .	—	1	1	12	—	—	14
	1/71st Foot .	—	2	1	9	—	—	12
	1/92nd Foot .	—	—	—	3	—	—	3
Byng's Brigade	1/3rd Foot . .	—	—	—	2	—	—	2
	1/57th Foot .	—	—	—	—	—	—	—
	2/31st Foot .	—	—	—	2	—	—	2
	1/66th Foot .	—	—	—	—	—	—	—
O'Callaghan's Brigade had no casualties								
Total		—	3	2	28	—	—	33
3rd Division [Picton]:								
Brisbane's Brigade	1/45th Foot .	1	14	9	106	—	2	132
	5/60th Foot .	—	4	2	35	—	1	42
	74th Foot . .	—	8	5	21	—	—	34
	1/88th Foot .	2	41	12	214	—	—	269
Keane's Brigade	1/5th Foot . .	1	5	—	31	—	3	40
	2/83rd Foot .	—	5	6	47	—	—	58
	2/87th Foot .	1	14	5	66	—	23	109
	94th Foot . .	—	1	1	12	—	1	15
Total		5	92	40	532	—	30	699
4th Division [Cole]:								
Anson's Brigade	3/27th Foot .	—	1	1	4	—	—	6
	1/40th Foot .	—	1	—	4	—	—	5
	1/48th Foot .	—	1	—	13	—	—	14
	2nd Provisional absent . .	—	—	—	—	—	—	—
Ross's Brigade	1/7th Foot . .	—	6	4	56	—	2	68
	1/20th Foot .	2	16	6	97	1	1	123
	1/23rd Foot .	—	16	3	69	—	—	88
Total		2	41	14	243	1	3	304
6th Division [Clinton]:								
Pack's Brigade	1/42nd Foot .	—	5	4	40	—	11	60
	1/91st Foot .	—	—	4	8	—	—	12
	1/79th absent .	—	—	—	—	—	—	—
Lambert's Brigade	1/61st Foot .	—	—	—	7	—	—	7
	1/32nd, 1/36th, 1/11th, no cas-ualties . .	—	—	—	—	—	—	—
		—	5	8	55	—	11	79

	Killed. Offi-cers.	Men.	Wounded. Offi-cers.	Men.	Missing. Offi-cers.	Men.	Total.
7th Division [Walker]:							
Gardiner's Brigade — 1/6th Foot	2	24	8	111	—	—	145
2/24th Foot	—	1	3	31	—	—	35
2/56th Foot	—	3	3	25	—	—	31
Brunswick-Oels	2	5	5	32	—	4	48
Inglis's Brigade — 68th Foot	—	3	1	27	—	—	31
1/82nd Foot	—	2	2	34	—	—	38
Chasseurs Britan-niques	1	2	5	20	—	12	40
51st absent	—	—	—	—	—	—	—
	5	40	27	280	—	16	368
Light Division [Alten]:							
1/52nd Foot	—	7	6	76	—	—	89
No casualties in the 95th	—	—	—	—	—	—	
Artillery	1	3	1	23	—	—	28
Engineers and sappers	1	—	—	1	—	—	2
General Staff	—	—	6	—	—	—	6
GENERAL TOTAL	14	197	108	1,265	1	60	1,645

PORTUGUESE LOSSES AT ORTHEZ

	Killed. Offi-cers.	Men.	Wounded. Offi-cers.	Men.	Missing. Offi-cers.	Men.	Total.
2nd Division.							
Harding's Brigade no casualties	—	—	—	—	—	—	—
3rd Division:							
Power's Brigade — 9th Line	—	11	2	36	—	—	49
21st Line	1	13	1	22	—	—	37
11th Caçadores	3	5	1	14	—	—	23
4th Division:							
Vascon-cellos's Brigade — 11th Line	1	44	9	78	—	16	148
23rd Line	1	36	5	77	—	3	122
7th Caçadores	—	8	1	16	—	—	25
6th Division:							
Douglas's Brigade — 8th Line	—	1	—	8	—	—	9
12th Line	—	—	1	4	—	—	5
9th Caçadores	—	3	—	7	—	—	10

	Killed.		Wounded.		Missing.		
	Offi-cers.	Men.	Offi-cers.	Men.	Offi-cers.	Men.	Total.
7th Division:							
Doyle's Brigade ⎰ 7th Line	—	—	—	—	—	—	—
19th Line	—	—	—	—	—	—	—
2nd Caçadores	—	—	—	3	—	—	3
Light Division:							
1st Caçadores	—	11	3	33	—	—	47
3rd Caçadores	—	13	—	13	—	—	26
17th Line	—	—	—	—	—	—	—
Le Cor's Division:							
Da Costa's ⎰ 2nd Line	—	2	—	1	—	—	3
14th Line	—	—	—	—	—	—	—
Buchan's Brigade ⎰ 4th Line	—	—	—	1	—	—	1
10th Line	—	—	1	—	—	—	1
10th Caçadores	—	3	1	6	—	—	10
Artillery. Da Silva's Battery	—	—	—	—	—	—	—
	6	150	25	329	—	19	529
GENERAL TOTAL:							
British and Portuguese	20	347	133	1,594	1	79	2,174

FRENCH LOSSES AT ORTHEZ. FEBRUARY 27, 1814

	Killed.		Wounded.		Prisoners.		Total.
	Offi-cers.	Men.	Offi-cers.	Men.	Offi-cers.	Men.	
Reille's Corps:							
Division Rouget	3	93	17	348	4	56	521
Division Taupin	8	69	19	444	5	46	591
Brigade Paris [of Harispe's division]	1	71	13	102	1	260	448
D'Erlon's Corps:							
Division Darmagnac	2	46	33	369	—	116	566
Division Foy	4	40	20	272	—	13	349
Clausel's Corps:							
Division Villatte	—	35	5	96	5	198	339
Division Harispe	2	95	5	129	4	599	834
Cavalry of P. Soult	2	58	5	150	1	50	266
Artillery	—	10	—	41	—	8	59
Engineers	—	—	—	4	—	—	4
État-Major Général	3	—	5	—	—	—	8
	25	517	122	1,955	20	1,346	3,985

NOTE. Tested by Martinien's invaluable lists the officer-casualties do not look far wrong. In the six infantry divisions the official 20 killed only differs by four from Martinien's 24, and in the wounded 112 is only less by three than Martinien's 115. I take it, therefore, that the total French loss was only very slightly over 4,000. This does not, of course, include the large number of deserters after the battle. The 'prisoners' undoubtedly include many wounded left on the field, as the proportion of dead to wounded in some units is much too high—e. g. in Paris's brigade 72 to 115, in Harispe's division 97 to 134. The wounded corresponding to this very high proportion of dead must be sought among the 'prisoners' to make the statistics credible. It will be noted that there are no figures for 'train' and other minor auxiliary services which generally occur in a French return, nor for the battalions of the 'Toulouse Reserve' which came up during the battle.

X

TOULOUSE, APRIL 10, 1814

WELLINGTON'S ARMY AT TOULOUSE

INFANTRY

2nd Division (W. Stewart):
British Brigades of Barnes,
Byng, and O'Callaghan . 4,838
Harding's Portuguese . 2,102
————
6,940

3rd Division (Picton):
British Brigades of Brisbane
and Keane . . . 3,157
Power's Portuguese . . 1,409
————
4,566

4th Division (Cole):
British Brigades of Ross and
Anson 3,539
Vasconcellos's Portuguese . 1,824
————
5,363

6th Division (Clinton):
British Brigades of Pack and
Lambert . . . 3,803[1]
Douglas's Portuguese . . 1,890
————
5,693

Light Division:
British 2,799
Portuguese . . . 1,476
————
4,275

Le Cor's Division:
Brigades of Buchan and
Almeida . . . 3,952
Total Anglo-Portuguese
Infantry . . . 30,789
Of which British . . 18,136
Portuguese . 12,653

Freire's Spaniards:
Marcilla's Division . . 3,959
Espeleta's Division . . 3,576
Sappers, &c. . . . 381
————
7,916

Morillo's Spaniards . . 2,001
Total Infantry . . 40,706

CAVALRY[2]

C. Manners's Brigade . . 1,426
Bülow's Brigade . . 701
Fane's Brigade . . . 816
Vivian's Brigade . . 939
Somerset's Brigade . . 1,717
Clifton's Brigade . . 891
————
Total Cavalry . . 6,490

[1] The 1/32nd of Lambert's brigade was absent.

[2] The Adjutant-General, George Murray, says that owing to the detachments in the rear and convoy guards, the real force of the cavalry was on April 10th much lower. He gives as present C. Manners's brigade, 1,111, Vivian's 895, Somerset's 1,611. Clifton and Fane were on the other side of the Garonne, with Hill's Corps.

ARTILLERY
British 1,510
Portuguese . . . 440
_____
1,950

N.B. It is impossible to give the numbers of engineers, train, &c., as the figures in the returns include all those present at the siege of Bayonne and at Bordeaux. The total must have been under 500:

Total Infantry	.	. 40,706
Cavalry	.	. 6,490
Artillery	.	. 1,950
		_____
		49,146

SOULT'S ARMY AT TOULOUSE

Morning States of April 1, 1814

1st Division, DARICAU:
Fririon's Brigade: 6th Léger, 76th Line (1 batt. each), 69th Line (2 batts.) . . . . 1,840 ⎫
Berlier's Brigade: 36th and 65th Line (2 batts. each), 39th Line (1 batt.) . . . . 1,999 ⎭ 3,839

2nd Division, DARMAGNAC:
Leseur's Brigade: 31st Léger, 75th Line (2 batts. each), 51st Line (1 batt.) . . . . 2,387 ⎫
Menne's Brigade: 118th and 120th Line (3 batts. each) . 2,635 ⎭ 5,022

4th Division, TAUPIN:
Rey's Brigade: 12th Léger, 32nd and 43rd Line (2 batts. each) . . . . 3,039 ⎫
Gasquet's Brigade: 47th Line (2 batts.), 55th and 58th Line (1 batt. each) . . . . 2,416 ⎭ 5,455

5th Division, MARANSIN:
Barbot's Brigade: 40th Line (2 batts.), 4th Léger, 50th Line (1 batt. each) . . . . 2,045 ⎫
Rouget's Brigade: 27th, 34th, 59th Line (1 batt. each) . 1,672 ⎭ 3,717

6th Division, VILLATTE:
St. Pol's Brigade: 21st Léger, 86th, 96th, 100th Line (1 batt. each) . . . . 2,658 ⎫
Lamorandière's Brigade: 28th Léger, 103rd Line (1 batt. each), 119th Line (2 batts.) . . . . . 1,951 ⎭ 4,609

8th Division, HARISPE:
Dauture's Brigade: 9th Léger, 25th Léger, 34th Léger (2 batts. each) . . . . 2,198 ⎫
Baurot's Brigade: 10th Line (2 batts.), 45th, 81st, 115th, 116th, 117th (1 each) . . . . . . 2,886 ⎭ 5,084

Reserve Division, TRAVOT'S:
Brigades Pourailly and Vuillemont, conscript battalions of new levy 7,267

Total Infantry 34,993

Cavalry. Division PIERRE SOULT:

Berton's Brigade 2nd Hussars, 13th and 21st Chasseurs	1,339 ⎫
Vial's Brigade: 5th, 10th, 15th, 22nd Chasseurs . .	1,361 ⎭ 2,700
Artillery and Train, and 2 companies pontoniers . . .	3,603
Engineers and Sappers	541
Gendarmerie	206

GENERAL TOTAL   42,043

[*Équipages militaires*, &c., omitted, as non-combatants.]

TOULOUSE. APRIL 10, 1814
BRITISH CASUALTIES

	Killed.		Wounded.		Missing.		
	Offi-cers.	Men.	Offi-cers.	Men.	Offi-cers.	Men.	Total.
2nd Division:							
Byng's Brigade . . .			no casualties.				
Barnes's Brigade ⎰ 1/50th Foot . .	—	2	2	8	—	—	12
1/71st Foot . .	—	3	—	13	—	—	16
⎱ 1/92nd Foot . .	—	—	—	—	—	—	—
O'Callag- ⎰ 1/28th Foot . .	—	3	3	25	—	—	31
han's ⎰ 2/34th Foot . .	—	2	1	11	—	—	14
Brigade ⎱ 1/39th Foot . .	—	—	1	4	—	—	5
Divisional Total . .	—	10	7	61	—	—	78
3rd Division:							
. ⎰ 1/45th Foot . .	1	7	8	72	—	5	93
Brisbane's ⎰ 1/74th Foot . .	—	32	7	72	2	—	113
Brigade ⎰ 1/88th Foot . .	—	8	2	76	—	—	86
⎱ 5/60th Foot . .	—	11	3	48	—	—	62
⎰ 1/5th Foot . .	—	—	—	3	—	—	3
Keane's ⎰ 2/83rd Foot . .	—	—	—	1	—	—	1
Brigade ⎰ 2/87th Foot . .	1	7	2	17	—	—	27
⎱ 94th Foot . .	—	1	—	5	—	—	6
Divisional Total . .	2	66	22	294	2	5	391
4th Division:							
Anson's ⎰ 3/27th . . .	2	23	5	76	—	—	106
Brigade ⎰ 1/40th Foot . .	—	7	8	71	—	—	86
⎱ 1/48th Foot . .	—	5	4	39	—	—	48
2nd Provisional (2nd & 2/53nd Foot) .	—	2	4	27	—	—	33
Ross's ⎰ 1/7th Foot . .	—	1	—	3	—	—	4
Brigade ⎰ 1/20th Foot . .	—	2	—	7	—	3	12
⎱ 1/23rd Foot . .	—	1	—	7	—	—	8
	2	41	21	230	—	3	297

		Killed. Offi-cers.	Men.	Wounded. Offi-cers.	Men.	Missing. Offi-cers.	Men.	Total.
6th Division:								
Pack's Brigade	1/42nd Foot . .	4	50	22	337	1	—	414
	1/79th Foot . .	3	16	15	179	—	1	214
	1/91st Foot . .	—	18	6	87	—	—	111
Lambert's Brigade	1/11th Foot . .	1	14	6	121	—	—	142
	1/36th Foot . .	1	38	9	100	—	4	152
	1/61st Foot . .	1	16	18	136	—	—	171
Divisional Total . .		10	152	76	960	1	5	1,204
Light Division:								
	1/52nd Foot . .	—	—	—	5	—	—	5
	1/95th Foot . .	—	7	1	11	—	—	19
	3/95th Foot . .	—	3	—	29	—	—	32
	No casualties in 1/43rd & 2/95th .	—	—	—	—	—	—	—
Divisional Total . .		—	10	1	45	—	—	56
CAVALRY:								
No casualties in Fane's, Bülow's and Clifton's Brigades.								
C. Manners's Brigade	5th D. G. . .	—	1	1	2	—	—	4
	3rd Dragoons .	—	—	1	5	—	—	6
	4th Dragoons .	—	2	1	5	—	—	8
Somerset's Brigade	7th Hussars .	—	—	—	—	—	—	—
	10th Hussars .	1	4	1	6	—	—	12
	15th Hussars .	—	—	—	4	—	—	4
Vivian's Brigade	1st Hussars K.G.L.	—	1	1	14	—	—	16
	18th Hussars .	—	—	—	—	—	—	—
Total Cavalry . .		1	8	5	36	—	—	50
Horse Artillery . . .		—	1	—	7	—	—	8
Field Artillery . . .		—	6	—	5	—	—	11
K.G.L. Artillery . . .		1	2	—	5	—	—	8
Total Artillery . .		1	9	—	17	—	—	27
Total British Casualties .		16	296	132	1,643	3	13	2,103

PORTUGUESE CASUALTIES

No casualties in Le Cor's divisions [brigades Almeida and Buchan] nor in Harding's brigade [2nd Division].

		Killed. Officers.	Men.	Wounded. Officers.	Men.	Missing. Officers.	Men.	Total.
3rd Division:								
Power's Brigade	9th Line	—	—	—	—	—	—	—
	21st Line	1	4	1	14	—	—	20
	11th Caçadores	—	8	3	12	—	—	23
4th Division:								
Vascon-cellos's Brigade	11th Line	1	5	—	16	—	—	22
	23rd Line	—	25	2	25	—	—	52
	7th Caçadores	—	7	2	25	—	—	34
6th Division:								
Douglas's Brigade	8th Line	2	32	3	65	—	—	102
	12th Line	1	30	3	139	—	—	173
	9th Caçadores	—	7	2	32	—	—	41
Light Division:								
	17th Line	—	—	—	5	—	—	5
	1st Caçadores	—	7	—	28	—	—	35
	3rd Caçadores	—	5	—	13	—	—	18
Artillery		—	3	1	4	—	—	8
	Total Portuguese	5	133	17	378	—	—	538[1]
	Total Spaniards	12	193	86	1,631	—	—	1,922
	Total British	16	296	132	1,643	3	13	2,103
	GENERAL TOTAL	33	622	235	3,652	3	13	4,558

TOULOUSE. FRENCH CASUALTIES

It is unfortunate that we have no regimental details, except for officer-casualties. But the totals were as follows in the official report:

killed 322, wounded 2,373, missing 541 = 3,236.

Undoubtedly the 'missing' include at least 100 killed, as Wellington claimed very few prisoners, except the large number captured in the hospitals of Toulouse on the 12th, when Soult evacuated the city. The

[1] As in the battles of the Pyrenees, the proportion between killed and wounded among the Portuguese seems abnormal—1 to 3 instead of the 1 to 5 among the British. Wellington's summary report gives a quite different percentage—with 60 less killed, and 250 more wounded. The revised Portuguese returns *must* be correct as to the killed—I can only conclude that as regards the wounded many slight cases did not get into the revised returns, though they had been entered in the summary report, while 60 mortally wounded were transferred from the second to the first column.

proportion of only 1 killed to 8 wounded is undoubtedly too low. In Wellington's army on this day it was 1 to 5·7.

The relative losses of the divisions may be roughly estimated by their officer-casualties in the subjoined table, extracted from Martinien's invaluable book.

	Killed.	Wounded.	Total.
Taupin's Division	5	23	28
Maransin's Division	1	11	12
Daricau's Division	5	18	23
Darmagnac's Division . . .	9	32	41
Villatte's Division	1	20	21
Harispe's Division	10	54	64
Travot's Conscripts	—	3	3[1]
Cavalry	2	12	14
Artillery	—	6	6
Engineers and Train	—	3	3
État-Major	2	14	16
	35	196	231

These officer-casualties, 231 in all out of a total of 3,236 casualties of all ranks, are 1 to 15, when we have deducted the 16 État-Major casualties. The British proportion was 1 to 14.

XI
BRITISH LOSSES IN THE BAYONNE SORTIE OF APRIL 14, 1814

Corps.	Killed. Offi-cers.	Men.	Wounded. Offi-cers.	Men.	Missing. Offi-cers.	Men.	Total.
General Staff . . .	2	—	3	—	3	—	8
1st Division. [Stopford's, Howard's, and Hinüber's Brigades]:							
1st Batt. 1st Foot Guards .	—	1	—	6	—	—	7
3rd Batt. 1st Foot Guards .	—	2	2	31	1	17	53
1st Batt. Coldstream Guards .	2	32	5	122	—	84	245
1st Batt. 3rd Guards . .	—	35	5	106	1	57	204
1st Light Batt. K.G.L. . .	—	7	3	17	—	1	28
2nd Light Batt. K.G.L. . .	—	20	2	39	1	28	90
1st Line Batt. K.G.L. . .	—	4	—	5	—	—	9
2nd Line Batt. K.G.L. . .	2	11	2	21	—	4	40
5th Line Batt. K.G.L. . .	2	7	2	11	—	—	22
Carried forward	8	119	24	358	6	191	706

[1] These 3 officers may not have been the only casualties among Travot's conscript battalions. Several of them were high-number battalions of regiments whose senior battalions were present; the three enumerated above belonged to regiments which had no unit present except one of these conscript battalions.

	Killed.		Wounded.		Missing.		
	Offi-cers.	Men.	Offi-cers.	Men.	Offi-cers.	Men.	Total.
Brought forward	8	119	24	358	6	191	706
5th Division [Hay's Brigade]:							
3/1st Foot	—	8	1	12	—	21	42
1/9th Foot	—	2	—	8	—	—	10
1/35th Foot	—	2	2	5	—	—	9
2/47th Foot	—	3	2	11	—	10	26
Company 5/60th attached to 5th Division . . .	—	—	1	4	—	5	10
Royal Artillery . . .	—	—	2	2	—	—	4
Royal Engineers . . .	—	—	2	—	—	—	2
Portuguese (5th Caçadores and 13th Line) . . .	—	8	2	19	—	—	29
	8	142	36	419	6	227	838

The French loss was, killed 11 officers 100 men, wounded 42 officers 736 men, missing 16 men, or in all 905. The regiment which suffered most was the 94th Line, which had 5 officers killed and 13 wounded out of 30 present. The apparent discrepancy between killed and wounded on the two sides —1 to 3 as against 1 to 7—is partly to be explained by the fact that the 233 British 'missing' were mostly wounded men, left on the ground when the pickets were driven in.

SPANISH TROOPS EMPLOYED BY WELLINGTON, AUGUST 1813–APRIL 1814

	Strength Aug. 31.	Strength Nov. 10.	Strength April 14.	Position in April.
I. The 'Fourth Army'. General Freire				
1st Division [Morillo] .	4,845	5,021	4,409	½ with Hill's corps, ½ at Navarrenx.
2nd Division [Carlos de España] .	4,342	4,580	3,963	Before Bayonne.
3rd Division [Losada, then Del Barco].	5,176	5,866	4,991	½ at Toulouse, ½ before Bayonne.
4th Division [Barcena, then Espeleta] .	4,488	4,149	4,085	At Toulouse.
5th Division [Porlier] .	2,355	4,544	3,729	½ at Toulouse, ½ before Bayonne.[1]
6th Division [Longa] .	2,607	2,507	left in Spain	Sent back to Spain after the Nivelle.
7th Division [Mendizabal] .	2,137	left in Spain	left in Spain	Left in Spain.
Cavalry, all left on the Ebro				Left in Spain.
Artillery and Engineers .	560	856	965	200 at Toulouse, rest before Bayonne.
Mina's Troops [or 8th Division] .	8,000	8,472	8,608	Blockading St. Jean-Pied-du-Port.
	34,510	35,995	30,750	
II. The 'Army of Reserve of Andalusia'. General Giron.				
1st Division [Virues] .	5,410	4,123	5,008	Sent back to Spain after the Nivelle.
2nd Division [Creagh, La Torre, Creagh] .	4,750	3,720	4,286	Ordered up to Bayonne late in February.
Cavalry all left on the Ebro .				
	10,160	7,843	9,294	

III. The 'Third Army', under the Prince of Anglona, only crossed the Pyrenees and occupied Pau in April 1814. It was 12,000 strong in August, 17,000 strong in December, 21,000 in April.

The total of Spanish troops used in the field by Wellington was 44,000 in August, 43,000 in November, 40,000 in April; the Third Army, never employed, being omitted, and the Cavalry, Longa, and Mendizabal having been left behind.

[1] Porlier's division, originally only one brigade, had been given a second brigade by November. The 'Composite Division' under Marcilla, which served at Toulouse, consisted of one brigade of Porlier's and one of Del Barco's division.

INDEX

Abbé, Louis Jean, general, engaged in the combat of Urdax, 52–3; contest of, with the 2nd Division at the Nivelle, 199–200; attacks Hill at St. Pierre, 269–72; left in garrison at Bayonne, 283, 326, at the sortie of Apr. 14, 508.

Adam, Colonel Frederic, defeated and wounded at Ordal, 100–2.

Admiralty, British, the, *see* Melville, Lord.

Adour, river, British passage of the, 335; construction of the great boat-bridge, 337, 338.

Agar, Pedro, Spanish Regent, dealings of, with Wellington, 142; arrested by King Ferdinand, 428.

Ainhoue, combat of, 53; evacuated by the French, 197.

Aire, combat of, 383–5.

Alava, Miguel, general, his toast to Wellington at Toulouse, 498.

Alten, Charles, major-general, commanding the Light Division, at the crossing of the Bidassoa, 128–9; at the battle of the Nivelle, 172–84; at Arcangues, 240–2; at Orthez, 357–67; at Vic-Bigorre, 445.

Alten, Victor, cavalry brigadier, 168, 225.

Alzate Real (or 'Boar's Back'), stormed by Light Division on Oct. 9, 129.

Amotz, the bridge of, stormed by the 3rd Division, on Nov. 6, 187.

Amposta, combat of, 86–7.

Andrade, José, colonel, in command at the combat of the Gorospil, 203–4.

Anglet, combat of, 236.

Anglona, the Prince of, general, replaces Del Parque in command of the 3rd Army, 311; ordered into France, 450.

Angoulême, François Antoine, Duke of, his arrival at Wellington's Head-quarters, 389; his propaganda among Royalists, 390; rides to Bordeaux, 396; assumes governmental power there, 397; rebuked by Wellington, 398; reviews the French army after Toulouse, 513.

Anson, William, major-general, at the Nivelle, 186; at Orthez, 358; at Toulouse, 475, 480.

Arabin, Captain Frederick, R.A., his battery at Ordal, 103.

Arcangues, combat of, 239–43; topography of, 261.

Arentschildt, Frederic Augustus, commands K.G.L. cavalry brigade, 468, 499.

Arentschildt, Victor, colonel, his battery at Toulouse, 474, 477.

Arriverayte, combat of, 327.

Ascain, Soult's Head-quarters at, 162, 173; evacuated, 201; becomes distributing centre for British Army, 219.

Ashworth, Charles, Portuguese brigadier, fine behaviour of his troops at battle of St. Pierre d'Irrube, 269; wounded there, 274.

Aylmer, Matthew, Lord, general, his brigade formed, 7; at San Marcial, 43; at the storming of Urrogne, 172; at the first combat of Barrouillet, 249; left before Bayonne, 333.

Barbot, brigadier-general, defends the Little Rhune, 177–9; at Toulouse, 486; wounded, 494.

Barcelona, Suchet's operations in front of, 414; the French army quits its vicinity, 412–13; sallies from, 430–1, 503.

Barcena, Pedro, Spanish general, at the battle of San Marcial, 43; at the crossing of the Bidassoa, 127.

Barnard, Andrew, colonel, wounded at the Nivelle, 194.

Barnes, Edward, major-general, at the battle of St. Pierre, 269–72; wounded, 273; and again at Aire, 386.

Bassussary, combats at, 239.

Bathurst, Henry, Earl, Secretary of War, correspondence of Wellington with, 111, 142, 216, 285–6; suggests the use of militia in France, 148; suggests transference of Wellington's army to another sphere, 308.

Baurot, French brigadier-general, his brigade at the Nivelle, 184, 185, 187; and at Toulouse, 486; wounded there, 488.

Baygorry, Val de, combats in, 118, 289.

Bayonette Ridge, the, stormed by the Light Division, 130–1.

Bayonne, topography of the fortress, 232–3.

Bentinck, Colonel Lord F., covers

INDEX 571

Menne, general, his brigade at Toulouse, 482.

Mequinza, Suchet's garrison at, 78; besieged, 98; captured by Van Halen's treachery, 419.

Meyer, French cavalry brigadier, his personal combat with Lord F. Bentinck, 106.

Militia, British, schemes for use of in the Peninsula, 148–9; a brigade reaches Bordeaux, 404.

Miller, James, colonel, commands a Portuguese brigade at San Marcial, 50–1.

Mina, Francisco Xavier, guerrillero chief, in Aragon, 76–7; his raids into France, 118, 289; takes charge of the Roncesvalles Passes, 167; captures Jaca, 322; blockades St. Jean-Pied-du-Port, 347; his after career, 522.

Mint, Wellington's clandestine establishment at St. Jean de Luz, 288–9.

Molins de Rey, combat of, 414.

Mont de Marsan, occupied by Wellington's army, 382.

Monzon, Suchet's garrison thereat besieged, 78, 88; captured by the treachery of Van Halen, 419.

Morillo, Pablo, general, joins the main army, 171; his division at the Nive, 175, 195, 200; his operations against Paris, 230, 260; rebuked by Wellington, 218; at combat of Garris, 323–4; besieges Navarrenx, 347.

Mouguerre, fighting on the hill of, at battle of St. Pierre, 267, 270, 272.

Mouiz forts, the, stormed by Colborne, 183–4.

Napier, William, colonel, volunteers for the storm of St. Sebastian, 17; his exploits at the storm of the Little Rhune, 181, 183; his controversies with Beresford, 525.

Napoleon, the Emperor, his policy of leaving large garrisons in Germany disastrous, 70; receives queries from Soult and Suchet, 95; his rejection of the Frankfurt propositions, 214; his orders to burn the palace of Marrac, 233; requisitions two divisions from Soult, 309–10; and two more from Suchet, 311–12; directs Soult to take the offensive at all costs, 377–8; authorizes Suchet, too late, to withdraw his garrisons, 412; attempts to cajole King Ferdinand, 298–300; concludes with him the Treaty of Valençay,

304; his self-deception as to its results, 307–9; abortive orders to Soult and Suchet, 422–3; rebukes Soult for indecision, 436; his abdication, 497–8; his views on Wellington and the British army, 519.

National Guards, French, a failure in the field, 292–3.

Navarrenx, besieged by Morillo's Spaniards, 343, 434.

Nive, battles of the, 223, 270.

Nivelle, Soult's defensive lines on the, 162–6; battle of the, 174–200.

O'Donnell, Henry, Conde d'Abispal, his dissensions with Wellington, 5; returns to the Front, 279; concurs in the restoration of Ferdinand VII, 429; his after career, 522.

O'Donoju, Juan, general, Spanish Minister of War, his disputes with Wellington, 143–4; disgraced by the Cortes, 143.

Ordal, combat of, 101–3.

Orthez, battle of, 356–70.

Oswald, John, general, criticizes the plan of the storm of St. Sebastian, 16; wounded at the assault, 25.

Pack, Denis, general, his brigade at Orthez, 363–5; and at Toulouse, 480, 482, 486–7.

Palafox, José, counsellor of Ferdinand VII, 303; his useless mission to Madrid, 306; at Saragossa, 425.

Pampeluna, blockade of, 150–5; surrender of, 156–7.

Paris, Marie-Auguste, general, evacuates Saragossa, 75; his retreat to France, 76–7; operations of, against Morillo, 224, 230, 260; at Orthez, 366–8; at Aire, 385.

Passages, Port of, its importance, 2, 4; and drawbacks, 11.

Peacock, Sir Nicholas, colonel, his disgraceful behaviour at St. Pierre, 270; cashiered, 280.

Penrose, Charles, admiral, his activity on the Biscay coast, 330, 336–7, 400–1, 404.

Peyrehorade, Soult's Head-quarters at, 283; occupied by the British, 345.

Picton, Sir Thomas, general, commanding the 3rd Division, at the combat of Sauveterre, 343–4; his operations at Orthez, 359–60; his rash attacks at Toulouse, 473–4, 483–4; his death at Waterloo, 526.